Educating for Mental Health

A BOOK OF READINGS

Educating for
Mental Health

A BOOK OF READINGS

JEROME M. SEIDMAN

Montclair State College

THOMAS Y. CROWELL COMPANY

New York / Established 1834

Preface

It is a truism that America's schools play a vital role in fostering the mental health and wholesome personal adjustment of our youth. The teacher, as well as the counselor or administrator, who likes and understands children, truly enjoys the teacher-pupil relationship, and is genuinely equipped to counsel boys and girls as they grow and learn, can contribute most importantly to developing soundness of personality, individual fulfillment, and responsible citizenship. Recognition of this fact, and of the need therefore to improve the preparation of teachers and their colleagues in related fields, has given rise to a great number of university course offerings in mental hygiene, mental health and education, human relations in education, the psychology of adjustment, and the like. It is for use in such courses that this book of readings is intended.

Understanding the problems of children and helping them solve their problems more effectively—these are the two major themes that shape the purpose and underlie the organization of this volume. The selections in Part One deal with the socialization process; with characteristics not only of children and adolescents, but of teachers as well; and with concepts that broaden our understanding of mental health, teaching-learning processes, and human development. Part Two seeks to demonstrate the extent to which everyday classroom practices can aid the teacher in stimulating thinking and the learning of wholesome attitudes and behavior. Part Three aims to show how the efforts of parents and teachers can be made more effective when joined with school and community programs. In its organization and coverage of topics, then, *Educating for Mental Health: A Book of Readings* follows closely the most widely used textbooks, as an examination of the table of correlations (p. 563ff.) will bear out.

In selecting the fifty-six articles for this collection from the vast amount of literature dealing with mental health and education, I have been guided by three criteria: (1) their competence and authoritativeness in treating the important problems that confront teachers, counselors, and administrators in their schools and classrooms; (2) the extent to which they show that educational practices are major forces in the improvement of mental health; and (3) their appeal—in form, content, and style—to students.

It is, of course, impossible within the confines of a single volume to represent all specialized areas and interests. The authors I have included, however, are those repeatedly cited in texts. Here, moreover, their contributions are presented in original form with minimal abridgments, and in some instances (selections 4, 10–12, 14, 21, 36, and 37) I have appended materials, which did not appear when the selections were originally published, that instructors will find useful. I have also retained the bibliographical references of the originals, compiling them conveniently in a single section in the back of the book, in the hope students will wish to pursue further the many problems being investigated.

The articles are in the main the most up-to-date available, all but four having been published since 1955, and over half since 1960. I admittedly have given little space to the too-often neglected early writers in the field, nor have I attempted to include writings on theories of personality, varieties of adjustive behavior, organic factors in personality, or psychotherapy. On the other hand, I have made the selection without regard to the boundaries of academic disciplines, having included anthropological and sociological as well as psychological and educational studies.

Educating for Mental Health: A Book of Readings can be used as a basic text by those instructors who prefer having their students read primary sources, and who, through their lectures and class discussions, elaborate upon and integrate the readings. Or, when used as a supplementary reader, it eliminates the necessity of compiling lists of assignments for outside readings and simplifies the student's task of fulfilling these assignments—especially when library facilities are limited or course enrollments large. However used, such a collection is invaluable in giving students the flavor of primary sources and an awareness of the way hypotheses are made and tested and research conducted.

Many persons have helped make this book possible. During a period of several years, the worth of many of the selections has been explored by obtaining student's evaluations of them. And I am especially grateful to the following colleagues for their generous and expert advice during my search for authoritative and readable material: David P. Ausubel, Eli M. Bower, Stuart W. Cook, Martin Deutsch, Robert F. DeHaan, Helen L. Gillham, Ira J. Gordon, Robert J. Havighurst, Ernest R. Hilgard, James G. Holland, Louis Kaplan, Mary E. Keister, Howard H. Kendler, Gerald T. Kowitz, Eleanor Leacock, Irving Lorge, Irving Maltzman, Lloyd McCleary, Alberta Munkres, Vincent Nowlis, Thomas F. Pettigrew, Ralph C. Preston, Abraham Shumsky, Lois M. Smith, John Thibaut, Willa V. Tinsley, J. Lloyd Trump, and James W. Vander Zanden.

I wish to acknowledge the courtesy of the authors and publishers for permission to reprint their material in this volume; specific acknowledgment accompanies each selection. I also wish to thank my students, Carolyn Abazia, Beverly Sorrentino, Sandra Swagler, and Muriel Wilson, for their very able proofreading. Finally, to my wife and sons—Cindy, Robert, and Alan—for their interest, understanding, and help, I affectionately dedicate this volume.

JEROME M. SEIDMAN

Upper Montclair,
New Jersey

Contents

PART TWO / HELPING CHILDREN

AND ADOLESCENTS

Cognitive Abilities, 285

Personality Development, 340

Social Behavior, 400

PART THREE / IMPROVING PARENT AND

TEACHER EFFECTIVENESS

School Practices, 435

Community Practices, 488

References Cited in Selections, 543

Correlations Table, 563

Index, 569

Part One

UNDERSTANDING CHILDREN

AND ADOLESCENTS

The Socialization Process

1 / Image of the Teacher by Adolescent Children in Four Countries: Germany, England, Mexico, United States

Harold H. Anderson, Gladys L. Anderson,
Irwin H. Cohen, and Frances D. Nutt

Socialization is the continuous process of learning—the shaping of individual characteristics and behavior through the training provided by the social environment. Children differ in interests, attitudes, ideals, values, and social behavior in ways that can be ascribed to differences in the cultural and subcultural settings in which they grow and develop. And specifically, as found in this study, children reared in more "dominating" or "authoritarian" cultures hold images of the teacher significantly different from those held by children in less "dominating" or more "democratic" cultures. The authors of this selection are Harold H. Anderson and Gladys L. Anderson of Michigan State University, Irwin H. Cohen of the Mental Health Institute, Independence, Iowa, and Frances D. Nutt.

A. PURPOSE

This report is based upon the *Lost Composition*, one of the 11 *Anderson Incomplete Stories* which were administered to over 9,000 fourth- and seventh-grade children in the seven countries of Germany, England, Norway, Sweden, Finland, Mexico, Puerto Rico and continental United States, during the period from 1952–1957. The purpose of the research

Reprinted from the *Journal of Social Psychology*, 1959, *50*, 47–55, with the permission of the authors and the Journal Press.

3

was twofold: to develop and test an instrument that would be sensitive to cross-national similarities and differences, and to examine children's responses in the light of certain hypotheses.

B. MATERIALS AND PROCEDURE

The Lost Composition. The children were asked to write a completion to the following story:

Betty often handed in her homework composition late to the teacher. This time it was an especially important composition and she had, moreover, finished it. On the way to school she lost her composition book and could not find it anywhere.

What does Betty say to her teacher?

What does the teacher say?

Think about these questions and finish this story with a few sentences.

The children's story completions in other languages were translated into English. The reliability of translation has been studied by Geierhaas (1955) [1] and shown to be adequate. From the content of the children's stories, a coding manual of 118 categories has been prepared and each protocol has been coded into categories. Independent coders of this story, using these content categories, demonstrated percentages of agreement of 89.1 and 90.09.

In coding the story completions distinction has been made between "check items" and "code items" (1957). A group of check items contains mutually exclusive categories in one of which each story must be checked. A code item is a category which is used only when the corresponding item appears in the child's story. In the coding manual for this story there are three sets of check items which provide answers to the questions: (a) Who initiated the contact, the child or the teacher? (b) Did the child tell the truth? (c) Did the teacher believe the child? The analysis presented in this paper is based on the three sets of check items and on 13 coding categories of punishment.

As shown in Table 1, the subjects were 3,178 seventh-grade children from Karlsruhe, Hamburg, and Munich, Germany; Birmingham, England; Mexico City; Benton Harbor, Michigan, and Knoxville, Tennessee.[2]

[1] [For citation of references, see References Cited in Selections, p. 543ff.]

[2] We are grateful for the cordial cooperation of many persons in the several locations in which we have gathered data. Specific acknowledgments for assistance in Karlsruhe and Hamburg, Germany; Birmingham, England; Knoxville, Tennessee, and Mexico have been made in previous reports (Anderson and Anderson, 1954; Anderson, et al., 1957).

For assistance in Munich, Germany, we are grateful to Städt. Oberschulrat Ederer, Professor Dr. Philip Lersch, Director, and Dr. Heinz-Rolf Lückert, Psychologisches Institut, University of Munich, and to the university students who served as members of our research team: Flne. Ilse Garbsch, Doris Hoberg, Beate Liller, Ilsabe Reese, Gabriele Schiller, Christel Zumsande, and Herren Hermann Brandstätter, Erich Harrer, Ludwig Krause, Lothar Schubert.

For permission to gather data in Benton Harbor, Michigan, we wish to thank Mr.

These locations were chosen for this report because it was assumed that, among our samplings, Germany (McGranahan, 1946) and Mexico (Diaz-Guerrero, 1955; de Leonard, 1956) represented the more dominative and authoritarian cultures and England and the United States represented the more integrative or democratic cultures.

Table 1. Numbers of Seventh-Grade Children Responding to Story
Number 6, *The Lost Composition,* of the *Anderson
Incomplete Stories*

Location	Abbreviation	Number
Karlsruhe, Germany	Kar.	621
Hamburg, Germany	Ham.	471
Munich, Germany	Mun.	325
Mexico City	Mex.	866
Birmingham, England	Bhm.	397
Knoxville, Tennessee	Knx.	214
Benton Harbor, Michigan	BnH.	284
		3178

It was further assumed that there will be found examples of integrative relating in the most dominating or authoritarian cultures and examples of domination in the presumed democratic cultures, as indeed our own research has already suggested (Anderson and Anderson, 1954, 1956, 1957; Heber, 1955).

C. HYPOTHESES

The hypotheses grew out of previous research on democratic and dictatorial teacher-child relations in American school rooms (Anderson, 1939, 1943; Anderson and Brewer, 1945, 1945a; Anderson, Brewer, and Reed, 1946). It was assumed that the same differences in child behavior reported in American dominative and integrative school rooms would be found to exist in more extensive samplings of dominative and integrative cultures.

The over-all hypothesis concerning Creativity in human relations is that democratic or integrative relationships facilitate Creativity and that dominative or authoritarian relationships restrict it.

Meryl A. Bird, Superintendent of Public Schools, and the principals of the public and parochial junior high schools. The data were gathered by Mary Ann Daugherty, Maryanne L. Myers, and Justin Lee Smith, who were recipients of Social Science Research Council Undergraduate Research Stipends, 1956, for work on this study, and H. H. Anderson.

A private grant has accelerated the coding and interpretation of the cross-national data as part of a five-year program of research in the area of Creativity.

The principal hypotheses of the cross-national research program that concern this story are:

1. Children brought up in a more dominating or authoritarian culture are different in their interpersonal relations from children in less dominating (more democratic) cultures.

2. In the *Lost Composition* story, valid communication will be lower in dominating cultures, that is, children in dominating cultures will show lower frequencies of telling the teacher the truth and higher frequencies of telling the teacher a lie.

3. Children in dominating cultures will be less ready to face reality and will thus show lower frequencies of the child's initiating contact with the teacher.

4. In the *Lost Composition* story, children in more dominating cultures will show the following characteristic images of the teacher: (a) More stories will have the teacher initiate the contact with the child. (b) More stories will have the teacher disbelieve the child. (c) More stories will have the teacher punish the child.

Conversely, the image of the teacher in stories from more integrative or democratic cultures will show significantly lower frequencies in these characteristics.

D. RESULTS

Table 2 shows that over four-fifths of the children in each location wrote stories in which the child initiated contact with the teacher. The Chi-square test revealed no significant differences between locations. The

Table 2. Mutually Exclusive Percentages of Children Indicating Which Member of the Teacher-Child Interaction Initiated the Contact

Child initiated—% (Cat. 21–1)		Teacher initiated—% (Cat. 21–2)		No information—% (Cat. 21–3)	
Kar.	87.9	Ham.	11.5	BnH.	9.5
BnH.	87.7	Mex.	11.1	Knx.	8.4
Mun.	87.4	Kar.	9.3	Mun.	7.7
Knx.	86.4	Bhm.	8.3	Mex.	6.1
Bhm.	85.6	Knx.	5.1	Bhm.	6.0
Ham.	83.6	Mun.	4.9	Ham.	4.9
Mex.	82.8	BnH.	2.8	Kar.	2.7
Chi² not sig.		Chi² sig. .01		Chi² sig. .01	

remaining children either had the teacher initiate the contact or gave no information from which the initiation of the contact could be inferred. Although the frequencies of stories in which the teacher initiated the contact were very low, the percentages were significantly different between locations. Three of the four samplings which have been assumed to come from more dominating or authoritarian cultures were highest in teacher-initiated contacts. The Munich sampling which fell between Benton Harbor and Knoxville represents an exception to our hypothesis.

Table 3. Mutually Exclusive Percentages of Total Children Indicating Whether the Child Told a Truth or a Lie

Truth—% (Cat. 23–1)		Lie—% (Cat. 23–2)		No information—% (Cat. 23–3)	
Mex.	89.5	Kar.	12.7	Knx.	9.8
Bhm.	89.2	Mun.	8.9	BnH.	9.2
BnH.	88.0	Ham.	8.1	Ham.	6.8
Ham.	85.1	Bhm.	6.3	Mun.	6.8
Knx.	85.0	Knx.	5.1	Mex.	6.8
Mun.	84.3	Mex.	3.7	Bhm.	4.5
Kar.	83.6	BnH.	2.8	Kar.	3.7
Chi² sig. .05		Chi² sig. .01		Chi² sig. .01	

Table 3 shows that 83 per cent or more of the children in each location had Betty tell the teacher the truth; the range of percentages is very small, though the over-all Chi-square was significant at the .05 level. Less than 13 per cent in each location had Betty tell the teacher a lie. Although the percentages were small, the differences between locations were significant. Consistent with the hypothesis, the three German locations were highest in having Betty tell a lie. Not consistent with the hypothesis was the Mexico City sampling which fell between Benton Harbor and Knoxville at the bottom.

In Table 4, the mutually exclusive check items of *Teacher believed, Teacher disbelieved,* and *No information* each differentiated between locations at the .01 level.

Table 4. Mutually Exclusive Percentages of Total Children Indicating Whether the Teacher Believed or Did Not Believe the Child's Story, Regardless of Whether It Was the Truth or a Lie

Believed—% (Cat. 22–1)		Disbelieved—% (Cat. 22–2)		No information—% (Cat. 22–3)	
Knx.	53.7	Kar.	48.9	BnH.	26.1
Bhm.	52.1	Ham.	47.6	Knx.	25.7
BnH.	50.7	Mun.	44.6	Mex.	22.2
Mun.	42.5	Mex.	42.1	Kar.	20.3
Ham.	36.9	Bhm.	32.2	Bhm.	15.6
Mex.	35.7	BnH.	23.2	Ham.	15.5
Kar.	30.8	Knx.	20.6	Mun.	12.9
Chi² sig. .01		Chi² sig. .01		Chi² sig. .01	

The hypothesis was that in an integrative or democratic culture there would be higher expressions of confidence in the child by the teacher as indicated by high frequencies of the item, *Teacher believed*. In Table 4, the children's images of the teacher consistently support this hypothesis. The three allegedly more democratic samplings were not significantly different from each other in percentages of stories in which the teacher believed the child. They were, however, significantly different at the .01 level from the three German samplings, and from the Mexico City sampling at the .05 level.

In the *Teacher disbelieved* category, Knoxville and Benton Harbor, lowest in percentages, were not significantly different from each other, yet were each significantly different at the .01 level from all other samplings. Karlsruhe, Hamburg, and Munich, highest in *Teacher disbelieved*, were not significantly different from each other, yet in turn were each significantly higher at the .01 level than the three samplings from the hypothesized democratic locations.

The ratios of percentages of *Teacher believed* to *Teacher disbelieved* ranging from Knoxville (2.9) to Karlsruhe (.54), were for all samplings consistent with the hypotheses. The ratio was highest, that is, higher percentages of *Teacher believed* than of *Teacher disbelieved*, in the democratic samplings of Knoxville, Benton Harbor, and Birmingham in that order. The relationship was reversed, that is, the frequency of *Teacher believed* was lower than the frequency of *Teacher disbelieved*, in the more dominating samplings of Munich, Mexico City, Hamburg, and Karlsruhe.

There was no systematic relationship between the teacher's belief or disbelief and the child's having told the truth or a lie.

Tables 5 and 6 are based upon categories of the teacher's punishing the child. Punishing is defined as: threatening, scolding, admonishing, advising, hitting, referring to the child's past unsatisfactory behavior or reputation, giving an inferior mark, assigning extra hours, assigning extra work, depriving of recreation, expelling or isolating, a negative statement of the teacher's unpleasant thought or act, or generically punishing. These represent the range of punishment items found in the story completions. The category of "Teacher has child rewrite the composition" was not included in the composite punishment category for two reasons, even though it was a frequently used category. Many children did not perceive this as punishment, and also, rewriting the composition was assumed to be a teacher's legitimate expectation of a school child. To simplify presentation and interpretation of data, Tables 5 and 6 give percentages of children in each location who wrote one or more of the punishment items.

Since more than four-fifths of all children produced stories in which a truth was told, only these stories are used in the punishment tables. To include children telling a lie would introduce a small though confounding variable. We asked the following questions of the data: when the child told the truth, what percentages of teachers were reported to have punished? What percentages when the teacher believed the child? What percentages when the teacher did not believe the child?

Table 5 Of Those Stories in Which the Child Told the Truth, Percentages in Which the Teacher Was Perceived as Punishing Regardless of Whether the Teacher Believed or Disbelieved the Child

Location	%	Location	%
Mex.	69.7	Kar.	47.2
Bhm.	68.4	BnH.	44.0
Ham.	60.8	Knx.	32.4
Mun.	57.7	Chi^2 sig. .01	

The rank order percentages of children who perceived the teacher as punishing are given in Table 5. Mexico City was highest in rank order with 69.7 per cent of the stories having one or more punishing items. Mexico City and Birmingham were significantly higher than all other locations, although not significantly different from each other. Knoxville was lowest in frequency, significantly lower than all other locations, including Benton Harbor at the .05 level. The low ranking of Knoxville and Benton Harbor and the higher ranking of the German and Mexico City samplings were consistent with the hypotheses. Birmingham's high position was consistent with reports of "canings" and of other physical punishment in some of the other stories.

Another perspective of punishment is given in Table 6 which shows the percentages of punishment when the teacher believed and when the teacher disbelieved the child's story. In all locations more teachers were perceived as punishing when they disbelieved than when they believed.

Table 6. Of those Stories in Which the Child Told the Truth, Percentages in Which the Teacher Was Perceived as Punishing When the Teacher Believed the Child, and When the Teacher Disbelieved the Child

(a) Teacher believed and punished *		(b) Teacher disbelieved and punished *	
Mex.	64.0	Bhm.	84.4
Ham.	59.9	Mex.	76.0
Bhm.	57.8	Mun.	63.6
Mun.	50.4	BnH.	60.6
Kar.	40.1	Ham.	60.1
BnH.	33.8	Kar.	54.2
Knx.	33.3	Knx.	37.8
Chi^2 sig. .01		Chi^2 sig. .01	

* Rank order correlation 6a—6b. $r' = .643$; $p. = .13$, not significant.

The largest difference was in Benton Harbor, where nearly twice as many teachers were perceived as punishing when they disbelieved as when they believed. Hamburg showed the least difference: as many teachers believed and punished as disbelieved and punished.

Table 6a shows the rank order percentages of teachers who believed the child but nevertheless punished. Mexico City was significantly higher than all other locations except Hamburg and Birmingham. Knoxville and Benton Harbor, lowest, were significantly lower than all others except Karlsruhe. Table 6b shows rank order percentages of teachers who disbelieved and punished. Birmingham and Mexico City were significantly higher than all other locations. Knoxville, again lowest, was significantly lower than all others except Karlsruhe. Benton Harbor was relatively high, in this unique instance, significantly higher than Knoxville.

Rank order percentages in Tables 5 and 6 were generally consistent with the hypotheses with the exception of Benton Harbor which was relatively high in punishment when the teacher disbelieved.

E. SUMMARY AND CONCLUSIONS

1. The purpose of the research program, of which this report is a part, was to develop and test an instrument that would be sensitive to cross-national similarities and differences, and to examine children's responses in the light of certain hypotheses about integrative and dominative cultures. The story-completions to one of the *Anderson Incomplete Stories* given by 3,178 children in Germany, England, Mexico, and the United States were analyzed to determine the children's image of the teacher.

2. The story involved a child with a reputation for handing in homework late to her teacher, who this time completed her composition on time, but lost it. Content categories were established to determine: (a) Who initiated the contact, the child or the teacher? (b) Whether the child told the truth or a lie? (c) Whether the teacher believed or disbelieved the child? (d) Whether the teacher punished the child in any way?

3. The hypotheses tested were that responses from children in a more dominating or authoritarian culture will be different from those of children in a more integrative or more democratic culture. Specifically, that in more dominating cultures there will be relatively higher frequencies of the teacher's initiating contact with the child, of the child's telling a lie, of the teacher's disbelieving the child, and of the teacher's punishing the child.

4. For purposes of this research the samplings from Hamburg, Karlsruhe, and Munich, Germany, and from Mexico City were assumed to come from more dominating or authoritarian cultures; sampling from Benton Harbor, Michigan; Knoxville, Tennessee; and Birmingham, England, were assumed to come from less authoritarian, that is, from integrative or more democratic cultures.

5. In all locations there were more child-initiated contacts than teacher-initiated contacts, and more truths than lies told. The hypotheses regarding teacher-initiated contacts and lies told were supported with but minor exceptions. In the more dominative or authoritarian locations, without exception the children wrote stories in which the teacher more frequently did not believe the child; conversely, in the more integrative or democratic samplings without exception the children wrote stories in which the teacher more frequently did believe the child. The hypotheses regarding punishment were supported with some exceptions: e.g., Birmingham, which was higher than expected, and Karlsruhe, which was lower than expected.

6. It is concluded that the *Anderson Incomplete Stories* is an instrument sensitive to cross-national similarities and differences, and that children reared in allegedly more authoritarian and dominating cultures hold images of the teacher that are significantly different from those held by children in less dominating, that is, more integrative or democratic cultures.

2 / The Changing American Child:
A Speculative Analysis [1]

Urie Bronfenbrenner

In what ways have parent-child relationships in the United States changed over the past twenty-five years? What are the present-day trends and what aspects of the culture contribute to the changes? How do variations in parental treatment effect child behavior? These are some of the provocative questions explored by Urie Bronfenbrenner of Cornell University.

A QUESTION OF MOMENT

It is now a matter of scientific record that patterns of child rearing in the United States have changed appreciably over the past twenty-five years (Bronfenbrenner, 1958). Middle class parents especially have moved

[1] This paper draws heavily on results from a program of research being conducted by the author in collaboration with Edward C. Devereux and George J. Suci. The contribution of these colleagues to facts and ideas presented in this paper is gratefully acknowledged. The research program is supported in part with grants from the National Science Foundation and the National Institutes of Health.

Reprinted from the *Journal of Social Issues*, 1961, *17* (1), 6–18, with the permission of the author and the Society for the Psychological Study of Social Issues, a Division of the American Psychological Association.

away from the more rigid and strict styles of care and discipline advocated in the early Twenties and Thirties toward modes of response involving greater tolerance of the child's impulses and desires, freer expression of affection, and increased reliance on "psychological" methods of discipline, such as reasoning and appeals to guilt, as distinguished from more direct techniques like physical punishment. At the same time, the gap between the social classes in their goals and methods of child rearing appears to be narrowing, with working class parents beginning to adopt both the values and techniques of the middle class. Finally, there is dramatic correspondence between these observed shifts in parental values and behavior and the changing character of the attitudes and practices advocated in successive editions of such widely read manuals as the Children's Bureau bulletin on *Infant Care* and Spock's *Baby and Child Care*. Such correspondence should not be taken to mean that the expert has now become the principal instigator and instrument of social change, since the ideas of scientists and professional workers themselves reflect in part the operation of deep-rooted cultural processes. Nevertheless, the fact remains that changes in values and practices advocated by prestigeful professional figures can be substantially accelerated by rapid and widespread dissemination through the press, mass media of communication, and public discussion.

Given these facts, it becomes especially important to gauge the effect of the changes that are advocated and adopted. Nowhere is this issue more significant, both scientifically and socially, than in the sphere of familial values and behavior. It is certainly no trivial matter to ask whether the changes that have occurred in the attitudes and actions of parents over the past twenty-five years have been such as to affect the personality development of their children, so that the boys and girls of today are somewhat different in character structure from those of a decade or more ago. Or, to put the question more succinctly: has the changing American parent produced a changing American child?

A STRATEGY OF INFERENCE

Do we have any basis for answering this intriguing question? To begin with, do we have any evidence of changes in the behavior of children in successive decades analogous to those we have already been able to find for parents? If so, we could take an important first step toward a solution of the problem. Unfortunately, in contrast to his gratifying experience in seeking and finding appropriate data on parents, the present writer has, to date, been unable to locate enough instances in which comparable methods of behavioral assessment have been employed with different groups of children of similar ages over an extended period of time. Although the absence of such material precludes any direct and unequivocal approach to the question at hand, it is nevertheless possible, through a series of inferences from facts already known, to arrive at some estimate of what the answer might be. Specifically, although as yet we have no comparable data on the relation between parental and child behavior for different families at successive points in time, we do have facts on the influence of parental treatment on child behavior at a given point in time; that is, we know that certain variations in parental behavior tend to be accompanied by systematic differences in the personality characteristics of children. If we are willing to assume that these same relationships obtained not only at a given moment but across different points in time, we are in a position to infer the possible effects on children of changing patterns of child rearing over the years. It is this strategy that we propose to follow.

THE CHANGING AMERICAN PARENT

We have already noted the major changes in parental behavior discerned in a recent analysis of data reported over a twenty-five year period. These secular trends may be summarized as follows:

1. Greater permissiveness toward the child's spontaneous desires
2. Freer expression of affection
3. Increased reliance on indirect "psychological" techniques of discipline (such as reasoning or appeals to guilt) vs. direct methods (like physical punishment, scolding, or threats)
4. In consequence of the above shifts in the direction of what are predominantly middle class values and techniques, a narrowing of the gap between social classes in their patterns of child rearing.

Since the above analysis was published, a new study has documented an additional trend. Bronson, Katten, and Livson (1959) have compared patterns of paternal and maternal authority and affection in two generations of families from the California Guidance Study. Unfortunately, the time span surveyed overlaps only partially with the twenty-five year period covered in our own analysis, the first California generation having been raised in the early 1900's and the second in the late '20's and early '30's. Accordingly, if we are to consider the California results along with the others cited above, we must make the somewhat risky assumption that a trend discerned in the first three decades of the century has continued in the same direction through the early 1950's. With this important qualification, an examination of the data cited by Bronson, Katten, and Livson (1959) points to still another, secular trend—a shift over the years in the pattern of parental role differentiation within the family. Specifically:

5. In succeeding generations the relative position of the father vis-à-vis the mother is shifting with the former becoming increasingly more affectionate and less authoritarian, and the latter becoming relatively more important as the agent of discipline, especially for boys.

"PSYCHOLOGICAL" TECHNIQUES OF DISCIPLINE AND THEIR EFFECTS

In pursuing our analytic strategy, we next seek evidence of the effects on the behavior of children of variations in parental treatment of the type noted in our inventory. We may begin by noting that the variables involved in the first three secular trends constitute a complex that has received considerable attention in recent research in parent-child relationships. Within the last three years, two sets of investigators, working independently, have called attention to the greater efficacy of "love-oriented" or "psychological" techniques in bringing about desired behavior in the child (Sears, Maccoby, and Levin, 1957; Miller and Swanson, 1958, 1960). The present writer, noting that such methods are especially favored by middle class parents, offered the following analysis of the nature of these techniques and the reasons for their effectiveness.

Such parents are, in the first place, more likely to overlook offenses, and when they do punish, they are less likely to ridicule or inflict physical pain. Instead, they reason with the youngster, isolate him, appeal to guilt, show disappointment—in short, convey in a variety of ways, on the one hand, the kind of behavior that is expected of the child; on the other, the realization that transgression means the interruption of a mutually valued relationship. . . .

These findings [of greater efficacy] mean that middle class parents, though in one sense more lenient in their discipline techniques, are using methods that are actually more compelling. Moreover, the compelling power of these practices is probably enhanced by the more permissive treatment accorded to middle class children in the early years of life. The successful use of withdrawal of love as a discipline technique implies the prior existence of a gratifying relationship; the more love present in the first instance, the greater the threat implied in its withdrawal (Bronfenbrenner, 1958).

It is now a well established fact that children from middle class families tend to excel those from lower class in many characteristics ordinarily regarded as desirable, such as self-control, achievement, responsibility, leadership, popularity, and adjustment in general.[2] If, as seems plausible, such differences in behavior are attributable at least in part to class-linked variations in parental treatment, the strategy of inference we have adopted would appear on first blush to lead to a rather optimistic conclusion. Since, over the years, increasing numbers of parents have been adopting the more effective socialization techniques typically employed by the middle class, does it not follow that successive genera-

---

[2] For a summary of findings on social class differences in children's behavior and personality characteristics, see Mussen and Conger (1956).

tions of children should show gains in the development of effective behavior and desirable personality characteristics?

Unfortunately, this welcome conclusion, however logical, is premature, for it fails to take into account all of the available facts.

SEX, SOCIALIZATION, AND SOCIAL CLASS

To begin with, the parental behaviors we have been discussing are differentially distributed not only by socio-economic status but also by sex. As we have pointed out elsewhere (Bronfenbrenner, 1961), girls are exposed to more affection and less punishment than boys, but at the same time are more likely to be subjected to "love-oriented" discipline of the type which encourages the development of internalized controls. And, consistent with our line of reasoning, girls are found repeatedly to be "more obedient, cooperative, and in general better socialized than boys at comparable age levels." But this is not the whole story.

. . . At the same time, the research results indicate that girls tend to be more anxious, timid, dependent, and sensitive to rejection. If these differences are a function of differential treatment by parents, then it would seem that the more "efficient" methods of child rearing employed with girls involve some risk of what might be called "over-socialization" (Bronfenbrenner, 1961).

One could argue, of course, that the contrasting behaviors of boys and girls have less to do with differential parental treatment than with genetically-based maturational influences. Nevertheless, two independent lines of evidence suggest that socialization techniques do contribute to individual differences, *within the same sex,* precisely in the types of personality characteristics noted above. In the first place, variations in child behavior and parental treatment strikingly similar to those we have cited for the two sexes are reported in a recent comprehensive study of differences between first and later born children (Schachter, 1959). Like girls, first children receive more attention, are more likely to be exposed to "psychological" discipline, and end up more anxious and dependent, whereas later children, like boys, are more aggressive and self-confident.

A second line of evidence comes from our own current research. We have been concerned with the role of parents in the development of such "constructive" personality characteristics as responsibility and leadership among adolescent boys and girls. Our findings reveal not only the usual differences in adolescents' and parents' behaviors associated with the sex of the child, but also a striking contrast in the relationship between parental and child behaviors for the two sexes. To start on firm and familiar ground, girls are rated by their teachers as more responsible than boys, whereas the latter obtain higher scores on leadership. Expected differences similarly appear in the realm of parental behavior: girls receive more affection, praise, and companionship; boys are subjected to

more physical punishment and achievement demands. Quite unanticipated, however, at least by us, was the finding that both parental affection
and discipline appeared to facilitate effective psychological functioning in
boys, but to impede the development of such constructive behavior in
girls. Closer examination of our data indicated that both extremes of
either affection or discipline were deleterious for all children, but that the
process of socialization entailed somewhat different risks for the two
sexes. Girls were especially susceptible to the detrimental influence of
over-protection; boys to the ill effects of insufficient parental discipline
and support. Or, to put it in more colloquial terms: boys suffered more
often from too little taming, girls from too much.

In an attempt to account for this contrasting pattern of relationships,
we proposed the notion of differential optimal levels of affection and
authority for the two sexes.

The qualities of independence, initiative, and self-sufficiency, which
are especially valued for boys in our culture, apparently require for their
development a somewhat different balance of authority and affection than
is found in the "love-oriented" strategy characteristically applied with
girls. While an affectional context is important for the socialization of
boys, it must evidently be accompanied by and be compatible with a
strong component of parental discipline. Otherwise, the boy finds himself in the same situation as the girl, who, having received greater affection, is more sensitive to its withdrawal, with the result that a little
discipline goes a long way and strong authority is constricting rather
than constructive (Bronfenbrenner, 1958).

What is more, available data suggest that this very process may already be operating for boys from upper middle class homes. To begin
with, differential treatment of the sexes is at a minimum for these
families. Contrasting parental attitudes and behaviors toward boys and
girls are pronounced only at lower class levels, and decrease as one moves
up the socio-economic scale (Kohn, 1959; Bronfenbrenner, 1958). Thus
our own results show that it is primarily at lower middle class levels that
boys get more punishment than girls, and the latter receive greater
warmth and attention. With an increase in the family's social position,
direct discipline drops off, especially for boys, and indulgence and protectiveness decrease for girls. As a result, patterns of parental treatment
for the two sexes begin to converge. In like manner, we find that the
differential effects of parental behavior on the two sexes are marked only
in the lower middle class. It is here that girls especially risk being over-
protected and boys not receiving sufficient discipline and support. In
upper middle class the picture changes. Girls are not as readily debilitated
by parental affection and power; nor is parental discipline as effective in
fostering the development of responsibility and leadership in boys.

All these trends point to the conclusion that the "risks" experienced
by each sex during the process of socialization tend to be somewhat different at different social class levels. Thus the danger of overprotection
for girls is especially great in lower class families, but lower in upper

middle class because of the decreased likelihood of overprotection. Analogously, boys are in greater danger of suffering from inadequate discipline and support in lower middle than in upper middle class. But the upper middle class boy, unlike the girl, exchanges one hazard for another. Since at this upper level the more potent "psychological" techniques of discipline are likely to be employed with both sexes, the boy presumably now too runs the risk of being "oversocialized," of losing some of his capacity for independent aggressive accomplishment.

Accordingly, if our line of reasoning is correct, we should expect a changing pattern of sex differences at successive socio-economic levels. Specifically, aspects of effective psychological functioning favoring girls should be most pronounced in the upper middle class; those favoring boys in the lower middle. A recent analysis of some of our data bears out this expectation. Girls excel boys on such variables as *responsibility* and *social acceptance* primarily at the higher socio-economic levels. In contrast, boys surpass girls on such traits as *leadership, level of aspiration,* and *competitiveness* almost exclusively in lower middle class. Indeed, with a rise in a family's social position, the differences tend to reverse themselves with girls now excelling boys.[3]

TRENDS IN PERSONALITY DEVELOPMENT: A FIRST APPROXIMATION

The implications for our original line of inquiry are clear. We are suggesting that the "love-oriented" socialization techniques, which over the past twenty-five years have been employed in increasing degree by American middle class families, may have negative as well as constructive aspects. While fostering the internalization of adult standards and the development of socialized behavior, they may also have the effect of undermining capacities for initiative and independence, particularly in boys. Males exposed to this "modern" pattern of child rearing might be expected to differ from their counterparts of a quarter century ago in being somewhat more conforming and anxious, less enterprising and self-sufficient, and, in general, possessing more of the virtues and liabilities commonly associated with feminine character structure.[4]

At long last, then, our strategy of inference has led us to a first major conclusion. The term "major" is appropriate since the conclusion takes as its points of departure and return four of the secular trends which served as the impetus for our inquiry. Specifically, through a series of empirical links and theoretical extrapolations, we have arrived at an estimate of

---

[3] These shifts in sex difference with a rise in class status are significant at the 5% level of confidence (one-tailed test).

[4] Strikingly similar conclusions were reached almost fifteen years ago in a provocative essay by Green (1946). With little to go on beyond scattered clinical observations and impressions, Green was able to detect many of the same trends which we have begun to discern in more recent systematic empirical data.

the effects on children of the tendency of successive generations of parents to become progressively more permissive, to express affection more freely, to utilize "psychological" techniques of discipline, and, by moving in these directions to narrow the gap between the social classes in their patterns of child rearing.

FAMILY STRUCTURE AND
PERSONALITY DEVELOPMENT

But one other secular trend remains to be considered: what of the changing pattern of parental role differentiation during the first three decades of the century? If our extrapolation is correct, the balance of power within the family has continued to shift with fathers yielding parental authority to mothers and taking on some of the nurturant and affectional functions traditionally associated with the maternal role. Again we have no direct evidence of the effects of such secular changes on successive generations of children, and must look for leads to analogous data on contemporaneous relationships.

We may begin by considering the contribution of each parent to the socialization processes we have examined thus far. Our data indicate that it is primarily mothers who tend to employ "love-oriented" techniques of discipline and fathers who rely on more direct methods like physical punishment. The above statement must be qualified, however, by reference to the sex of the child, for it is only in relation to boys that fathers use direct punishment more than mothers. More generally, . . . the results reveal a tendency for each parent to be somewhat more active, firm, and demanding with a child of the same sex, more lenient and indulgent with a child of the opposite sex . . . . The reversal is most complete with respect to discipline, with fathers being stricter with boys, mothers with girls. In the spheres of affection and protectiveness, there is no actual shift in preference, but the tendency to be especially warm and solicitous with girls is much more pronounced among fathers than among mothers. In fact, generally speaking, it is the father who is more likely to treat children of the two sexes differently (Bronfenbrenner, 1958).

Consistent with this pattern of results, it is primarily the behavior of fathers that accounts for the differential effects of parental behavior on the two sexes and for the individual differences within each sex. In other words, it is paternal authority and affection that tend especially to be salutary for sons but detrimental for daughters. But as might be anticipated from what we already know, these trends are pronounced only in the lower middle class; with a rise in the family's social status, both parents tend to have similar effects on their children, both within and across sexes. Such a trend is entirely to be expected since parental role differentiation tends to decrease markedly as one ascends the socio-economic ladder. It is almost exclusively in lower middle class homes that fathers are more strict with boys and mothers with girls. To the extent

that direct discipline is employed in upper middle class families, it tends
to be exercised by both parents equally. Here again we see a parallelism
between shifts in parental behavior across time and social class in the
direction of forms (in this instance of family structure) favored by the
upper middle class group.

What kinds of children, then, can we expect to develop in families
in which the father plays a predominantly affectionate role, and a relatively low level of discipline is exercised equally by both parents? A
tentative answer to this question is supplied by a preliminary analysis of
our data in which the relation between parental role structure and
adolescent behavior was examined with controls for the family's social
class position. The results of this analysis are summarized as follows: . . .
Both responsibility and leadership are fostered by the relatively greater
salience of the parent of the same sex . . . . Boys tend to be more responsible when the father rather than the mother is the principal dis-
ciplinarian; girls are more dependable when the mother is the major
authority figure . . . . In short, boys thrive in a patriarchal context, girls
in a matriarchal . . . . The most dependent and least dependable adolescents describe family arrangements that are neither patriarchal nor
matriarchal, but equalitarian. To state the issue in more provocative
form, our data suggest that the democratic family, which for so many
years has been held up and aspired to as a model by professionals and
enlightened laymen, tends to produce young people who "do not take
initiative," "look to others for direction and decision," and "cannot be
counted on to fulfill obligations" (Bronfenbrenner, 1958).

In the wake of so sweeping a conclusion, it is important to call attention to the tentative, if not tenuous character of our findings. The results
were based on a single study employing crude questionnaire methods and
rating scales. Also, our interpretation is limited by the somewhat "at-
tenuated" character of most of the families classified as patriarchal or
matriarchal in our sample. Extreme concentrations of power in one or
another parent were comparatively rare. Had they been more frequent,
we suspect the data would have shown that such extreme asymmetrical
patterns of authority were detrimental rather than salutary for effective
psychological development, perhaps even more disorganizing than equalitarian forms.

Nevertheless, our findings do find some peripheral support in the
work of others. A number of investigations, for example, point to the
special importance of the father in the socialization of boys (Bandura
and Walters, 1959; Mussen and Distler, 1959). Further corroborative
evidence appears in the growing series of studies of effects of paternal
absence (Bach, 1946; Sears, Pintler and Sears, 1946; Lynn and Sawrey,
1959; Tiller, 1958). The absence of the father apparently not only affects
the behavior of the child directly but also influences the mother in the
direction of greater over-protectiveness. The effect of both these tendencies is especially critical for male children; boys from father-absent
homes tend to be markedly more submissive and dependent. Studies

dealing explicitly with the influence of parental role structure in intact families are few and far between. Papanek (1957), in an unpublished doctoral dissertation, reports greater sex-role differentiation among children from homes in which the parental roles were differentiated. And in a carefully controlled study, Kohn and Clausen (1956) find that "schizophrenic patients more frequently than normal persons report that their mothers played a very strong authority role and the father a very weak authority role." Finally, what might best be called complementary evidence for our inferences regarding trends in family structure and their effects comes from the work of Miller, Swanson, and their associates (1958; 1960) on the differing patterns of behavior exhibited by families from *bureaucratic* and *entrepreneurial* work settings. These investigators argue that the entrepreneurial-bureaucratic dichotomy represents a new cleavage in American social structure that cuts across and overrides social class influences and carries with it its own characteristic patterns of family structure and socialization. Thus one investigation (Gold and Slater, 1958) contrasts the exercise of power in families of husbands employed in two kinds of job situations: (a) those working in large organizations with three or more levels of supervision; (b) those self-employed or working in small organizations with few levels of supervision. With appropriate controls for social class, equalitarian families were found more frequently in the bureaucratic groups; patriarchal and, to a lesser extent, matriarchal in the entrepreneurial setting. Another study (Miller and Swanson, 1958) shows that, in line with Miller and Swanson's hypotheses, parents from these same two groups tend to favor rather different ends and means of socialization, with entrepreneurial families putting considerably more emphasis on the development of independence and mastery and on the use of "psychological" techniques of discipline. These differences appear at both upper and lower middle class levels but are less pronounced in higher socio-economic strata. It is Miller and Swanson's belief, however, that the trend is toward the bureaucratic way of life, with its less structured patterns of family organization and child rearing. The evidence we have cited on secular changes in family structure and the inferences we have drawn regarding their possible effects on personality development are on the whole consistent with their views.

LOOKING FORWARD

If Miller and Swanson are correct in the prediction that America is moving toward a bureaucratic society that emphasizes, to put it colloquially, "getting along" rather than "getting ahead," then presumably we can look forward to ever increasing numbers of equalitarian families who, in turn, will produce successive generations of ever more adaptable but unaggressive "organization men." But recent signs do not all point in this direction. In our review of secular trends in child rearing practices we detected in the data from the more recent studies a slowing up in the headlong rush toward greater permissiveness and toward reliance on indirect methods of discipline. We pointed out also that if the most recent editions of well-thumbed guidebooks on child care are as reliable harbingers of the future as they have been in the past, we can anticipate something of a return to the more explicit discipline techniques of an earlier era. Perhaps the most important forces, however, acting to redirect both the aims and methods of child rearing in America emanate from behind the Iron Curtain. With the firing of the first Sputnik, Achievement began to replace Adjustment as the highest goal of the American way of life. We have become concerned—perhaps even obsessed—with "education for excellence" and the maximal utilization of our intellectual resources. Already, ability grouping, and the guidance counsellor who is its prophet, have moved down from the junior high to the elementary school, and parents can be counted on to do their part in preparing their youngsters for survival in the new competitive world of applications and achievement tests.

But if a new trend in parental behavior is to develop, it must do so in the context of changes already under way. And if the focus of parental authority is shifting from husband to wife, then perhaps we should anticipate that pressures for achievement will be imposed primarily by mothers rather than fathers. Moreover, the mother's continuing strong emotional investment in the child should provide her with a powerful lever for evoking desired performance. It is noteworthy in this connection that recent studies of the familial origins of need-achievement point to the matriarchy as the optimal context for development of the motive to excel (Strodtbeck, 1958; Rosen and D'Andrade, 1959).

The prospect of a society in which socialization techniques are directed toward maximizing achievement drive is not altogether a pleasant one. As a number of investigators have shown (Baldwin, Kalhorn and Breese, 1945; Baldwin, 1948; Haggard, 1957; Winterbottom, 1958; Rosen and D'Andrade, 1959), high achievement motivation appears to flourish in a family atmosphere of "cold democracy" in which initial high levels of maternal involvement are followed by pressures for independence and accomplishment.[5] Nor does the product of this process give ground for reassurance. True, children from achievement-oriented homes excel in planfulness and performance, but they are also more aggressive, tense, domineering, and cruel (Baldwin, Kalhorn and Breese, 1945; Baldwin, 1948; Haggard, 1957). It would appear that education for excellence if pursued single-mindedly may entail some sobering social costs.

But by now we are in danger of having stretched our chain of inference beyond the strength of its weakest link. Our speculative analysis has become far more speculative than analytic and to pursue it further

[5] Cold democracy under female administration appears to foster the development of achievement not only in the home but in the classroom as well. In a review of research on teaching effectiveness, Ackerman reports that teachers most successful in bringing about gains in achievement score for their pupils were judged "least considerate," while those thought friendly and congenial were least effective. (Ackerman, 1954.)

would bring us past the bounds of science into the realms of science fiction. In concluding our discussion, we would re-emphasize that speculations should, by their very nature, be held suspect. It is for good reason that, like "damn Yankees" they too carry their almost inseparable sobriquets: speculations are either "idle" or "wild." Given the scientific and social importance of the issues we have raised, we would dismiss the first of these labels out of hand, but the second cannot be disposed of so easily. Like the impetuous child, the "wild" speculation responds best to the sobering influence of friendly but firm discipline, in this instance from the hand of the behavioral scientist. As we look ahead to the next twenty-five years of human socialization, let us hope that the "optimal levels" of involvement and discipline can be achieved not only by the parent who is unavoidably engaged in the process, but also by the scientist who attempts to understand its working, and who—also unavoidably—contributes to shaping its course.

3 / New Patterns of Relationships between the Sexes among Preadolescents [1]

Carlfred B. Broderick and Stanley E. Fowler

New behaviors in the relationships between the sexes among youth from ten to thirteen years of age, such as the increase in friendly relations and romantic attachments and more flexibility and similarity in sex roles, are emerging. This pattern of preadolescent boy-girl relations, seemingly based on greater understanding and sharing of value orientations, is documented by Carlfred B. Broderick of the Pennsylvania State University and Stanley E. Fowler of the University of Georgia. It may be asked: How widespread are these changes in America? How do they relate to the learning of sex roles, sexual experimentation, marital happiness, child-rearing practices?

The first purpose of this paper is to document the emergence of new norms for cross-sex interaction among preadolescent children. The second is to offer an interpretation of this new development. The need for new research in this area can be appreciated if one compares descriptions of

[1] We wish to acknowledge our indebtedness to the University of Georgia General Research and to the Institute of Mental Health, National Institutes of Health, for their generous financial support of this study.

Reprinted from *Marriage and Family Living*, 1961, 23, 27–30, with the permission of the authors and the National Council on Family Relations.

preadolescent social life written in the 1930's with the findings of a survey published in 1958 by the U.S. Office of Education.

Furfey (1930, p. 101) [2] summarized his careful and systematic observations of boy-girl relations at this age as follows:

". . . girls are rigorously excluded from participation in masculine activities. The girl, however, does not feel the affront very keenly since she . . . has the same negative attitude toward boys that they have toward her."

This observation is reinforced by Campbell's (1939) [3] finding that:

(The boy), ". . . becomes sufficiently conscious of sex so that he does not wish to touch girls or show them any attention except under socially approved conditions such as in games or dancing."
(The girl), ". . . begins to be sufficiently conscious of sex so that she will not deliberately touch boys except under conventional circumstances as in games or dancing. She classifies games according to sex—boys play this, girls play that."

By contrast in a recent national survey, fourth, fifth, and sixth grade teachers gave quite a different picture:

". . . in some schools boys and girls do not seem to feel a strong need to separate. In fact, as low as the 4th grade and continuing through the 6th, they frequently ask for activities such as folk dancing and table games *together,* and dating begins in some cases . . . in 5th grade . . . Boys seem to do more personal grooming (some begin in the 4th), carrying a comb and using it, washing hands voluntarily, even occasionally wearing a tie. Girls begin to wear lipstick and nail polish and to dress up their hair. A few children wear 'steady rings,' and some date. . . . In grade 6, . . . 'They show they like each other in a friendly way.' 'They aren't so antagonistic as formerly.' 'They don't pick on each other so much.' 'They get along better.' 'Their social relations are much more mature.' " (Lewis, 1958, pp. 30–31) [4]

It will be seen that although the old pattern of avoidance may still be a potent factor in many groups, new patterns are emerging which promise to revolutionize boy-girl relationships at these ages.

In order to gain more information on these developments, in the spring of 1958 we studied the cross-sex interaction patterns of 264 fifth, sixth, and seventh graders in an elementary school located in a middle class district in a Southern urban community. Although detailed socio-

[2] This study is based upon systematic and longitudinal observations of 75 boys who were members of a club group and also interviews and observations of 450 grade school and high school boys.
[3] This study is based on carefully analyzed observations of 53 girls and 59 boys aged 5 to 17 who were members of a social club set up with this research in mind.
[4] "The study reported here was begun in 1955 . . . The purpose was to find out and report . . . what educators say about today's children in grades 4, 5, and 6. . . . Forty 1-day conferences were held, including approximately 1,300 persons from 415 school systems in 68 communities of 35 States and the District of Columbia. Large and small urban schools, consolidated and rural schools, and schools made up of different racial and socio-economic groups were represented. . . . The present bulletin, then, is the result of a survey of research, conferences, observations, and interviews." (From the Foreword)

economic data were not available, the school records of parental occupations indicate that a large majority of these children come from homes in the upper lower to upper middle class range. The age range of the entire sample was 9 to 13 years for girls and 9 to 14 years for boys. With relatively few exceptions the 108 fifth graders were 10 or 11, the 79 sixth graders 11 or 12, and the 77 seventh graders 12 or 13 years of age. Although our sample is drawn from a single community, it is representative in that it reflects the trends reported in the previously mentioned national survey.

THE EMERGING PATTERN

Nothing better illustrates the thawing of relationships between the sexes over the past quarter of a century than a comparison of friendship choices at these ages. Studies done in the twenties and thirties report univocally that the percentage of friendship choices extended across the sex barrier dropped to near zero in about the third or fourth grade and remained there through about the eighth, after which a slight rise was discernible. (See for example Hsia, 1928, Segoe, 1933, and Moreno, 1934.) By contrast, Table I shows that when the children in our sample were asked whom they liked best of all the children they knew (four choices were permitted) the choices across sex lines ranged from 19.7 per cent in the fifth grade to 14.6 per cent in the seventh. If we look at the percentage of children who chose at least one of four friends across sex lines (Table II), we find even more dramatic evidence of the new look in boy-girl relations at this age. From 51.9 per cent of the children in the fifth grade to 37.7 per cent of the children in the seventh grade chose one or more friends of the opposite sex. It would seem from this that although most boys and girls still prefer the companionship of their own sex, many have bridged the gulf between the sexes.

In addition to this increase in cross-sex friendship, there has been an increase in romantic interest among these children. Most probably ro-

Table I. Friendship Choices by Sex of Friend Chosen and by Grade *

| | Per Cent | | | |
Grade	Cross-Sex Choices	Same-Sex Choices	Total	Total Number
5th	19.7	80.3	100.0	350
6th	16.0	84.0	100.0	256
7th	14.6	85.4	100.0	253
TOTAL	17.1	82.9	100.0	859

* Each child had up to four choices. The units in this table are choices.

mance has always been an element for some children of this age. For example, in 1930 Furfey described Max, a 12 year old boy, who openly and ardently declared his affection for his sweetheart. In commenting on

Table II. Frequency of Choosing at Least One Friend of the Opposite Sex, by Grade *

| | Per Cent | | | |
Grade	One or More Cross-Sex Choices	No Cross-Sex Choices	Total	Total Number
5th	51.9	48.1	100.0	108
6th	41.8	58.2	100.0	79
7th	37.7	62.3	100.0	77
TOTAL	44.7	55.3	100.0	264

* Each child had up to four choices. The units in this table are children.

the situation, however, Furfey wrote, "Although love affairs are common enough among 12 year olds in fiction, a case like Max's is very rare in real life. This devotion to a girl is uncommon before adolescence and is a distinctly precocious trait" (Furfey, 1930, p. 125). Campbell (1939), in describing the typical 12 to 13 year old girl wrote, "She would not admit that a certain boy is attractive to her, though she begins to take a covert interest." This picture of generally disinterested boys and covertly interested girls contrasts sharply with the situation our study reveals. In our sample the great majority of children in each grade claimed to have a sweetheart (Table III), and most of these expected reciprocation (see in Table IV the responses to the question, "Does Sweetheart like you too?"). Moreover the majority of them apparently do not keep their feelings to themselves (see in Table IV, "Does Sweetheart know?", "Do your friends know?", "Do your folks know?"). That these children in fact do discuss their romances with others is borne out by the ability of their classmates to list the sweetheart pairs in their schoolroom with consider-

Table III. Frequency of Sweetheart Choice, by Grade and Sex

| | Per Cent | | | | | |
| | Have a Sweetheart | | No Sweetheart | | Total Number | |
Grade	Boys	Girls	Boys	Girls	Boys	Girls
5th	86.8	94.5	13.2	5.5	53	55
6th	86.4	97.1	13.6	2.9	44	35
7th	74.4	86.8	25.6	13.2	39	38
TOTAL	83.1	93.0	16.9	7.0	136	128

able accuracy, especially in those cases where the relationship was reciprocal or believed by one member to be reciprocal.

Table IV. Frequency of "Yes" Answers to Sweetheart Questions

| | Per Cent * | |
Question	Boys	Girls
Does sweetheart like you too?	62.2	51.3
Does sweetheart know?	68.1	68.9
Do friends know?	63.7	73.1
Do folks know?	62.0	74.8

* Per cents based on 113 boys and 119 girls who made a sweetheart choice.

Apparently, the question of dating was not investigated during the
period which we have used for comparison (1930–1939). In 1949, Hollingshead (1949, pp. 224–25) found that the most "adventurous" youngsters begin to date at the age of 12, and that among the 13 year olds in
Elmtown about 15 per cent of the boys and 20 per cent of the girls had
begun to date. Later studies by Smith (1952), Lowrie (1956), and Cameron
and Kenkel (1960) indicate the increasing incidence of dating at early
ages. The 1958 Office of Education survey previously mentioned indicated
that in some schools dating may begin as early as the fourth grade. Our
own data illustrate this trend (Table V), for in the fifth grade (10 and
11 year olds) 45 per cent of the boys and 36 per cent of the girls claim
to have had dating experience. By the seventh grade (12 and 13 year
olds) nearly 70 per cent of the boys and 53 per cent of the girls claim to
have had at least one date.

Table V also indicates that some experience with kissing is common
at these ages. Unfortunately we know of no comparable data from the
earlier period.

Table V. Dating and Kissing Experience, by Grade and Sex *

	Per Cent					
			Kissed Opposite Sex		Been Kissed by Opposite Sex	
Grade	Dated					
	Boy	Girl	Boy	Girl	Boy	Girl
5th	45.3	36.4	58.5	32.7	66.0	65.5
6th	52.3	28.6	79.5	34.3	72.7	54.3
7th	69.2	52.6	89.7	44.7	87.2	86.8
TOTAL	54.4	39.1	74.3	36.7	74.3	68.8

* These percentages based on full sample (see Table III for marginals).

Although the data we have seen so far are impressive, some of the most convincing evidence that times have changed comes from another portion of our study. Children were asked to rank the desirability of a companion of the same sex, a companion of the opposite sex, or of no companion at all in three different situations (eating, taking a walk, going to a movie). They could rank the cross-sex companion as first, second, or third choice. Table VI shows the results. In the sixth and seventh grades, the majority of boys and girls felt that when taking a walk or going to a movie, the companionship of the opposite sex is to be preferred above either of the alternate arrangements. Both sexes are more conservative when choosing an eating companion, but in the 7th grade the proportion preferring the opposite sex rises to nearly one-half even in this setting.

EXPLANATION OF DATA

In order to account for the changes which we have noted it may be profitable to look at the reasons that are generally put forth to explain the mutual withdrawal of the sexes when it occurs. Blair and Burton

Table VI. Preference for Opposite Sex Companion in Three Situations, by Grade and Sex *

| Situation | Grade | Per Cent | |
| | | Prefer Opposite Sex Companion | |
		Boys	Girls
Eating	5th	35.0	30.9
	6th	34.9	31.4
	7th	46.2	47.4
Walking	5th	49.0	50.9
	6th	69.8	51.4
	7th	71.8	68.4
Movie	5th	58.5	45.5
	6th	68.2	51.4
	7th	74.3	65.7

* Percentages based on full sample (see Table III for marginals).

(1951, pp. 38–39) summarize the conclusions of most writers in this field when they list three explanations for cross-sex antagonism. Let us consider each in its turn.

1. ". . . it is probably partially based on the differences in physical and intellectual development of boys and girls . . . ," referring to the fact that at this stage girls are approximately six months more mature

physically and mentally, and often a year or more advanced socially. These differences in themselves are considered to be less important as causes of hostility than the differences in interests and activities which they engender. Since these differences are continuing ones, we must assume that they exert an influence toward the separation of boys and girls of the same age today as they did a generation ago. Therefore, we must look elsewhere to find the factors which have given impetus to the changes in boy-girl relations.

2. ". . . antagonism is partly due to the effort of individuals to identify themselves more closely with their own sex." Through mutual withdrawal each group provides support for the values distinctive of its own sex roles. This is reinforced through the systematic rejection of the competing values of the opposite sex role. Boys would seem to have additional motivation for withdrawal, for at this age it is particularly difficult to maintain the superiority of the masculine role in the face of the double threat presented by the superior status of mothers and female teachers, and the superior academic and social achievements of girls the same age. The traditional masculine tactic seems to be disdain for the feminine values and withdrawal from competition with females into a world of strictly masculine interests. There is time enough to emerge when he may assert his superiority from a stronger position in adolescence. Many of these same elements are involved in Blair and Burton's third explanation of antagonism also.

3. "Perhaps it is a result of instilling into children the difference between boys' and girls' roles almost before birth." Traditionally boys and girls have had such different behavior and values expected of them that a period of role-training and practice in relative isolation from the opposite sex was a necessary preliminary to their attempt to fulfill these roles later in a heterosexual setting.

These last two explanations for cross-sex antagonism during pre-adolescence are based on differences in both the *status* and the *content* of traditional male and female roles. There is considerable evidence, however, that in large segments of our society these differences are diminishing. For example the 1955 Purdue Opinion Panel and a 1958 study by Landis and Landis both indicate that in the last generation the sex roles have become much more flexible and now overlap in many areas. The contents of the two sets of expectations are becoming more similar as women have achieved many masculine prerogatives and men have begun to share many traditionally feminine responsibilities. As these roles converge and the experiences and values of the two sexes become more similar, cross-sex hostility becomes less appropriate. Rejection of the values of the opposite sex loses much of its purpose when their values are very similar to one's own. Similarly, as the social statuses of the two sexes approach each other many boys seem to feel less need to defend a shaky claim to superiority during this period.

In addition to the negative effect of lessening the need for defensive withdrawal, increasing consensus in important values has been shown to provide a positive impetus to the development of friendly relations between the sexes.[5]

CONCLUSION

We set ourselves the task of documenting the emergence of new norms in the relationships between the sexes among youth 10–13 years of age and to interpret the trend. While old patterns of hostility and withdrawal are not dead, new behaviors and relationships are developing, based on greater understanding and sharing of value orientations. Further research must determine how widespread or unequal these changes may be throughout the nation. Yet if our interpretation of our findings is correct we may expect continued changes in the direction of greater cross-sex interactions and friendships, including romantic attachments at this age. With these may be expected more early cross-sex sexual experimentation, an increase in early marriage rates and greater difficulties in finding clearly defined and generally accepted social sex roles.

4 / Perception of the Parent-Child Relationship and Its Relation to Child Adjustment

Naomi M. Serot and Richard C. Teevan

This study by Naomi M. Serot and Richard C. Teevan of Bucknell University shows that a child's adjustment is related to his perception of his relationship with his family and not as has usually been thought, to the parents' perception of the relationship or the actual parent-child relationship. Focus on the child's perception of his home life extends our horizons toward understanding the dynamics of child development and personality.

One of the basic tenets of developmental psychology is the thesis that the early familial environment of the child, especially the pervading parental attitude or emotional tone of the parent-child relationship, is a fundamental factor influencing the development of personality. Clinical

[5] For the most sophisticated and up-to-date expression of this principle, see Newcomb (1956).

Reprinted from *Child Development*, 1961, *32*, 373–78, with the permission of the authors and the Society for Research in Child Development.

data offer strong support to the theory of a correlation between parent-child relationships and the nature of children's personality or relative adjustment (Jackson, Klatskin, and Wilkin, 1952; Martin, 1942–1943; Newell, 1934; Symonds, 1939). Much research has been effected for the purpose of isolating the particular attitudes which affect the child (Brown, 1942; Chwast, 1956; Hattwick and Stowell, 1936–1937; Zucker, 1943) and the qualities of personality that are the result of the specific attitudes determined (Radke, 1946). Often, however, this research has been inadequate or contradictory, leaving a confused picture of the relationships involved.

A review of the research offers a few explanations for the meagerness of results on this problem: Ausubel's (1954) study suggests that the essential relation is that which exists between the child's perception of his familial environment and his adjustment and not, as has been thought, between expressed parental attitudes and childhood adjustment. Based on evidence in Swanson's (1950) study of delinquents, it was thought that, rather than use attitudes as good indicators of the nature of the parent-child relationship, it might be more useful to measure the proximity of a given child's relationship to the theoretical ideal relationship. These two possibilities suggested a third: if it is the child's perception of his familial relationships which affects his adjustment, then parental perception of the parent-child relationship may well disagree with the child's perception of the same, and, if so, the former is unlikely to be related to the child's adjustment. On the basis of these suggestions, the following hypotheses were constructed:

1. A child's perception of his parent-child relationship is correlated to his adjustment: the well adjusted child will perceive his parent-child relationship as relatively happy and close to the theoretical ideal, whereas the maladjusted child's perception of his relationship will be far from ideal.

2. There is little agreement between parental perception of the parent-child relationship and the child's perception of the same.

3. Parental perception of the parent-child relationship, therefore, does not correlate with the offspring's adjustment.

METHOD

Subjects

The sample of children consisted of 102 boys and girls, 9 and 10 years of age, who attended the fourth grade in public schools. The schools used were chosen because of the variability in the socioeconomic level of the parents and because of a reputed range of student adjustment. Fourth graders were used because they are young enough not to be involved in adolescent dynamics and old enough to comprehend the tests, and, also, it was thought that they might be more willing to respond truthfully than older children, more aware of social meanings, would be. The mean number of siblings was three.

The parents were those of the selected children, excluding those of children who obtained the mean adjustment score. Seventy sets (both mothers and fathers) were contacted. Most of the parents were of upper-lower and lower-middle class, with about one-sixth of lower-lower and one-sixth of middle- or upper-middle class.

Instruments

The California Test of Personality (CTP), Elementary Series AA, was used to measure the children's adjustment. A high score on the CTP indicates relatively good adjustment.

The Swanson (1950) Child-Parent Relationship Scale (CPRS) [1] was used to measure perception of the parent-child relationship. Swanson, using the scale on adolescents, found that it did not discriminate well at the ideal end of the test, but that it was a good discriminator at the other end of the scale. Since other relationship measures have proven to be so inadequate, the CPRS seemed to be the most usable measure in spite of this difficulty. The language and concepts of the scale were sufficiently elementary to be comprehended by fourth graders, and the form of the items was such that they could be reworded to provide a parallel measure for the parents' perception and, thus, afford a means of comparison. Consequently, the parents' scale [2] contained the same questions, but they were reworded so that each item asked the parent for his perception of the relationship. A high score on the CPRS indicates a poor parent-child relationship as perceived by the subject.

In addition to the two tests, a short information questionnaire was used for each student. It included such items as name and address, whether or not the child lived at home with both real parents, father's occupation, and number of children in the family.

Procedure

The teachers of the three chosen classes distributed letters asking for parents' permission to use their children. The children were given no information previous to the testing time. The day the tests were administered, the children were told that the purpose of the tests was to gather information about fourth graders as a whole and that the tester was not interested in individual people. No names were requested, and the fact that names would remain anonymous was emphasized. Each test was coded so that the two tests and questionnaire of a given subject could be identified. The children were also told that their true feelings were being sought and that there were no right or wrong answers: they were

[1] [Appended to the selection.]   [2] [Appended to the selection.]

to answer as they really felt. These facts were reiterated, and it was suggested that they ask questions when they had difficulty recognizing words. It was found that those children who could not recognize words could, however, understand them when they were pronounced for them. The CTP was administered first, according to the standardized instructions in the manual. Each child was allowed to finish the test at his own rate of speed. The CPRS was given next, again with no names requested and with reminders about answering according to true feelings with no fear of being identified. Thirdly, after all the tests were collected, the children filled out the information questionnaire.

The parents were sent letters explaining, nebulously, the nature of the study, requesting their participation, and giving instructions for taking the tests. Two copies of the parental form of the CPRS were included. Mothers and fathers were asked to participate individually. Names were not requested, and, again, the tests were coded so that they could be matched with children's tests. Two weeks after the letters and tests were mailed, a letter of reminder was sent out, requesting that those who had not done so return their questionnaires. Thirty-one sets of parents and five additional mothers replied adequately. Fifty-one per cent of the mothers, therefore, and 44 per cent of the fathers participated. The percentage of returns, compared to other studies (Stogdill, 1934–1935; Stott, 1940), was quite high, as much of the past research has been based on less than 20 per cent returns. The mean adjustment score of the children whose parents participated in the study was the same as the total child sample. The returns, therefore, were considered adequate.

The final parent sample consisted of 31 fathers and 36 mothers. Ten of the original children were absent the day the tests were given, one did not receive permission to participate, and three were omitted because they did not live at home with both real parents; thus, the total child sample consisted of 88 children, 44 boys and 44 girls.

RESULTS

The Pearson product-moment correlation coefficient between the children's CPRS and their scores on the personal Adjustment part of the CTP was −.77; the Social Adjustment scale of the CTP, minus the Family Relationship component (one group of items on the scale which is similar to the CPRS), correlated −.84 with the CPRS; the correlation of the CPRS with the Total Adjustment score, minus the Family Relationship component, was −.80. All three correlations are significant beyond the 1 per cent level of confidence.[3] A negative correlation means that a low score on the CTP (poor adjustment) correlates with a high score on the CPRS (perception of the parent-child relationship as far from ideal). Thus, there is significant support for the first hypothesis: the well-

---

[3] All correlations in this paper were calculated on two-tailed tests.

adjusted child perceives his parent-child relationship as relatively happy and close to the theoretical ideal, and the maladjusted child's perception of his parent-child relationship is far from ideal.

The correlation between mothers' and offsprings' CPRS scores was .17; between the fathers' and offsprings' scores, it was .19. Both correlations are insignificant and, therefore, support the second hypothesis: there is very little agreement between parental perception of the parent-child relationship and the child's perception of the same.

A correlation of .04 was found between mothers' CPRS scores and their children's scores on Total Adjustment, minus the Family Relationship component of the CTP. The correlation between the fathers' CPRS scores and the children's adjustment was .16. Both correlations are insignificant and support the third hypothesis: the parents' perception of the parent-child relationship is not related to their children's adjustment.[4]

DISCUSSION

In an attempt to discover the limitations of the results, a chi square was determined between socioeconomic status of the family (measured by occupation) and the children's adjustment. There was no significant relation. The means for the CTP and the CPRS were the same for children in large families as they were for those in small families. Socioeconomic status and the number of children in the families were excluded as factors that could have affected the correlations. There seemed to be no other common contaminating factor which could have influenced the test results. Because of the young age of the children and the manner in which the tests were administered, it is fair to assume that the children responded truthfully. It is highly improbable that a child of 9 or 10 years of age could so alter his responses as to make his scores on both tests correlate, and it is even more improbable that a large enough part of the sample could have seen through the tests. It also seems justifiable to assume that the parents were honest, for had they not been sincere they need not have participated. Also, they often added comments to the test questions, indicating thoughtfulness and concern. Based on information given by the teachers, it is obvious that ability to answer discriminatively did not correlate with IQs.

The only indicated limitation to the test results is the skewed discriminating character of the CPRS. It differentiated more adequately on this sample of children than it did on Swanson's sample, although it still was a better discriminator at the upper end of the scale. As the test was a reliable indicator of a poor parent-child relationship, it seemed that, in-

---

[4] The product-moment correlation coefficient for an agreement score between mothers and fathers and their children's CTP scores was .21, which is not significant. For the same sexed parent and the CTP, the coefficient was −.47; for the opposite sexed parent and CTP, it was .20. It must be remembered that two-thirds of the parents who responded were parents of boys and that boys had lower adjustment scores than did girls.

stead of negating the validity of the correlations, the broad rather than precise differentiating characteristic of the scale merely decreased the size of the correlation. In defense of this conclusion, it is noted that, when the correlations were determined for each class separately, the greatest correlation came from the class with the most maladjusted children (independently determined).

The major implications of the results focus on the child's perception of his home life. It seems that an important developmental step has been underemphasized in theory and almost absent from research. Previous experiments have tried to relate parental attitudes or the quality of the parent-child relationship (measured by questionnaires or interviews) directly to the nature of child adjustment. They have not discovered definite one-to-one relations, for they have failed to take into account the fact that the child reacts to his perception of the situation and not directly to the situation itself. The results of this study imply that, when this fact is recognized, the expected correlations appear.

The parent-child relationship of a family, which includes parental attitudes toward childrearing, involves many subtleties which have individual, often subconscious, meanings for all concerned. These meanings influence each individual's perception of the relationship. The child's perception of the relationship is of extreme importance to him, for it is directly related to his adjustment; the actual parent-child relationship is only indirectly related to a child's adjustment. Studies of the dynamics of child psychology must, therefore, discover the course of development of children's perception of their familial environment and the factors that allow parental perception of the same environment to be so very different. Only then will it be feasible to discover more exactly the relation between child adjustment and parental attitudes.

SUMMARY

A review of the research performed within the area of parent-child relationships and child adjustment led to the formulation of three hypotheses: (a) a child's adjustment is related to his perception of his relationship with his family; (b) the child's perception of the relationship is unrelated to his parents' perception of the same; and (c) the parents' perception of the relationship is unrelated to his offspring's adjustment. The method used to test these hypotheses was described. The statistical results obtained significantly support the hypotheses.

CHILD-PARENT RELATIONSHIP SCALE (CPRS)

The following sentences are arranged to find out how *you* feel about *your* life at home. The right answers will be your true feelings about each sentence.

You are *not* asked to sign your name to this paper.

Please circle an answer for every question. "Y" means "Yes," "N" means "No," and the "?" mark means "Uncertain" or "Not Sure."

1. It is hard for me to feel pleasant at home.   Y   N   ?
2. My parents criticize me too much.
3. My parents have faith in me.
4. As far as ideas are concerned, my parents and I live in different worlds.
5. My parents get angry easily.
6. I get a "square deal" at home.
7. When they make me mind, my parents are nice about it.
8. As I have known it, family life is happy.
9. My parents nag at me.
10. My parents are mean to me.
11. I find more understanding at home than elsewhere.
12. My parents are fair with me in money matters.
13. My parents quarrel with me a lot.
14. It is hard for me to be pleasant and happy when my parents are around.
15. I am happy and contented at home.
16. My parents tell other people things about me that I think they should not mention.
17. I have to keep quiet or leave the house to keep peace at home.
18. I am "picked on" at home.
19. My parents take an interest in the things I like.
20. My parents are what I think ideal parents should be.
21. I believe that my parents think I will not "amount to much."
22. I feel that my parents do not trust me.
23. There is real love and affection for me at home.
24. My parents try to understand my problems and worries.
25. My parents compare me unfavorably with other children.
26. My parents irritate me.
27. We have good times together at home.
28. I feel contented at home.
29. I talk over important plans with my parents.
30. I often have good times at home with my family.
31. I wish that I had different parents than the one I have.
32. My friends have happier homes than I do.
33. I feel that my parents try to deceive me.
34. My parents take the attitude of "Oh, you don't want to do that," to the things I would like to do.
35. I enjoy going out with my parents.
36. My parents criticize me unjustly.
37. I feel nervous at home.
38. Other people understand me better than my parents do.

39. My parents say that I am not as nice to them as I should be.
40. My parents expect too much from me.
41. My parents point out my faults to my friends.
42. I think that my parents try to "slip things over" on me.
43. I feel like leaving home for good.
44. I feel that my parents are pleased with me.
45. My parents usually treat me fairly and sensibly.
46. When I ask my parents if I may do something, they say, "No."
47. My parents can be completely trusted.
48. I change from loving my parents to hating them and back again.
49. I feel "close" to my parents.
50. I know that my parents are my friends.

PARENT-CHILD RELATIONSHIP SCALE (PCRS)

The following sentences are arranged to find out how *you* feel about *your* relationships with your child. The right answers will be your true feelings about each sentence.

You are not asked to sign your name to this paper.

Please circle an answer for every question. "Y" means "Yes," "N" means "No," and "?" means "Not Certain" or "Unsure."

1. I make our home a pleasant place for our child.   Y N ?
2. I criticize my child too much.
3. I have faith in my child.
4. As far as ideas are concerned, my child and I live in different worlds.
5. I get angry easily.
6. I give my child a "square deal" at home.
7. When I make my child mind, I am nice about it.
8. Our family life is happy.
9. I nag at my child.
10. I am often mean to my child.
11. I give my child more understanding at home than he gets elsewhere.
12. I am fair with my child in money matters.
13. I quarrel with my child a lot.
14. I make it easy for my child to be pleasant and happy when he is around me.
15. I make my home a place where my child is happy and contented.
16. I tell other people things about my child that he might think I should not mention.

17. In our home, my child has to keep quiet or leave to keep things peaceful.
18. I "pick on" my child at home.
19. I take an interest in the things my child likes.
20. I am what I think an ideal parent should be.
21. I often think my child will not "amount to much."
22. I believe my child is trustworthy.
23. I offer my child real love and affection at home.
24. I try to understand my child's problems and worries.
25. I sometimes compare my child unfavorably with other children.
26. I often feel as though I am irritating my child.
27. We have good times together at home.
28. I ordinarily make my home a place where my child can feel contented.
29. My child talks to me about plans that are important to him.
30. My child often has good times at home with his family.
31. I think my child sometimes wishes he had different parents than the ones he has.
32. My child's friends have happier homes than he does.
33. I sometimes find it necessary to try to deceive my child.
34. I often take the attitude of "Oh, you don't want to do that," to the things my child wants to do.
35. My child enjoys going out with me.
36. I sometimes feel I criticize my child unjustly.
37. I believe there are things about our home which might make our child nervous there.
38. Sometimes I think other people understand my child better than I do.
39. I sometimes tell my child that he is not as nice to me as he should be.
40. I sometimes feel that I expect too much from my child.
41. I sometimes criticize my child in the presence of his friends.
42. I sometimes try to "slip things over" on my child.
43. I think that my relationships with my child sometimes get so bad that he might want to leave home for good.
44. I am usually pleased with my child.
45. I usually treat my child fairly and sensibly.
46. When my child asks for permission to do something, I often say "No."
47. My child can trust me completely.
48. Sometimes I do things that might make my child hate me, other times I do things that might make him love me.
49. My child feels "close" to me.
50. I am a friend to my child.

5 / Achievement, Striving, Social Class, and Test Anxiety

Martin L. Hoffman, Spiro B. Mitsos,
and Roland E. Protz

Recent research in American communities demonstrates that such factors as sex, social class, and race effect the child's development and behavior. This study compares working-class and middle-class high school juniors and seniors in test performance under financial incentive. The results indicate that whereas working-class performance tends to rise uniformly in response to material reward, middle-class performance either rises or touches off anxiety responses that lower performance. "The source of this anxiety is a problem for further research." The authors are Martin L. Hoffman of the Merrill-Palmer School, Spiro B. Mitsos of Evansville State Hospital, and Roland E. Protz of the Beatty Memorial Hospital.

Need Achievement scores of middle-class, as compared to working-class, adolescents have been found by Douvan (1956) and Rosen (1956) to be high under ordinary test conditions; and by Douvan (1956) to remain at the same level even when a desired prize is offered for superior performance. Thus, achievement striving in the middle class appears to be highly internalized and relatively unaffected by external reward.

On the assumption that achievement striving relates positively to performance, it was hypothesized that middle-class performance would also be relatively unaffected by external reward; more specifically, that compared to working-class Ss, middle-class Ss would show little improvement in test performance under financial incentive. Two studies were done, one using a simple motor test (Study A) and the other, a written intelligence test (Study B).

METHOD

Social Class

The details of the class measure are presented by Douvan (1956). In brief, Ss designated as working class were those who identified with the

Reprinted from the *Journal of Abnormal and Social Psychology*, 1958, *56*, 401–3, with the permission of the authors and the American Psychological Association.

working class and whose fathers did manual work; those designated as middle class identified with the middle class and their fathers' occupations largely involved dealing with people.

STUDY A

The procedure of Study A followed that used by Douvan (1956). Students in their regular high school classrooms performed a simple number-tracing task under a time limit that guaranteed that no one would finish. In five classes the test was introduced simply as a measure of "visual-motor coordination, how well your hands and eyes work together." For six other classes it was added that in order to encourage the students to try their hardest, a five-dollar reward would be offered to everyone scoring above "a certain point." In order to minimize competitive motivation, the possibility of everyone's getting the reward was emphasized.

The Ss in Study A were high school juniors and seniors in a medium sized midwestern city (population about 80,000). From a pool of 271 students, 122 were selected who clearly fit the middle-class criteria and 37 who clearly fit the working-class criteria. It turned out that 68 middle-class and 24 working-class Ss had taken the test under the financial reward condition while 54 middle-class and 13 working-class Ss had performed under the no-reward condition.

STUDY B

In Study B, a before-after design was used. Alternate forms of the Otis Quick Scoring Mental Ability Test were given the same Ss under the two conditions. The setting in each case was a large assembly hall in which all students took the test together. Gamma Test Form C was administered first. The procedure given in the Manual of Directions was followed except that the students were allowed to work for only ten minutes. The instructions to the students stated that the test measured one's "ability to think." Gamma Test Form C was given one week later with no advance notice that there was going to be a retest. No information was provided regarding previous level of performance. The instructions included mention that the test was similar to the one taken previously, that we were now interested in how much they could improve their scores, and that five dollars would be given to "those of you who do a good deal better on the test than they did a week ago." To minimize competitive motivation, it was added that "all sizeable improvements would be rewarded."

A questionnaire asking each S to estimate (a) the extent of his desire for a five-dollar prize and (b) how hard he would work for this sum, was used to provide an index of conscious motivation aroused by the reward offer.[1]

The Otis was scored in the standard manner, i.e., adding the num-

[1] [Appended to the selection.]

ber of items answered correctly. To take into account changes in the number of errors, the tests were also scored in terms of right minus wrong.

The Ss in Study B were high school seniors in a small midwestern city (population about 15,000), none of whom had ever taken the Otis before. From a pool of 150 students, 47 middle-class and 27 working-class Ss were selected using our dual criterion.

RESULTS AND DISCUSSION

STUDY A

The data for Study A (Table 1) confirm the hypothesis that the performance differential under the two test conditions would be smaller for the middle class than for the working class. The working class improved significantly in the reward condition while middle-class scores declined slightly.

STUDY B

In Study B, with either total-correct or right-minus-wrong scoring of the Otis, both the middle- and working-class Ss obtained significantly higher scores in the reward than in the non-reward condition (Table 2). The middle class showed less improvement, as expected, but the difference is not significant ($p < .3$ with total-correct scoring and $p < .2$ with right-minus-wrong scoring). The hypothesis of less improvement in the middle class receives statistical support, however, when we disregard the amount of improvement and consider only the percentage of Ss who show any improvement at all. Thus, with total-correct scoring, 85.2 per cent of the working-class and 61.7 per cent of the middle-class Ss showed an improvement ($p < .02$). With right-minus-wrong scoring the percentage of working- and middle-class Ss showing improvement are 77.8 and 55.3 respectively ($p < .03$).

Results of the questionnaire on the desirability of the five-dollar reward indicate, as also reported by Douvan (1956), that there was no class difference in conscious desire for the reward. Apparently the reward was large enough to elicit a high degree of motivation from the Ss regardless of class position. Therefore, the greater number of working-class Ss showing improvement can not be attributed simply to the fact that money is scarcer in their environment.

Achievement striving and test anxiety. A greater percentage of middle-class than working-class Ss obtained *lower* scores on the second testing when the reward was offered than on the first testing when there was no reward—25.5 per cent compared to 11.1 per cent with total-correct scoring ($p < .1$), and 38.3 per cent compared to 14.8 per cent with right-minus-wrong scoring ($p < .02$). These Ss did more poorly in the reward condition even though (a) they were as motivated as the others to obtain the

Table 1. Middle-Class and Working-Class Performance on a Motor Task under Two Reward Conditions

| | MATERIAL REWARD | | | | |
| | Absent | | Present | | |
Class	N	Mean	N	Mean	p
Middle	54	20.11	68	19.87	. .
Working	13	16.00	24	20.00	.01

Table 2. Middle-Class and Working-Class Improvement from No-Reward to Reward Condition

| | | Number of Items Correct | | | Right Minus Wrong | | |
Class	N	No Reward	Reward	t	No Reward	Reward	t
Middle	47	29.7	32.4	3.84 ***	23.8	25.4	1.83 *
Working	27	26.2	29.5	5.35 ***	17.1	19.9	3.52 ***

* $p < .05$.   *** $p < .001$.

Table 3. Percentage of Middle-Class and Working-Class Ss with Low, Middle, and High Improvement

Class	Low [a]	Middle [a]	High [a]
Total correct			
Middle	46.8	21.3	31.9
Working	25.9	48.2	25.9
Right minus wrong			
Middle	46.8	19.2	34.0
Working	18.5	55.5	25.9

[a] Low, middle, and high cut-off points obtained by trisecting the total distribution based on all 150 Ss in the initial pool.

five dollar prize, as indicated by their questionnaire responses, (b) they had as much room for improvement, i.e., their initial scores were comparable to the initial scores of the others, and (c) they should have shown at least some improvement due to practice effect, since the two test forms were given only a week apart and contained items of highly similar content and level of difficulty. It therefore seems necessary to conclude, in line with recent test anxiety research, that the Ss whose scores went down actually increased their strivings in response to the reward offer, but in so doing touched off efficiency-reducing emotional responses such as fears and expectations of failure.

Increased striving can also be inferred on the part of most of the remaining middle-class Ss, since all but four of them made some improvement, especially since the middle-class improvers actually improved to a greater extent than the working-class improvers ($p < .1$ for total correct and $p < .2$ for right-minus-wrong scoring).

This analysis suggests that (a) most middle-class Ss, contrary to the finding by Douvan mentioned earlier, increase their achievement strivings under external reward conditions and (b) the effect of such an increase in striving in the middle class is either to improve performance or to impair it. It would follow that the distribution of improvement scores for the middle class should be bimodal and highly variable. Both these expectations are borne out in our data. The middle-class distribution shows tendencies toward bimodality (Table 3) and it is more variable than the working-class distribution (F ratio significant at the .05 level with either total-correct or right-minus-wrong scoring).

McClelland (1953) suggests that fantasy verbalization as well as test performance is depressed by anxiety about achievement and failure, and that as a result an S who is high on achievement striving may obtain spuriously low scores on his projective need Achievement measure if he is also high on anxiety. If such anxiety about achievement and failure can be aroused, or perhaps intensified, by an increase in striving induced by external reward, and if this occurs mainly in the middle class as the present study suggests, a number of middle-class Ss should be expected to obtain lower need Achievement scores in reward than in non-reward conditions. This reason could explain Douvan's (1956) finding that the mean need Achievement score for the middle class does not rise in the reward condition.

CONCLUSIONS

Both studies support the hypothesis that middle-class test performance is more highly generalized and less subject to improvement through increased striving for material reward than working-class performance. Study B, with before-after data, suggests further that although middle-class Ss may have achievement strivings that are relatively highly internalized and thus generalized to situations which have no external reward, they are like the working-class Ss in that these strivings *do* increase when a reward is offered. *The main difference between the two groups seems to be that while working-class striving and performance tend to rise uniformly in response to reward stimuli, in the middle-class reward-induced increases in striving may either raise the level of performance or touch off anxiety responses that lower it.* The source of this anxiety is a problem for further research. The literature on social class would suggest that, whether or not a prize were offered, the attempt to improve one's performance on a task designated as measuring the "ability to think" might readily engage the self-esteem needs of many middle-class Ss; moreover, for some *S*s, attempting to improve may have this effect even with less ego-involving tasks. The resulting anxiety, which might be called "improvement anxiety" to distinguish it from other kinds of test anxiety, could have resulted in the performance decrements found here. Another possible explanation of these decrements is that the offer of a prize produced guilt feelings in those *S*s for whom competition with siblings and peers for adult rewards is synonomous with the expression of unacceptable hostile impulses. Such *S*s might have felt competitive despite the announcement by the adult that it was possible for everyone to win the prize. Doing poorly under these conditions could function as a guilt-avoiding mechanism.

QUESTIONNAIRE

Place a check mark in front of the words that describe best how you feel. Choose one statement for each sentence. Please do not sign your name.

1. I would like to win a $5.00 prize.
   ____a. very much ____b. quite a lot ____c. a little more than average ____d. a little less than average ____e. not very interested ____f. not at all interested

2. I think most students in this school would like to win it.
   ____a. very much ____b. quite a lot ____c. a little more than average ____d. a little less than average ____e. would not be very interested ____f. would not be at all interested

3. Compared with other students, I would like to win a $5.00 prize.
   ____a. much more than most ____b. more than most ____c. about the same as most ____d. less than most ____e. much less than most

4. How hard would you try for such a prize?
   ____a. my very hardest ____b. pretty hard ____c. harder than most ____d. not as hard as most ____e. not very hard ____f. not at all

5. How much time would you spend trying for a $5.00 prize?
   ____a. 5 hours or more ____b. 3 to 5 hours ____c. 2 to 3 hours ____d. 1 to 2 hours ____e. ½ to 1 hour ____f. up to half an hour ____g. none

Teacher Personality
and Behavior

6 / Teachers' and Clinicians' Attitudes
toward the Behavior Problems of Children:
A Reappraisal [1]

Harry Beilin

*Research in the last thirty years on differences in the attitudes of teachers
and clinicians toward child behavior reveals that although at present
there is greater congruence between them, the teacher's role remains
primarily task-oriented, the clinician's adjustment-oriented. These
differences as well as the relationships of the sex and age of the child
and teacher attitude toward behavior problems are discussed
from the standpoint of role theory in the following article by
Harry Beilin of Brooklyn College.*

The contrast between contemporary American education and that of
40 or 50 years ago is striking in at least one respect, the influence of psychology, in particular, clinical psychology.[2] It would require little effort
to detail the many and diverse ways teacher training, parent education
and child care reflect the consequences of psychology's influence. The

[1] The author is indebted to Martin Hamburger and Louis Rosenzweig for their
critical reading of this paper.

[2] Although the period following the first World War saw the impact of the testing
movement and the effects of Behaviorism, it was not till the 1930's and 1940's that
clinical psychology became a part of the child development and educational scene in a
major way.

Reprinted from *Child Development*, 1959, *30*, 9–25, with the permission of the author
and Society for Research in Child Development.

future historian will undoubtedly dwell upon the part played by E. K. Wickman's (1928) Commonwealth Fund monograph, "Children's Behavior and Teachers' Attitudes" in this development. Wickman's report, which contrasts teachers' and "mental hygienists'" attitudes toward the behavior problems of children evoked an assault upon the teacher's mode of dealing with children when it made evident that teachers' attitudes were widely at variance with those of clinicians. The effect of its publication is still felt. The contiguity of events might suggest to some a causal relationship between widespread knowledge of the Wickman findings and the emergence of clinical psychology as a force in contemporary education. However, a more temperate and realistic appraisal would accept the ubiquitous penetration of psychology into American life and not as a condition unique to education. The impact of the monograph was in actuality only one of a series of challenges to the values and attitudes of educational personnel. But irrespective of its true role—whether as reflection, or as initiator of a Zeitgeist—the place of the Wickman study in education and child psychology has been significant and will probably continue to be.

Wickman's results, in the main, suggest that mental hygienists were primarily concerned with *withdrawing* and other nonsocial forms of behavior in children of elementary school age, whereas teachers of these same children were more concerned with *classroom management, authority,* and *sex problems.* The results influenced many (starting with Wickman) to urge teachers to adopt a hierarchy of attitudes closer to that of the clinician. This view presumed that the clinician's judgment should be accepted as the criterion for adequate and inadequate behavior. Few have challenged this thesis.

The intent of the present review is to examine what the result of 30 years of research suggests for continued acceptance of this point of view. To anticipate, it will be suggested that Wickman's findings be reinterpreted and his prescription for change in educational policy modified.

THE WICKMAN STUDY

The Wickman studies were begun in Minneapolis in 1924, but a more ambitious program was undertaken in Cleveland in 1925–1926, where the following was done:

1. In a single pilot school, teachers' characterizations of undesirable behavior, with indications of "sensitiveness" to their occurrence, were elicited by questionnaire.

2. Teachers' attitudes toward various types of problems were obtained by three measures (detailed in part below).

3. On rating scales, teachers noted their reactions to problems themselves, then to pupils in whom the problems were observed, and finally to the total adjustment of their pupils.

4. Subsequently, the teachers from 13 schools in six communities and

two additional teacher groups enrolled in graduate school were studied using the rating scale method developed for the pilot study. The most important feature of this involved the rating of a number of behaviors obtained from the teachers' original freely-given characterizations of problem behavior. The results are reported as mean ratings and rankings of mean ratings.

5. Finally, 30 "mental hygienists" (8 psychiatrists, 4 psychologists, 13 psychiatric social workers and 5 teachers with social work background) from child guidance clinics in three cities were studied for their attitudes toward 50 of the same behaviors rated by teachers. The mean ratings and rankings of ratings were then contrasted and correlated with those of teachers.

The rating instructions for teachers stressed: (a) *present* problems, (b) "seriousness" of the problems or "difficulties" created by them, and (c) rapid responses to the rating scale. With clinicians, the emphasis was on (a) relevance of the problem behavior for *future* adjustment, (b) though "seriousness" and "difficulty" were retained, the focus was on the "importance" of the behavior, and (c) no time limit was imposed for response to the rating scale.

The principal results can be summarized as follows:

1. Teachers were most aware of overt and aggressive behaviors, inattention to school tasks, and behaviors which violated their standards of morality. They were much less concerned with behaviors indicative of social or emotional maladjustment not directly related to school routine.

2. Boys were reported more frequently than girls for behavior problems.

3. Teachers preferred the less active, more compliant behavior of girls to the more aggressive behavior of boys. Desirable conduct for teachers, then, took on the distinguishing characteristics of girl behavior.

4. "Mental hygienists" considered withdrawing and other nonsocial forms of behavior most serious and discounted the teachers' stress on antisocial behavior and violations of school rules.

5. There was a rank order correlation of $-.22$ between the rankings by mental hygienists of 50 behavior problems and the original Cleveland teachers' ($N = 28$) rankings of the same behaviors. The correlation was $-.11$ when the full sample was used ($N = 511$).

These findings were interpreted by Wickman in Thorndikian stimulus-response terms. The teachers distinguish, he said, between the attacking and withdrawing types of behavior problems. Their attitudes are principally determined, however, by the attacking nature of the child's conduct. The aggressive behaviors are identified and considered more serious because the teacher is aroused to counterattack by virtue of the frustration in him. On the other hand, the responses to withdrawing forms of behavior are modified by sympathy and protective feelings.

On the basis of these findings Wickman then proposed that:

1. Teachers' attitudes should be influenced to become more like the "ideal" clinicians. (Clinicians' attitudes are considered ideal because their

judgments are (ostensibly) based upon knowledge of research in child adjustment.)

2. Teacher attitudes should be changed not by exhortation but by (a) information about child behavior through seminars and other learning experiences; and (b) practice in therapy with children.

3. Teachers' functions be less concerned with intellectual learnings and more with life adjustment.

After the appearance of the 1928 monograph some serious limitations in method and conception were pointed out by G. Watson (1933) in a critical note [3] which are as cogent now as when first offered. The majority of efforts to rectify the deficiencies have concerned only some of the criticisms. The others, however, may be of as great issue as those treated.

Watson's objections were:

1. *The procedures themselves are open to criticism.*
   a. The directions given teachers and clinicians were not the same. Teachers were instructed to rank behaviors for *present* seriousness; clinicians, for *future* adjustment.
   b. The time given to respond to the questionnaires was not identical. Teachers were under the control of the experimenter; clinicians were allowed an extended period to respond.
   c. No definitions were given for the behavioral terms to be rated leaving to each subject the interpretation of the terms, and thus further reducing comparability of the results.

The issues raised by Watson's concern with methodology are intimately related to other criticisms.

2. *The choice of mental hygienists' attitudes toward the behavior problems of children as a criterion for evaluating teachers' attitudes toward the same problems is open to question.*

The Wickman study and others that follow (though not all) accept the clinicians' judgments as a criterion either implicitly or explicitly. Watson observes that there is no reason to suppose clinicians to be "correct" and teachers not, rather than vice versa. Wickman is questioned for not even considering this possibility.

3. *There has been too ready an acceptance of a causal relationship between withdrawing behavior in childhood and maladjustment in adulthood.*

In addition to questioning whether the term "withdrawing" means the same thing to teachers and clinicians, Watson questioned whether withdrawing behavior in childhood is casually related to, or predictive of, maladjustment in adulthood. Although this is contended in more than one theoretical position, there was very little evidence for the validity of this claim in 1928, and little more is available now. In

---

[3] One writer has even wondered how the study could have been so widely and uncritically accepted with these limitations. The answer probably rests in the fact that its thesis was part of a powerfully developing movement.

Watson's paper there is reference to a pilot study which, for all its limitations, casts some doubt on the aforementioned assumption.

THE LITERATURE

After the Watson critique there was concern for the validity of the results and replications were undertaken with one or another modification in design, ultimately making comparability difficult.[4]

The studies, in the main, fall into the following groupings according to procedures used:

A. *Studies employing descriptions of problem behavior.*
    1. Teacher nomination of children with problems, followed by description and classification of problem behaviors.[5]
        a. In addition to all or part of the above, some use is made of a rating scale of problem behaviors.[6]
    2. Teacher description of problem behavior (with no reference to specific children) from which a rating scale is developed or the descriptions themselves are used.[7]
    3. Children identified and described as problems by a social or therapeutic agency (Blanchard and Paynter, 1924; Rogers, 1942a).

B. *Studies employing the Wickman rating scales.*
    1. With Wickman's direction (Beilin, 1958; Hurlock and McDonald, 1934; Schruppe and Gjerde, 1953).
    2. With modifications of Wickman's directions.[8]

Confirmation of Wickman Findings

Early studies that made use of the Wickman scales "confirmed" what Wickman had found in that the rankings made by the teachers in other communities approximated those of Wickman's teachers. Boynton and McGaw (1934) obtained a correlation of .87 between Wickman's and their own teacher ratings. Dickson (1932), Laycock (1934), Young-Masten (1938) and Yourman (1932) gave similar results as did the Epstein (1941) and Snyder (1934) studies. Thompson (1940) offered the added information that teachers were more nearly in agreement with the rankings made by

[4] We shall consider all studies found that bear upon the problems focused on by Wickman and his critics in spite of the lack of comparability. Some studies are included which antedate Wickman because the data they offer are relevant.

[5] Beilin (1958), Beilin and Werner (1957a), Hildreth (1928), Peck (1935), Wandt (1952).

[6] Boynton and McGaw (1934), Epstein (1941), MacClenathan (1934), McClure (1929), Snyder (1934), Ullmann (1957), Young-Masten (1938), Yourman (1932).

[7] Clark (1951), Del Solar (1949), Laycock (1934), Seidman and Knapp (1953), Stouffer and Owens (1955), Thompson (1940), Wickman (1928).

[8] Ellis and Miller (1936), Hunter (1957), Mitchell (1942), Sparks (1952), Stouffer (1952, 1956).

parents than with the rankings of child psychologists. In Young-Masten's study (1938), in addition to securing conduct reports for nominated problem children, she observed a group of 28 problem children and a control group of the same number. From the classification of behavior records for each child observed, she obtained a statistically significant difference between the groups for behavior "which from the standpoint of the teacher, was annoying, and upset the order and peace of the classroom, and interfered with the other children" (p. 180).

Five years after the appearance of the Wickman report Bain (1934) assessed the attitudes of teachers enrolled in graduate work using the original directions for teachers. The resulting rankings showed higher correlations with Wickman's mental hygienists than had been true for the original teacher sample. The correlations reflected greater teacher concern with *recessive, withdrawing behaviors* than with *active offenses* and *sex problems*.[9]

Replication of the Wickman study, employing the same directions, was undertaken in 1951 by Schruppe and Gjerde (1953). They concluded that teachers' attitudes in 1951 agreed more closely with the "ideal criterion" (clinicians' attitudes) than did 1927 teacher's attitudes (a correlation of .57 (1951) compared with −.04 (1927) using means of teachers' and clinicians' ratings). None of the traits listed as most serious by one group was listed as least serious by the other. Wickman had five such differences. Griffiths' (1952) study, although not a replication of Wickman's, was similar to some features of it. He found that behavior difficulties most reported by teachers relate to violations of classroom rules and work rules. However, he indicated that teachers have changed over the years as evidenced by their awareness that a child who is easy to manage is not necessarily well adjusted.

Del Solar's (1949) study is a report of interviews with parents and teachers which details the joys and problems of child rearing. It was the shy and withdrawing, rather than aggressive, behaviors which concerned this group of teachers and parents. These findings contradict Wickman and most other investigators. Del Solar's findings may result however, from the nature of the questions asked in the interview (only one, concerning liabilities of students, is cited), the small size of the sample (6 teachers rating 28 children), and the atypical nature of the subjects (all teachers had advanced study and were employed in a school of above average socioeconomic status).

We would conclude from these studies (holding the question of the validity of Wickman's methodology aside for the moment) that there is considerable evidence to indicate agreement with Wickman's original findings. Furthermore, there has been an observable shift in the intervening years in the attitudes of teachers in the direction of being more like those of "mental hygienists." In spite of greater congruence, how-

---

[9] In another part of the study Bain reports that one semester of instruction had little effect in changing attitudes toward problem behaviors. Whether the differences reported in the Bain study result from the select character of the sample is not known.

ever, a sizeable difference remains between the attitudes of teachers and clinicians toward behavior problems of children.

The Methodical Issue

Modifications as a rule have aimed at introducing uniformity in the administration of the problem rating scales. This has meant either modifying the directions given clinicians or teachers so that both groups could respond under the same stimulus conditions.

In Ellis and Miller's (1936) investigation the instructions used were those originally given clinicians. In this study they were administered to teachers. With this change in method ratings of teachers correlate .49 with Wickman's mental hygienists (and .65 with Wickman's teachers). Again, the change is the result of increased realization of the seriousness of *withdrawing* and *recessive* personality traits. The investigators note, however, that teachers "still consider" *violations of general standards of morality* and *transgressions against authority* as the most seriously rated types of behavior.

Sparks' (1952) investigation made use of both the Wickman teacher and clinician directions and scales. These were administered to teachers and graduate students (in education). Teachers' ratings made in terms of seriousness for future adjustment (the mental hygienist form) were different from the kinds of ratings made when the directions stressed "troublesomeness" in the classroom, although in both cases they were still different from psychologists' ratings. The correlation of ratings (for teachers) between the original teacher form and the mental hygienist form of the scale was .05.

Mitchell's (1942) study was conducted in the same cities where Wickman had done his 13 years earlier. The scales and directions were both modified, the scales but slightly. The directions given teachers and mental hygienists were the same: they were asked to rate behavior traits keeping in mind the behaviors of fifth and sixth grade children they had observed. (No such grade specification was made by Wickman.) The directions given the 1940 group were "almost" identical with those given by Wickman and these we presume were the instructions originally given clinicians. The correlation between means of ratings of 1927 and 1940 mental hygienists was .80. Some mental hygienists had apparently become more "conservative" in their ratings. They no longer considered *unsocial, withdrawing,* and other traits as extremely grave—in fact, no traits were now so considered. Whereas, the correlation in 1927 between the means of teachers and mental hygienists' ratings was .08 (by the rank difference method), the correlation in 1940 was .70. Mitchell interprets this to mean that either the identity in directions accounts for these results or teachers and clinicians have moved closer in their judgments.

In Stouffer's (1952) investigation teachers were first given the original instrument for teachers; later, the original scale for mental hygienists. A group of mental hygienists were then administered the original mental hygienists' scale. Stouffer reports a correlation of .52 between the teachers' ranking of problem behaviors and mental hygienists' ranking of the same, employing different directions (the original Wickman procedure). A correlation of .61 was obtained when the instructions (those of mental hygienists) were the same for both groups. A rank order correlation of .87 was obtained between the rankings of Stouffer's and Wickman's mental hygienists.

Stouffer concluded that while teachers' attitudes toward the behavior problems of children have changed there has been little change in the attitudes of mental hygienists.[10] The changes in teachers' attitudes reflect again the reduced importance of problems related to *honesty, sex, truancy,* and *classroom order,* and increased importance of *withdrawing* and *recessive* personality traits.

Stouffer's (1956) study is of particular interest because it recognizes that a difference may exist between teachers of different grade levels. In contrast to his 1952 study the later one deals with secondary school teachers. The instructions were those for clinicians. The results were contrasted with those of elementary teachers in the prior study and with Wickman's (elementary) teachers. The rank order correlation of secondary teachers' rankings and elementary teachers' rankings was .88; between the same secondary teachers' and mental hygienists' ratings, .49. As reported in the earlier study, the correlation between elementary teachers' and mental hygienists' rankings was .61. Elementary teachers are, then, in greater agreement with mental hygienists than secondary school teachers. In terms of children's behaviors, elementary teachers are more concerned with withdrawing tendencies; secondary school teachers, with classroom management and problems related to class work and school routines.

The findings that the criteria of adjustment and maladjustment differ depending upon age and grade level is given support in a study by Beilin (1958). In this instance, the procedure involves teacher nomination of maladjusted children, descriptions of their distinguishing characteristics, and content analysis of the descriptions. In general, an age trend (from elementary grades to young adulthood) was found with a concern (in elementary grades) for social-interpersonal aspects of adjustment (e.g., *withdrawal, aggressiveness, emotional instability*) to later concern (in high school) with character traits (e.g., *reliability, dependability*) and finally (young adulthood) with *achievement* and *integration into the community.*

In the 1957 study by Hunter, elementary and secondary school teachers were sent the Wickman mental hygienists' rating scale and instructions. His results are similar in direction to Mitchell's and Stouffer's though not in size of correlations. The correlation between teachers' and mental hygienists' rankings of mean ratings was .22. *Aggressiveness* is still rated more highly by teachers than by mental hygienists.

Using a procedure which raises some doubts, Ullmann (1957) had

[10] Note that Mitchell (1942) suggests such a change although the correlation for the same relationship differs from Stouffer's by only .07.

teachers nominate well and poorly adjusted children who were then rated on a 144-item rating scale. Discrimination indices were computed for each item. The check list was then submitted to a group of mental hygienists who rated the extent to which each item was indicative of good or poor adjustment. The discrimination indices were correlated with the means of clinicians' ratings of the items. The correlation was .86. For favorable items it was .69; unfavorable, .50. These results are interpreted by Ullmann as confirming the Mitchell findings that teachers have moved closer to clinicians in their judgments (in spite of the considerable difference in procedure from Mitchell). Ullmann reports, however, that these correlations may be too high by virtue of some of his procedures.

At this point it appears that the differences in directions that were a part of the Wickman procedure quite clearly contributed to the differences demonstrated between teachers and mental hygienists. When this is controlled, however, differences still emerge and these are of the kind originally observed.

It is also apparent that there has been a change in the direction of greater congruence between the attitudes of teachers and clinicians. That that congruence is not consistent for all levels of teachers has been made explicit in recent studies. It is likely that differences between elementary and secondary teachers have always existed vis-à-vis the matters here reviewed, but, where teacher and clinician attitudes appear to be the same, differences in meaning may still attach to the behaviors.

Teacher "Expertness"

The specific criteria employed by teachers and clinicians in assessing maladjustment in children have been mentioned. As already indicated, most investigators have shown teachers to be most concerned with children's behaviors that are *aggressive, disruptive of school routines,* or generally reflecting *lack of interest in school activities.* In addition, teachers are, or have been, less concerned with *withdrawing* and other nonsocial behaviors. Some investigators have characterized this as indicative of a middle class value pattern; e.g., *stealing* is the teacher's consistent concern in MacClenathan's (1934) study. The emphasis upon these school disrupting traits has not been unanimous, however. Peck (1935) found *undesirable personality traits* to be the greatest concern of the teacher, *regressive* traits somewhat less so, and *aggressive* behaviors least. Of only moderate import were *violations of school work demands.* Clark (1951) differs from the usual view, too, in concluding that teachers are actually more annoyed by children's behaviors which annoy other children than by behaviors which affect teachers themselves.

In most of the cited studies it is implied or explicitly stated that the teacher is "wrong" in reacting as she does to the problems of children. Teachers have been criticized as untutored in the scientific facts concerning child development and are thus seen as generally being incapable of assessing children's adjustment.

Stewart (1949) rejects this thesis. With 184 boys and 193 girls as subjects, a comparison was made between ratings of problem students and non-problem students. Identification was also attempted of those with and without "whole life"problems. From ratings of these youngsters she concludes that teachers are capable of distinguishing between problems as school problems or "whole life" problems. She insists that teachers possess much more insight into children's behavior than they are credited with by some investigators.

In spite of the few studies that report different patterns of teachers' attitudes, the hierarchy of attitudes seems to be quite close to Wickman's formulation. The Stewart report is important not so much because it rejects this hierarchy but rather in its highlighting the difference between clinicians and teachers as not being a matter of ignorance. What the difference is attributable to remains to be discussed.

Sex Differences

There seems to be universal agreement that boys are more likely to be identified as maladjusted or behavior problems than girls.[11] The proportion of boys (in contrast to girls) so identified ranges in these reports from 66 to 88 per cent. Not only is there a difference in proportion but behaviors which form the bases for these identifications are in part different for each sex (Beilin and Werner, 1957a; Epstein, 1941; Wickman, 1928). Ullmann's (1957) interpretation is of some interest. It is *not*, he says, that "desirable conduct for teachers takes the distinguishing characteristics of girl behavior as suggested by Wickman but rather teachers assign girls more favorable ratings because they lack awareness of the manner in which girls are making their adjustment" (p. 39). Ullmann explains that boys' patterns of adjustment are more manifest to the observer, whereas girls deal with problems on an intrapsychic level. This interpretation is in the tradition of imputing lack of insight to teachers. Stewart's (1949) results are again cogent. Her data do not suggest that teachers lack insight into their adjustment, but rather that they distinguish a different *kind* of adjustment for girls. Another study with young adults suggests the same (Beilin and Werner, 1957a). In this instance, sex differences in degree of adjustment are supplemented by differences in the types of behavior identified with the maladjustments of each sex.

Why should the nature of adjustment be different for boys and girls? Whatever the *ultimate* reasons (whether biological or social), the temptation is to say that the differences, in an *immediate* sense at least, result from different *expectations*. It is evident from the cited studies that boys and girls are expected to act in prescribed ways in our culture. The rea-

[11] Blanchard and Paynter (1924), Boynton and McGaw (1934), Epstein (1941), Griffiths (1952), Hildreth (1928), Hurlock and McDonald (1934), McClure (1929), Neumeyer (1949), Peck (1935), Rogers (1942), Snyder (1934), Wickman (1928), Young-Masten (1938), U.S. Children's Bureau (1949).

sons girls are considered better adjusted by teachers is that teachers have certain expectations of what good adjustment *in school* should be and the prescription for girls' adjustment is more consistent with these expectations than the prescription for boys' good adjustment. As Wickman makes evident, the teacher is concerned with getting what she is teaching "across," and behaviors which facilitate this are more likely to be valued. The behaviors of girls are of this kind.

This approach is more acceptable to us, from the evidence, than the interpretation that teachers' attitudes are based on a lack of sophistication.

There is some evidence that men and women teachers evaluate the problems of children differently. Women are found by one investigator to rate problem behaviors as more serious than do men (Ellis and Miller, 1936). Another study (Hunter, 1957) reports, however, that specific problem behaviors are treated differently by each sex. Men teachers consider *sex* problems as less serious than do women; women consider *appearance* and *destruction of property* as less serious than do men. Others (Beilin and Werner, 1957; Stouffer and Owens, 1955) report similar findings, although in the former case it is emphasized that the similarities are greater than the differences.

Age and Grade Influences

The sixth grade appears to be modal for the nomination of children with problems, with the first and second grades offering the least. The fifth, seventh, and eighth grades also give the teacher some difficulty (Hildreth, 1928; Hurlock and McDonald, 1934; McClure, 1929; Snyder, 1934). Difference in maladjustments of elementary and secondary school youngsters were reported early in the literature (Hildreth, 1928) and somewhat neglected till recently. Hildreth (1928) observed that maladjusted elementary school children are more likely to be identified as *unstable, nervous* or *shy;* the secondary school pupil, as *aggressive* or demonstrating *poor study habits.* Peck (1935) finds the differential effect of sex of students in these identifications, however. Grade differences in problem type are reported by others as well (Beilin and Werner, 1957a; Stouffer, 1956; Stouffer and Owens, 1955). The differences found by Stouffer (1956) have already been described. Griffiths (1952) states that certain behavior difficulties (as reported by teachers and parents) increase with age; others decrease.

Socioeconomic Status

There are limited data relating socioeconomic status of the child to his identification as a problem. Levy (1931) finds "socially high grade children have personality or emotional problems . . . children of lower classes have social problems" (p. 158). Yourman (1932) reports a larger proportion of problem children are of lower socioeconomic status. Snyder (1934) found that schools differentiated by their level of socioeconomic status yielded different numbers of problems with more from the lower groups. There was no statistically significant difference, however, in socioeconomic status between a problem group and a control group.

The study by Griffiths (1952) makes the most ambitious attempt to relate socioeconomic status to the identification of behavior problems. There were few significant differences among children of different socioeconomic levels in teachers' ratings of their problems. More differences appear, however, according to the parent's ratings and the child's own ratings. Griffiths concludes that some differences exist between middle socioeconomic level children and others. In particular, they are more submissive and less aggressive.

It is apparent that few data are available as to the relationship between socioeconomic status and the behavior problems of children.

DISCUSSION

The studies reviewed suggest strongly that differences in teachers' and clinicians' attitudes existed in 1927. From that time to the present changes appear to have taken place among teachers' attitudes so that they approximate more closely those of clinicians. There is some possibility that clinicians have tempered their evaluations as well.

Despite the shift toward congruence, teachers' attitudes remain different, and different in ways not dissimilar from what they were in Wickman's day. Why? First, let us recall that Wickman and others made much of this difference. It was suggested, even insisted, that the teacher should change. Such an injunction could rest only on the premise that the clinician's attitudes were more legitimate or more correct. This view was accepted though G. Watson was the first and not the last to question it. Watson's position was not that the clinician was necessarily incorrect or that he should not serve as a criterion. Rather, Wickman was chided for not even considering the alternatives to accepting the clinician as criterion. For Wickman, the virtue of choosing the clinicians' attitudes as an ideal was recommended by his expert knowledge of children's adjustment. Let us examine this claim.

For one, Wickman asked clinicians to rate behaviors in light of their possible future consequences. Would the clinician, with any validity, know the future consequences of the appearance of a behavior in childhood? The answer is doubtful. In 1927 there were few if any studies which had indicated with even low degrees of certainty the outcome in adolescence or adulthood of a child's particular behavior (e.g., *withdrawing* behavior). In fact, if anything, there was some doubt that this could be done (Preston and Shepler, 1931; Watson, 1933). Evidence since then leads to even greater uncertainty (Beilin, 1957; Ives, 1949). According to some theories a withdrawn child is more likely to become maladjusted than one who is not. Yet the proof of how true this is and in what proportion for any population is almost nonexistent. Although it has been shown that in an adult *psychotic* group (Witmer, 1934) there was a tendency for maladjustive behaviors to be present in childhood (information was obtained from retrospective reports), this tells us little about the prevalence of withdrawing behavior in a population of children or about the likelihood of such behaviors resulting in maladjustment, neurosis, or psychosis in adulthood.

However, there is a more important issue, in light of the functions of the therapist qua therapist: withdrawing behaviors present a problem to be dealt with at the time of their appearance. Such behaviors can be a basis for a visit to a therapist—in childhood as well as adulthood. The clinician is more likely to attempt some therapy than to postpone action till adolescence or adulthood (although, in some instances, this might reasonably be done). The clinician is often forced to act by immediate criteria; for he cannot wait for ultimate validation. It is thus part of his role as a therapist to be concerned about these behaviors. In essence, the behaviors with which a clinician is concerned are related to his status and the functions that accompany that status. If these behaviors were of equal relevance to the functions of the teacher, they would be equally valued. However, they are not. This has been so even in the period of "life-adjustment" programs and through the era of the "whole child," except possibly for some special groups of teachers. In spite of much pressure, teachers on the whole continue to be concerned with behaviors that facilitate or interfere with their teaching. A number of investigators recognize the difference in function between clinician and teacher [12] even though the teacher's role is not simple to define. It is, after all, a reflection of an educational philosophy. The prevailing philosophy of education in 1927, whether explicit or implicit, was oriented to the training of intellectual skills. In the interim the function of the teacher has broadened considerably to include training in social and other skills. There has been much pressure on the teacher to be a counselor and in some ways something of a psychotherapist as well—but, at the least, to focus more on the emotional life and adjustment of the child. The question of which role is "better" is a question of values. At present, the trend is back again toward the training of intellectual skills. The trend of increasing teacher sophistication in psychology will probably continue, and will probably not revert to the level of 1927. To urge (e.g., Stouffer, 1952, 1956) that the teacher's attitudes approximate the clinician's is unrealistic unless the teacher's role becomes one with the clinician—and this seems unlikely.

Other considerations recommend themselves as well. The teacher has a vital role in the socialization of the child. She is, after all, a culture carrier and to some extent a parental surrogate. Her own behaviors are significant in the child's development of self-control, character traits, values, and work habits. These functions are certainly as important as any. There is no question that the teacher needs to be aware of withdrawing and other undesirable personality characteristics. What is ques-

[12] Davis and McGinnis (1939), Hildreth (1928), MacClenathan (1934), Schrupp and Gjerde (1953), Stewart (1949), Watson (1933), Yourman (1932).

tioned is the need for the teacher to concern herself with them to the same extent and in the same way as the clinician.

To summarize, the difference reported by Wickman in attitudes toward the behavior problems of children should be interpreted as reflecting differences in the roles of teachers and clinicians and the discharge of functions of the role incumbents (Brim, 1957; Sarbin, 1954). The efforts of many have been directed to alter the prescription of the teacher's role and performance in this role. This effort has in part been successful, as witnessed by the greater congruence in attitudes between teacher and clinician. In spite of the partial change in prescription, the teacher's role remains principally task-oriented; the clinician's, more adjustment-oriented. It seems unrealistic and possibly even undesirable to expect the teacher's behaviors reflected in her attitudes and values to become congruent with those of clinicians. Other results reviewed here are consistent with this thesis. The reported disparity between elementary and secondary teachers results from differences in role. The high school teacher is even more subject matter-oriented than the elementary school teacher. The greatest impact of the "child-oriented" or "life-adjustment" philosophy in turn has been in the elementary school. This has resulted in a modification of role prescription for the elementary school teacher which is reflected in greater similarity between the attitudinal hierarchies of elementary teachers and clinicians. The observed differences are due not only to the teacher's role but result from the actions of the children themselves. The pupil's role-related behaviors change with progress through school as the youngster assumes new responsibilities and loses old ones. Behavior differences are not only bound to their age but also their sex. The same behavior is not expected or demanded of boys and girls. The attitudes of teachers in turn will reflect differences in age and sex role expectations.

SUMMARY AND CONCLUSIONS

The studies concerning teachers' and clinicians' attitudes toward the behavior problems of children, which have emerged principally from the initiative of the Wickman 1928 monograph, are reviewed. The following conclusions are drawn:

1. Differences existed in 1927 between the attitudes of teachers and clinicians toward the behavior problems of children. This seems to have been true in spite of the methodological limitations of the Wickman study.

2. Since 1927 there has been a shift in the hierarchy of teachers' attitudes to approximate more closely those of clinicians. This shift is not due to an artifact of research methodology. Those studies which incorporate adequate controls and consistent instructions show even greater congruence between the attitudes of the two groups.

3. There has been some change in the attitudes of clinicians although this is based upon the conclusions of one study.

4. Criteria employed in evaluating the behavior problems of children differ for elementary and secondary school teachers.

5. More boys are identified as maladjusted than girls and the criteria of maladjustment (and adjustment) differ in part for each sex.

6. The sex of the teacher affects, in part, attitudes toward children's problems.

7. Studies of the relationship of socioeconomic factors to the evaluation of children's behavior problems are inadequately dealt with in the literature.

Differences in attitudes between teachers and clinicians are interpreted in the framework of role theory. The attitudinal hierarchies of teachers and clinicians are seen as reflecting their respective roles and the ways these roles influence the organization of their respective experiences. Wickman's findings of 1927 are interpreted as indicative of the role of the teacher in that era. The role expectations of teachers have changed. Replications of the Wickman study indicate these changes have resulted in greater congruence between teachers' and clinicians' attitudes. It is suggested by virtue of the teachers' essential task-orientation and the clinicians' adjustment-orientation that complete or nearly complete congruence is not likely to be achieved.

The relationship of sex and age to attitudes toward behavior problems is also explained in the light of role theory.

7 / Student Attitudes toward Child Behavior Problems

Robert M. Porter

One approach in helping adults to understand children is to assist them in becoming aware of their attitudes toward child behavior. In this study Robert M. Porter of the State University Teachers College, Oneonta, New York, reports on the conceptions held by high school seniors, college students, and teachers of the best way to handle children with problems.

The look-for-the-cause approach is accepted by mental hygienists as the method of preference in dealing with child behavior problems. That teacher attitudes toward their pupils' behavior have been moving closer

Reprinted from the *Journal of Educational Research*, 1959, 52, 349–52, with the permission of the author and Dembar Publications, Inc.

to a mental hygiene point of view during the past thirty years has been chronicled by such researchers as Ellis and Miller (1936), Mitchell (1942), Stouffer (1952), Schrupp and Gjerde (1953), and Hunter (1957). Undoubtedly much of this improvement can be attributed to Wickman's (1928) study of 1928 which had shown that teachers and clinical psychologists were some distance apart in rating the seriousness of various kinds of behavior. The former stressed overt, objective behavior while the latter emphasized more subjective manifestations of maladjustment.

Wickman's work touched off numerous subsequent investigations. Another impetus has arisen from the increasing emphasis that teacher-preparing institutions have given to child growth and development and educational psychology courses. Sparks (1952) found that teachers with training beyond the bachelor's degree more closely approached the mental hygienists' position than did those with less training. The purpose of the present study was twofold: (a) to ascertain how undergraduate students in teacher education felt that certain child behavior problems should be handled, and (b) to ascertain the extent of improvement in student attitudes as they progressed through their four years of college. At what point are these students when the college gets them and how much growth toward clinicians' attitudes occurs in their subsequent undergraduate career?

PROCEDURE

In an effort to obtain some answers to these questions an investigation was undertaken at the State University Teachers College at Oneonta, New York during the fall of 1956. Data were obtained from about sixty students in each of the four classes: freshman, sophomore, junior and senior. This study was widened to include sixty-four seniors of the local high school and sixty in-service teachers who were members of extension courses being given by the College in Albany, New York.

The data collection instrument was a test devised by Celia B. Stendler (1949) which contained twenty-five response statements describing various behavior patterns in children. Stendler had used the test to examine the problem of teacher insight into pupil behavior from a different angle than had Wickman, et al. She attempted to discover how teachers thought certain kinds of behavior should be dealt with. She queried one hundred fifty-seven elementary teachers in the midwest. Persons being questioned were asked to complete the statement by describing what they considered to be the best way of treating the particular problem. They were not required to sign their names. The test was as follows:

PROBLEMS OF CHILD BEHAVIOR

Here are some statements about children which are not complete. Each statement describes a particular kind of behavior problem. For example, the first statement says, "I think the child who never finishes on time should—" You are to finish the statement by describing what you think would be the best way of treating his particular problem.

1. I think the child who never finishes on time should
2. I think the child who continually fights with other children should
3. I think the child who continually steals should
4. I think the child who bites his fingernails should
5. I think the child who daydreams most of the time should
6. I think the child who relies on the teacher too much should
7. I think the child who does his work over and over until it is just right should
8. I think the child who never works up to his capacity should
9. I think the child who never pays attention should
10. I think the child who is always late should
11. I think the child who always lies should
12. I think the child who always talks back to the teacher should
13. I think the child who is easily discouraged should
14. I think the child who continually shows off in class should
15. I think the child who always feels everyone is picking on him should
16. I think the child who loses his temper when he doesn't get his way should
17. I think the child who uses vulgar language should
18. I think the child who tries to cheat on exams should
19. I think the child who is always unhappy and moody should
20. I think the child who continually plays truant should
21. I think the child who is a bully should
22. I think the child who wastes school materials should
23. I think the child who continually disobeys should
24. I think the child who is disliked by other children should
25. I think the child who is timid and shy should

Table I. Percentage of Responses for Six Categories in Twenty-five Items

Number	1 Take Punitive Measures	2 Talk to the Child	3 Send Him to a Doctor
64 High School Seniors	38.4	21.3	.35
60 College Freshmen	22.01	32.1	.34
61 College Sophomores	20.2	25.6	.46
60 College Juniors	13.5	28.1	.47
63 College Seniors	10.7	25.3	.59
60 In-Service Teachers	17.3	19.9	1.9
157 Stendler Teachers	13.9	33.4	2.7

Answers to the test were categorized by Stendler under six different categories. They were as follows:

1. Take punitive measures.
2. Talk to him. Moralize. Be shown the error of his ways.
3. Send him to a doctor.
4. Adjust the work. This included increasing or decreasing the work, or recommending any kind of project.
5. Praise or encourage him.
6. Study him to find the cause of behavior and plan a course of action accordingly.

FINDINGS

The percentage of the total responses of each of the six groups that fell in each category is shown in Table I. The figures obtained by Stendler are given for comparative purposes. It is readily apparent that the technique most used by the high school seniors was Category 1, Take Punitive Measures. Over a third of them elected this category. Resort to this method was decreasingly elected by the four college classes, progressing from freshmen to seniors.

About one fifth of the freshmen, but only about one ninth of the seniors, chose to take punitive measures to deal with behavior problems.

The teachers in the field reversed this trend slightly, however. This may have been due to the fact that many of them, now middle-aged, did their teacher-training work before the causal approach was stressed as much as it is today. Another explanation may well be that once away from the classroom of theory and into the classroom of reality they found that a punitive measure is the easiest "solution" to an uprising in the ranks.

For what behavior problems was Category 1 more frequently chosen than any other category? More high school seniors chose it than any other technique for fifteen of the twenty-five problems on the test. These figures dropped to five for college freshmen and six for sophomores. Behaviors for which both groups very frequently use it included being always late,

Describing Pupil Behavior Made by Six Groups Tested

4 Adjust the Work	5 Praise or Encourage	6 Study Him to Find Cause of Behavior	No Answer
18.5	10.7	5.9	4.4
16.8	14.1	10.6	4.3
22.7	12.5	12.3	6.2
20.3	14.5	17.6	5.6
25.0	14.8	19.2	4.6
23.7	14.9	17.9	4.6
22.5	9.1	14.6	3.8

talking back, showing off, bullying, and disobeying. Juniors preferred it for only two problems—the show-off and the disobedient. There were no instances in which college seniors preferred it to any other technique. In-service teachers, however, chose it very frequently to deal with the child who doesn't pay attention, is always late, talks back, loses his temper, wastes materials, or disobeys. The Stendler teachers would use it especially for tardiness, bullying, and disobedience.

These are overt behaviors disruptive of class routine and management, and the Wickman and subsequent, e.g., Stouffer, studies indicate that teachers view these as more serious behavior problems than do clinicians. (Harry Rivlin (1936) makes an interesting distinction between conduct and behavior. The former, he says, is the chief concern of the teacher, while the term "behavior problem" is more correctly applied to the area of concern of the psychiatrist.) Of interest would be a follow-up study to ascertain the views of the same college seniors tested after they have been employed in the classroom for a couple of years.

The high schoolers would do considerably less "talking to" than punishing. Category 2, Talk to the Child, was, however, the technique most chosen by all four college classes. It was the preferred technique for all groups except the high schoolers (who chose punishment) to deal with cheating, vulgar language, temper tantrums, or wasting of materials.

Very few persons in any group tested (less than two per cent) chose Category 3, Send the Child to a Doctor. It is gratifying to note that students and teachers alike apparently realize that attributing behavior problems to physical disorders very often fails to hit the mark. Stendler reported that only for fingernail biting would more teachers use this category than some other techniques. Of the groups tested in this study, the high school seniors would deal with this problem by punishment. The college classes preferred Talking to the Child or Adjusting the Work. The in-service teachers would Look for the Cause.

Category 4, Adjust the Work, would be used by a majority of the persons in each group tested in this study, and by the Stendler group, to handle the child who daydreams, relies on the teacher too much, or is timid and shy. These are not problems disrupting classroom routine; they involve personality maladjustment. For them, Category 4 was turned to by all groups. There was a slight tendency toward increased use of this technique the higher the group on the educational ladder.

Only about 11 per cent of the high school seniors turned to Category 5, Praise or Encourage, to handle the problems presented on the test. This figure rose to about 14 per cent for the college classes and the in-service teachers. Stendler had reported that about 9 per cent of her group had recourse to this method. All of the groups in the present study, and the Stendler group would use this category for the child who is easily discouraged—an obvious choice, of course. The younger groups would use it for the child who does his work over and over until it is just right. It appears significant that college seniors, and the in-service teacher groups used in this and the Stendler study, would Talk to the Child and point out the error of his ways (Category 2). With added training and experience, it seems, comes a realization that this behavior is not as praiseworthy as it at first appears.

Mental hygienists feel that Category 6, Study the Child to Find the Cause of Behavior, is the best answer for all twenty-five problems, and in the answers given by the various groups tested, recourse to this technique increased steadily from the high schoolers (nearly 6 per cent) to the college seniors (nearly 20 per cent). (See Table I.) One may reasonably assume, therefore, that instruction in the college investigated emphasized an understanding of causal factors of behavior and that the instruction had some effect.

For what behavior problems was Category 6, Study to Find the Cause, chosen more than was any other technique? The high school seniors preferred it for one item, the child who is disliked by other children. There were no problems for which the majority of college freshmen would study the cause. College sophomores, juniors, seniors, and the in-service teachers would have very frequent recourse to this method to handle problems involving children who fight, steal, are moody and unhappy, play truant, and/or are disliked. The teachers in the Stendler study felt that stealing, truancy and tardiness especially would call for handling by this category.

SUMMARY

This study endeavored to measure the growth in attitudes toward handling certain child behavior problems as students progressed through a representative teacher-preparing institution. Data were collected from a sampling of high school seniors, the four classes of a teachers college, and teachers taking in-service courses with that college.

Findings seemed to indicate that:

1. The technique most selected by high school seniors to handle the behavior problems presented was punishment. All four college classes favored talking to the child, as did the Stendler teachers. The in-service teachers of the current study favored adjusting the work.

2. There was a sharp drop in the election of the use of punishment from high school seniors to college seniors.

3. Punishment was especially chosen to deal with overt behaviors which disrupt the classroom.

4. Very seldom would any of the groups tested seek to handle a behavior problem by sending the child to a doctor.

5. There was a tendency to handle problems of a more subjective nature, involving perhaps some personality maladjustment, by adjusting the work. The older the group, the more this method was chosen.

6. The older groups recognized that it was not praiseworthy for the child to do his work over and over to seek perfection.

7. There was a decided tendency for older groups to move more and

more toward the mental hygienist view that the best technique for behavior problems is to seek the cause.

8. The general consensus of the six groups tested was that the most
serious behavior problems involved unhappiness and moodiness, stealing,
being disliked by others, fighting and truancy.

Further study could well be made to follow the same college seniors
as they go out into their first jobs, and to attempt to see just how much
carryover there is of their college-inculcated attitudes, and just how much
these attitudes are bent when they meet the reality of the outside world.

8 / Explorations in Classroom Management

Jacob S. Kounin, Paul V. Gump,
and James J. Ryan, III

*A fundamental question about teacher-pupil interaction is
explored in this article: What is the effect of teacher behavior
on motivation and learning? The research is of the "projected
experiment" type, directed at understanding the network of
interpersonal relationships in the classroom. The authors are
Jacob S. Kounin and Paul V. Gump of Wayne State University and
James J. Ryan, III, of the University of Nevada.*

The origins of the researchers to be summarized here lay in the authors'
feeling of inadequacy in trying to help teachers, especially beginning ones,
with problems of importance to them. Discipline is one problem frequently verbalized by teachers. Teachers' questions about "what to do
when Johnny disturbs" have been shrugged off with impatience, or have
been answered with slogans or "principles." Scientific research about the
technology and theory of controlling misbehavior in a classroom is either
lacking or inadequate.

Consequently, we turned our attention to a study of the practical
problem of classroom management, from the standpoint of technology.
We wanted to see whether there is not some lawfulness about discipline
in classrooms or, on the other hand, whether the variety of variables involved is so great as to preclude the possibility of predicting pupils' reactions from the qualities of disciplinary techniques employed.

Since the teacher must work with groups or, at least, "aggregates" of

Reprinted from the *Journal of Teacher Education,* 1961, *12,* 235–46, with the permission
of the authors and the National Commission on Teacher Education and Professional
Standards of the National Education Association.

pupils, we shifted the focus from the effects of disciplinary measures upon an individual child to that of the audience reactions, or the "ripple effects."

Specifically, how does a teacher's method of handling the misbehavior of one child (henceforth to be referred to as a *desist-technique*) influence *other* children who are audiences to the event but not themselves targets?

The factors to be discussed can be grouped into two major classifications: (1) variables operating at the time of the desist-technique (e.g., the qualities of the desist-technique, the social position of the target) and (2) prevailing variables (e.g., the audience-pupils' intensity of motivation to learn and their liking for the teacher).

I. VARIABLES OPERATING AT THE TIME OF THE DESIST-TECHNIQUE

A. Threatening vs. Supportive Desist-Techniques

In a fashion characteristic of psychologists, we started with an experiment using college students (these are "captive subjects" that do not require administrative clearances and parental approvals). Four classes of students in a college of education were used as subjects. Two classes were taught by a young instructor of educational methods; two classes were taught by an older professor of psychology.

The experiment was conducted as follows:

1. At the second meeting of the class a researcher, posing as a graduate student, obtained questionnaire data on the attitudes of students regarding their instructors, the degree of seriousness of classroom misbehaviors (including "coming late to class") and causes of racial prejudice. The student reports were anonymous.

2. The two instructors of each of the four classes began the third class period with a lecture which gave "his own evidence" that the single most important cause of racial prejudice was repressed hostility toward punitive parents that is displaced upon minority groups.

3. A male student, previously informed about the experiment, arrived late to class—toward the end of the instructor's lecture.

4. The instructor directed either a threatening or a supportive desist-technique at the late-comer. Both desist-techniques stated that coming late interfered with the instructor's presentation and should cease. The supportive desist-technique went on to offer the late-comer help in acquiring the lecture material he had missed. The threatening one stated coldly that "this cannot help but affect my evaluation of you and your grade."

5. The "graduate student" readministered his attitude questionnaire.

Two conclusions emerged from this preliminary experiment:

1. Students who are not themselves targets of a desist-technique *are* affected by it.

2. The *two methods* of handling misbehavior in a classroom *produce* statistically significant *different results*. That is, there is a degree of predictability from some dimensions of desist-techniques to some effects upon audience students.

Threatening-desist-techniques, for both instructors, resulted in significantly lowered judgments of the instructors' helpfulness, likeability, freedom from authoritarianism, and fairness; threatening techniques also raised ratings of the amount of classroom tension.

For the young instructor—but not for the professor—differences between the two desist-techniques produced significant changes in ratings of the instructor's competence in his subject-area and in the freedom of the students to communicate with the instructor.

Students in none of the groups changed their attitudes about the seriousness of the deviancy (coming late), and all groups shifted significantly towards the position of the instructors about the causes of racial prejudice.

It would seem, then, that differences in the effects of certain qualities of desist-techniques are more marked in some areas than in others; that the prestige of the emitter of the desist-technique makes some difference; and that some norms of classroom behavior are so well established in colleges as to be rather resistant to change by an instructor's stand on the issue. Influence attempts of instructors that are directly related to course content are not readily changed in relation to a single example of their desist-technique style.

However, another finding may well serve to limit the generalizability of the above results. Although 97 per cent of the students reported that they did *not* perceive that the event was contrived, the students who witnessed either technique were surprised that a college instructor would take time out to correct a student for coming late, even though they rated coming late as a serious misbehavior. Most of them, especially those who witnessed the threatening desist-technique, felt that the behavior was *not* typical for the instructor. There were frequent comments on a post-incident questionnaire such as: "He must have had an argument with his wife," or "He probably got caught in a traffic-jam." This reaction to an unexpected behavior of an instructor, in a sense "excusing it away," may actually function to reduce the changes produced by differences in desist-techniques. From the viewpoint of research methodology and strategy these findings also point to the advisability of using teacher-style variables that are within expectations and that have some ecological prevalence.

B. Punishing vs. Reprimanding vs. Ignoring

In an experiment with eighth and ninth graders (for whom teachers' use of desist-orders is not unexpected) Ryan, Gump, and Kounin (in preparation) investigated whether qualities of a desist-technique make any difference in audience-pupils' reactions.[1] Volunteer paid subjects were recruited from three metropolitan junior high schools during the summer months to come to a university campus for the purpose of participating in a research studying different methods of teaching. Volunteers were randomly assigned to groups of about twenty-five each where they were asked to consider themselves as being in a regular classroom.

After each group assembled it experienced the following sequence of events: the experimenter introduced the activities of the day; a female teacher (the same for each group) introduced herself to the class; the subjects filled out a questionnaire containing mostly ratings of their first impression of the teacher; the teacher taught a lesson, using slides, about Turkey; a pretrained pupil (also the same person for all groups) misbehaved (got up and sharpened a pencil while the slides were being shown); the teacher issued a desist-technique; the subjects filled out another questionnaire about the activities, the teacher, and the deviancy-event.

Three desist-techniques were used: (1) punitive and intense (walked toward him, saying "Hey you, who do you think you are?" in a firm, irritated voice, put her arm on his shoulders in a gesture of pushing him into his seat, saying, "Now sit down! If you ever do that again, I'll really make trouble for you."); (2) simple reprimand (saying in a matter-of-fact tone: "Don't do that again. Please sit down in your seat now."); and (3) ignoring (indicated awareness of the behavior, but did nothing).

The "take" of the experimental manipulation was evidenced by the existence of a significant difference between all groups in the predicted direction regarding the subjects' ratings of the teacher's meanness, anger, and degree of determination to stop the misbehavior.

Compared to the others, the punitive technique resulted in the subjects' rating the *deviancy* as "most serious," the degree of *interference* with attention to the task as "greatest," the *teacher* as "making too much of an issue" over the event, the experience "most discomforting," and the *teacher* "best able to maintain order in a class of 'tough kids.' "

The simple reprimand produced the highest ratings for teacher fairness and also resulted in the subjects' reporting their paying more attention to the lesson following the event and to the teacher being judged as best able to maintain order in "most classes."

Subjects witnessing "ignoring" as the desist-technique thought the misbehavior most likely would recur, but rated the teacher highest in her degree of liking for pupils.

There were no differences between the groups in subjects' ratings of how much the teacher knew about the subject or how well she could explain it. When equivalent effects are considered (likeability, fairness, felt discomfort) it should be noted that the results of punitiveness in this

---

[1] This experiment was actually started at a later time in the sequence of explorations in order to study the effects of pupil-motivation. (It will be referred to later as the "high-school experiment.") We are referring to it here because it does show that qualities of the desist-technique make some predictable differences in audience-pupils' reactions.

experiment are quite similar to the results obtained from the threatening desist-technique in the college experiment.

C. Clarity, Firmness, and Roughness

In one study by Kounin and Gump (1958) fifty observers were trained to record critical incidents in Barker and Wright's (1954) specimen-record style. These were incidents in which an audience-child was aware of a teacher directing a desist-technique at another child. Twenty-six kindergarten classes were selected to represent the range of socio-economic and ethnic neighborhoods in a large city. All observations were made during the first four days of beginning kindergarten. The observers were instructed to record: (1) what the deviant and the audience-child were doing immediately before the teacher intervened, (2) the full content and manner of the desist-technique and the deviant's immediate reaction, and (3) the behavior of the audience-child during and for two minutes following the desist-technique.

When the resulting 406 incidents were analyzed, it was possible to reliably characterize both the teachers' desist-techniques and the behavior of the audience-children.

The qualities of the desist-technique were rated along dimensions of: (1) clarity (defining the deviancy and stating what to do to stop it); (2) firmness (this included items conveying an "I mean it" quality—walking closer to the deviant, or continuing to look at the deviant until he stopped); and (3) roughness (angry remarks and looks, or punishment).

The reactions of the audience-child were classified as (1) no reaction (no overt behavior which the coder could interpret as related to the desist-technique incident); (2) behavior disruption (overt signs of negative emotionality such as fear, anxiety, and restlessness or a shift away from an originally constructive direction); (3) conformance (stops a deviancy of his own or behaves even better, i.e., sitting more "correctly" himself); (4) nonconformance (engages in a misbehavior of his own); and (5) ambivalence (both conforms and misbehaves).

Statistically significant differences were obtained in the overt behavior of the audience-children as related to the desist-technique used by the teacher. Techniques increasing "clarity" resulted in increased "conformance," but had no effect upon "behavior disruption." Techniques increasing "roughness," on the other hand, had no effect on "conformance or nonconformance," but did increase "behavior disruption." The effects of "firmness" differed from both.

Some of the conclusions of this study are as follows:

1. What teachers *do* makes a difference. There is some lawfulness about the effects of techniques. It was not necessary to obtain personality ratings or IQ tests of the teachers as persons; it was only necessary to find out what they do and how they do it. (Whether teachers with personality factor-x can or cannot *do* things certain ways is another issue.)

2. There are contextual or prevailing variables that also effect how an audience-child will react to an event. Two such contextual variables stand out from the kindergarten study. One refers to the degree of familiarity the pupil has with the teacher and the situation. (Such familiarity, of course, relates to the amount of time one has spent in a particular experience. For example, there were more "no reactions" on the *last* three days than on the first day.) The other contextual variable is the audience-child's orientation at the time of the incident. Techniques high in "firmness," for example, produced increased "conformance," but *only* for audience-children who were themselves oriented toward, or interested in deviancy at the time of the event.

3. "Roughness" is not an increased degree of "firmness." In terms of their effects, it is evident that these are different dimensions.

Although it does not deal specifically with the ripple effect, we would like to summarize another study on the effects of "punitiveness" since it is closely related to the dimension of "roughness." In a study by Kounin and Gump (1961) we attempted to determine the influence of teachers judged to be punitive upon childrens' attitudes toward misconduct. Three pairs of first-grade teachers, each pair from the same school, were *selected*. One of a pair was rated as "punitive" (anti-child, ready to threaten and inflict harm) by principals, assistant principals, the two investigators, and a supervisor of student teachers; the other member of the pair was rated as "nonpunitive." All teachers were rated as having good organization and as achieving the learning objectives for their grade. Children from these classes were interviewed individually during the third month of attendance at school. The interview consisted of the question: "What is the worst thing a child can do at school?" and, following the reply, "Why is that so bad?" The misconducts talked about were coded for content and for certain qualities. The following was found:

1. Children with teachers judged to be punitive showed more pre-occupation with aggression—their misconducts were more serious, their targets suffered more harm; they more frequently cited physical assaults on others as misconduct, and their replies contained more gory—or "blood and guts"—phrases.

2. Children with punitive-rated teachers had more conflicts and were more unsettled about misbehavior in school. They selected misconducts to talk about for which they expressed abhorrence and yet which required premeditation, or "malice aforethought."

3. The children with nonpunitive teachers gave more "reflexive justifications" as explanations for why given misconducts were bad. This was coded when a child gave no consequence for either himself or others in his explanation of why the misconduct was bad—the reason given being "because it's not nice" or "because it's bad." We suggested two interpretations for this finding: (a) that children with nonpunitive teachers have less conflicts about misconduct than have children with punitive teachers—to say "you don't do x because it's not nice" reflects a settled

issue; and (b) a sort of naive faith and trust in the teacher is reflected by children with nonpunitive teachers—a reflexive justification for a school misconduct is like, say, "x is bad because teacher says so."

4. Punitiveness of teachers detracts from childrens' concern with school-unique values and results in less internalized socialization. Children with punitive teachers talked more about physical attacks on peers—misconduct by no means unique to the classroom setting. Children with nonpunitive teachers talked more about learning, achievement losses, and violations of school-unique values and rules.

D. Task-focus vs. Approval-focus

Since discipline is centrally related to problems of power and influence and methods of exerting power and influence, another study was undertaken in which Alden (1959) dealt with some variables pertaining to these factors. Following French (1956), she hypothesized the following bases for teacher power and influence: the coercive role (the teacher as one who can punish); the "legitimate" role (the teacher as an official leader); reward; and pupils' liking for a teacher and teacher expertness.

The base of a new teacher's power (specifically, "expertness" and "liking") was manipulated by varying the experimenter's introduction of the teacher. All classes were given a lesson in secret writing. A "high expert" was introduced as knowing all about codes and as having a high position in the military intelligence for coding and decoding secret codes; the "low expert" was introduced not as an expert but simply as a teacher who had agreed to teach the lesson. The "high liking" new teacher was introduced as being very fond of children and the "low liking" as not caring about children one way or another.

The desist-techniques used by the teacher were related to these concepts. Some desist-techniques focused upon liking and teacher approval ("I see a boy playing with some paper clips. I just don't like a boy who plays with things when he should be paying attention."). Other desist-techniques related to expertness and focused upon the task ("I see a boy playing with some paper clips. Because secret writing demands concentration, I don't see how he can learn much about it when he plays with things instead of paying attention.").

Fifth graders were divided randomly into eight classes in which a new teacher taught a lesson (in a pedantic, "academic" manner) about secret writing. In this manner, both "high" and "low expert" and "high" and "low liking" teachers used both approval-focused and task-focused desist-techniques. In each group three desist-orders were directed at three children who had been trained to act the role of misbehaving pupils. In four of the groups, the desist-technique focused upon teacher liking and approval and in four groups the desist-technique focused upon the task.

One of Alden's most impressive findings was the following: in all cases, desist-techniques focusing upon the task were more effective in eliciting desirable student reactions than desist-techniques focusing upon the teacher's approval. (With the exception of scores on a test of how much was learned from the lesson, measurements of results were all based upon differences between measures given before the lesson and measures given after the lesson.) For some effects, the superiority of the task-focused desist-techniques held, regardless of whether the introduction of the teacher focused upon her expertness or her liking for children. Thus, in all groups, task-focused desist-techniques increased audience-childrens' ratings of the teacher's skill in handling children and increased their rated degree of interest in secret writing.

For some effects, the use of a task-focused desist-technique combined with the teacher's expertness to effect the pupils' reactions. Thus, when an expert teacher used a task-focused technique it increased the children's judgment of how much she liked pupils and would be inclined to reward pupils; it resulted in the pupils considering the deviances she corrected as being more serious and feeling less inclined to misbehave themselves; and it led to a greater amount of information recalled by the pupils from the lecture itself. The influence of being introduced as having high liking for children made a significant difference on one measurement: a teacher with high liking for children *and* high expertness using task-focused desist-techniques resulted in pupils feeling more inclined toward discussing personal matters with her.

E. The Deviant's Reaction and Prestige

An experiment by Gnagey (1960) was directed at two questions: (1) What is the effect of the deviant's reaction to a teacher's desist-technique upon audience-pupils? (Specifically, does whether the deviant submits to or defies the teacher's desist-order make any difference on how audience-children react to the event?) (2) Does the prestige of the deviant among his classmates influence audience-pupils' reactions to a desist-order event?

In this study, four intact classes of fifth graders were shown a science film during which a male classmate "misbehaved" (saying aloud, "Hey, is this film about over?"). This deviant boy then became the target of a desist-order exerted by the teacher. This teacher, who was new to the class, directed the deviant to leave the room and report to the principal. The deviants were preselected on the basis of sociometric scores. (Of course, their classmates didn't know that the deviancies were part of an act.) Two male deviants had high attributed influence among their classmates and two had low influence. Two (one high-influence and one low-influence) were trained to behave in a *submissive* manner (saying, "Yes ma'am, I'm sorry," on leaving the room) and two were trained to react in a *defiant* manner (saying belligerently, "I'll leave the room, but I won't go to the principal's office. The heck with you!").

Gnagey found that the target's reaction did make a predictable difference in audience-pupils' reactions. Compared to pupils who saw the deviant defy the teacher, pupils who witnessed the deviant submit to the teacher rated the teacher as "more capable of handling kids" and as more expert in showing films; they rated the desist-technique as fairer; and they recalled more facts from the film. The magnitude of the differences between the effects of the two kinds of deviant reactions was greater for boys than for girls and was greater for boys who were audience to a high-influence deviant than boys who were audience to a low-influence deviant.

The Gnagey study also points up one reason for an audience-person to be affected by a desist-order directed at someone else, namely, some sort of linkage with the deviant. In this case it is a sociometric linkage— the linkage of an audience-pupils' motivation to identify with a same-sexed person in a high prestige position. Hence, the finding, for boys only, of a greater effect of a high-influence male's reaction than that of a low-influence male's reaction. Another sort of linkage—to the deviancy event—was illustrated by the previously mentioned kindergarten study. Here, when the audience-child was either deviant himself or was watching the deviancy, he was more likely to react to the desist-technique than if he had no such relationship to the deviancy. In both the Gnagey study and the kindergarten study, then, linkages are shown to be important: linkages to the deviant person, and linkages to the deviancy event.

II. THE INFLUENCE OF PREVAILING VARIABLES

With the exception of the kindergarten study, all the studies previously referred to dealt with contrived conditions and with audience-pupils' reactions to qualities of desist-orders as these were emitted by teachers unknown to them except for that one time. As such, they may be loaded in favor of discovering a ripple effect. For a desist-order may have an effect on a nontarget classmate because something in it contains new information for him concerning the teacher or the rules of the setting. This is probably the reason for the finding in the kindergarten study that the degree of clarity of a desist-technique makes a difference in the conforming behavior of an audience-child, especially on the first day of school attendance when the situation is not completely structured. Except for the facts pertaining to learning scores in the Alden and in the Gnagey studies, most of the effects dealt with attitudes and judgments.

Research conducted in other contexts shows that judgments of others are subject to selective perception and perceptual distortion on the basis of the receiver's motivations as well as on the basis of the receiver's relationship to the emitter of behavior (relative prestige, liking for, etc.).[2] Accordingly, it seemed pertinent to investigate audience-pupils' reactions to naturally occurring desist-techniques in actual classrooms with regular teachers. The design employed here was similar to that used in the kindergarten study but with two differences: older children were used as subjects and interviews were utilized in order to study judgments and attitudes. The research sought to determine the influence of variables

[2] Some examples are Pepitone (1950) and Hurwitz, Zander, and Hymovitch (1960).

"within" audience-pupils as such influences affected their reaction to desist-orders. These "within" variables were: (1) the degree of intensity of students' motivation to learn the subject-matter and (2) students' degree of liking for their teacher.

The subjects, randomly selected, included sixty-three boys and sixty-two girls who were just entering high school. They were interviewed between the fourth and tenth day of their attendance at the school and again three months later. One high school was located in a predominantly lower-class neighborhood, one in a lower-middle-class area, and the third in a middle-middle-class neighborhood.

The interview centered around students' descriptions of a most-recent incident when another student engaged in a misbehavior which the teacher did something about. A complete description of the deviance and of the teacher's method and manner of handling it was obtained. The students' open-ended evaluations of the incidents and how they were handled and their reports of how the incidents affected them also were obtained. Finally, students' responses to prestructured, forced-choice items (relating to the teacher's fairness, his own inclination to behave better or worse afterwards, etc.) were secured. Reports of two such incidents were obtained from each student: one based on the academic class in which he said he was "most determined to learn" and one relating to the class in which he said he was least determined to learn the subject-matter. (Gym, music, and shop were excluded.) For the first interview descriptions of, and reactions to, 250 desist-order incidents involving sixty-four different teachers were obtained. (The second interview included eight fewer subjects.)

The first focus of this study was upon audience-pupils' intensity of motivation to learn as it affected their reactions to desist-orders. Assuming that most high-school teachers concentrate on subject matter,[3] we hypothesized that pupils highly motivated to learn would see desist-orders as facilitating their goals, would be more inclined to perceive desist-orders in terms of task-salient dimensions, would see deviances as more interfering and more serious, would react more favorably (in respect to teachers' intents) to desist-orders, would attribute more power and influence to teachers, and so on.

Ofschus (1960) developed codes for various aspects of the reported incidents. He scored the responses of the pupils and compared the reactions of pupils reporting a desist-incident in the class in which they were "highest in determination to learn" with their reactions when reporting a desist-incident in a class in which they were lowest in motivation to learn.[4] He found that audience-pupils' intensity of motivation to learn the subject *did* predict reaction to a desist-event. In high-motivation classes deviancies were rated as more disturbing to the class and more

---

[3] A study by Hilton (1955) indicates this is a tenable assumption.

[4] Most of these were found to be run-of-the-mill incidents—most of the deviancies were coded as quite mild (mainly talking or noise and laughter) and most of the desist-techniques seemed to involve either no harm, or only mild harm, to the deviant.

serious, desist-techniques were rated as more fair, students tended to take more of the teacher's side as opposed to that of the deviant, and the students tended to report acting even better themselves after the incident. In low-motivation classes, students tended to report more teacher-punitiveness and anger and to judge more of the teachers as "making too much of an issue" of the incident. In evaluating the desist-technique, more of those in the high-motivation group evaluated it on the basis of its effectiveness in stopping the misbehavior, whereas more in the low-motivation group used teacher-manner (anger, fairness) as a basis for evaluating the incident.

In line with this finding, Osborne (in preparation) coded pupils' responses to a request to describe the teacher. More of those in the high-motivation group talked about task-relevant attributes (competence in explaining, homework properties) while more in the low-motivation group talked about non-task teacher-attributes (fairness, personal qualities, etc.). It would appear, then, that "motivation to learn" may operate to select saliencies in what pupils perceive about teachers and to influence judgments about, and reactions to, teachers' desist-techniques. However, other findings show that such a viewpoint may be over-simplified. When talking about teachers in classes where pupils were highly motivated to learn, only a small number of pupils felt neutral to or disliked the teacher; in the low-motivation classes more than three times as many pupils felt neutral towards or disliked the teacher. Evidently intensity of motivation to learn is highly associated with liking for the teacher. Are these prevailing variables separable? And which gives rise to which?

By comparing the reaction of pupils in classes with both high-motivation and liking for the teacher with the same pupils' reaction in classes with low-motivation and high-liking and separately with classes with low-motivation and low-liking Ryan (1959) was able to separate the effects of motivation and liking for the teacher. In general, it was found that "motivation to learn" was associated with degree of attention paid to the task and tendency to behave even better after a desist-event. Judgments about the desist-technique, however, varied with liking for the teacher. Liking for the teacher predicted judgments of fairness and siding with the teacher; disliking the teacher was associated with seeing teacher anger, punitiveness, and overreacting to the deviancy. It appears, then, that knowledge of both motivation to learn and liking for the teacher help predict reactions to a desist-event, but they may relate to different facets: "motivation" predicts reactions regarding the task and behavior conformance; "liking" predicts evaluative judgments regarding the teacher's behavior in the event.

The above comparisons were made for the total population of desist-events. Do these findings hold for all types of desist-events or only for certain kinds? Is the predictability of a pupil's reaction improved by knowing the qualities of the desist-event in addition to knowing the pupil's motivation to learn and liking for the teacher?

In order to answer the above questions the pupils were divided into four categories: (1) high motivation to learn and high liking for the teacher (HiM HiL); (2) high motivation to learn and low liking for the teacher (HiM LoL—this group was not included in the statistical analysis for the first interview because of the small number of cases); (3) low motivation to learn and low liking for the teacher (LoM LoL); and (4) low motivation to learn and high liking for the teacher (LoM HiL).

Two questions may be asked regarding any of the above comparisons: (1) *Within* any one group, does it make any difference whether a desist-technique does or does not have a certain quality? For example, do the pupils in the HiM HiL group react differently to a desist-technique that contains punishment than to one that does not? (2) Are there differences *between* groups in how the pupils react to a desist-technique involving a certain quality? For example, do the pupils in the LoM HiL group react differently to a desist-technique containing punishment than do the pupils in the LoM LoL group?

One of the organizing concepts in this study focused on the concept of commitment. Pupils in the HiM HiL group may be thought of as committed in a positive direction to both the task and the teacher. Pupils in the LoM LoL are committed in a negative direction to both the task and the teacher. Pupils in the LoM HiL have a mixed commitment—they are committed in a negative direction to the task and in a positive direction to the teacher.

The audience-pupils' reactions in this research were categorized as follows: (1) reactions relating to the task (these relate to the inclination to pay more attention, or not to, and to behave better, or not to, following a desist-order); (2) reactions involving evaluations of the teacher (these have to do with whether the teacher is judged as making too much of an issue of the deviancy or not, whether she was fair to the deviant or not, and whether the audience-pupil tended to take the teacher's or the deviant's side in the event); and (3) reactions in which an evaluation of the teacher is not involved. (The data here dealt with how *serious* the pupil rated the misbehavior.)

In general, the results of Ryan's study supported the following hypotheses regarding the task-related dimensions of attention and behavior conformance:

1a. Hypothesis: When there is a *clear prevailing commitment* to the task, *negative or positive,* variations in desist-techniques will not produce shifts in task-related reactions of an audience pupil to a desist-event. In *none* of the four within-group comparisons did the presence or absence of punishment, of anger, or of strong firmness make a difference in whether pupils reported an inclination to pay more attention to the task or to behave better themselves.

1b. Hypothesis: When there is a low or negative task-commitment, task-related reactions to desist-technique qualities that manifest the teacher's intent will be effected by whether the pupil likes the teacher or not. In the LoM groups only, pupils who witnessed desist-techniques involving strong firmness, anger, or punishment shifted in a direction of paying more attention and behaving better if they liked the teacher but not if they were neutral toward or disliked the teacher. When the desist-techniques did not contain anger, punishment, or firmness (when teacher-intent was not signalled) there were no differences between the LoM HiL and LoM LoL groups.

1c. Hypothesis: When there is high positive commitment to the task, task-related reactions to desist-technique qualities that manifest the teacher's intent will not be effected by difference in liking for the teacher. There were no significant differences between the HiM HiL and HiM LoL groups in attention and behavior-change reactions to desist-techniques containing punishment, anger, or firmness.

In order to account for the results involving judgments that evaluate the teacher's behavior, we have looked to Heider's (1958) theory of balance. Briefly, Heider postulates forces to avoid imbalance and maintain balance between our perception of people and their acts. Thus, to perceive a liked person to do something "bad" is an unbalanced perception: an example of a balanced perception is to perceive a person who is liked as doing good things. Assuming "unfair" to be bad, we would expect pupils who like the teacher to judge her desist-techniques as fair. Accordingly, we proposed and tested several hypotheses (see 2a and 2b in the following paragraphs) regarding evaluations of the teacher.

2a. Hypothesis: When there is a clear prevailing commitment to the teacher, variations in desist-techniques or in motivation to learn will not produce shifts in those teacher evaluations that have clear good-bad connotations.

In none of the four *within* group comparisons, did the presence or absence of anger, punishment, or firmness make a difference in whether pupils rated a desist-technique as fair or unfair.

2b. Hypothesis: When there is a clear prevailing commitment to the teacher, judgments of a desist-technique having clear good-bad connotations will be in balance with this commitment irrespective of the quality of the technique or the commitment to the task.

HiL groups judged desist-techniques as more fair than LoL groups whether or not the desist-technique contained punishment, anger, or firmness, and this held true for both HiM and LoM groups.

Assuming that taking the teacher's side versus the deviant's side also tends to follow the balance theory, but perhaps not as closely, since this judgment does not have such clear good-bad connotations as does fairness, we further hypothesized that:

2c. Hypothesis: When desist-techniques contain some strong property, commitment to the teacher will influence how pupils evaluate the event in evaluations not having clear good-bad connotations.

When desist-techniques contained punishment, anger, or strong firmness, HiL groups differed significantly from LoL groups; HiL groups were more on the teacher's side and LoL groups were more on the deviant's side. When the desist-technique did not contain anger, punishment, or strong firmness the HiL groups did not react differently from the LoL groups.

Judgments which did not involve evaluations of the teacher were re-lated to the nature of pupil commitment by hypotheses pertaining to the kinds of cues that influence a pupil when he judges the seriousness of a deviancy (see 3a and 3b which follow).

3a. Hypothesis: When there is a clear commitment to both the task and the teacher, judgments of deviancy-seriousness will not be dependent upon whether or not the desist-technique manifestly signals the teacher-value.

Within neither the HiM HiL nor LoM LoL groups did the teachers' using or not using punishment, anger, or firmness make any difference in how the pupils rated the degree of seriousness of the deviancy.

3b. Hypothesis: Where there is no commitment to the task, but where there is commitment to the teacher, pupils will utilize the teachers' manifest-value to judge the seriousness of the deviancy.

Only within the LoM HiL group did the teachers' use of punishment, anger, or firmness relate to pupils' ratings of the seriousness of the de-viancy. In this group, when the teachers signalled their value by anger, punishment, or firmness the pupils increased their ratings of the serious-ness of deviancy. Differences between LoM LoL and LoM HiL in judgments of the seriousness of the deviancy were significant when the desist-techniques contained anger, punishment, or firmness, but were not when the desist-techniques did not contain these teacher-message prop-erties.

In summary, certain variables an audience-pupil carries "within" him do appear to influence how he reacts to a desist-event directed at a target other than himself. The pupil's intensity of motivation to learn is one. This commitment to the task, positive or negative, is mainly in-fluential in affecting how much attention he focuses on the task and how much he is inclined to behave even better after witnessing a desist-event—both being task-related variables. The pupil's liking for the teacher is another relevant variable. This commitment to the teacher, positive or negative, is mainly influential in determining how the student arrives at evaluative judgments about the event. These judgments follow the laws of balance, i.e., a liked person tending to be perceived as doing good things and a disliked person tending to be perceived as doing bad things. Thus, the desist-techniques of liked teachers tend to be seen as more "fair," those of disliked teachers as more "unfair." In addition, when a teacher signals his intent or value in the desist-technique the pupil who likes him takes his cue about the deviancy from him.

One study mentioned earlier and one additional research may be re-ferred to here to illustrate efforts that were made to determine whether motivation to learn effects liking for the teacher or whether liking for the teacher effects motivation to learn.

In the high-school experiment previously mentioned in 1b, we at-tempted to create experimentally conditions which would result in high and low motivation. Considerable difficulty was experienced in creating low motivation for the paid volunteers who came to a university campus to participate in research. After four experimental failures to create a low motivation condition, we finally produced comparatively lower motivation in one group than in another. Although there were significant differences in reactions to desist-technique qualities, the reactions of the "high" and "low" motivation groups did not differ. This failure to replicate some aspects of the "interview study" leaves the issue unsettled; the results may mean that motivation to learn follows liking of the teacher, or merely that only relatively lower motivation rather than actual low motivation was produced in the low-motivation condition, or, still again, that there are differences in commitment in an experimental setting as compared to an actual classroom.

In another study we obtained, by use of questionnaires, estimates of pupils' "premotivation to learn world history" two weeks prior to their attendance in high school. About one to two weeks after their attendance in the high school we replicated the "interview study" with questionnaires in which classes of pupils described some desist-events and rated their reactions to it. While "premotivation to learn" did predict (r = .49) "post-motivation to learn," it did not predict students' reactions to the desist-event in the post situation. Both "post-motivation to learn" and "post-liking for the teacher" were significantly related (as were motivation and teacher-rated ability to explain and to make the subject interesting). Allowing for differences between questionnaire and interview methods (results from the questionnaire, as might be expected, contained much more sparse descriptions of the events and the teacher which were more difficult to code reliably), the results seem to indicate that motivation to learn is not solely determined by what a pupil brings to the class but is effected, even in one week, by what happens in the class and by whatever it is that teachers do that leads to their being rated as being liked and as being able to explain and make the subject interesting.

III. WHAT ABOUT LIKING FOR A TEACHER?

While liking for the teacher stands out as an important variable, we must pause to ask what this means. Do the same behaviors that contribute to teachers being liked account for persons in other roles being liked? Or does the teacher role carry its unique properties as far as "being liked" is concerned?

The questionnaire study showed a relationship between ratings of "explains well" and "makes interesting" and pupils' liking for the teacher. The Alden (1959) study showed a relationship between task-focus desist-techniques and rated liking for the teacher. When Osborne (in preparation) compared the pupils' descriptions of teachers in "high"- and "low-liked" groups, the differences were about the same as the differences obtained when "high" and "low" motivation groups were compared. When describing "high-liked" teachers, task-property descriptions were predominant, e.g., "explains well," "assigns the right amount of home work," "helps you learn." (Seventy per cent of the pupils mentioned this dimension when talking about "high-liked" teachers.) Only 19 per cent of the pupils mentioned "friendliness" or "meanness" (more of the "low-liked" teachers being included when this non-task dimension was described). In contrast, in a study by Polansky and Kounin (1956) in which adults and college students were asked to describe a professional helper (physician, social worker, college counselor) they had just seen for the first time, the majority talked about "friendliness," "helpfulness." "Understanding" was referred to by 49 per cent of the clients when talking about professional helpers, compared to 7 per cent of the high-school students who used this term when describing teachers.

In a study of the ripple effect in a camp milieu Gump and Kounin (1959–60) also asked campers to describe camp counselors. The most frequently used dimension was that which we called "gratuitous giver": 63 per cent of the campers (ranging from seven to thirteen years of age) described their counselor with statements illustrated by "gives us candy" and the like. Only 2.3 per cent of the campers used terms that might be equivalent to "explaining well," e.g., "taught us how to play ball better." It also was found that concepts of misbehavior (obtained from the question, "What's the worst thing to do?" and "Why is that so bad?") also differed, depending upon whether the camper was talking about camp, home, or school milieus. The role of the central adult (parent, teacher, counselor) as a sufferer from childrens' misbehaviors and as a retributor also differed as between milieus.

All the above leads us to believe that the salient dimensions used to analyze adult-child relationships probably differ for parents, camp counselors, teachers, and other adult-child role figures. Equivalences may be theoretically possible at a higher level of abstraction, but concrete techniques cannot be directly extrapolated from one adult-child role to another.

It would seeem, further, that studies of the attributes of teachers as such, whether obtained from projective and inventory-type measures or from boy-scout-type lists of characteristics (trustworthy, loyal, helpful, friendly) are inadequate to the task of analyzing what constitutes teachership. We need to know what teachers *do* that makes a difference for the learning and behavior of *pupils* in *classrooms*. Not only do we need to know what teachers do to manage misbehavior, but we must know what they *do* to evolve and sustain motivation to learn and to become "liked." What *are* the really significant dimensions of what we call teaching? (We are inclined to believe that the "desist-style" dimension here discussed is not as important as some others.)

What is more, studies are needed to better inform us about what constitutes the nature of the classroom as a unique setting distinct from other kinds of settings for children's groups. For, television or not, the locus of necessity of educational practice and the point of application of learning theory or group dynamics theory or other psychological theories is the classroom with a teacher in charge of a group of children or adolescents. And what we know of teachers or students, separately or together, must be relevant to this basic context if it is to be of benefit to those doing the job.

Researchers should get into the classrooms; and teachers and administrators should let them in.

9 / The Influence of Teachers on Aspirations of Students [1]

Howard Rosenfeld and Alvin Zander

This article explores the influences of teachers on the aspirations of students to achieve in the classroom. Among the findings are: Students tend to accept teacher-attempts to motivate them when they perceive the acts as rewarding and legitimate. Students tend to ignore teacher-influences that they perceive as indiscriminate and coercive. Students distinguish between two forms of coercion by teachers and two forms of reward. The authors are Howard Rosenfeld of the University of Kansas and Alvin Zander of the University of Michigan.

Early studies of goal setting have shown that a person usually selects a level of aspiration which represents a mild challenge for him, given that he has knowledge of his past performances (Lewin, Dembo, Festinger, and Sears, 1944). In general, he attempts to reach the most rewarding goal that he feels he can reasonably attain. It is also known that aspirations are often influenced by sources external to the persons who set them (Festinger, 1942). Little evidence however is available concerning the nature of this influence process.

The interest of this study in the effects of teachers on a student's aspirations was stimulated by the above problem and by the awareness that appropriate goal setting by a student is an important practical issue. A salient dimension on which a pupil can hardly avoid setting a level of aspiration, and can hardly avoid being influenced by his teacher when doing so, concerns his grades in school. We define a student's level of aspiration as that level of achievement, indicated by a grade, which a pupil realistically expects to attain in a given course.

For the purposes of this investigation, we assume that teachers attempt to influence pupils to work up to their capacities, and that these pressures are guided by professional norms that students should not be

[1] The research reported herein was performed pursuant to a contract with the Office of Education, United States Department of Health, Education, and Welfare.

Reprinted from the *Journal of Educational Psychology*, 1961, 52, 1–11, with the permission of the authors and the American Psychological Association.

expected to work beyond or below their capacities. We assume that any given student is reasonably confident he knows the level of his best possible performance (his capacity) and that he believes his teacher knows his capacity equally well. We further assume that students are aware of the pressures from teachers and that students believe they should not be pressed to aspire either beyond or below their capacities.

The attempts of teachers to influence students are usually based upon assumptions as to what will motivate pupils to accept these inductions, such as rewards, punishments, provision of relevant information, and so on. French and Raven (1959) have proposed five separate bases of social power whose effectiveness depends upon the degree that they stimulate forces in the recipient of the influence attempts to act in accord with these inductions, minus the degree they generate forces in the recipient to resist these inductions. A summary of studies on the consequences of these different forms of social power is provided by French and Raven (1959) and by Cartwright (1959). The hypotheses considered in the present investigation are in large part suggested by French and Raven. The derivations of these hypotheses are described by those authors and will not be discussed here.

A secondary concern of this study is in the students' perceptions of the valence and the probability of performing up to his capacity, and how these variables intervene between influence attempts by teachers and the setting of aspirations by students. This interest in the consequences of perceived valence and probability stems from assumptions in Lewin's theory of aspiration setting that the level of aspiration is a function of the positive valence of succeeding, the negative valence of failing, and the probability of succeeding or failing. Probability is measured here in terms of the perceived difficulty of achieving a capacity performance.

Finally, we consider the effects of different forms of social power upon attitudes toward teachers and the subject matter of the course. Hypotheses tested here were, for the most part, proposed by French and Raven.

The present theoretical orientation may be summarized in the following model, the terms of which are explained below.

Act of teacher	Decision making by Student	Decision of student
Form of influence	Valence of capacity	Congruence be-
	Difficulty of capacity	tween student's
		aspirations and
		capacity

By form of influence we refer to the bases of social power proposed by French and Raven: reward, coercion, expert, legitimate, and referent. Each of these is defined in the presentation of the results. Valence of capacity is the degree that a student perceives the attainment of his capacity grade as an attractive goal. Difficulty refers to his perception of the probability that the goal is attainable. It is assumed that the degree of difficulty perceived by a student is determined not only by his personal ability, but also by external barriers such as the competence of teachers and the sufficiency of time and help in doing assignments. Degree of congruence between aspired grade and capacity grade is the distance between the aspired grade and the capacity grade, divided by 1.

METHOD

Due to the exploratory nature of this research and the large number of concepts involved, a written questionnaire was selected as the basic instrument. Although it is difficult to specify with confidence the direction of causality in our correlational results, hypotheses and empirical evidence developed in other settings can be used in interpreting the most probable direction of causality. Conclusions will be stated in terms of hypotheses deemed worthy of study under more controlled conditions.

The relevant concepts were measured with questions utilizing Likert-type scales. Preliminary versions of this questionnaire were developed and revised on the basis of intensive interviews with students. The questionnaire focused on the aspirations of students in mathematics classes and on the relationship of students to teachers of mathematics. Mathematics was selected since this course is required of all respondents and because there should be little ambiguity in students' minds over the nature of a good performance compared to courses using more subjective criteria for evaluation of their progress. The questions were repeated for English courses in order to examine the effects of a different course content and the consequences of the greater social emphasis upon achievement in mathematics which supposedly characterizes contemporary society.

Four-hundred male students, 100 from each of four junior high schools comprised the sample. Tenth graders were selected because they include the oldest group with a wide distribution of ability. The four schools were chosen to provide a wide range of socioeconomic status and ability of students. A comparison of results for the predicted relationships within each of the four schools revealed that no important differences exist among the schools insofar as the present data are concerned.

Respondents in each school filled out the questionnaire during a 1.5-hour period while teachers were absent from the testing room. The administration of the questionnaire uniformly occurred shortly after students had received their grades for the fourth of six marking periods. The recent knowledge of their grades provided the students with stable evidence of their present level of performance while permitting the possibility of future changes in the grades and in the students' aspirations for grades.

Validation of Assumptions

The interpretation of results in this study rests upon assumptions stated earlier about teachers' intentions and students' perceptions of teachers' acts. The results, on the whole, support the reasonableness of these assumptions.

It was assumed that students believe their capacity is known by teachers. Evidence suggesting that this assumption is warranted for the purposes of this study is provided by the pupils' answers to the query: "Do you think your teacher is a good judge of your ability?" In the responses 67 per cent of the students described their teachers as "quite good" or "very good" judges of their abilities. It was also assumed that students are aware of their own capacities and that they support the norm that they should not be expected to perform at levels beyond capacity. Support for these assumptions is found in responses to the question: "How reasonable is your teacher in how well he expects you to do?" Seventy-nine per cent of the students replied that their teacher "expects about the right amount from me," 14 per cent felt that the teacher required "too much," and 7 per cent answered "too little." These percentages also provide indirect support for the assumption that teachers are guided by professional norms holding that students should not be expected to work beyond or below capacity.

A further assumption was that teachers expect pupils to work up to their capacity level. Over 80 per cent in each of the schools perceived their teacher as expecting they could perform at the level of their capacity, while less than 1 per cent said that they had no idea what their teacher expected of them. Most students, however, did not view these as strong demands. In response to the question: "Has your math teacher 'pushed' you to work toward this [capacity] grade?" 55 per cent said that they felt "little or no pressure" while only 14 per cent said that they felt "quite a lot" of pressure.

The aspirations of students may be strongly determined by their confidence in themselves. We felt it was important, therefore, to determine what effect this personality characteristic might have upon students' attitudes toward influence attempts by teachers as well as students aspirations and achievements. A standardized measurement of test-anxiety prepared by Mandler and Sarason (1952) was administered to all subjects. High scores on this measure indicate a high fear of failure.

While text-anxiety was not correlated with students' perceptions of teachers' influence, it was related to aspirations setting in a way consistent with findings in previous research on the level of aspiration. Atkinson has found that persons with high test-anxiety tend to avoid moderate risks (Atkinson, 1957). The present data show that students with high test-anxiety set aspirations farther from their present level of performance than do students with low test-anxiety. The goals set by the more anxious students were often unrealistically high. The high goals are taken to be unrealistic since it was noted that the farther students set their aspirations from their current grades in mathematics, the less they were likely to attain their levels of aspiration in their final grades for the course $(r = -.63 \, **).$[2]

---

[2] Correlation coefficients reported in text and tables are marked by asterisks to indicate the probability values at the .05 (*) and .01 or less (**) levels of significance, two-tailed test.

RESULTS

How much were the students committing themselves when they stated their levels of aspiration? To answer this question, aspired grades were compared with the grades actually received by students at the end of the semester. The substantial relationship between aspired grades and those received at the end of the semester ($r = .66$ **) suggests that the aspirations were realistic among a majority of students. The aspired grades usually were set from one-third to one whole letter grade higher than grades received for immediately past performances, a typical phenomenon in setting aspiration levels indicating a desire for future improvement.

Our principal concern is in the relationships of the separate forms of power exerted by teachers (as students view these matters) with the congruence between students' stated aspirations for grades and their perceived capacities.

Perceived level of capacity was measured by the query:

Not everyone can get A for a final grade in mathematics. Many students know that they must get something less because everyone has an upper limit to his ability. What final grade do you think you could get if you worked to the limit of your ability and did the best you could in mathematics for the rest of the semester?

Aspired grade was obtained by the query:

Students do not always feel like doing their best in a certain class. Sometimes they are willing to accept a grade which is not as good as they *could* get if they really tried. The final grade you will get in your math class this semester will depend partly on how hard you are going to work for the rest of this semester. Considering how hard you plan to work, what final grade do you think you should get in math this year?

Effects of Separate Bases of Power

The most direct attempts to influence students are based on the use of sanctions: by rewarding or coercing. Rewards are given or promised for behavior which is in accord with the wishes of the inducer. Coercion, based upon the ability to punish, is exerted or threatened for behavior that is not in accord with the wishes of the inducer. In a school, a teacher may administer sanctions in many ways: by the grades he gives, by comments or signs made to students, by exclusion from the group or assignment of responsibilities in class, by reports to authorities or parents, and the like. In order to encompass this variety of approving or disapproving cues, it was found necessary to cast questions about sanctioning acts by teachers in terms of the approval or disapproval that students perceived teachers have toward them. A general measure of the degree that sanctioning was perceived as rewarding or coercive was sought with the query: "On the whole, how much do you feel that your math teacher is pleased (or displeased) with you compared to the rest of the class?" It was expected that the greater the relative approval received by the student, the greater would be the congruence between his aspired grade and his capacity grade. In the first row of Table 1 it can be seen that this expectation is supported.

Table 1. Correlations between Forms of Power and Congruence ($N = 415$)

Form of power attributed to teacher	Congruence of student's aspirations and capacity
Comparative degree of rewarding sanction	.21 **
Discriminate reward, frequency	.07
Indiscriminate reward, frequency	.03
Discriminate coercion, frequency	.09
Indiscriminate coercion, frequency	−.14 **
Legitimacy of grading	.21 **
Expertness in grading	.09
Referent status of teacher	.13 **

** $p < .01$.

Although reward and coercion can be conceived as the extreme ends of a single dimension, French and Raven note that "the distinction between these two types of power is important because the dynamics of them are different." Extreme punishment of a person, for example, may lead him to avoid or escape the whole situation in which it operates, while receipt of a valued reward may make the situation more attractive to him. Thus, measures were made of the degree that teachers reward ("Does your math teacher seem to be pleased when you do your best?") and of the degree that teachers coerce ("Does your math teacher seem displeased when you don't try very hard and your work is not as good as it could be?"). Each of these questions was answered on a frequency scale. Because the reward and coercion in these instances are being given where they are ordinarily taken to be appropriate reactions, they are designated as discriminate sanctions to distinguish them from indiscriminate sanctions, discussed in a moment. On the second and fourth lines of Table 1 are shown correlations between frequency of discriminate sanctions and congruence. The low and nonsignificant correlations suggest that the degree of discriminate reward or coercion that teachers were perceived to use do not affect the degree of congruency between aspirations and capacity.

Two further concepts relevant to sanctioning behavior were investigated. The first is indiscriminate reward: "Is your math teacher ever pleased with your work even when you don't try hard?" The second is indiscriminate coercion: "Does your math teacher ever seem to be dis-

pleased with you even when you do your best in class?" It can be seen
in Table 1 that indiscriminate reward has no apparent effect upon congruence while indiscriminate coercion is inversely related to congruence.

This last finding suggests that indiscriminate coercion arouses
stronger tendencies to resist the teacher's inductions, than to accept them.

**Table 2. Correlations between Forms of Sanction and Power,
and Desire to Conform and Legitimacy ($N = 415$)**

Form of power attributed to teacher	Desire to conform	Legitimacy
Discriminate coercion	.13 **	.06
Indiscriminate coercion	—.19 **	—.24 **
Difference **		
Discriminate reward	.29 **	.31 **
Indiscriminate reward	—.11 *	—.03
Difference **		

* $p < .05$.   ** $p < .01$.

To test such an hypothesis, students were asked: "How often do you feel
like doing the things your math teacher wants you to do?" Results relevant to this hypothesis are shown in the first column in Table 2. It is
plain that students perceived themselves as less ready to conform to a
teacher's desires when coercion was indiscriminate than when it was
discriminate.

It has been found in other research that resistance to influence becomes greater as legitimacy of influence decreases (see French and Raven).
The legitimacy of social sanctioning stems from the perception, in those
being influenced, that the influencer is behaving in accord with the internalized values of the ones being influenced. The degree of legitimacy
attributed to teachers' behavior was measured by the query: "How fair is
your mathematics teacher about most things?" The correlations between
legitimacy and the separate forms of sanctioning are shown in the second
column of Table 2. It can be seen that discriminate reward is reliably related to legitimacy but indiscriminate reward has no relationship with
legitimacy. Furthermore, indiscriminate coercion is reliably associated
with nonlegitimacy while discriminate coercion has almost no association
with legitimacy. We conclude that teachers who are considered discriminate in rewards are likely to be seen as "fair," while those who are
indiscriminate in coercion are likely to be seen as "unfair."

French and Raven hypothesize that coercion arouses strong resistance
in the recipient of it so that the inducer's desires are not always acted
upon by the recipients and, depending upon the strength of the resistance
aroused, the recipients may instead be stimulated to do the opposite of
what has been asked of them. This hypothesis has been corroborated by

Zipf (1958) and Sampson (1960). The present findings (and those to be seen in Table 3) suggest that resistance to coercion in the school setting may more readily generate negativism when the coercion is indiscriminate.

Legitimate power, we have seen, stems from the perception that an influencer is behaving in accord with the values of the person being influenced. In some instances acts by a teacher may be perceived as legitimate or nonlegitimate without their being direct attempts to influence the student. An example of this type of legitimacy concerns the fairness of the teacher in evaluating the student's work. The degree of this form of legitimacy attributed to teachers was measured by the question: "If you did your best in math class would your teacher actually give you the grade that describes your ability?" It was expected that students who perceived their teacher as more legitimate would tend to set levels of aspiration closer to their perceived capacities since the risk of failure from unfair treatment by the teacher would be minimal. Evidence reported in the sixth row of Table 1 supports this prediction. Confidence, then, that one will receive the grade he earns if he works up to capacity (and not necessarily a high grade) is associated with tendencies to aspire to attain capacity.

Expert power is based upon the perceived reliability of the influencer's information. The more an informer is perceived as knowing what he is talking about, the more the informer is likely to influence the recipient of the information. Since we are assuming that teachers' inductions are often placed upon the student in the direction of working up to capacity, it is evident that the teacher's attempts to influence will be more acceptable if the student perceives that the teacher knows what the student's capacity is. Thus, expertness of the teacher was measured in one way with the following question: "Do you think your math teacher is a good judge of your ability in mathematics?" It was expected that greater attribution of expertness to the teacher would be associated with greater congruence between aspiration and capacity. In the realm of teaching, however, expertness is also conceived as skill in the substantive content of the course being taught. A measure of this type of expertness is the following: "How much do you think your math teacher knows about the mathematics he is supposed to teach?" Results reported in Table 1 concern only expertness in judging the ability of students, since the results with the previous measure (expertness in math) were not different in any important respects. The nonsignificant correlations in the seventh row of Table 1 suggest that the expertness of the teacher does not generate greater congruence between aspirations and capacity. The failure of expertness to be related to congruence might be explained by French and Raven's (1959, p. 163) statement that

expert power results in primary social influences on the person's cognitive structure and probably not on other types of systems. Of course, changes in the cognitive structure can change the direction of forces and hence of locomotion, but such a change of behavior is secondary social influence.

Referent power exists in an influencer when others desire to be like him. Students who are highly attracted to a teacher are likely to behave in ways of which he would approve, although they may not be aware of doing so. It was found offensive to students in pretests to inquire how much they desired to associate with or be like teachers. Therefore, measurement of this form of power was by means of the question: "In general, how much do you like your mathematics teacher as a person?" The prediction that greater referent power attributed to a teacher would be associated with greater congruence between aspiration level and perceived capacity was supported, as shown in the eighth row of Table 1.

The effects of the various forms of power may be summarized by noting the positive effects of rewarding sanctions, legitimate power, and referent power on the congruence between aspirations and capacity, and the negative effect of indiscriminate coercion. It is noteworthy that the first three forms are also significantly positively related to one another, indicating that they often appear simultaneously in the teacher's behavior and often supplement one another, as proposed by French and Raven. Indiscriminate coercive power, on the other hand, is negatively related to each of the other forms. The first three forms of power, we may add, are attributed to teachers more often by students who attribute high capacity to themselves, while coercive power is attributed to teachers more often by students who assign low capacity to themselves. Nevertheless, when perceived capacity is controlled, the relationships in Table 1 are not substantially lowered and retain their statistical significance—students with high ability not differing greatly from those with low ability.

Student Performance

An important consequence of social power is the degree that the separate forms of power motivate students to *perform* at the level of their aspirations. The relationship between the closeness of the aspired grades to the *actual grade* the student received at the end of the year, and the attribution of reward power to the math teacher was $r = .24$ **. This relationship is significantly greater than its relationship to coercive power ($r = -.08$). Thus, positive forms of influence appear to stimulate attainment of aspirations more than do coercive forms of influence.

Valence and Difficulty of Attaining Capacity

According to the theory of aspiration setting proposed by Lewin et al. (1944) one specific aspiration level, out of a number of possible alternatives, is likely to be chosen depending upon the degree that it is attractive but not too difficult to attain. We thus expected to find students placing their levels of aspiration closer to their perceived capacity the more the capacity grades were valent for them and the less achievement of them was perceived as difficult. Valence of capacity was measured by the question: "How good do you think you would feel if you did get this grade?" Difficulty was measured with the query: "How hard would you have to work in order to receive this grade?" The expectation just stated was supported: valence of capacity grade is positively related to congruence ($r = .12$ *), and difficulty of attaining capacity grade is negatively related to congruence ($r = -.27$ **). It is noteworthy that valence and difficulty are positively related to each other ($r = .26$ **), supporting the Lewin et al. (1944) and the Atkinson (1957) findings that a difficult goal tends to be more attractive than easy ones.

We had expected to find that different forms of power would have different degrees of relationship to the valence the student attributed to the achievement of his capacity grade. A teacher who rewards a student for working at capacity, for example, might generate a greater desire in him to achieve capacity than a teacher who punishes him for not doing so. The statistical relationships between each form of influence and valence of reaching capacity were, however, consistently too low to be considered reliable. But the teachers' total amount of power in attempting to influence students appears to affect students' perceptions of the valence of the capacity grade. When all forms of power are considered together in a multiple correlation with valence, the multiple correlation between power and valence of the capacity grades is .27 **. The nature of the contributions made by the separate forms of power, moreover, makes it appear likely that a teacher who employs several positive bases of power simultaneously, to support his inductions on a student to work up to capacity, will have greater effect upon the valence of doing so than a teacher who employs only one positive basis of power. Why and how social power can have effects upon the valence of a goal are problems worthy of future attention.

It seems reasonable that the closer a student sets his aspired grade to his perceived capacity, the more he will be satisfied in attaining this established aspiration. This contention was supported by a correlation of .32 ** between congruence and valence of success, the latter measured by the query: "How good would you feel if you were given the grade you intend to get?"

Desire to Conform

A direct determination of the readiness of students to be influenced by teachers was sought by the use of two related concepts: perceived desire to conform and perceived desire negatively to conform. The former was measured with the question: "How often do you feel like doing the things your math teacher wants you to do?" The latter was measured by the query: "How often do you feel like doing the opposite of what your math teacher wants you to do?" All forms of power together are strongly related to desire to conform (multiple $R = .56$ **). Desire to conform, in turn, is related to congruence ($r = .20$ **).

The relationships between the separate forms of power and the desire to conform, or to do the opposite, are shown in Table 3. Consistent with Table 1, indiscriminate coercion was related to nonconforming desires, indiscriminate coercion and reward were negatively related to conforming desires, and all other forms of power (including expertness) were positively associated with conforming desires.

Attitudes of Students toward Teacher and Course

A final interest of this investigation was in the relations between types of power and attitudes toward relevant aspects of the social setting. Two variables were considered here. One query asked about changes in attitudes toward the teacher ("Has your opinion of your mathematics teacher changed from what it was at first?"). The other inquired about changes in attitude toward the content of the course ("Do you feel any different about mathematics now than you did before you took this math course?"). Both items were scored in terms of direction of attitude change

Table 3. Correlations between Forms of Power and Motivation to Conform ($N = 415$)

Form of power attributed to teacher	Desire to conform	Desire negatively to conform
Comparative degree of rewarding	.35 **	—.24 **
Discriminate reward, frequency	.29 **	—.15 **
Indiscriminate reward, frequency	—.11 **	.09
Discriminate coercion, frequency	.13 **	.00
Indiscriminate coercion, frequency	—.19 **	.16 **
Legitimacy of grading	.33 **	—.24 **
Expertness in grading	.30 **	—.20 **
Referent status of teacher	.53 **	—.29 **

** $p < .01$.

as well as intensity of change. In Table 4 correlations are presented between these two attitudes and the different forms of power attributed to teachers. The evidence indicates that each form of power affects both of these attitudes in directions similar to the effects we have seen for grade aspirations, and desires to conform, and in directions suggested by French and Raven.

Results from English Classes

The results we have thus far observed concerning teachers in mathematics were not completely replicated when students were queried about their English teachers. Similar correlations were found in mathematics and English when relating forms of power to desires for conformity and to attitude changes toward the teacher and the course content. Only legitimate power, however, was significantly related to the congruence of aspired and capacity grades in the English classes. The fact that legitimate

Table 4. Correlations between Forms of Power and Changes in Attitudes ($N = 415$)

Form of power attributed to teachers	Change in attitude toward teacher	Change in attitude toward math.
Comparative degree of rewarding	.27 **	.30 **
Discriminate reward, frequency	.30 **	.23 **
Indiscriminate reward, frequency	—.05	—.08
Discriminate coercion, frequency	.07	.01
Indiscriminate coercion, frequency	—.22 **	—.21 **
Legitimacy of grading	.17 **	.17 **
Expertness in grading	.37 **	.29 **
Referent status of teacher	.57 **	.40 **

** $p < .01$.

power appears to have positive effects in both mathematics and English is understandable since legitimacy was rated by the students as the most effective source of a teacher's power in response to an inquiry into the relative importance of teachers, parents, and peers as power figures.

The failure of the other bases of power among English teachers to be related to congruence, however, requires further explanation. The original reason for the inclusion of questions about English teachers was the expectation that students would be less certain of the nature of good performance in English courses than in mathematics courses. We anticipated that influence might be more effective in English classes because students would be less clear about their capacities in that subject matter and therefore less confident of appropriate aspirations for themselves, thus being more vulnerable to influences from teachers (cf. Festinger, 1954). Contrary to our expectations, more uncertainty about the appropriateness of their aspirations was shown in mathematics than in English, as indicated by responses to the question: "Do you think you are aiming for too high or too low a grade?" Comparisons, furthermore, of responses to questions concerning the degree that teachers reveal their reactions to good or bad performances and the adequacy of help rendered by teachers showed no differences between mathematics and English classes. We were led, therefore, to suspect that the apparent ineffectiveness of influence attempts in English classes was due not to the course material itself or to the methods of teaching, but to the motivations of students.

An indicator of student concern over performance was available in the previously mentioned measure of valence of success. In mathematics classes, all forms of influence except coercion were significantly related to the valence of successfully achieving the aspired grades. In English classes, however, only referent power showed this relationship to a significant degree. It appears, then, that the students were more eager to do well in mathematics than in English. Further weight is lent to this interpretation by responses to the question: "Which class do you think is more important for your future?" In the replies, 34 students favored English, 152 preferred mathematics, and the rest saw them as equally important.[3] It is interesting to note that in the literature on level of aspiration, experimental predictions are better supported the more that subjects have ego involvement in their tasks (Lewin, et al., 1944; Stotland, et al., 1957).

SUMMARY AND CONCLUSIONS

A questionnaire was used to explore the effects of teachers' influences upon students' aspirations for achievement in school. Hypotheses drawn from earlier work on the differential consequences of separate types of social power were tested in a correlational analysis.

1. Tendencies to accept a teacher's influences are aroused in students who are subject to reward, legitimate, referent, or expert power; while tendencies to ignore or oppose what teachers desire are aroused in students subject to indiscriminate coercive influences.

2. With the possible exception of expert power, these tendencies affect the degree to which students set their aspired grades congruent with their perceived capacities.

3. Two forms of coercion are distinguished by students: disapproval of inadequate performance, which appears to have no effect on aspirations or future performance, and disapproval even when performance is as good as the student feels he can do, which seems to have negative effects on aspiration setting as well as future performance.

4. Two forms of reward are also discriminated by students. Tendencies to accept a teacher's influences are lowered under indiscriminate reward but increased by reward for adequate performances.

5. The positive or negative forces set up by the separate bases of power affect the favorableness or negativeness of student attitudes toward teachers and course content.

6. The separate bases of power are effective in determining aspirations to the degree that the students are ego involved in the performances on which they are setting aspirations.

[3] The questionnaire was administered to students during the spring of 1959, that is, during the post-Sputnik emphasis on mathematics and physical science.

10 / Test Anxiety and Classroom Observations [1]

Kenneth S. Davidson and Seymour B. Sarason

(1) Test anxiety scores serve as effective predictors of boys' but not girls' school behavior. (2) Defensiveness scores serve as effective predictors of girls' but not boys' school behavior. (3) Feeling and admitting to anxiety tends to be disturbing to boys but may be helpful motivationally for girls. (4) Teachers show differential treatment of boys and girls. These are some of the findings of this research with second-grade children by Kenneth B. Davidson of Wayne University and Seymour B. Sarason of Yale University.

In a previous publication (Sarason et al., 1960) we have described a variety of studies comparing high anxious (HA) and low anxious (LA) children. The measure primarily used for the assessment of anxiety level was the Test Anxiety Scale for Children (TASC).[2] The pattern of these previous findings has been clearly and extensively less favorable for the high anxious children, particularly for the high anxious boys.

In one study (Sarason et al., 1958) classroom observations were made of HA and LA children matched for grade, sex, and intelligence. Those observations described the HA children (particularly the boys) as less secure, task-oriented, and academically adequate than the LA subjects. Because those classroom observations were primarily exploratory and one of a series of procedures for studying 32 matched pairs of HA and LA children, each child was observed for only one hour. The data obtained from these observations were necessarily limited in scope and could not clarify the nature of dynamics and changes occurring in children that would aid in understanding the process by which anxiety interferes with scholastic effectiveness. In that study the process of subject selection did not permit assessment of the effects resulting from differences in teachers and classroom atmospheres.

As a result of these considerations the classroom observations in the present studies had two purposes: (a) to determine the relation of anxiety

---

[1] The research reported herein was performed pursuant to a contract with the United States Office of Education and a grant from the National Institute of Mental Health, Department of Health, Education, and Welfare.

[2] [Appended to the selection.]

Reprinted from *Child Development*, 1961, 32, 199–210, with the permission of the authors and the Society for Research in Child Development.

about school to a wide variety of personality and behavior variables measured in the classroom and (b) to explore the effects of differences in classroom atmosphere upon those relations.

PROCEDURE

The present study was carried out in the three second grade classrooms of a North Haven, Connecticut, elementary school. The choice of
the second grade also permitted study of the important question of how
early high anxious children can be detected in order to intiate early steps
towards prevention of negative effects of anxiety on learning and development. The TASC can be administered in the usual group procedure
to most children at the end of first grade. In the last month of the previous
school year the TASC and a similarly constructed and administered questionnaire, the Defensiveness Scale for Children (DSC),[3] were given to the
first grade children.

The DSC includes the 11 Lie items formerly found in the General
Anxiety Scale for Children (GASC) [4] and 29 other items. Children who
give "Yes" answers to questions of the DSC are saying in effect that they
can admit and communicate to others about a variety of reactions such
as anxiety, shame, aggression, insecurity, and concern about themselves
and their relations with others. Children who answer "No" more frequently would generally be more "defensive." The interest in a "defensiveness" score was an exploratory one and stemmed from various considerations. For example HA children were able to admit to feelings of
anxiety on the TASC and GASC, but parental interview findings (Davidson, 1959; Sarason, et al., 1960) indicated that they did not communicate
freely about their feelings to their parents. Also, some LA children with
high Lie scores seemed to communicate in a defensive manner that was
more typical of HA children. Finally, the TASC discriminated very
effectively between HA and LA boys but significant results were much
less frequent for girls. The hope was that the DSC would differentiate
among girls more effectively or aid in understanding the limited results
obtained for girls with the TASC. For these reasons the defensiveness
scores were obtained and correlated, in an exploratory manner, with the
same measures of personality and classroom behaviors as were the TASC
scores.

All of the children in the three second grade classrooms were observed by two trained observers who made notes spontaneously. They
observed all morning or all afternoon daily for four months beginning
the first day of school. In the original plan one observer sat in one room,
the other in a second room. Both observed the children in the third room
in order to provide a measure of the adequacy of inter-observer agreement in rating children on personality and classroom behavior variables.
After a few observation sessions in this third room, both independently
reported that the children expressed themselves much less freely in the

[3] [Appended to the selection.]   [4] [Appended to the selection.]

third room than the children in the other rooms. Each felt they were not getting to understand the children in the third room as well, which indicated that, unless more freedom of expression occurred in those children, the inter-observer reliability in evaluations of those children could be inadequate for subsequent analyses.

As a result, beginning about the third week, both observers sat, at different times, in each of the three second grade rooms and took notes on all the children. The number of children in the study varied because families moved, but the maximum number of subjects in any aspect of the study was 96, including 53 boys and 43 girls, of whom 40 boys and 37 girls had received the TASC and the DSC in first grade.

In order to assess the subjects' personality and classroom behavior, a check list of 25 variables [5] was formed with definitions provided for each of the items. After three months both observers rated all 96 children, and each teacher rated the children in her class on a 10-point scale of each of the 25 items. A number of the items were selected because they had yielded significant results when parents of HA and LA subjects had rated their own child on those qualities (Davidson, et al., 1958; Sarason, et al., 1960). Other items dealing with daydreaming, level of achievement, speed of learning, memory, and attention to school-work were included because of their possible significance for both anxiety and classroom effectiveness. However, predictions were not made for these items because children's behavior in school may vary considerably from their behavior at home and because parents and teachers may differ in their values, expectations, and sanctions regarding children's behavior and personality.

RESULTS

There were two phases in the analysis of the data obtained in this study. In the first phase the observers' and teachers' check-list ratings were analyzed to determine the degree of inter-observer and teacher-observer agreement. Also, the children's TASC and DSC scores were correlated with the check-list ratings given them by the observers and their teacher In the second phase the observers' classroom notes were analyzed to compare the teachers' methods of handling children's needs and the teachers' expression of emotions and value judgments.

Personality Check List

Inter-observer reliability. The check-list study began with an assessment of the inter-observer reliability. The two observers' ratings of the children were correlated for each of the 25 items of the check list. These correlations were computed for the following six groups: all 96 subjects, the 53 boys, the 43 girls, and each of the three separate classrooms with boys and girls combined. The results of this analysis are presented in

[5] [Appended to the selection.]

Table 1. All subsequent analyses involving check-list ratings utilized only those 18 items with inter-observer reliability levels of at least .40 for boys and girls both separately and combined. Two major findings emerge from this assessment of reliability: First, there is significantly greater agreement between observers in evaluating boys as compared with girls. On 21 of the 25 items, the reliability coefficient is higher for boys than for girls ($p < .01$). Second, the inter-observer agreement for the children in rooms 2 and 3 is similarly greater than for the children in room 1, which was the room originally chosen for the reliability check. It should also be noted that there are uniformly low levels of agreement between observers about children's anxiety, tension, and fear of failure in comparison to their very adequate agreement on variables such as emotional expression, cautiousness, maturity, speed of learning, retention, and responsibility.

Table 1. Inter-Observer Reliabilities *

Item	Children $N = 96$	Boys $N = 53$	Girls $N = 43$	Room 1 $N = 32$	Room 2 $N = 32$	Room 3 $N = 32$
1. Anxiety §	.27	.36	.23 ‡	.20 ‡	.28 ‡	.32 †
2. Anxiety facilitates §	.48	.65	.08 ‡	.47	.68	.31 †
3. Independent	.48	.51	.41	.29 ‡	.59	.54
4. Hides emotion	.61	.66	.56	.47	.67	.71
5. Difficulty in communicating	.49	.50	.53	.58	.60	.52
6. Submissive	.70	.79	.54	.60	.73	.80
7. Cautiousness	.69	.71	.58	.58	.66	.71
8. Not sensitive	.46	.50	.50	.13 ‡	.22 ‡	.78
9. Relaxed §	.23 †	.33 †	.12 ‡	.38 †	.25 ‡	.09 ‡
10. Unambitious	.47	.44	.50	.30 †	.53	.49
11. Set in ways §	.64	.79	.30 †	.65	.59	.72
12. Net well liked	.56	.77	.42	.39 †	.64	.67
13. Immature	.61	.63	.63	.57	.67	.58
14. Sociable §	.66	.75	.33 †	.35 †	.66	.85
15. Does not daydream	.47	.45	.50	.39 †	.60	.42
16. Inactive	.62	.74	.46	.63	.73	.46
17. Underachievers	.49	.49	.50	.17 ‡	.76	.71
18. Learns quickly	.88	.74	.83	.74	.86	.82
19. Forgets	.78	.78	.75	.65	.83	.83
20. Does not fear failure §	.33	.31 †	.10 ‡	−.09 ‡	.09 ‡	.52
21. Does not pay attention	.72	.87	.57	.65	.56	.81
22. Weak conscience	.73	.78	.55	.66	.70	.85
23. Masculine	.75	.66	.56	.51	.96	.78
24. Optimistic §	.46	.54	.39	.16 ‡	.60	.57
25. Not responsible	.78	.84	.62	.78	.74	.84
Mean (25 items)	.60	.65	.48	.44	.65	.67
Mean (18 items)	.65	.68	.57	.48	.70	.71

* All correlations are significant (one-tail test) beyond the .01 level except as noted.
† $p < .05$.   ‡ Not significant.
§ These items were not used in later analyses or in computing means in the bottom row.

Teacher-observer agreement. As part of this phase of the analysis, teacher-observer agreement was assessed by correlating the teachers' ratings of the children with those by each observer for each of the 18 selected items. These correlations were computed for the three separate rooms with the boys and girls combined in each room. The results are presented in Table 2.

Table 2. Correlations between Observers' and Teachers' Check-List Ratings *

	Teacher 1 $N = 32$		Teacher 2 $N = 32$		Teacher 3 $N = 32$	
	Rater A	Rater B	Rater A	Rater B	Rater A	Rater B
1. Independent	.13 ‡	−.06 ‡	.55	.80	.02 ‡	.12 ‡
2. Hides emotions	.16 ‡	.58	.30 †	.47	.45	.45
3. Difficulty in communicating	.67	.60	.58	.73	.32	.60
4. Submissive	.67	.62	.74	.66	.70	.60
5. Cautious	.69	.37 †	.59	.72	.76	.68
6. Not sensitive	.25 ‡	.36 †	.50	.35 †	.53	.59
7. Unambitious	.69	.52	.54	.32 †	.60	.52
8. Not well liked	.52	.36 †	.65	.54	.60	.22 ‡
9. Immature	.23 ‡	.34 †	.61	.66	.78	.65
10. Does not daydream	.14 ‡	.50	.27 ‡	.49	−.04 ‡	.35 †
11. Inactive	.53	.67	.78	.80	.71	.39 †
12. Underachievers	.04 ‡	.45	.56	.64	.31 †	.51
13. Learns quickly	.68	.65	.79	.84	.73	.78
14. Forgets	.44	.55	.86	.82	.67	.70
15. Does not pay attention	.69	.56	.74	.73	.80	.74
16. Weak conscience	.69	.61	.78	.81	.86	.79
17. Masculine	.83	.73	.91	.71	.68	.72
18. Not responsible	.67	.47	.79	.80	.81	.77
Mean	.52	.51	.68	.69	.62	.59

* All correlations are significant (one-tail test) beyond the .01 level except as noted.
† $p < .05$.   ‡ Not significant.

The observer-teacher correlations are higher for room 2 than for room 1 for 15 of the 18 items in the case of each observer. Comparing rooms 3 and 1 the correlations are larger in room 3 for 13 of the 18 items in the case of observer A and larger for 10 of the 18 items for observer B. The means of the 18 correlations for each teacher-observer combination show that, for each observer, agreement with the teachers' ratings was greatest for room 2, smaller for room 3, and least for room 1. The difference in mean teacher-observer agreement between room 2 and room 1 was significant for both observers ($p < .01$). Thus, not only the inter-observer reliability but also the teacher-observer agreement is significantly less for the check-list ratings of the children in room 1.

It will be recalled that both observers remarked very early in their observations that the children in room 1 seemed to express themselves less

freely than the other boys and girls. This suggested that the observers'
and teachers' ratings might be more constricted for the children in room 1
as compared with rooms 2 and 3. Thus, for each item, the standard deviations were computed for each observer's and the teacher's ratings of
the children in the separate rooms. Fourteen of the standard deviations
for observer A are larger than the corresponding sigmas obtained from
the teacher's ratings in room 1. For observer B, 13 of the 18 standard
deviations are larger than those obtained for this teacher. However, the
outstanding finding is obtained by comparing the standard deviations of
the ratings by the three teachers. For all 18 items, the teacher in room 1
constricted her ratings more than the other two teachers and often did
so to a marked degree. While the observers tended—observer A only
slightly—to constrict their ratings of the children in room 1 more than
the other children in the other rooms, the teacher in room 1 constricted
her ratings of her pupils more than either observer and much more than
the other two teachers.

Relationship of ratings to test anxiety and defensiveness. The last

Table 3. **Significant Mean Correlations between Subjects' TASC Scores
and Ratings by Observers and Teachers**

Variable *	Room 1 N = 27	Room 2 N = 24	Room 3 N = 26	Boys N = 40	Girls N = 37	Children N = 77
1. Independent	..	..	..	+.24 ‡	−.26 ‡	..
2. Hides emotions	..	+.25 ‡	..	+.27 ‡	−.19 †	..
3. Difficulty in communi- cating	..	..	..	+.20 †	..	..
4. Submissive	..	+.54 ‡	..	+.23 †	..	+.15 †
5. Cautious	..	+.47 ‡	..	+.30 ‡	..	+.14 †
6. Not sensitive	..	−.30 †	..	..	−.28 ‡	−.16 †
7. Unambitious	..	..	..	−.20 †	..	..
8. Not well liked	..	..	..	..	..	..
9. Immature	..	..	..	..	+.22 †	..
10. Does not daydream	..	..	..	..	..	+.14 †
11. Inactive	..	+.34 ‡	..	+.25 ‡	..	..
12. Underachievers	..	−.26 †	..	−.25 ‡	..	−.17 †
13. Learns quickly	..	..	+.31 ‡	..	..	..
14. Forgets	..	..	+.30 †	..	..	..
15. Does not pay attention	..	−.47 ‡	..	−.26 ‡	..	−.18 ‡
16. Weak conscience	..	−.58 ‡	..	−.26 ‡	..	−.21 ‡
17. Masculine	..	−.45 ‡	+.24 †	..	..	−.16 †
18. Not responsible	..	−.39 ‡	..	−.29 ‡	..	−.14 †

NOTE. Mean correlations were computed through z transformations and tested for
significance using a two-tail test and the formula, $t_z = M_z \sqrt{3(N-3)}$, with $df =
3(N-3)$.

    * Positive correlations mean that anxiety is directly related to the variables as listed,
while for negative correlations anxiety is inversely related to the listed variables.

    † $p < .05$.   ‡ $p < .01$.

phase of the check-list analysis concerned the relation between the observers' and teachers' check-list ratings of the children and the subjects' TASC and DSC scores. For the children in each room and for the boys and girls separately and combined in all rooms, TASC and DSC scores were correlated with each observer's and the teacher's ratings. For each grouping of children, three correlations for each item were obtained between ratings—the two observers' and the teachers'—and the TASC scores. The means of these three correlations which were significant are presented in Table 3. The same procedure was followed for the DSC, and these results are presented in Table 4.

Aside from the specific relations between anxiety or defensiveness and the characteristics and behaviors measured by the ratings, two findings are clearly shown. First, TASC scores relate significantly to a whole series of personality characteristics for boys, but not for the girls, while the reverse is true for the DSC. Second, in room 2 anxiety correlates significantly with a number of variables but not defensiveness. The reverse

Table 4. Significant Mean Correlations between Subjects' DSC Scores and Ratings by Observers and Teachers

Variable *	Room 1 N = 27	Room 2 N = 24	Room 3 N = 26	Boys N = 40	Girls N = 37	Children N = 77
1. Independent	+.37 ‡	..	−.26 †	..	..	..
2. Hides emotions	+.34 ‡	−.32 ‡	..	..	..	..
3. Difficulty in communicating	+.36 ‡	..	..	..	+.28 ‡	+.16 †
4. Submissive	+.40 ‡	−.31 †	..	..	..	..
5. Cautious	+.54 ‡	−.28 †	−.33 ‡	..	..	..
6. Not sensitive	+.35 ‡	..	..	+.22 †	..	..
7. Unambitious	..	..	+.36 ‡	..	..	+.17 †
8. Not well liked	..	..	..	..	+.27 ‡	+.14 †
9. Immature	−.40 ‡	..	+.50 ‡	..	..	..
10. Does not daydream	..	..	..	..	−.23 †	..
11. Inactive	+.26 †	..	..	..	..	..
12. Underachievers	..	..	+.46 ‡	..	+.20 †	..
13. Learns quickly	..	..	−.27 †	..	−.26 ‡	−.22 ‡
14. Forgets	..	..	+.43 ‡	+.19 †	+.32 ‡	+.25 ‡
15. Does not pay attention	..	..	+.58 ‡	..	+.20 †	+.18 ‡
16. Weak conscience	−.42 ‡	..	+.54 ‡	..	..	+.13 †
17. Masculine	..	..	..	..	+.23 †	+.22 ‡
18. Not responsible	−.31 ‡	..	+.54 ‡	..	+.23 †	+.17 †

NOTE. Mean correlations were computed through z transformations and tested for significance using a two-tail test and the formula, $t_z = M_z \sqrt{3(N-3)}$, with $df = 3(N-3)$.

* Positive correlations mean that defensiveness is directly related to the variables as listed, while for negative correlations defensiveness is inversely related to the listed variables.

† $p < .05$.   ‡ $p < .01$.

is true in both rooms 1 and 3. The first finding indicates that anxiety about school is related to a variety of personality traits and behavior patterns among boys but only to a few such qualities among girls. On the other hand, high defensive (HD) and low defensive (LD) girls differ in many respects while HD and LD boys tend not to differ much. In other words, anxiety level, as measured by the TASC, is an effective predictor of boys' personality and behavior patterns in school, whereas defensiveness, as measured by the DSC, performs in the same manner for girls.

In view of the variation in both inter-observer and teacher-observer agreement on the check-list ratings, one would expect corresponding results in correlating those ratings with both the TASC and DSC scores. However, in room 1, where there was the least agreement about ratings, the DSC yielded significant results for 10 of the 18 items and no significant results for any of the TASC items. In room 2, where there was greatest agreement about ratings, the TASC yielded significant results for 10 of the 18 items, but the DSC yielded significant results for only three items. In other words, in spite of the lower reliability for ratings of children in room 1, those ratings are significantly correlated with defensiveness. These findings suggest that either anxiety or defensiveness may be the meaningful variable for different classrooms.

Classroom Observation Notes

This phase of the study was concerned with the teachers' methods of coping with the children's needs and personality characteristics. The analysis focused on teachers' handling of children's dependence, cautiousness, fear of failure, motivation, failure and success, and behavior problems (shyness, anxiety, aggression). Instances in which the teacher expressed strong emotions or value judgments were also noted.

The observers independently culled examples from their notes for each teacher for each of these categories. For each incident or note, two clinicians independently indicated by favorable (+) or unfavorable (−) ratings whether the teachers' efforts had helped the children by meeting their needs or had interfered with or reduced the children's effectiveness. Some notes were rated as favorable with unfavorable tones (+ −) or as more unfavorable (− +) while others were given ?'s when both qualities were equal. The clinicians agreed completely on 628 or 70 per cent of their 892 ratings, while disagreeing completely on less than 4 per cent of the ratings. On 745 or 84 per cent of their ratings they agreed about the favorable or unfavorable direction of the rating.[6]

With this exensive agreement the two clinicians held conferences to arrive at a single rating for those notes on which they disagreed. Thus, for each note there was one rating on which the judges were in agree-

[6] The authors wish to express their appreciation to Dr. Wayne Owen for his assistance in these detailed evaluations. In addition the reader may wish to refer to the parental interview study (Davidson, 1959; Sarason, et al., 1960, pp. 222–25) in which the same general procedure of "favorable-unfavorable" ratings was used.

ment. The frequencies of favorable (+ and + −) and unfavorable (− and − +) ratings for each variable are given for the three teachers in Table 5.

Table 5. Frequencies of Positive and Negative Ratings of Observers' Notes

	Teacher 1		Teacher 2		Teacher 3	
	+	−	+	−	+	−
Dependency	18	72	98	16	37	31
Caution	5	29	40	9	17	16
Fear of failure	5	11	24	4	13	7
Motivation	11	31	24	5	16	19
Failure and success	16	37	40	1	29	13
Shyness, anxiety, aggression	7	10	29	2	12	26
Emotion and value judgment	2	33	28	7	2	14
TOTAL	64	223	283	44	126	126

For all seven categories, the teacher in room 2 received more favorable evaluations by far than either of the other two teachers. For the teacher in room 3, one half of the incidents were rated favorably and one half unfavorably, while only one quarter of the ratings for the teacher in room 1 were favorable. This pattern of results is especially clear with respect to the three teachers' handling of the children's dependence, cautiousness or impulsiveness, and failures or successes, as well as the teachers' expression of emotions and value judgments.

DISCUSSION

While these analyses yielded a series of significant results, there are really two general findings of importance for the study of child behavior and personality in the classroom. First, the evidence indicates that the teacher is a prime variable in such studies, and, second, different patterns of results can be expected for boys as compared with girls.

With respect to the first point, differences were found between teachers with respect to levels of reliability and constriction of check-list ratings, correlation of those ratings with TASC and DSC scores, and the evaluations of observers' notes on the teachers' methods and behavior. In the case of room 1 there was low inter-observer and teacher-observer reliability, constriction, especially by the teacher in rating the children, and unfavorable evaluations of the teacher's behavior. In comparison, for rooms 2 and 3, there was greater inter-observer and teacher-observer agreement and less constriction in the rating of those children, as well as more favorable evaluations of the teachers.

It is distinctly possible that in room 1 the teacher's ineffective handling of the dependence, cautiousness or impulsiveness, failures and suc-

cesses of her pupils, as well as her negatively evaluated expressions of
affect and value judgments, were important determinants of the lack of
spontaneous expression and behavior of those children. The notes of each
observer and even casual or untrained observations describe this teacher
as authoritarian, punitive, and rejecting of needs to be dependent or
cautious. As a result, these children did conform to their teacher's rules
and suppressed expression of their needs and feelings in a variety of ways.

It should be pointed out that the mean TASC scores were nearly identical for the three rooms. However, the mean DSC score for room 1 was
higher, though not significantly, than the means for the other two rooms.
Also, the mean Lorge-Thorndike IQ was lowest for room 1, though the
difference was not significant. There is the possibility that the greater
defensiveness and lower intelligence, in combination, acounts for their
less spontaneous expression. It is our own opinion, however, that the
greater defensiveness in room 1 may be an effect of the tendencies of the
teacher to de-emphasize differences among her children (constriction of
ratings) and to misperceive or misinterpret their behavior. That is to say,
a teacher with such tendencies may not only be responding ineffectively
and inappropriately to the needs and behavior of the children but also
may be engendering in them greater defensiveness, i.e., the tendency to
suppress the expression of personal feeling. We are not dealing here with
a type of teacher-child interaction which occurs infrequently in this particular classroom, but one which goes on over long periods of time. It is
also likely that, as this pattern of interaction goes on over time, the defensive behavior of the children affects the teacher in a way so as to reinforce her tendency to misperceive and misinterpret the significance of
the behavior of her children.

The final difference between teachers showed defensiveness but not
test anxiety related to a whole series of check-list items for the children in
rooms 1 and 3, while the reverse was true for room 2. It is possible to
speculate on the reasons for this pattern, but, in any event, it suggests
that teachers who vary in their methods and behavior may stimulate
different feelings and needs in their pupils which then determine their
classroom behavior and characteristics. In rooms 1 and 3, receiving expressions of rejection or acceptance, respectively, seemed a central issue
for the children, while in room 2 the teacher showed acceptance of all
children, though not all behavior, and the central issue seemed to be
academic achievement and improvement.

In view of the fact that anxiety was the meaningful variable for
boys and defensiveness for the girls, it is possible that an important determinant of the similar result found among the teachers is differential reactions and relations to boys and girls by the teachers. Observers frequently commented that the teacher in room 1 tended to favor girls and
the room 3 teacher tended to favor boys, while there was no apparent
difference for boys and girls in room 2. In any event, when teachers differ
markedly, it seems highly likely that measures of different variables will
yield different results for the children in their rooms.

The content of the above paragraph is but an instance of the more general finding of differential results for boys and girls. There was greater inter-observer and teacher-observer agreement in rating boys on the check-list items, and the observers and teachers did not constrict their ratings of the boys as much as they did those of the girls. Since both observers and all three teachers were women, it might be expected that, if anything, they would show more agreement and less constriction of their ratings for girls. That the reverse occurred is probably related to the fact that the observers and teachers agree that, in school, boys give more overt and spontaneous expression to a wider range of feelings and impulses than do girls. This finding does suggest that observation of children as a basis for measurement is likely to be more effective for a wider range of variables for boys than for girls.

The main difference between boys and girls, however, was the finding that test anxiety scores serve as predictors of boys' but not girls' school behavior and characteristics, while the pattern was reversed for the defensiveness scores. The fact is that differences between HA and LA have been found much more frequently for boys than for girls, and these results have generally showed the LA boys in a more favorable light. This led to speculation that feeling and admitting to anxiety is an ego-alien and disturbing state of affairs for boys, but may be ego-syntonic, not disturbing, and perhaps helpful in a motivational sense for girls (Sarason, et al., 1958). There are some other observations which bear upon this notion. Frequently, in giving the questionnaires, one sees girls nodding delightedly as they answer "Yes" to TASC items. Boys express pleasure in this situation only if they are shaking their heads sideways as they answer "No." Boys who answer these items "Yes" seem quiet and tense and often smile and express relief when they can give a "No" answer. These behaviors clearly fit in with the notion that being test anxious can be ego-alien for boys and ego-syntonic for girls.

There is no clear-cut behavior difference between boys and girls when they are responding to the DSC. However, this scale generally measures freedom to express feelings of anxiety, shame, aggression, and concern about the feelings of others when such expression is appropriate. Responding "Yes" means to the LD—in one sense—that their behavior is appropriate or "good" (i.e., concerned about others, accepting responsibility for oneself, etc.). "No" answers describe one as being able to cover up feelings or unconcerned about being aggressive or others' reactions—in a sense—a picture of a strong, silent, masculine person. Clearly, behaving in a "good" or appropriate manner would be ego-syntonic for both boys and girls. However, being unconcerned about others' feelings, masculine, or aggressive would be ego-syntonic for boys and ego-alien for girls.

While these points remain in the realm of speculation, nevertheless, they do indicate that the TASC may well measure ego-alien feelings for boys and ego-syntonic feelings for girls while the DSC measures ego-syntonic qualities of boys and ego-alien qualities of girls. If boys or girls can accept equally being high or low with respect to a given variable, that characteristic may be relatively meaningless as a determinant of their behavior and personalities. However, being high or low on a trait that is unacceptable is the difference between having a lot or a little of a disturbing quality or feeling. Anxiety, apparently ego-alien for boys and ego-syntonic for girls, is an effective predictor for the former but not the latter. Defensiveness, which may well measure ego-syntonic qualities for boys and ego-alien traits for girls, is an effective predictor of the behavior and personality characteristics of girls.

TEST ANXIETY SCALE FOR CHILDREN (TASC)

Instructions

My name is _____. I'm going to be asking you some questions—questions different from the usual school questions for these are about how you feel and so have no right or wrong answers. First I'll hand out the answer sheets and then I'll tell you more about the questions. . . .

Write your name at the top of the first page, *both your first and your last* names. . . . Also write a B if you're a boy or a G if you're a girl. (For the 4th, 5th and 6th grades, 'Write the name of the school you attended last year and year before last year.')

As I said before, I am going to ask you some questions. No one but myself will see your answers to these questions, not your teacher or your principal or your parents. These questions are different from other questions that you are asked in school. These questions are different because there are no right or wrong answers. You are to listen to each question and then put a circle around either 'Yes' or 'No.' These questions are about how you think and feel and, therefore, they have no right or wrong answers. People think and feel differently. The person sitting next to you might put a circle around 'Yes' and you may put a circle around 'No.' For example, if I asked you this question: 'Do you like to play ball?', some of you would put a circle around 'Yes' and some of you would put it around 'No.' Your answer depends on how you think and feel. These questions are about how you think and feel about school, and about a lot of other things. Remember, listen carefully to each question and answer it 'Yes' or 'No' by deciding how you think and feel. If you don't understand a question, ask me about it.

Now let's start by everybody putting their finger on Number 1. Here is the first question. Number 1. Do you worry when _____. (Repeat this procedure of introducing the questions for several of them and continue throughout to say the number of the question before reading it.)

1. Do you worry when the teacher says that she is going to ask you questions to find out how much you know?
2. Do you worry about being promoted, that is, passing from the ____ to the ____ grade at the end of the year?

3. When the teacher asks you to get up in front of the class and read aloud, are you afraid that you are going to make some bad mistakes?
4. When the teacher says that she is going to call upon some boys and girls in the class to do arithmetic problems, do you hope that she will call upon someone else and not on you?
5. Do you sometimes dream at night that you are in school and cannot answer the teacher's questions?
6. When the teacher says that she is going to find out how much you have learned, does your heart begin to beat faster?
7. When the teacher is teaching you about arithmetic, do you feel that other children in the class understand her better than you?
8. When you are in bed at night, do you sometimes worry about how you are going to do in class the next day?
9. When the teacher asks you to write on the blackboard in front of the class, does the hand you write with sometimes shake a little?
10. When the teacher is teaching you about reading, do you feel that other children in the class understand her better than you?
11. Do you think you worry more about school than other children?
12. When you are at home and you are thinking about your arithmetic lesson for the next day, do you become afraid that you will get the answers wrong when the teacher calls upon you?
13. If you are sick and miss school, do you worry that you will do more poorly in your school work than other children when you return to school?
14. Do you sometimes dream at night that other boys and girls in your class can do things you cannot do?
15. When you are home and you are thinking about your reading lesson for the next day, do you worry that you will do poorly on the lesson?
16. When the teacher says that she is going to find out how much you have learned, do you get a funny feeling in your stomach?
17. If you did very poorly when the teacher called on you, would you probably feel like crying even though you would try not to cry?
18. Do you sometimes dream at night that the teacher is angry because you do not know your lessons?

In the following questions the word 'test' is used. What I mean by 'test' is any time the teacher asks you to do something to find out how much you know or how much you have learned. It could be by your writing on paper, or by your speaking aloud, or by your writing on the blackboard. Do you understand what I mean by 'test'—it is any time the teacher asks you to do something to find out how much you know.

19. Are you afraid of school tests?
20. Do you worry a lot *before* you take a test?
21. Do you worry a lot *while* you are taking a test?
22. *After* you have taken a test do you worry about how well you did on the test?
23. Do you sometimes dream at night that you did poorly on a test you had in school that day?

24. When you are taking a test, does the hand you write with shake a little?
25. When the teacher says that she is going to give the class a test, do you become afraid that you will do poorly?
26. When you are taking a hard test, do you forget some things that you knew very well before you started taking the test?
27. Do you wish a lot of times that you didn't worry so much about tests?
28. When the teacher says that she is going to give the class a test, do you get a nervous or funny feeling?
29. While you are taking a test do you usually think you are doing poorly?
30. While you are on your way to school, do you sometimes worry that the teacher may give the class a test?

I've asked you a lot of questions, and I will ask you some more questions soon. But, in the meantime, let's do something different. Turn to the next page—it's a blank page. Draw a picture of a man on this page. Just take a couple of minutes to draw it. I'll tell you shortly before you're to stop. Draw a picture of a man. . . .

(If questions are asked about what kind of drawing, answer 'Any kind of drawing you want'; if questions are asked about erasing, permit it; allow 2 minutes for the drawing; say after $1\frac{1}{2}$ minutes, 'You will have to stop soon.')

Turn to the next page. Draw a picture of a woman on this page. Again just take a couple of minutes to draw it. Draw a picture of a woman. . . .

Turn to the next page. Draw a picture of a house on this page. Again just take a couple of minutes to draw it. Draw a picture of a house. . . .

GENERAL ANXIETY SCALE FOR CHILDREN (GASC)

Turn to the last page. Write your name at the top of the page, both your first and your last name. I'm going to ask you some more questions about how you think and feel. Remember, there are no right or wrong answers. Listen carefully to each question and put a circle around either 'Yes' or 'No' after deciding how you think and feel. Number 1. When you are _____.

1. When you are away from home, do you worry about what might be happening at home?
2. Do you sometimes worry about whether (other children are better looking than you are?) (your body is growing the way it should?)
3. Are you afraid of mice or rats?
L 4. Do you every worry about knowing your lessons?
5. If you were to climb a ladder, would you worry about falling off it?
6. Do you worry about whether your mother is going to get sick?

7. Do you get scared when you have to walk home alone at night?

L 8. Do you ever worry about what other people think of you?

9. Do you get a funny feeling when you see blood?

10. When your father is away from home, do you worry about whether he is going to come back?

11. Are you frightened by lightning and thunderstorms?

L 12. Do you ever worry that you won't be able to do something you want to do?

13. When you go to the dentist, do you worry that he may hurt you?

14. Are you afraid of things like snakes?

15. When you are in bed at night trying to go to sleep, do you often find that you are worrying about something?

L 16. When you were younger, were you ever scared of anything?

17. Are you sometimes frightened when looking down from a high place?

18. Do you get worried when you have to go to the doctor's office?

19. Do some of the stories on radio or television scare you?

L 20. Have you ever been afraid of getting hurt?

21. When you are home alone and someone knocks on the door, do you get a worried feeling?

22. Do you get a scary feeling when you see a dead animal?

23. Do you think you worry more than other boys and girls?

24. Do you worry that you might get hurt in some accident?

L 25. Has anyone ever been able to scare you?

26. Are you afraid of things like guns?

27. Without knowing why, do you sometimes get a funny feeling in your stomach?

28. Are you afraid of being bitten or hurt by a dog?

L 29. Do you ever worry about something bad happening to someone you know?

30. Do you worry when you are home alone at night?

31. Are you afraid of being too near fireworks because of their exploding?

32. Do you worry that you are going to get sick?

L 33. Are you ever unhappy?

34. When your mother is away from home, do you worry about whether she is going to come back?

35. Are you afraid to dive into the water because you might get hurt?

36. Do you get a funny feeling when you touch something that has a real sharp edge?

L 37. Do you ever worry about what is going to happen?

38. Do you get scared when you have to go into a dark room?

39. Do you dislike getting in fights because you worry about getting hurt in them?

40. Do you worry about whether your father is going to get sick?

L 41. Have you ever had a scary dream?

42. Are you afraid of spiders?

43. Do you sometimes get the feeling that something bad is going to happen to you?
44. When you are alone in a room and you hear a strange noise, do you get a frightened feeling?
L 45. Do you ever worry?

DEFENSIVENESS SCALE FOR CHILDREN (DSC)

1. Do you love to play sports best of all?
2. Should girls be just as brave as boys?
3. Do you ever worry about knowing your lessons?
4. Do you sometimes dream about things you don't like to talk about?
5. Are you sometimes afraid of getting into arguments?
6. When someone scolds you does it make you feel badly?
7. Do you ever worry about what people think of you?
8. When you get mad do you ever tell anyone else about it?
9. Do you sometimes feel like hurting someone?
10. Do you ever worry that you won't be able to do something that you want to do?
11. Do you like to play in the snow?
12. Are you sorry for some of the things you have done?
13. When one of your friends won't play with you, do you feel badly?
14. When you were younger, were you ever scared of anything?
15. When someone makes you mad, do you ever tell them about it?
16. Do you feel cross and grouchy sometimes?
17. Are there some people that you don't like?
18. Have you ever been afraid of getting hurt?
19. Since you started school, have you ever felt like crying?
20. Do you feel it's important to think about how you can get people to like you?
21. Do you like to go to the beach in the summertime?
22. Do you ever worry about something bad happening to someone you know?
23. Sometimes when you get mad, do you smash something?
24. When you hurt somebody's feelings, does it make you feel badly?
25. Do you wish your teacher paid more attention to you?
26. Do you ever worry about what is going to happen?
27. Do you sometimes have arguments with your mother and father?
28. Are you ever unhappy?
29. Are there some things you just don't like to talk about?
30. If you think someone doesn't like you, does it bother you?
31. Do you like to go on trips with your mother and father?
32. Has anyone ever been able to scare you?
33. Do you feel terrible if you break something which belongs to somebody else?
34. Do you lose your temper sometimes?
35. Have you ever had a scary dream?

36. When you are worried about something, do you like to talk about it?
37. Does it bother you if the teacher chooses someone else instead of you to do something for her (or him)?
38. Do you every worry?
39. When you've done something wrong, is it hard for you to say you're sorry?
40. Is it hard for you to tell someone you're scared?

PERSONALITY CHECK LIST

The four-year survey which we are conducting in the Hamden elementary schools (by virtue of a grant from the United States Public Health Service) is concerned with several interrelated questions. One of these questions is: how early in a child's school career can one meaningfully predict a child's future status? In order to make this kind of prediction it is necessary that we obtain as comprehensive evaluation as possible of the present status of the child. In this undertaking it is obvious that the teacher is one of the very best sources of evaluation. Preliminary research which in previous years we have done in other school systems encourages us in the belief that a comprehensive evaluation by the teacher may be the best basis for prediction.

In asking you to render your professional opinion about certain children in your class, it is important to stress that we have chosen children in a way so as to have a representative sample of the elementary school population. The information we are requesting will, of course, be confidential. We earnestly request your cooperation. The information you can supply will be of great value in the attainment of the practical objectives of this project.

Seymour B. Sarason

Instructions

On the next page will be found a list of 24 paired terms. Each of these pairs contains contrasting personality characteristics. On each of the subsequent pages a pair of terms is defined. Read the definitions for each pair and then assign a rating for that child on that item.

In assigning a rating to a child for any one item, you will essentially make two decisions: (1) Which of the two terms more accurately describes the child and (2) to what degree does the child approach the extreme of the description of the term chosen from the pair for him. The same two decisions are involved in each rating. As an example for item #1:

Anxious   5 4 3 2 1   1 2 3 4 5   Unanxious

Decide for each child which term of the pair, "Anxious–unanxious," fits him best. Then circle one of the numbers from 1 to 5 on the side near that term. The numbers 1 to 5 have the following meanings:

1. slightly on this side
2. more than a little on this side
3. quite a bit on this side
4. a lot on this side
5. very much on this side

The higher the number circled and the closer the circled number to the term, the greater the child's tendency to behave or feel the way that term of the pair was defined. Of the ten numbers *only one number is circled for that child for that item,* but circle a number for each child even if you do not feel such confidence in your rating for any of various possible reasons. If you really lack confidence in any one particular rating for a child, put a question mark (?) next to the circle you made. For each item please feel free to make any comments you think would clarify your rating.

Make your ratings for an item without considering your ratings for any other item. Make your ratings for an item only in terms of the definition given for that item.

Items to be rated

1. Anxious	Unanxious
2. Dependent	Independent
3. Shows or expresses emotions	Hides or suppresses emotions
4. Communicates easily	Difficulty in communicating
5. Aggressive	Submissive
6. Impulsive	Cautious
7. Sensitive	Not sensitive
8. Tense	Relaxed
9. Ambitious	Unambitious
10. Adapts to changes	Set in ways
11. Well-liked	Not well-liked
12. Mature psychologically or emotionally	Immature psychologically or emotionally
13. Withdrawn	Sociable
14. Daydreams	Does not daydream
15. Active	Inactive
16. Overachievers	Underachievers
17. Learns slowly (new material)	Learns quickly (new material)
18. Retains material	Forgets material
19. Fears failure	Does not fear failure
20. Pays attention	Does not pay attention
21. Strong conscience	Weak conscience
22. Feminine	Masculine
23. Pessimistic	Optimistic
24. Responsible	Not responsible

1. Anxious   5 4 3 2 1   1 2 3 4 5   Unanxious

An "anxious" child is one who *expresses or shows* worry, apprehension, concern, nervousness, or fearfulness *overtly,* and an "unanxious" child *does not* show or express worry, etc. *characteristically.* Indicate by your rating whether or not each child *shows* anxiety characteristically. The anxiety may be about lessons or tests, curricular or extra-curricular school activities, as well as about relationships with parents, other children, and the teacher.

COMMENTS: *

2. Dependent   5 4 3 2 1   1 2 3 4 5   Independent

Children should be rated as "dependent" to the extent that they need, want, and try to get help, support, or guidance from others with the tasks or problems that face them. "Independent" children would seek to function or perform without that help, support, or guidance. Dependent behavior would include requests for assistance, relying on others for opinions, attitudes, and guided for action, responses showing need for support from others.

3. Shows or expresses   1 2 3 4 5   Hides or suppresses
   emotions   5 4 3 2 1   emotions

This is not a question of whether a child characteristically feels one particular way or another—such as happy or sad, angry or friendly, anxious or unanxious—or any other emotions. The issue here is whether the child *shows, expresses, and reveals openly his feelings*—or, on the other hand, *suppresses, hides, or prevents others from knowing* his feelings, whatever the feelings may be. Some children "act" as if they feel certain emotions, but do not actually feel them—or "say" they feel certain emotions when they do not. These behaviors are in the direction of "hiding" feelings, although the child may "act like" or "say" he is feeling some emotion. Feelings may also be suppressed by appearing indifferent or aloof, denial, and various methods of blocking communication, such as, withdrawal and silence. Which children tend to "show" or "express" their feelings and which tend to "hide or suppress" their emotions?

4. Communicates   1 2 3 4 5   Difficulty in com-
   easily   5 4 3 2 1   municating

The child who "communicates easily" *characteristically* speaks and converses steadily and without halting and *does not show* confusion, searching for words, or blocks, pauses, "uh's" and "um's" while speaking. The reverse would be true for children with "difficulty in communicating" —they would speak unsteadily, haltingly, and would *show* confusion, searching for words, blocks, etc. Children who speak only a little would be rated on the "difficulty in communicating" side. Children who talk

---

* [Each item is followed by Comments.]

quite a lot would be rated on the "communicates easily" side, *unless* they *show* confusion, searching for words etc. *characteristically,* in which case they would be rated on the "difficult" side.

5. Aggressive   5 4 3 2 1   1 2 3 4 5   Submissive

The "aggressive" child is one who competes, argues, fights, struggles to succeed, win, or dominate in his relations with others, whereas the "submissive" child is passive and accepts his lot without fight, struggle, argument, or vigorous effort. The "aggressive" child may be openly or physically hostile, angry, and the like, although not necessarily. The "submissive" child does not express physical aggression, and, while he may feel and show anger, the "submissive" child submits to the decisions and control of others.

6. Impulsive   5 4 3 2 1   1 2 3 4 5   Cautious

An "impulsive" child reacts, or responds without giving himself time to consider the situation sufficiently, while the "cautious" child responds and proceeds allowing himself more than enough time for consideration of the problem or situation at hand. The "impulsive" child tends to be unable to postpone his reaction and the "cautious" child tends to delay his response or reaction in order to have time for considering the situation. Correctness or inappropriateness of response or reaction or whether the impulsiveness or cautiousness gets the child into trouble or interferes with or helps the child are irrelevant. The question is how much does the child tend to respond immediately, "on-impulse," or to delay his response to consider the situation, regardless of the child's effectiveness.

7. Sensitive   5 4 3 2 1   1 2 3 4 5   Not sensitive

"Sensitive" children *show* that they are easily upset emotionally and *show* that their feelings are easily hurt. Children who are "not sensitive" *characteristically do not show* emotional upset or hurt feelings. Signs of emotional upset would include a child's easily becoming unable to cope with or control *his own* feelings *when something has happened which hurts his feelings.*

8. Tense   5 4 3 2 1   1 2 3 4 5   Relaxed

A "tense" child characteristically *shows* signs of *physical* and *bodily* tension, strain, and effects of being under pressure. "Relaxed" children characteristically tend *not to show* signs of physical and bodily tension, strain, and the effects of being under pressure.

9. Ambitious   5 4 3 2 1   1 2 3 4 5   Unambitious

The two goals in question here are success and accomplishment. The "ambitious" child strives and works for success and accomplishment in work and play and wants to win and be "on top." The "unambitious" child does not strive and work for success and accomplishment and tends to be indifferent, apathetic, or resigned to his lot about winning and being "on top."

10. Adapts to changes 5 4 3 2 1   1 2 3 4 5 Set in ways

In new situations and relationships, a child who "adapts to changes" tries new ways of adjusting or coping with problems. A child who is "set in his ways" rigidly retains old reaction or behavior patterns and ways of adjusting or coping with problems although those ways and patterns may be inappropriate or ineffective in the new conditions. The child who is "set in his ways" tends to be rigid and inflexible. The child who "adapts to changes" is flexible and not rigid, and can alter his ways and adapt to changes.

11. Well-liked 5 4 3 2 1   1 2 3 4 5 Not well-liked

The question here is whether a child's classmates *show* a liking and a preference for him *or show* indifference or dislike toward him. Whether anyone else likes or dislikes a child is *not* to be considered in these ratings.

12. Immature 5 4 3 2 1   1 2 3 4 5 Mature
                                         psychologically
                                         or emotionally

Behaviorally and emotionally, the "immature" child resembles children younger than himself, whereas the "mature" child resembles children older than himself, considering the child's actual chronological age. The "immature" child might be "babyish" or "babyish for his age" while the "mature" child might be described as "grown-up for his age." The physical maturity of the children is *not* a factor in this rating. In other words, whether a child is large or small or appears physically mature or immature should *not* be taken into consideration. The question only concerns the degree of *psychological and emotional maturity*.

13. Withdrawn 5 4 3 2 1   1 2 3 4 5 Sociable

A "sociable" child tends to interact freely with others and to enjoy and to prefer being with and interacting with others. The "withdrawn" child tends to be by himself and, when interacting with others, does so minimally and with difficulty rather than freely and he tends to end the interaction quickly. Quite possibly the child may prefer to be alone and may feel more comfortable alone. The "sociable" child has more and freer interpersonal interactions, or socializes more. The "withdrawn" child tends to socialize little and has fewer and less free interpersonal interactions.

14. Daydreams 5 4 3 2 1   1 2 3 4 5 Does not
                                              daydream

A child who "daydreams" tends easily to become lost in his thoughts and fantasies and children who "do not daydream" tend to react to, think about, and focus on events and objects in the world around them, although they *may or may not* be focusing their attention on their work.

15. Active 5 4 3 2 1   1 2 3 4 5 Inactive

The "active" child is one who *characteristically* expends much energy physically and moves vigorously or energetically. The "inactive" child expends little energy physically and moves little and *not energetically*.

16. Overachievers 5 4 3 2 1   1 2 3 4 5 Underachievers

On this item, for each child compare what the child achieves in school with what the child would be expected to achieve considering his intelligence and aptitudes. The "overachievers" learn and accomplish more than would be expected for them individually, the "underachievers" learn and recognize less. The question is *not* why *but* whether and how much the child "over" or "under" achieves.

17. Learns slowly 5 4 3 2 1   1 2 3 4 5 Learns quickly
                                                           (new material)

Here, the question is how fast or slow the child is in the learning of new material in school. Children who "learn quickly" tend to grasp the new material immediately on first presentation or with few experiences with the material, whereas children who "learn slowly" tend to need many experiences with and explanations of new material before they have learned it.

18. Retains   1 2 3 4 5 Forgets material
      material 5 4 3 2 1   (presented in class)

The question here is, regardless of how quickly a child may learn, how well the child retains material presented in class. The child who "retains well," is able to recall the material presented in class easily after time has passed. The child who "forgets material" has difficulty in recalling it after time lapses is rated as, "retains material." The children who recall less and only recall after shorter time lapses are rated as "forgets material." Children recall more, etc. if they are given hints and clues. Those who "retain" tend to need fewer hints; those who "forget" tend to need more hints.

19. Fears failure 5 4 3 2 1   1 2 3 4 5 Does not
                                                           fear failure

Indicate the extent to which each child *characteristically shows* fear of failure. Children who "do not fear failure" characteristically are willing to take the chance that they might fail or make mistakes *without showing* fear, concern, worry, or apprehension. Children who "fear failure" *show* fear, concern, anxiety, worry, or apprehension when faced with the chance that they may fail or make mistakes.

20. Pays attention 5 4 3 2 1   1 2 3 4 5 Does not pay
                                                           attention

The question here is whether attention is paid to the work or activity to which the child should be attending. The child who "does not pay attention" is distracted from his seat work, the teacher's instructions, or class or group activity to which he should be attending. The child's attention may be drawn to irrelevant external objects or events or he may become dreamy or involved in his own inner thoughts. Children who "pay attention" focus on the teacher's instruction, the class or group activity to which he should be attending. The child's attention may be drawn to irrelevant external objects or events or he may become dreamy or involved in his own inner thoughts. Children who "pay attention" focus on the teacher's instruction, the class or group activity or seat work to which they should be attending. To what extent does each child pay attention to or become distracted from the work, instruction or activity to which he should be attending.

21. Strong conscience 5 4 3 2 1   1 2 3 4 5 Weak
conscience

The child with a "strong conscience" will *characteristically* not permit himself to disobey or be "bad" and will show feelings of guilt for being bad. The child with a weak conscience permits himself to misbehave or disobey and will tend not to show feelings of guilt when he does so. This is primarily a question of whether the child permits himself to misbehave or not.

22. Feminine 5 4 3 2 1   1 2 3 4 5 Masculine

The question here concerns the extent to which each child's *behavior, attitudes,* and *interests* tend to be typical of those of boys *or* of girls of this age. The rating involves an evaluation of the balance of masculine and feminine behavior and interest. To the extent that one is very predominant in a child, the number circled would be higher in the dominant direction. The children whose masculine and feminine behaviors, attitudes, and interests are more evenly balanced would receive ratings of 1 or 2 in one direction or the other.

23. Pessimistic 5 4 3 2 1   1 2 3 4 5 Optimistic

The "optimistic" child *characteristically shows* a cheerful manner and outlook on life. The reverse is true for the "pessimistic" child, who tends to *show* that he expects things will turn out poorly or to *show* that he is discouraged about how things will turn out—he is the opposite of cheerful.

24. Responsible 5 4 3 2 1   1 2 3 4 5 Not responsible

The "responsible" child can be trusted with duties and obligations, and he accepts responsibility for himself, his actions, and for helping. The child who is "not responsible" or is irresponsible cannot be trusted to do what he is told or to accept and fulfill obligations and duties. He tends not to accept responsibility for himself, his actions, and for helping.

A. Do you feel that this child will progress normally through the elementary school grades?

(check one)   Yes ____ No ____

If your answer is "no," please explain.

If your answer is "yes," please answer the following question: Even though you feel this child will progress normally through the grades, have you ever observed this child to have any kind of learning difficulty? In other words, because a child progresses normally through the grades it does not necessarily mean that he does not have academic problems.

Child Development
and Behavior

11 / Classroom Social Structure
as a Mental Health Problem

Ronald Lippitt and Martin Gold

In this selection, Ronald Lippitt and Martin Gold of the University of Michigan reveal that the elementary-school child who is in a low position in the socio-emotional structure of the classroom contributes to unhealthy classroom situations by his negative self-evaluation and his response to this, his hostility toward others, his unskilled and unrealistic behavior, and his insensitive and defensive reactions to feedback from others. Classmates add to his difficulty by their rapid and rigid evaluative labeling, their inadequate skill for communicating sympathetic guidance, and their lack of group standards for support of deviancy. Teachers reinforce the unhealthy classroom situations by their lack of focused effort on human relations, lack of mental-health goals, and lack of constructive behavior toward low-status children.

One of the two most important and influential environments for the child is the classroom in which he lives during a part of each day. His relations with his teacher and with his peers are two major aspects of his school environment. These relations have a variety of important meanings for the child: "What is expected of me?" "What can I do and what can't I do?" "What will happen if . . . ?" "Who do I like?" "Who don't I like?" "Who likes me?" "Who doesn't?" "Who does the teacher like?"

Reprinted from the *Journal of Social Issues*, 1959, *15* (1), 40–49, with the permission of the authors and the Society for the Psychological Study of Social Issues, a Division of the American Psychological Association.

"Who's the strongest?" As clarification emerges about the meaning of such important questions, relations in the classroom develop a stable pattern or structure, which we are calling the classroom socio-emotional structure. Stratification becomes clear about those who are looked up to and down on in various ways. Each child finds he has a position, or several positions, in this socio-emotional structure. This social structure becomes a dominant aspect of his school environment and of his total life situation. His position in this structure becomes a very important determinant of his personal mental health situation, and of his motivation and ability to participate in classroom interaction.

This paper reports a research exploration of the development and maintenance of the classroom socio-emotional structure in a sample of 39 elementary classrooms.[1] The paper also explores some of the mental health correlates of the child's position in this socio-emotional structure, which in turn suggest focal points for diagnosis of socio-emotional problems in the classroom situation and formulation of therapeutic strategy in working toward the improvement of classroom mental health.

THE DEVELOPMENT OF THE SOCIO-EMOTIONAL STRUCTURE OF THE CLASSROOM

To what degree can we really talk about a social structure in the classroom? How much consensus is there among classmates about who belongs where in the structure? How stable is the structure over time?

All of the children in all of the 39 elementary school classrooms rated all their classmates on a four point scale, indicating the degree to which the ratee was perceived as able to get the others to do what he wanted them to do.[2] The resulting stratification is called the social power structure of the classroom. If we look at the consensus among the group members in making these ratings, we find that in the average primary grade the children in the top third of the power structure received 47 per cent of the high power (number 1) ratings from peers while the bottom third received 18 per cent high ratings and 46 per cent lowest ratings. Consensus is even higher among fourth, fifth, and sixth grades with 58 per cent of the highest ratings going to the top third and only 11 per cent to the bottom third. The agreement on who is liked most and who least is comparable. The most disliked third of the average class received over half of the strong dislike ratings.

Not only is there high consensus about who belongs where in the social structure, but there is high stability of the structure from early in the school year to the middle of the school year and to the end of the

    [1] The research reported in part in this paper was supported by Grant M–919 of the National Institute of Mental Health. Principal investigators were Ronald Lippitt, Robert Fox, and Douglas Blocksma. Sidney Rosen was Project Director. A book is in preparation reporting the total research program.
    [2] [See appended Sociometric Instructions.]

school year. Looking first at the social power structure we find that for the first, second, and third graders there is an average classroom correlation (Pearson r) of .73 between the social structure in early October and in the middle of January; between January and May the average correlation is .72; and from early fall until the end of the school year, the correlation in the primary grades is .63. All of the individual correlations are highly significant. For the fourth, fifth, and sixth grades the average correlation between October and January is .77; between January and May it is .78; and between early October and May, .75. The structures concerning who is liked and disliked and who is regarded as expert and inexpert in classroom activities have an even higher stability, with most of the correlations being above .80. The evidence is clear that the interpersonal social structure of the classroom forms rapidly and maintains a high degree of stability throughout the school year. The same children remain in positions of low power and isolation or dislike throughout the year, and the same children stay at the top of the totem pole.

But are the same children at the top and the bottom of all the totem poles? A partial correlation program was carried out for four different social structures in each classroom; the social power structure, the affective (like and dislike) structure, the expertness structure, and the coerceability (ability to use physical coercion) structure. These analyses were summarized separately for younger and older classrooms in the elementary grades, and also for the beginning and end of the year. We find that with the other variables controlled there is still a high relationship between the power structure and the affect structure, a correlation of .57 at the beginning of the school year and .65 at the end of the year. The correlation is significantly higher for older than for younger boys (.44 as compared to .69). There is a smaller but significant relationship between the power structure and the expertness structure (.21 in October and .29 in May). The relationship of the coercion structure to the power structure increases from a zero relationship in the fall to an average correlation of .27 in the spring, although there is a great variability between groups in this relationship, and the relationship is accounted for to a great extent by the boys in each classroom rather than the girls. There is a significant relationship (.40) between the affect structure and the expertness structure in the fall which drops somewhat during the school year (.21 in May). There is a scattering of insignificant positive and negative correlations between the coerceability structure and affect structure and between the coerceability structure and the expertness structure. It is clear then that the children are making differentiations in their judgments of one another, and that being highly liked or perceived as expert are both significant paths to social influence in the socio-emotional structure of the group.

But how do the children really think about each other when they have a chance to freely apply their own descriptive and evaluative labels? Are these dimensions we have been measuring really the central dimensions of the interpersonal structure as far as the children are concerned, or have they been somewhat imposed by measurement procedures? Gold (1958) has explored this question in a substudy of 152 children in kindergarten through the sixth grade. In a preliminary study he had fairly lengthy interviews with 21 children representing all the grade levels exploring with open ended questions their perceptions of their peers. From these interviews emerged seventeen characteristics or properties of children which seem to be matters of some concern as peers describe each other. These items fall into four areas: expertness characteristics (e.g. smart, has good ideas, good at making things); physical characteristics (e.g. fighting ability, strength, appearance); socio-emotional characteristics (e.g. friendliness, fun to be with, doesn't tease); and "associational" characteristics (e.g. likes to do same things I do). These open ended interviews clearly confirmed the previous researches in camp settings (Polansky, Lippitt, and Redl, 1950) concerning the salience of the dimensions of socio-emotional structuring studied in the classroom groups. In a second part of the study specific low power and high power children were compared as to their possession of the valued characteristics. Gold found that the children gave the highest value to socio-emotional characteristics, but also placed a high value on expertness and the lowest value on physical prowess. It was also found that highly valued characteristics were attributed significantly more often to children who were high in the power structure of the classroom group. It seems clear that children do perceive each other in terms of these characteristics, and that these characteristics are evaluated in such a way that they become resources relevant to the acquiring of high or low position in the social structure of the group.

MENTAL HEALTH CORRELATES OF POSITION IN THE CLASSROOM SOCIAL STRUCTURE

Let's turn from the perceptions of peers to the judgments and assessments of adults. Adults in the school environment who have an interest in mental health tend to perceive children in terms of adjustment and deviancy along similar socio-emotional dimensions. We might expect, therefore, that there would be some relationship between perceptions and evaluations by peers and mental health assessments by adults. Two explorations of this question have been carried out as part of a larger study. Douglas (1958) conducted a study of the responses of 115 children to frustration in a series of story completion situations where a child is frustrated by a loved adult. In these situations children use various types of psychological defenses against the expression of their feelings of aggression toward powerful loved adults. Working within a theoretical framework developed by Miller (Miller & Swanson, 1960), Douglas coded the primitivity or maturity of the defenses used by the children in coping with frustrating situations. Partialing out the effects of intelligence and age, Douglas found that the children who are lowest in the socio-emotional structure of the classroom more often used the most primitive defense of denial in the face of conflict than those children high in being liked and influential, who were more apt to use more mature defenses showing relatively minor distortions of the reality situation. In terms of clinical judgments, the use of the more primitive defenses is a symptom of poorer mental health in coping with conflict situations.

In a study of seven elementary classrooms, Echelberger (1959) analyzed cumulative teacher ratings of children on the Haggerty-Olson-Wickman Behavior Rating Schedule (1930). This schedule yields five scores: behavior problem symptoms, problems in intellectual functioning, problems of physical characteristics, social adjustment problems, and problems of emotional temperament. Echelberger correlated the position of the child in the socio-emotional structure in the classroom with the behavior problems scale (e.g. cheating, temper outbursts, truancy), the social adjustment scales (e.g. shyness, relation to authority, assertiveness), and the emotional adjustment scales (e.g. cheerfulness, excitability, suspiciousness). The tabulation below reports some relevant correlations (those .26 and greater are significant at the .05 level or better).

Table 1. Correlations (Pearson *r*) of Sociometric Ratings with Selected Haggerty-Olson-Wickman Ratings, by Grade

Grades	N	Behavior Problems	Social Adjustment	Emotional Adjustment
1–3	64			
Power x		—.28	.26	.21
Popularity x		—.46	.36	.27
4–6	72			
Power x		—.31	.36	.41
Popularity x		—.29	.35	.38

In every case it can be noted that the more influential and more popular children impress their teachers with a significantly more favorable mental health picture. They show fewer behavior problem symptoms, greater social adjustment, and more stable emotionality.

Jennings (1943) has proposed that an important dimension of personality health is the ability to make and maintain social connections, to have the capacity for friendships with others. In this context we might expect that the amount of positive affection, as compared to negative affect, which a child feels toward his peers might be considered a mental health criterion. In our classrooms each child indicated how much he liked or disliked other children in the class on a four point scale, with ratings 1 and 2 indicating two degrees of liking the other, and points 3 and 4 indicating two degrees of intensity of dislike. Table 2 indicates that in the older grades the children in high status positions express more positive affect in their ratings of peers than do low status children. (The differences of 8 per cent are significant beyond the .02 level.) Through the course of the school year, this difference becomes greater, the low status children increasing the proportion of negative feelings toward their fellow classmates.

Table 2. Comparison of Mean Percentages of Liking Choices (Spring) Made by High and Low Power Children, by Grade and Sex

	High Status		Low Status	
	Mean	N	Mean	N
Kindergarten to Grade 3				
Boys	60%	(79)	62%	(83)
Girls	60	(82)	61	(67)
Grades 4 to 6				
Boys	72	(103)	64	(77)
Girls	70	(73)	62	(78)

Direct observation of the children interacting in the classroom supports this conclusion about negative and positive affect. We recorded on quantitative behavior schedules an hour of classroom interaction in a standardized situation a few weeks after the school year began. The children participated in four activities designed to maximize the need for cooperation and coordination with others.[3] Each child interacted with every other child in the classroom in at least one of the activities. The data from these observations permit typing each child in terms of a behavioral output pattern.[4] In Table 3 we can see that those behavior patterns which indicate aggressive-assertive or passive-hostile activity output are more frequently characteristic of the low power children in the classroom social structure. Low status children tend to behave in ways that are likely to disrupt interpersonal friendships and also classroom functioning. (Differences of 5 per cent are significant beyond the .05 level.)

To summarize, then, we can say that children in low positions in the socio-emotional structure of the classroom tend to have mental health difficulties which are reflected both in inner psychological processes, in interpersonal relationship difficulties, and in behavior patterns which disrupt the life of the classroom group.

Table 3. Comparisons of Percentages of Low Power with Other Children in Behavior Output Type Categories

Behavior output type categories	Low Power (N = 311)	Other (N = 654)
1. Active-assertive, friendly	14%	25%
2. Active-assertive, unfriendly	27	22
3. Neutral or mixed	27	28
4. Passive, friendly	22	21
5. Passive, unfriendly	10	4
	100%	100%

[3] [See appended Standardization of Game Administration.]
[4] [See appended Behavior Output Form.]

THE IMPACT OF THE MILIEU ON
THE CHILD'S MENTAL HEALTH SITUATION

It becomes very important to consider the question: do the on-going processes of the classroom tend to aggravate or to alleviate the mental health problems of children low in the socio-emotional structure of the classroom? Looking first at the meaning of the on-going relationship with peers, we find that children who are low in the social structure have a continuing experience of social failure and rejection. For example, the success of each child's attempts to influence his peers during the standardized activity situation proved to be significantly correlated with his position in the social structure. Those low in the social structure experienced more failure of their own attempts and were more dominated by the behavior of others. This correlation increased during the course of the school year. Some of the low status children reacted to these behaviors from their peers by more withdrawal, and others reacted by more aggressive-assertive efforts to improve their position, which only resulted in still more failure.

That the children are sensitive to this incoming feedback from their peers is revealed by the self-evaluation index, which is a combination of self ratings on the social power and liking scales. Table 4 indicates that children's self evaluations tend to correspond to the feelings expressed by peers. (Differences between high and low power means are significant by T-test beyond the .05 level, except among the younger boys.) The younger boys seem to be less sensitive to the feelings of others about them, although their ratings also indicate some awareness of their status. It may be that they are more prone to make defensive self ratings to help them cope with their unhappy position in the group.

It is quite apparent to the children's teachers that high and low status pupils are treated differentially by their peers. We asked the teachers in the experimental classrooms to rate each child on the relative amount of warmth he received from others.[5] These ratings were significantly correlated with the peer ratings of social power and likeability. The

Table 4. Comparisons of Mean Self-Evaluation Score (Fall) of High and Low Power Children, by Grade and Sex

	High Power		Low Power	
	Mean	N	Mean	N
Kindergarten to grade 3				
Boys	3.47	(79)	3.86	(83)
Girls	3.23	(82)	3.91	(67)
Grades 4 to 6				
Boys	3.76	(103)	4.53	(77)
Girls	3.74	(73)	4.35	(78)

[5] [See appended Teachers' Rating Form. The amount of warmth received by the child is the seventh item.]

correlations were considerably higher in the spring than in the fall.

But peers are only part of the classroom milieu. The teacher is an important part of the environment. What about her contribution?

Table 5. Comparison of Percentages of Teacher Interaction with High and Low Power Children, by Sex

	N	Social Behavior Evaluation	Per-formance Evaluation	Total Content Tallies	Supportive Remarks	Critical Remarks	Total Supportive-Critical Tallies
Girls:							
High	43	16%	84%	104	57%	43%	104
Low	44	24%	76%	116	73%	27%	116
Boys:							
High	37	22%	78%	102	62%	38%	103
Low	35	30%	70%	176	42%	58%	176

Part of our study included observations of a sample of classroom activities by a team of graduate student observers. Each observer watched an individual elementary school child for an hour at a time, recording (1) with whom the child interacted and who initiated the interaction; (2) the affective quality of the interaction, whether friendly, neutral or unfriendly; (3) whether the content of the interaction was primarily social or was concerned with the performance of a learning activity.[6] None of the observers had any knowledge of the pupils' social status in the classroom. Each child was observed by two different observers. There were 318 child hours of observation in the sample of classrooms. Part of the analysis deals with pupil-teacher interactions which can be summarized only briefly here.

It will be noted from Table 5 that teachers pay attention to the social behavior, rather than the performance behavior, of low status pupils more often than of high status pupils. Evidently this aspect of

Table 6. Comparison of Affective Quality of Teachers' Interactions with High

	N	Teachers' Approaches to Pupils		
		Friendly	Neutral	Unfriendly
Girls:				
High	43	32%	48%	19%
Low	44	36%	51%	14%
Boys:				
High	37	36%	47%	18%
Low	35	28%	52%	20%

[6] [See appended Instructions for Observing Pupil-Teacher Behavior; Classroom Observation of Pupil-Teacher Behavior.]

their behavior leads to social evaluation and response more frequently on the teacher's part, just as it does for classmates. How the teacher responds depends on whether she is interacting with a low status girl or boy. Low status boys tend to receive more criticism than their high status boy classmates; but low status girls receive more support. In Table 6 we see that teachers were friendly slightly more often toward low status girls than other girls, but more often neutral or unfriendly toward low status boys. Differences in children's behavior probably evoke these different responses from teachers. Looking at the data on the children's approaches to their teachers, we note that low status girls are not only more warm in their relations with the teachers, but are relatively passive and withdrawing, while low status boys are more aggressive and troublesome than their higher status classmates.

This brief discussion of teachers' behavior should not be construed to mean that the teachers involved in the study were "playing favorites." Rather, we think that teachers, faced with the task of teaching youngsters in classroom groups and necessarily having to maintain order to do so must respond critically to disruptive behavior, and respond quite naturally with affection to little girls who seem to be asking for it and apparently getting little from their peers. But, we must ask, what are the implications of these findings for evaluating the classroom as a mental health milieu? What solutions to mental health problems do low status boys find from the generally critical and rejecting classroom relationships; or low status girls, who depend upon their relationships to teachers in the absence of satisfying give and take with their peers?

IMPLICATIONS FOR DIAGNOSTIC FOCUS AND THERAPEUTIC STRATEGY

When we try to close in on the locus of pathology which maintains and aggravates the unhealthy situation of certain children in the classroom group, it is apparent that the difficulties are created and maintained

and Low Power Pupils, by Sex

Total Teachers' Approaches	Pupils' Approaches to Teachers			Total Pupils' Approaches
	Friendly	Neutral	Unfriendly	
99	29%	66%	5%	111
111	49%	49%	2%	100
118	20%	66%	14%	64
167	17%	74%	9%	118

by a circular social process contributed to by the individual child, by his classmates, and by the teacher. If we focus on the individual child who is in difficulty we see that he contributes to the unhealthy situation by (1) his negative self evaluation and his response to this; (2) his hostility toward others; (3) his unskilled and unrealistic behavior output of assertive aggressiveness or withdrawing noncontribution; (4) his insensitive and defensive reception of feedback from others which might potentially give him more guidance for his own behavior.

If we look at the rest of the group as a source of difficulty for the individual child we see that there is (1) a very rapid evaluative labelling of a child and a strong tendency to maintain this evaluative consensus in spite of further information about the individual child as stimulus; (2) very inadequate skills of the group in providing the member with feedback which communicates sympathetic guidance rather than rejection or ignoration; and (3) a lack of group standards concerning the acceptance and support of deviancy.

If we look at the role of a teacher and her contribution to the situation we note (1) a lack of teaching effort focussed on developing personal attitude and group standards about good human relations; (2) a lack of interpersonal grouping practices and other procedures guided by mental health goals; (3) a lack of clear presentation of constructive behavior patterns toward low status children which could be imitated by her other pupils.

The conversion of these diagnostic insights into a mental health strategy is a challenging task. How much can one do by working directly outside the classroom group with the children in need of help, to assist them to initiate changes in the social process? How much can be done by working directly with the high power children who have the most influence on the socio-emotional structure of the classroom? What can be done by helping teachers to initiate curriculum content and training procedures which will have a direct influence on the socio-emotional structure of the class? These are the questions we are exploring with our collaborating classrooms.

SOCIOMETRIC INSTRUCTIONS

Today we're going to play a new kind of game. It's a secret game. That means that you can't let any of the other kids in the class see what you do with your pictures. You can't tell them about it either. Let's look at the sheet of pictures you have. There are pictures of everyone in the class. Find your own picture and draw a line under it. Now put the letter A at the top of the page. (If the child cannot do this, do it for him, or show him how.)

Question A: (for kindergarten and 1st grade). You all like to have kids do things for you, don't you? Raise your hands if you do. Have you ever done something for someone? Raise your hands if you have. Have you ever gotten another kid to do something for you? Raise your hands if you have. You all know that in any classroom some kids have an easier time than others in getting kids to do things for them. What we want to know is—what kids in *this* class have an easy time and what kids have a hard time getting *you* to do the things he wants you to do? Look at the pictures. Do you see the numbers on the side of each picture? (On the board is a chart which shows you what the numbers will mean for this set of pictures.) #1 on the top means *almost always*—that is, if the kid in the picture can *almost always* get *you* to do things for *him*. #2 right below it means *often*, that the kid can *often* get you to do things for him. #3 below that means *once in a while*, that the kid in the picture can get you to do things for him *once in a while*. #4 means *hardly ever*, that the kid can *hardly ever* get you to do things for him. Look at the first picture. If it's your own, skip it and we'll come to it later. When the rest of you come to your picture, skip over it and we'll do something special with it later.

Now we are looking at the first picture. If this kid can get you to do things for him (her) *almost always*, draw a line through #1. If you think he (she) can get you to do things *often*, draw a line through #2. If he can get you to do things *once in a while*, draw a line through #3. And if he can *hardly ever* get you to do things, draw a line through #4. Remember you have all four numbers to pick from and it's perfectly all right to use any of the numbers. This is a secret game. Remember none of the other kids are supposed to know what you are doing with your pictures. It's supposed to be a complete secret from them. (Note: if the children do not seem to understand the concept of the question, give them concrete examples.) Now let's go on to the next picture. (Repeat with illustrations.)

Now everyone find your own picture. We would like you to guess what the other kids think of you—whether they think you can get them to do things for you. If you think most of the kids marked your picture #1, draw a line through the #1 next to your picture. If you think they marked your picture #2, draw a line through the #2 next to your picture. If you think they marked your picture #3, draw a line through the #3 next to your picture. If you think they marked your picture #4, draw a line through the #4 next to your picture.

COLLECT THE PICTURES FOR QUESTION A. DISTRIBUTE THOSE FOR B AND HAVE THE CHILDREN UNDERLINE THEIR OWN PICTURE AND PUT THE LETTER B AT THE TOP OF THE PAGE.

Question B: In all classrooms some children are liked better than others. Each of you, I'm sure likes some kids more than others. We want to know whom *you* like in this class and whom you don't like. Let's look at the first picture. If it's yours skip it. The rest of you also leave your own 'til later when we come back to it.

If you like this kid very much, draw a line through the #1 on top (point to example). If you like this kid a little, draw a line through the

#2 here (point). If this kid is someone you don't like very much, draw a line through the #3 here (point). If this kid is someone you don't like at all, draw a line through the #4 here (point).

Number 1 means you like him very much, number 2 means you like him a little, number 3 means you don't like him very much and number 4 means you don't like him at all. Remember this is a secret game and none of the other kids are supposed to know what you do. Also you have all four numbers to choose from. Now let's look at the next picture (repeat instructions).

Now let's go back to your picture. We want you to guess how much the other kids in the class like you. We want you to mark your picture the way you think most of the other kids did. If you guess most of them marked #1 on your picture, draw a line through the #1 next to your picture. If you guess most of them marked #2 on your picture, draw a line through #2. If you guess most of them marked #3, draw a line through #3. If you guess most of them marked #4 on your picture, draw a line through #4.

(Break till next session for Kindergarten and 1st grade)

COLLECT THE PICTURES FOR QUESTION B. DISTRIBUTE THOSE FOR C AND HAVE THE CHILDREN UNDERLINE THEIR OWN PICTURE AND PUT THE LETTER C AT THE TOP OF THE PAGE.

Question C: Some kids know how to do things very well at school and some just don't know how to do these things as well. We want to know what kids in this class are good at doing things you do at school. Look at picture number 1. If it is your picture skip it and look at the next one. The rest of you also skip your own picture and we will come back to it later. Now if you think this kid is *very good* at doing things you do at school, draw a line through number 1 here (point). If you think this child is *good* at doing the things you do at school, draw a line through number 2 here (point). If this kid is *not so good* at doing the things you do at school, draw a line through number 3 here. If this kid is *poor* at doing the things you do at school, draw a line through number 4. Remember you have all four numbers to choose from. Number 1 means very good at doing things at school, number 2 means good, 3 means not so good and 4 means poor. Remember this is a secret game.

Now let's go back to your picture. We want you to guess how good the other kids think *you* are at doing things at school. If you guess most of them marked #1 on your picture, draw a line through number 1. If you guess most of them marked #2, draw a line through number 2. If you guess that most of them marked #3, draw a line through number 3 here. If you guess most of them marked #4, draw a line through number 4.

COLLECT THE PICTURES FOR QUESTION C. DISTRIBUTE THOSE FOR D AND HAVE THE CHILDREN UNDERLINE THEIR OWN PICTURE AND PUT THE LETTER D AT THE TOP OF THE PAGE.

Question D: You all know that there are some children in every class who can make the others afraid of what they might do or say to them and there are some kids who can't. We want to know who can make the kids in this room most afraid of him. Let's look at the first picture. If it's your own, skip it. The rest of you also leave your own 'til later. If this kid can make the rest of the kids *very afraid* of him, draw a line through number 1. If he can make them *afraid* of him, draw a line through number 2. If he *can't* make them very afraid of him, draw a line through number 3 and if he can't make them afraid of him *at all,* draw a line through number 4. #1 means he can make the rest of the kids very afraid, #2 means he can make them afraid, #3 means he can't make them very afraid and #4 means he can't make the kids afraid at all. (Go on to the next picture and repeat instructions with illustrations to the chart.)

Now let's go back to your picture. We want you to guess how much the other kids think you can make them afraid of *you.* If you guess most of them marked your picture #1, draw a line through number 1. If you think most of them marked your picture #2, draw a line through number 2. If you think most of them marked your picture #3, draw a line through number 3, and if you guess most of them marked your picture #4, draw a line through number 4.

STANDARDIZATION OF GAME ADMINISTRATION

First Visit

TEACHER: This is Mr. _____ who would like to talk to us for a few minutes.

LEADER: I'm here this morning to ask your help on something we are trying to find out. You see, I'm a teacher like (NAME OF CLASSROOM TEACHER). As teachers, we are interested in finding out what boys and girls of your age like to do. One of the things we know is that children like to play games, and that some children like certain games better than others. For example, if I asked each and every one of you what your favorite game is—you would probably say?????? (PAUSE AND WAIT FOR ANSWERS. IF THERE ARE NONE, THEN ASK A FEW CHILDREN.) That's fine— that's good—etc.

Now some of the games you mentioned are played outdoors, while some of them are played indoors. What we are interested in is in finding games that can be played in the classroom without disturbing—making too much noise for—the next room. So far, we have four games, *that we think children like to play.* The only way we can be sure that these games are fun is to have children play them and then ask which ones they like. This way we would know which of these games children really like best. When I talked to your teachers (HE *or* SHE) told me that this class likes to play games, so I decided to come in and ask you if you would help us. (WAIT FOR RESPONSE.) Since you decided to help us you should know that you are one of many classes, in many different schools, that will be helping us. What we would like to have you do is play the games, and then tell us which games you think are most fun. . . . There are four games, and it would take you one hour to play all of them. We also feel that it is important for every boy and girl to have the chance to play every game. To make this possible, we will divide the class into four groups—one group for each corner of the room. At the end of each game, we will change some children from one group and put them into a new group. Since we don't know all of your names, and since we don't want to say "Hey you, go to group two," we decided to give each of you a big number that you can wear. (AT THIS TIME, THE LEADER SHOWS THE HALTER AND DEMONSTRATES HOW TO PUT IT ON.) This way, when the game ends, all we have to do is to say "Numbers 1, 6, 9, 15 and 21 go to group 2."

Once you have been given a number and a group, you will go to one of the corners and start the first game; while you are playing there will be people who will be writing some of the things they see. This way we can keep a record of the way the games are being played and to make sure that everyone is in the right group.

I've talked for a long time, so I'll stop now and let you ask questions. (A QUESTION PERIOD)

We're very glad that you want to help us, but in return we feel you will have a good time—so if there are not any more questions, I'll see you all on __(date)__ at __(time)__ with all the games, numbers, and visitors.

(TO THE TEACHER BUT SO THE CLASS CAN HEAR) Thanks Mr. _____, for letting me come in. You have a nice class, and I'm going to enjoy working with them. 'Bye.

Final Administration of the Games

LEADER: When I talked to you __(date)__, I told you that today I would bring you the games, the numbers and the visitors. Well, here are the games (show the box), here are the numbers (show the numbers) and here are our visitors. If you remember, what we would like you to do is to play these four games, and then tell us which ones you liked. Since we feel that every child should play every game in small groups, we decided to divide the class into four groups—one group for each corner of the room. The way we will do it will be to read off your name and assign you to a group. Once you are at your group you will be given a halter like this to put on. Sometimes they are difficult to put on so it would be a good idea to help each other. Now group 1 will be in this corner (point), group 2 will be in this corner (point), etc. Listen carefully for your name and group. Wait until I have read all the names before you go to your group. All right, the children in group 1 are . . . The children in group 2 are . . . , etc.

DISTRIBUTE THE NUMBER—ASSIGN THE GROUPS—AND THEN HAVE EVERY CHILD SIT DOWN WITH HIS GROUP IN HIS CORNER.

Now that you belong to a group, it is very important that you stay with it. If, for some reason, you have to leave your group raise your hand and I'll come over and talk to you. This way I'll know where everybody is. Now, if you don't understand what to do, or if you have any questions, during this next hour, I want you to ask *me,* and not our visitors. Besides, our visitors will be busy watching games, and seeing that you get to the right group, while my job is to answer all of your questions.

The first game we will play is called Tinker Toys (Creative Construction from third grade up)—(Each Observer will have a box with all the games). What your group will do is to decide what *one* object (thing) your group would like to build. For example, some groups might like to build a house, ferriswheel, airplane, merry-go-round, an animal, etc. Once your group has decided what to build I want everyone in the group to raise their hands. Then I'll come over and you can tell me. It is important that I know what you are going to build before you start building it. You have about ten minutes for this game, and then we must stop. At the end of the game, I want each group to select one person to put the tinker toys away.

If there are no more questions, let us begin the first game. (AT THIS POINT, THE OBSERVERS WILL PUT THE TINKER TOYS ON THE TABLE.) Now remember, if you have any questions to ask, raise your hand and I'll come over to you and try to answer them.

AT THE END OF TEN MINUTES, THE LEADER CALLS TIME. HE COMPLIMENTS THE GROUP ON THEIR TASK, WHILE THE OBSERVER CLEARS OFF THE TABLE AND RETURNS THE GAMES TO THE BOX.

LEADER: It certainly seemed that you enjoyed yourselves so I think we better wait until you have played all the games before we discuss and vote on them. The next thing we have to do is to change groups.

Now, there will be some children who will remain in the same group, while the rest of you will go to a different one. Listen carefully for your number so that you will know where to go.

THE LEADER WILL READ OFF THE NUMBERS OF THE NEW GROUPS.

The second game we will play is called paper bag dramatics. It is a game where you can use your imagination. Each group will be given a paper bag containing six objects. What your group is to do is to make up one story between all of you while using all of the objects in the bag. The first story will be your practice story. Once your group has decided on the story and selected one person to tell your story to me, raise your hands. After your group has told me its practice story, they will makeup a better story to tell another group. This way, each group will hear three stories—two of their own, and one from another group. Remember, once you have finished making up your story, and have selected your story teller, raise your hand so I'll know when you are ready. You have about ten minutes to make up your two stories, and about three minutes to tell it, so it can't be too long but it can be real interesting. Any questions?

OBSERVERS PUT THE PAPER BAG ON THE TABLE.

AFTER EIGHT MINUTES HAVE PASSED, STOP THE GROUPS AND EXCHANGE
STORY TELLERS. AT THE END OF TWO MINUTES THE LEADERS CALL A HALT
TO ALL ACTIVITY AND COMPLIMENT THEM ON THEIR STORIES, WHILE THE
OBSERVER CLEARS OFF THE TABLE AND RETURNS THE GAME TO THE BOX.

LEADER: The last game made you use your imagination. The next will
make you use your hands. Before I explain it further, we better change
groups, so listen for your number. (THE LEADER READS OFF THE NUMBERS
OF THE NEW GROUPS.) Our next game is a construction game. What we
want your group to do is to make one building out of clay. Now there
are all kinds of buildings your group can make. There are the old log
cabins, schools, huts, sky scrapers, churches, etc. What your group is to
do is to make one house that everyone can help build. You have ten
minutes to construct your house. Also in this game, each group will select
one person to put away the clay after you have finished making your
building.

CHANGE GROUPS AND GIVE INSTRUCTIONS AS IN PREVIOUS GAMES.

There is an old saying that six heads are better than one when you
try to solve a problem. I wondered if that was true so when I taught
school I used to have my children play a game called Magic Mind, and
much to my surprise I had some groups that were wonderful. What I
would do would be to show them a bottle of beans and ask them how
many beans were in the bottle. They got so good at it, and had so much
fun doing it, we decided to try it out as a new game. What we will do
when we play Magic Mind is to put a bottle filled with beans on the
table. What your group will do is to sit on their chairs and try to decide
how many beans are in the bottle without touching the bottle. We want
you to stay in your chairs so nobody will get a better look. To make it
more difficult and more fun, each group will have only one answer to give.
This means you better talk it over and decide what you think the right
answer is. Remember, in this game, your answer may be the correct one.
Once your group has decided on its one answer, write it down on a
card and I'll come over and tell you the correct number of beans. Now
each group will get only four bottles and the best group will be announced at the end of the game, so take your time and don't rush since
you would want your group to be best. All right, as soon as you're ready
our visitors will put the first bottle on the table. Any questions?

The next thing we will do is to take off our numbers, put them on
the table, and then return to your regular seat.

Now that you played all four games, we would like to get your opinion on the ones you liked. I guess one way of doing it would be to vote
on them. If more than a half of the class votes for it we will consider the
game good for children of your age, OK?

HOLD A VOTING SESSION

Now that we have all the information that we want, we want to thank you for helping us. You have done a wonderful job, and we are real happy we decided to use your class. That is about all we have to say. If there are not any more questions then we'd better say "goodby."

BEHAVIOR OUTPUT FORM

Observer_____ Child Observed_____ Grade_____

Teacher_____ Date_____

A R F U V P   DESCRIPTION OF BEHAVIOR   (time)

A–*Approaches* other child

R–*Recipient* of approach from other child

F–the approach is *friendly*

U–the approach is *unfriendly*

V–the approach is verbal

P–the approach is physical

TEACHERS' RATING FORM

Teacher_____   Class_____

Date_____   School_____

We are interested in getting as good a picture of the children in your class as possible. In the following pages, we are asking you to tell us how the various members of the class behave *over the whole range of classroom activities*. We are asking you to put your judgments in the following form:

On each of the following pages is a question about some area of behavior. Beneath it is a list of the children in your class and five vertical columns, each column standing for some degree to which the behavior under consideration might be shown.

We want you to put a check mark (√) opposite each child's name, in the column which describes most accurately the extent to which that child shows the behavior under consideration.

In order to get more information about the children who show the greatest and the least degree of the behavior, *we are asking you to begin your ratings on each question by checking two and only two children in the extreme right and extreme left columns and by numbering the children in each extreme pair 1 and 2, to indicate which is the most extreme in these two columns.*

For example; a rating of the children in your class on some aspect of behavior might look like this:

	Most often	Often	Sometimes	Not often	Hardly ever
Albert Adams	2				
John Brown					1
Barbara Crenshaw	1				
Roberta Doe					
Harriet Jones					
Frank Moore					
Michael O'Hara				2	

Number *1* on the extreme left indicates that Barbara Crenshaw shows this behavior *most* often and number *2* on the extreme right indicates that Michael O'Hara shows this behavior *least* often.

If you find that you cannot rate a child in one of the areas of behavior, place a check in the margin next to his name so that we will know that you considered him.

1. Some children make only a few attempts to influence the other children in their class, but they are quite successful. Other children make a great many influence attempts but meet with little success.

Who is most successful at getting others to do things in your class? (What level of success does each child have in his attempts to get the others to do things for him? Of all the orders, suggestions and beseechments made, about how many are successful?)

	Almost always successful	Mostly successful	As successful as not	Mostly unsuccessful	Almost always unsuccessful

2. A large part of the interaction among children is in the nature of influence attempts in your class.

Who *tries most to get the others to do things* in the total range of class activity? (Who makes the most suggestions, gives orders, beseeches?)

	Most often	Often	Sometimes	Not often	Least often

3. Children tend to be more expert in some areas than in others, such as intellectual, physical and social (see next three ratings).

In your class, *who shows the best intellectual performance?* (How well do the children do on mental tasks?)

	High	Above average	Average	Below average	Low

4. *Who shows the most physical coordination and motor skill?* (Who demonstrates the most skill at manipulative tasks and physical activities?)

High	Above average	Average	Below average	Low

5. Some children have more *procedural skills* than others. That is, they serve to keep their group together and moving efficiently toward a goal rather than contributing technical skills or knowledge.

Who in your class *shows the most procedural skill?* (Who patches up arguments? Who asks for a vote or otherwise helps the group to reach a decision? Who coordinates work?)

A great deal	More than average	Some	Not very much	Almost none

6. Children differ in the amount of warmth they show one another. In your class, *who shows the most friendly behavior?* (Who says friendly things, makes friendly overtures and responses?)

Very much	A good deal	Some	Not much	Hardly any at all

7. Just as children differ in the amount of warmth they show one another, they also differ in the *amount of the warmth shown toward them.* A child may give out a lot of friendly behavior, but he is not necessarily the recipient of a lot of friendly behavior.

Toward whom do the children in your class show the most friendly behavior?

Receives the most	Receives a lot	Receives an average amount	Receives little	Receives almost none

8. Some children are more generally *dependent* than others. Further, while some may be relatively independent from the other children they lean heavily on their teacher for support; others may be fairly independent of the teacher but need the support of the other children. (See next question.)

Which children are most dependent on their teacher?

Most dependent	Fairly dependent	About average dependency	Fairly independent	Most independent

9. Some children are more generally *dependent* than others. Further, while some may be relatively independent from the other children they lean heavily on their teacher for support; others may be fairly independent of the teacher but need the support of the other children.

Which children are most dependent on the other children?

Most de-pendent	Fairly de-pendent	About average dependency	Fairly inde-pendent	Most inde-pend-ent

10. Some children are predominantly *egoistic* and some children predominantly *altruistic*. That is, some children seem to respond mainly to their own needs and to ignore the needs and wishes of others, while other children seem to act mainly out of consideration for the needs and wishes of others.

Which children in your class are *most highly egoistic* and which *most highly altruistic?*

Mainly egoistic	Egoistic but some-times al-truistic	About half egoistic & half al-truistic	Altruis-tic but some-times egoistic	Mainly altru-istic

11. Children respond differently to influence attempts made on them by other children. Some resist almost all of them and others accept almost all of them.

Which children in your class *resist influence attempts most often* and which *accept influence attempts most often* from the other children?

Almost always resist	Usually resist	Half the time resist & half the time accept	Usually accept	Almost always accept

12. Children try in many ways to influence one another. Some are very directive, giving orders; others make suggestions; others plead.

Which is the *predominant form of influence attempt* used by each child in your class?

Mainly orders	Orders but some-times suggests	Mainly suggests	Be-seeches but some-times sug-gests	Mainly be-seeches

13. Some children tend to use physical force more than others in order to get their peers to do the things they want them to do. This includes not only actually hitting the others and pushing them, but threatening them with menacing gestures as well.

To what extent does each child use physical force in influence attempts?

Fre-quent	Above average	Average	Below average	Almost never

14. Children show different degrees of control of their impulses to blurt out what they feel or to act without thinking. The *undercontrolled* child loses control easily and "lets go" without considering the consequences for himself or others. The *overcontrolled* child has strong internal restrictions to spontaneous expression. He can't "let go" even when it is appropriate to do so. He seems afraid to express his own wishes.

To what extent does each of the children show impulse control?

Very impulsive Very undercontrolled	More impulsive than controlled	About equal balance of control and impulse expression	Tends to inhibit impulses more than most	Very over controlled or inhibited

15. Some children seem to be the usual targets for one kind of influence attempt and not another. Some are ordered around, some get a lot of suggestions, some are begged to do things.

Which is the predominant form of influence attempt that each child in your class receives? (Check two children in each column and number each pair 1 and 2 as before.)

Receives mostly orders	Receives mostly beseechments

INSTRUCTIONS FOR OBSERVING PUPIL-TEACHER BEHAVIOR

As you know, a great variety of events do and can occur in the classroom. Some of these events are important and others are unimportant, and it is often difficult to decide in advance how important they actually are. Another difficulty resides in the fact that when observing we cannot register everything that goes on at a given time, even if we wanted to.

Therefore, it is often advisable to concentrate one's efforts on a limited front by focussing on only a limited number of categories of behavior.

Once these categories have been decided upon in advance we can proceed to note each occurrence during a specified time interval which can readily be classified into any of our predetermined categories.

The categories which will be described below are, we believe, important insofar as our research objectives are concerned. They have been constructed, in some cases, so that the observer need only make tallies to indicate the number of times that a given type of behavior occurred. In other cases, we are more interested in the actual content of the occurrence insofar as the event is concerned with standards about behavior. This will call for brief, written descriptions of the event in question.

I. *Types of Behavior*
   The Manner of Approach: The behavior to be noted concerns (a) The number of times and the manner in which the teacher approaches or is approached by specific children in the classroom; and (b) *Types of support:* The number of times that the teacher supports or withholds support from children for things they do in the classroom.
  A. *Manner of Approach*
    1. *Teacher approaches the child*
      Indicate by a tally on the observation sheet in the same row along which the child's name appears, *each time* that the teacher approaches any given child. Specify the manner of approach by entering the tally in one of three sub-categories, namely,
      (a) does the teacher approach the child with *affection* or
      (b) does the teacher approach the child in a *neutral* (work-oriented) way, or
      (c) does the teacher approach the child with *coolness* or *with anger.*
    2. *Teacher is approached by the child*
      Indicate by a tally on the observation sheet, in the same row along which the child's name appears, *each time* that a given child approaches the teacher. Specify the manner of approach by entering the tally in one of three sub-categories, namely,
      (a) does the child approach the teacher *with affection,* or
      (b) does the child approach the leader in a *neutral* (work-oriented) way, or
      (c) does the child approach the teacher with *coolness* or *with anger.*
  B. *Type of Support*
    1. *Teacher supports, encourages, praises behavior.*
      Indicate by a tally on the observation sheet, in the same row along which the child's name appears, *each time* that the teacher supports, encourages or praises a specific child for,
      (a) specific behavior which the child shows towards other children, or for

CLASSROOM OBSERVATION OF PUPIL-TEACHER BEHAVIOR

Observer _____ Grade Observed _____ Teacher _____ Date _____

I. Types of Behavior

	MANNER OF APPROACH			TYPE OF SUPPORT	
	Teacher Approaches [mark with slant (/)] or is Approached by the Child [mark with circle (o)]			Teacher Supports, Encourages, Praises [mark with plus (+)] or Withholds Approval, Discourages, Criticizes [mark with minus (−)]	
Identity of Children	With Affection	In Neutral Manner	With Coolness or Anger	Behavior Toward Other Children	Individual Work, Individual Performance

II. Types of Standards about Behavior (write down each incident as it occurs)

A. *What kinds of behavior standards, if any, does the teacher explicitly encourage and support?*

  1.
  2.
  3.

B. *What kinds of behavior standards, if any, does the teacher explicitly discourage, criticize, etc.?*

  1.
  2.
  3.

(b) individual work, and performance.
2. *Teacher withholds approval, discourages, criticizes.*
Indicate by a tally on the observation sheet, in the same row along which the child's name appears, *each time* that the teacher withholds approval from, or discourages or criticizes a specific child for,
(a) specific behavior which the child shows toward other children, or for
(b) individual work and performance in working with things.
II. *Types of Standards About Behavior*
A. *What kinds of behavior standards, if any, does the teacher explicitly encourage and support?*
For example: (Mrs. X) praised Sally for sharing her things with other children.
B. *What kinds of behavior standards, if any, does the teacher explicitly discourage?*
For example: (Mrs. X said to Johnny): "It isn't nice to tease people, Johnny." Or: Teacher stops fight without explanation.

BE SURE TO LABEL EVERY OBSERVATION SHEET SO THAT IT CAN BE IDENTIFIED LATER ON.

12 / Psychological Health and Classroom Functioning: A Study of Dissatisfaction with School among Adolescents [1]

Philip W. Jackson and Jacob W. Getzels

Dissatisfaction with school appears to be part of a larger picture of psychological discontent rather than a direct reflection of inefficient functioning in the classroom. Dissatisfied boys tend to project the causes of their discontent on others whereas girls are more likely to be self-critical, turning blame for their dissatisfaction inward. Rosenzweig's (1934) concepts of "intropunitiveness" and "extrapunitiveness" are applied to these findings, and a theoretical framework is proposed by Philip W. Jackson and Jacob W. Getzels of the University of Chicago.

[1] This study was supported by a research grant from the United States Office of Education. The present report is an expanded version of a paper read at the American Psychological Association meeting, Cincinnati, Ohio, September 1959.

Reprinted from the *Journal of Educational Psychology*, 1959, *50*, 295–300, with the permission of the authors and the American Psychological Association.

The problem of dissatisfaction with school among children is of theoretical and practical significance to both psychologists and educators. At the theoretical level dissatisfaction with school becomes part of a broader area of inquiry which aims at an understanding of the individual's functioning in an institutional setting and which includes studies of staff morale, role conflict, productivity, and the like. At a practical level the question of why children like or dislike school is directly related to the immediate problems of school dropouts, grouping procedures, planning for the gifted child, and the like.

As might be expected, a social phenomenon as important as dissatisfaction with school is not without its explanatory hypothesis. Some of these spring from empirical findings, while others appear to be part of our cultural ethos. Educational studies that point to an empirical linkage between school failure and school dropouts, and industrial studies that demonstrate a relationship between low morale and decreased output, lead one to suspect that reduced effectiveness in school (i.e., low scholastic achievement) would be a natural concomitant of dissatisfaction with the institution. Thus one would expect to find heightened dissatisfaction among students who have low ability or who are unable for one reason or another to deal adequately with scholastic material.

More recently it has been suggested (although never adequately demonstrated) that many successful students with high ability are dissatisfied with their school experiences; the term "boredom" is often linked with the term "gifted child" in current expositions by educators. The boredom problem among "gifted" combined with the failure experiences of the low ability child suggests that the greatest number of dissatisfied students is to be found among extreme ability groups. Those who are low in ability and achievement would be expected to show dissatisfaction because of the numerous frustrations they experience in the classroom. Those who are high in ability and achievement would be expected to show dissatisfaction because of the relative lack of stimulation which they experience in the classroom.

Both of these explanations (or, more accurately, hypotheses) contain the implication that dissatisfaction with an institution arises out of the individual's interaction with that institution. An alternative explanation might be that the individual brings a set toward satisfaction or dissatisfaction *to* the institution—that it is a reflection of a more pervasive personal orientaton and that success or failure experiences within the institution have a limited influence upon it. This hypothesis obviously places more emphasis than do the earlier ones upon psychological variables, as opposed to environmental variables, in understanding dissatisfaction with school. The research described here was designed to test the relative merit of these alternative views.

PROBLEM

The purpose of this investigation is to examine the differences in psychological functioning and classroom effectiveness between two groups of adolescents—those who are satisfied with their recent school experiences and those who are dissatisfied.

SUBJECTS AND PROCEDURE

The Ss of this investigation were two groups of adolescents identified from among 531 students enrolled in a Midwestern private school. These students were divided into five class groups ranging from the prefreshmen to the senior year of high school. In this institution a single grade, the prefreshmen, is substituted for the usual seventh and eighth grades. The instrument used to select the experimental groups, called the Student Opinion Poll,[2] was a 60-item opinionnaire designed to elicit responses concerning general satisfaction or dissatisfaction with various aspects of school—viz., the teachers, the curriculum, the student body, and classroom procedures.

The instrument was scored by giving one point each time the S chose the "most satisfied" response to a multiple-choice item. Thus, the possible range of scores was from 0 to 60. For the total school population the mean score on the Student Opinion Poll was 37.30; the standard deviation was 9.57. The experimental groups were chosen as follows:

Group I—the "dissatisfied" group—consisted of all students whose score on the opinionnaire was at least one and a half standard deviations *below* the mean of the entire student body. This group contained 27 boys and 20 girls.

Group II—the "satisfied" group—consisted of all students whose score on the opinionnaire was at least one and a half standard deviations *above* the mean of the entire student body. This group contained 25 boys and 20 girls.

The experimental groups were compared on the following variables:

1. *Individual intelligence tests.* In most cases this was the Binet. A small number of children were given the Henmon-Nelson, the scores of which were converted by regression equation into equivalent Binet scores.

2. *Standardized verbal achievement test.* The Cooperative Reading Test was used. Prefreshmen and freshmen were given Test C_1, Form Y; older students were given C_2, Form T.

3. *Standardized numerical achievement tests.* Because of differences in the curricula of the various grade groups it was not possible to administer the same test of numerical achievement to all Ss. The following tests were given according to grade placement:

Prefreshmen—Iowa Everypupil Arithmetic Test, Advanced Form O.

Freshmen—Snader General Mathematics Test.

[2] [Appended to the selection.]

Sophomores—Cooperative Elementary Algebra Test, Form T.

Juniors—Cooperative Intermediate Algebra Test.

Seniors—Cooperative Geometry Test, Form 2.

4. *California Personality Test.* Two forms of this instrument were used. The intermediate form was given to prefreshmen; the secondary form was given to all of the older groups. Two subscores were obtained, "personal adjustment" and "social adjustment."

5. *Direct Sentence Completion Test.*[3] Ss were asked to complete 27 sentences of the type: "When I saw I was going to fail I _____," or, "I think my father is _____." Each sentence was given a plus or minus score depending upon the presence or absence of morbid fantasy, defeatism, overt aggression, and the like. The total score was the summation of the individual sentence scores.

6. *Indirect Sentence Completion Test.* This instrument was identical with the Direct Sentence Completion Test except that proper names were inserted for the pronoun "I," thus changing it from a "self-report" to a "projective" instrument. Boys' names were used in the male form of the instrument and girls' names in the female form. The instrument was presented as a "thinking speed" test. To reinforce this notion Ss were asked to raise their hands when they were finished and the elapsed time was written on their test booklet. This instrument was administered approximately two weeks prior to the administration of the Direct Sentence Completion Test.

7. *Group Rorschach.* Cards III, IV, IX, and X were projected on a screen. For each picture the S was presented with 10 responses and was asked to choose the three which he thought to be most appropriate. Each list of 10 contained four "pathological" responses. The S's score was the number of nonpathologic responses among his 12 choices. This group technique follows that described by Harrower-Erikson and Steiner (1945).

8. *Teacher ratings.*[4] Each student was given three ratings by his present teachers. These ratings included: (*a*) his general desirability as a student; (*b*) his ability to become involved in learning activities; and (*c*) his possession of leadership qualities. Teachers were required to place all of their students on a five-point scale so that Categories 1 and 5 each contained one-twelfth of the students; Categories 2 and 4 each contained one-fourth of the students; and Category 3 contained one-third of the students. The values 5, 8, 10, 12, and 15 were assigned to the categories and were used in quantifying the ratings.

9. *Adjective Check List.*[5] From a list of 24 adjectives each student was asked to choose the six which best described his characteristic feelings while attending classes in particular school subjects. The list contained 12 "positive" (e.g., confident, happy, eager, relaxed) and 12 "negative" adjectives (e.g., bored, restless, misunderstood, angry). The use of the negative adjectives by the experimental groups was analyzed both quantitatively and qualitatively.

RESULTS

With the exception of the adjective check list the results of all comparisons are shown in Table 1. Contrary to popular expectations the "satisfied" and "dissatisfied" students did *not* differ from each other in

[3] [Appended to the selection.]   [4] [Appended to the selection.]
[5] [Appended to the selection.]

Table 1. Mean Scores, Standard Deviations, and _t_ Statistics for Satisfied and

	BOYS			
	Dissatisfied (N = 27)		Satisfied (N = 25)	
	_x_	_s_	_x_	_s_
IQ	134.85	14.58	136.44	14.59
Verbal Achievement	49.96	8.69	50.68	7.87
Numerical Achievement	50.35	9.75	52.17	10.52
Calif. Personal Adjust.	45.58	9.82	53.40	7.63
Calif. Social Adjust.	44.85	11.37	51.84	8.93
Direct Sentence Comp.	46.93	10.58	49.25	10.02
Indirect Sentence Comp.	47.19	9.61	51.29	6.95
Group Rorschach	48.35	10.66	47.44	10.30
Teacher Rating I:				
Desirability as a student	8.94	1.83	10.35	1.70
Teacher Rating II:				
Leadership qualities	9.01	2.08	10.13	1.96
Teacher Rating III:				
Involvement in learning	9.09	2.14	10.23	1.69

* Significant at the .05 level.
** Significant at the .01 level.

either general intellectual ability or in scholastic achievement. Those differences which did appear were linked to psychological rather than scholastic variables. More specifically, each of the test instruments designed to assess psychological health or "adjustment" was effective in distinguishing "satisfied" from "dissatisfied" students within one or both sex groups.

For both sexes the experimental groups were differentiated by their scores on the California Test of Personality. The experimental groups of boys were further differentiated by their responses to the Indirect Sentence Completion Test. For girls additional differences appeared in their responses to the Direct Sentence Completion Test and the Group Rorschach.

On all of these test variables the "satisfied" group attained the "better" score—i.e., the score signifying a more adequate level of psychological functioning. It is also worthy of note that whenever a significant difference appeared, the mean score of the total student population fell between the mean scores of the experimental groups. Thus, the variables that differentiate the experimental groups tend also to distinguish them from the total population of students.

In addition to showing differences on psychological health variables, "satisfied" and "dissatisfied" boys were perceived differently by their teachers. On all three of the teachers' ratings the "satisfied" boys received more favorable judgments than did "dissatisfied" boys. The fact that this

Dissatisfied Adolescents on Dependent Variables [a]

	GIRLS				
	Dissatisfied (N = 20)		Satisfied (N = 20)		
t	x	s	x	s	t
ns	128.45	15.06	128.00	11.45	ns
ns	50.63	9.11	52.28	6.76	ns
ns	47.78	8.61	48.50	10.26	ns
3.18 **	47.90	13.03	54.76	9.25	1.86 *
2.45 **	47.00	13.15	55.76	7.89	2.50 **
ns	46.65	12.01	54.00	5.73	2.53 **
1.75 *	49.60	10.35	53.47	7.97	ns
ns	47.35	11.35	54.16	8.32	2.15 **
2.85 **	9.84	1.91	10.05	1.59	ns
2.00 *	9.91	2.37	10.04	1.24	ns
2.14 **	9.67	2.32	10.33	2.11	ns

[a] With the exception of IQ, all scores were based upon parameters of the total student body from which the experimental groups were drawn. The scores of all tests were transformed to T scores with a mean of 50 and a standard deviation of 10. For the total population the teacher ratings have a mean of 10 and a standard deviation of 2. The mean IQs for the total school population are: boys, 132, and girls, 128.

result does not appear to be true for girls lends support to the popular expectation that boys are more likely to express their negative feelings publicly than are girls. This hypothesis receives some confirmation from the results of the adjective check list which are described below.

In Table 2 are shown the number of Ss who chose negative adjectives when asked to describe their typical classroom feelings. As they are arranged in Table 2 the adjectives reflect the rankings of four judges who were asked to rank the words on the degree to which they involved an implicit or explicit criticism of others. The 12 adjectives were typed on separate cards and were accompanied by the following directions:

On the following cards are a number of negative adjectives which a person might use to describe himself. Rank these adjectives on the degree to which they involve an implicit or explicit criticism of others. For each adjective ask the question: If a person used this adjective *to describe himself* would he also be implicitly or explicitly criticizing others? Give a rank of 1 to the adjective which would be *least* critical of others and a rank of 12 to the adjective which would be *most* critical of others.

Four psychologists served as judges. The average rank order correlation among the four sets of judgments was .84. The adjectives are presented in Table 2 according to the ranked sum-of-ranks of the judges.

**Table 2. Number of Subjects Choosing Negative Adjectives when Asked
to Describe Typical Classroom Feelings**

| | BOYS | | | GIRLS | | |
Adjective	Dissatisfied ($N = 27$)	Satisfied ($N = 25$)	Chi Square	Dissatisfied ($N = 20$)	Satisfied ($N = 20$)	Chi Square
Inadequate	19	16	ns	17	7	10.42 **
Ignorant	19	13	ns	15	3	14.54 **
Dull	25	16	6.36 *	16	9	5.60 *
Bored	24	13	8.61 **	20	13	8.48 **
Restless	20	15	ns	19	9	11.90 **
Uncertain	20	21	ns	17	13	ns
Angry	15	4	8.76 **	13	4	8.29 **
Unnoticed	19	5	13.25 **	7	4	ns
Unhelped	18	8	6.24 *	9	6	ns
Misunderstood	16	5	8.31 **	5	2	ns
Rejected	12	3	6.66 **	4	0	ns
Restrained	17	2	16.91 **	9	3	4.29 *

* Significant at the .05 level.
** Significant at the .01 level.

The adjective "inadequate" was judged as being most free of criticism of others, while the adjective "restrained" was judged as involving the greatest amount of criticism of others.

As might be expected, the use of negative adjectives was far more frequent among dissatisfied students than among satisfied students. Four adjectives seemed to discriminate equally well between the experimental groups for both sexes; these were: "bored," "angry," "restrained," and "dull."

An examination of Table 2 also suggests the existence of sex differences in the students' description of their typical classroom feelings. Remembering the classificatory scheme by which the adjectives are ranked in Table 2, it appears that dissatisfied girls are somewhat less likely than dissatisfied boys to use negative adjectives involving implicit criticism of others. Dissatisfied boys, on the other hand, are less likely than dissatisfied girls to be distinguished from their satisfied counterparts by the use of adjectives *not* involving implicit criticism of others. If one thinks of criticism directed towards others within Rosenzweig's schema of "intropunitiveness" and "extrapunitiveness" (Murray, 1938), then the observed sex differences may be conceptualized by saying that dissatisfied girls are more *intropunitive* than satisfied girls; dissatisfied boys are more *extrapunitive* than satisfied boys.

This difference in the direction of aggression may provide a context for the obtained differences in teacher ratings discussed earlier. If the dissatisfied boy is more likely than his female counterpart to lay the blame for his dissatisfaction upon others in his environment, particularly school authorities, it is reasonable to expect that he would be viewed as some-what less than completely desirable by the classroom teacher. The dis-satisfied girl, on the other hand, seems more willing to direct her negative feelings inward, thus avoiding the additional risk of counter-aggression by school authorities or by other adults.

DISCUSSION

Two major conclusions are suggested by the findings of this study. First, dissatisfaction with school appears to be part of a larger picture of psychological discontent rather than a direct reflection of inefficient func-tioning in the classroom. It is almost as if dissatisfaction were a product of a pervasive perceptual set that colors the student's view of himself and his world. Second, it appears that the "dynamics" of dissatisfaction operate differently for boys and girls. Boys seem to project the causes of their discontent upon the world around them so that adults are seen as rejecting and lacking in understanding. This tendency to blame adults may be one reason why these boys are seen as less attractive by teachers than are satis-fied boys. Girls, on the other hand, are more likely to be self-critical, turn-ing blame for their dissatisfaction inward. Feelings of inadequacy, igno-rance, and restlessness more sharply differentiate satisfied and dissatisfied girls than is the case with boys. This tendency to be intropunitive may partially explain why teacher ratings fail to distinguish between our two experimental groups of girls.

The atypicality of the sample population used in this research places a number of limitations upon the inferential statements which can be made on the basis of these findings. Fortunately, however, the major por-tion of the investigation has recently been replicated using seventh and eighth grade lower-class Negro adolescents as Ss (Spillman, 1959). The findings of the latter study are essentially the same as those reported here. Again the psychological rather than the intellectual or scholastic variables discriminated between satisfied and dissatisfied students. The findings with respect to the use of negative adjectives were not as clear-cut but, again, every intropunitive adjective was used more frequently by dis-satisfied girls as compared with dissatisfied boys, while the latter exceeded the girls in their use of extrapunitive adjectives.

It should be noted that even the most satisfied students made some use of negative adjectives when asked to describe their typical feelings in the classroom. Also, the average member of the satisfied group expressed some dissatisfaction on one-sixth of the questions in the Student Opinion Poll. These two observations should serve as ample cautions against the danger of interpreting any sign of dissatisfaction with school as symptomatic of deeper psychological difficulties. Apparently, some degree of dissatisfac-tion is the rule rather than the exception. Nonetheless, the responses of the extremely disgruntled group of students leaves little doubt that dissatisfaction with school, like beauty, is frequently in the eye of the be-holder.

SUMMARY

This investigation examines the differences in psychological func-tioning and classroom effectiveness between two groups of adolescents—those who are satisfied with their recent school experiences and those who are dissatisfied. The major findings point to: (a) the relevance of psy-chological health data rather than scholastic achievement data in under-standing dissatisfaction with school; (b) the importance of differentiating the attitudes of dissatisfied girls from those of dissatisfied boys, the former being characterized by feelings of personal inadequacy, the latter by feel-ings critical of school authorities. Rosenzweig's concepts of intropunitive-ness and extrapunitiveness are applied to these findings and a relevant theoretical framework is proposed.

STUDENT OPINION POLL

As you probably know, there has been considerable public discussion during the past few months concerning American education. In order to cut through the haze of arguments and counter-arguments, a research team supported by the United States Office of Education is interested in obtaining information from the students themselves. While student opinion is not the only factor to be considered in planning for better schools, it is clearly a very important factor and one which has been overly neglected in the past.

The U.S. Office of Education researchers recognize the difficulty of questioning students concerning education "in general." For this reason, the questions which follow focus upon your experiences in the school in which you are now studying. Wherever the words "school," "teacher," "student," and the like, appear on this form, they refer to *this* school, the teachers you have had while studying *here*, your past and present classmates in *this* school, and so forth.

All of the information obtained from this questionnaire will be treated confidentially. It will never be shown to teachers or other school personnel in a form which will allow them to identify you. We are asking you to place your name on the questionnaire, however, so that the re-sponses may be related to other information available on the school.

ANSWERS ARE TO BE PUT ON THE SEPARATE ANSWER SHEET. DO NOT MARK THIS BOOKLET!

Answer the following questions by placing an "X" in the appropriate box on the answer sheet.

1. In determining the basic nature of its program, the school   a. pays too much attention to the wishes of parents.   b. pays just about the

right amount of attention to the wishes of parents.   c. pays too little attention to the wishes of parents.

2. In my opinion the variety of subjects offered in the school is   a. too broad.   b. just about right.   c. not broad enough.

3. While there are some differences among them, most teachers in this school are   a. very inspiring.   b. quite inspiring.   c. somewhat inspiring.   d. not inspiring.

4. In some schools the administrators (principals, superintendents, etc.) have close contacts with students, while in other schools, such contacts are rare. It seems to me that in this school   a. the administrator keeps such close contact with student affairs that they frequently involve themselves in matters that do not require their attention.   b. the contacts between administrators and students are about right.   c. the administrators have contacts with students so rarely that they are unaware of many student problems.

5. The freedom to contribute something in class without being called upon by the teacher is   a. discouraged more than it should be—students do not get enough opportunity to have their say.   b. encouraged more than it should be—students seem to be rewarded just for speaking even when they have little to say.   c. handled about right.

6. The things that I am asked to study are   a. of great interest to me.   b. of moderate interest to me.   c. of limited interest to me.   d. of little interest to me.

7. Concerning the opportunities for getting together socially with other students in this school, my opinion is that   a. there are altogether too many things going on, so that you are continually distracted from homework and other individual activities.   b. the opportunities for getting together socially are about right.   c. there are not nearly enough opportunities for getting together with other students.

8. In terms of *adequate* preparation for college I believe the program of the school is   a. more severe and rigorous than it needs to be.   b. about right.   c. less severe and rigorous than it should be.

9. The content of different courses from years to year is   a. too repetitious—the same material seems to be reworked again and again.   b. repeated just enough to allow for a feeling of continuity.   c. so unrelated that new material does not seem to build on earlier work.

10. In this school the teachers' interest in students' *academic work* might best be described as   a. too great—they intrude upon the privacy of the student.   b. just about right.   c. not great enough—teachers are not concerned enough with the work of students.

11. When school-work activities requiring full teacher support occur, my feeling is that   a. nearly all teachers cooperate.   b. most teachers cooperate.   c. some teachers cooperate.   d. few teachers cooperate.

12. It is a common practice in many classrooms to allot some class time for individual study. I find this study time allotment   a. so generous as to be somewhat wasteful.   b. adequate enough so that most stu-

dents can get at least a good start on their work.   c. so sparing as to be relatively worthless for any constructive activity.

13. The students in this school who receive poor grades are likely   a. to receive more sympathy from their fellow classmates than they deserve. b. to be respected by their classmates more than they should be. c. neither a nor b.

14. From the standpoint of intellectual ability, students in this school are a. too bright—it is difficult to keep up with them.   b. just bright enough.   c. not bright enough—they do not provide enough intellectual stimulation.

15. On the whole the school program places   a. less emphasis on *artistic training* than it should.   b. about the right emphasis on *artistic training*.   c. more emphasis on *artistic training* than it should.

16. Most of the subjects taught in the school are   a. interesting and challenging.   b. somewhat above average in interest.   c. somewhat below average in interest.   d. dull and routine.

17. In this school the teachers' interest in the students' *private life* might best be described as   a. too great—they intrude upon the privacy of the student.   b. just about right.   c. not great enough—teachers are not concerned enough with the personal life of their students.

18. The student who displays a sense of humor in class is generally   a. admired by teacher more than he should be.   b. penalized by teachers more than he should be.   c. neither admired nor penalized by teachers more than he should be.

19. There is often a feeling that teachers "go too fast" to permit students to really understand what is going on. In this school, the rate at which teachers usually present materials is   a. too slow.   b. about right. c. too fast.

20. Students who are outstanding athletes in their school are   a. respected more than they should be by their fellow students.   b. respected less than they should be by their fellow students.   c. neither a nor b.

21. The relative emphasis upon competition and cooperation among students in this school seems to be   a. too much emphasis upon competition to suit me.   b. too much emphasis upon cooperation to suit me.   c. a satisfactory balance between competition and cooperation.

22. All things considered the school program   a. puts too much emphasis on *scientific training*.   b. emphasizes *scientific training* in about the right degree.   c. puts too little emphasis on *scientific training*.

23. The present overall curriculum of the school   a. is about right. b. requires only minor revisions to make it about right.   c. requires considerable revision.   d. should be abandoned and replaced with a different program.

24. In general, the teachers I have had in this school seem to know their subject matter   a. very well.   b. quite well.   c. fairly well.   d. not as well as they should.

25. In evaluating the written and oral work of students a. too much emphasis is placed upon grammar and style and not enough upon the value of what the student is trying to say. b. the balance between style of expression and content is about right. c. so little emphasis is placed upon grammar and style that students have difficulty learning how to express themselves.

26. Students may work either by themselves or in groups. The amount of work done in *groups* is a. too great. b. about right. c. too small.

27. My observation has been that students from different economic, social, racial, and religious backgrounds get along together in this school a. very well. b. moderately well. c. less well than is desirable. d. very poorly.

28. As compared with what I feel to be desirable, the amount of "school spirit" at this school is a. more than enough. b. about right. c. not enough.

29. In its total program the school a. puts too much stress on intellectual matters. b. gives intellectual matters about the right emphasis. c. does not put enough stress on intellectual matters.

30. The extracurricular program of the school is a. very responsive to the needs and interests of the student body. b. quite responsive to the needs and interests of the student body. c. somewhat responsive to the needs and interests of the student body. d. very unresponsive to the needs and interests of the student body.

31. In matters relating to students, teachers in this school seem to be a. fair at all times. b. generally fair in their practices. c. occasionally unfair in their practices. d. often unfair in their practices.

32. In general classroom procedures are a. often so unorganized that it is difficult to get things done. b. flexible enough to meet most situations. c. often so rigidly organized that it is difficult to make changes.

33. Classroom seating arrangements in this school are a. too flexible to suit me; you can never be sure where you will sit and who will sit next to you. b. just about right. c. too rigid to suit me; it is difficult to arrange the furniture to meet special needs.

34. The students who receive top grades in this school are likely to be a. admired more than they should be by fellow students. b. rejected more than they should be by fellow students. c. neither admired nor rejected by fellow students.

35. In my opinion, student interest in social organizations, such as clubs, fraternities, and sororities is a. too great. b. about right. c. not great enough.

36. In general the subjects taught are a. too easy. b. about right in difficulty. c. too difficult.

37. When students are in need of special help, teachers in this school are a. always available. b. generally available. c. available if given special notice. d. available only in cases of extreme need.

38. The ability of the teachers in this school to present new material seems to be a. very superior. b. good. c. average. d. poor.

39. As compared to other methods of teaching, the practice of having students join discussion groups is   a. used more than I feel it should be.   b. used in about the right proportion with other methods.   c. used less than I feel it should be.

40. The time spent in homeroom activities is   a. always well spent.   b. generally well spent.   c. rarely well spent.   d. wasted.

41. In general, students in this school take their studies   a. too seriously.   b. too casually.   c. in a right proportion between a and b.

42. In some schools a lot of emphasis is placed upon student government, honor societies, and other types of formal social organization. In my opinion, the emphasis upon such activities in this school is   a. too great.   b. about right.   c. not great enough.

43. The *physical training* program of the school is   a. emphasized too much.   b. about right.   c. not emphasized enough.

44. Some things that we learn are of little use to us now but will become useful in the future; other things can be used as soon as we learn them. In this school teachers seem to   a. focus too much upon learning that will not become useful for some time to come.   b. focus too much upon learning that is useful to us now, neglecting things that we might need later.   c. achieve a nice balance between things of immediate and future usefulness.

45. When it comes to grading students, teachers in this school are generally   a. too "tough."   b. just "tough" enough.   c. not "tough" enough.

46. As compared to other methods of teaching, the practice of having the teacher give a lecture is   a. used more than I feel it should be.   b. used in about the right proportion with other methods.   c. used less than I feel it should be.

47. Homework assignments in the school are usually   a. carefully thought through by the teacher and clearly related to classroom work.   b. consistent with what is going on in the classroom but not related to it in any systematic way.   c. given without much thought and having little bearing on the classroom work.   d. unrelated to classroom work and chiefly of a "busy work" nature.

48. The student who differs from the crowd in this school is likely to find that   a. most students will tend to ignore or reject him for being different.   b. most students do not particularly care whether or not a person differs from the group.   c. most students admire the person who is different.

49. In my opinion, the emphasis which students in this school place upon grooming and appearance is   a. too great.   b. about right.   c. not great enough.

50. As an objective of the curriculum, *social skills,* i.e. training on how to get along with other people, is   a. not given enough emphasis.   b. given just about the right amount of emphasis.   c. given too much emphasis.

51. Some teachers are friendly and accepting to students; others are more detached and aloof. In general, the teachers in this school are   a. very friendly and accepting.   b. quite friendly and accepting.   c. somewhat friendly and accepting.   d. only occasionally friendly and accepting.

52. Individual pupils differ in their abilities and interests. Some teachers tend to ignore these differences. Other teachers pay too much attention to these differences. In general, teachers in this school   a. focus too much upon individual differences, giving undue attention to those who happen to be most different from the group.   b. do not focus enough upon individual differences, so that students with special talents or problems are frequently unrecognized.   c. pay just enough attention to individual differences.

53. In general, my attitude towards the grades I have received in this school is   a. I always receive the grades that I deserve.   b. I generally receive the grades that I deserve.   c. I sometimes receive the grades that I do *not* deserve.   d. I frequently receive the grades that I do *not* deserve.

54. Teaching aids such as films, T.V., and the like   a. are used more than I feel they should be.   b. are used as much as they should be.   c. are used less than I feel they should be.

55. Judging from the types of students who are my classmates, I believe that the admissions policy of this school is   a. too restrictive; the students are too much alike.   b. just about right.   c. not restrictive enough; there are many students in this school who should not be here.

56. In the typical class, memory work and the learning of important facts are   a. given too much emphasis.   b. given about the right emphasis.   c. not given enough emphasis.

57. In some classes the teacher is completely in control with the students having little to say about the way things are run. In other classes the students seem to be boss with the teacher contributing little to the control of the situation. In general, teachers in this school seem to take   a. too much control.   b. about the right amount of control.   c. too little control.

58. In addition to teachers, some schools employ persons who are specially trained to help students with personal, vocational, and educational problems. In my opinion, this type of service in this school is   a. so plentiful that it is sometimes forced upon you whether you want it or not.   b. adequate to meet the needs of the students.   c. so meager that it is difficult to obtain even when you want it.

59. When a newcomer enters this school, chances are that other students will   a. go out of their way to accept him.   b. are quite willing to accept him.   c. tend to ignore him.   d. openly reject him.

60. In general, my attitude toward school may best be described as   a. very favorable—I like it as it is; no changes are necessary.   b. more favorable than unfavorable—a few changes are necessary to

make me entirely happy. c. more unfavorable than favorable—many changes are necessary before I can be entirely happy. d. unfavorable—I frequently feel that school is pretty much a waste of time.

DIRECT SENTENCE COMPLETION TEST[6]

This is a test to find out how you behave in certain situations or when certain things happen to you. In this test you are given the first part of a sentence, and you are to finish the sentence so that it tells something about you. There are no right or wrong answers, but what you say will tell something about the kind of a person you are. Don't worry about spelling, but write as legibly as you can. Don't waste time.

Example: When I am given a gift, I _____.

One person might write: *am very happy*. Another person might write: *feel sorry since I can't give one back*. Or a third person might write: *try it on right away*. And so on. The answer you write should tell how you feel or act in the situation.

1. When I have something to say and others are around, I
2. My reputation is that I
3. When told that I failed the test, I
4. My family
5. Whenever I feel myself to be on trial, I
6. I feel that most people who meet me for the first time think I am
7. When they asked me to be in charge, I
8. From past experience, I know that my teacher's opinion of me is
9. Most jobs with responsibility make me feel
10. Compared with other people, I feel myself to be
11. My mother
12. Working with others all the time makes me
13. My opinion of most teachers is that
14. When I see others doing better than I am, I
15. I believe most grown-ups think of me as being
16. When I think the odds are pretty much against me, I
17. I feel my family thinks I am
18. From past experience, I feel most people are
19. From past experience, no matter what others think, I myself know that I
20. My father
21. I believe most people work because they
22. I often think of myself as
23. When I try to do the lesson and can't, I
24. Like most people, I sometimes think my family is

[6] [The full test contains 60 items. Only the 27 items used in the study are included here.]

25. I think most people think of me as
26. When told I have to do the whole thing by myself, I
27. When I think the job is too much for me, I

TEACHER RATINGS

The child's behavior in the classroom setting cannot be understood without reference to observations and reactions by his teachers. The teacher is the best qualified person—indeed, he is in many ways the only person—to provide this material. Accordingly, we are asking teachers to make three observations: one dealing with teacher preferences, one with the child's social behavior, and one with the child's ability to become involved with the learning task.

Item I. This is a student whom the teacher especially enjoys having in class. When asked what kind of person you prefer as a member of your class, this is the student who comes most readily to mind. He may or may not be the one who gets along best in the classroom situation, he may or may not be the brightest child in the class, and he may or may not be the one who gets the best grades. But he is *liked* by you and is the sort of person about whom you are most likely to say, "Of all the children in my class, this is the one I most *enjoy*."

INSTRUCTIONS: Please rate the students listed here according to the following scheme (all the students are in your classes this quarter):

1. Mark *H* next to the _____ students whom you would rate higher than the others on this list for the quality described in this item.
2. Mark *L* next to the _____ students whom you would rate lower than the others on this list for the quality described in this item.
3. Mark *M* for all the others—this is the middle group.
4. Now, circle the *H* next to the _____ students who are especially high.
5. Circle the *L* next to the _____ students who are especially low.

Item II. This is a student who gets along exceptionally well in interpersonal relationships. He may or may not be the brighest child, and he may or may not be the outstanding scholar. *But* he is outstanding in his ability to function harmoniously within the formal and informal social relationships of the class. He has high prestige among peers, and is likely to be sought out as a "leader" and "opinion-maker" by other students, although he may not necessarily hold student offices. The implication here is not of course that he is the "campus politician," but that he is generally liked and respected by other children.

INSTRUCTIONS: [Same as for Item I.]

Item III. This is the student who is most involved in (excited about) the learning task. Given a problem to be solved, an issue to be investigated, a work to be appreciated, he seems to get genuine pleasure from the educational experience. Learning is *fun* for this child. This does not mean that he is necessarily the brightest student or highest achiever, although he may be. He may not even be best liked by his teachers or peers, although again he may well be. *But* there is no doubt that he is interested in the new, enjoys the pursuit of discovery, gets pleasure out of knowing, and is, of all the children in your classes, *most eager to learn.*

INSTRUCTIONS: [Same as for Item I.]

ADJECTIVE CHECK LIST

Even before we have attended a new class in a certain subject, we have developed expectations on the basis of our previous experience with that subject. On the second page of your answer sheet, you will find a number of adjectives in the margin of the paper and the names of a number of school subjects listed across the top. Imagine that you are to attend a class in each of these subjects next year. In the column under each subject you are to check, in the appropriate boxes, the *six* adjectives most nearly describing your probable feelings when attending class in that subject. After you have chosen these six, place a "1" beside the check for the adjective which you would use if your choice were limited to one word, a "2" beside the check for the adjective which you would use next, and so on until you have numbered your adjectives from one to six.

When you have finished, each column should have six checks with a number from one to six beside them.

	English	*Math.*	*Phys. Educ.*	*Science*	*Art & Music*	*Social Studies*	*Foreign Language*
contented							
ignorant							

The remainder of the list is as follows: encouraged, angry, knowledgeable, inadequate, stimulated, unnoticed, benefited, dull, confident, unhelped, appreciated, alert, uncertain, restless, understood, bored, friendly, misunderstood, accepted, restrained, rejected, effective.

13 / A Study of Validity and Constancy of Choices in a Sociometric Test [1]

Eugene Byrd

Several selections in this volume use the sociometric technique, which aims to explore the interpersonal relationships of groups in terms of the extent to which members accept one another. How valid are sociometric results? In the following study of a group of fourth-grade pupils over a two-month period, Eugene Byrd of Miami, Florida finds a high degree of relationship between sociometric choices and real life choices.

PROBLEM

The purpose of this study is to investigate the constancy of choice behavior as expressed on Moreno's sociometric tests and in a life situation. The degree to which observed choices in the life situation agree with reported choices on the sociometric test, when the criterion of choice is held constant, may be considered a measure of validity. In an effort to determine the degree of change in choice behavior that is known to occur over a period of time, the original sociometric test was readministered shortly following the observation of choosing in the life situation. Lack of validity would be indicated by a change greater than that expected and measured by the test-retest method.

BACKGROUND AND SETTING OF THE PROBLEM

The Moreno test has found extensive and intensive use in the fields of sociology, psychology, and education. Its fundamental purpose is to measure the social structure of a specified group. The sociometric test accomplishes this by requiring each individual of a specified group to select one or more individuals in that group on the basis of a stipulated criterion of choice. The standard method of obtaining choices in a sociometric test is the question-and-answer method (i.e., the individuals are asked to name their choices). These choices are usually written by the in-

[1] This study was made in connection with a research project being carried on under a grant from the Research Council of Florida State University.

Reprinted from *Sociometry*, 1951, *14*, 175–81, with the permission of the author and J. L. Moreno, M.D., Editor, Beacon House, Inc., publishers.

dividual or, in cases of young children, may be written by the experimenter. Thus, by simply counting the total number of choices each individual receives from the other members of the group a rank order can be obtained and each individual's relative position in that group may readily be ascertained. This is the basis of the group structure in sociometric studies.

The basic structure may be subdivided into groups of individuals on the basis of the number of choices received. Those individuals who receive the largest number of choices have been designated as *leaders, stars, most-chosen,* and *most-accepted.* Individuals receiving few or no choices have been called *isolates, unchosen, rejected, least-chosen,* and *least-accepted.* These names refer only to their sociometric status and may or may not agree with other behavioral criteria. One should use caution when using these terms to describe an individual as they are always relative to the group measured and the specific choice criteria used to determine the status. The status of an individual may also change and so an individual who is classified as an isolate on one sociometric test may not be so classified on another test or on the same test at a later date. It is important then to be able to know the degree of stability in sociometrically determined group status.

The following experiment was designed to investigate the validity of a sociometric test as measured by the degree to which observed choices agree with reported choices when the criterion of choice is held constant. In an effort to determine the expected degree of change in choice behavior the original sociometric test was readministered shortly following the observation of choosing in the life situation.

SUBJECTS

The subjects used in this experiment consist of twenty seven pupils in the fourth grade class of the Florida State University Demonstration School. All subjects used in computing data were present at the administration of the sociometric tests.

METHODOLOGY

1. A sociometric test was administered to determine the group status. This test was of the paper and pencil type and the pupils wrote down their choices "privately." A single criterion of positive choice was used. No limit was set on the number of choices that could be expressed.

2. The subjects were next given the opportunity to make their choices in the life situation using the original choice criterion. On the basis of these choices group status was determined as in the sociometric test.

3. After all the subjects had expressed their choices in the life situa-

tion the original sociometric test was readministered and group status again determined.

PROCEDURE

Prior to administration of the first sociometric test the examiner was introduced to the class and with the help of the teacher discussed some of the things the children liked to do. Although the selection of presenting short psychodramas had been pre-selected by the examiner the suggestion of "doing some plays" came from the children themselves. The class then discussed some of the mechanics and manners that would be necessary for such plays. It was decided that the plays could be presented in the classroom with those not participating to act as an audience.

Situation I—The Sociometric Test

The examiner asked all the children to indicate the persons they would choose to be in their play.

When you give your play what classmates would you like to have in it? I want you to write down their names because you know them much better than I do. You may choose anyone you like and as many as you like. Write their names on the piece of paper you have. Miss B____ or I will help you spell any names you need help with.

After the papers had been collected they were told:

You can be thinking about the play you would like to give. It may be about something you have done, something you are going to do, or about something you would like to do if you had the chance. It isn't necessary to write it all out but know what you want to do in case your turn comes first.

No further mention was made of their original choices.

Situation II—The Life Situation

After an interval of four days the dramas were presented at the average rate of two per one hour session; two sessions per week. No sessions were held when there were absences. Each child in turn was asked his choices privately by the examiner in order to obtain a higher degree of individual spontaneity and to avoid influence of a few individuals who exhibited obvious signs of wanting to be chosen in every play. No child with the exception of the last few knew when his turn would come.

After the choices were given, the examiner read off the names and those individuals chosen met in the corner of the room where the theme of the play and assigning of roles were given by each child who did the choosing. The play was then presented to the class. This procedure extended over an interval of eight weeks.

Situation III—The Sociometric Retest

One week after the last drama was presented a second sociometric test was given. The children were told they would have an opportunity to give another play. The original sociometric test procedure was then repeated.

RESULTS

The choices made in all three situations are presented in Table 1. The subjects are listed in rank order of choices received on the first sociometric test in Situation I. The vertical columns contain the choices received. The horizontal rows contain the choices expressed. The numbers 1, 2, and 3 indicate the situation in which a choice was expressed. For example, pupil AA chose pupil B in all three situations. These choices are indicated by 1-2-3- under B's name. Since B also chose AA in all three situations these choices are indicated with 1-2-3- under AA's name. Individual totals in each situation, of choices received, and choices made are indicated.

CONSTANCY OF CHOICE EXPRESSION

The total number of choices made by the group are: Situation I, 155; Situation II, 160; Situation III, 166. As a group the *number* of choices made tends to remain constant over a two month period.

In order to determine the extent to which the subjects choose the *same* individuals in any two situations a ratio was computed between the number of choices repeated in any two situations and the total number of choices expressed by the group in one of those situations. These results are presented in Table 2.

Of 155 choices expressed in the original sociometric test (Situation I) 73 (47 percent) were reexpressed for the same individuals in the life situation (Situation II). Of 155 choices expressed in Situation I 89 (57 percent) were reexpressed for the same individuals on the readministration of the sociometric test (Situation III). Of 160 choices expressed in the life situation 93 (58 percent) were expressed for the same individuals on the sociometric retest. Of 155 choices on the original sociometric test 58 (37 percent) were expressed for the same individuals in *both* the life situation and the sociometric retest.

These figures show that as a group about half of the choices expressed are for the same individuals from one situation to another regardless of whether they are written on paper or expressed in a life situation. This would suggest that the choice criterion was not psychologically different between the two situations as reflected by the group. How does this change in expression of choices affect the group status?

Table 1. The Expression of Choices by a Fourth Grade in Three Situations Having the Same Choice Criterion

		CHOICES RECEIVED — PUPILS																											TOTAL CHOICES EXPRESSED SITUATION		
	AA	A	B	C	D	E	F	G	H	I	J	K	L	M	N	O	P	Q	R	S	T	U	V	W	X	Y	Z	I	II	III
AA		3						123	1		1 3			123	1 3	2	23	12										8	7	9
A	1 3		123	1 3	123	123	123	1		1 3	1 3	123		123	123	2	23	2					23					3	4	8
B	123	1		1 3	23	23			23	1 3	23	23		23	3		2	1						23			23	4	8	6
C	1 3	1 3			1	2	1		2	2	2				1 3	1	3		1									6	5	6
D	23	23	23	123	123	123	2	23	23	123	123	123	1 3	12				2	1									4	8	5
E	123	2	2	123	1 3	123	123	23	23	1 3	2	23	1 3	23			23	23	1									5	8	4
F	12	1	123		1 3	1 3				13		2	3	23		1		23										5	10	7
G	2	1														1												3	5	3
H	123	12		23	23	23	1	123		2	3		2	123	123	123	1	3		2							2	4	5	4
I	1 3	1 3	1 3	1	1 3	1 3	1 3	1 3	2	3	1 3	1 3	3	23	123		123	3	3	3		3			3		2	10	4	12
J	1	3	3	1 3	12	2		1 3			1 3	1 3			12		12	12		12								7	4	6
K	123	1 3	23	123	1	1	123	1 3	1	23	123	1		23	12			12										6	5	6
L	123	3	2	123		1				1	3	3		2	23	2				3		3			2			4	6	6
M	1 3	123	1 3	123	123	123	123	123	1	2	123	23	23		2		23	23			3	123	123		2			10	6	7
N	123	123	1 3	3					23	2	23	23	3			2				123		123	123					5	7	6
O	1 3	123	1		1				23	23	23	23																5	5	7
P	123	123	123	23	23	12			3	123	123	23	3	1	2	2				123			123		123	2	23	4	8	6
Q	3	23	1 1	123	2	1	2		123				3	1 3	1	123	123	2	2	2	12				3			6	6	7
R	1	123	1 1	123	1		23	12	12	12	12	12	123	13	1	123	123	23	123	123	12	3		2	3		23	9	6	6
S	1 3	123	3 1						2		1	1	1	2	1	123	2	2	123	123	3	3				3	3	4	3	5
T	3	123	1 1		1			123	12	3	3	3	3	2	3	123	23	2	2	2	2	3	2	2				6	5	6
U	1 3	1 3	123	23		23	1		2	2	2	2			2		2	2	2	1 3	1 3	3		2				5	5	7
V	123	1 3	2		3				3	3	3			1	3	123	23	2		3 1	2 1	2	1 3	13	13	3		5	6	5
W	1	12	12						12		2		3										1	2	3			5	7	5
X	1 3	123	1 3	2	2	2		1		123	3	1	3	1	2	123	23	2	2	1 1	3 1	1	1	2			3	5	7	7
Y	123	123	12	3	3				3			2		1	2	3	23	2	2	2	4	4	4	2	3			3	5	5
Z	123	123							123						123	123	123			12						2		12	5	7
TOTAL CHOICES REC'D I	21	19	15	11	9	9	7	6	6	6	6	10	5	5	4	3	3	3	3	3	1	1	1	1	1	0	0	**155**		
II	12	18	11	5	11	9	8	3	6	4	10	2	2	4	4	4	7	11	1	2	2	2	4	2	3	1	4	**160**		
III	21	20	15	6	10	10	6	4	5	6	11	5	3	3	4	2	5	4	2	4	4	2	2	2	3	1	3	**166**		

Table 2. Constancy of Choice Expression as Measured by Repeated Choices

Situation *	Total Number of Choices Made by Group	Choice Repeated		
		In Situation	Number	Percent
I	155	II	73	47
I	155	III	89	57
I	155	II & III	58	37
II	160	I	73	46
II	160	III	93	58
II	160	I & III	58	36
III	166	I	89	54
III	166	II	93	56
III	166	I & II	58	35

* Situation I—Sociometric Test; Situation II—Life Situation; Situation III— Sociometric Retest

CONSTANCY OF CHOICE STATUS

In order to measure the degree of constancy of the group status from one situation to another the Spearman Rank-Difference correlation method was used.[2] Tied scores were given a common rank equal to the mean of the ranks involved. The coefficients found are as follows:

Situation I and II   Rho $= .76 \pm .09$
Situation II and III   Rho $= .80 \pm .08$
Situation I and III   Rho $= .89 \pm .04$

If a t ratio of 2.0 is allowed then these three coefficients are not statistically significantly different. The coefficient of $.89 \pm .04$ between the sociometric test-retest is relatively high. It also reflects the change in choice behavior we might expect from the changes observed in the expression of choices. Group status cannot change unless individuals change in their expression of choices. However, it is conceivable and likely that status is more stable than expression of choices. Leaders tend to remain leaders even though their choosers may vary. No attempt is made to demonstrate this hypothesis in this study.

It was stated that in order to measure validity of a sociometric test by observing the choice behavior in the life situation one must be prepared to measure the expected change in choice behavior that would occur during the interval between measurements. If the correlation be-

[2] This method yields a coefficient designated by the Greek letter rho. For all practical purposes it is equivalent to the Pearson r. In no case does r exceed rho by more than .018. For the formulae and computation of rho and its standard error see Guilford (1942, pp. 227-31).

tween the sociometric test-retest is taken as a measure of this change then any increase in change in choice behavior due to lack of validity would tend to lower the coefficients of correlation between the sociometric tests and the life situation. It can be seen that these are lower but, as stated, not significantly so. This data suggests that there is little indication that change in choice behavior as measured by a sociometric test is due to lack of validity in the test. The greater part of the change is probably due to the dynamic aspect of choice behavior *per se*. This study should only be considered as exploratory. Only one group of children and one choice criterion were used. Further study is needed using other choice criteria and other groups differing in degree of cohesion before more decisive conclusions regarding the validity of sociometric tests are reached. Other methods of measuring validity that are not influenced by the intrinsic change should be investigated.

SUMMARY AND CONCLUSIONS

This study investigates the constancy of choice behavior as expressed on Moreno tests and in a life situation using the same choice criterion. This method is offered as an approach to the study of validity in sociometric tests. The sociometric test was readministered after choices were expressed in the life situation to determine the degree of expected change in choice behavior. The results of this study suggest that when a choice criterion has real meaning to the subjects, the degree of change in choice behavior between a sociometric test and a life situation is not significantly greater than that which occurs between a sociometric test and later re-administration of the same test. The writer feels that the results of this study support the hypothesis that a sociometric test is valid insofar as the choice criterion has reality value for the subjects.

14 / Personality Characteristics of Socially Accepted, Socially Neglected, and Socially Rejected Junior High School Pupils [1]

Norman E. Gronlund and Loren Anderson

On the basis of a "guess who" measure, sociometrically accepted, neglected, and rejected seventh- and eighth-grade pupils differ in

[1] This study was supported by a grant from the Bureau of Educational Research, College of Education, University of Illinois.

Reprinted from *Educational Administration and Supervision*, 1957, *43*, 329–38, with the permission of the authors.

personality characteristics: Accepted pupils are characterized by their peers as good looking, tidy, friendly, likable, enthusiastic, cheerful; rejected pupils are described as not good looking, untidy, not likable, restless, talkative; neglected pupils as quiet and not talkative, and receive relatively few mentions on either positive or negative characteristics. The authors, Norman E. Gronlund of the University of Illinois and Loren Anderson of Junior High School, Mt. Zion, Illinois, suggest several practical classroom methods to assist neglected and rejected pupils to improve in social acceptability.

A recent study (Gronlund and Whitney, 1956) has shown that the extent to which junior high school pupils are accepted by their classmates is related to the degree to which they are accepted throughout the school and in their neighborhoods. This pervasiveness of pupils' social status among their peers has increased the importance of identifying factors related to their social acceptability. Why is it that some pupils are highly accepted by their peers while others are neglected, or even actively rejected by them? Are there distinct personality patterns that characterize the socially accepted, the socially neglected, and the socially rejected pupils? Answers to such questions as these should enable teachers to better understand their pupils' social relations. Even more important, a study of the personality factors related to social acceptability should provide suggestions for improving the status of those pupils who are socially neglected or socially rejected.

Several research studies (Kuhlen and Lee, 1943; Laughlin, 1954; Tryon, 1939) have been concerned with the aspects of personality preadolescent and adolescent pupils consider most desirable in each other. In general, high social acceptability was found to be associated with positive personality characteristics such as cheerfulness, enthusiasm, friendliness, and the like. Pupils with low social acceptability were characterized as lacking in positive personality traits and possessing some negative characteristics, such as restlessness, talkativeness, fighting, and so forth. These studies have made valuable contributions concerning the factors related to social acceptability. However, none of the investigators separated the characteristics of the socially neglected pupils from those of the socially rejected pupils. Although both groups of pupils have low social acceptability, it is expected that they would have quite different personality patterns. Northway's (1944) clinical study of pupils with low social acceptability bears directly on this point. She found that some of the pupils who lacked social acceptance among peers were shy, withdrawing, socially uninterested persons, while others were noisy, boastful, socially ineffective individuals. Common sense would indicate that pupils in the first category would probably be socially neglected by their peers and those characterized as having undesirable, aggressive traits would in all probability be socially rejected. Testing this common-sense relationship between personality patterns and the two categories of pupils having low social acceptability is the main concern of this study. Specifically, the personality characteristics of the socially neglected and the socially rejected pupils will be compared and contrasted with those of the socially accepted pupils.

METHOD OF INVESTIGATION

The social acceptability of the pupils participating in this study was determined by means of a sociometric test. This test requested choices of pupils on three positive criteria and one negative criterion. Each pupil was asked to indicate the five classmates he *most* preferred as work companion, the five classmates he *most* preferred as play companion, and the five classmates he *most* preferred as seating companion. The negative criterion required the names of the five classmates the pupil *least* preferred as seating companion. This criterion was used as a measure of rejection. It was felt that one negative criterion was sufficient for the purpose and that a larger number might place unnecessary emphasis on the rejective aspects of the sociometric choosing.

This sociometric device was administered to all of the seventh- and eighth-grade pupils in a small city located in central Illinois. There were one hundred and fifty-eight pupils with approximately an even number of boys and girls. The six classroom groups ranged in size from twenty-five to twenty-eight pupils. The regular classroom teacher administered the sociometric test to each classroom group. All data were obtained during the second semester of the school year.

In addition to making choices on the sociometric test, each pupil responded to a social analysis form based on the "guess who" technique. This form presented brief positive and negative descriptions of eighteen personality traits and instructed the pupils to indicate which of their classmates best fitted each description. The following items illustrate the positive and negative descriptions for *friendliness*.[2]

1. Here is someone who is very friendly, who has lots of friends, who is nice to everybody.
2. Here is someone who does not care to make friends, who is bashful about being friendly, or who does not seem to have many friends.

Similar positive and negative items were included for each of the other personality traits. After each descriptive sketch, spaces for six names were provided. The pupils were encouraged to write as many names as they desired after each description and to use each classmate's name as often as needed. Thus they had complete freedom in assigning the behavior descriptions to their classmates.

---

[2] The complete form, entitled Social Analysis of the Classroom, is appended to the selection.

ANALYSIS OF DATA AND RESULTS

The sociometric results were analyzed by totaling the number of choices each pupil received on each of the sociometric criteria. In accord with the findings in a previous study (Gronlund, 1955), there was considerable overlap in the choosing on the three positive criteria. If a pupil was highly chosen as seating companion he also tended to be highly chosen as work companion and play companion. Consequently, choices on these three criteria were combined into a single measure of social acceptability. These scores ranged from 0 to 46 with a mean of 15. The social rejection scores, obtained on the single negative criterion, ranged from 0 to 21 with a mean of 5.

These sociometric results were used to select the socially accepted, the socially rejected, and the socially neglected groups. There were ten boys and ten girls in each category. The twenty pupils in the most *socially accepted* group received an average of 29 choices on the positive sociometric criteria. The twenty pupils in the most *socially rejected* group received an average of 12 rejection choices. The twenty most *socially neglected* pupils were those receiving the smallest number of choices on both the positive and the negative criteria. They had an average of 4 acceptance choices and 2 rejection choices. It should be noted that the larger number of acceptance choices received is due to the fact that these are based on three sociometric criteria while the rejection choices are based on one sociometric criterion.

The Social Analysis form was scored for each pupil by totaling the number of mentions he received on each item and then algebraically summing the positive and negative scores for each personality characteristic. Thus if a pupil received 10 mentions as being friendly (+) and 2 mentions as being unfriendly (−) his score for friendliness would be 8. Positive scores indicate socially desirable traits and negative scores indicate their opposites. The strength of the personality trait in the individual is assumed to be roughly equivalent to the number of mentions he receives on that trait.

Social acceptability and personality characteristics of girls. The personality characteristics most closely associated with the three social acceptability categories for girls are presented in Table I. These characteristics are self-explanatory, with the possible exception of those on humor. *Humor (self)* means she enjoys a joke on herself. *Humor (jokes)* means she enjoys hearing jokes. Only those traits receiving an average of 3 or more mentions are included in the analysis. The numbers of mentions received have been rounded off to the nearest whole number.

It will be noted that the socially accepted girls were characterized as being attractive, neat, and in general possessing aggressive and out-going behavior. These findings are similar to the results of other studies (Bonney, 1943; Kuhlen and Lee, 1943). Our main interest here, however, is

Table I. Average Number of Mentions Received on Social Analysis Form by Most Accepted, Most Neglected, and Most Rejected Girls (N = 30)

Characteristic	Accepted	Neglected	Rejected
Good-looking	14		−8
Tidy	13		−4
Friendly	10		
Likable	8		−4
Enthusiastic	8		
Cheerful	7		
Quiet (not restless)	7	3	−4
Interest in dating	6		
Humor (self)	4		
Initiative	4		
Humor (jokes)	3		
Talkative	3	−3 *	5

* Minus sign (−) means opposite of trait.

to contrast the socially neglected and the socially rejected groups with that of the socially accepted group.

The socially neglected girls received neither positive nor negative mention on most of the personality traits. They were characterized as being quiet and *not* talkative. In general then, they seemed to attract neither favorable nor unfavorable attention. They apparently were the neutral personalities who were overlooked, rather than disliked, by their classmates. This low social acceptability group appears to be similar to the quiet withdrawing pupils identified by Northway's (1944) clinical analysis.

The socially rejected girls also received little mention on the positive traits. However they were not overlooked on the negative items. Since they were rated as being *not* good looking, untidy, *not* likable, restless, and talkative, it would appear that they were aggressive enough to attract attention. However the attention they attracted to themselves was generally unfavorable. The resemblance between this group and Northway's (1944) "socially ineffective" category is quite obvious. Apparently these rejected girls were attempting to make social contact with their peers but lacked the necessary grooming and social skill.

The characteristic "talkative" deserves special attention. It will be noted that both the accepted and the rejected groups were characterized as being talkative, while the neglected group was rated as being *not* talkative. This seems to indicate that although talkative girls gain recognition they do not necessarily gain social acceptance. It is probably the nature of their conversation, as well as other personality characteristics, rather than the talking itself, that determines whether they will be accepted or rejected by their peers.

There were six personality traits omitted from the above analysis, since they did not receive sufficient mention in any of the three social acceptance categories. These traits are those of being bossy, fighting, seeking attention, being active in games, being a tomboy, and being daring. Apparently these characteristics are not related to social acceptability among these junior high school girls.

Table II. Average Number of Mentions Received on Social Analysis Form by Most Accepted, Most Neglected, and Most Rejected Boys (N = 30)

Characteristic	Accepted	Neglected	Rejected
Good looking	7	3	−6
Good-looking	7		−7 *
Tidy	7		−3
Friendly	5		
Likable	7		−3
Enthusiastic	4		
Cheerful	5		
Quiet (not restless)		3	−6
Interest in dating			
Humor (self)	4		
Initiative			
Humor (jokes)	5		
Talkative			6
Active in Games	12		

* Minus sign (−) means opposite of trait.

Social acceptability and personality characteristics of boys. In order to make the analysis for boys comparable to that for the girls, the same twelve personality characteristics have been listed in the same order in Table II. In addition, a thirteenth characteristic has been added to the list, since it has been shown to discriminate among the boys. As in the case of girls, only those traits receiving an average of 3 or more mentions are recorded in the table.

In general, the socially accepted boys were characterized as possessing personality traits similar to those of the socially accepted girls. However, there are some important differences. Four of the traits that were characteristic of the socially accepted girls, are not descriptive of the socially accepted boys. These are those of being quiet, having an interest in dating, showing initiative, and being talkative. In addition, one trait, not significant in the case of girls, was indicated as being the trait most closely related to boys' social acceptability, that is, being active in games. These differences between boys and girls seem to reflect developmental differences characteristic of this age level. The boys' previous interests in active pursuits (Tryon, 1939) are carried over into the junior high school, while the earlier-maturing girls' are concerned with quiet activities, dating, etc., which are characteristic of more advanced social adjustments.

The differences between the socially accepted boys and the socially accepted girls should not distract attention from the characteristics they had in common. The socially accepted pupils of both sexes were characterized as being good-looking, tidy, friendly, likable, enthusiastic, cheerful, and having a good sense of humor. These results are similar to those found for boys and girls at both the sixth and the twelfth grade levels by Kuhlen and Lee (1943).

The socially neglected boys were overlooked on practically all of the personality traits. They received an average of 3 mentions as being quiet. Their lack of mention on both the positive and the negative items verifies the similar findings for girls. Apparently socially neglected pupils of both sexes lacked social stimulus value. They were members of the classroom group but in a sense were "social islands" unto themselves. Members of this low social acceptance group were truly socially *neglected* by their peers.

The characteristics of the socially rejected boys are identical to those of the socially rejected girls. Both groups had the reputation of being *not* good-looking, untidy, *not* likable, restless, and talkative. It should be pointed out that in addition to possessing these negative traits, they lacked the positive characteristics associated with social acceptability. Thus, the socially rejected pupils attracted attention among their peers, but it was primarily negative attention. This is in contrast to the positive attention directed toward the socially accepted pupils and the lack of attention rendered the socially neglected pupils.

The personality traits which did not receive sufficient mention to discriminate among the three social acceptability types for boys are, interest in dating, initiative, being bossy, fighting, seeking attention, being a sissy, and being daring. Apparently the undesirable aggressive behavior, indicated by several of these characteristics, loses its prestige value (Bonney, 1944) by the time boys reach the junior high school age.

IMPLICATIONS FOR THE CLASSROOM TEACHER

The results of this study clearly indicate that strong, positive personality characteristics are associated with social acceptability among junior high school pupils. Probably more important, the results suggest that pupils with low social acceptability cannot be placed in a single category. The socially neglected pupils appear to be ignored or overlooked by their classmates while the socially rejected pupils are actively disliked. These findings should provide implications for improving the social acceptability of pupils.

The emphasis placed on appearance and friendly, aggressive behavior seems to indicate the importance of good grooming and social skills at the junior high school level. Assisting pupils in these areas may help improve their social acceptability. A special unit could be included in the home-room program. This unit need not be restricted to grooming and social skills but could include other aspects of social acceptability. One effective method of beginning such a unit is to present to the pupils a list of the personality characteristics related to social acceptability. This list could be obtained from published studies, or, more effective for discussion purposes, it might be based on a study of the teacher's own classroom. Just making the pupils aware of the factors related to social acceptability is sometimes helpful. In addition, a discussion of such factors serves to motivate pupils to want to learn how to improve their grooming and social skills. This approach is, of course, most effective with pupils who lack the knowledge of what is important in social relations and are awkward in their use of social skills. It is not expected that such an approach, by itself, is sufficient to improve the peer acceptance of the socially neglected and the socially rejected pupils.

Somehow, the neglected pupils must be brought to the attention of their peers. Interaction with classmates may be facilitated through small group work, through minor positions of responsibility in the classroom, through working on class projects, and through other avenues of social contact with fellow pupils. It is important that the introduction to group activities be gradual and that the pupil's social skills are sufficient to cope with the new social activity. It should be noted that increased aggressiveness, on the part of the socially neglected pupil, can lead to social rejection as well as to social acceptability. If their social status is to be improved, rather than made worse, careful guidance is needed in developing socially effective aggressiveness.

Improving the social acceptability of the rejected pupil is a special problem. Before he can be helped to gain social status, it is first necessary to remove or modify the characteristics causing rejection. This cause may be as simple as being untidy or it may involve a complicated pattern of traits that is difficult, if not impossible, to modify. Where possible, the teacher should attempt to identify the causes of rejection and remove them. In some cases individual counseling, or other outside help, may be necessary to modify the behavior of the rejected pupil.

In addition to changing the behavior of the rejected pupil, the teacher must make a special effort to change the child's reputation among his classmates. Changes in behavior are not automatically accompanied by changes in reputation. The child who was once thought of as *not* likable remains *not* likable until experience proves otherwise. Since rejected children are generally avoided, these *new* experiences do not readily occur unless the teacher takes an active rôle. Seating the rejected child near those who reject him least and having him work with small groups of pupils will help him get reëstablished. From this vantage point he can gradually be integrated into the larger group. Casual comments by the teacher, concerning his improved behavior, may also help. However, it should be recognized that the classroom teacher cannot give the rejected child social acceptance among his peers. She can only help him develop the characteristics, and arrange for the necessary social interaction that leads to social acceptability.

In addition to providing implications for improving the social acceptability of individual pupils, the results of this study indicate the shortcomings of the "guess who" technique for obtaining the personality characteristics of pupils. Since the neglected pupils seldom receive either positive or negative mention on the behavior characteristics, a description of their personality is either very sketchy or completely lacking. In the present study the neglected pupils were characterized as being quiet, but even on this characteristic they received relatively few mentions. Thus, although the "guess who" technique may be a useful method for obtaining behavior descriptions of aggressive pupils, it is of little value in determining the characteristics of pupils who lack sufficient aggressiveness to attract the attention of their classmates.

SOCIAL ANALYSIS OF THE CLASSROOM[3]

Directions

Below are some word pictures of members of your class. Read each statement and write down the names of the persons whom you think the descriptions fit.

REMEMBER: One description may fit several persons. You may write as many names as you think belong under each.

The same person may be mentioned for more than one description. Write "myself" if you think the description fits you.

If you cannot think of anyone to match a particular description, go on to the next one.

You will have as much time as you need to finish. Do not hurry.

NOW YOU ARE READY TO BEGIN

1. Here is someone who finds it hard to sit still in class; he (or she) moves around in his (or her) seat.
2. Here is someone who can work very quietly without moving around in his (or her) seat.
3. Here is someone who likes to talk a lot, always has something to say.
4. Here is someone who doesn't like to talk very much, is very quiet, even when nearly everyone else is talking.
5. Here is someone who plays active games like football and basketball a great deal, or who likes to run and jump and so on.
6. This person seldom plays active games like football and basketball, but prefers to read or sit and play quiet games.
7. Here is someone who is always ready to take a chance at things that are new or unusual, and is never worried or frightened.

[3] Reprinted from Ruth Cunningham, *Understanding Group Behavior of Boys and Girls.* Bureau of Publications, Teachers College, Columbia University, 1951. By permission.

8. Here is someone who is always worried or scared, who won't take a chance when something unexpected or unusual happens.

9. Here is someone who always knows how to start games or suggests something interesting to do so that others like to join in.

10. Here is someone who waits for somebody else to think of something to do and always likes to follow the suggestions which others make.

11. This person always seems to have a good time and seems to enjoy everything he (or she) does no matter where it is—in school, on the playground, at a party, everywhere.

12. This is someone who never seems to have a good time, who never seems to enjoy very much anything he (or she) does.

13. This is someone who is always cheerful, jolly, and good-natured, who laughs and smiles a good deal.

14. Here is someone who always seems rather sad, worried, or unhappy, who hardly ever laughs or smiles.

15. This is someone who is thought to be very good-looking.

16. Here is someone who is thought not to be good-looking at all.

17. Here is someone who always tries to keep himself (or herself) neat and clean and tidy looking.

18. This is someone who never tries to keep himself (or herself) neat and clean and tidy looking.

19. Here is someone whom everybody likes; people are always glad to have him (or her) around.

20. Here is someone whom nobody seems to care much about; people do not notice when he (or she) is around.

21. Here is a girl who likes to read boys' books, play boys' games, or would prefer to be a boy.

22. Here is a boy who prefers girls' books or girls' games, or would prefer to be a girl.

23. Here is a girl who often goes out with boys, or a boy who often goes out with girls. He (or she) likes to go to parties or dances.

24. Here is a girl who isn't much interested in going out with boys, or a boy who isn't much interested in going out with girls. They do not care to go to parties or dances.

25. Here is someone who can enjoy a joke and see the fun in it even when the joke is on himself (or herself).

26. Here is someone who can never appreciate a joke when it is on himself (or herself).

27. This person is very fond of a good joke, is the first to laugh and always sees the point.

28. Here is a person who doesn't care much for jokes or who has to have them explained before he (or she) sees the point.

29. Here is someone who enjoys a fight; he (or she) often fights rather than let the other person have his (or her) way.

30. Here is someone who never fights but lets the other person have his (or her) way.

31. This is someone who is always trying to get others to watch what

he (or she) can do or to listen to him (or her) tell about all the things he (or she) can do.

32. Here is someone who does not care whether or not he (or she) is the center of attention.

33. This is someone who is always telling others what to do, bossing them.

34. Here is someone who does not mind being told what to do, who does not mind being bossed.

35. Here is someone who is very friendly, who has lots of friends, who is nice to everybody.

36. Here is someone who does not care to make friends or who is bashful about being friendly, or who does not seem to have many friends.

15 / The Psychodynamics of Social Mobility in Adolescent Boys

Elizabeth Douvan and Joseph Adelson

What does research say about the motivational sources of upward mobility and downward mobility? This study of a national sample of adolescent boys analyzes some of the psychic accompaniments of mobility and presents a theory of the personality determinants of social mobility. The authors are Elizabeth Douvan and Joseph Adelson of the University of Michigan.

There is a large and growing body of literature on social mobility, and the significance of the topic is generally acknowledged; so it is surprising to find that only limited attention has been given to studying the motivational sources of mobility. What we do find is a general disposition to treat *upward* mobility in a vaguely invidious fashion. It would seem that, in this country, the Horatio Alger tradition and the "dream of success" motif (Lynn, 1955) have been pervasive and distasteful enough to have alienated, among others, a good many social scientists. The upwardly aspiring individual has apparently become associated with the pathetic seeker after success or with the ruthless tycoon. This image of success is, much of it, implicit—assumption and attitude, and not quite conviction —but it seems to have dominated the thinking of our intellectual community.

Or so it has been until recently. Newer empirical findings have encouraged a more differentiated view of mobility. We begin to get some

Reprinted from the *Journal of Abnormal and Social Psychology*, 1958, *56*, 31–44, with the permission of the authors and the American Psychological Association.

sense that varying motivations may underlie social striving; we become aware that the direction, the rapidity, and the absolute extent of mobility may reflect differing psychodynamic sources and thus require separate analytic treatment.

In this paper, a first effort is made to explore and clarify one problem in this complex area—to analyze some of the psychic accompaniments of upward and downward mobility strivings among adolescent boys. In the following section, a theory of the personality determinants of mobility is presented; the paper as a whole is devoted to testing some of these formulations.

THEORETICAL CONSIDERATIONS

Upward Mobility

We can distinguish at least three separate patterns of motivation which are implicit in discussions of upward social mobility: fear of failure, ambivalence toward success, and hope of success.

The first pattern—perhaps the most common image of the mobile individual—is of the desperately scrambling Philistine, exhausted in his pursuit of status. He has defined his identity and personal worth exclusively by the criteria of success. Perhaps a typical genetic source of this pattern has been described by Ackerman and Jahoda (1950, pp. 88–89). Competitiveness is taught by the family: "Most of the mothers of our cases . . . apparently did not tell their children 'be happy' but rather 'make money'. . . ." "Success is measured by comparison with others rather than by actual achievement. . . . There are always some who have done better, who have more money and more social prestige; and there is always the danger of being pushed down the social ladder by a competitor."

In the second pattern—ambivalence toward success—the dynamics are more complex. The individual aspiring upward is here seen as responding to the dominance and prestige of the more privileged stratum through a defensive identification with this group and by denying and decrying his own background and status. The genetic sources of this choice of mechanism may be sought in the aspirer's early encounters with authority and status in the original family setting. We discover in the family scene a harsh and forbidding parent, one who allows the child no hostility; we find a child who has accommodated to parental strength through identification. In this formulation, we see the mobile individual showing many of the characteristics of the "authoritarian personality": a conscious over-idealization of the parent and of authority together with unconscious rebellion and hostility, rigidity, conformity, and anti-intraception. As regards mobility, we find the following dynamics: the motive for upward aspiration arises out of the need to emulate the parents; at the same time mobility arouses conflict since it implies a struggle with this powerful authority figure (Adorno, et al., 1949).

Without question, both of these mobility types occur (perhaps frequently) in our society. Yet the recent literature on mobility has suggested that the most common pattern is the one we have called "hope of success" (McClelland, 1953). Here we find interest in success directed by a rational ego: the individual who can mobilize his energies effectively, whose aspirations are realistic. The mobility goals are moderate or, in those cases where aspiration is toward a substantial status move, they are nevertheless realistic in view of the individual's talents.

We find a family milieu which encourages autonomy, is not obsessed by status, yet accepts and transmits without ambivalence the culturally central value of achievement. Moreover, the shifts in identity required do not implicate the child in conflict: the family has provided or permitted the child a model for identity consistent with the goal of mobility.

In a society which holds upward mobility to be a central value, which provides opportunity for it, and in which it is, apparently, a very common occurrence, we can expect that the dominant motivational pattern informing upward aspiration is not a defensive one—does not necessitate a personally damaging flight from one's past; rather, we would expect it to accompany effective ego functioning and successful socialization by a family which is transmitting a cultural value of which it approves.[1]

Downward Mobility

What about the adolescent boy whose aspirations are downward in direction? Here we have someone whose goals are atypical; indeed, they contradict directly a strongly held cultural value. To be sure, the same novelistic tradition which associates upward mobility with Babbittry has sometimes offered us a sentimental image of the downward mobile type, presenting him as an unfettered, romantically sullen child of nature. Our own view is considerably darker.

We see downward aspiration as representing, in many areas, the psychodynamic opposite of upward mobility. If we are correct, these

[1] One may speculate about those social situations in our culture where upward aspiration necessitates a good deal of emotional stress or induces personal conflict. Generally, we would say, these are situations where a change in status requires a decisive modification of behavior or necessitates a sharp shift in identity models. A number of such situations come to mind: (a) where the status change involves a concomitant ethnic (including religious) shift; (b) where it involves a gross movement up the status ladder; (c) where there has been a limited opportunity to learn the status behavior of the higher status group; (d) at certain points in the status continuum, where the defining criteria of the higher status group are realistically difficult to achieve; e.g., in the movement from lower-upper to upper-upper status, in those cases where a defining criterion is ancestry; (e) where the group-of-origin is ambivalent or hostile to the mobility of its members, necessitating a decisive abandonment of the past as a condition of mobility. Under these conditions, mobility upward will require an unusually high degree of personal motivation.

adolescents are demoralized, alienated, anomic. An ambivalent relationship to the parents produces an impoverished ego, vulnerability to conflict, a failure to internalize general cultural values. Ambivalence is, of course, an almost universal outcome of the socialization process; but we conjecture that it is especially acute among the downward mobile. We expect to find a relationship to the parents which is infantile, that is, dependent and hostile. Dependency and aggression accompany, reinforce, and conceal each other. The child who is captured in an infantile tie to his parents has too much of his energy committed in ambivalence; ego functions remain immature and conflict-ridden; the ego is unable to cope adequately with impulses, internalized morality, and the more complex aspects of reality. At its best, the ego enforces a harmony among the psychic institutions and the outside world. But the downward mobile boy, if our formulation is correct, is at the mercy of his impulses, which continually threaten to overwhelm brittle controls. The superego drives are equally primitive and frightening; parental prohibitions are not sufficiently internalized, in part because of their very intensity; superego functioning is consequently immature, in that there is an inadequate fusion of ego and superego processes; the superego stands at some distance from the ego, so that questions of morality are not so much matters of right and wrong as of escape and pursuit. As regards the ego's operations vis-a-vis the outer world, we do not hypothesize that the downward mobile show any gross pathology of reality testing. And yet we feel that the more complex and articulated ego processes—judgment, rapport, control, time-binding—are poorly or unevenly developed.

Hypotheses

In the research reported here, a study of the mobility aspirations of adolescent boys, we test a number of hypotheses based on these conceptions of the sources of mobility strivings. Specifically, the following predictions were made about upward- and downward-aspiring boys.[2]

1. *Energy level.* The upward-mobile boys possess a high degree of available energy for use in social and work activities. Downward-mobile boys, on the other hand, show a diminished vitality.

2. *Achievement mode.* The boys aspiring to higher status show a pervasive achievement orientation and a secure sense of their own effectiveness in reaching goals. The downward mobile are less oriented toward achievement and dominated by a concern with security.

3. *Orientation toward the future.* The time perspective of the upward mobile tends to be extended, while the downward mobile tend to have a constricted orientation in time.

4. *Personal standards.* The upward mobile boys manifest well inter-

---

[2] In this paper we will use the terms "upward aspiring" and "upward mobile" interchangeably. It should be clear that we do not assume that upward aspiration will necessarily lead to successful social mobility.

nalized moral values and standards of personal behavior. Internalization is relatively incomplete among the downward mobile.

5. *Autonomy.* The upward aspiring display a precocious independence from the family, and a strong sense of autonomy in choosing values and goals. Downward mobile boys, on the other hand, are tied in a dependent relationship to the family.

6. *Orientation toward the self.* Upward-mobile boys are realistic in assessing themselves, and show a high degree of self-confidence. The downward aspiring reveal ambivalence toward the self and a lack of poise in social situations.

7. *Family milieu.* In this area, our predictions were firmer and more specific about the downward mobile group. Previous research (Gough, personal communication, 1955) led us to expect a pattern of ambivalent dependency in the downward mobile boys' relations with their families. Rebellion and rejection of parental values combined with a strong dependency stem from inconsistent and punitive treatment at the parent's hand: in short, we anticipated an authoritarian family setting.

In addition to these specific predictions, we were interested in inquiring whether the relationship to the family, in upward mobile boys, is characterized by an ambivalent rejection of family values or by a conflict-free differentiation of the self from the family.

METHOD

Subjects

The data for our analysis derive from a national sample survey of adolescent boys conducted by the Survey Research Center.[3] The sample for the total study consisted of a thousand boys in the 14- to 16-year age range selected by probability sampling methods. Each boy was given a personal interview at school by a member of the research center's field staff. Open-ended questions and projective questions were used, and interviews lasted from one to three hours.

In the present analysis, we have used as the base sample the interviews taken with urban nonfarm youth whose fathers' occupations fell in any of the following categories: small business owners, self-employed artisans, white collar, sales, and clerical workers; skilled and semi-skilled manual workers. The reason for excluding the sons of men occupying positions at the two extremes of the skill hierarchy becomes apparent when the mobility measure is discussed.

[3] The survey was sponsored by the Boy Scouts of America. The complete questionnaire used in the study has been deposited with the American Documentation Institute. Order Document No. 5422 from ADI Auxiliary Publications Project, Photoduplication Service, Library of Congress, Washington 25, D.C., remitting in advance $1.75 for 35 mm. microfilm or $2.50 for 6 by 8 in. photocopies. Make checks payable to Chief, Photoduplication Service, Library of Congress.

Mobility Aspiration

Each of our youthful respondents was asked the following questions:

a. What kind of work would you like to do as an adult?
b. Are you pretty sure about this or do you think you're just as likely to go into something else?

Each boy's aspiration was classed on the occupational scale and compared to his father's position to determine whether it was equivalent to or higher or lower than the father's job in the hierarchy of skills and status.

The distribution of aspiration types by father's occupation is presented in Table 1 for all urban youth in the original sample. An obvious

Table 1. Distribution of Aspiration Types by Father's Occupation

Aspiration	Father's Occupation			
	1 Professional, Managerial (N = 136) %	2 White Collar a (N = 183) %	3 Manual Skilled b (N = 335) %	4 Manual Unskilled (N = 70) %
Upward		46	58	84
Stable	67	29	34	16
Downward	33	25	08	

NOTE. Ten per cent of the total urban sample of boys was lost in the process of rating the boy's aspiration in relation to father's occupation. These were Ss who had not decided what they wanted to be, who gave vague answers, or who wished to be farmers.

a This category includes small business owners in addition to sales and clerical workers.
b This category includes both skilled and semi-skilled workers.

fact is illustrated in this table. Boys whose fathers currently occupy jobs in the top category are by definition limited to equivalent or lower status aspirations, just as those whose fathers are unskilled workers are barred from downward aspiration.

Because of this limitation on the relative freedom of direction in the aspirations of boys from families in Groups 1 and 4, and because we were interested ultimately in both upward and downward mobility, the sample was restricted to those boys from the two middle categories. The aspiration behavior of boys from the extreme groups may reflect in part a statistical artifact. That is, assuming that by chance a certain proportion of boys will aspire to a status-skill level different from the parent's, the direction of deviation is automatically determined for boys in Groups 1 and 4. In the middle groups, on the other hand, deviation is possible in either direction, and the selection of one or the other type should reflect certain specific motivational factors. One might maintain that the fact of aspiring to a level other than the father's in itself reflects unique psychological characteristics, but since the direction of deviation is a focus of our present concern, opportunity for choice in both directions was controlled.[4]

RESULTS

In the following pages we show contrasts among upward, downward, and stable groups. In most cases, we find linear relationships between status aspiration and other variables: the upward mobile are particularly high or low on a variable, the downward mobile are at the opposite extreme, and the stable group falls somewhere in between. Occasionally we find that either the upward or downward aspiring group clearly distinguishes itself from the other two groups. And in a few relationships, the stables stand out, the linear relationship gives way to a curvilinear one.

Since our predictions all concern the mobility categories and there was uncertainty about the exact position of the stable group, chi square was used to test the significance of variation among the three groups.

Energy Level

We see here a sharp contrast between upward and downward subjects (Ss): while the upward mobile boy is unusually lively and energetic, the downward aspirer is inactive and apathetic. On all of our measures, the upward group reveals a high commitment of energy to social and recreational pursuits, and yet not at the expense of work involvement; they also seem to show a spirited and enthusiastic love of activity. The downward mobile boy, in contrast, shows an impoverished vitality: he does not participate energetically or enthusiastically in recreational activities.

Looking first at boys' memberships in organizations (Table 2, Item 1), we find that three quarters of the upward mobile Ss belong to some organized group; while slightly less than half of the downward aspiring boys report membership. The upward mobile also have a relatively high proportion of multiple memberships, compared to the other two groups. A similar relationship appears in the area of general leisure activities: almost half the upward mobile report having tried twenty or more separate activities while only about one quarter of the downward mobile

[4] The group used for analysis consisted of 335 boys from working-class background and 183 from white-collar families. Since the upward mobile group contained a disproportionate number of boys from blue-collar backgrounds, we ran all mobility analyses separately for the two broad occupational groups (Categories 2 and 3 in Table 1). Relationships were of approximately the same order within each of these groups. Analysis is presented for the combined group in order to avoid complicating tables unnecessarily, but in all cases relationships reported also held within each of the two background groups.

fall in this category; the stable group is approximately midway between the other two (Table 2, Item 2). There is a small difference in dating, the upwards being slightly more likely, and the downwards least likely to date (Table 2, Item 3).

Table 2. Relationships between Mobility Aspiration and Indices of Level of Energy

Item	Upward (N = 277) %	Stable (N = 168) %	Down-ward (N = 73) %	χ^2 *	p Level
	Mobility				
1. Number of group memberships [a]					
a. none	25	33	52	26.91	.01
b. one	32	38	22		
c. two	23	20	17		
d. three or more	20	09	09		
2. Number of leisure activities					
a. fewer than 20	52	65	67	11.65	.01
b. 20 or more	48	35	33		
3. Dating					
a. do date	66	59	52	5.67	.10–.05
b. do not date	34	41	48		
4. Employment					
a. have jobs	49	47	51	.44	.90
b. do not have jobs	51	53	49		
5. Leisure reading					
a. do not read	17	27	25	7.93	.05
b. fiction-novels, mysteries	32	23	11	12.31	.01
c. travel and adventure	31	20	18	10.52	0.1
d. technical, scientific	09	04	01	11.13	.01
e. sports and hobby books	10	09	04	2.44	.30–.20
f. history, biography	08	07	05	.27	.90–.80
g. animal stories	05	04	05	.73	.70–.50
h. comics, joke books	21	26	27	1.95	.50–.30
i. newspapers, magazines	19	16	19	.96	.70–.50
6. Proportion of activities enjoyed					
a. fewer than half	45	41	59	6.09	.05
b. one half or more	55	59	41		
7. Additional activities desired					
a. suggest activity	63	31	10	87.67	.01
b. do not suggest activity	37	69	90		

* Unless noted, the chi square was derived from a 3 × 2 table with two degrees of freedom.

[a] In this case, the chi square was derived from a 3 × 4 table with six degrees of freedom.

Although they more commonly engage in leisure pursuits, the aspiring boys are not significantly different from others in having job commitments. One might expect that the reason the downward-aspiring boys play less is that they work more. But this does not seem to be the case (Table 2, Item 4), the three groups being approximately equal in the percentage who hold jobs. The more active social life of the upward mobile boy represents an increment in total activity rather than a substitute for work activity. The upward mobile boy is more likely to report leisure reading. He has a more diversified reading pattern, and his reading includes more demanding material. The downward aspiring boy much less often reads novels and mysteries, travel and adventure stories, and technical, scientific literature. Stable boys fall between the other two groups on all specific categories of reading, but are like the downward mobile in the proportion of nonreaders. The single case in which the trend favors the downward mobile boy is in the category "comics, joke books" (Table 2, Item 5).

Upward mobile boys are not only more active currently but also seem to be more enthusiastic about their activities and more receptive to new experiences. After our Ss had checked the leisure pursuits they had experienced within the last year, they were asked to check the ones they had especially enjoyed. In general, the two indices bear a low negative relation to each other—that is, boys who do more things are more selective in naming those they "particularly enjoy." Despite this tendency for a negative association, we find that the upward aspiring boys (who take part in more leisure activities) are nevertheless enthusiastic about the things they do. They are like the stables in the proportion of their leisure pursuits that they designate as particularly enjoyable; while the downward mobile, who have tried relatively few leisure activities, are much less enthusiastic about these few (Table 2, Item 6). When asked if there are other activities they would like to try, aside from those appearing on the list, almost two-thirds of the upward group name something else they would enjoy. This responsiveness contrasts sharply to the other groups: a third of the stable group, and only one tenth of the downward group suggest any additional unlisted activities that appeal to them (Table 2, Item 7).

Achievement Mode

We expected that the degree of striving reflected in a boy's job aspiration would be part of a general achievement orientation, that upward occupational aspiration would be associated with the pattern of behavior which McClelland, et al. (1953) have termed the "achievement syndrome," and that the upward mobile boy would show concern with achievement as against security and would be interested in meeting self-imposed standards of excellence. The downward aspiring boy, on the other hand, should show the same lack of vigor, the same constriction in setting other goals that we have seen in his choice of a future occupation.

The most direct evidence on these points is found in response to other questions in the occupation area. The Ss were asked to choose among criteria for judging the attractiveness of a job, to choose the two most and the two least important dimensions. Compared to the stable and

Table 3. Relationships between Mobility Aspiration and Indices of Achievement Mode

Item	Mobility			χ^2 *	p Level
	Upward $(N = 277)$ %	Stable $(N = 168)$ %	Downward $(N = 73)$ %		
1. Job criteria selected [a]					
a. interesting work	56	51	33	15.74	.01
b. status achievement	44	28	36	22.15	.01
c. security	50	59	65	5.84	.10
2. Reasons for job choice [a]					
a. status	20	09	03	11.65	.01
b. ease of job or ease of obtaining job	04	12	32	15.27	.01
c. interest of work	70	78	58	5.99	.05
3. Preference: success or security					
a. success	52	35	33	12.00	.01
b. security	48	65	67		
4. Savings					
a. do save	30	21	18	6.16	.05
b. do not save	70	79	82		
5. Education plans					
a. beyond high school	69	42	12	140.06	.01
b. not beyond high school	31	58	88		

* Unless noted, the chi square was derived from a 3×2 table with two degrees of freedom.

[a] Categories here are not exhaustive. Tests are run on the presence or absence of particular answers.

downward groups, upward mobile boys stress interesting work and have a less dominating concern about security. They are highest of all three groups in desire for status achievement. The downward mobile also strongly wish for status, but their status drive is not bound to a demand for interest in the content of the job; rather, they would most like to have status combined with security. The answers of our stable group are interesting on this item; relatively unattracted by status and fame, they stress security and interesting work (Table 3, Item 1).

When we ask boys to rationalize their own job choices, the upward aspiring S emphasizes interest in the work itself, while the downward mobile more often adduces the ease of the work, or the ease of obtaining employment in the field (Table 3, Item 2).

It would seem, then, that the upward mobile Ss are more willing to yield security for the sake of achievement. In answer to a forced-choice question: "Which would you rather have—a job where you're sure you won't be laid off or one you can't be so sure of but where you have a chance to be a big success?" the striving boys choose the challenging, less secure job significantly more often than boys in either of the other groups (Table 3, Item 3).

Achievement orientation is often inferred from the willingness to forego immediate gratification for long-term goals. One indication of this appears in answer to the question, "What do you spend your own money for?" The boys who aspire high are more likely to say they save their resources for education or other long term goals (Table 3, Item 4). As we would expect, boys aspiring to higher occupations also reveal more extensive educational plans than do other boys (Table 3, Item 5).

Orientation toward the Future

The upward mobile boys have an extended time perspective and a marked interest in attaining adult status; while the downward group shows constriction in time, as in other aspects of the life space. We asked our Ss what decisions they would have to make in the next few years; the answers were rated for the breadth of time perspective. The upward aspiring boys are more likely to mention decisions in the more distant future, such as adult roles and goals. The downward mobile more often name immediate decisions, those within the high school period (Table 4, Item 1).

In answer to the question "What things that you do—at home, in school, or with your friends—make you feel important and useful?" the upward striving boy more often states instances in which he has assumed adult roles. He is less likely than the downward mobile S to mention peer acceptance as a source of self-esteem. An interesting finding here is that the stable group is highest of all three in choosing "belonging, being part of a group," one of the few occasions where this group does not fall somewhere between the other two. We suggest, though very tentatively, that this may reflect a concern with maintaining stable interpersonal ties.

We may also point to the apparently greater social maturity of the upward mobiles. As we have seen, they are somewhat more likely to date. They are also more eager for heterosexual social activities; when asked to choose between an all-boy or a coed social club, the upward aspiring less often prefer the former (Table 4, Item 3).

Table 4. Relationships between Mobility Aspiration and Indices of Orientation toward the Future

Item	Upward (N = 277) %	Stable (N = 68) %	Down-ward (N = 73) %	χ^2 *	p Level
		Mobility			
1. Time perspective on decisions [b]					
a. within high school	17	18	29	5.21	.10
b. beyond high school	78	73	77	1.75	.50
c. distant future	53	51	26	16.51	.01
2. Sources of self-esteem [b]					
a. assuming adult role	31	23	16	6.91	.05
b. belonging, being part of a group	46	56	32	11.34	.01
c. being accepted by peers	03	07	14	10.90	.01
d. nothing	04	08	11	6.39	.05
3. Preference for coed or all-boy club [a]					
a. all boy	39	48	59	10.60	.05
b. neutral	23	16	14		
c. coed	38	36	27		

* Unless noted, the chi square was derived from a 3 × 2 table with two degrees of freedom.

[a] In this case, the chi square was derived from a 3 × 3 table with four degrees of freedom.

[b] Categories here are not exhaustive of responses given to open questions, and more than one response was often given. Tests are run on the presence or absence of particular answers.

The Internalization of Personal Standards

Another point of difference between the groups concerns the interiorization of standards. Upward mobile boys consistently show a more complete internalization of personal controls. Downward mobile boys show a tendency to externalize standards and to rebel against them.

A set of projective pictures showed an adolescent boy in conflict between a promise made to his parents (to be home at a certain time) and peer pressure (to stay out later). Our Ss were asked what the boy would do and how he would feel about it.

In all of our groups, approximately two thirds of the respondents say that the boy will go home. However, the motives attributed to the boy differ sharply. The upward mobile boys more often have the boy go home because "he promised" or because "his parents trust him," whereas the downwards say he will go because of a fear that the parents will find out and punish the transgression (Table 5, Item 1).

Regardless of their responses to these questions, all Ss were asked: "If the boy decided to stay with his friends awhile, do you think he'd tell his parents about it later?" The upward aspiring group answer "yes" more frequently than other boys (Table 5, Item 2).

Another series of questions concerned boys' conceptions of and general reactions to rules. Here, again, the upward mobile group reveals a greater degree of internalization. When asked why a boy might break a rule, they focus on uncontrollable emergency situations and those in which a boy is old enough (i.e., responsible enough) to guide his own behavior. On the other hand, the downwards more frequently give responses fitting the categories of "rebellion against the parent," "irresistible impulse," and "when parental authority is not present" (Table 5, Item 3). When asked what kind of a rule they would never break, upward mobile Ss more often mention those which involve responsibility to others; they less frequently say that there is no rule, or no rule that comes to mind, which they wouldn't break (Table 5, Item 4).

Table 5. Relationships between Mobility Aspiration and Indices of Internalization of Personal Standards

	Mobility				
Item	Upward (N = 277) %	Stable (N = 168) %	Down-ward (N = 73) %	x^2 *	p Level
1. Reaction to parent-peer conflict [a]					
a. adheres to promise because of sense of trust	37	19	16	24.03	.01
b. adheres to promise because of fear of punishment	04	06	14	6.38	.05
2. Honesty with parents					
a. would tell parents	55	42	44	9.15	.05
3. Conditions for breaking a rule [a]					
a. emergency	18	10	10	6.56	.05
b. boy mature enough	11	07	01	6.49	.05
c. rebellion	10	14	22	10.11	.01
d. impulse	05	11	16	11.41	.01
e. parental authority absent	05	10	27	31.50	.01
4. Unbreakable rule					
a. no unbreakable rule	03	17	21	10.85	.01

* Unless noted, the chi square was derived from a 3 × 2 table with two degrees of freedom.

[a] Categories here are not exhaustive of responses given to open questions, and more than one response was often given. Tests are run on the presence or absence of particular answers.

Autonomy

We saw earlier that the striving boys are interested in assuming adult-like roles, those, that is, in which they themselves are responsible for their behavior and for a job. We see here a seemingly greater drive towards independence and responsibility. In contrast, the downward mobile, though they show signs of rebellion against the parents, are also more dependent on them.

In one series of items, our Ss were asked whose advice they would prefer to take on particular problems—their parents' or friends'. The issues ran from such central ones as what time to be in at night to matters of taste, such as personal grooming. While there were no very striking differences in the proportions who would heed their parents on any of these topics, one interesting difference appears in the proportion of boys who inject a note of independence while discussing these issues. Thirty per cent of the striving group spontaneously assert that they would follow their own ideas on at least one of the six issues, and only three per cent of the downwards give such a response (Table 6, Item 2).

We find another indication of independence from the family in response to the question, "Can a friend ever be as close as a family member?" The upward mobile Ss most often agree to this idea (Table 6, Item 3).

When our Ss are asked what the role of a club leader ought to be, we again find that the aspiring boys desire independent direction of their behavior. They limit the leader's function to that of a helper (Table 6, Item 4). A coder rating based on this question and on one which asked the S to describe an adult leader he had liked, revealed that the downward mobile S is more authority reliant than other boys (Table 6, Item 5).

Finally, a crucial index of independence from the family is yielded when Ss are asked to choose an adult ideal. As we would expect, the stable group, which includes all boys who choose the same occupation as the father's, also has the largest proportion of boys who choose the father as an ideal. The upwards more often choose a model outside the family, or describe a composite of characteristics from several people. More often than other boys, downward mobiles say there is no adult they wish to be like. And despite the fact that they choose the father less often than stable boys, they give the largest proportion of within-family models of any group, particularly choosing grandfathers and uncles. Here again we can observe the ambivalence of the downward mobile boys; though they are covertly rebellious toward family authority, they cling to within-family models. Another way of viewing this finding is to see in it a reflection of the downward mobile boys' narrowed and immature life space. Havighurst, Robinson, and Dorr (1946) have found that the tendency to choose within-family models characterizes the earlier years of adolescence. Our downward mobile boys retain the more infantile, more restricted image of the adult world.

The upward mobile boys, on the other hand, tend to a certain precocity in the loosening of family ties. Yet we have seen in the previous section on internalization that this is not associated with rebellion from or rejection of the family. Further evidence along these lines appears in the discussion of family milieu.

Table 6. Relationships between Mobility Aspiration and Indices of Autonomy

Item	Mobility			χ^2 *	p Level
	Upward (N = 277) %	Stable (N = 168) %	Down-ward (N = 73) %		
1. Independence in allocating funds					
a. no independence	01	01	19	59.27	.01
2. Advice on decisions					
a. interjects own opinions	30	21	03	24.69	.01
3. Intimacy of friendship					
a. can be as close as family relationship	59	54	34	9.92	.01
4. Role of adult leader [a]					
a. helper	58	51	38	9.71	.01
b. decision maker	40	43	51	3.67	.20
5. Authority reliance					
a. high	38	47	54	6.06	.05
b. moderate	62	53	47		
6. Adult ideal [a]					
a. family member	41	50	55	5.99	.05
b. unrelated adult acquaintance and composite	31	24	18	6.74	.05

* Unless noted, the chi square was derived from a 3×2 table with two degrees of freedom.

[a] Categories here are not exhaustive of responses given to open questions, and more than one response was often given. Tests are run on the presence or absence of particular answers.

Until now evidence has been presented bearing on the *sense* of autonomy. Some other data suggest that these differences are related to the objective degree of autonomy permitted upward and downward boys by their parents. We asked: "What are your parents' ideas about the way you spend your money?" One fifth of the downward mobile respondents replied that they do not have funds of their own but ask their parents for money as they need or want some special thing. In the upward mobile group, fewer than one per cent gave this answer (Table 6, Item 1). Since there is no difference between the groups with respect to actual spending of money, we may infer that the difference resides in the *control* of spending.

Orientation toward the Self

Upward mobile boys show a high degree of self-acceptance, and a confidence in social situations. The downward mobile is more ambivalent toward himself and more unsure and conflicted in social interaction.

Interviewers rated boys on a number of variables, among which were self-confidence, humour, and the clarity with which they organized and presented their opinions and attitudes. We may interpret these ratings, with caution, as reflecting the boy's social skill and ability to handle himself in social interaction with an adult. On each of the ratings, the upward mobile are high; they are more self-assured, show humour more often, and are better organized in the interview. The downward mobile are relatively unconfident, humorless, and disorganized (Table 7, Items 1, 2, and 3).

We find signs of self-rejection and demoralization in the downward mobile boys' answers to the question, "What would you like to change

Table 7. Relationships between Mobility Aspiration and Indices of Orientation toward the Self *

| | Mobility | | | | |
Item	Upward (N = 277) %	Stable (N = 168) %	Down-ward (N = 73) %	χ^2 *	p Level
1. Self-confidence [a]				7.93	.10
a. high	30	23	18		
b. average	52	57	57		
c. low	18	20	25		
2. Humour				7.14	.05
a. present	74	67	58		
b. absent	26	33	42		
3. Organization of ideas [a]				7.31	.10
a. high	60	53	50		
b. average	22	27	20		
c. low	18	20	30		
4. Desired changes [b]					
a. self rejecting, major	04	10	15	6.36	.05
b. changes that are impossible	06	07	23	11.33	.01
c. changes within boy's own power	37	29	05	14.10	.01

* Unless noted, the chi square was derived from a 3 × 2 table with two degrees of freedom.

[a] In this case, the chi square was derived from a 3 × 3 table with four degrees of freedom.

[b] Categories here are not exhaustive of responses given to an open question, and more than one response was often given. Tests are run on the presence or absence of particular answers.

about yourself if you could—about your looks or your life or your personality?" They more often desire changes so gross or so central as to indicate alienation from the self; and they more often wish for changes that are unlikely to occur. The upward mobile boy more often refers to changes he has the power to effect himself. He is more realistically critical of himself, and less self-rejecting (Table 7, Item 4).

Family Milieu

The reader may recall that we felt far more confident of our predictions about the downward than the upward mobile in this area. We believed that the downward group would show a pattern of ambivalence towards the parent, a mingling of dependency and hostility; and we further held that this pattern would arise out of inconsistent, overly harsh methods of discipline. We did not, however, feel we could make any

Table 8. Relationships between Mobility Aspiration and Indices of Family Milieu

Item	Mobility			χ^2 *	p Level
	Upward $(N = 277)$ %	Stable $(N = 168)$ %	Down-ward $(N = 73)$ %		
1. Punishment ª					
a. physical	02	08	15	19.12	.01
b. deprivational	66	69	65		
c. psychological	32	23	20		
2. Portrayal of parental figures					
a. harsh	27	35	48	11.59	.01
b. non-harsh	73	65	52		
3. Disagreements with parents					
a. have disagreements	66	56	49	6.39	.05
b. do not have disagreements	34	44	51		
4. Parents' attitudes toward way boy spends money					
a. disapproval	19	16	05	8.58	.05
b. no disapproval	81	84	95		
5. Leisure activities with parents ª					
a. share many	19	11	09	17.23	.01
b. share some	73	74	68		
c. share none	08	15	23		

* Unless noted, the chi square was derived from a 3 × 2 table with two degrees of freedom.

ª In these cases the chi square was derived from a 3 × 3 table with four degrees of freedom.

specific statement about the upward mobile: here we were interested in discovering what we could about the family milieu, in particular whether upward aspiration is associated with a rejection of family values, or a defensive identification with a forbidding parental authority, or by that relatively amiable relationship to the parent which permits the growth of autonomy.

To begin with, we find that deprivation seems to be the dominant method of discipline for all groups; differences here are not significant. Striking differences appear, however, in the relative frequency of "psychological" and "corporal" methods of punishment. Only one in fifty of the upwards says that their parents use physical punishment; approximately one in ten of the stables and one in seven of the downwards report this method. In contrast, the use of "psychological" techniques (such as "given a good talking to") occurs in more than one quarter of the upward mobile responses, about one in five of the stables, and only one in eighteen of the downwards (Table 8, Item 1). We find that the parents of the upward aspirers avoid the harshest method of punishment; the "psychological" methods, which we suspect encourage the child's internal controls, are infrequently used by the parents of downward mobile boys.

Are our mobile Ss presenting an over-idealized picture of their families? We looked for the pattern of repressed hostility and surface idealization which has been shown to characterize defensive identifiers (Adorno, et al., 1949; Hoffman, 1953; Sarnoff, 1952). But our data reveal that the opposite is true: in the projective materials—where the Ss are not discussing their own parents and where they have an opportunity to discharge repressed hostility without danger—the upward aspiring portray parents as less harsh than do the other groups (Table 8, Item 2). And as we shall see, they are more aware of differences between themselves and their parents. They more commonly report that their parents have some "old-fashioned ideas, or ideas they disagree with" (Table 8, Item 5), and that their parents in some respect disapprove of the way in which they spend their own money (Table 8, Item 6). We saw previously (Table 6, Item 3) that they are not likely to feel that family relationships are necessarily more intimate than friendships; and they less often choose an ideal adult from within the family group (Table 6, Item 6). The upward mobile boys are, then, more sensible of differences with parents.

Do the aspiring boys have a detached rather than congenial relationship to their parents? The single bit of evidence on this question suggests that this is not the case: they more often report engaging in leisure activities with their parents (Table 8, Item 5).

The downward mobile boy's family relationship is, as we expected, marked by ambivalence: the pattern is one of conscious idealization accompanied by unconscious suspicion and hostility.

We have already seen that the parents of this group are more often severe in their punishment. And in this group we find evidence of repressed hostility: in the projective stories, the downward mobile boys picture parental figures as both harsh and suspicious (Items 3 and 4, Table 8). Yet consciously they are more likely to deny differences with their parents. Some of our findings on autonomy have shown this; and in addition we find that these boys most often say they have no disagreements with their parents (Table 8, Item 5), and they least often say their parents disapprove of their handling of funds (Table 8, Item 6). The downward mobile boy shares leisure activities with his parents somewhat less than do boys in the other two groups (Table 8, Item 7).

Alternative Hypotheses

Before we discuss the possible meanings of these findings, we must consider briefly alternative hypotheses which might account for them. These are: (a) An age differential among the three groups; thus, the upward aspiring Ss might have given "little boy" job hopes, while the non-mobile group presented more mature aspirations; (b) a difference among the groups in frame of reference, so that the upward aspirers may have understood the interviewer to be asking for "fantasy" aspirations while other boys took the question to mean "realistic expectations"; (c) objective differences in the social status of the groups: perhaps the upward mobile boys' families are at the upper end of their group in income or education, and so provide their sons with an objectively greater opportunity for mobility; (d) a difference in intelligence among the groups.

First, on the question of realism. There were in our total sample fewer than one per cent of the boys who gave us their job choices distinctly "little boy" or "glamour" occupations. Among boys in the mobility analysis sub-sample, there were no aspirations listed which were obviously or totally based on ideas of glamour. When the boys are asked how sure they feel about the job they've chosen, we find that very few of them say they're not at all sure; more important, the variation that does occur is not related to the type of aspiration they express. Boys in the three groups show approximately equal certainty that they will *get* the jobs for which they are aiming (Table 9, Item 1).

Furthermore, we find a difference in educational plans, one which is appropriate for the difference in job aspirations; this indicates at least a minimal degree of realism in our Ss' understanding of work preparation (Table 3, Item 5).

The groups differ neither in age (Table 9, Item 2) nor in present socioeconomic status. The upward mobile boys are not from homes which are higher economically or in educational background (Table 9, Items 3, 4).

The two rough measures of intelligence available both show the striving group to be somewhat superior. The upward aspiring boy is more likely to report leisure reading (Table 2, Item 5), and he is rated by coders as more facile verbally (Table 9, Item 5). The downward mobile are rated low on verbal skills, but their reading pattern does not differ significantly from that of the stable group ($\chi^2 = .10$; $p > .90$ with 1 df). We will defer a consideration of this until the discussion.

Table 9. Relationship of Mobility Aspiration to Age, Certainty about
Aspiration, Family Income, Father's Education and Intelligence

	Mobility				
Item	Upward (N = 277) %	Stable (N = 168) %	Down-ward (N = 73) %	x^2 *	p Level
1. Certainty about aspiration					
a. high	57	58	54	3.22	.70
b. moderate	34	33	33		
c. low	09	09	13		
2. Age					
a. fourteen	33	29	31	1.94	.80
b. fifteen	30	36	33		
c. sixteen	37	35	36		
3. Family economic status [a]					
a. high average	32	35	31	2.76	.70
b. average	53	49	52		
c. low	15	16	17		
4. Father's education					
a. grade school	32	27	25	3.07	.70
b. high school	50	58	55		
c. college	18	15	20		
5. Verbal ability					
a. high	25	11	03	33.92	.01
b. average	69	75	74		
c. low	06	14	23		

* Unless noted, the chi square was derived from a 3 × 3 table with four degrees
of freedom.
[a] The measure used for economic status was the Remmers House and Home Scale.

DISCUSSION

We may interpret our data on the upward aspiring boy in relation to
ego structure and functioning. We did not, of course, make a direct investigation of intrapsychic processes; furthermore, our understanding of
"normal" ego functioning is, at present, limited and tentative. Nevertheless, it may be of some interest to attempt a formulation of our results in
the current vocabulary of ego psychology.

Among upward aspiring boys we find a high level of diversified activity, suggesting that energy is available to the ego for focused use in
work and play. We may infer that the antecedent condition for this ac-
cessibility is in the ego's having at its disposal a relatively high degree of
neutralized energy. If we assume that both groups, mobile and non-
mobile, do not differ in primary energy resources, we may conjecture

that the aspiring Ss have less energy tied to the resolution of conflict, and consequently gain in neutralized, disposable energy.[5]

Another sign of the comparative effectiveness of ego functioning among aspiring boys is seen in the greater degree of cohesion among the three major systems within the personality. On the one hand, ego processes in the mobile boy are less likely to be imperiled by the breakthrough of impulses (When would a boy break a rule?); on the other hand, he is less likely to show evidence of an excessively punitive superego. The greater degree of internalization of moral values among aspiring boys suggests a more harmonious articulation between the ego and superego systems. Our data show that this integration is not purchased at the expense of an unusual quantity of guilt.

A consideration of the intelligence factor is relevant here. Although we had no direct measure of intelligence, we saw that the upward mobile boys read more and read more difficult things; and they are judged on the basis of the interview to be more verbally skilled. In all likelihood there *is* an intellectual difference among our groups; one plausible interpretation of many of our findings is that they merely reflect group differences in IQ. We feel, however, that such a formulation assumes an overly simple causal sequence—for one thing it fails to clarify the mechanisms which mediate between IQ and other indices of successful ego functioning. A good deal of recent data points to a high degree of association between intelligence and variables which indicate effective ego functioning. The direction of causality and connection among these variables is by no means understood. Furthermore, to explain our data as a function of intelligence alone would not allow us to generate predictions in the area of family relations. If we assume, however, that our data are best understood by positing differences in intrapsychic organization— and particularly in ego structure and functioning—we may then posit specific expectations about family milieu.

We would expect—on the basis of the higher energy level and the more refined control of impulsivity among upward mobile Ss—that they have relatively good relationships within the family and have successfully resolved infantile object ties. We mean by this that there is a relative absence both of covert hostility toward the parents, and of overt dependence upon them, together with a relatively high degree of objectivity about family relations.

We have seen that this is, in fact, the case. The mobile boy asserts (and probably has been encouraged toward) greater independence of judgment and behavior. It will be recalled that he expresses a desire for equalitarian rather than dependent relationships with adults. He frequently uses his own convictions as authority in making decisions.

The aspiring boy more often admits differences between himself and

---

[5] Cf. Rapaport (1953, p. 353): "In other words, the amount of energy which the person can dispose by investing it in objects, by becoming interested in activities, even when essential drive-aims and drive-objects are in abeyance, is an indicator of ego-autonomy and ego strength."

his family. He seems able to assert the legitimacy of an autonomous self-definition—to the extent, at least, of selecting an ego ideal outside the family setting.

The independence we have observed has not occurred through rebellion from or rejection of the family. Despite their ability to differentiate themselves from their parents, the upward aspirers give evidence of a congenial relationship with them. They share their leisure activities; in response to a projective measure they reveal relatively little covert hostility toward parental figures.

Their parents are, in fact, comparatively lenient; they are more likely to employ mild and essentially verbal discipline and use physical punishment infrequently.

We have seen, then, that the upward aspiring boy is characterized by a high energy level, the presence of autonomy, and a relatively advanced social maturity. These attributes may be viewed as derivatives of a generally effective ego organization, one which has developed out of the successful resolution of infantile object-ties and conflicts. We would expect, on theoretical grounds, that this development would be most likely to occur in a family setting where the parents allow the child a nonambivalent connection with them, where autonomy can emerge without conflict. As we have seen, the data we have suggest that this is the case.

We have already presented, in the introductory section, our view of the internal psychic processes which characterize downward mobile boys. From the specific perspective of ego functioning, we see an apparent blocking or impoverishment of energy which should, ideally, be available to the ego. We may infer that neutralization is not being successfully accomplished. There is a relatively poor articulation among the psychic systems: impulses threaten the ego's integrity; the superego seems overly severe and yet incompletely incorporated. These boys seem humourless, gauche, disorganized—relatively so, at least. Perhaps the most telling and poignant datum which the study locates is their response to the possibility of personal change, their tendency to want to change intractable aspects of the self, and the degree of alienation revealed by their desire to modify major and fundamental personal qualities. As we have seen, this pattern is associated with a certain quality of family interaction: the boy gives evidence of an ambivalent tie to the parent, a mixture of overt dependency and covert aggression. One of the determinants of this ambivalence, we may infer on theoretical grounds, is in the parents' relatively punitive style of discipline which fails to establish self-governing controls in the child.

A final point concerning the mechanisms through which the differing aspirations become established: In the case of upward aspiration we assume a direct connection between the socialization process and the aspiration to social mobility. That is, we assume that the parents transmit the value on mobility during socialization, and that the child incorporates this as part of a complex of values which includes autonomy and general achievement. In contrast, we conjecture that the process in downward

aspiration may be more indirect: the rebellion engendered by an ambivalent family atmosphere may be directly expressed in a rejection of
general social goals; or we may have a diffuse demoralization which causes
(and prepares the child for) failure and isolation in social situations. In
turn, these failures result in a general narrowing of goals, and a retreat
from success; a central expression of this is the lowering of occupational
goals.

SUMMARY

We have only recently begun to recognize that prevalent views of the
dynamics of mobility, based as they are largely on literary sources and on
extreme instances, require refinement and differentiation. The paper begins by distinguishing varieties of mobility behavior. There is presented a
model of the psychodynamics of upward and downward aspiration, which
is tested with data from a national sample of adolescent boys. The general
formulation holds that upward mobility is found among boys with effective, autonomous ego functioning; downward mobility is seen as a
symptom of demoralization. Psychoanalytic ego theory provides the
framework from which we make specific predictions of differences in the
areas of activity level, achievement mode, time perspective, internalization of values, autonomy, self-esteem, and family milieu. The findings reveal sharp differences, in the predicted directions, between upward and
downward aspiring groups.

Fostering Understanding

16 / The Goals of Mental-Health Education Commonly Selected by a Group of Experts

Gwen Andrew and Esther L. Middlewood

The basic goals or objectives of a program in mental-health education according to a group of experts should be to develop understanding of mental-health principles, promote and maintain good mental health in children, develop community programs, and promote professional training in mental health. A number of practical suggestions for implementing these objectives are listed in the following selection by Gwen Andrew and Esther L. Middlewood of the Michigan Department of Mental Health.

Concomitant with the mushrooming growth of interest in mental-health education, there has been constant pressure from many sources to evaluate the effectiveness of such programs. Serious and sincere questions have come from members of all disciplines in the field of mental hygiene, including those engaged in educational efforts, those in a clinical setting, and those representing other areas of endeavor closely related to the education programs. Further, equally pressing and sincere questions are already appearing from the sources of financial support.

As a part of its preventive program, the Michigan Department of Mental Health has for approximately five years maintained an education division which is engaged in a state-wide program of mental-health education. Cognizant of the importance of questions regarding the effectiveness of such education, this division, in collaboration with the research division of the department, set out to develop a series of projects designed to evaluate the various aspects of the program within the framework of a

Reprinted from *Mental Hygiene*, 1953, 37, 596–605, with the permission of the authors and The National Association for Mental Health.

continuing practical service. This latter point was considered important if the evaluations were to be of use to those actively engaged in education efforts.

At the outset, it was assumed that such education is worth while and necessary in view of the widespread mental-health problem, the limited clinical facilities available to deal with the problem, and the commonly accepted premise that therapy *per se* is not necessary or advisable for all people or for all problems. Furthermore, many aspects of mental-health problems seem more amenable to mass-education techniques and perhaps more immediately solvable through such procedures. Thus, we were interested in developing projects designed to evaluate the various techniques used, with particular emphasis on their effectiveness in changing the level of information, and if possible in changing the attitudes and the behavior of people. Which people were reached most effectively was also to be a primary consideration.

It immediately became obvious that a major problem involved in evaluative studies was the suspected variability and lack of integration of the objectives of the many professionals working in the field. Without a reasonably concise pattern of goals to be achieved, attention to techniques becomes comparable to the development of a well-designed experiment, the results of which have no application beyond the experiment itself. The means to an end become the end in itself, and the pressing basis for the whole program becomes lost in a discussion of the procedures, or at least in a series of studies difficult to relate to one another or to a comprehensive program. One cannot peruse the psychological literature without recognizing that this situation is not unique to the field of mental-health education.

Therefore, it appeared to us that a very important primary project was a determination of the basic goals or objectives of a program in mental-health education. It seemed that the most feasible means to make this determination was to consult a selected group of professional people, including not only mental-health educators, but also practicing clinicians and those producing materials. We assumed that if experts from all disciplines were consulted, a list of objectives could be compiled that would be based both upon theory and upon experience and that would attain objectivity through the common goals listed independently by these experts. In other words, if several experts independently listed a certain goal for mental-health education, we felt it could be considered an objectified goal because it commonly appeared in the thinking of those qualified to discuss both the theoretical and the experiential aspects of the problem. This procedure is essentially the commonly used experimental technique of the agreement of independent observers.

To execute the plan, eighty-six experts were requested by letter to enumerate and discuss those objectives which they believed important for a mental-health-education program. The letter of request explained the plan to establish a list of goals that might ultimately contribute to a basic unified approach for the field of mental-health education. It was further explained that the list established in this manner might be used in developing evaluation projects. Thirty-six of the requests went to psychiatrists, twenty to psychologists, eight to social workers, and twenty-two to mental-health educators.

For purposes of this study, members of disciplines other than these four were considered as mental-health educators and were contacted because of their contributions in that area. We do not pretend, of course, to have contacted all or even most of the expects in the field, and we made our selection without regard to the number of participants included from a particular discipline. We attempted to get some balance between those with a more theoretical orientation and those more immediately concerned with the practical aspects, and we wanted at least some representation from the various orientations involved. The selection of names was made by consulting the membership lists of the American Orthopsychiatric Association, the American Psychiatric Association, the American Psychological Association, the American Association of Psychiatric Social Workers, and the publishers of lists of mental-health-education materials. An "expert" is defined for this project as one who is a member of one of the above groups and who has attained some prominence in his area of specialization. The selection of these people was made by a committee of three, who pooled their judgments on whether or not to include a name.

Sixty-four of the eighty-six experts replied to the letter, in some instances after a follow-up letter had been sent. A tabulation of the requests sent and the replies received gave the following results:

Discipline of addressee	Number of requests	Number of replies
Psychiatrists	36	29
Psychologists	20	14
Social workers	8	7
Mental-health educators	22	14
	86	64

We were somewhat amazed at the enthusiastic response our request received from the experts we consulted. There were those, of course, who did not reply at all, and there were some who did not believe the project was feasible. These, without exception, stated that a committee of key people could perhaps develop a list of goals. We had previously rejected this suggestion because such a measure could not give us the independent opinions based on personal experience which we were seeking from this preliminary investigation. It seemed to us that a first step was to determine the common objectives selected *independently* by a group of experts practicing in the various facets of the field of mental hygiene. Even experts react to the pressures of group discussions, and it has been common experience that some members of the group will be heard only rarely, that others will be vocal enough to direct the entire group, that some ideas will be discussed beyond the point of fruitful contribution, and that in the process of the discussion many ideas will be lost or never expressed at all.

It is the authors' hope that this first report may contribute the framework from which a committee of experts may begin to discuss and elaborate the objectives of the mental-health-education program. As a result of such discussion, it is hoped that a long-range program can be developed, with concomitant plans for the ultimate evaluation of our success in achieving the goals for which we strive.

The analysis of the replies presented a further problem in relation to objectivity. If we were to assume that any set of goals we derived from the letters was objectified because of common mention by a group of experts, we had to analyze the responses in some manner that would reflect the overlap of ideas and not the bias of the person making the analysis. To circumvent this possibility, two members of the research staff read all the letters and noted the objectives discussed in them. Each staff member then combined the results of his first analysis into the major goals or areas that evolved in his notes. Sub-goals which further elaborate the major goals were also compiled from the original analyses. The results obtained by these two staff members were then compared and combined into a master list of major goals, each with a list of sub-goals related to the major area. Identical objectives appeared in the analyses of both staff members.

The next step was to have all the letters read again, tallying each reference to a major goal and also tallying a reference to any of the sub-goals. In this way the five major goals and the elaborative sub-goals most commonly selected by the experts were determined. A commonly selected goal is defined here as a goal suggested by at least twenty of the experts. This figure was arbitrarily selected with two considerations in mind. The first was the purpose of the project—to determine *common* objectives of mental-health education—and the second was the desire not to eliminate objectives recognized as important by many, but not a majority of the experts. By the use of this method,[1] the following objectives were defined:

I. Disseminate knowledge about and develop understanding of the underlying principles of mental health (with emphasis on the aspects related to the individual adult):
   A. Stimulate optimal personal development through knowledge of existing information and understanding of self.
   B. Improve the capacity of individuals for successful interpersonal relationships.
   C. Develop awareness of the importance and attainability of mental health and its influence on the total life pattern.
   D. Disseminate knowledge of the principles of personality development.

[1] There are no quotations from the letters since we did not request such permission, and because in some instances we were asked not to publish or quote the material offered.

   E. Develop understanding of the rôle of unconscious motivation in
      determining behavior.
   F. Promote understanding of the interrelationship of environmental
      and personal factors in determining personality development.
   G. Disseminate knowledge of basic needs and means through which
      individuals and society can provide for meeting these needs.
   H. Develop publications to inform the public about various aspects
      of mental health.
   I. Help individuals to seek professional treatment and consultation
      freely. (It was frequently cautioned that this objective must be
      realistically related to the available facilities as well as to the
      need for such services.)
II. Promote the development and maintenance of good mental health in
    children:
   A. Inform parents and others responsible for child care about the
      generally accepted theories of child development and help them
      understand problem behavior as indicative of a need for help.
   B. Inform parents and teachers of the importance of environmental
      influence on child development.
   C. Teach parents the rôle of the family in forming personality, em-
      phasizing the importance of satisfying parent-child relationships,
      especially with regard to giving children assurance of love and
      security.
   D. Train teachers and school administrators in child-development
      theory, in the elements of the psychology of adjustment
      necessary to recognize children with problems, and in devel-
      oping the ability to maintain a mentally healthy classroom at-
      mosphere.
   E. Promote screening of personnel as a part of school administra-
      tion in an attempt to assure well-adjusted teachers.
   F. Develop mental-health curricula in school systems to help chil-
      dren make satisfactory adjustments (including guidance courses,
      art-of-living courses, marriage-and-the-family courses, pupil dis-
      cussion groups, guidance services), and, in general, adjust school
      practices to children's emotional needs.
   G. Develop mental-health literature appropriate for school children
      of all ages.
III. Create informed public interest in the problems of mental illness:
   A. Develop public understanding of the incidence and nature of
      mental illness and eliminate misconceptions about it.
   B. Teach the public that mental illness is preventable and curable
      and promote early treatment. (Several experts stressed the im-
      portance of not misleading people with regard to the curability of
      all mental illnesses.)
   C. Inform the public about existing facilities for the care of the
      mentally ill and develop interest in expanding such facilities,
      with an understanding of the economic factors involved.

     D. Help people understand how to live with and coöperate with those who are recovering from mental illness.

IV. Develop the community aspects of the mental-health program:

     A. Teach the relationships between cultural values and mental health and ways to modify social concepts not conducive to mental health.

     B. Coöperate with groups attempting to remove cultural and social detriments to good adjustment, such as prejudice, insufficient recreation, poor housing, and insecure employment situations.

     C. Develop the local facilities that attempt to help people maintain mental health and create public support of these facilities.

     D. Influence the welfare of individuals by indoctrinating in the principles of mental health those at the policy-making level in the community's various institutions.

     E. Develop inter-agency and inter-group coöperation among those carrying out programs concerned with mental health, including both the clinical and the educational aspects.

V. Promote training of personnel:

     A. Develop more training in psychiatric information for physicians.

     B. Teach mental-health principles to members of allied professions, including nurses, ministers, judges, parole officers, educators, and hospital administrators.

     C. Teach principles of mental health to publishers of children's books and producers of radio, television, and theater programs.

     D. Develop interdisciplinary understanding of the contribution each can make in coöperative efforts for mental-health education.

     E. Further develop training in mental-health education as a profession and give clinicians more training in educational techniques.

     F. Train volunteer workers for those aspects of mental-health programs which they can handle adequately.

Referring to the tabulation of replies received, the reader will note that most responses came from psychiatrists, which in effect means that any list of goals developed will emphasize their opinions. Should they differ from others in the field, this emphasis will have an important effect in that the point of view of other experts may be obscured. Because of this situation, we attempted a simple breakdown of the results according to disciplines. The problem of the percentage obtained when using a small number was recognized—i.e., when there are only five people in a group, the opinion of one person makes a difference of 20 per cent in the results. Therefore, we have presented the number of respondents selecting each goal instead of giving percentages which might be misleading. Regardless of this circumstance, there is considerable agreement among the members of these related fields, since limited differences were found between groups. The number of respondents in each group who listed each of the goals was as follows:

NUMBER OF EACH DISCIPLINE SELECTING EACH MAJOR GOAL

GOAL	Psychiatrists (N-25) *	Psychologists (N-9)	Social workers (N-5)	Mental-health educators (N-9)	All groups combined (N-48)
I	13	6	2	8	29
II	16	7	3	6	32
III	11	2	3	6	22
IV	11	4	3	6	24
V	9	3	4	4	20

* The number for each discipline may not agree with the number shown in the tabulation on page 198, since in some cases it was impossible to summarize or otherwise interpret the response.

It will be seen that marked agreement exists between disciplines, although, comparatively speaking, the mental-health educators emphasize promoting knowledge of mental-health principles and the psychologists underemphasize promoting knowledge of the problems of mental illness. The social workers are somewhat more concerned with professional training than the others, but it appears to be training for allied professions, which may be due to their more extensive work with these groups. The psychiatrists show no marked deviations from the results obtained for the members of other disciplines.

The five major goals that were developed appear to break into separate areas motivated by the different forces that underlie the entire mental-health-education program. Goals I and II (develop understanding of mental-hygiene principles and develop good mental-health in children) may be based on the underlying principle that education, as preventive mental-hygiene, attempts to reduce or prevent anxiety through the development of the individual's insight into his motivations and through the relaxation of superego function. That this is possible through mass education is apparently assumed, or at least hoped for, by most of those engaged in the mental-health movement. Threatening or "scare" literature seems to have been produced as a part of the effort to develop these primary goals; consequently we would like to stress the importance of presenting fundamental concepts to the public constructively and with as little threat as possible. The use of threat to gain support for the mental-health program is an example of defeating the effort to reach a long-term goal—anxiety reduction—in order to reach an immediate and perhaps more superficial goal.

Goals III and IV (informing the public about problems of mental illness, and development of the community aspects of mental hygiene) apparently are considered important partially because of the continuing need professionals find to inform the public about practical aspects of the mental-hygiene problem in order to enlist public support for already developing programs, for new programs, and for various projects undertaken to solve some of the mental-health problems. This might be called a drive for public understanding and, thereby, support of the mental-health movement.

Goal V (promoting professional training) is a practical goal that may have become apparent to the experts in their efforts to achieve the other objectives which seem more related to a fundamental philosophy. In a sense this goal must be reached, at least to some degree, before it will be possible to achieve the more fundamental objectives of mental-health education.

A well-defined education program should without doubt consider all of these goals in terms of the available staff and the particular skills of members of this staff. To achieve some objectives might require a minimum of staff effort and time might be allotted accordingly. Some objectives might be best attained through coöperation with other programs rather than through the direct service of a mental-health-education staff.

Mental-hygiene societies and allied lay groups are doubtless key sources of personnel to attain some goals and they are certainly the groups in which much of the education program will first take effect.

With the objectives outlined and with the development of an integrated approach by coöperating groups and agencies, it should be possible to conduct an effective mental-health program. Such an organized effort should make it possible to determine periodically the measure of success achieved. The present problem for research, then, is to develop practical and meaningful measures of the effectiveness of the various techniques used to obtain the objectives and to apply these measures to the continuing education program.

17 / What Psychology Can We Feel Sure About?

Goodwin Watson

Goodwin Watson of Teachers College, Columbia University presents fifty propositions about children and learning on which psychologists tend to agree. A careful study of the propositions may help us to understand better teaching-learning processes, which may lead to improvement of educational practices.

Educators and others who wish to apply psychology in their professional work have long been troubled by controversies among psychologists themselves. Behaviorism arose to challenge the introspective method; Thorn-

Reprinted from *Teachers College Record*, 1960, *61*, 253–57, with the permission of the author and the Bureau of Publications, Teachers College, Columbia University.

dike's connectionism was controverted by Gestalt concepts; psychoanalysts talked an almost completely different language. It was natural for teachers to say, "Let's wait until the psychologists themselves straighten out their various systems!" It looked for a while as if one could support almost any educational practice by choosing which psychologist to cite.

Gradually, however, a body of pretty firm facts has accumulated. While it remains true that research findings will be somewhat differently expressed and explained within different theoretical frameworks, the findings themselves are fairly solid.

A workshop of educators [1] recently asked me to formulate for them some statements of what we really know today about children and learning. To my own surprise, the list of propositions with which few knowledgeable psychologists of any "school" would disagree, grew to fifty.

In no science are truths established beyond the possibility of revision. Einstein modified thinking about gravity, even though Newton's observations were essentially correct. Psychology is much younger and more malleable than physics. New facts are constantly accumulating in psychological research, and these will doubtless introduce some qualifications and modifications—conceivably even a basic contradiction. The educator who bases his program on these propositions, however, is entitled to feel that he is on solid psychological ground and not on shifting sands.

What follows is a listing of fifty propositions, important for education, upon which psychologists of all "schools" would consistently agree. These are presented in twelve classifications.

NATURE-NURTURE

1. Every trait in human behavior is a product of the interaction of heredity (as determined at conception by genes) and environmental influences. Some traits (preferences in food or clothing, for example) are easily influenced by nurture; others (height, rate of skeletal ossification) seem to be affected only by extreme differences in environment.

2. There are specific stages in individual development during which certain capacities for behavior appear. The manner in which these capacities are then utilized sets a pattern for later behavior which is highly resistant to change. If unutilized then, they are likely not to develop later (for example, visual perception, mother attachment, language pronunciation, sports skills, peer relations, independence from parents, heterosexuality).

3. The significance of the important biological transformations of pubescence (growth of primary sex organs, development of secondary sex characteristics, skeletal and muscular growth, glandular interaction) lies mainly in the *meaning* which cultural norms and personal history have given to these changes.

[1] The New Jersey State Curriculum Workshop, Atlantic City, November 12, 1959.

LEARNING PROCESS

4. Behaviors which are rewarded (reinforced) are more likely to recur.

5. Sheer repetition without indications of improvement or any kind of reinforcement is a poor way to attempt to learn.

6. Threat and punishment have variable and uncertain effects upon learning; they may make the punished response more likely or less likely to recur; they may set up avoidance tendencies which prevent further learning.

7. Reward (reinforcement), to be most effective in learning, must follow almost immediately after the desired behavior and be clearly connected with that behavior in the mind of the learner.

8. The type of reward (reinforcement) which has the greatest transfer value to other life-situations is the kind one gives oneself—the sense of satisfaction in achieving purposes.

9. Opportunity for fresh, novel, stimulating experience is a kind of reward which is quite effective in conditioning and learning.

10. The experience of learning by sudden insight into a previously confused or puzzling situation arises when: (a) there has been a sufficient background and preparation; (b) attention is given to the relationships operative in the whole situation; (c) the perceptual structure "frees" the key elements to be shifted into new patterns; (d) the task is meaningful and within the range of ability of the subject.

11. Learners progress in any area of learning only as far as they need to in order to achieve their purposes. Often they do only well enough to "get by"; with increased motivation they improve.

12. Forgetting proceeds rapidly at first—then more and more slowly; recall shortly after learning reduces the amount forgotten.

MATURATION: LIFE TASKS

13. The most rapid mental growth occurs during infancy and early childhood; the average child achieves about half of his total mental growth by the age of five.

14. Ability to learn increases with age up to adult years.

15. During the elementary school years (ages six to twelve) most children enjoy energetic activity—running, chasing, jumping, shouting, and rough-house. For most staid adults this is uncomfortable. Boys are generally more vigorous, active, rough, and noisy than girls.

16. Not until after eleven years of age do most children develop the sense of time which is required for historical perspective.

17. Readiness for any new learning is a complex product of interaction among physiological maturation, prerequisite learning, the pupil's sense of the importance of this lesson in his world, and his feeling about the teacher and the school situation.

INDIVIDUAL DIFFERENCES

18. No two children make the same response to any school situation. Differences of heredity, physical maturity, intelligence, motor skills, health, experiences with parents, siblings, playmates; consequent attitudes, motives, drives, tastes, fears—all these and more enter into production of each child's unique reaction. Children vary in their minds and personalities as much as in their appearance.

19. Pupils vary not only in their present performance but in their rate of growth and the "ceiling" which represents their potential level of achievement. Some "late bloomers" may eventually surpass pupils who seem far ahead of them in grade school.

20. Gains in intelligence test scores by children are positively related to aggressiveness, competitiveness, initiative, and strength of felt need to achieve.

21. Pupils grouped by ability on any one kind of test (age, size, IQ, reading, arithmetic, science, art, music, physical fitness, and so forth) will vary over a range of several grades in other abilities and traits.

LEVEL OF CHALLENGE

22. The most effective effort is put forth by children when they attempt tasks which fall in the "range of challenge"—not too easy and not too hard—where success seems quite possible but not certain.

23. According to some studies, many pupils experience so much criticism, failure, and discouragement in school that their self-confidence, level of aspiration, and sense of worth are damaged.

TEACHING METHOD

24. Children are more apt to throw themselves wholeheartedly into any project if they themselves have participated in the selection and planning of the enterprise.

25. Reaction to excessive direction by the teacher may be: (a) apathetic conformity, (b) defiance, (c) scape-goating, (d) escape from the whole affair.

26. Learning from reading is facilitated more by time spent recalling what has been read than by rereading.

27. Pupils *think* when they encounter an obstacle, difficulty, puzzle or challenge in a course of action which interests them. The process of thinking involves designing and testing plausible solutions for the problem as understood by the thinker.

28. The best way to help pupils form a general concept is to present

the concept in numerous and varied specific situations, contrasting experiences with and without the desired concept, then to encourage precise formulations of the general idea and its application in situations different from those in which the concept was learned.

"DISCIPLINE" AND LEARNING

29. Over-strict discipline is associated with more conformity, anxiety, shyness and acquiescence in children; greater permissiveness is associated with more initiative and creativity in children.

30. When children (or adults) experience too much frustration, their behavior ceases to be integrated, purposeful and rational. Blindly they act out their rage or discouragement or withdrawal. The threshold of what is "too much" varies; it is lowered by previous failures.

GROUP RELATIONS

31. Pupils learn much from one another; those who have been together for years learn new material more easily from one of their own group than they do from strangers.

32. When groups act for a common goal there is better cooperation and more friendliness than when individuals in the group are engaged in competitive rivalry with one another.

33. At age six, spontaneous groups seldom exceed three or four children; play groups all through childhood are smaller than school classes.

34. Children learn that peer consensus is an important criterion; they are uncomfortable when they disagree with their peers, and especially when they find themselves in a minority of one against all the others.

35. Groups which feel some need (internal coherence or external pressure) to work together try to influence deviates toward the group norm. If there is no felt need to stay together, the deviate may be ignored and thus excluded.

36. Leadership qualities vary with the demands of the particular situation. A good leader for a football team may or may not be a good leader for a discussion group, a research project, or an overnight hike; leadership is not a general trait.

37. In most school classes, one to three pupils remain unchosen by their classmates for friendship, for parties, or for working committees. These "isolates" are usually also unpopular with teachers.

SUBJECT MATTER

38. No school subjects are markedly superior to others for "strengthening mental powers." General improvement as a result of study of any

subject depends on instruction designed to build up generalizations about principles, concept formation, and improvements of techniques of study, thinking, and communication.

39. What is learned is most likely to be available for use if it is learned in a situation much like that in which it is to be used and immediately preceding the time when it is needed. Learning in childhood-forgetting and relearning when needed is not an efficient procedure.

40. Television is the most frequently reported activity of elementary school pupils, occupying about the same number of hours per week as are given to school—far more than would voluntarily be given to school attendance.

ATTITUDES AND LEARNING

41. Children (and adults even more) tend to select groups, reading matter, TV shows, and other influences which agree with their own opinions; they break off contact with contradictory views.

42. Children remember new information which confirms their previous attitudes better than they remember new information which runs counter to their previous attitudes.

SOCIAL STRATIFICATION

43. Attitudes toward members of "out-groups" are usually acquired from members of one's "in-group."

44. Children who differ in race, nationality, religion, or social class background, but who play together on a footing of equal status and acceptance, usually come to like one another.

45. Children who are looked down upon (or looked up to) because of their family, school marks, social class, race, nationality, religion, or sex tend to adopt and to internalize this evaluation of themselves.

46. Two-thirds of the elementary school children of America come from lower-class homes; the one-third who come from the lower-lower class usually find school very uncongenial.

47. Children choose most of their "best friends" from homes of the same socioeconomic class as their own.

48. More girls than boys wish, from time to time, that they could change their sex.

EVALUATION

49. If there is a discrepancy between the real *objectives* and the *tests* used to measure achievement, the latter become the main influence upon choice of subject matter and method.

50. The superiority of man over calculating machines is more evident in the formulation of questions than in the working out of answers.

18 / Controlled Experimentation in the Classroom

Julian C. Stanley

To enable us to gain further understanding of how children learn, this article by Julian C. Stanley of the University of Wisconsin stresses the need for teacher participation in controlled experimentation conducted in the classroom. Examples of two types of classroom research are illustrated by a speech study and a study of attitude change as a function of role-playing. The author is of the opinion that much more experimentation should be done in the classroom and urges teachers to collaborate with "experts" in experimental design.

My thesis is that much more controlled experimentation under classroom conditions should be done. "Experimentation" as used here is *not* meant to include uncontrolled experimentation, important though such experimental analysis undoubtedly is. Nor do I include status studies unless they are imbedded in an experimentally controlled design.

There are two general types of controlled experimentation in classrooms. One of these is the "methods" study in which two or more ways of doing something are compared in an unbiased fashion. The other is so-called "fundamental research," whose intent is to derive general principles applicable beyond the immediate situation in which they are found. We need far more of both types of research.

THE SPEECH STUDY

Consider the following example of the many methodological decisions teachers must make virtually every day. Recently I had the pleasure of helping several high-school teachers set up an experiment to determine the effectiveness of observing seventh graders unobtrusively in the natural context of the classroom and then telling them in writing specifically which speech faults they needed to correct, and how to correct them. Logically and intuitively, it was apparent to the speech teachers that this procedure should be quite effective, far better than just instructing students in the speech class or having no formal instruction at all. They were scientifically minded, however, and therefore decided to subject their hunch to empirical test. The design of their study should serve to illuminate several aspects of careful experimentation.

Reprinted from the *Journal of Experimental Education*, 1957, 25, 195–201, with the permission of the author and Dembar Publications, Inc.

They might have taken the students in each speech class at the beginning of the semester and divided them *randomly* into two groups, one of whom would be "followed" in other classes during the semester and notified of speech imperfections. The other group would not be "followed." If the extra attention was effective in improving speech behavior, then the "followed" group should be the better speakers and oral readers by the end of the semester. Having both groups in intermixed order speak and read orally for judges who do not know to which group a given individual belongs is a means of securing unbiased ratings that can then be separated for the two groups and compared. If the average rating of the "followed" group is significantly larger than the average rating of the "not followed" group, then we would conclude that the extra attention is having some positive influence upon speaking. Of course, the influence still might not be great enough to warrant the expenditure of time and money, but at least "following" would be shown to be having *some* effect.

In this sort of experiment it is easy to test additional hypotheses without using any more students than are necessary for the simple comparison of the "followed" and "not-followed" group. One might, for instance, hypothesize that "following" would work better for girls than for boys. By dividing the students first by sex and then randomly by followed vs. non-followed group (see Table I), we can answer two new questions: (1) Do boys differ from girls on the ratings? (2) Are there differences between the sexes with respect to the value of "following"?

Going still further, we might include in the experiment both those persons who are taking speech and those taking English, dividing all the speech students into two sex groups and subdividing each of these into the "followed" vs. the "non-followed." Similarly, we would separate the English students into boys and girls, then dividing the boys into "followed" vs. "non-followed" and the girls likewise. See Table II.

This arrangement results in eight groups: boys taking speech who are followed, boys taking speech who are not followed, girls taking speech who are followed, girls taking speech who are not followed, boys taking English who are followed, boys taking English who are not followed, girls taking English who are followed, and girls taking English who are not followed. It enables us to answer seven different questions, contrasted with only one for the two-group design and three for the four sex-method groups, and yet requires no more students than the two-group setup. The seven questions that can be answered are: Do boys differ from girls with respect to speaking or oral reading ability? Do those persons taking speech differ from those taking English? Does the "followed" group differ from the "non-followed" group? Are there interactions of sex, subject, and method, sex and subject, sex and method, or subject and method? [1]

---

[1] If there are no significant interactions, the "main effects" are additive. Suppose, for example, that girls are superior to boys, persons taking speech are superior to those taking English, and the "followed" group is superior to the "non-followed" group. Then, if interactions are nil, the best speakers will be the girls taking speech and

The four- and eight-group arrangements shown in Tables I and II are both "factorial designs." We have two levels of each factor—sex, subject, and method—combined in all possible ways with each other to yield eight different sex-subject-method groups in Table II. The huge advantages of factorial designs are that they allow several variables to be manipulated simultaneously and then to be evaluated independently of each other and that they make the testing of interactions possible. Frequently heard objections to the artificiality of controlled experimentation

Table I. A Four-Group (Sex-Method) Factorial Design *

	Method	
Sex	Not followed	Followed
Boys		
Girls		

* There are n students in each of the four groups, or $4n$ students in the entire experiment. Half of the $2n$ boys are assigned *randomly* to the "not followed" group and the other half to the "followed" group. Similarly, half of the $2n$ girls are assigned *randomly* to the "not followed" group.

Table II. An Eight-Group (Sex-Subject-Method) Factorial Design *

		Method	
Sex	Subject	Not followed	Followed
Boys	Speech		
	English		
Girls	Speech		
	English		

* Each boy is assigned *randomly* to one of four groups (speech-not followed, speech-followed, English-not followed, or English-followed). Likewise, each girl is assigned *randomly* to one of the four groups. Preferably, each of the eight groups will contain the same number of students; in the speech study there were six students in each of the eight groups.

being followed. The worst speakers will be the boys taking English and not being followed. However, if, despite the general superiority of girls, speech, and following, the boys taking English and not being followed were the best speakers, we would have a triple interaction (sex, speech, and method).

Two-factor interactions may also occur. Girls taking English might be superior to girls taking speech, despite the overall superiority of the speech group over the English group. Also, boys being "followed" might be better speakers than the followed girls, despite the overall speaking superiority of the girls. Or those persons taking English and being followed might be better speakers, regardless of sex, than those taking speech and being followed, even though for the experiment as a whole the speech group is superior to the English group.

Table III. A Factorially Designed Change-of-Opinion Experiment Involving 16 Groups *

		Role			
Sex	Initial Opinions	Congruent with Initial Opinions	Opposite to Initial Opinions	First-Row Observer	Outside Control
Men	Internationalist Isolationist				
Women	Internationalist Isolationist				

* There were two persons in each of the 16 groups, a total of 32 in the experiment, not counting the 30 raters. Each man was assigned randomly to one of the four role groups; women were assigned similarly.

involving the manipulation of a single variable in a sort of vacuum, with other factors held as constant as possible, are not applicable to the factorial design. It permits us to approximate a natural setting in our experimentation, while at the same time testing several possible factors with nearly as much efficiency as if we were considering only a single variable such as "followed" vs. "non-followed." As yet, this design is seldom employed in educational research, though it is of wide utility.

In Table II we have the outline of a methods experiment actually conducted. Results were all negative. The boys and girls spoke and read equally well, the speech classes did not do appreciably better than the English classes, the "followed" students were no better speakers or readers at the end of the semester than the "non-followed" group, and none of the four interactions was significant. Therefore, within the limitations of our experimental procedure we are forced to conclude at least tentatively that "following" students is a waste of time and money.

It is essential to remember the conditions under which we experimented, however. Having used only seventh graders in a certain rather atypical type of school, we cannot generalize our conclusions to other grades or other schools. The method of "following" we used is the only one for which we have information; another method might be effective. Our findings are limited by the nature of the speech and oral reading ratings secured, and by the competencies and idiosyncrasies of the 10 particular raters involved. Furthermore, the rating situation itself may be too formal and unlifelike to elicit natural speech behavior from the students. Finally, we gathered our data at the end of the first semester and consequently cannot make statements applicable to the whole year. Nevertheless, there is certainly no positive evidence in this carefully controlled study that being followed is worthwhile. Henceforth, the burden of proof is upon proponents of "following" rather than upon its opponents. They may want to launch new experimentation to test further hypotheses, such as the following: another well defined method of following is effective;

following works better in other grades than it does in the seventh; following is more effective in other schools than here; other measures of speaking and oral reading ability reveal the effectiveness of following.

Where possible, we try to design methods experiments so as to answer questions more general than the purely local problem under consideration. Relating the study to a conceptual scheme or theory from which results can be deduced in advance enables us to test important aspects of the theory while we are getting our specific information. How well this can be done depends largely upon how advanced conceptually the field in which we are working is. If speech theorists have devised definite frameworks to unify their field, then we can test deductions based upon these. For example, if one theory emphasizes changing the individual's self-concept in a certain way, we can use a method of "following" that is congruent with it. Or, if another theorist emphasizes giving the student successful experiences in a speaking situation, we can try to accomplish that. Because of the numerous ways to assist or tutor a student, we must select the ones for trial on the best possible logical and empirical grounds, rather than just picking at random.

THE OPINION-CHANGE STUDY

The methods experiment of Table II constituted action research, since it was designed by actual teachers of speech to determine whether or not they should continue following their students. Its results were of immediate practical value to these teachers in their school. Some research is less related to action and more to general speculation. A study conducted by Herbert Klausmeier and myself (1957) may illustrate this semi-theoretical type of experiment.

We were interested in whether or not role playing changes extreme opinions. Our subjects were 145 beginning graduate students, 62 in my advanced educational psychology class and 83 in his. Thirteen days before the beginning of the experiment itself we obtained ratings of attitude toward world government on a four-question opinionnaire. Then for my experiment I chose low scorers ("isolationists") and high scorers ("internationalists"), leaving the middle scorers to rate secretly the quality of the role playing. One-fourth of the extreme scorers were assigned to play a role opposite to their initial opinions, one-fourth play a role congruent with their initial opinions, one-fourth to play no role but to serve as first-row observers, and one-fourth to go to the library before the experiment began and work on unrelated material. Thus there were four "role" groups: different role, same role, observer, and outside control. Each of the four role groups contained an equal number of men and women, and each had half of its persons whose initial opinions were "isolationist" and half who were initially "internationalist." In all, there were 16 role-sex-initial opinion groups, as shown in Table III. Seven hypotheses can be tested with this design, using change-of-opinion scores based upon differences between the first opinionnaire and a similar opinionnaire administered the day after the experiment.

Are the differences among the four roles significant? Do the changes of men differ from those of women? Does it make any difference with respect to opinion change whether the person was originally "isolationist" or "internationalist"? Are any of the interactions among sex, initial opinion, and role significant?

Klausmeier's design was identical with mine, except that where I used a "sex" classification he used "age": 31 or less vs. 32 or more. Under our conditions, role playing had no effect upon opinion. We had hypothesized that persons playing a role in line with their initial opinions should change little, while persons playing an opposite role should shift in the direction of that point of view, but this did not happen. Nor did the persons playing a compatible role change significantly less than the persons who left the room without even observing the role playing. Our only positive finding was a slight tendency for the women in my study to get more world-minded and the men less world-minded; this interaction of sex with initial opinions may be atttributable merely to chance.

IMPLICATIONS

Since both of the studies I have outlined yielded essentially negative findings, you may wonder whether these experiments were worth performing. Obviously, it is valuable to know that following students to observe and record their speech errors for their information is not effective. It is probably of even greater importance to learn that confident claims for the opinion-modifying influence of role playing do not hold up in a controlled experiment.[2] Both experiments highlight the fact that hypotheses *must* be tested empirically as well as logically. Our best brain-children may be worthless or downright pernicious. Expert opinions, pooled judgments, brilliant intuitions, and shrewd hunches are frequently misleading. Ultimately, they must be tested by the careful gathering of evaluative data if education is to advance on the basis of sound principles.

We badly need educational experimentation of the controlled variety. Too much of our research effort has been directed toward questionnaires, statistical compilations, and dead-end correlational studies. We have shied away from designing and executing studies involving the manipulation of pertinent variables. Our colleagues in agriculture and the behaviorial sciences such as psychology have forged far ahead of us experimentally.

[2] As in the speech study, one must not overgeneralize the results of the Stanley-Klausmeier investigations. Definite limitations were set by the type and small number of subjects used, the formal nature of the role playing situation, and the opinion area involved. Janis and King (1954), studying "The Influence of Role Playing on Opinion Change," with small groups under non-classroom conditions, found evidence for such change. For a recent review article that contains 22 references, see Mann (1956).

Yet we cannot rely upon psychologists, sociologists, and anthropologists to do our experimentation. They provide much relevant theory and many enticing hypotheses for us, but we must hoe our own garden; they cannot be expected to do this.

OBSTACLES TO CONTROLLED EXPERIMENTATION

In my opinion, one of the major reasons why experimentation in education has languished is that our graduate schools have been confused by a false practitioner versus research distinction. This has lead in most schools of education to the training of few, if any, persons in educational experimentation as such. Whereas almost no psychology major can earn a Ph.D. degree in a reputable university without prolonged exposure to experimental psychology, statistics, and measurement, we let the great majority of our doctoral candidates get through their dissertations with hardly the basic rudiments of training for experimentation. And training is essential. While it is true that many persons who receive such training will actually engage in little experimentation, untrained individuals are virtually certain to do none or to do it ineptly.

Another reason for the paucity of educational experimentation is that university professors in schools of education typically do very little themselves. Until they provide the training for experimentation and set appropriate examples for their students, improvement is unlikely.

Few public school administrators and even fewer parents realize the dire necessity for continual experimentation. Some equate experimentation with vivisection. Others protest against the use of control groups, saying that if a given method is likely to be of value they want all the students to have it, not realizing that in this way they make it difficult, if not impossible, ever to assess the worth of the method. Perhaps the widely publicized tests of Salk's polio vaccine will be a salutary antidote to this attitude, though it is doubtful that many persons not already aware of the need for controls in experimentation will perceive the similarity between the polio study and, say, the introduction of a new method for teaching handwriting.

Two essential ingredients of controlled experimentation are difficult to incorporate into our thinking. One is the imperative need for *designing* experiments "from scratch." Experiments do not "just grow." They must be planned in advance down to the finest detail. The final analysis of data must be anticipated and worked through abstractly or in a pilot study before the experiment itself begins. This preplanning phase will usually require more time than the actual experiment. Once all aspects of the design have been thought through and refined as much as possible, the experiment must be run off exactly as planned, allowing only for unavoidable disasters. We hear a great deal about "flexible experimentation," but once set in motion a controlled experiment is completely rigid and inflexible. Flexibility must be reserved for the preplanning and postplanning phases. The experimental findings almost invariably suggest new hypotheses that can be tested experimentally.

The second difficult concept to put over is the crucial need for randomization. The very notion of randomization is hard to grasp, since it implies chaos for the single case and a high degree of order for the group. Suppose that you have 30 pupils in a class and that you want a control group of 15 and an experimental group the same size. How shall you divide the class into halves in order not to give an undeserved lead to one group or the other? If there were five seats to a row, you might consider taking all students in the first three rows for one group and all in the last three rows for the other group. Would this procedure yield two groups of equal ability for, say, an arithmetic experiment? Not in most classes, for seating is hardly likely to be random. If mostly girls sit near the front of the room and mostly boys near the rear, and if one sex surpasses the other in arithmetic skill, results of the experiment will be biased at the very beginning.

We might put all 30 names into a hat, each on a separate slip, shuffle them *thoroughly,* and then draw out 15. Or, somewhat less defensibly, we might alphabetize the 30 names and put the odd-numbered persons (1, 3, 5, . . . , 29) in one group and the even-numbered persons (2, 4, 6, . . . , 30) in the other. The best method is to number the children from 1 through 30 (or from 0 through 29) and draw 15 numbers within this range from a table of random numbers. In all three instances—shuffling slips, alphabetizing, and random numbers—it is essential to decide *in advance* which will be the control group and which the experimental. We cannot wait until we note into which group our prize pupil happens to fall and then call this the experimental group. Experiments must be without bias if they are to yield unambiguous conclusions.

I cannot stress too heavily the need for getting *fresh* data specifically designed to answer the questions you pose. Too often a researcher, particularly a thesis-driven graduate student, is tempted to exhume some moribund material he finds stored away in a convenient mausoleum and perform a statistical autopsy on it. This "seeing what the data died of" is good clinical medicine but rarely worthwhile research. The persons who originally collected the data did not have the present problem in mind, so it would be quite unusual for the data to bear directly on the current hypotheses. About all you can get out of this post-mortem analysis is a crazy patchwork quilt of guarded conclusions and tortuous qualifying statements. The customary upshot is to say that "more research is needed." Of course it is, but not research of this foredoomed variety.

Almost as culpable is the person who gathers mountains of data as he goes along, without any particular experimental design, in the hope that eventually it will serve to test some hypotheses he gets around to formulating. In many instances this is a collossal waste of time and energy, harking back to the exploratory days of the late nineteenth century and the biometrical approach of Karl Pearson. Since 1925, and particularly since 1935, when R. A. Fisher's *The Design of Experiments* appeared, we have known about the inefficiency of this "sawed-off shotgun" approach. No longer do we need huge numbers of experimental subjects in order to reach valid conclusions. Small-sample theory enables us to emphasize the rigor of the experimental design instead of the size of the sample itself. Ten thousand subjects in an ill-planned study may yield results more equivocal than 40 subjects in a carefully designed experiment.

PREPARATION FOR CLASSROOM EXPERIMENTATION

There are many experiments you can do in the classroom. Most of these probably fall within the category of action-method studies, but some may be of more general import. Remember that the generality of your findings is inextricably bound up with the formulation of the problem; if you strive for generality of application rather than viewing your investigation as answering a merely local problem, you can make a contribution beyond the confines of your school.

You will want to have the necessary training in statistics (particularly the analysis of variance) and research methods before trying to design an experiment, and/or you will want to work closely from the *beginning* with a specialist who understands these matters well. Unfortunately, there are not many such persons available, perhaps no more than 100 educationalists in the whole United States. A possible solution is to take statistics and experimental design courses in the psychology department of a major university. Collaboration is the desirable plan, however, even though you do acquire considerable technical sophistication.[3] Cooperative efforts such as the speech study I described earlier benefit all persons involved immensely.

In any event, it is essential that you design your experiment thoroughly before beginning to "turn the crank" and that all collaboration be started at the very beginning, rather than after the data are in. As the statistician must nearly always say to the researcher who consults him too late, after the experiment has been mismanaged badly, "Of all sad words of tongue or pen, the saddest are these, it might have been." Ordinarily, the specialist in experimental design does not know your subject matter field as well as you, but he can point out logical flaws and methodological imperfections that might nullify all your otherwise commendable efforts.

RECAPITULATION

This paper has been concerned entirely with controlled experimentation in the classroom, which I believe we have neglected to our great

[3] Even the experimental-design "experts" in education and psychology consult each other and the mathematical statisticians frequently.

detriment. Most decisions about methods have been based upon colloquial, anecdotal, or administrative considerations rather than experimentation. Seldom are adequate control groups incorporated into classroom
experiments. The necessity for long-range experimental design is not usually appreciated by teachers and administrators. The principle of random-
ness is often misunderstood or ignored in favor of elaborate matching,
which has several disadvantages. Worst of all, few teachers, including
those with doctoral degrees, get even minimal training for modern experimentation. Our professional literature is virtually devoid of well controlled experimental studies in the classroom. We continue to pool igno-
rance via conferences, questionnaires, rating scales, opinionnaires, and
ineffective correlational studies, all of which are valuable for certain purposes but not sufficient in themselves.

If we are to advance beyond the dark ages of educational pre-science,
we must emulate the experimental proficiency and zeal of colleagues in
other behaviorial sciences. Ours is a distinctive task; education has its own
problems to solve. Only by close collaboration between experimentally
aware persons at all levels in a widespread research partnership can we
hope to make headway against the vast complexities of the teaching-
learning process.

19 / Basic Approaches to Mental Health: The Human Relations Program at the State University of Iowa

Ralph H. Ojemann

*Aiming toward an increase in self-understanding and improvement in
mutually satisfying social relationships, Ralph H. Ojemann is working
on programs designed to help parents, teachers, other school personnel,
and children to extend their insight into and appreciation of the causes
of behavior from a surface approach to an approach that takes account
of the dynamics of behavior. This selection explains the Preventive
Psychiatry Research Program of the State University of Iowa.*

Some years ago when we were making observations of parental and
teacher behavior toward children, it was observed that parents and teachers tended to deal with child behavior as a surface phenomenon instead
of taking account of the factors underlying or causing the behavior. Observation also tended to indicate that such an approach to behavior

Reprinted from *Personnel and Guidance Journal*, 1958, 36, 198–206, with the permission
of the author and the American Personnel and Guidance Association.

tended to produce conflicts and emotional strains in both adult and child.

For example, if a child attempted to overcome a feeling of inadequacy by "pushing" to be first so often that it interfered with class activity, the teacher who approached this behavior as a surface phenomenon would try to stop it by such methods as reprimanding the child, making him go to the end of the line, or sending him out of the room. She tended to do this without thinking about or inquiring as to the causes of the behavior. Since the feeling of inadequacy remained in spite of the scolding, going to the end of the line, or leaving the room, the child would still be under a strain and would attempt more vigorous action or a different approach. The teacher would soon observe that her attempts to stop the behavior were not successful. She would tend to intensify her attempts to stop the pupil's interfering behavior and the whole round of strains would rise to a new level.

Observation of the behavior of parents toward children tended to reveal a similar situation. Analyses of parental behavior often revealed a sequence somewhat as follows. In the early years of the child's life, parents would try to control him by telling him what to do, punishing him, coaxing him, and so on. When these procedures failed after years of trial some parents would give up. This left the child to his own devices for meeting problems and he often failed to find satisfying and cooperative solutions. Other parents would doggedly persist, only to meet with increasing resistance and conflict.

WHAT THE EARLY OBSERVATIONS SUGGESTED

An analysis of such behavior on the part of parents and teachers suggested that if they could extend their insight into and appreciation of the causes of behavior and change from a surface approach to an approach that takes account of the dynamics of behavior, the chances blocking strong motivations in the child (and also in themselves) would be lessened and the chances for cooperative or mutually satisfying interaction would be increased.

A test of this hypothesis was made in the case of teachers in a study by Wilkinson (1929). Through the use of an experimental and control group it was shown that as the teacher acquired more insight into the backgrounds, ambitions, worries, and concerns of pupils, conflict between teacher and pupil tended to lessen and the pupils' attitudes toward school tended to change in a more favorable direction.

A close examination of the idea that teachers and parents can guide children more effectively and produce less emotional conflict if they approach the child's behavior in dynamic terms suggested that we were dealing with two cases of the larger problem of the relation of one person to another. The reactions of a teacher toward a child or a parent toward a child are essentially reactions of one person toward another. This observation suggested the question, will the hypothesis hold in any human relationship? If we change children to approach behavior dynamically, will that help them in getting along with adults and with their associates?

When we examined the whole problem still more closely we noted another aspect. After a child learns about the factors that underlie behavior, theoretically he could apply this learning not only to the behavior of others but also to his own actions and to the guiding of his own development. For example, if he learned that over-aggressive behavior is often motivated by a feeling of inadequacy, and if he learned something about how feelings of inadequacy develop and how they can be overcome, he would have something to help him interpret his own over-aggressive behavior or his own feelings of inadequacy. The question then became, if we change children so that they appreciate the differences between the surface and dynamic approaches to behavior, will that affect their relationships with others and their relationship to themselves?

This question had two parts. (1) Can children acquire an appreciation of the differences between the surface and dynamic approaches to behavior and apply the dynamic approach in their relations with their parents, teachers, other adults, in their relations with their associates, and in guiding their own development? (2) If they can learn and can be motivated to apply, will that reduce the emotional conflicts and increase the amount of mutually satisfying interaction in these relationships?

This question, with varying emphases on the several aspects, was studied in the investigations by Morgan and Ojemann (1942), McCandless (1941), Bate (1948), and Stiles (1950). In summary, these investigations showed that children in the elementary and secondary grades can learn the beginnings of the dynamics of behavior, that they can learn to apply this knowledge in their relations with others, and that the process of learning about human behavior can be greatly extended on the school level.

THE PLACE OF EDUCATION IN
HUMAN RELATIONS IN THE SCHOOL

When it became fairly clear that children can learn to approach behavior in terms of its causes, considerable thought was given to the next problem that suggested itself, namely, how can the material about behavior be inserted into the school curriculum?

Two approaches could be made. One would be to introduce a separate course on human relations. This is perhaps the first suggestion that occurs. When we studied the problem, however, several questions arose.

When we looked over the various "core" areas in the school curriculum we noted several that dealt rather directly with human behavior. Examples are social studies, English (human behavior in literature and writing), home economics (family relationships), and guidance. How did

it happen that in spite of these opportunities to study human development people grew up with a surface approach to behavior as in the case
of the parents and teachers we had observed? Why is the surface approach
so apparent in our culture?

A careful study of this question led to an examination of the content
and method of the several subjects as now taught in school, and this
revealed an interesting situation. It can perhaps best be described by an
example from community civics. When we examine the discussion in the
ordinary civics book of such a problem as crime, for example, we find a
discussion of how the police force is organized, its functions as prescribed
by law, methods for detecting and apprehending the criminal, and the
system of courts, training schools, and prisons that have been developed.
We may find a short discussion of the fact that crime is somewhat associated with economically underprivileged conditions.

But all of this approaches crime as a "surface" phenomenon. We can
show this by considering the questions we would ask if we approached
criminal behavior in terms of its causes. If we do that we would ask such
questions as these: Are the ways in which the police and the courts handle
a criminal such that after they apprehend him they try to find out what
caused the behavior and then take the causes into account in their reactions toward him? Do they try to find out in a given case whether the
causes are such that the criminal can be rehabilitated into a self-respecting
cooperating citizen and not be a constant threat to other members of
society, or if he cannot be rehabilitated is he then effectively isolated? In
other words, do the present systems that society has set up study the
criminal to find out the causes of his behavior and base their treatment of
him on those findings?

Furthermore, if criminal behavior is caused, then real protection from
the criminal requires that the community find out and change those conditions that produced him. Real protection—both in the sense of protection from direct damage to life and property which the criminal may
inflict and also in the sense that taking care of criminals is a drain on
the other citizens—comes when people in the community are aware of
the forces that tend to produce crime and seek to change those forces.

In considering what the forces are we will have to go beyond the
observations that poverty and similar conditions are somewhat correlated
with crime and ask the more penetrating question—How does it happen
that some persons living in a given environment become criminals, while
other persons living in the same home and same neighborhood do not?
But these questions are not considered in the usual text. The treatment
is largely surface in character.

We could give other examples illustrating the same point. In short,
much of the treatment of human problems in civics teaches the "surface"
approach. What is true for civics also tends to hold true for the other
social studies. Stiles (1947), for example, found in analysis of the material
on human behavior in fifteen social studies readers used in the elemen-

tary school that less than one per cent of the selections treated human behavior in the dynamic way. Much of the treatment is of the surface variety.

The question now becomes—Under what arrangement do we have the most effective learning conditions? Do we have it if (a) we have a surface approach to behavior in the usual school subjects and a dynamic approach in a separate course on human behavior, or (b) if we have a dynamic approach wherever human behavior is discussed?

It is well known from studies on learning that changes are made most effectively when that which the child learns is applied consistently in a variety of situations. This suggested to us that we may profitably experiment further with the possibility of changing the content of school subjects from a surface to a dynamic treatment. Accordingly, studies were undertaken to determine how the material on the dynamics of behavior could be integrated into such areas as social studies, English, guidance, home economics, and others. Also, studies were undertaken to see how and to what extent the child could apply the dynamic approach in his relations with his associates and in guiding his own development.

In addition to school influences, there are the home influences. A child learns from the way his parents act toward him. Just as in the case of the teacher, the parent can work with the child using a surface approach or a more causal approach. If he uses principally a surface approach he is demonstrating to the child a non-causal method of working with others which the child will also tend to adopt. We have evidence (Ojemann, 1946) that children learn early in life a surface approach to behavior.

Such an analysis of the problem indicated to us that if we wanted to develop causally-oriented children, we needed classrooms equipped with teachers who both teach causally-oriented content materials and practice the causal approach in the daily relations with pupils. It would also help if the home environments of these children practiced the causal approach at least in some measure. We have attempted to develop such classrooms and homes.

Under our general plan, the program, by arrangement with a school system, provides summer fellowships so that selected teachers can attend an intensive training program. This program is designed to familiarize the teacher-students with the differences between surface and causal approaches, to help them apply the causal approach to the daily activities in the classroom, and to develop skill in teaching causally-oriented materials.

A supervisor of teachers, on the Preventive Psychiatry staff, works with the teachers throughout the year, holding a series of conferences with each. During the summer training program, each teacher assists in the preparation of teaching materials for his own classroom. With the supervisor's help he continues this adaptation of materials for classroom purposes throughout the year. We thus obtain a group of classrooms for our laboratory, each equipped with a causally-oriented teacher and appropriate curricular content.

EXAMPLES OF CURRICULAR EXPERIENCES

To provide a more detailed picture of the integrated program as presently conceived, it may be helpful to examine some of the actual learning experiences that are provided at several age levels. Examples for this purpose will be drawn from two age levels, namely, primary and intermediate.

1. Examples of experiences at the primary level

A. *Demonstrations furnished by the teacher's behavior.* At each age level, as has been indicated, the child is influenced by the behavior of the teacher as well as by what he hears or reads. How the teacher handles the day-to-day social situations that arise in the classroom and on the playground, the extent to which the teacher seeks to know the child's ambitions, concerns, and abilities and makes use of this information in planning his program of work and understanding his behavior before dealing with it, are examples of experiences that affect the growth of a causal orientation.

This training of the teacher to practice the causal approach is an important part of the program at all age levels and the primary level is no exception.

Furthermore, as soon as the child has some appreciation of why a situation has to be understood before it can be reacted to logically, the teacher can take the simpler situations that arise and work them out with the class to involve the children in a practical application of a causal orientation. It is important that the teacher choose only the simpler situations at the beginning, for a careful grading as to difficulty is as important in learning human behavior concepts as it is in learning other concepts.

B. *Use of narratives.* To help the primary child develop an appreciation of the differences between the non-causal and causal approaches (at the primary levels the teachers have labeled the approaches the "non-thinking" and "thinking" ways), a variety of materials have been developed which can be read to the child and discussed with him. One type of material consists of stories in which the non-causal and causal procedures are contrasted. Listening to the narratives and discussing them provide vicarious experiences for learning the differences between the two ways of living.

Each narrative describes some behavior situation. After the situation has been set forth, some character in the story begins to make a surface approach to it, then rethinks his proposed reaction and makes a more causal approach. Some of the ways in which the behavior may have developed come out and one of the characters in the narrative acts in the light of these data. The situation has a reality about it in that someone begins to make a surface approach which children in our culture experience quite frequently. But, it also introduces a new way of living—a way that takes account of the meaning or the causes of behavior instead of its overt form.

For example, in one situation a boy gets into so many fights that something has to be done. The teacher in the story is about to deal with this in the usual way when he recalls that such things do not occur of their own accord. He does a little probing and before long it comes to light that this boy has been teased a great deal because he had to go home immediately after school each day to help take care of his baby sister and didn't have time to play with the other children. When the teacher learns this, he takes measures to work out this basic problem.

To help the child develop a more generalized conception and to prevent him from thinking only of incidents involving himself, situations were developed involving children older and younger than himself and children from quite different environments. There is some observational evidence that situations involving people different from the child tend to be less emotionally charged and therefore less difficult for the child to consider causally in the early discussions.

Each narrative is preceded by a short introduction for use by the teacher. After the reading of the story there is a discussion. The purpose of this discussion is not only to recall the incidents of the story, but also to bring out the differences in procedure when one thinks of causes as contrasted with principal attention to the overt form of behavior. The discussion is also designed to consider alternative ways of meeting situations and some of the probable effects of these alternatives.

It is suggested to the teacher that this material furnish part of the offering in the regular "story period." Under usual school conditions, the material read in the story period deals with various objects and events in the child's environment. Some of it deals with people. It is suggested that material dealing with people be heavily weighted with the causally-oriented materials described. The causally-oriented stories are thus part of the primary child's story period content.

C. *Use of expositions to help understand and appreciate the work of the teacher and other persons with whom the child interacts directly.* An example of this type of material is a leaflet entitled "The Work of the Teacher." This is a simplified discussion contrasting the conception of the teacher as "someone whose main job is to check up on you" with the conception of "a guide to help you learn." This material is designed to be read by the teacher to the class and talked over with them. The logical implications of the "guide to help you" concept are described, including what alternatives are available to the child and their respective probable consequences when he finds his learning experiences not challenging. Included also is a discussion of how it may help the teacher to "tell her when something is worrying you."

The purpose of the material is to help the child gain some understanding of the behavior of the teacher, her feelings, and her methods.

It is also designed to help the child begin learning that he has a part in arranging his social environment.

Similar material has been prepared to help the child gain some appreciation of the work of parents and other adults in his social environment.

2. Examples of experiences at the intermediate level

A. *The behavior of the teacher.* Since pupils at the intermediate levels can read syllabi, work sheets and other material to be read by pupils can be prepared. However, at this level as at the primary level, the pupil also learns from what he observes of the behavior of the teacher in the daily interactions with the class. Hence, it is recognized in the integrated program that the teacher's daily behavior is an important part of the learning experience at the intermediate level as well as at the primary level, and the plan includes training of teachers at this level also in practicing the causal orientation. A pamphlet prepared for the National Education Association for use by teachers reflects this recognition (Ojemann, 1954). In its full development, the integrated plan expects that all teachers will apply the principles of human development in their daily work in the classroom.

At this level there is also the opportunity to help the pupil take some responsibility for his own development. The discussion of the work of the teacher, referred to in the description of sample materials at the primary level, is extended to include a consideration of how the pupil can help to build up his cumulative record for the school, in what areas he can keep the teacher informed about his attitudes and feelings, and how he can apply what he is learning to his own behavior.

At this level also there is the possibility of using the room council as a laboratory in which the child can apply the causal orientation in a real life situation. Since in the integrated plan the subject matter areas of social studies, health, and reading incorporate material designed to enrich a pupil's conception of the dynamics of behavior, and since he is encouraged to apply the enriched conception to situations arising in the room council, it will be helpful to indicate how the subject matter areas make their contribution before describing the use of the room council in detail.

B. *Teaching causally-oriented social studies.* In elementary social studies each of the major topics can be developed in terms of the basic factors operating in the behavior of the people involved.

The following examples will illustrate this. As an introduction to the fifth grade social studies, two teachers [1] prepared the following introduction:

I. INTRODUCTION TO FIFTH GRADE SOCIAL STUDIES

This year we are going to try to look at Social Studies in a little different way. In Social Studies we discuss problems about people. It will help

[1] Appreciation is expressed to Ann Pavlovsky and Marian Kennedy.

us to understand these problems more fully if we know something about why people act as they do.

This little booklet is to be used with your textbook in Social Studies to make it possible for you to learn more about the behavior of people and what the effects of their behavior are.

We will want to find out how situations come about that cause people to act the way they do.

1. What are the needs the people are trying to satisfy?
2. What methods are they using to work out their feelings?
3. What are the effects on other people as a result of the methods chosen to work out those needs or feelings?
4. What might happen if other methods were used?

These questions are then developed in the discussion of historical events in subsequent units.

ATTITUDES OF PARTICIPATING TEACHERS

Our program brings up two groups of questions. The first group relates to procedures: How does the plan work? What is the attitude of the teacher toward it? Can teachers be interested in cooperating in such an enterprise? Do the teachers resist training in mental health principles?

Thus far, we have worked with primary, intermediate, and secondary school teachers. At the present writing, we have a group of 15 primary, 15 intermediate, 11 secondary teachers, and 3 counselors drawn from three school systems. They have participated in the summer program and have helped to revise various aspects of the curriculum to develop in the child a sensitivity to the causes and consequences of behavior. For instance, instead of being content with the usual textbook statement that, unlike boundaries between many European countries, the United States-Canadian border has never been fortified, they prepared a discussion, based on available studies of conflict and cooperation, on some of the probable underlying factors in producing the United States-Canadian relationships. The counselors have helped the secondary teachers extend their knowledge of the children in their classes.

The fact that we have had more requests for inclusion in the program than we can accommodate indicates that the teachers on the whole have a positive attitude toward it. Those who have been accepted have cooperated enthusiastically.

Something we learned in our early work may provide a clue to at least part of this cooperation. While most presentations of mental health for teachers today stress the motivating forces operating in the child, little emphasis is given to the problem of how these forces can be expressed constructively under classroom conditions and how the teacher can accept her past mistakes. One of the hypotheses underlying the approach in our program is that much of the resistance appearing in work with teachers arises from the frustration a teacher feels when she learns about a child's needs but does not see how she can meet them under classroom conditions. In our work with teachers we point out these problems early in the program, on the theory that if the teacher realizes we are aware of his problems and are interested in helping him resolve them he will feel less frustrated. As the program has progressed we have found this to be true. Always we attempt to increase the security and self-respect of each individual member of the program by working with the teachers rather than telling them.

Can a teacher help children in elementary and secondary schools take a more understandable approach to social situations? If so, what effect does this have on the children? Does it make them more, or less, secure? More, or less, able to develop satisfying relations with others? We have evidence that significant changes have been produced throughout the primary and intermediate grades. This evidence has been reported in several studies (Levitt, 1953; Ojemann, et al., 1955; Snider, 1957).

A typical example may be found in some of the data obtained from our experiments with the fourth, fifth, and sixth grades. At each level a causally-trained teacher was matched with a teacher without such training from a nearby school, who served as a control. The matching was according to sex, age, training, and years of experience. Similarly, the children in the respective classes were equated as to intelligence. The experimental group was like the control group except that the control teacher did not participate in the summer training program and did not use causally-oriented curricular materials.

At the beginning of the school year all the children were given two causal-orientation tests. In one of the tests, the child was presented with a series of social situations to which he was asked to suggest a solution. The possible reactions ranged from arbitrary, judgmental, and punitive, such as: "It serves him right—he should be made to stay in"; to an awareness of possible complexity, such as: "The teacher should find out more about this."

In the second test, another series of social situations was presented, each followed by a series of statements with which the pupil was asked to indicate agreement or disagreement. Some examples are: "It wouldn't make much difference what method the teacher used to make him stop (bothering others) so long as he stopped bothering others." "Since these boys do the same things (described in the situation) they are probably all alike in most ways." "If another boy disobeyed his father the same way, his reason would be the same as Jack's."

The children were given tests again in the spring and the results of the experimental and control classes compared. In all grades a statistically significant change appeared in the experimental group but not in the control group.

Thus it appears that our laboratory, which consists of a teacher trained to be sensitive to the dynamics of behavior and to demonstrate this sensitivity in the daily living in the classroom and using a curriculum which incorporates these principles, is producing a degree of causal orientation among children.

Does the new orientation help causally-oriented children make more satisfying adjustments to their environment? We have various kinds of data to throw light on this question. For example, children from both the experimental and control groups were given the anti-democratic tendency scale test developed by Gough, et al., (1950). This is essentially a measure of authoritarianism.

A detailed analysis of the results (Levitt, 1955) obtained from the experimental and control groups showed a significant difference between the two groups on both scales. The causally-oriented children showed significantly less authoritarianism. It thus appears that as children become more aware of the dynamic complexities of human motivation and behavior, their attitudes toward others begin to change from an authoritarian relationship to a more democratic relationship. In all of the analyses the effects of intelligence were eliminated by various statistical procedures.

ROLE OF CAUSAL ORIENTATION IN MENTAL HEALTH

A great many questions need answering before we can determine what role a causal orientation toward behavior plays in the prevention of mental illness and development of mental health. For example, we want to know what happens in later years to the child oriented causally through his school experiences. We want to know what kinds of behavior disturbances an "inoculation" with a causal orientation will prevent, if any, both during school age and in later years. Already, our laboratory enables us to study the relationships that develop between teachers and pupils in the causally-oriented classroom as compared to the relationships in a non-causally-oriented classroom. It also points the way for a study of a host of questions that arise in the investigations of the causes of emotional breakdowns and the avenues by which mental health in its full measure may be achieved.

ASSUMPTIONS UNDERLYING THE PROGRAM

As we look over the whole program, what are the assumptions that underlie it? It seems that there are two or perhaps three. The first is that we can describe the differences between a surface and a causal approach to behavior. From the numerous occasions in which we have attempted to communicate the meaning of these concepts, it appears that it is possible to distinguish these approaches in their major aspects. We expect that a gradual refinement in meaning will take place (Levitt, 1953).

A second assumption is that a careful study using methods that can be duplicated and repeated by others so that the results can be checked is the only way in which we will be able to discover what degree of causal orientation can be developed at the various age and intelligence levels and what the effect is when a thorough going causal orientation appears. It will be noted that we are not assuming that a causal orientation appears. It will be noted that we are not assuming that a causal orientation will relieve all mental strains or prevent all mental breakdowns. Rather we are asking the question, to what extent will an "inoculation" with a causal orientation prevent various types of mental illness and increase the amount of emotionally satisfying and creative uses of human energy? In our tests of the effects of the causal orientation, we are interested not only in measuring degree or extent of prevention but we are also interested in measuring degree or extent to which human energies are released in "creative" and "satisfying" achievement.

Finally, in the early stages of our work we had to assume that learning a causal orientation was not so incompatible with the individual goals of the teachers, children, and parents with whom we worked that it produced long-enduring conflict and frustration. Both observation and test results have indicated that this is no longer entirely an assumption but may be considered a generalization that has a degree of support.

Our program, which goes under the title of The Preventive Psychiatry Research Program, is an example of teachers, guidance workers, and other school personnel joining hands with research investigators to study not only whether changes in learners can be made but also what the effects are of these changes in the lives of the learners. Teaching is viewed as a way of creating a new pattern or way of living, the effects of which can then be studied (Ojemann, 1948).

20 / Under-achievement: Concept or Artifact?

Gerald T. Kowitz and Charles M. Armstrong

Under-achievement and over-achievement have long been focal points of interest and research. The problem receives a new direction in this report by Gerald T. Kowitz and Charles M. Armstrong of the New York State Education Department. Their research suggests that under-achievement and over-achievement are related more to school policies than to characteristics of students.

What can be done for the under-achiever? School administrators and teachers ask this question again and again. While many solutions have been proposed, none has been wholly successful.

If we ask who is the under-achiever, the answer is often a simple

Reprinted from *School and Society*, 1961, *89*, 347–49, with the permission of the authors and the Society for the Advancement of Education.

definition: he is the pupil who is not working hard enough to achieve to the limits allowed by his abilities. But what causes the condition? Is the under-achiever maladjusted? Is he ill or perhaps suffering from a specific nutritional deficiency? Is his problem the result of poor teaching? Is he a slothful sinner? A program for a maladjusted child must be quite different from one for a child who is physically ill. Still another approach would be needed if the child has not acquired the basic academic skills. Unless the diagnosis is able to distinguish among the several causes, successful treatment cannot be expected.

Striving toward scientifically defensible procedures, professional educators have developed definitions of under-achievement that are quantifiable. Some are relatively crude, such as the idea that a pupil should "read up" to his mental age. Other and more complex formulas have been devised. Nearly every one has been attacked and demolished both through the logic and the statistics involved. Nonetheless, as Gallagher (1959) points out, the idea has great appeal and there is a great desire for some formula regardless of whether it can be defended scientifically.

A related problem is that the formulas do not specify the direction of the discrepancy. As long as the difference between the scores is large enough, it does not matter which score is larger. It is just as logical to declare a child an over-achiever because his achievement score exceeds his ability score as to declare him an under-achiever because his ability score exceeded his achievement score. If one category has a diagnostic significance, the other should, too. While there is general acceptance of the idea of under-achievement, there is resistance to the idea of over-achievement. Many are willing to believe that, while it is sinful for a child's scores to be warped in one direction, an equal warp in the opposite direction is virtuous. A correct interpretation of the score patterns would be that no warp represents virtue, while a significant warp in either direction is an indicator of some sort of trouble. Specialists in mental hygiene have recognized that it is not good for a child to achieve beyond his ability. He can do so only at the expense of some other facet of his life.

Many of the problems in the study of over- and under-achievement can be traced to the use of group tests. While, admittedly, it is unwise to use group tests for individual diagnostics, it is often and commonly done. Before the procedure can be evaluated, even as an operational expedient (and what is being done to provide better techniques?), several fundamental questions must be examined.

What is measured by the tests? Since both intelligence and achievement tests are based upon the ability of the child to reproduce and manipulate facts that he has learned, would the conditions contributing to discrepant score patterns be more likely to exist in the student or in the test? To what extent are discrepancies between the scores on achievement and ability tests the results of problems in test reliability and validity? To what extent can they be explained by statistical regression?

What forces are involved in determining the location of a student's score within the distribution of scores of all students? Tiedeman and McArthur (1956), in examining this question, pointed out that the fundamental component of the normal curve is chance. They question the "magic" that converts differences defined as chance into differences of diagnostic significance for the educational life of the child. In their research they made some progress toward demonstrating that the conventional methods of identifying under- and over-achievers selected individuals who were not truly different from the other members of the group.

In an earlier study, Kowitz and Armstrong (1961) found that school policy could result in some pronounced accelerations in patterns of academic achievement. If these shifts produced discrepancies that met the operational criterion for over-achievement, a new facet of the problem might be opened for investigation.

By assuming that a pattern of discrepancy scores between group tests can be used to diagnose under- and over-achievement, the problem can be explored on an individual and on an institutional basis. While educators have assumed that it is an individual problem, requiring corrective programs for individual pupils, more than one parent has expressed the belief that his child would have achieved more if the school had been run properly.

To study the problem, the writers selected two schools, one in which promotion from grade to grade was automatic and one in which promotion largely depended upon academic attainment. The schools were closely matched in terms of pupil ability and community characteristics.

Longitudinal records were used. Discrepancy scores were calculated for each pupil at the third grade, the sixth grade, and the ninth grade. Because of the statistical nature of the tests, some discrepancies must be expected. Using the commonly accepted criterion of 1.96 standard deviations between the scores, for example, about five per cent of the scores could appear discrepant by chance alone. These should be equally split with 2.5 per cent appearing as under-achievers and 2.5 per cent appearing as over-achievers.

Contrary to expectations, there was little consistency in the proportion of pupils showing discrepancy scores at the several grade levels. In the third grade, both schools showed a significant group of under-achievers in reading but not in arithmetic. In the school where promotion depended upon achievement, there was an unusually large group of over-achievers in both reading and arithmetic in the sixth grade. In the ninth grade, neither school varied from the expectation. Since these were longitudinal records, with the same children in each grade group, the instability of the proportion with discrepant scores suggests that discrepant achievement is not a function of the pupil's nature, but that discrepant scores as indexes of under- and over-achievement have received much more attention than they deserve. They are not stable, apparently responding quite readily to school policy.

To explore the possibility of school generated differences, test scores on 77 school districts, involving about 12,000 students, were used. Expectancy tables were developed for discrepancy scores in arithmetic and reading in the fourth grade and the proportion of discrepant scores in each subject was calculated for every school. Over half the school showed solid evidence of over-achievement, while only about 15 per cent showed under-achievement in reading and less than 10 per cent showed it in arithmetic.

Some evidence was found for the idea that school policy has a material effect upon the pattern of achievement of its students. By far, achievement in excess of measured ability appears to be a more prevalent problem than what is commonly called under-achievement. In fact, the evidence for the idea of under-achievement as a characteristic of a child was, at best, weak and shaky.

Support for this position can be seen in the report on changing values of college students (Riesman, Jacob, and Sanford, 1959), where the social atmosphere of the institution is identified as a determiner of student change. Further support on the high-school level is seen in the work of Coleman (1960), who showed that the proportion of top marks going to the most able students is a function of the value system within the institution.

When viewed from these facts, it is not surprising that special programs to treat under-achieving individuals have not found great success.

21 / Attributed Social Power and Group Acceptance:
A Classroom Experimental Demonstration [1]

Alvin Zander and Arthur R. Cohen

The forces at work in group interaction, specifically, the effects of social power on group acceptance, are demonstrated in the following selection by Alvin Zander of the University of Michigan and Arthur R. Cohen of New York University. By participating in a class demonstration such as this, the student can experience, examine, and discuss his own behavior and that of the group. He may learn that people tend to react differently to persons to whom they attribute much power or little power. High-power persons tend to be received with more interest and attention, and they in turn tend to emphasize more the attractive qualities of the group. Experience with such demonstrations, learning

[1] This demonstration is a by-product of a program of studies on social position and interpersonal relations supported by a research grant MH-325 (C) from the National Institute of Mental Health, of the National Institutes of Health, Public Health Service.

Reprinted from the *Journal of Abnormanl and Social Psychology*, 1955, *51*, 490–92, with the permission of the authors and the American Psychological Association.

firsthand through individual and group activity, the student may gain
further understanding of his own behavior and the behavior of others.

This paper describes a classroom demonstration which illustrates the reaction of group members to the communications and behavior they receive from others, when the nature and direction of the communications
are influenced by the amount of power attributed to special members.

The exercise is based on the assumption that individuals are likely to
be sensitive and alert toward persons to whom they attribute much power,
and relatively less concerned with those who are viewed as having little
power. Attributed power is here defined as the perception of a person's
ability to influence or determine the fate of the perceiver whenever the
powerful person wishes to do so. The unique feature of power, as distinguished from prestige, authority, or status (and the probable cause of
the sensitivity it generates in subordinates), is that the powerful person
is typically perceived as a potential source of either need gratification or
deprivation by those with little power. The latter individuals in turn behave toward superiors in a fashion which maximizes the possibility that
the powerful persons will facilitate the subordinates' need gratification.

Such alertness has been noted in various studies. The more that
power is attributed to a person, the greater is the likelihood that he will
be the target of communication from subordinates (Hurwitz, et al., 1953;
Jackson, 1952; Thibaut, 1950), receive more deferential or solicitous behavior from them (Lippitt, et al., 1952), and be perceived as friendly toward
the observer (Pepitone, 1950). Assuming that the subordinates are not able
or willing to avoid interaction with the one to whom they attribute high
power, it has been reported that their behavior toward the superior may
be either an attempted substitute for upward mobility (Thibaut, 1950),
or an effort to win support and rewards from the superior (Hurwitz, et al.,
1953; Lippitt, et al., 1952).

Since deferential, solicitous, and attentive behavior is more often directed toward persons with high attributed power, it may be derived,
other things being equal, that a member who is treated as though he were
a powerful person will have greater attraction to the group and higher
self-evaluation than one who is treated as though he were a subordinate.
He will be attracted to the group because he views his position as secure
(Kelley, 1951), and because he feels wanted and valued by the group (Jackson, 1952). His self-evaluation will be positively influenced by the same
perceptions.

The demonstration is a procedure for illustrating these notions. It
precedes any class discussion of power, group structure, position, or
related concepts and serves as an insight-producing experience which provides a readiness to explore such subject matter. The exercise is so designed that the persons to whom high and low power is attributed are not
aware that they have a unique position in the eyes of the others in the

group. This is done in order to prevent the development of any confounding expectations arising from perceptions of own power.

METHOD

The students are instructed to form into groups of seven persons each. They are told in somewhat more detail than is necessary here that each circle is to think of themselves as constituting a committee which has been appointed by the vice-president of the University and to ignore the existence of the other similar committees in the room. Each group has the hypothetical task of preparing advice for the vice-president as to the most suitable policy for the use of a large sum of money which has been given to the school by an anonymous donor. The man who provided the funds has stipulated only that students have at least some voice in determining how the money should be expended, and that the money be used for student welfare. They are informed that each committee is to assume that it has already met once prior to this occasion but at that time felt that their group was too small and unrepresentative of the relevant viewpoints. Thus, they have asked the vice-president to appoint several additional members to their group.

Each subgroup is then requested to select two persons to send out of the room. These are to be the new members just appointed by the vice-president at the committee's request. This step makes it possible to state a reasonable but false purpose by asserting that the objective of the demonstration is to show how it feels to be a newcomer to a group which has been previously organized. The persons sent into the hall are given further instructions, asked to select a partner different from the one with whom they had left the room, and to return on signal to a group different from the one they had both left. They are told that they will be interviewed in front of the class, after their meeting with a committee, concerning how it feels to be a new member. They are not informed that they will have unusual social positions attributed to them when they arrive at the meeting, nor is anything said about the behavior expected of them by their groups. Thus, in effect, they are induced to be students in the role of late arrivers to an organized group.

Meanwhile the groups in the classroom are given the information that the vice-president has selected two new committee members in accordance with their request, that one is the Dean of the School of Education (the subjects are mostly Education majors) and the other is a college freshman. They are instructed to be very sure that they do not tell the newcomers about these positions in the subsequent meeting. They are asked to decide as a group which location in the circle (when occupied by a new member) will be considered to be the Dean and which the freshman, and are given a few minutes to develop some history so that they can properly act as though they have had a meeting prior to the arrival of the new members. They are not told to treat the newcomers differently, nor is anything said as to how they should act toward the new members.

The persons who have been sent out of the room are then asked to join the committee of their choice and the meetings begin. Typically the "Deans" are received with much interest and attention by the groups, while the "freshmen" are greeted with more detachment and given less notice. The discussion is usually directed toward the newcomers in large part, but primarily to the Dean. After ten minutes the discussion is stopped by the instructor and all class members are asked to fill out a brief questionnaire [2] which is introduced as a means to gather their private thoughts about the meeting. The completed questionnaires are then set aside for the moment and various newcomers are interviewed before the class concerning their feelings while they had been participating as group members. These oral reports illustrate for the students that the Deans and the freshmen react differently to the group experience. The Deans tend to emphasize the attractive qualities of the group and the interest the members displayed in his ideas. The freshman's remarks are quite the opposite.

The demonstration is concluded by simultaneous discussions within each group. During this time the manipulation is revealed to the newcomers, the new members are reassured, told how they were chosen for the two levels, and the members discuss the reasons for their behavior toward the Dean and the freshman in their group. Finally, before the questionnaires are handed in, each participant is asked to indicate on it whether he had been a Dean, a freshman, or a group member.

QUESTIONNAIRE RESULTS

Data concerning reactions to the meeting are available from the reflection questionnaires completed by the Deans and the freshmen in 21 subgroups before they had been told of their unwitting roles and prior to any group discussion concerning the nature of their interpersonal relations. This instrument, which is very brief for practical reasons, contains five graphic rating scales (eight points). On two of the questions there are data from only 13 groups since these items were added after the demonstration had been tried in one class containing eight groups.

Table 1. Average Reactions of "Deans" and "Freshmen" to Their Group Experiences

Measure	N in each role	Deans Mean	Freshmen Mean	t	p
Attraction of group for member	13	6.2	4.1	3.79	.001
First impression made on group	13	5.0	3.9	2.41	.03
Social validity given to opinions	21	5.4	3.9	2.63	.02
Degree of influence on group	21	6.8	4.4	4.49	.001
Ease felt in group	21	5.8	5.2	.87	.20

[2] [Reflection Questionnaire, p. 236.]

REFLECTION QUESTIONNAIRE

Please place a check on the following rating scales at the point which best describes your feelings *during the meeting* you just experienced.

1. How much were you "at ease"?

1 —— 2 —— 3 —— 4 —— 5 —— 6 —— 7 —— 8

1	3	6	8
very uncomfort-able, uneasy	a bit uncom-fortable	somewhat comfortable	very com-fortable, relaxed

2. How much general influence did you feel you had in this group?

1 —— 2 —— 3 —— 4 —— 5 —— 6 —— 7 —— 8

1	3	6	8
what I said seemed very unimportant to them	what I said seemed a bit unimportant	what I said seemed some-what important	what I said seemed very important

3. How good an impression do you think you made upon first coming into the group?

1 —— 2 —— 3 —— 4 —— 5 —— 6 —— 7 —— 8

1	3	6	8
extremely poor	not as good as I usually do	better than I usually do	extremely favorable

4. As far as you could determine, how much did you find that the other members in the group were in agreement with your opinion, judgments or beliefs?

1 —— 2 —— 3 —— 4 —— 5 —— 6 —— 7 —— 8

1	3	6	8
almost no agreement	not much agreement	a great deal of agreement	almost complete agreement

5. To what extent can people in general be expected to look forward to or avoid such situations?

1 —— 2 —— 3 —— 4 —— 5 —— 6 —— 7 —— 8

1	3	6	8
definitely avoid them	tend to avoid them	tend to look forward to them	look for-ward to them a great deal

It is apparent in Table 1 that the Deans felt attracted to their group, perceived that they had made a good first impression, that the group agreed with their ideas, and believed that they had had a stronger influence in the group than did the freshmen. All of these differences are statistically significant at acceptable levels of confidence. The two new members were not significantly different in the degree to which they were at ease during the meeting, although the findings are in the direction one might expect.

These results may be interpreted to mean that the Deans were more attracted to the group and evaluated themselves more highly than did the freshmen. They suggest that the group members tended to treat the two newcomers in quite different fashions since this is the most probable cause of the discrepancy in the reactions of the late arrivers.

Experience with this demonstration (and others like it) in classrooms and audience settings indicates that persons will readily differentiate in their behavior toward others to whom they are asked only to attribute some characteristic such as high or low power. In regard to the person whom they perceive in a high power role they will be attentive and appreciative, or appear to feel that way. They will appear less interested in one to whom they assign little power. The behavior of the group, in turn, will usually be interpreted by the person who is the target of such actions as an indication of his value to the group since he is not aware of the power being attributed to him by the members. (If he had known about his power, this may have caused him to perceive and evaluate the group's behavior differently.) The exercise vividly illustrates for the students that their own behavior made one person feel that he was given attention and was appreciated, while the other felt ignored and unwanted —all of this because of the members' direct reaction to the power attributed to the newcomers.

The demonstration of these phenomena in the classroom provides an opportunity to experience, examine, and discuss forces at work in hierarchical groups which otherwise remain at a verbal level of awareness.

22 / Developing Creativity in Children

Robert C. Wilson

A major quest in education focuses on what the teacher can do to stimulate creativity in the classroom. Robert C. Wilson of Portland State College suggests a wide range of activities to encourage creative

Reprinted from *Education*, 1960, *81*, 19–23, with the permission of the author and the Bobbs-Merrill Company, Inc. Copyright 1960 by The Bobbs-Merrill Company, Inc., Indianapolis, Indiana.

*expression. Some of the activities can be used to identify talented
children for programs aiming to develop their capabilities to the fullest.*

"By the time we get children in high school, their creativity has been
killed. They all want to be told what to do."

"I feel that I ought to do more to make my pupils creative, but I
don't know how to do it."

These are typical remarks of secondary and elementary school teachers. They feel that schools destroy children's creativity and that they,
as teachers, have an obligation to attempt to develop it. What can
teachers do?

First of all, what is creativity? One might define it as the process by
which something new is produced—an idea or an object, including a new
form or arrangement of old elements. The new creation may contribute
to the solution of some problem, or it may be the production of an
aesthetic effect or the clarification of a concept. Indeed it may be any
intellectual, emotional, or social problem with which an individual in
our society is interested or concerned. The creative solution is aimed primarily at solving a problem which concerns the person engaged in the
process. It may or may not solve a problem for someone other than the
creator.

It is realized that the foregoing is not a complete definition, but
further connotations of the term "creativity" will appear in the remainder
of the article. This definition stresses the purposes of the creator and the
problem he is trying to solve rather than the purposes and problems of
some social group. It also stresses the wide range of problems of daily
living, the solutions of which may require creativity.

CREATIVITY IN THE CLASSROOM

One study of the primary abilities in creative thinking revealed
several abilities which seem to be important in creativity in science, engineering, and invention (Wilson, 1954). Another study carried on in the
Department of Art Education at The Pennsylvania State University
found similar abilities to be important for creativity in art (Lowenfeld,
1958). These two studies have led to the following suggestions for encouraging "new ideas" in the classroom (Wilson, 1958). The validity of
the suggested methods has not been established in any systematic research
studies. Such merit as they may have rests upon their content validity and
the reports of teachers who have employed them.

BRAINSTORMING

Alex Osborn (1953) has described a procedure for group thinking
sessions designed to provide an atmosphere permissive of new ideas. This

procedure, dubbed "brainstorming," can be used effectively in the classroom.

The purpose of brainstorming is to obtain as many ideas as possible in relation to a given problem. There are four simple rules which must be followed:

1. *Judgment is ruled out.* Criticism of ideas must be withheld until later.

2. *Free-wheeling is welcomed.* The wilder the idea, the better; it is easier to tame down than to think up.

3. *Quantity is wanted.* The greater the number of ideas, the more likelihood of finding a successful solution.

4. *Combinations and improvements are sought.* In addition to contributing ideas of their own, participants should suggest how ideas of others can be combined into still another idea.

A problem may be written on the board, and the pupils may be asked to suggest as many ideas as possible, with the teacher listing these ideas on the board. No idea is rejected; every idea is accepted. Each idea stimulates others. At times, the ideas will tumble out so fast that the teacher will have difficulty keeping up.

Only after the ideas have been written down does evaluation take place. The class goes over the list, selecting those ideas that seem most likely to work; modifying some ideas into workable form; and rejecting those ideas that seem unworkable. Next, those ideas that seem workable may be tried out.

Brainstorming may be used with school and classroom problems such as the following: (a) "What can we do to make our schoolroom more interesting and comfortable?"; (b) "How can we make the line in the lunchroom move more rapidly?"; and (c) "What questions would be most interesting to study in this unit?"

On the other hand, brainstorming may be used with personal problems. For example: "What can each of us do to make our home more happy?" or "How can we earn extra money?"

Another possibility involves brainstorming first a list of problems and then a list of suggested solutions for each of the more important problems. For example, "Let's list as many problems as we can that sixth graders must face." Then, in regard to each problem, "Let's list as many ways as we can for solving this problem."

SENSITIVITY TO PROBLEMS

A primary mental ability which seems to be important in creative thinking is sensitivity to problems. To solve a problem creatively, one must be aware of the existence of the problem. This ability involves approaching problem situations with such questions as, "What is the problem here?"; "Is the apparent problem the real problem?"; "What would happen if such and such were changed?"; and "How can this situation be improved?"

We are unaware of certain types of problems, because we do not observe the world around us. We are unaware of other types of problems, because we make unconscious assumptions. We take things for granted about our world and its problems. Many creative acts have had their beginnings, because someone questioned an assumption that previously had been taken for granted.

Pupils may be encouraged to make better use of their senses by observation trips. For example, they may be asked to walk around the building; on their return, they may be asked to list the things they saw. Then they may repeat the trip, looking for things they overlooked the first time; after the second trip, they can make a second list.

Other trips can be made to look for objects colored red, for round objects, or for things that one wouldn't see during another season of the year. The children may be asked to look for unrecognized problems or for things which need to be improved.

Pupils may be encouraged to question some of the things that they take for granted and to consider what things might be like if some basic assumptions in their lives were different. Questions of the "What-would-happen-if—" or "What-would-it-be-like-if—" variety may serve to develop sensitivity to problems. The following are a few examples: What would happen if (a) everyone in the world were suddenly to become deaf; (b) everyone always told the truth about everything; (c) we had only three fingers; (d) we all lived by the Golden Rule; (e) we knew when we would die; (f) the air all over the world became radioactive?

IDEATIONAL FLUENCY

A satisfactory solution to a problem is most easily found when one is choosing from a large number of ideas. Individual and group activities, which have as their aim getting as many ideas as possible, are probably helpful in encouraging a second primary mental ability, ideational fluency. Brainstorming is one such activity.

The following list contains some suggestions for helping individual pupils to increase their flow of ideas. The time limits are arbitrary and may be changed to suit the group.

1. List on a piece of paper all the uses you can think of for a brick. You will have five minutes.

2. List as many things as you can think of that are square in shape. You will have five minutes.

3. When students have trouble thinking of ideas to write about in a report or theme, suggest that they first list all the things that might possibly be related to the topic. If pupils do this, uncritically, for fifteen or twenty minutes, they usually will come up with an abundance of ideas from which they may choose.

4. List all the ways you can think of in which you might entertain yourself if you had an evening to spend alone at home.

5. Fluency in creative writing may be encouraged by allowing fifteen or twenty minutes each morning for pupils to write whatever they wish to write. At first, some children may have difficulty in getting started. It may be well to suggest that they write about something that happened yesterday (real or imaginary) or about something that they saw on the way to school.

The teacher may look over the work of four or five pupils each day. It should be emphasized that, during this particular writing exercise, spelling, punctuation, and grammar are not the concern. The important thing is for the children to write anything they feel like writing. Free and fluent development of an idea is the aim.

ENCOURAGING ORIGINALITY

A third important primary mental ability is originality, the ability to have unusual, uncommon, or clever ideas and to see relationships between things that are only remotely connected.

Classroom activities in this area may encourage a deliberate effort to give uncommon or unusual responses, to look for a different or new way of doing something. The following are some suggested activities:

1. In presenting reports, as in connection with a social studies unit, the pupils may be instructed to use any method other than the obvious ones of reading to or telling the class. Pupils may decide to use dramatizations, quiz sessions, opaque projectors, tape recorders, interview techniques, etc.—the possibilities are innumerable.

2. An adaptation of the first technique is "selling a book." Instead of presenting a book report, a pupil may be told that his problem is to put himself in the position of a salesman. He may use any technique he wishes in an effort to arouse the interest of the class in reading the book.

3. Let the pupils pretend that they are going to write a poem about spring (or any season of the year). "Everyone will have an opportunity to go to the window and look outside for four minutes. When you come back to your seats, you will list all the things you saw that you would not see on a rainy day. If you list something that no one else lists, your score on that idea will be *ten*. If only two or three people in the room put down the same idea, your score will be *five*. If four or five people list the same idea, your score will be *three*. If more than five people list it, your score will be *one*. You will note that the closer you observe and the more uncommon your responses, the higher your score will be."

This activity may be followed by a discussion of creative thinking and the function of unusual or uncommon ideas.

STRONG INTERESTS NEEDED

Studies of the childhood backgrounds of eminent scientists indicate one thing which many of them had in common: They possessed strong interests at an early age, and they have carried these interests into their adult lives so that they have worked at their jobs with persistent intensity and single-minded devotion. For these men, time spent on other activities usually is spent reluctantly and, then, chiefly because of outside pressure. Most of these scientists are happiest when they are working; moreover, they achieve their greatest personal satisfactions through their work.

Many teachers and parents are concerned lest a child will not develop into a well-rounded individual. The evidence seems to indicate that to be a highly productive or creative adult, one cannot be well rounded. One must devote a very great amount of time to one area of interest. In other words, one must be somewhat lopsided.

Teachers, therefore, who feel that creativity is important should not try to force pupils to be well rounded, nor should they force children to play down their strong interest. On the contrary, it would seem that one way to develop creativity might be to encourage pupils to develop some strong interests. The capacity to have a strong interest in something may be an important prerequisite to creativity.

FIGURING THINGS OUT

Another interesting finding is that the capacity for intense concentration on a problem accompanies the development of an understanding of the concept of research. That is, at some point in his school career, the more creative individual becomes aware of the possibility of finding things out, firsthand, for himself.

The implication is that creativity may be promoted by situations in which the pupil is encouraged to work out his own solutions to problems. The teacher's task is to provide materials for students to work with; to provide sufficient time for them to manipulate ideas and toy with the elements of a solution; and to provide for problems which do not have pat answers. Obviously, it is not easy to furnish these things for a class of thirty pupils in an already crowded curriculum, which may require that pupils shift to a new subject every forty or fifty minutes.

It is, of course, much easier to tell a student what to do, what to read, and what to think than it is to set up a situation in which he must figure out these things for himself. Perhaps not all students can learn to work on their own. Nevertheless, it seems evident that we, as teachers, have an obligation to encourage them to try.

23 / Perception of Self and Others in the Helping Relationship

Arthur W. Combs

The need to study teacher behavior in a context of theory is a recurring theme in psychological and educational literature. In this selection, Arthur W. Combs of the University of Florida hypothesizes that persons who are effective in helping relationships can be distinguished from those who are ineffective on the basis of their characteristic ways of perceiving. "The difference between the good teacher and the bad one seems to lie, not in the methods but, in the perceptions he has about the youngsters with whom he is working." Forty-one sub-hypotheses are listed and the reader is invited to start exploring some by putting them to experimental check.

The nature of the helping relationship and the kinds of people who are likely to be effective helpers is an important problem for medicine, psychology, education, social work, the ministry, as well as training schools for administrators, supervisors, foremen, and many more. For a long time most of the agencies have been in the grip of the so-called "competencies" approach to training helpers. This approach calls for the accumulation of trait descriptions of helpers and of their behavior on the one hand, and the attempt to teach newcomers to the field how to behave in these ways, on the other. This is a straightforward and logical approach to the problem and the literature of almost any one of the helper training agencies includes long lists of traits and methods to be learned by the aspiring helper trainees.

Despite the apparent logic of this way of determining what needs to be taught, the competencies approach has proven to be a bitter disappointment to most helper training agencies for two reasons:

First, it appears to be a fallacy that the methods of experts can be effectively taught to neophytes. The expert, it seems, is not a neophyte with better methods. He is a different breed of fish altogether. I had an interesting illustration of this years ago while teaching a How-To-Study course at Ohio State University. The purpose of this course was to try to save the students who were having difficulty making their way in our academic jungles. In the determination of what to teach these young

I wish to thank Dr. Combs for permission to include his unpublished report. J.M.S.

people, it quickly became apparent that we could *not* use the results of our surveys on the better students for, almost without exception, we found that better students typically went to the movies often, were involved in all kinds of campus activities, studied by fits and starts as the mood struck them, and, even, frequently found it unnecessary to study at all! Teaching such methods to our failing students would have been like throwing a rock to a drowning man!

Second, the competencies approach assumes good helpers can be clearly distinguished from poor ones on the basis of traits or of methods they use. This relationship, however, is of a disappointingly low order. Apparently a wide variety of types of people can become effective helpers and the methods they use may be equally diverse. Some good teachers lecture; some others never do. Some are tough, while others, equally good, are lenient. Some counselors talk a great deal; some counselors talk very little. Yet both are judged as good by their clients. Methods, it seems, are deeply personal—arising from the personality of the helper and tailored to the situations and persons with whom he is dealing. Like the clothes he wears they must fit who he is.

Helper training institutions need much more dynamic descriptions of the nature of the helper than trait approaches have provided. Useful descriptions of helpers must be couched in dynamic terms which are more or less directly translatable into goals and objectives for the training program. It seemed to a number of us at Florida, therefore, that an approach to the problem from a perceptual orientation might provide us with more effective leads for constructing our teaching, counseling, and school psychology training programs.

From the research of Fiedler (1950, 1950a), Heine (1950), Quinn (1950), and others, there seemed to be good reason to believe that there is such a thing as a helping relationship and that the characteristics of this relationship may be well nigh universal. Fiedler (1950), for example, found that expert therapists from various schools of thought were more alike in their conception of the helping relationship than beginning therapists and expert therapists in the same school. What is more, he also found that the man-in-the-street could apparently describe the ideal helping relationship about as well as the experts!

To determine if other kinds of helpers would see ideal relationships in this fashion we first applied Fiedler's Ideal Relationship Q-Sort to a group of good teachers in our University Laboratory School. We did this by simply changing the word "therapist" to "teacher" and "patient" to "student" in each of the items of the Fiedler scale. Sure enough, when we did this, we found a correlation of .85 between our good teachers' conception of the ideal relationship and that of the expert therapists (Soper and Combs, publication pending). We next tried the Q-sort on "good" and "poor" teachers. One panel of "good" and "poor" teachers was nominated by students who gave us the names of the "very best teacher I ever had" and "the worst one I ever had." A similar panel was nominated by supervisors. Contrary to our expectations, we found that both "good" and "poor" teachers agreed with the expert therapists with correlations in the neighborhood of .85 (Soper and Combs, publication pending). Apparently you cannot tell the difference between good teachers and bad teachers on the basis of what they *know* they ought to do.

At this point we tried looking at helpers from a perceptual frame of reference and came to the conclusion that the outstanding characteristic of these people was that they had somehow learned to use themselves as highly effective instruments for carrying out their own and society's purposes. Their superiority was not so much a question of behaving in mechanical terms, "like a robot" or an adding machine. Rather, the model was more like a Univac capable of taking in all kinds of data, passing it through a formula, and arriving at the best or more appropriate answer in the light of all the factors involved. The "formula" in this case was the perceptual or phenomenal field of the helper himself. It seemed to us, if we could find the characteristic ways in which good helpers perceived we would have a more stable and accurate description of their differences, on the one hand, and a more immediate usable frame of reference for the construction of a curriculum for helpers, on the other. Our question became: Can we describe good helpers and poor helpers better in terms of their perceptions than we can in terms of their behavior?

From the very beginning of our attempt to look at the problem in this way it began to produce results. It checked on every hand with our common sense observations. Furthermore, it helped us to explain some of the wide variations we found in our explorations of good and bad teaching. For example, one of the things that had puzzled us was that toughness or leniency was ascribed about equally to both "good" teachers and "poor" ones. Rogers (1961) points out in a review of some research on the helping relationship that the most important single factor having to do with the establishment of such relationships seems to be the *intent* of the helper. Our observations were similar. The moment we looked at "good" teachers and "poor" ones in terms of how they perceived the children with whom they worked, the problem above disappeared for the teacher who believes his students *can*, may make them work like crazy because "he knows they can do it," or, he may send them off to the library unsupervised to work by themselves, also because "he knows they can do it." The difference between the good teacher and the bad one seems to lie, not in the methods, but in the perceptions he has about the youngsters with whom he is working.

This approach seemed so promising that we set up a seminar consisting of interested staff members and graduate students to examine the helping relationship and to define a series of research hypotheses which might be explored. You will find these hypotheses in Table 1.

As a consequence of our discussions of the helping relationship in phenomenological or perceptual terms, it seemed to us that effective helpers could be described in terms of their perceptions in five major areas:

1. the general frame of reference, or point of view, from which the helper approached his problem
2. the ways in which the helper perceived other people
3. the ways in which the helper perceived himself
4. the ways in which the helper perceived the task with which he was confronted
5. the ways in which the helper perceived appropriate methods for carrying out his purposes.

Under each of these headings we listed a series of probable continua with respect to the ways in which the helper saw events under that heading. For example, under the heading "Seeing other people and their behavior" it seemed to us, helpers would more often perceive those they worked with as "capable" rather than "incapable," as "trustworthy" rather than as "untrustworthy" and so on down the list.

We have not yet been able to push forward as rapidly as we would like to explore these hypotheses. . . . We are hopeful, however, that during the coming year it may be possible to subject a number of these hypotheses to experimental check. Meanwhile, there are plenty of hypotheses here to go around and it is our hope that perhaps others in this audience or elsewhere may be interested in exploring these matters as well. If these concepts prove to have the empirical validity suggested by theoretical analysis and practical observation, we believe that could prove of great significance to our thinking and practice in the future.

Table 1. Sample Hypotheses for Exploring the Perceptual Organization of "Helpers" and "Non-Helpers"

Compiled by a Graduate Seminar on the Helping Relationship, College of Education, University of Florida, Spring, 1959. Arthur W. Combs, Seminar Chairman

The basic assumption. The seminar members believe that persons who have learned to use themselves as effective instruments in the production of helping relationships can be distinguished from those who are ineffective on the basis of their characteristic perceptual organizations. More specifically, "helpers" can be distinguished from "non-helpers" with regard to their characteristic ways of perceiving:

A. General Frame of Reference
B. Seeing People and Their Behavior
C. The Helper's Self
D. The Helping Task and Its Problems
E. Appropriate Methods for Helping

Under each of the above headings, the seminar formulated a series of perceptual continua that seemed fruitful for investigation. In each instance the perceptual organization presumed to be characteristic of the helper is stated first.

A. *General Frame of Reference*
Internal   .   .   .   .   .   .   External
Growth orientation .   .   .   .   Fencing in or controlling

Perceptual meanings	Facts, events
People	Things
Hopeful	Despairing
Causation oriented	Mechanics oriented

B. *Seeing People and Their Behavior*

As capable	Incapable
As trustworthy	Untrustworthy
As helpful	Hindering
As unthreatening	Threatening
As respectable	No account
As worthy	Unworthy

C. *The Helper's Self*
Sees self as:

Identified with people	Apart from people
Enough	Not enough
Trustworthy	Not trustworthy
Liked	Not liked
Wanted	Not wanted
Accepted	Not accepted
Feels certain, sure	Doubt
Feels aware	Unaware
Self revealing	Self concealing

D. *The Helping Task and Its Problems*
Purpose is:

Helping	Dominating
Altruistic	Narcissistic
Larger	Narrower
Understanding	Condemning
Accepting	Rejecting
Valuing integrity	Violating integrity

Approach to problems is:

Positive	Negative
Open to experience	Closed to experience
Process oriented	Ends oriented
Relaxed	Compulsion to change others
Awareness of complexity . . .	Oversimplification
Tolerant of ambiguity	Intolerant

E. *Appropriate Methods for Helping*
Sees helping methods superior to manipulating methods
Sees cooperation superior to competition
Sees acceptance superior to appeasing
Sees acceptance superior to rejecting (attacking)
Sees permissive methods superior to authoritarian
Sees open communication superior to closed communication
Sees giving methods superior to withholding
Sees vital methods superior to lifeless

24 / Teaching Machines

B. F. Skinner

*From the experimental study of learning come devices such as teaching
machines, which aim to provide optimal conditions for self-instruction
and to free the teacher from the more routine tasks so that he can give
added attention to students who need remedial or advanced help,
individually and in groups. B. F. Skinner is at Harvard University.*

There are more people in the world than ever before, and a far greater
part of them want an education. The demand cannot be met simply by
building more schools and training more teachers. Education must become more efficient. To this end curricula must be revised and simplified,
and textbooks and classroom techniques improved. In any other field a
demand for increased production would have led at once to the invention of labor-saving capital equipment. Education has reached this stage
very late, possibly through a misconception of its task. Thanks to the
advent of television, however, the so-called audio-visual aids are being
reexamined. Film projectors, television sets, phonographs, and tape recorders are finding their way into American schools and colleges.

Audio-visual aids supplement and may even supplant lectures, demonstrations, and textbooks. In doing so they serve one function of the
teacher: they present material to the student and, when successful, make
it so clear and interesting that the student learns. There is another function to which they contribute little or nothing. It is best seen in the
productive interchange between teacher and student in the small classroom or tutorial situation. Much of that interchange has already been
sacrificed in American education in order to teach large numbers of
students. There is a real danger that it will be wholly obscured if use of
equipment designed simply to *present* material becomes widespread. The
student is becoming more and more a mere passive receiver of instruction.

PRESSEY'S TEACHING MACHINES

There is another kind of capital equipment which will encourage
the student to take an active role in the instructional process. The possibility was recognized in the 1920's, when Sidney L. Pressey designed

Reprinted from *Science*, 1958, *128*, 969–77, with the permission of the author and the
American Association for the Advancement of Science.

several machines for the automatic testing of intelligence and information. . . . In using the device the student refers to a numbered item in a multiple-choice test. He presses the button corresponding to his first choice of answer. If he is right, the device moves on to the next item; if he is wrong, the error is tallied, and he must continue to make choices until he is right.[1] Such machines, Pressey (1926) pointed out, could not only test and score, they could *teach*. When an examination is corrected and returned after a delay of many hours or days, the student's behavior is not appreciably modified. The immediate report supplied by a self-scoring device, however, can have an important instructional effect. Pressey also pointed out that such machines would increase efficiency in another way. Even in a small classroom the teacher usually knows that he is moving too slowly for some students and too fast for others. Those who could go faster are penalized, and those who should go slower are poorly taught and unnecessarily punished by criticism and failure. Machine instruction would permit each student to proceed at his own rate.

The "industrial revolution in education" which Pressey envisioned stubbornly refused to come about. In 1932 he expressed his disappointment. "The problems of invention are relatively simple," he wrote. "With a little money and engineering resource, a great deal could easily be done. The writer has found from bitter experience that one person alone can accomplish relatively little and he is regretfully dropping further work on these problems. But he hopes that enough may have been done to stimulate other workers, that this fascinating field may be developed."

Pressey's machines succumbed in part to cultural inertia; the world of education was not ready for them. But they also had limitations which probably contributed to their failure. Pressey was working against a background of psychological theory which had not come to grips with the learning process. The study of human learning was dominated by the "memory drum" and similar devices originally designed to study forgetting. Rate of learning was observed, but little was done to change it. Why the subject of such an experiment bothered to learn at all was of little interest. "Frequency" and "recency" theories of learning, and principles of "massed and spaced practice," concerned the conditions under which responses were remembered.

Pressey's machines were designed against this theoretical background. As versions of the memory drum, they were primarily testing devices. They were to be used after some amount of learning had already taken place elsewhere. By confirming correct responses and by weakening responses which should not have been acquired, a self-testing machine does, indeed, teach; but it is not designed primarily for that purpose. Nevertheless, Pressey seems to have been the first to emphasize the importance of immediate feedback in education and to propose a system in which each student could move at his own pace. He saw the need for

---

[1] The Navy's "Self Rater" is a larger version of Pressey's machine. The items are printed on code-punched plastic cards fed by the machine. The time required to answer is taken into account in scoring.

capital equipment in realizing these objectives. Above all he conceived of a machine which (in contrast with the audio-visual aids which were beginning to be developed) permitted the student to play an active role.

ANOTHER KIND OF MACHINE

The learning process is now much better understood. Much of what we know has come from studying the behavior of lower organisms, but the results hold surprisingly well for human subjects. The emphasis in this research has not been on proving or disproving theories but on discovering and controlling the variables of which learning is a function. This practical orientation has paid off, for a surprising degree of control has been achieved. By arranging appropriate "contingencies of reinforcement," specific forms of behavior can be set up and brought under the control of specific classes of stimuli. The resulting behavior can be maintained in strength for long periods of time. A technology based on this work has already been put to use in neurology, pharmacology, nutrition, psychophysics, psychiatry, and elsewhere (Skinner, 1957).

The analysis is also relevant to education. A student is "taught" in the sense that he is induced to engage in new forms of behavior and in specific forms upon specific occasions. It is not merely a matter of teaching him *what* to do; we are as much concerned with the probability that appropriate behavior will, indeed, appear at the proper time—an issue which would be classed traditionally under motivation. In education the behavior to be shaped and maintained is usually verbal, and it is to be brought under the control of both verbal and nonverbal stimuli. Fortunately, the special problems raised by verbal behavior can be submitted to a similar analysis (Skinner, 1957a).

If our current knowledge of the acquisition and maintenance of verbal behavior is to be applied to education, some sort of teaching machine is needed. Contingencies of reinforcement which change the behavior of lower organisms often cannot be arranged by hand; rather elaborate apparatus is needed. The human organism requires even more subtle instrumentation. An appropriate teaching machine will have several important features. The student must *compose* his response rather than select it from a set of alternatives, as in a multiple-choice self-rater. One reason for this is that we want him to recall rather than recognize —to make a response as well as see that it is right. Another reason is that effective multiple-choice material must contain plausible wrong responses, which are out of place in the delicate process of "shaping" behavior because they strengthen unwanted forms. Although it is much easier to build a machine to score multiple-choice answers than to evaluate a composed response, the technical advantage is outweighed by these and other considerations.

A second requirement of a minimal-teaching machine also distinguishes it from earlier versions. In acquiring complex behavior the student must pass through a carefully designed sequence of steps, often of considerable length. Each step must be so small that it can always be taken, yet in taking it the student moves somewhat closer to fully competent behavior. The machine must make sure that these steps are taken in a carefully prescribed order.

Several machines with the required characteristics have been built and tested. Sets of separate presentations or "frames" of visual material are stored on disks, cards, or tapes. One frame is presented at a time, adjacent frames being out of sight. In one type of machine the student composes a response by moving printed figures or letters (Skinner, 1954). His setting is compared by the machine with a coded response. If the two correspond, the machine automatically presents the next frame. If they do not, the response is cleared, and another must be composed. The student cannot proceed to a second step until the first has been taken. A machine of this kind is being tested in teaching spelling, arithmetic, and other subjects in the lower grades.

For more advanced students—from junior high school, say, through college—a machine which senses an arrangement of letters or figures is unnecessarily rigid in specifying form of response. Fortunately, such students may be asked to compare their responses with printed material revealed by the machine. . . . Material is printed in 30 radial frames on a 12-inch disk. The student inserts the disk and closes the machine. He cannot proceed until the machine has been locked, and, once he has begun, the machine cannot be unlocked. All but a corner of one frame is visible through a window. The student writes his response on a paper strip exposed through a second opening. By lifting a lever on the front of the machine, he moves what he has written under a transparent cover and uncovers the correct response in the remaining corner of the frame. If the two responses correspond, he moves the lever horizontally. This movement punches a hole in the paper opposite his response, recording the fact that he called it correct, and alters the machine so that the frame will not appear again when the student works around the disk a second time. Whether the response was correct or not, a second frame appears when the lever is returned to its starting position. The student proceeds in this way until he has responded to all frames. He then works around the disk a second time, but only those frames appear to which he has not correctly responded. When the disk revolves without stopping, the assignment is finished. (The student is asked to repeat each frame until a correct response is made to allow for the fact that, in telling him that a response is wrong, such a machine tells him what is right.)

The machine itself, of course, does not teach. It simply brings the student into contact with the person who composed the material it presents. It is a labor-saving device because it can bring one programmer into contact with an indefinite number of students. This may suggest mass production, but the effect upon each student is surprisingly like that of a private tutor. The comparison holds in several respects. (i) There is a constant interchange between program and student. Unlike lectures, textbooks, and the usual audio-visual aids, the machine induces sustained activity. The student is always alert and busy. (ii) Like a good tutor, the machine insists that a given point be thoroughly understood, either frame by frame or set by set, before the student moves on. Lectures, textbooks, and their mechanized equivalents, on the other hand, proceed without making sure that the student understands and easily leave him behind. (iii) Like a good tutor the machine presents just that material for which the student is ready. It asks him to take only that step which he is at the moment best equipped and most likely to take. (iv) Like a skillful tutor the machine helps the student to come up with the right answer. It does this in part through the orderly construction of the program and in part with techniques of hinting, prompting, suggesting, and so on, derived from an analysis of verbal behavior (Skinner, 1957a). (v) Lastly, of course, the machine, like the private tutor, reinforces the student for every correct response, using this immediate feedback not only to shape his behavior most efficiently but to maintain it in strength in a manner which the layman would describe as "holding the student's interest."

PROGRAMMING MATERIAL

The success of such a machine depends on the material used in it. The task of programming a given subject is at first sight rather formidable. Many helpful techniques can be derived from a general analysis of the relevant behavioral processes, verbal and nonverbal. Specific forms of behavior are to be evoked and, through differential reinforcement, brought under the control of specific stimuli.

This is not the place for a systematic review of available techniques, or of the kind of research which may be expected to discover others. However, the machines themselves cannot be adequately described without giving a few examples of programs. We may begin with a set of frames (see Table 1) designed to teach a third- or fourth-grade pupil to spell the word *manufacture*. The six frames are presented in the order shown, and the pupil moves sliders to expose letters in the open squares.

The word to be learned appears in bold face in frame 1, with an example and a simple definition. The pupil's first task is simply to copy it. When he does so correctly, frame 2 appears. He must now copy selectively: he must identify "fact" as the common part of "manufacture" and "factory." This helps him to spell the word and also to acquire a separable "atomic" verbal operant (Skinner, 1957a). In frame 3 another root must be copied selectively from "manual." In frame 4 the pupil must for the first time insert letters without copying. Since he is asked to insert the same letter in two places, a wrong response will be doubly conspicuous, and the chance of failure is thereby minimized. The same principle governs frame 5. In frame 6 the pupil spells the word to complete the sentence used as an example in frame 1. Even a poor student is likely to do this correctly because he has just composed or completed the word five times, has made two important root-responses, and has learned that two letters occur in the word twice. He has probably learned to spell the word without having made a mistake.

Teaching spelling is mainly a process of shaping complex forms of behavior. In other subjects—for example, arithmetic—responses must be brought under the control of appropriate stimuli. Unfortunately the ma-

Table 1. A Set of Frames Designed to Teach a Third- or Fourth-Grade Pupil to Spell the Word *manufacture.*

---

1. **Manufacture** means to make or build. *Chair factories manufacture chairs.* Copy the word here:

   □ □ □ □ □ □ □ □ □ □

2. Part of the word is like part of the word **factory**. Both parts come from an old word meaning *make* or *build*.

   m a n u □ □ □ □ **u r e**

3. Part of the word is like part of the word **manual**. Both parts come from an old word for *hand*. Many things used to be made by hand.

4. The same letter goes in both spaces:

   □ □ □ □ **f a c t u r e**

5. The same letter goes in both spaces:

   m □ **n u f** □ **c t u r e**

6. **Chair factories** □ □ □ □ □ □ □ □ □ □ **chairs.**

   m a n □ **f a c t** □ **r e**

---

terial which has been prepared for teaching arithmetic [2] does not lend itself to excerpting. The numbers 0 through 9 are generated in relation to objects, quantities, and scales. The operations of addition, subtraction, multiplication, and division are thoroughly developed before the number 10 is reached. In the course of this the pupil composes equations and expressions in a great variety of alternative forms. He completes not only $5 + 4 = \square$, but $\square + 4 = 9$, $5 \square 4 = 9$, and so on, aided in most cases by illustrative materials. No appeal is made to rote memorizing, even in the later acquisition of the tables. The student is expected to arrive at $9 \times 7 = 63$, not by memorizing it as he would memorize a line of poetry, but by putting into practice such principles as that nine times a number is the same as ten times the number minus the number (both of these being "obvious" or already well learned), that the digits in a multiple of nine add to nine, that in composing successive multiples of nine one counts backwards (*nine, eight*een, twenty-*seven*, thirty-*six*, and so on), that

[2] With the assistance of Susan R. Meyer.

nine times a single digit is a number beginning with one less than the digit (nine times *six* is *fif*ty something), and possibly even that the product of two numbers separated by only one number is equal to the square of the separating number minus one (the square of eight already being familiar from a special series of frames concerned with squares).

Programs of this sort run to great length. At five or six frames per word, four grades of spelling may require 20,000 or 25,000 frames, and three or four grades of arithmetic, as many again. If these figures seem large, it is only because we are thinking of the normal contact between teacher and pupil. Admittedly, a teacher cannot supervise 10,000 or 15,000 responses made by each pupil per year. But the pupil's time is not so limited. In any case, surprisingly little time is needed. Fifteen minutes per day on a machine should suffice for each of these programs, the machines being free for other students for the rest of each day. (It is probably because traditional methods are so inefficient that we have been led to suppose that education requires such a prodigious part of a young person's day.)

A simple technique used in programming material at the high-school or college level, by means of the machine . . . is exemplified in teaching a student to recite a poem. The first line is presented with several unimportant letters omitted. The student must read the line "meaningfully" and supply the missing letters. The second, third, and fourth frames present succeeding lines in the same way. In the fifth frame the first line reappears with other letters also missing. Since the student has recently read the line, he can complete it correctly. He does the same for the second, third, and fourth lines. Subsequent frames are increasingly incomplete, and eventually—say, after 20 or 24 frames—the student reproduces all four lines without external help, and quite possibly without having made a wrong response. The technique is similar to that used in teaching spelling: responses are first controlled by a text, but this is slowly reduced (colloquially, "vanished") until the responses can be emitted without a text, each member in a series of responses being now under the "intraverbal" control of other members.

"Vanishing" can be used in teaching other types of verbal behavior. When a student describes the geography of part of the world or the anatomy of part of the body, or names plants and animals from specimens or pictures, verbal responses are controlled by nonverbal stimuli. In setting up such behavior the student is first asked to report features of a fully labeled map, picture, or object, and the labels are then vanished. In teaching a map, for example, the machine asks the student to describe spatial relations among cities, countries, rivers, and so on, as shown on a fully labeled map. He is then asked to do the same with a map in which the names are incomplete or, possibly, lacking. Eventually he is asked to report the same relations with no map at all. If the material has been well programmed, he can do so correctly. Instruction is sometimes concerned not so much with imparting a new repertoire of verbal responses as with getting the student to describe something accurately in any available terms. The machine can "make sure the student understands" a graph, diagram, chart, or picture by asking him to identify and explain its features—correcting him, of course, whenever he is wrong.

In addition to charts, maps, graphs, models, and so on, the student may have access to auditory material. In learning to take dictation in a foreign language, for example, he selects a short passage on an indexing phonograph according to instructions given by the machine. He listens to the passage as often as necessary and then transcribes it. The machine then reveals the correct text. The student may listen to the passage again to discover the sources of any error. The indexing phonograph may also be used with the machine to teach other language skills, as well as tele-graphic code, music, speech, parts of literary and dramatic appreciation, and other subjects.

A typical program combines many of these functions. The set of frames shown in Table 2 is designed to induce the student of high-school physics to talk intelligently, and to some extent technically, about the emission of light from an incandescent source. In using the machine the student will write a word or phrase to complete a given item and then uncover the corresponding word or phrase shown here in the column at the right. The reader who wishes to get the "feel" of the material should cover the right-hand column with a card, uncovering each line only after he has completed the corresponding item.

Several programming techniques are exemplified by the set of frames in Table 2. Technical terms are introduced slowly. For example, the familiar term "fine wire" in frame 2 is followed by a definition of the technical term "filament" in frame 4; "filament" is then asked for in the presence of the non-scientific synonym in frame 5 and without the syn-onym in frame 9. In the same way "glow," "give off light," and "send out light" in early frames are followed by a definition of "emit" with a synonym in frame 7. Various inflected forms of "emit" then follow, and "emit" itself is asked for with a synonym in frame 16. It is asked for with-out a synonym but in a helpful phrase in frame 30, and "emitted" and "emission" are asked for without help in frames 33 and 34. The relation between temperature and amount and color of light is developed in several frames before a formal statement using the word "temperature" is asked for in frame 12. "Incandescent" is defined and used in frame 13, is used again in frame 14, and is asked for in frame 15, the student receiving a thematic prompt from the recurring phrase "incandescent source of light." A formal prompt is supplied by "candle." In frame 25 the new response "energy" is easily evoked by the words "form of . . ." because the expression "form of energy" is used earlier in the frame. "Energy" appears again in the next two frames and is finally asked for, without aid, in frame 28. Frames 30 through 35 discuss the limiting tem-peratures of incandescent objects, while reviewing several kinds of sources. The figure 800 is used in three frames. Two intervening frames then per-mit some time to pass before the response "800" is asked for.

Unwanted responses are eliminated with special techniques. If, for

Table 2. Part of a Program in High-School Physics. (The machine presents one item at a time. The student completes the item and then uncovers the corresponding word or phrase shown at the right.)

Sentence to be completed	Word to be supplied
1. The important parts of a flashlight are the battery and the bulb. When we "turn on" a flashlight, we close a switch which connects the battery with the ____.	bulb
2. When we turn on a flashlight, an electric current flows through the fine wire in the ____ and causes it to grow hot.	bulb
3. When the hot wire glows brightly, we say that it gives off or sends out heat and ____.	light
4. The fine wire in the bulb is called a filament. The bulb "lights up" when the filament is heated by the passage of a (n) ____ current.	electric
5. When a weak battery produces little current, the fine wire, or ____, does not get very hot.	filament
6. A filament which is *less* hot sends out or gives off ____ light.	less
7. "Emit" means "send out." The amount of light sent out, or "emitted," by a filament depends on how ____ the filament is.	hot
8. The higher the temperature of the filament the ____ the light emitted by it.	brighter, stronger
9. If a flashlight battery is weak, the ____ in the bulb may still glow, but with only a dull red color.	filament
10. The light from a very hot filament is colored yellow or white. The light from a filament which is not very hot is colored ____.	red
11. A blacksmith or other metal worker sometimes makes sure that a bar of iron is heated to a "cherry red" before hammering it into shape. He uses the ____ of the light emitted by the bar to tell how hot it is.	color
12. Both the color and the amount of light depend on the ____ of the emitting filament or bar.	temperature
13. An object which emits light because it is hot is called "incandescent." A flashlight bulb is an incandescent source of ____.	light
14. A neon tube emits light but remains cool. It is, therefore, not an incandescent ____ of light.	source
15. A candle flame is hot. It is a (n) ____ source of light.	incandescent
16. The hot wick of a candle gives off small pieces or particles of carbon which burn in the flame. Before or while burning, the hot particles send out, or ____, light.	emit
17. A long candlewick produces a flame in which oxygen does not reach all the carbon particles. Without oxygen the particles cannot burn. Particles which do not burn rise above the flame as ____.	smoke
18. We can show that there are particles of carbon in a candle flame, even when it is not smoking, by holding a piece of	

Sentence to be completed (cont.)	*Word to be supplied*
metal in the flame. The metal cools some of the particles before they burn, and the unburned carbon _____ collect on the metal as soot.	particles
19. The particles of carbon in soot or smoke no longer emit light because they are _____ than when they were in the flame.	cooler, colder
20. The reddish part of a candle flame has the same color as the filament in a flashlight with a weak battery. We might guess that the yellow or white parts of a candle flame are _____ than the reddish part.	hotter
21. "Putting out" an incandescent electric light means turning off the current so that the filament grows too _____ to emit light.	cold, cool
22. Setting fire to the wick of an oil lamp is called _____ the lamp.	lighting
23. The sun is our principal _____ of light, as well as of heat.	source
24. The sun is not only very bright but very hot. It is a powerful _____ source of light.	incandescent
25. Light is a form of energy. In "emitting light" an object changes, or "converts," one form of _____ into another.	energy
26. The electrical energy supplied by the battery in a flashlight is converted to _____ and _____.	heat, light; light, heat
27. If we leave a flashlight on, all the energy stored in the battery will finally be changed or _____ into heat and light.	converted
28. The light from a candle flame comes from the _____ released by chemical changes as the candle burns.	energy
29. A nearly "dead" battery may make a flashlight bulb warm to the touch, but the filament may still not be hot enough to emit light—in other words, the filament will not be _____ at that temperature.	incandescent
30. Objects, such as a filament, carbon particles, or iron bars, become incandescent when heated to about 800 degrees Celsius. At that temperature they begin to _____ _____.	emit light
31. When raised to any temperature above 800 degrees Celsius, an object such as an iron bar will emit light. Although the bar may melt or vaporize, its particles will be _____ no matter how hot they get.	incandescent
32. About 800 degrees Celsius is the lower limit of the temperature at which particles emit light. There is no upper limit of the _____ at which emission of light occurs.	temperature
33. Sunlight is _____ by very hot gases near the surface of the sun.	emitted
34. Complex changes similar to an atomic explosion generate the great heat which explains the _____ of light by the sun.	emission
35. Below about _____ degrees Celsius an object is not an incandescent source of light.	800

example, the second sentence in frame 24 were simply "It is a(n) _____ source of light," the two "very's" would frequently lead the student to fill the blank with "strong" or a synonym thereof. This is prevented by inserting the word "powerful" to make a synonym redundant. Similarly, in frame 3 the words "heat and" preempt the response "heat," which would otherwise correctly fill the blank.

The net effect of such material is more than the acquisition of facts and terms. Beginning with a largely unverbalized acquaintance with flashlights, candles, and so on, the student is induced to talk about familiar events, together with a few new facts, with a fairly technical vocabulary. He applies the same terms to facts which he may never before have seen to be similar. The emission of light from an incandescent source takes shape as a topic or field of inquiry. An understanding of the subject emerges which is often quite surprising in view of the fragmentation required in item building.

It is not easy to construct such a program. Where a confusing or elliptical passage in a textbook is forgivable because it can be clarified by the teacher, machine material must be self-contained and wholly adequate. There are other reasons why textbooks, lecture outlines, and film scripts are of little help in preparing a program. They are usually not logical or developmental arrangements of material but strategems which the authors have found successful under existing classroom conditions. The examples they give are more often chosen to hold the student's interest than to clarify terms and principles. In composing material for the machine, the programmer may go directly to the point.

A first step is to define the field. A second is to collect technical terms, facts, laws, principles, and cases. These must then be arranged in a plausible developmental order—linear if possible, branching if necessary. A mechanical arrangement, such as a card filing system, helps. The material is distributed among the frames of a program to achieve an arbitrary density. In the final composition of an item, techniques for strengthening asked-for responses and for transferring control from one variable to another are chosen from a list according to a given schedule in order to prevent the establishment of irrelevant verbal tendencies appropriate to a single technique. When one set of frames has been composed, its terms and facts are seeded mechanically among succeeding sets, where they will again be referred to in composing later items to make sure that the earlier repertoire remains active. Thus, the technical terms, facts, and examples in Table 2 have been distributed for reuse in succeeding sets on reflection, absorption, and transmission, where they are incorporated into items dealing mainly with other matters. Sets of frames for explicit review can, of course, be constructed. Further research will presumably discover other, possibly more effective, techniques. Meanwhile, it must be admitted that a considerable measure of art is needed in composing a successful program.

Whether good programming is to remain an art or to become a scientific technology, it is reassuring to know that there is a final authority—

the student. An unexpected advantage of machine instruction has proved to be the feedback to the *programmer*. In the elementary school machine, provision is made for discovering which frames commonly yield wrong responses, and in the high-school and college machine the paper strips bearing written answers are available for analysis. A trial run of the first version of a program quickly reveals frames which need to be altered, or sequences which need to be lengthened. One or two revisions in the light of a few dozen responses work a great improvement. No comparable feedback is available to the lecturer, textbook writer, or maker of films. Although one text or film may seem to be better than another, it is usually impossible to say, for example, that a given sentence on a given page or a particular sequence in a film is causing trouble.

Difficult as programming is, it has its compensations. It is a salutary thing to try to guarantee a right response at every step in the presentation of a subject matter. The programmer will usually find that he has been accustomed to leave much to the student—that he has frequently omitted essential steps and neglected to invoke relevant points. The responses made to his material may reveal surprising ambiguities. Unless he is lucky, he may find that he still has something to learn about his subject. He will almost certainly find that he needs to learn a great deal more about the behavioral changes he is trying to induce in the student. This effect of the machine in confronting the programmer with the full scope of his task may in itself produce a considerable improvement in education.

Composing a set of frames can be an exciting exercise in the analysis of knowledge. The enterprise has obvious bearings on scientific methodology. There are hopeful signs that the epistemological implications will induce experts to help in composing programs. The expert may be interested for another reason. We can scarcely ask a topflight mathematician to write a primer in second-grade arithmetic if it is to be used by the average teacher in the average classroom. But a carefully controlled machine presentation and the resulting immediacy of contact between programmer and student offer a very different prospect, which may be enough to induce those who know most about the subject to give some thought to the nature of arithmetical behavior and to the various forms in which such behavior should be set up and tested.

CAN MATERIAL BE TOO EASY?

The traditional teacher may view these programs with concern. He may be particularly alarmed by the effort to maximize success and minimize failure. He has found that students do not pay attention unless they are worried about the consequences of their work. The customary procedure has been to maintain the necessary anxiety by inducing errors. In recitation, the student who obviously knows the answer is not too often asked; a test item which is correctly answered by everyone is discarded as nondiscriminating; problems at the end of a section in a textbook in mathematics generally include one or two very difficult items; and so on. (The teacher-turned-programmer may be surprised to find this attitude affecting the construction of items. For example, he may find it difficult to allow an item to stand which "gives the point away." Yet if we can solve the motivational problem with other means, what is more effective than giving a point away?) Making sure that the student knows he doesn't know is a technique concerned with motivation, not with the learning process. Machines solve the problem of motivation in other ways. There is no evidence that what is easily learned is more readily forgotten. If this should prove to be the case, retention may be guaranteed by subsequent material constructed for an equally painless review.

The standard defense of "hard" material is that we want to teach more than subject matter. The student is to be challenged and taught to "think." The argument is sometimes little more than a rationalization for a confusing presentation, but it is doubtless true that lectures and texts are often inadequate and misleading by design. But to what end? What sort of "thinking" does the student learn in struggling through difficult material? It is true that those who learn under difficult conditions are better students, but are they better because they have surmounted difficulties or do they surmount them because they are better? In the guise of teaching thinking we set difficult and confusing situations and claim credit for the students who deal with them successfully.

The trouble with deliberately making education difficult in order to teach thinking is (i) that we must remain content with the students thus selected, even though we know that they are only a small part of the potential supply of thinkers, and (ii) that we must continue to sacrifice the teaching of subject matter by renouncing effective but "easier" methods. A more sensible program is to analyze the behavior called "thinking" and produce it according to specifications. A program specifically concerned with such behavior could be composed of material already available in logic, mathematics, scientific method, and psychology. Much would doubtless be added in completing an effective program. The machine has already yielded important relevant by-products. Immediate feedback encourages a more careful reading of programmed material than is the case in studying a text, where the consequences of attention or inattention are so long deferred that they have little effect on reading skills. The behavior involved in observing or attending to detail—as in inspecting charts and models or listening closely to recorded speech—is efficiently shaped by the contingencies arranged by the machine. And when an immediate result is in the balance, a student will be more likely to learn how to marshal relevant material, to concentrate on specific features of a presentation, to reject irrelevant materials, to refuse the easy but wrong solution, and to tolerate indecision, all of which are involved in effective thinking.

Part of the objection to easy material is that the student will come to depend on the machine and will be less able than ever to cope with the inefficient presentations of lectures, textbooks, films, and "real life." This is indeed a problem. All good teachers must "wean" their students, and the machine is no exception. The better the teacher, the more explicit must the weaning process be. The final stages of a program must be so designed that the student no longer requires the helpful conditions arranged by the machine. This can be done in many ways—among others by using the machine to discuss material which has been studied in other forms. These are questions which can be adequately answered only by further research.

No large-scale "evaluation" of machine teaching has yet been attempted. We have so far been concerned mainly with practical problems in the design and use of machines, and with testing and revising sample programs. The machine . . . was built and tested with a grant from the Fund for the Advancement of Education. Material has been prepared and tested with the collaboration of Lloyd E. Homme, Susan R. Meyer, and James G. Holland.[3] The self-instruction room . . . set up under this grant . . . contains ten machines and was recently used to teach part of a course in human behavior to Harvard and Radcliffe undergraduates. Nearly 200 students completed 48 disks (about 1400 frames) prepared with the collaboration of Holland. The factual core of the course was covered, corresponding to about 200 pages of the text (Skinner, 1953). The median time required to finish 48 disks was 14½ hours. The students were not examined on the material but were responsible for the text which overlapped it. Their reactions to the material and to self-instruction in general have been studied through interviews and questionnaires. Both the machines and the material are now being modified in the light of this experience, and a more explicit evaluation will then be made.

Meanwhile, it can be said that the expected advantages of machine instruction were generously confirmed. Unsuspected possibilities were revealed which are now undergoing further exploration. Although it is less convenient to report to a self-instruction room than to pick up a textbook in one's room or elsewhere, most students felt that they had much to gain in studying by machine. Most of them worked for an hour or more with little effort, although they often felt tired afterwards, and

[3] Dr. Homme prepared sets of frames for teaching part of college physics (kinematics), and Mrs. Meyer has prepared and informally tested material in remedial reading and vocabulary building at the junior high school level. Others who have contributed to the development of teaching machines should be mentioned. Nathan H. Azrin cooperated with me in testing a version of a machine to teach arithmetic. C. B. Ferster and Stanley M. Sapon (1958) used a simple "machine" to teach German. Douglas Porter (1958), of the Graduate School of Education at Harvard, has made an independent schoolroom test of machine instruction in spelling. Devra Cooper has experimented with the teaching of English composition for freshmen at the University of Kentucky. Thomas F. Gilbert, of the University of Georgia, has compared standard and machine instruction in an introductory course in psychology, and with the collaboration of J. E. Jewett has prepared material in algebra. The U.S. Naval Training Devices Center has recently contracted with the University of Pennsylvania for a study of programs relating to the machine instruction of servicemen, under the direction of Eugene H. Galanter.

they reported that they learned much more in less time and with less effort than in conventional ways. No attempt was made to point out the relevance of the material to crucial issues, personal or otherwise, but the students remained interested. (Indeed, one change in the reinforcing contingencies suggested by the experiment is intended to *reduce* the motivational level.) An important advantage proved to be that the student always knew when he stood, without waiting for an hour test or final examination.

SOME QUESTIONS

Several questions are commonly asked when teaching machines are discussed. Cannot the results of laboratory research on learning be used in education without machines? Of course they can. They should lead to improvements in textbooks, films, and other teaching materials. Moreover, the teacher who really understands the conditions under which learning takes place will be more effective, not only in teaching subject matter but in managing the class. Nevertheless, some sort of device is necessary to arrange the subtle contingencies of reinforcement required for optimal learning if each student is to have individual attention. In nonverbal skills this is usually obvious; texts and instructor can guide the learner but they cannot arrange the final contingencies which set up skilled behavior. It is true that the verbal skills, at issue here are especially dependent upon social reinforcement, but it must not be forgotten that the machine simply mediates an *essentially verbal* relation. In shaping and maintaining verbal knowledge we are not committed to the contingencies arranged through immediate personal contact.

Machines may still seem unnecessarily complex compared with other mediators such as workbooks or self-scoring test forms. Unfortunately, these alternatives are not acceptable. When material is adequately programmed, adjacent steps are often so similar that one frame reveals the response to another. Only some sort of mechanical presentation will make successive frames independent of each other. Moreover, in self-instruction an automatic record of the student's behavior is especially desirable, and for many purposes it should be fool-proof. Simplified versions of the present machines have been found useful—for example, in the work of Ferster and Sapon (1958), of Porter (1958), and of Gilbert—but the mechanical and economic problems are so easily solved that a machine with greater capabilities is fully warranted.

Will machines replace teachers? On the contrary, they are capital equipment to be used by teachers to save time and labor. In assigning certain mechanizable functions to machines, the teacher emerges in his proper role as an indispensable human being. He may teach more students than heretofore—this is probably inevitable if the worldwide demand for education is to be satisfied—but he will do so in fewer hours and with fewer burdensome chores. In return for his greater productivity he can ask society to improve his economic condition.

The role of the teacher may well be changed, for machine instruction will affect several traditional practices. Students may continue to be grouped in "grades" or "classes," but it will be possible for each to proceed at his own level, advancing as rapidly as he can. The other kind of "grade" will also change its meaning. In traditional practice a *C* means that a student has a smattering of a whole course. But if machine instruction assures mastery at every stage, a grade will be useful only in showing *how far* a student has gone. *C* might mean that he is halfway through a course. Given enough time he will be able to get an *A;* and since *A* is no longer a motivating device, this is fair enough. The quick student will meanwhile have picked up *A*'s in other subjects.

Differences in ability raise other questions. A program designed for the slowest student in the school system will probably not seriously delay the fast student, who will be free to progress at his own speed. (He may profit from the full coverage by filling in unsuspected gaps in his repertoire.) If this does not prove to be the case, programs can be constructed at two or more levels, and students can be shifted from one to the other as performances dictate. If there are also differences in "types of thinking," the extra time available for machine instruction may be used to present a subject in ways appropriate to many types. Each student will presumably retain and use those ways which he finds most useful. The kind of individual difference which arises simply because a student has missed part of an essential sequence (compare the child who has no "mathematical ability" because he was out with the measles when fractions were first taken up) will simply be eliminated.

OTHER USES

Self-instruction by machine has many special advantages apart from educational institutions. Home study is an obvious case. In industrial and military training it is often inconvenient to schedule students in groups, and individual instruction by machine should be a feasible alternative. Programs can also be constructed in subjects for which teachers are not available—for example, when new kinds of equipment must be explained to operators and repairmen, or where a sweeping change in method finds teachers unprepared (Menger, 1958). Education sometimes fails because students have handicaps which make a normal relationship with a teacher difficult or impossible. (Many blind children are treated today as feebleminded because no one has had the time or patience to make contact with them. Deaf-mutes, spastics, and others suffer similar handicaps.) A teaching machine can be adapted to special kinds of communication— as, for example, Braille—and, above all, it has infinite patience.

CONCLUSION

An analysis of education within the framework of a science of behavior has broad implications. Our schools, in particular our "progres-

sive" schools, are often held responsible for many current problems—
including juvenile delinquency and the threat of a more powerful foreign
technology. One remedy frequently suggested is a return to older techniques, especially to a greater "discipline" in schools. Presumably this
is to be obtained with some form of punishment, to be administered
either with certain classical instruments of physical injury—the dried
bullock's tail of the Greek teacher or the cane of the English school-
master—or as disapproval or failure, the frequency of which is to be increased by "raising standards." This is probably not a feasible solution.
Not only education but Western culture as a whole is moving away from
aversive practices. We cannot prepare young people for one kind of life
in institutions organized on quite different principles. The discipline of
the birch rod may facilitate learning, but we must remember that it also
breeds followers of dictators and revolutionists.

In the light of our present knowledge a school system must be called
a failure if it cannot induce students to learn except by threatening them
for not learning. That this has always been the standard pattern simply
emphasizes the importance of modern techniques. John Dewey was speaking for his culture and his time when he attacked aversive educational
practices and appealed to teachers to turn to positive and humane methods. What he threw out should have been thrown out. Unfortunately he
had too little to put in its place. Progressive education has been a tem-
porizing measure which can now be effectively supplemented. Aversive
practices can not only be replaced, they can be replaced with far more
powerful techniques. The possibilities should be thoroughly explored
if we are to build an educational system which will meet the present
demand without sacrificing democratic principles.

25 / A New Look at Classroom Discipline [1]

David P. Ausubel

*Many beginning teachers regard classroom discipline as an area in which
they have received little or no practical instruction and the problem
that worries them most in their day-to-day teaching. David P. Ausubel
of the University of Illinois discusses the attributes of democratic
classroom discipline, critically examines "permissiveness doctrines"*

[1] The concepts of classroom discipline advocated here are adapted from Ausubel
(1952, pp. 101–91, 465–71; 1954, pp. 235–38, 480–81; 1958, pp. 374–76, 440–43).

Reprinted from *Phi Delta Kappan*, 1961, *43*, 25–30, with the permission of the author
and Phi Delta Kappa.

which misinterpret and distort the ideal of democratic classroom
discipline, and suggests correctives.

A few years ago, in one of our better New England high schools, two members of the school's counseling staff happened to be walking in the building when their attention was drawn to sounds of a disturbance in an adjoining corridor. Investigating further, they found that two boys, surrounded by a knot of curious onlookers, were engaged in an all-out switchblade fight. One counselor quickly whispered to the other, "We'd better break this up in a hurry before there's bloodshed." The latter replied heatedly, "For heaven's sake leave them alone or you'll ruin everything! Do you want the kids to think we are *disciplinarians?*" Fortunately, however, the native common sense of the first counselor prevailed over the doctrinaire permissiveness of his colleague, and a near-tragedy was averted.

This true story is admittedly a bit extreme and unrepresentative of disciplinary attitudes in American public schools. Nevertheless, somewhat less extreme versions occur frequently enough to suggest that American teachers are more confused and disturbed about matters of discipline today than at any previous time in the history of our public school system.

It is true that superficial observation does not support this conclusion. On the surface, practically everything *appears* the same as it was ten years ago when, except in the so-called "Blackboard Jungles," these same teachers seemed supremely confident that the ideal of democratic discipline had been achieved in the American classroom. Substantially the same disciplinary philosophy is still preached in our teachers' colleges; and teachers, by and large, still practice the same kind of discipline they practiced a decade ago.

To be sure, there is still an appreciable gap between the theory of discipline as taught in colleges of education, and discipline as it is actually conceived and practiced in the schools. For example, in a recent survey conducted by the National Education Association, 72 per cent of the responding classroom teachers favored the judicious use of corporal punishment in the elementary school. But the gap is no greater now than it has ever been. In everyday disciplinary practice, American teachers have never gone along completely with the more extreme ideas of educational theorists. Elementary and high school teachers, after all, have to be realistic in handling problems of discipline because they encounter them daily in doing their jobs. Unlike professors of education who, rarely if ever, have to cope with disciplinary problems in the classroom, they can ill afford to be starry-eyed about these matters.

Why then should teachers be suddenly confused and disturbed about issues of discipline? Closer scrutiny reveals that everything is not *really* the same as it used to be. One important factor in the situation has undergone significant change: Although educational theory in the field of classroom discipline has remained virtually unchanged over the past two decades, the pendulum of public opinion in recent years has been swinging further and further away from the formerly fashionable cult of permissiveness. As a result, a growing estrangement has arisen between the general public, on the one hand, and educational and psychological theorists, on the other—with the classroom teacher and the rank-and-file school administrator caught squarely in the middle. Teachers, of course, were also in the middle throughout the entire period of approximately 1935–1955 when American classroom discipline underwent a process of extensive democratization. But this middle position was decidedly more comfortable then than it is now, because all three groups—educational theorists, teachers, and the public at large—were moving toward the same culturally desirable goal of a less authoritarian classroom climate.

It is true that these three groups were moving toward this goal at quite different rates. Permissiveness, nondirective guidance, and the cults of extroversion, conformity, and social adjustment were much more extreme among child-centered educators, client-centered counselors and psychoanalytically trained child study experts than among American parents and teachers generally. By 1955, however, the entirely laudable objective of more democratic pupil-teacher relationships had been reached, and perhaps overreached. Public opinion began moving away from permissiveness, but educational and psychological theorists and professors of education, with few exceptions, stood their ground tenaciously. The same relatively extreme permissive doctrines of discipline are still dominant in teachers' colleges, even though educational philosophy in the post-Sputnik era has generally become less permissive in most other areas such as curriculum.

Now, it was one thing for teachers to swim in the middle of two streams moving in the same historically necessary direction, and to enjoy the approbation of both the general public and of their own professional leaders. It is quite another for them to be caught between two opposing streams, and to be faced with the problem of having to choose between the spirit of the times, on the one hand, and the historically obsolete ideological extremism of their former professors, on the other.

HISTORICAL AND CULTURAL PERSPECTIVE

Before examining how particular concepts and practices of discipline have gone astray, it might be profitable first to view the problem in historical perspective within a broader cultural context. The revolution in classroom discipline that swept American schools between 1935 and 1955 was as necessary as it was inevitable. Teacher-pupil relationships had to be brought into closer alignment with the general spirit of adult egalitarianism in American society; and a more desirable balance had to be achieved between the actual dependence of children on adult direction and their realistic capacities for exercising self-direction and self-discipline. It was inevitable, of course, that we would go too far in redressing the balance—in overdoing the permissiveness and in cutting back adult control and guidance too drastically. Much more serious, however, were the deplorable consequences of de-emphasizing certain other traditional American values in the enthusiasm of democratizing adult-child relationships.

Thus, in stressing the inherent right of children to receive the consideration to which they are entitled, we have neglected the equally valid claims of age and maturity. In debunking superficial and unilateral forms of etiquette, we have lost sight of the importance of genuine courtesy in human relationships. And in attacking despotic and abusive adult rule, we have failed to culivate appropriate respect for just and rightful authority.

By respect for age I do not mean uncritical veneration or ancestor worship, but simply the consideration that is due all human beings at any stage in the life cycle. Yet our cultural attitude toward middle-aged and elderly persons tends to be patronizing and slightly contemptuous. Because they quite understandably lack the exuberance and venturesomeness of youth they are often cavalierly dismissed as "has-beens" or as bumbling, ineffectual "fuddy-duddies."

Courtesy is another of our most valuable cultural assets that was overlooked in the frenzy of extending democracy to home and school. It is fashionable in many quarters—not only among the younger set—to regard good manners and the more subtle amenities of interpersonal relationships as hollow formalities. But even the highly stylized bowing ceremony of the Japanese is far from being an empty gesture. It symbolizes deep and culturally ingrained respect for the dignity of the individual and genuine concern for his pride and feelings. Although bowing is obviously incongruous with our modern way of life, concern for the pride, feelings, and dignity of every human being is one of our most cherished American values. Hence, since courtesy is basically an institutionalized set of rules designed to safeguard and implement this legitimate cultural concern, those who sneer at courtesy, whether they realize it or not, sneer at nothing less than human dignity.

Finally, our culture has tended to put authority figures in an anomalous and untenable position, particularly in the school environment. We have assigned them the necessary and often distasteful task of authority figures the world over, that is, to enforce certain basic standards of conduct; but in too many instances we have failed to give them the respect, the authority, and the protection commensurate with this responsibility. When they conscientiously attempt to apply without fear or favor the community approved sanctions for violating these standards, we accuse them of being punitive, vindictive, and authoritarian. School administrators, of course, are not above criticism and reproach when they use poor judgment or exceed their authority; but society has an obligation to protect them from disrespect and abuse for simply doing their duty and exercising their just and necessary disciplinary prerogatives. In our present cultural climate, therefore, it is small wonder that many principals and superintendents of schools are more concerned with courting general popularity than with enforcing desirable norms of pupil behavior.

THE BRIGHTER SIDE OF THE COIN

In pointing out some of the failings of our recent approach to discipline, I do not mean to detract in any way from our genuine accomplishments. The latter are extremely impressive when compared with disciplinary practices in many other countries. I recently had an opportunity to study secondary schools in New Zealand, an English-speaking welfare state of British origin with a pioneering tradition not unlike our own. School discipline in New Zealand high schools connotes explicit subjection to authority and implicit habits of obedience that are enforced by a very heavy-handed set of controls and punishments. It implies a very identifiable atmosphere of classroom control which the teacher maintains with much deliberate effort—in much the same sense that he strives to have his pupils understand and assimilate the subject-matter he teaches.

By contrast, the American approach to discipline seems laudably incidental. Our teachers tend to feel that the cause of discipline is adequately served if pupils exercise sufficient self-control and observe a minimum set of rules with sufficient decorum to enable classroom work to proceed in an orderly, efficient manner. They do not, in other words, strive deliberately for discipline as an explicit goal in its own right. They assume instead that good discipline is *ordinarily* a natural by-product of interesting lessons and of a wholesome teacher-pupil relationship; that the vast majority of pupils respond positively to fair and kindly treatment; that respect for the teacher is a usual accompaniment of the latter's superior knowledge, experience, and status as a leader, and does not have to be reinforced by such artificial props and status symbols as differences in clothing, mode of address, and fear of the strap. Hence they treat adolescents as maturing young adults rather than as unruly children, and implicitly expect them to respond in kind—which they usually do. And it was a very gratifying experience to discover that despite the absence of strict authoritarian controls, American high school students, on the whole, behave more decorously than their New Zealand counterparts—particularly when not under direct supervision.

SCIENCE OR OPINION

Discipline today is much less a science than a matter of opinion. It not only shifts in response to various social, economic, and ideological factors, but also manifests all of the cyclical properties of fads and fashions. Objective scientific evidence about the relative merits of different types of discipline is extremely sparse. Indeed it is highly questionable to what extent valid empirical data are obtainable and even relevant in matters of discipline. Whether or not particular disciplinary practices are appropriate depends, in the first place, on the particular values, institutions, and kinds of personal relationships prevailing in a given culture; and, second, any definitive empirical test of appropriateness would have to be conducted over such an extended period of time that its conclusions would tend to be rendered obsolete by intervening changes in significant social conditions. For all practical purposes, therefore, the choice of disciplinary policy involves taking a rationally defensible and self-consistent position based on value preferences, relevant considerations of child development, and on individual experience and judgment.

Because discipline cannot be placed on a largely scientific basis, however, does not mean that one position is as good as another or that no public policy whatsoever is warranted. Society is continually obliged to resolve issues of much greater moment with even less objective evidence on which to base a decision. Under the circumstances all we can reasonably expect is greater humility and less dogmatism on the part of those engaged in formulating disciplinary policy. Thus, the most disturbing aspect of the entire problem is not the fact that there is precious little scientific evidence to support the disciplinary doctrines expounded in our colleges of education and educational journals and textbooks, but rather the ubiquitous tendency to represent purely personal opinions and biases, as if they were incontrovertibly established findings of scientific research.

THE DEFINITION AND FUNCTIONS OF DISCIPLINE

By discipline I mean the imposition of *external* standards and controls on individual conduct. Permissiveness, on the other hand, refers to the absence of such standards and controls. To be permissive is to "let alone," to adopt a laissez-faire policy. Authoritarianism is an excessive, arbitrary, and autocratic type of control which is diametrically opposite to permissiveness. Between the extremes of laissez-faire permissiveness and authoritarianism are many varieties and degrees of control. One of these, to be described in greater detail below, is democratic discipline.

Discipline is a universal cultural phenomenon which generally serves four important functions in the training of the young. First, it is necessary for socialization—for learning the standards of conduct that are approved and tolerated in any culture. Second, it is necessary for normal personality maturation—for acquiring such adult personality traits as dependability, self-reliance, self-control, persistence, and ability to tolerate frustration. These aspects of maturation do not occur spontaneously, but only in response to sustained social demands and expectations. Third, it is necessary for the internalization of moral standards and obligations or, in other words, for the development of conscience. Standards obviously cannot be internalized unless they also exist in external form; and even after they are effectively internalized, universal cultural experience suggests that external sanctions are still required to insure the stability of the social order. Lastly, discipline is necessary for children's emotional security. Without the guidance provided by unambiguous external controls, they tend to feel bewildered and apprehensive. Too great a burden is placed on their own limited capacity for self-control.

DEMOCRATIC DISCIPLINE

The proponents of democratic classroom discipline believe in imposing the minimal degree of external control necessary for socialization, personality maturation, conscience development, and the emotional security of the child. Discipline and obedience are not regarded as ends in themselves but only as means to these latter ends. They are not striven for deliberately, but are expected to follow naturally in the wake of friendly and realistic teacher-pupil relationships. Explicit limits are not set routinely or as ways of showing "who is boss," but only as the need arises, i.e., when they are not implicitly understood or accepted by pupils.

Democratic discipline is as rational, nonarbitrary, and bilateral as possible. It provides explanations, permits discussion, and invites the participation of children in the setting of standards whenever they are qualified to do so. Above all it implies respect for the dignity of the individual, and avoids exaggerated emphasis on status differences and barriers between free communication. Hence it repudiates harsh, abusive, and vindictive forms of punishment, and the use of sarcasm, ridicule, and intimidation.

The aforementioned attributes of democratic classroom discipline are obviously appropriate in cultures such as ours where social relationships tend to be egalitarian. This type of discipline also becomes increasingly more feasible as children become older, more responsible, and more capable of understanding and formulating rules of conduct based on concepts of equity and reciprocal obligation. But contrary to what the extreme permissivists would have us believe, democratic school discipline does not imply freedom from all external constraints, standards, and direction, or freedom from discipline as an end in itself. And under no circumstances does it presuppose the eradication of all distinctions between pupil and teacher roles, or require that teachers abdicate responsibility for making the final decisions in the classroom.

DISTORTIONS OF DEMOCRATIC DISCIPLINE

Many educational theorists have misinterpreted and distorted the ideal of democratic discipline by equating it with an extreme form of permissiveness. These distortions have been dogmatically expressed in various psychologically unsound and unrealistic propositions that are considered sacrosanct in many teachers' colleges. Fortunately, however, most classroom teachers have only accepted them for examination purposes—while still in training—and have discarded them in actual practice as thoroughly unworkable.

According to one widely held doctrine, only "positive" forms of discipline are constructive and democratic. It is asserted that children must only be guided by reward and approval; that reproof and punishment are authoritarian, repressive, and reactionary expressions of adult hostility which leave permanent emotional scars on children's personalities. What these theorists conveniently choose to ignore, however, is the fact that it is impossible for children to learn what is *not* approved and tolerated, simply by generalizing in reverse from the approval they receive for behavior that *is* acceptable. Even adults are manifestly incapable of learning and respecting the limits of acceptable conduct unless the distinction between what is proscribed and approved is reinforced by punishment as well as by reward. Furthermore, there is good reason to believe that acknowledgment of wrong-doing and acceptance of punishment are part and parcel of learning moral accountability and developing a sound conscience. Few if any children are quite that fragile that they cannot take deserved reproof and punishment in stride.

A second widespread distortion of democratic discipline is reflected in the popular notion that there are no culpably misbehaving children in the classroom, but only culpably aggressive, unsympathetic, and punitive teachers. If children misbehave, according to this point of view, one can implicitly assume that they must have been provoked beyond endurance by repressive and authoritarian classroom discipline. Similarly, if they are disrespectful, then the teacher, by definition, must not have been deserving of respect. It is true, of course, that much pupil misconduct *is* instigated by harsh and abusive school discipline; but there are also innumerable reasons for out-of-bounds behavior that are completely independent of the teacher's attitudes and disciplinary practices. Pupils are also influenced by factors originating in the home, the neighborhood, the peer group, and the mass-media. Some children are emotionally disturbed, others are brain-damaged, and still others are aggressive by temperament; and there are times when even the best behaved children from the nicest homes develop an irresistible impulse—without any provocation whatsoever—to test the limits of a teacher's forbearance.

Both of the aforementioned distortions of classroom democracy are used to justify the commonly held belief among educators that pupils should not be reproved or punished for disorderly or discourteous conduct. I have, for example, observed classrooms where everybody talks at once; where pupils turn their backs on the teacher and engage in private conversation while the latter is endeavoring to instruct them; and where pupils verbally abuse teachers for exercising their rightful disciplinary prerogatives. Some educators contend that all of this is compatible with wholesome, democratic teacher-pupil relationships. Other educators deplore this type of pupil behavior but insist, nevertheless, that punishment is unwarranted under these circumstances. In the first place, they assert, reproof or punishment constitutes a "negative" and hence axiomatically undesirable approach to classroom management; and, secondly, the misbehavior would assuredly have never occurred to begin with, if the teacher's attitudes had been less autocratic or antagonistic. I have already answered the second group of educators, and to the first group I can only say that I am still sufficiently old-fashioned to believe that rudeness and unruliness are not normally desirable classroom behavior in any culture.

When such misconduct occurs, I believe pupils have to be unambiguously informed that it will not be tolerated and that any repetition of the same behavior will be punished. This action does not preclude in any way either an earnest attempt to discover why the misbehavior occurred, or suitable preventive measures aimed at correcting the underlying causes. But, by the same token, the mere fact that a pupil has a valid psychological reason for misbehaving does not mean that he is thereby absolved from moral accountability or rendered no longer subject to punishment.

Still another related distortion of democratic discipline is reflected in the proposition that it is repressive and authoritarian to request pupils to apologize for discourteous behavior or offensive language. However if we take seriously the idea that the dignity of the human being is important, we must be willing to protect it from affront; and apology is the most civilized and effective means mankind has yet evolved for accomplishing this goal. In a democratic society nobody is that important that he is above apologizing to those persons whom he wrongfully offends. Everybody's dignity is important—the teacher's as well as the pupil's. It is no less wrong for a pupil to abuse a teacher than for a teacher to abuse a pupil.

If apologies are to have any real significance in moral training, however, it is obvious that, even though they are explicitly requested, they must be made voluntarily, and must be reflective of genuine appreciation of wrong-doing and of sincere regret and remorse. Purely formal and mechanical statements of apology made under coercion are less than worthless. Apologies are also without real ethical import unless their basis is reciprocal, i.e., unless it is fully understood that under comparable circumstances the teacher would be willing to apologize to his pupils.

A final distortion of democratic classroom discipline associated with the extreme child-centered approach to education is the notion that children are equipped in some mysterious fashion for knowing precisely what is best for them. Empirical "proof" of this proposition is adduced from the fact that nutrition is adequately maintained and existing deficiency conditions are spontaneously corrected when infants are permitted to select their own diet. If the child can successfully choose his diet, runs the argument, he must certainly know what is best for him in *all* areas of development, including curriculum and classroom management.

This doctrine, however, has even less face validity than the three other distorted concepts of school discipline. Because the human being is sensitive in early childhood to internal cues of physiological need, we cannot conclude that he is similarly sensitive to complex intellectual and moral needs, or that he has sufficient experience, perspective, and judgment to make intelligent decisions in these latter areas. Even in the field of nutrition, self-selection is a reliable criterion of need only during early infancy. The current interests and opinions of immature pupils can hardly be considered reliable guideposts and adequate substitutes for seasoned judgment in designing a curriculum or in formulating rules of classroom behavior. Hence, while it is reasonable to consider the views of pupils in these matters, teachers and school administrators cannot abdicate their responsibility for making the final decisions.

WHAT NEEDS TO BE DONE

In seeking to correct these undesirable permissive distortions of classroom democracy, it would be foolhardy to return to the equally undesirable opposite extreme of authoritarianism that flourished in this country up to a quarter of a century ago, and still prevails in many western nations. Democratic school discipline is still an appropriate and realistic goal for American education; hence there is no need to throw away the baby with the bath water. It is only necessary to discard the aforementioned permissivist doctrines masquerading under the banners of democracy and behavioral science, and to restore certain other traditional American values that have been neglected in the enthusiasm of extending democracy to home and school.

More specifically, we first have to clear up the semantic confusion. We should stop equating permissiveness with democratic discipline, and realistic adult control and guidance with authoritarianism. Permissiveness, by definition, is the absence of discipline, democratic or otherwise. We should cease instructing teachers that it is repressive and reactionary to reprove or punish pupils for misconduct, or to request them to apologize for offensive and discourteous behavior.

Second, we should stop misinterpreting what little reputable evidence we have about discipline, and refrain from misrepresenting our personal biases on the subject as the indisputably established findings of scientific research. The available evidence merely suggests that in our type of cultural setting, authoritarian discipline has certain undesirable effects—*not* that the consequences of laissez-faire permissiveness are desirable. As a matter of fact, research studies show that the effects of extreme permissiveness are just as unwholesome as are those of authoritarianism. In the school situation a laissez-faire policy leads to confusion, insecurity, and competition for power among pupils. Assertive pupils tend to become aggressive and ruthless, whereas retiring pupils tend to withdraw further from classroom participation. The child who is handled too permissively at home tends to regard himself as a specially privileged person. He fails to learn the normative standards and expectations of society, to set realistic goals for himself, and to make reasonable demands on others. In his dealings with adults and other children he is domineering, aggressive, petulant, and capricious.

Third, we should stop making teachers feel guilty and personally responsible for all instances of misconduct and disrespect in the classroom. We do this whenever we take for granted, without any actual supporting evidence, that these behavior problems would never have arisen in the first place if the teachers involved were truly deserving of respect and had been administering genuinely wholesome and democratic discipline.

Finally, teachers' colleges should terminate the prevailing conspiracy of silence they maintain about the existence of disciplinary problems in the public schools. Although discipline is the one aspect of teaching that the beginning teacher is most worried about, he receives little or no practical instruction in handling this problem. Colleges of education, as pointed out above, rationalize their inadequacies in this regard by pretending that disciplinary problems are relatively rare occurrences involving the disturbed child, or more typically the disturbed teacher. Due respect for the facts of life, however, suggests that prospective teachers today not only need to be taught more realistic propositions about the nature and purposes of democratic discipline, but also require adequately supervised, down-to-earth experience in coping with classroom discipline.

26 / The Whole Child: A Fresh Look

Harold Taylor

Harold Taylor, former president of Sarah Lawrence College, believes that a fresh look at "the whole child" is needed and proposes that "the educator must have an image of the child in the reality of his school and his society."

The real quarrel between the conservatives and the liberals in education is about the kind of society they wish to live in. The conservatives want more control over children and more stability in the society; the liberals want more freedom and more change.

But the issue between them is seldom put in these terms. Instead, each is inclined to attack and defend abstractions. Attacks are made on "progressive education" and the "philosophy of John Dewey," which is equated with "life adjustment," "doorbell ringing," "play projects,"

Reprinted from the *Saturday Review*, December 16, 1961, *44*, 42–43, 57–58, with the permission of the author and Saturday Review, Inc.

"citizenship courses," and the "child-centered school" where it is said precious time is wasted on the child's psyche while he gropes for his own conclusions and his own identity. He should be taught the hard subjects under strong discipline.

On the other hand, progressive ideas and programs are too often defended by their proponents as if critics had no right to raise questions, as if the ideas and practices on which their theories rest were valid for all time. The progressives must again become progressive.

For example, there is merit in the criticism of the kind of false liberalism that tries to overcome intellectual and social inequality by smothering it in sentiment. There are differences in the capacities of children and there are differences in their social status. They know it, their parents know it, their teachers know it. The task of the educator, liberal or otherwise, is to deal directly with these differences and to take the children where they are. If children are slow learners, it is no kindness to them to act as if they weren't. Nor does it help them to hold the others back in order not to damage the confidence of the slow. This may have the opposite effect if what they really need is to learn how to learn. If children are culturally undernourished, have little vocabulary, come from poor and broken homes, what they need is not merely liberal sentiment but direct action by teachers who understand how to deal with their deficiencies.

The conservative's program of higher academic standards and more subject matter misses the entire point; the problem of the slum child is a total problem. If the slum child is also a Negro, Puerto Rican, a Mexican, in America he is segregated socially, economically, physically and mentally all at once. The problem is poverty, poverty of every kind—cultural, intellectual, economic, and emotional.

The educator must go to the root of the matter, and he must deal with the whole child. The root is in the social and economic conditions in which the child exists. The educator must deal bluntly with those who support the residential segregation of the colored people and the poor. He must fight those who wish to profit in real estate at the expense of the children. He must think of education as a total process, in which the conditions of society deeply affect the child's mind, the level of his achievement, and the range of his possibilities. The curriculum, the classroom, the guidance office are instruments for dealing with one part of the child's life. But they do not and cannot function in a social vacuum.

Nor is it permissible any longer to say that the social environment of the child is not the problem of the educator, that it belongs to city planners, social workers, economists, housing experts, or society. It belongs to everyone, but most of all to the educator. The educator is not a personnel manager, an administrator, an organization man, although his work involves organizing, managing, and administering. He is a social and intellectual leader, and he begins to exercise his leadership when he recognizes the conditions of his society and brings to bear upon them the force of a humanitarian philosophy.

It is in exactly this matter that the conservatives and the liberals alike have failed; the conservatives by turning their backs on it and concerning themselves with the "gifted," the intellectually well-to-do, and cultivation of an elite; the liberals by failing to extend into practice the implications of their own philosophy. The conservatives have been quite clear in their view that education is a stabilizing force, concerned with the transmission of the culture from generation to generation, and acting as a sorting device for the social classes. The liberals have been equally clear that education is an instrument of social change, through which a society may reform itself upon the initiative of its citizens.

But in practice, the liberals and the progressives have addressed themselves of late, not to the deeper questions of social and cultural change, but to a fairly narrow range of emotional problems to be found in the young, and to the development of new techniques for learning. They have tended to equate democracy with tolerance and good feeling, while the real questions have to do with the radical extension of democracy itself. The work of the progressives has for the most part been carried out in the suburbs where they have been content to accept the *status quo* of a segregated, white, and affluent society while they adapt their methods and ideas to the needs of a suburban clientele.

These community needs have become more and more directed to the improvement of status and are expressed in the desire, sometimes mounting to compulsion, to have children attend schools, colleges, and universities that confer that status. The tendency of the progressives has been to accept without a struggle the legitimacy of all such values, provided they are held by a suitable number of people of respectable means and appropriate social position. The educators have joined the establishment.

At a time when conservatives are becoming more conservative, and often turning into radical reactionaries, the liberals have thus lost their initiative and have been drawn along in the wake of their adversaries. The progressives, that educational wing of the liberal movement, have stayed behind the line of battle.

There are many reasons for this, among them a national confusion about where the line of battle really is. It is too often put at that point where the antagonisms between the United States and the Soviet Union intersect, and educators have been pressed into the role of civilian-soldiers on our side of the line. We are at present so absorbed in competition with the Russians that Americans are now using the Russian arguments for a controlled educational system, including the argument that more scientific and technical subject matter applied more stringently to all will produce high school and college graduates who will strengthen the national security.

At a time when education is publicly regarded as an instrument of national policy (in itself a dangerous and misleading assumption), it follows that we place our main emphasis on classifying and selecting for special treatment those students who are already scholastically able, rather than tackling the bigger question of how to correct the social and economic conditions that stunt children's intellectual growth in the first place. There is no more dramatic instance of this neglect of the main issue than in our failure to provide even a minimal basis for financing the American educational system through federal aid. We have put the money into a $50 billion military budget, because that is where we think the national interest lies.

In fact, our national interest lies in the construction of a strong and vigorous educational system, reaching into the entire range of the country's population for the discovery and encouragement of every kind of talent that exists there. Some of the most promising of the young are to be found in the city slums, in the Negro ghettos of the Southern states, in the industrial areas of the north where only half the children finish high school. Some of the most talented are not in school at all. We have the money and we must spend it in massive amounts to clear out the educational slums, to take the action that will give us schools and communities across the country which are truly integrated in a racial, economic, and social democracy. Once we tackle the educational question head-on we are on the way to solving the social problem.

At the present time our policies are constructing a class system, not a democracy. We lack a social dimension in our educational planning, and we work almost exclusively in terms of the academic curriculum, the measurement of I.Q., the pressure for academic achievement. An education has come to be considered as a way of moving into a higher social class than the one into which a person is born; it is a means of increasing personal income.

The time has come for a new progressive movement that can push once more to the front edge of educational and social change. There are some who are already there, educators like those who began their pioneer work at the George Washington High School in New York, where the education of the child in a depressed area was considered a total problem, not merely a lack of high I.Q. levels in the student body.[1]

The main effort was to enrich the child's total experience by using the whole of New York City and its arts and culture as the educational environment, by extending the range of possibility for all the children beyond the limits of their local streets, by reaching out to the children and their parents with sympathetic guidance and improved instruction in every segment of the curriculum. The success of that project, now grown to the Higher Horizons program and spreading through similar efforts around the country, is a clear sign of the direction we must go. The success is to be measured, not simply by how many children who were formerly deprived of good education are now able to attend universities, but by how all of the children in school have been educated up to the limits of their particular talent, and how the community itself has been enriched and changed by the increase in knowledge and the lift in attitude. The recruitment, on a national scale, of hundreds of young college

[1] [See selection 56 in this volume.]

graduates to teach in these communities, and to enter into the life of the community itself, would have an immediate effect on the improvement of these areas. We need a Peace Corps for our own educational system.

There are others who form the vanguard for a new progressive movement to be found among those who are pressing toward a new conception of the child's mind and his capacity to learn. These are men and women who, like Jerome Bruner in his experimental work at Harvard, are dealing directly with children to find the best ways in which they can learn, and who collaborate actively with scholars from the university and teachers from the schools to infuse the subject-matter of the school curriculum with ideas drawn from modern discoveries in science, mathematics, literature and the arts.

Too often in the past, those progressives who worked with the concept of the whole child made their own separation of the intellect from the emotions, and the child from his society, by placing primary emphasis on the child's psychic security and emotional comfort. The particular contribution of the "whole child" concept to education in this century has been to turn the educator's attention to the psychic development of the child and to the way in which his personal relations, his emotions, his ability to learn and to build a character are directly affected by the social and psychological environment of the classroom and the school. In part this was a reaction against the rigidity and insensitivity of traditional school practices. In part it was a new and fascinating theory of learning and of personality development which has dominated modern thought since the century began.

But the original concept of the whole child has become corrupted by use and misuse into something no longer recognizable in the original. There are many who have accepted modern ideas without understanding them, and have developed a simple-minded psychology which holds that as long as there is good feeling and "warm" relationships there is healthy emotional development. Or, conversely, that in order to preserve the sense of worth and the feeling of confidence in the child it is necessary never to express or convey negative judgments or to carry out direct instruction.

What may very well happen here is that you get neither emotional nor intellectual maturity, but instead sloppy work, under-achievement, and unstable emotions. Freud's point was that neuroses in later life could be traced back to traumatic experiences in childhood. He did not argue that all negative experiences and prohibitions in childhood are traumatic. In fact, the removal of authority and of critical judgment on the part of the teacher may leave the child to wallow in a mass of indecision, or, in the case of the adolescent, to spend so much time in self-concern, question-raising and in rationalizing his indolence that there is no longer any inclination toward responsibility. The child may begin to feel that he must be forgiven everything, and failure to meet sensible standards may be called by dozens of forgiving psychological names.

The conservatives are now legitimate in their criticism of that kind of "adjustment" which adjusts moral and intellectual scruples right out of the educational situation. It is wise for a child to know that there are certain things to which a teacher and a society should not be expected to adjust. A recent statement from a group of psychiatrists describes an effort on their part to develop drugs which will, they hope, lead to the control of disgust, pique, resentment and other emotions, and in the long run instill "altruism, brotherly love and scientific creativity." For certain situations and certain actions there can be no more healthy emotion than that of disgust, and I would hate to see it done away with.

Some of those who equate modernism in education to the necessity of being permissive in every situation are using their personal response to children as a kind of drug in exactly this sense. True learning comes from engaged effort in the right circumstances. It does not spring full-blown from the unconscious, nor should it be overly protected from the reality into which it goes. The necessity for meeting clear criteria of achievement is one of the spurs to creative effort. The student who is not measuring himself against a set of standards appropriate to himself and his situation cannot gain the strength he needs no matter how desperately friendly everyone is. He will gain in personal stature and emotional size more from engaging in serious intellectual tasks to meet the expectations of a sensitive and discerning teacher than he will from undiluted tender loving care.

On the other hand, the conservatives who argue for more discipline, harder subjects and more of them, seldom pause to think about actual consequences as far as the children are concerned. What they are likely to get is the elimination of a large number of children who simply can't do the work. This converts the subjects into testing devices to screen out those who can't do them well. It may also assure that these subjects will contain little nourishment for the intellectual life of the children who can.

As a result there are extraordinary pressures on the child from all sides—from his parents who urge him to work harder and "get good grades," from the community where his status is involved, from the testing program of the school, that mechanical monster which decides his fate. But such pressures do little more than to destroy the possibility of his genuine intellectual growth, since the necessities of test-passing inhibit the enjoyment of ideas and the deeper consideration of their meaning.

The child gains no benefit from constant admonition unless the urging is accompanied by sensitive help in learning. The stance is wrong. The child who is unable to do well in mathematics or in English does not need goading or the threat of a bad grade. He needs good teaching and a curriculum of the kind which does not badger him with difficulties but helps him to overcome them.

The conservatives, after calling for more discipline, denounce the progressives for wanting the opposite, for wanting to pamper children, cater to their interests, and leave them undisciplined. The denunciations are valid in those cases where teachers assume that anything which is not exciting and interesting to the child is therefore bad for him. This kind of teaching is not particularly progressive, it is simply bad teaching, and there are many kinds of bad teaching.

Progressive theory does not call for sacrificing intellectual achievement to emotional well-being or to superficial game-playing. It calls for intellectual activity to which the child can commit himself, it calls for practical experience with the arts, sciences and society, it calls for consideration of the child's capacity to learn and of the stage of learning which he has presently reached. It holds that the subject-matter of the curriculum must be designed in such a way that it nourishes the intellectual growth of the child and gives him a chance to handle ideas for himself.

The trouble with much of the elementary and high school curriculum is not that it has been constructed by progressives, but that it has not kept pace with the child's ability to learn. It has fallen behind that ability, partly because too little attention has been paid to the child as an individual, thus striking an average of standard material which has neither lifted the slow nor challenged the fast, and partly because too little attention has been paid to the intellectual content of the curriculum itself.

Beneath this is a deeper cause—the lack of sustained attention by scholars in the sciences and the arts to the intellectual quality of the entire public school curriculum. This is also true of the college curriculum, an apparatus consisting mostly of standard textbooks, a pre-arranged syllabus and a content which goes unrevised from year to year except for occasional change in the textbooks. The scholars in the universities have been interested almost exclusively in their own subject-matter and not in education. Therefore the content of the curriculum in the schools and in the colleges has seldom been refreshed by the contributions of first-rate minds in contemporary scholarship.

The establishment of a strong curriculum with serious intellectual content is not a question of adding more subject-matter in order to give children more to do, or to make the curriculum "harder," so that the mind will be trained. It is a question of holding in one's mind a double image of what the curriculum must be and what it must do, just as the composer writes down what he is composing and hears his own sounds as he writes. A curriculum is a composition in just this sense, and it consists not merely in textbooks and readings, but in questions, experiences, atmosphere, attitudes, remarks, interests. A true curriculum can only be made by one who knows intuitively what his plan of education will be like in action, what kind of response it can evoke in the learner.

The educator must therefore have an image of the child in the reality of his school and his society, at a particular stage in the child's life, and in relation to all the parts of that life. Once endowed with this empathy, the educator must then be a scholar who is deeply educated in a field of knowledge he has mastered, and must be concerned that the learner be enabled to come to terms with that field. Progressive theory calls for experimental work of the kind now being done in mathematics by those scholars who are finding new ways to overcome the unnecessary difficulties standing between the child and mathematical concepts. The problem of these educators is not simply to make things easy for the child, but rather to build a curriculum in such a way that the child is able to learn from it, to enjoy it, to work with it. Out of such work comes intellectual discipline.

We must be very clear about this. It is the deepest point of difference between liberal and conservative ideas, and it goes to ultimate questions of social and moral philosophy. In effect, the conservatives say, teach the sciences, foreign languages, mathematics, history, literature, teach them straight, teach them early. There are facts, ideas and subjects which everyone must know; the children who grasp these readily should be recognized and rewarded, should be assigned to the best teachers, while the rest should be recognized for what they are—inferior in mental ability.

What the conservative is really arguing against is the compassion of the liberal, who wishes to shield the child from punitive devices, from the strictures of authority and the destructive effects of competition, both intellectual and social, until the child is strong enough to establish a true character of his own. He may then be discovered to have become tough-minded, disciplined in independence, while retaining his sensitivity.

To this end, the curriculum must be a means through which each child may become engaged in serious intellectual action; the curriculum is the substance on which his growth is nourished.

Serious intellectual effort is a joy to the child, the discovery of facts and the creation of one's own conclusions are the ultimate joys of learning. The kind of society which makes this possible is one which respects the child for what he can do and does all that can be done to help him to do it.

Part Two

HELPING CHILDREN

AND ADOLESCENTS

Cognitive Abilities

27 / Discrimination Learning in Children as a Function of Reinforcement Value[1]

Yvonne Brackbill and Donald Jack

Teachers tend to depend principally on one incentive—grades. Yvonne Brackbill of Johns Hopkins University and Donald Jack demonstrate that since no two children will have exactly the same needs, they will not always be equally reinforced by the same rewards. When kindergarten children are permitted some choice in the incentive for which they would strive, variability of performance is reduced. In practical application, since for some children grades do not serve as incentives, meaning psychologically that these children are motivated by needs that are not satisfied by attaining high grades, teachers might obtain better achievement and behavior by offering them other, individually determined incentives.

The present study is concerned with the influence of reinforcement *value* on learning. Reinforcement *value* is defined as the individual S's relative preference for various types of reinforcers, when amount of reinforcement and probability of occurrence of reinforcement are held constant.[2]

[1] The authors wish to express their thanks and gratitude for the cooperation and assistance received from the following persons: Neal Royer, Superintendent, Campbell Elementary School District; Peter Franusich, School Psychologist; Duane Beaubien, Principal, Dover School; and Wayne Fontes, Principal, Hamilton School.

[2] From a conceptual point of view, *reinforcement value* might be considered as roughly analogous to *incentive motivation* (K), insofar as the latter intervening variable is used to account for performance differential as a function of differences in quality of reinforcement (Spence, 1956). There are operational differences, however, since the present procedure does not involve a consummatory response, the classical conditioning of which is assumed to be the basic mechanism underlying incentive motivation.

Reprinted from *Child Development*, 1958, *29*, 185–90, with the permission of the authors and the Society for Research in Child Development.

The results of several studies show that, on the average, different types of reinforcers are differentially effective for learning (Abel, 1936; Terrell and Kennedy, 1957). For example, Terrell and Kennedy (1957) found that children learn faster when rewarded with candy rather than with praise. However, despite the fact that children as a *group* learn more effectively on candy reinforcement, it is hardly conceivable that any one type and amount of reinforcement has an exactly equal reinforcing effect for all Ss of any such group. Given one group of Ss and one type of reinforcement, there must still be some intragroup variability in effectiveness of that reinforcement as a function of variability in value of the reinforcer for the Ss. In other words, for different people, the same objective or external reinforcer may have different reinforcement values, and if so, the within-group variability in reinforcement value should be reflected statistically as a large standard deviation in number of trials to learning criterion.

The present experiment used a discrimination learning situation to compare the relative effects of two experimental treatments: identity of reinforcement *value* vs. identity of external reinforcing object. Ss run under the first condition (group RV) were allowed to choose the most preferred one of three reinforcers: M & M candies, varicolored marbles, or varicolored plastic trinkets. Ss of the second experimental group (group R) were reinforced with candies. It was predicted that although there would be no significant mean difference between the two treatment groups in trials to criterion, group RV would show greater within-group homogeneity than group R, i.e., there would be a significantly smaller standard deviation for group RV.

Candy was used as the standard reinforcer for group R in order to make the experimental comparison a conservative one. The reasoning behind this was as follows: First, from a logical consideration, it would seem that if sigma were to vary in size at all with differences in *average* reinforcement value, it should be smallest for that reinforcer having the highest average value (and hence, the greatest facilitating effect on learning). (See, for instance, the relative sizes of standard deviations in Terrell and Kennedy's [1957, p. 259] Table 1.) Second, from a statistical consideration, if means and standard deviations are positively correlated in size, that treatment producing lowest mean number of trials to criterion should also show the smallest standard deviation.

METHOD

Subjects

The Ss were 60 male children. They were obtained from the eight kindergarten classes of two elementary schools within a single school district. Mean age of Ss was 63.6 months, *SD*, 3.4. The sample was relatively homogeneous in terms of race (white) and socioeconomic status (middle class). Mean California Mental Maturity Scale IQs for second graders at each school was 106. Goodenough Draw-A-Man tests were available for all kindergartners, and were used in the selection process to eliminate potential Ss of subnormal intelligence, as follows: The school psychologist submitted a list of names of children with extremely low scores on the Goodenough test. A short-form WISC was then administered to these 17 children. Using a cutting score of 70 IQ, eight of the 17 were eliminated from the total pool from which Ss were drawn.

Selection of Ss and placement into one of the two experimental groups was in alphabetical order. In order to have the total RV group composed of equal numbers of Ss preferring each of the three reinforcers, a quota was established of 10 Ss per type of reinforcer. This quota imposed no practical difficulties, since, on the average, the three reinforcers were approximately equal in attractiveness. Only two potential Ss were discarded because they chose a reinforcer (trinkets) for which the quota had already been reached.

Experimental Procedure

S was seated opposite E, at a small table on which were three boxes, the discriminative stimuli. The boxes were of different colors (dark red, light red, and red-orange). Two boxes, No. 1 and No. 2, were the same size but different in size from the third box.[3] Color and size, however, were irrelevant cues, as was also the presence of box No. 3, since the correct response was a simple position alternation sequence of the reinforcement between boxes No. 1 and No. 2. For presentation, the boxes lay open side down on a large piece of brown felt approximately four inches distant from each other; the end boxes, No. 1 and No. 3, were equidistant from S. Position of the boxes was constant for all trials.

On a second table, to S's right, lay a small pillow on which S rested his head between trials. This served two purposes: (a) it eliminated the necessity of placing a screen in front of S while E reloaded the boxes, and (b) it reduced sound localization in the event of any auditory cues during reloading.

As soon as S entered the experimental room, E gave the following instructions:

(group R) Do you know what these are? (E paused and indicated an open box of M & M candies.) They're candy; they're chocolate. I have something very special for you to do, and if you can do it you can have some of the candy.

(group RV) Here are some marbles; here are some charms; here are some candies. (E paused and indicated the appropriate boxes; placement and naming

[3] The boxes were of ordinary heavy cardboard construction. Box No. 1 measured 4¼ by 3½ by 1⅛ in., and was painted with a mixture of 2 parts red Dope to 1 part white Dope. Box No. 2 had the same dimensions as Box No. 1, and was painted with a mixture of 1 part red Dope to 2 parts white Dope. Box No. 3 measured 3⅛ by 2¼ by 1⅜ in., and was painted with orange Dope.

order were rotated by Ss.) Now I have something very special for you to do, and if you can do it you can have some of the charms OR some of the candies OR some of the marbles. You can't have some of all of them, just some of one kind. Now THINK HARD: if you could have JUST ONE KIND, which kind would you rather have —would you rather have some candies OR would you rather have some charms OR would you rather have some marbles?

(Both groups) I'm going to put one _____ at a time under one of these boxes. And every time you pick up the box that has the _____ under it, you can keep the _____. Understand? Now! THERE IS A WAY TO FIND THE RIGHT BOX EVERY SINGLE TIME. SEE IF YOU CAN FIND THE WAY.

Put your head down on that pillow and wait until I say "ready." . . . Ready. Pick up the box that you think has the _____ under it. . . . Now every time you get a _____, pick it up and put it in this envelope, and all the _____ that you put in there will be for you to keep. . . . Head down. . . . Ready.

(After the last trial, the following statement was repeated until S indicated agreement. The purpose of the statement was to "jam" inter-S communication.)

Well, you found the way, didn't you? You found out that the candy was always under the RED box. (E indicated simultaneously all boxes.) Yes, the candy was always under the RED box.

Two learning criteria were used: (a) number of trials taken before S no longer chose the irrelevant or never-reinforced box No. 3; and (b) the number of trials taken to a run of 10 consecutive correct choices. An experimental session ended either when S reached the second criterion or after the 150th trial. In the latter case, the score assignment was 150. Session length ranged from 10 to 25 minutes per S, depending upon time taken to reach the second criterion.

Table 1. Means and Variance Estimates for Discrimination Learning Criteria

	First Criterion: number of trials to eliminate irrelevant box GROUP		Second Criterion: number of trials to and including 10 consecutive correct responses GROUP	
	R	RV	R	RV
N	30	30	30	30
M	58.30	43.57	72.47	60.97
σ_{DM}		11.15		10.55
t		1.32		1.09
p		.19		.27
σ^2	2503.96	1351.25	2283.13	1167.34
F		1.85		1.96
p		.05 *		.05 *

* One-tailed test.

RESULTS

Table 1 shows the means and standard deviations for both groups on both learning criteria. As predicted, there were negligible differences between means and relatively large differences between standard deviations. That is, on both measures, the RV group showed significantly less variability than did the R group. Although the evidence is by no means overwhelming in support of the hypothesis, it ought to be pointed out that the experimental comparison was a conservative one in two ways. The first—the use of a high average value reinforcer for group R—was mentioned above. Second, the true variability was underestimated by assigning to nonlearners the limiting score of 150. This restriction worked against the hypothesis since there was a disproportionately larger number of nonlearners in group R than in group RV (six as compared to one).

The correlation between CA and number of trials to the second criterion was $-.12$. The insignificant size of this correlation is no doubt attributable to restriction of age range in the sample. Last, there was no significant difference in mean performance between the 10 candy reinforced Ss of group RV and the 30 candy reinforced Ss of group R.

DISCUSSION

The results of the present study are relevant to some common methodological problems. First, an experimenter who employs a simple analysis of variance design, using children as Ss frequently finds that between-group differences are large, but that the size of the within-group variability is even more impressive. The present findings suggest that the use of individually determined reinforcers will reduce such error variance.

Second, experimenters working with young children often report some difficulty in maintaining sufficient motivation to ensure Ss' cooperation or even to keep them in the experimental room. The method of allowing S to choose that reinforcer he would most like to work for probably maximizes motivation as a function of high incentive value.

A third methodological problem concerns the fact that the effectiveness of any given type of reinforcer varies with age. For example, Sturgis (1957) has reported that trinkets are not effective reinforcers at age $2\frac{1}{2}$, but are effective at age 4. What is needed, then, is a "methodological cookbook" of normative data, listing relative effectiveness of all possible reinforcers by successive age levels. But this information is not available, except for the limited data provided by Terrell and Kennedy (1957). At present, selection of the most effective reinforcer for a given problem and age group depends on a good guess or a pilot study. The present results suggest that it would be less hazardous and/or time-consuming to hold reinforcement value constant for any experimental group rather than reinforcement type, i.e., to offer Ss a selection of reinforcers.

The above data may also lend themselves to practical application. For example, in the classroom situation, teachers depend principally on one type of reinforcement—the grade. However, grades are not equal in reinforcement value for all students. In view of this, teachers might obtain better academic results from their poorer students by offering other, individually determined, incentives. As an incidental note, one of the authors has tried informal remedial training with a few children deficient in either arithmetic or reading. In all cases, the under-achievement appeared to be a function of insufficient motivation, not of inability. Rapid improvement was noted when the procedure included (a) reinforcement with individually determined reinforcers, and (b) a combined reward-punishment technique (Brackbill and O'Hara, 1958).

SUMMARY

A comparison was made of the relative effects on discrimination learning of two experimental treatments: identity of reinforcement value vs. identity of external reinforcing object. Reinforcement value was defined as S's relative preference for various types of reinforcers, with amount of reinforcement and probability of occurrence of reinforcement held constant. Results supported the expectation that, although the two groups would not differ in mean trials to criterion, the reinforcement value group would show significantly less variability in trials to criterion.

28 / Effects of Group Experience on Individual Problem Solving

Bryce B. Hudgins

> Do elementary school children working together in groups learn
> techniques of problem solving which they apply later in individual
> problem solving? This problem in transfer is experimentally investigated
> by Bryce B. Hudgins of Washington University, using fifth-grade
> pupils working on arithmetic problems.

A number of investigators (Gurnee, 1937; Klugman, 1944; Perlmutter and de Montmollin, 1952; Taylor and Faust, 1952) have examined the relative effectiveness of problem solving by groups and by individuals. In

Reprinted from the *Journal of Educational Psychology*, 1960, *51*, 37–42, with the permission of the author and the American Psychological Association.

general, they have found that groups furnish more correct solutions to problems than comparable subjects do working as individuals. The present inquiry continues in this tradition, and attempts to extend knowledge in the area by providing experimental answers to two questions related to the problem solving behavior of elementary school children. First, do children working together in groups learn techniques of problem solving which they can apply later in similar situations, and secondly, does interaction, as herein defined, contribute to the superiority of group problem solving? A casual inspection of elementary school principles of teaching texts would suggest that this transfer and the conditions under which it occurs are demonstrated facts rather than unanswered problems.

Answers to these questions hinged on the assumption that groups of children would be more successful in solving problems than their counterparts working individually. This result had been so well demonstrated in the past that there seemed little reason to doubt that it could be replicated in a school situation.

Additional significance of the study lies in the use of "natural groups." The use of ad hoc groups has been criticized in a survey of investigations of group and individual performance.

A common and dangerous practice is to generalize the principles valid for ad hoc groups to traditioned groups. The ad hoc group is treated as a microscopic model of the traditioned group. This might be true, but has not been experimentally validated. It is equally possible that ad hoc and traditioned groups behave in accordance with their individual principles (Lorge, et al., 1958).

The groups used in this study were ad hoc in the sense that they were organized for purposes of the investigation. It seems to the writer that what constitutes a traditioned group depends upon the context in which the group is found. It can be argued that groups which operate for three consecutive days, as in the present study, approximate traditioned groups as they exist in the classroom. The analogy here is between the experimental groups and others which are formed for a specific activity within the classroom.

HYPOTHESES AND RATIONALE

Three hypotheses were formulated to provide a basis for answering the questions asked above:

1. The first hypothesis was that problem solving experience in a group improves individual ability more than does individual experience.

It was hypothesized that when subjects (Ss) who had worked on arithmetic problems as members of a group were tested individually, their mean score would be significantly higher than the mean of Ss who had worked individually throughout the experiment. This answers the first question above, concerning the carry-over from the group situation to a subsequent individual one.

2. The second hypothesis was that individual ability to solve arithmetic problems improves as a result of specifying the steps involved in arriving at solution.

Specification consisted of providing written answers to a series of questions which were intended to lead Ss toward problem solution. There were four questions which specification subjects had to answer in connection with the solution of each problem:

1. What are you asked to find?
2. What information are you given that will help you find the answer?
3. What do you have to do to find the answer?
4. What is the answer?

It was predicted that the mean score of Ss who had worked under the condition of specification would be significantly higher than the mean of Ss who had not used specification.

Underlying this hypothesis was the reasoning that disagreement among group members about a solution initiates a review process during which the attention of individual members is directed to the various critical steps in problem solution. The group's contribution to successful problem solving, then, lies in "instructing" the participants in proper problem solving procedure. If this is true, the student working alone who is required to specify the steps by which progress is made toward problem solution will improve much as if he were exposed to the influence of the group. Thus, the group influence may be an artifact, seemingly important, but only because it invokes a process which one ordinarily would not use, but would be capable of using, in isolation.

3. A final hypothesis was that the improvement of problem solving ability as a result of group experience stems from the relevancy of intragroup communication to the processes involved in problem solution.

That is, students tested individually following a period of time in which they had worked as members of a group using specification would solve significantly more problems than subjects who worked initially in nonspecification groups. By systematizing the "instruction" process in the group situation, presumably even greater gains in individual problem solving success will be realized.

In short, is there carry-over in the form of higher individual performance as a consequence of the group experience, and does a structuring of problem solving procedures account for a portion of the variation in pupil performance?

METHOD

Sample

The Ss of the investigation were 128 fifth-grade students selected in equal numbers from each of four public schools in the city of St. Louis.

Controls

A measure of each *S*'s general mental ability and arithmetic problem solving ability was made immediately prior to the experiment. The general mental ability test used was the California Test of Mental Maturity, Short Form. Arithmetic ability was measured by the California Arithmetic Test, Elementary, Grades 4-5-6, Form W.

The 32 *S*s in each classroom were matched by fours on the basis of their general ability and arithmetic test scores, and assigned to one of four experimental groups. The assignment of the 8 *S*s in each group to an experimental condition was done by reference to a table of random numbers. Following the final assignment there was no significant difference in either general mental ability or arithmetic ability among the groups prior to the experiment.

During the experiment, the groups from two of the classes were taken to a room other than their regular classroom. In the other two classes, *S*s working individually were taken to another room, while the groups remained in their homeroom. This was done in order that the novelty of a new working environment would not exercise a systematic influence on any one of the experimental conditions.

Tasks

The arithmetic problems from Forms J, K, L, and M of the Stanford Achievement Test, Intermediate, were used as experimental materials. The following are two problems out of the total 120 which *S*s were asked to solve.

Bill jumped 13 feet, 5 inches on Tuesday. On Thursday, he jumped 11 feet, 9 inches. How much farther did he jump on Tuesday than on Thursday?

The butcher says to cook a turkey 20 minutes for each pound. At what hour should a 15 pound turkey be started in order to be done at twelve o'clock noon?

Procedures, Phase 1

The first phase consisted of three consecutive days of problem solving using Forms J, K, L of the Stanford. The 128 pupils worked as follows: Thirty-two pupils (called *AS*s) worked in subgroups of four students. Each subgroup had to agree on a single answer to each question in the specifications.

Another 32 pupils (*BS*s) also worked in four member groups. Within each group, members were free to develop their own methods for solving the problems. The only restriction imposed upon them was that the group must arrive at one answer to each problem.

Half of the 64 pupils working individually (CSs) used the method of specification. The other half (DSs) were simply instructed to solve the problems and to record each solution in the appropriate space on the problem sheets.

Procedures, Phase 2

This portion of the experiment consisted of the 128 students solving individually the 30 problems in Form M of the Stanford. To ascertain the possible effects of differential retention, all the Ss from one classroom (i.e., one-fourth of the total sample) were tested on each of the following days after the completion of Phase 1—the first, second, fifth, and twelfth day. In this way, one-fourth of the A, B, C, and DSs were tested on each day of Phase 2.

RESULTS

Phase 1

Throughout the three days of Phase 1, Ss who worked in groups made higher scores than Ss working individually. On the first day the mean score of Ss working in groups (A and B) was 18.82; that for Ss working individually (C and D) was 12.80. The mean score for individuals rose on the second day to 13.13, while the groups' mean was only 17.69. On the final day, group Ss had a mean of 20.18 correct responses as compared with 14.91 for individuals. The difference for each of the three days of Phase 1 was significant beyond the .01 level. If these differences had not occurred, there would have been no basis for testing the hypotheses in Phase 2. Any reason for expecting that transfer might result from the group experience, or that specification might be useful as an explanatory concept, would have been lacking. It is for these reasons that Phase 1, which simply demonstrated an already well established finding, was an essential part of the experiment. It confirmed the condition upon which the appropriateness of tests of the three hypotheses depended.

The mean of the Ss using specification (Conditions A and C) was 13.88 for the first day. The mean of the B and DSs (conditions of nonspecification) for the same day was 17.74. This difference was significant beyond the .05 level. On the second and third days of the first phase, there was no significant difference between the specification and nonspecification conditions. However, the BSs (who worked in groups without specification) achieved higher scores during Phase 1 than Ss working under any of the other three experimental conditions.

Phase 2

Table 1 gives the mean scores for Phase 2 of Ss who had worked under each of the four experimental conditions, and the mean of each class

Table 1. Mean Score on Arithmetic Problems for Each Phase 1
Experimental Condition and Each Day of Phase 2

	Day on which Phase 2 Was Administered				
Phase 1: Experimental Condition	1 ($N = 32$)	2 ($N = 32$)	5 ($N = 32$)	12 ($N = 32$)	Mean
A: Groups with specifi-					
cation	15.25	17.25	10.75	15.25	14.63
B: Groups without speci-					
fication	17.38	19.38	14.25	13.75	16.19
C: Individuals with speci-					
fication	16.25	14.63	16.38	13.25	15.13
D: Individuals without					
specification	19.13	15.75	12.88	12.75	15.13
MEAN	17.00	16.75	13.57	13.75	15.27

Table 2. Summary Table of Analysis of Variance of Phase 2 Scores

Source	df	Mean Square	F	p
X: Groups versus individuals	1	2.53	.09	>.05
Y: Specification versus non-				
specification	1	19.53	.70	>.05
Z: Retention groups	3	111.03	3.99	>.05
XY: Interaction	1	19.54	.70	>.05
XZ: Interaction	3	48.28	1.73	>.05
YZ: Interaction	3	19.87	.71	>.05
XYZ: Interaction	3	27.84	.89	>.05
Within	112	31.31		
TOTAL	127			

which received Phase 2 on a given day, respectively. As revealed by Table 2, none of the differences among Ss in Phase 2 was significant.

These findings indicated that, although groups of students working cooperatively solve more problems than comparable students working alone, there is no significant improvement in the problem solving performance of the former Ss because of this group experience. Consequently, the first hypothesis was rejected. Nor were the other two hypotheses supported; that is, practice in specifying the steps used in solving a problem did not improve performance any more than in the case where such specification was not made. This was true whether specification was used by individuals or by small groups.

DISCUSSION

One problem undertaken by this investigation was an attempt to offer a valid explanation of the superiority of the group over individual problem solving activity. It was hypothesized that this superiority must somehow grow out of the interaction among members working together in the group.

The results of the experiment are clearly opposed to the acceptance of such an hypothesis. However, it must be remembered that the interaction used in this investigation was of a particular type which has been designated specification. It cannot be said with certainty that interaction per se does not affect the quality of the group product. It is possible that, in another form, interaction may contribute to the group superiority.

For example, two interaction patterns were observed in the nonspecification groups during Phase 1. In some of the groups there was a tendency for one S to determine the answer and to communicate it to the other group members. If this person had status as a class leader, his solutions were accepted unquestioningly by the other group members. If he did not have such status, the correctness of his solutions had to be demonstrated before they were accepted.

The second pattern was a more cooperative one which approximated the pattern of the specification groups except for one difference. In these groups each S read the problem and solved it independently. The answers were then compared. If all the answers were identical, the solution was accepted; but if there was disagreement, one person usually took the initiative to demonstrate the appropriateness of the solution to the deviant member or members.

A point of interest arose from the way in which these solutions were determined. Suppose the problem under consideration to be the following: "Our team scored sixteen points in the first game, six points in the second, and fourteen in the third. How many points did we score in all three games?" If there was disagreement about the answer, one person would try to remove the confusion. The usual form of this was to say, "Sixteen and six are twenty-two and fourteen are thirty-six." Such unarguable logic was usually enough to convince the deviant member. On rare occasions the individual said, "You have to add to solve this problem." This remark was followed by the computation.

At no time was there any evidence of attention being given to the first two questions assigned to the specification groups. Such specification as occurred was related to the questions of deciding upon a process appropriate for the solution, and of finding the answer itself. No student was observed justifying his reason for selecting a particular process. Obviously when an incorrect process was selected and agreed upon, the resulting wrong answer tended to receive enthusiastic if misguided support.

Why did the group Ss fail to make higher scores than the C and DSs on the final test? The answer to this question seems to lie in understanding how the Phase 1 tasks were approached by the members of both kinds of groups. Specification, which was used by half of the groups in Phase 1, provides a systematic means of attacking arithmetic problems. It was assumed that the correct answer to a problem would be found if Ss followed the prescribed steps and if the appropriate computational skills were known and could be used by them. It was also assumed that Ss who used specification in Phase 1 would see the applicability of the method when they were later confronted by similar problems, i.e., in Phase 2. The Phase 2 scores of "groups with specification" Ss lead to the conclusion that there was no transfer from the group to the individual situation of the steps which were used in the training period.

As for members of nonspecification groups, it is probable that little if any problem solving skill was acquired in the training period. Their attention seems to have been focused upon accomplishing the task at hand with little regard for developing skills which would be useful in subsequent cases.

The importance for transfer of generalized experience has been demonstrated by Judd (1908) and by Hendrickson and Schroeder (1941). Furthermore, Kingsley and Garry (1957, p. 508) point out "that the mere knowledge of the principle will not insure transfer of training to new situations. Its general applicability must be realized, and the learner must be able to see the possibility of its application to the new situation."

This is a significant point for the present discussion. Prior to the experiment, Ss were told the nature of the condition under which they would work. They were also informed that at a later time they would be asked to solve additional problems by themselves. Little emphasis was placed upon this statement, and no attempt was made to instruct specification Ss that the task given them was one which might help them later in solving problems.

Despite the failure of specification to account for the superiority of groups over individuals, it is still possible, as indicated above, that interaction is related to this superiority. The most reasonable hypothesis at this point appears to be that the problem solving superiority of small groups depends upon the efforts of the most able member of the group to communicate his knowledge to others, and upon the degree to which he achieves acceptance of his solutions. If this hypothesis proves tenable, transfer from the group to the individual situation would not be expected to occur.

SUMMARY

This study inquired (a) whether specification (citing the steps leading to solution) is related to the problem solving superiority of small groups over individuals and (b) whether individual problem solving ability improves as a result of group experience.

Subjects were 128 fifth-grade girls and boys. The first phase of the study lasted three days during which subjects worked on sets of arithmetic problems under an experimental condition. Half worked as group members; half as individuals. Group members solved significantly more problems than subjects who worked alone.

In Phase 2, all subjects worked individually. No differences were found among subjects' scores in this second phase. It was concluded that specification is not related to group problem solving effectiveness and that group experience does not enhance individual problem solving.

29 / Homework and Achievement in Plane Geometry

Vynce A. Hines

A review of experimental research on home study concludes that "regularly assigned homework favors higher academic achievement," and "statements that homework may have adverse psychological effects are unsupported by research" (Goldstein, 1960, pp. 221, 222). In this one-year study of the effect of homework on achievement in plane geometry, Vynce A. Hines of the University of Florida matches pairs of students on chronological age, mental age, and previous performance in algebra. Scores on seventeen tests, including a readministration of the initial achievement test in plane geometry, favor the homework group over the no-homework group. The limitations of the study are noted and the suggestion made that the experiment be repeated and improved using similar and different subject areas.

After surveying the related literature and research on homework, Ruth Strang (1955) comments, "Although many opinions exist on the effect of homework on scholastic success, there has been little research on the subject." Such research has often been of short duration and has lacked adequate controls. This study is an effort to answer the question of the value of out-of-class study for achievement in plane geometry.

MATCHING OF GROUPS

Two classes were formed using the matched-pairs technique and included all pupils who had registered for plane geometry. The experimental group did no home study; the control group did do home study.

Reprinted from *Mathematics Teacher*, 1957, 50, 27–29, with the permission of the author and the National Council of Teachers of Mathematics.

Pairing was done on the basis of chronological age, intelligence quotients, and point averages for two semesters of beginning algebra. The groups were later compared on scores on the Co-operative Achievement Tests in Algebra and in Plane Geometry which were given during the first days of the experiment. The groups were found to be quite similar on these tests, but these data were not used in forming the original pairs. Nineteen pairs were formed, and the two participating teachers took turns drawing from each pair for members of their respective classes.[1]

Peters and VanVoorhis' (1940, p. 165) Formula 95 was used to calculate standard errors of differences between means in terms of the differences between paired measures. The differences found were small ones and could have occurred by chance from forty-five to ninety-seven per cent of the time. Sixteen of the nineteen pairs finished the year and were used for the experiment, and for calculating the matching results just reported. Standard deviations were comparable for the two groups. Both groups had a higher mean IQ—120.1 and 119.2—than would be found ordinarily in a high school class. However, IQs ranged from 91 to 147 in the experimental group and from 81 to 144 in the control group, in the original nineteen pairs, and from 99 to 144 in both groups among the sixteen pairs who finished. The algebra test scores indicate a high level and almost equal retention over the summer by the two groups. The initial plane geometry test scores indicate very little knowledge of plane geometry and for many of the pupils the scores were accountable by chance.

The two teachers agreed to follow the same textbook (Mallory, 1943) closely. The book was divided into eight units. An objective test booklet accompanied the text. At the end of each unit, both groups took this test on the unit. The following day, beginning with the end of the second unit, pupils took a cumulative review test, also from the booklet. The teachers planned their work so that each group spent the same number of days on each unit covered.

The experiment ran from September until June, approximately 180 school days. Teaching procedures were kept as uniform as possible by the two teachers. Both groups met at the same hour, 8:10 A.M., for a class which lasted a full sixty minutes. Both groups devoted part of most periods to supervised study, so that often the control group had its outside study started before it left class. Both groups were taught by student teachers for identical periods during the second semester—teachers who received identical grades from the same three judges. The principal difference between the two groups was that in the control group homework was assigned two or three times a week. While records were not kept, it was thought that the average pupil would take from forty minutes to one hour for assignments.

The nature and purpose of the experiment were explained to both classes at the beginning of the year and the resulting pupil co-operation was thought to be excellent by the two teachers.

[1] The writer taught the no-home-study group; Miss Mary Iball taught the home-study group. The study was made several years ago at the University High School, University of Illinois, Urbana, Illinois.

Students from the control group worked slightly faster than those in the experimental group on the unit tests and cumulative review tests. More pupils from the control group were able to finish these tests during the sixty-minute period than were able to finish from the experimental group. Whether this was because of extra, outside-of-class practice is not known.

At the end of the first semester both groups took an objective test prepared by the high school mathematics staff. At the end of the year both groups were tested on the Co-operative Plane Geometry Test, Form N—the same test administered at the beginning of the year.

For the purpose of the experiment, the only evaluation attempted was that which measured achievement in plane geometry as measured by the scores on unit tests, cumulative review tests, a semester examination, and a standardized geometry test.

It might be pointed out that if there is an advantage in out-of-class study, then the design of the experiment meant that any "cheating," i.e., study outside of class by members of the experimental group, or failure to study outside of class by members of the control group, should serve to reduce any differences found between the two groups.

Absences from the two classes were about the same. Any make-up work was done in class by members of the experimental group during supervised study periods. Neither group received appreciable out-of-class help from the teachers. So far as is known, no additional tutoring was done outside of class for members of either group.

EXPERIMENTAL DATA

Means, standard deviations, differences of means, critical ratios, and the probabilities of the critical ratios were determined for the two groups on the eight unit tests, seven cumulative review tests, the semester examination, and the Co-operative Achievement Test in Plane Geometry. Peters and VanVoorhis' (1940, p. 165) Formula 95 was used to calculate the standard errors of differences between means in terms of the differences between paired scores. This formula makes unnecessary the tedious calculation of correlations between matching variables, here, multiple Rs.

Table 1. Comparison of Experimental (E) and Control (C) Groups on Co-operative Achievement Test in Plane Geometry

	Initial Test		Final Test		Gains		Difference in Gains
	E	C	E	C	E	C	
X	35.5	35.8	55.6	61.1	20.1	25.3	5.2
s	8.9	7.0	10.5	7.4			
D		.3		5.5			
t		.10		1.50			1.55
p		.95		.16			.15

Every one of the seventeen comparisons favored the control group. Nine of the differences are statistically significant at or beyond the five per cent level, three others at or beyond the ten per cent level. Variability of performance tended to increase in both groups on both the unit tests and the cumulative review tests. During the first semester—Units I through IV—the experimental class tended to be more variable; during the second semester, more variability was observed in the control group. Although no strong trend is apparent in the size of ts, the size of the differences between the groups increased. During the first semester the mean differences were 4.0 and 2.4 on the unit and review tests. During the second semester the mean differences were 5.0 and 6.2, increases in spread of 1.0 and 3.8 points.

Differences on the Co-operative Achievement Test give approximately the same t value whether they are calculated on differences in final scores or differences in gains. These scaled-score differences are equivalent to about a 25-percentile spread. Translated into letter grades, the typical experimental-group pupil made a C, while his control matchee received a B.

CONCLUSIONS

1. Out-of-class study, usually written work, increases achievement in plane geometry.

2. The differences in achievement tend to be cumulative.

3. Differences tended to be slightly greater on cumulative review tests than on unit tests covering recent material.

4. If a traditional grading system were used—A, B, C, D, E—and if students were graded only on the tests reported here, home study would increase the grade of the average student by one letter.

LIMITATIONS

It is possible that the differences found could be accounted for by differences in skill or zeal on the part of the two teachers involved. Hence, it would be desirable to repeat the experiment with other classes and with the home-study situation reversed.

While the groups were well matched, they were small. Further, they were somewhat superior in intelligence to most plane geometry classes. These factors make it a little hazardous to generalize the findings to larger and less able classes. Further, the small number of cases makes it futile to study differentials by intelligence levels.

The experiment does point out, however, a design by which future studies can obtain more adequate research from which to generalize. It is suggested that pairs of teachers in many schools use this design in classes in different subject areas, those in which homework is primarily written and those in which assignments emphasize reading or other activities. It would be well to accumulate results for groups of varying ability and also for classes of different sizes. A few dozen such studies would give definitive answers to some questions in the homework versus no-homework argument.

30 / The Transfer Effects of a How-to-study Course upon Different IQ Levels and Various Academic Subjects

Salvatore G. DiMichael

We can improve our study habits. There are some tried and proven ways such as setting up a study routine, being properly motivated, and using a technique for effective study such as the Survey Q3R Method (Robinson, 1961), which includes five specific steps labeled Survey, Question, Read, Recite, and Review. In this study of ninth grade students, Salvatore G. DiMichael of the U.S. Department of Health, Education, and Welfare, New York City, demonstrates that instruction in how to study has value chiefly for the middle group of mental ability. This conclusion is supported by other studies on the effectiveness of study-skills courses (Entwisle, 1960).

In another article (DiMichael, 1943), the writer presented data which demonstrated that the how-to-study course as taught in the experiment could be expected to increase substantially the knowledge of efficient study skills of ninth-grade pupils. It was found, over the period of one term, that students of average mental ability did not acquire more knowledge about better study techniques as a by-product of the regular subject-matter classes. Students of superior mental ability did obtain such knowledge in an incidental way. On the other hand, students who were given the special how-to-study course learned significantly more about effective study techniques than matched pupils. These increases can be termed the direct results of a how-to-study course, and the data proved the direct effects of such training to be appreciable.

However, the crucial test of the efficacy of the course in how-to-study must lie in its ability to bring about higher accomplishment in the scholastic achievement of the pupils. This refers to the transfer effects of the course. By transfer is meant the extension and application of what was learned in the how-to-study classes to other subjects in the curriculum.

Reprinted from the *Journal of Educational Psychology*, 1943, *34*, 166–75, with the permission of the author.

The transfer effects which may have carried over to other subjects would include ideas, understandings, ideals, attitudes, techniques, and the like. In this follow-up report of the same experiment some of the possible transfer effects of the special instruction will be inferred from results on achievement tests in the regular subjects of the high school.

The broad purpose of the present part of the investigation is to evaluate experimentally the transfer effects of a how-to-study course upon the achievement of pupils of different levels of intelligence and upon achievement in several academic subjects. The more specific questions which this study seeks to answer are:

1. Will the increased knowledge of efficient study skills be translated into actual practice and be observed objectively in superior achievement scores?

2. Which level of intelligence will derive the most benefit from the instruction given in such a course?

3. In what academic subject—history, Latin, or algebra—is the greatest amount of transfer observed?

The ninth grade, in which this experiment was conducted, has seemed to be an especially promising level to teach study skills. Educators generally believe that the ". . . art of study ought in theory to be acquired as early in the student's career as possible . . ." (Whipple, 1929, p. 2). Most previous experiments have inferred that the how-to-study classes met the test of usefulness. However, each of these studies was deficient in one or more of the following respects: pupils in the groups were not closely matched on significant factors inherent in the experimental situation such as mental age, IQ, chronological age, curriculum, and school year; more important, teacher efficiency was not controlled; the number of cases were in some studies too small for reliability; objective, standardized tests were not used to measure the amount of transfer; the results were not related to different levels of intelligence, nor were results related to different subjects in the curriculum. The present study has sought to avoid these shortcomings.

The investigation included one hundred ninety-two cases in a matched-group, control-type experiment. The subjects were matched individually on the basis of seven criteria: IQ, MA, chronological age, sex, school year, curriculum, and teacher. On the basis of these criteria two groups were formed, one of one hundred two and the other of ninety subjects. The first was called the 'Superior' group, composed of those students whose IQ ranked them above the median of the class; the second was termed the 'Average' group (because their IQ's placed them in the average range according to IQ classifications) and was made up of those students who ranked below the median of their class in mental ability. The mean IQ of the Superior group was 112.4, and of the Average group, 97.5. Table I contains the information pertinent to the comparability and description of the groups. It can be seen that a very close matching has been accomplished.

The IQ's of the pupils had been obtained as a routine school procedure just two months before the experiment began. The Otis Self-Administering Test, Higher Examination: Form *A*, was given. It has a reported reliability of .917. The Cooperative Medieval History Test, Provisional Form 1935, was used for that subject; it has a reliability of .94 as determined by the Spearman-Brown formula. For the subject of Latin, the Cooperative Latin Test, Revised Series, Form *Q*, with a reliability of .95 was employed as the initial test, and Form *R* was used as the final test. The Cooperative Algebra Test, Elementary Algebra Through Quadratics, Form *Q*, was given for the pre-test, and Form *R*, was administered at the close of the experiment. Their reliability is .86 at the single grade level.

Table I. Comparability and Description of Groups

Group	N	Aver. IQ	SD IQ	Age Yrs.—Mos.	SD Mos.
Superior					
Exp.	51	112.84	6.10	14—1	6.00
Con.	51	112.02	5.68	14—2	6.44
Average					
Exp.	45	96.96	4.86	14—6	8.92
Con.	45	98.00	4.79	14—6	8.48

The instruction in how-to-study was given to the experimental students in two forty-five-minute periods each week throughout the Spring term of 1942, totaling twenty-seven class sessions. The instructor frequently made use of the lecture method and also other methods when they were deemed appropriate to most effective learning; even blackboard games were utilized to heighten class interest. The instructor conducted the class informally, and occasionally spoke with the students outside of class about their school work, attitudes, ambitions, and the like. No outside preparation was required for this non-credit course.

The experimenter took a broad point of view on the concept of study in his instructional efforts. Emphasis was laid upon study and study techniques as necessary not only for school but for present and future life activities as well. Study was always considered as a real life activity of value and importance, to be used in factory, home, community, and school. This broad view of study was purposely adopted because the investigator considered it to be a good medium for obtaining maximum transfer. The emphasis in the teaching was on the development of a clearer understanding of, and a desire to use, the superior study skills.

Pupils of superior and average intelligence were instructed similarly in the how-to-study class. While the experimental group was given the special instruction, the control group remained in their regular 'study' class to work on daily class assignments. After the special instruction the experimental group returned to their regular class where similar influences acted upon both groups alike. The investigator wishes to call attention to the fact that this experimental set-up has made it possible to control such variables as teacher efficiency, class size, equipment, books, and assignments.

In planning the units of the course, the experimenter used the results of the study by Laycock and Russell (1941) as an objective basis for validating the contents of the course. The purpose was to provide instruction both in those topics most frequently mentioned in how-to-study manuals for secondary-school pupils and also suited to the needs of the particular students. The following twelve units were explained in class: the effect of attitudes upon scholarly efficiency; concentration and the control of attention; planning a time schedule; increasing speed of reading; increasing comprehension; increasing vocabulary; outlining; notebooks and note-taking; writing a term paper, theme, or report; remembering and memorizing more efficiently; reviewing; and preparing for and taking examinations.

The 't' ratios were derived by the method credited to Student and explained by Ezekiel (1932, p. 449). These ratios may be interpreted in terms of the null hypothesis and levels of confidence (Lindquist, 1940, p. 52). When the 't' ratio lies beyond the five-per-cent-level of confidence one may be reasonably certain that the difference is not due to chance alone; at the one-per-cent-level one may be practically certain of a true difference in the compared statistics. The per cents refer to the number of chances in one hundred that a greater difference will be obtained by mere chance sampling.

RESULTS

When the transfer effects of the course were determined for the groups differentiated by IQ and MA into Superior and Average, only one gain was observed to be statistically significant. This gain was made by the Superior experimental group in the subject of history which showed a superiority of 5.74 points over its control group. This improvement yields a 't' ratio of 2.72 which is significant at the one-per-cent-level, so that there is practical certainty that the difference is not due to chance sampling. This same Superior group exhibited a very slight, insignificant increase over the matched group in the subjects of Latin and elementary algebra. The Average experimental group showed slight, insignificant losses in history and algebra, but a gain over the control group in Latin which resulted in a 't' ratio found beyond the twenty-per-cent-level of confidence. Thus, the transfer effects of the how-to-study course were found objectively to have affected favorably the history achievement of pupils of superior intelligence. There was some positive transfer effect also upon the Latin achievement of the Average group, but this was not statistically reliable. In algebra the noticeable differences in achievement could be attributed to mere chance sampling.

Table II. Transfer Effects of the How-to-study Course

Groups	N Pairs	Net Gain	SE$_{NG}$	't' Ratio	Level of Confidence (Per Cent)
History					
Sup. Exp.-Con.	48	5.74	2.11	2.72	1
Aver. Exp.-Con.	41	—2.12	2.37	— .90	40
Latin					
Sup. Exp.-Con.	51	.25	.95	.26	80
Aver. Exp.-Con.	45	1.59	1.08	1.47	10
Algebra					
Sup. Exp.-Con.	49	.17	1.06	.16	90
Aver. Exp.-Con.	41	— .36	1.45	— .25	90

TRANSFER EFFECTS UPON QUARTER GROUPS

In the above analysis the groups were one hundred two and ninety in number. It was decided to split each of these larger groups in half and note whether the results of the matched groups differentiated into quarters on the basis of mental ability would yield more exact interpretations of the effects of the how-to-study class. The quantitative descriptions of this quartile classification and the comparability of the matching have been presented in Table III. Considering both control and experimental groups together, the highest quarter had an average IQ of 116.8, which means that on the average they are at the 84th percentile in intelligence

Table III. Comparability and Description of the Matched Groups Divided into Quarters According to Levels of Intelligence

Group	N	Mean IQ	SD	Mean Age Yrs.—Mos.	SD
Highest Quarter					
Exp.	23	117.4	5.86	14— 0	5.75
Con.	23	116.2	5.47	14— 0	5.88
Second Quarter					
Exp.	28	108.9	2.98	14— 2	5.86
Con.	28	108.7	2.70	14— 3	6.52
Third Quarter					
Exp.	22	100.5	2.60	14— 4	7.92
Con.	22	101.5	2.33	14— 3	6.30
Lowest Quarter					
Exp.	23	98.6	3.56	14—10	8.30
Con.	23	94.7	4.18	14—10	8.96

(Freeman, 1939, p. 302); the second quarter had an average intelligence of 108.8 which is at the 69th percentile; the third quartile had an average IQ of 101, at about the 50th percentile; and the lowest quarter had an average of 94.2 which is found at the 36th percentile of a normal distribution of IQ scores.

The results in Table IV definitely reveal that the previous data can be satisfactorily refined. In the subject of history it was found that the second-quarter group made the greater contribution to the observed significantly improved achievement of the total Superior group. The 't' ratio of 2.49 obtained from the differences between the means of the experimental over the matched control group is beyond the two-per-cent-level of confidence. This may be accepted as a practically reliable difference between the observed mean scores.

In the subject of Latin, the division of the two large groups into quarters manifests another interesting trend. The third quarter now shows a statistically significant gain although in the analysis of the total Average group there was only a statistically unreliable gain for the experimental students. This quarter, whose mean IQ was 101, has proved its capacity to achieve a definite positive transfer from the how-to-study course to the Latin test. On the other hand, the first, second, and lowest quarters show no differences worthy of notice because they are so unreliable.

In algebra the special course does not seem to have affected achievement scores of the pupils even when the means of the quarter groups are examined. The very small difference between the large Average control and experimental groups, as seen in the previous section, turns into opposite directions when the Average group is divided in half on the basis of mental ability. The change tends to be favorable to the third-quarter

Table IV. Transfer Effects of the How-to-study Course upon Different Levels of Intelligence in History, Latin, and Algebra

Academic Subject	IQ Level	Mean Gain Exp.–Con.	SE_{MG}	't' Ratio	Level of Confidence
History	116.8	3.20	3.02	1.06	30%
	108.8	7.41	2.97	2.49	2%
	101.0	− .96	3.74	− .26	80%
	94.2	−4.25	3.01	−1.41	20%
Latin	116.8	− .48	1.56	− .31	80%
	108.8	.86	1.15	.75	50%
	101.0	3.73	1.27	2.94	1%
	94.2	− .47	1.61	− .29	80%
Algebra	116.8	− .20	1.40	− .14	90%
	108.8	.44	1.55	.28	80%
	101.0	2.55	1.72	1.48	20%
	94.2	−3.74	2.26	−1.66	20%

students who were enrolled in the how-to-study class, and unfavorable to the experimental students of the lowest quarter. These latter differences have to be interpreted cautiously, since neither of the results approaches statistical significance.

If the trends shown in the 't' ratios of the various quarter groups are inspected in Table IV, there is observable a tendency for the middle experimental groups, with mean IQ's of 108.8 and 101, to manifest the most benefit from the how-to-study course. The comparisons in the three academic subjects demonstrate a positive gain for the middle experimental groups in five out of six comparisons (one being statistically reliable at the one-per-cent-level of confidence, and the other at the two-per-cent-level); whereas for the highest and lowest groups, it is the control students who maintain a very slight superiority in five out of six comparisons (but none of these even approached statistical significance).

CONCLUSIONS

In subsequent paragraphs, the results of this experiment will not be considered solely by themselves; rather, the interpretations of the present data will be examined in the light of the more important results obtained by other investigators who have reported on the effectiveness of a how-to-study course.

1. The data of this experiment have led the investigator to conclude that the course, as taught in this study, has proved its value for the middle groups of mental ability. One of these middle groups benefited significantly in history and the other made a significant, positive transfer in Latin achievement. Moreover, the middle quartile groups made a statistically significant gain in knowledge of study skills as was described in the first report (DiMichael, 1943). Of the other investigators in this field, Pressey (1928), Jones (1927), Bird (1931), Wagner and Stabel (1935), Book (1927), Moore (1934), Gatchel (1931), and Crawford (1926), agree with this investigator on the value of the course. Mills (1934) absolutely disagrees. Turrell (1937) maintains that such a course was unnecessary in the junior college where he conducted his investigation. However, he found that the middle-third group in intelligence who took the one-unit how-to-study course made a superior showing in seventy-one per cent of the comparisons with the control group. Winter (1936) believes in its short-term but not its long-term effects.

2. The present study lends weight to the conclusion formulated by Pressey (1928) and also by Bird (1931) that students of very poor ability, that is, below the first quartile in intelligence, do not profit noticeably from the course.

3. The how-to-study course has not demonstrated its value objectively for the students in the highest quarter of mental ability. These very superior students did make a significant gain in the knowledge of proper

study skills as a result of the course (DiMichael, 1943), but such additional knowledge did not noticeably transfer to other subjects in the curriculum to any appreciable degree. Only in the subject of history did the very superior experimental pupils show any advantage, but this gain in achievement was not by itself statistically reliable. The data of the present experiment partially contradict the conclusion formulated by Bird (1931) which states that the course will benefit the student in direct proportion to his ability level provided it precedes academic defeat. Such a conclusion seems to be only partly true.

4. Though the how-to-study course will improve the achievement of some groups, the improvement will not be enough to enable how-to-study pupils of a lower quarter group to compete on an equal plane with students in the next higher quarter in intelligence who have not been given the special instruction. In other words, the instruction in best methods of study may result in greater returns in proportion to one's ability, but it will not materially compensate for lack of mental ability. This is stated as a general rule; individual exceptions have been noted in most experimental reports. In this experiment the various quarter intelligence groups maintained without exception a corresponding rank in achievement within the different academic fields. This conclusion agrees with studies by Eckert and Jones (1935) and Bird (1931).

5. The special instruction in how-to-study transferred in varying amounts to the different academic subjects of history, Latin, and algebra. Some differences observed between the experimental and the control groups were positive, others slightly negative, others were insignificant. It is possible, then, that the gains in any one subject may be averaged out by being combined with scores in other subjects in which there may appear no gain, or even a slight loss. For this reason, the transfer effects of the how-to-study course should be judged with reference to a particular subject, and not with reference to the total average grade of the student in all subjects together.

6. The transfer effects upon the different academic subjects have not been similar from study to study. Jones (1929) is probably correct in implying that the different results are due to the dissimilar materials employed in the how-to-study courses.

7. It was observed that the instruction in how-to-study transferred in varying amounts upon the achievement of pupils on different levels of intelligence. Because of this fact, the effects of the course upon pupils of a certain level of intelligence may be obscured by being averaged out in the achievement scores of different levels of intelligence. Therefore, the transfer effects must be determined with reference to the level of intelligence of the students to whom the course is given.

31 / The Development of Understanding in Arithmetic by a Teaching Machine [1]

Evan R. Keislar

An automated teaching device or teaching machine presents information and questions, requires an overt and measurable response, and provides knowledge of results usually immediately following each response. The machine enables the experimenter to control and manipulate with laboratory precision such factors as presentation methods, problem sequence, immediacy of reinforcement, and amount of practice, in order to maximize the transfer of previous learning to new situations. Using a multiple-choice teaching machine which graphically records each step of performance, in this study Evan R. Keislar of the University of California (Los Angeles) finds that fourteen fourth- and fifth-grade pupils understand areas of rectangles significantly better than do their matched control group who receive no planned instruction on this topic. The principles of programming are described and illustrated and suggestions are given for revising the program.

The use of teaching machines for the teaching of spelling and arithmetic combinations has already been shown to have merit (Skinner, 1954; Pressey, 1927). And studies have demonstrated that automated teaching can result in more than simple rote learning (Porter, 1957; Ferster and Sapon, 1958). In this study, the problem was to explore the possibility of using a multiple-choice method for the automated teaching of "understanding," specifically, an understanding of areas of rectangles. By *understanding* is meant the ability to answer a variety of questions different from those encountered during training but belonging to the same general class; the broader this class is, the greater is the understanding.

Essentially, the paper describes an attempt to devise a program for the teaching of understanding, together with the principles underlying its construction and weaknesses that were encountered in the use of the program. No information is available as to what a comparable group of pupils would have learned in regular classes. To have provided such in-

[1] Appreciation is expressed to the staff of the University Elementary School of the University of California, Los Angeles, and to Mrs. Pauline Bart for their cooperation in this study.

Reprinted from the *Journal of Educational Psychology*, 1959, *50*, 247–53, with the permission of the author and the American Psychological Association.

formation would have required a fairly large sample of teachers and classes. But more important is the fact that, at this writing, it is premature to compare the teaching machine approach with regular classroom instruction. Programs for use with such machines need improvement before such studies can have much meaning.

APPARATUS

The teaching machine used in this study was an extensive adaptation of the Film Rater used by the Navy for teaching aircraft identification. Multiple-choice items on a Kodachrome strip-film were projected in sequence upon a viewing plate. The learner responded to each item by pressing one of five buttons. If the answer was correct a green light was turned on and the next item could be brought into view by pressing a special button. But if this answer was wrong a red light came on; only after turning off his red light could the learner try again. To proceed to the next item the learner had to answer correctly.

A special device recorded a graph of all right and wrong answers for each item. If the wrong answer was given the pen moved to the right one-twentieth of an inch. For each correct answer the pen moved vertically an equal distance to a new line. Hence the subject's performance for any item could be read from the horizontal line on the graph corresponding to this item number.

THE ITEM SET

The total program consisted of 120 items, 10 of which instructed the learner how to operate the machine and informed him of the goal to be attained. The remaining 110 items were constructed to provide a sequence beginning with concepts of squares, rectangles, length, and width. Following items requiring the pupil to indicate the number of square units in rectangles, the concept of area was presented. Applications included paint coverage, rug size, and tile laying, followed by practical problems of adding and subtracting areas and finding the length or width of rectangles. The set concluded with items involving cost.[2]

PRINCIPLES OF PROGRAMMING

Several of the principles outlined by Skinner (1958) and illustrated in his completion-item set were applied to this multiple-choice approach.

[2] This program, consisting of a Kodachrome strip film of 120 frames, has been deposited with the American Documentation Institute. Order Document No. 6080, from ADI Auxiliary Publication Service, Library of Congress, Washington 25, D.C., remitting in advance $2.00 for microfilm, $16.25 for 35-mm. enlargement prints. Make checks payable to Chief, Photoduplication Service, Library of Congress.

To illustrate the principles discussed below, a short sequence from the program, Items 18 through 29, is presented in Fig. 1. The original program was in color.

1. The step from each item to the next in the sequence should be small enough so that the learner almost always gets each item right. Although Homme and Glaser (1958) and Coulson and Silberman (1959) found that smaller steps resulted in better learning and took less time per step than larger steps, definitive evidence on this issue has not yet been obtained. In this study it was assumed that if a pupil selected the wrong alternative to an item he did so either because he was improperly selected for the program or because of inadequate prior learning in the program itself. The programmer should make sure that a pupil learns enough before an item is presented so that generalization to this item is practically assured.

In opposition to this line of reasoning is the argument in favor of higher item difficulty that the learner is encouraged to "formulate his own hypotheses and try them out." This procedure may have merit if information is supplied to the student showing why the alternative is incorrect (Crowder, 1958) or if branching in the program permits special remedial instruction. But where, as in this study, the pupil is informed only that he is wrong when he makes an error, he is given no more information than when he gets the item correct. One fifth grade subject, after completing the program in this study, commented, "It's hard to know why you get something wrong. When I got it right, I knew it. When I got it wrong, I didn't know why." Since the absence of an explanation is likely to heighten the aversive consequences of failure, it appeared most desirable to adopt a minimum difficulty level for the items in this study. If it seemed helpful to emphasize that certain responses were wrong, instead of having the student learn this by "being wrong," special items were constructed for this purpose, e.g., "Which of the following figures is NOT a rectangle?"

2. Skinner's use of the vanishing stimulus and the prompt facilitates the occurrence of the correct response. For example, in Items 25 and 26 colored rows of squares encourage the right answer. In Item 27 these become merely dotted lines which vanish completely in Item 28. In Item 20 the correct answer "1 ft." is prompted by the dimension "1 ft." in the diagram.

3. To promote generalization within a broad class of items, a process necessary for understanding, the learner should acquire a variety of verbal responses which might later be used, through intraverbal associations, to evoke other appropriate responses. This is simply a process of mediated or secondary generalization, a complex example of which is found in Judd's theory of transfer through verbal principles. For instance, it was judged that if the pupil learned to group squares within a rectangle by rows, as in Items 25 through 28, he would acquire intraverbal associations which would promote the correct response in learning later in the program to multiply the length by the width to find the area and, still later, to divide

18. Squares can be large or small. But if each side on a square is one foot long, this is called a square foot. Which figure is one square foot?

A. [□ 4 ft.] 4 ft.

B. [□ 5 ft.] 5 ft.

C. [□ 1 ft.] 1 ft.

D. [▭ 1 ft.] 2 ft.

E. [▯ 2 ft.] 1 ft.

19. Here are two squares; [□ □] They are exactly the same size. Suppose I put the squares together side by side like this.

[□□]

What kind of a figure will the two squares together make if I leave out the middle line like this?

[▭]

A. Another bigger square.
B. A rectangle.

20. Here is a rectangle. It is 2 feet long and 1 foot wide.

1 ft. [▭] 1 ft.
   2 ft.

Suppose I draw a line in the middle, like this; I will make 2 squares. How long will each side of each square be?

1 ft. [□│□] 1 ft.
     2 ft.

A. 1 ft.   B. 2 ft.   C. 3 ft.

21. Suppose you have a rectangle which is 3 feet long and 1 foot wide like this

      3 ft.
1 ft. [│ │ │] 1 ft.
      3 ft.

How many squares, 1 ft. long on each side, can I make out of this rectangle?
A. One   B. Two   C. Three

22. How many square feet are in a rectangle which is two feet high and one foot wide like this:

A. One
B. Two
C. Three
D. Six

      1 ft.
[┆ ┆] 2 ft.
      1 ft.

23. How many square feet are in a rectangle which is 2 feet wide and 4 feet long?

[grid figure]

A. Two   B. Four   C. Six   D. Eight

24. Each side of this square is one inch long. This is called one square inch. How many square inches are in this rectangle which is one inch wide and five inches long?

1 in. [□] 1 in.

      1 in.
[▭] 5 in.

A. One B. Two C. Three D. Four E. Five.

25. Here is a rectangle which is 2 inches wide and 4 inches long. How many square inches are there in this rectangle?

[grid figure]

There are 2 rows with 4 squares in each row. How can we write the total number of square inches?
A. 2 + 2   C. 2 + 4 + 2 + 4
B. 2 + 4   D. 4 + 4

26. This rectangle is 4 inches wide and 7 inches long. How many square inches are in this rectangle?

[figure]

A. There are 4 rows with 4 squares in each row.
B. There are 8 rows with 4 squares in each row.
C. There are 4 rows with 7 squares in each row.
D. There are 4 rows with 14 squares in each row.

27. This rectangle is 5 inches long and 3 inches wide.

      5 in.
3 in. [▭ grid]

There are 3 rows of squares. In each row there are 5 square inches. How many square inches are there in the rectangle?
A. 5 + 5   B. 5 + 5 + 5   C. 5 + 5 + 5 + 5

28. Here is a rectangle which is 5 in. wide and 9 in. long. How many square inches are there in the rectangle?

[black figure]

A. 9 + 9 + 9 + 9 + 9   B. 5 + 5 + 5 + 5 + 5
C. 9 + 5 + 9 + 5   D. 5 + 5 + 9 + 9 + 9

29. A rectangle which is 5 in. wide and 9 in. long contains 9 + 9 + 9 + 9 + 9 square inches. What is a quick way of finding how many square inches this is?
A. Add 9 and 5.
B. Add 9 and 9 and 9 and 9 and 9.
C. Multiply 9 by 5.
D. Divide 9 by 5.

Fig. 1. A Sample Sequence of Items, Nos. 18–29, to Illustrate Programming Principles

the area by the length to find the width. In other words, with these items the pupil is being prepared to "gain insight into why" you multiply in one case and divide in the other. Appropriate intraverbal associations, such as verbal principles, definitions, or characteristics, should function to extend the pupil's learning to entirely new items which involve the same principle or concept. If this indeed can be accomplished, the use of multiple-choice items in automated teaching results in something more than "mere recognition" of the right answer.

4. Procedures or concepts which are not otherwise involved in the sequence of items should be reviewed periodically. For example, a review of the process of grouping squares into rows, originally presented in Items 25–28, was provided later by six items occurring at intervals throughout the program.

5. Other techniques included the repetition of the correct answer on the succeeding item (as in Item 29), the irregular appearance of "interesting" colored pictures accompanying the item, and the use of a variety of forms of the multiple-choice item.

SUBJECTS

Fourteen experimental Ss and 14 controls, individually matched on the basis of intelligence, sex, reading ability, and pretest scores, were selected from the fifth and low sixth grades. All Ss showed competence in multiplication and division but little acquaintance with the topic of area. A fifteenth S who had completed the program was dropped from the study because of an automobile accident prior to the posttest. The control Ss were given no special instruction of any kind. They were used to control for the effects of incidental learning such as that which might result from the administration of the pretest.

PRETEST AND POSTTEST

Both of these tests were of the free-answer or essay type. The pretest consisted of 12 problems involving multiplication and division, in addition to 8 problems dealing with areas of rectangles. The posttest consisted of the same eight problems of the pretest on area plus another eight most of which were more difficult. Sample problems on the posttest were:

1. A gallon of paint will cover an area of 200 sq. ft. How long a stretch of fence could you paint with 2 gallons if the fence is 5 feet high?

2. A sheet of cardboard is 3 feet long. It weighs exactly 4 ounces. What is the area of this cardboard if it is 2 feet wide?

3. A sheet of paper is 10 in. wide and 12 in. long. This sheet of paper is cut into strips. The strips are laid end to end and then joined with Scotch tape. This long strip now looks like this:

Can anyone tell what the area of this long strip is?
If so, what is it?

PROCEDURE

Experimental Ss operated the machine for two or three periods on successive days. The total time spent with the machine ranged from one hour and 30 minutes to slightly over two hours. The posttest was given the day following the end of such machine instruction to each experimental S and his control.

RESULTS

The mean score of the experimental group on the posttest was 12.4, with a standard deviation of 5.6. The corresponding control mean was 5.4, with a standard deviation of 3.7. Since the posttest scores for the experimental group showed a much greater variance than did the control, a sign test was used. All except one of the experimental Ss showed a higher posttest score than did their matched controls, a difference which is significant at the .01 level. Although the experimental group answered every item, except one, of the posttest better than the control group, most of these pupils missed several items which were similar to those presented in the program; they learned far less than what had been expected.

The total errors on the program ranged from 3 to 118 with a mean of 54. Jane's record, presented in Fig. 2, was the poorest performance and indicates very little learning as measured by the posttest. Part of her problem may have been inadequate ability in computation, since her computation score was relatively low. Even for a typical student like Kenneth, whose record is shown in Fig. 3, the program was too difficult; 40 mistakes is entirely too many according to the criterion adopted. The program appeared to be ideal for Byron, whose record appears in Fig. 4. Although he showed little ability in the field of area on the pretest, Byron's performance on the posttest was outstanding. He was able to generalize from his training so well that on the posttest he solved completely new problems of obtaining the area of a parallelogram and a triangle.

The rank order correlation between total number of errors on the program and the gain on the posttest was −.83. While this of course supports the hypothesis that the optimum difficulty level of each item should be low, it does not permit, in itself, any such conclusion. The rank order correlation of mental age was .52 with gain on the posttest and −.79 with number of program errors. On the basis of this limited sample it appears that the program was more appropriate for the brighter children.

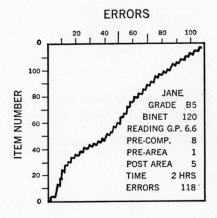

Fig. 2. Graphic Record of the Poorest Performance

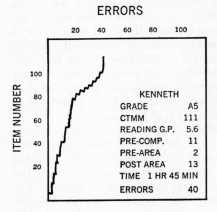

Fig. 3. Graphic Record of a Typical Pupil

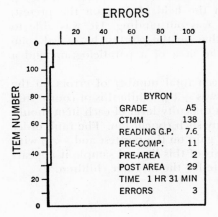

Fig. 4. Graphic Record of the Best Performance

DESIRABLE REVISIONS IN THE PROGRAM

In the absence of definitive evidence on the question, it appears that the major weakness of this program was that it was too difficult for most of the pupils. Revisions should be made along the following lines:

1. Since the reading load was probably a major obstacle for many pupils, sentences should be shorter and the total amount of reading less for each item. Possibly several versions of the program, at different reading levels, would be desirable.

2. The steps in many if not most cases could be smaller. For example, Item 22, which was missed by three pupils, could be preceded by items analogous to 19 and 20. Item 24, also missed by three pupils, could be divided into two items, the first introducing the concept of square inch only. Item 25 could be rewritten as two or even three items.

The greatest misapplication of the principle of small steps occurred in the latter part of the program. For the group of 15 pupils who performed the item set, on the first 10 items there was a total of five errors on the first attempt (out of a possible 150). On succeeding sets of 10 items this number of first-attempt failures increased until it reached 66 for the last set of 10 items. The relatively high difficulty of the items in the latter part of the program appeared to result from the fact that these more complex items required a diversity of other understandings, abilities which were not tested for in the pretest. For example, although pupils were selected on the basis of their ability to divide, many failed to relate division to the process of successive subtraction. The program failed to provide adequate introduction or review of these concepts.

Faced with this type of problem a programmer can either use a more adequate pretest to provide for better selection or he can add the additional items as required. When a great variety of item sets in arithmetic become available, the problem largely disappears. The prerequisites to any item set can be stated in terms of the successful completion of previous item sets. Conversely, the record obtained for a pupil with one item set might be used diagnostically to indicate what the next set, remedial, optional, or otherwise, might be.

3. A wider variety of items should be used for each new process. For instance, Items 25–28 should be supplemented with items which provide verbal statements as alternatives and more familiar illustrations of the problem. As another example, on many of the posttest questions asking for an area, Ss wrote only the correct number failing to indicate the square units involved. Although six items had been presented in the program to reduce this kind of error, these items unfortunately were all stated in exactly the same way. The item stem called for an area and among the alternatives one distractor listed only the correct number. Although completion items may be necessary to teach this type of behavior, better results in this program could probably have been obtained if, instead of the

single form, a variety of multiple-choice forms had been used, e.g., use of "none of these" as an alternative, asking "What is left out in this answer?" or asking for the appropriate rule.

CONCLUSION

The use of multiple-choice items in automated teaching appears to have some effectiveness under these conditions in teaching understanding, as herein defined, even though the criterion was a free-answer test. Although the average pupil did not show as high a degree of competence on the posttest as expected, the program was also far more difficult than intended. Since there appeared to be a strong relationship between success on the program and gains on the posttest, before the limitations and advantages of the multiple-choice method used in this study may be assessed, the program should be revised to include smaller steps and a greater variety of items. Whether the best performers on the present program would have learned more from such a longer and simpler revision remains to be determined; to accommodate individual differences in ability two or three versions of the program may be desirable.

SUMMARY

Fourteen elementary school pupils responded individually to a set of 110 multiple-choice items in a teaching machine. The performance of each child was graphically recorded. Subjects performed significantly better on a test of understanding of areas of rectangles than did their matched controls who received no planned instruction on this topic. The principles of programming are discussed and illustrated. Suggestions given for the revision of the program, which appeared to be too difficult for most pupils, include the introduction of smaller steps and a greater variety of types of multiple-choice items.

32 / Priming Creative Thinking in the Primary Grades

E. Paul Torrance

Teachers can help children in the primary grades to produce more and better ideas than they would without training. How this is done is depicted in this article by E. Paul Torrance of the University of Minnesota.

Reprinted from the *Elementary School Journal*, 1961, *62*, 34–41, with the permission of the author and the University of Chicago Press. Copyright 1961 by the University of Chicago.

Many methods are being offered for evoking more and better creative ideas from individuals and groups (Clark, 1958; Osborn, 1957; Wilson, 1958). A few of these methods are being evaluated objectively through controlled experiments (Parnes and Meadow, 1959), though reports have been limited to research with adult groups. The experiment reported here was undertaken to encourage creative thinking among young children.

Osborn has suggested a set of questions or principles for stimulating new ideas. The questions can be applied in a variety of situations but are most directly applicable in developing ideas for improving a product, a procedure, or group performance. We used the questions to stimulate children to think of ideas for improving a toy. Among the questions we asked were these:

What would happen if we made it larger? (Magnification)

What would happen if we made it smaller? (Minification)

What could we add? (Addition)

What would happen if we took something away? (Subtraction)

What would happen if we took something away and put something else in its place? (Substitution)

What would happen if we took it apart? (Division)

How could we rearrange it? (Rearrangement)

What would happen if we multiplied it? (Pairs, sets, etc.) (Multiplication)

What would happen if we changed its position? (Reversal)

What would happen if we made it out of a different kind of material? (Material)

What would happen if we gave it motion? (Sensory appeal: motion)

What would happen if we gave it odor? (Odor)

What would happen if we gave it light? (Light)

What would happen if we gave it sound? (Sound)

What would happen if we changed the color? (Color)

What would happen if we changed the shape? (Shape)

What would happen if we made it stronger? (Adaptation)

What would happen if we put it to other uses? (Other uses)

The first objective of our experiment was to determine whether children in the primary grades can be taught to use these questions.

Our second objective was to compare the effects of two approaches. In the first approach we instructed children to think of as many ideas as possible without attention to the quality of the ideas. In the second approach we urged the children to think of the most interesting, the most clever, the most unusual ideas they could.

Motivation to produce a large number of ideas has had an important place in training programs designed to help individuals and groups develop new ideas. Osborn and others contend that the more ideas produced, the greater the chances of obtaining "good ideas" (Osborn, 1957).

The subjects of our experiment were 375 pupils enrolled in Grades 1 through 3 in two elementary schools—204 pupils in School X and 171 pupils in School Y. All the pupils in two classrooms in each of the three grades in each school were included in the experiment.

The pupils in each classroom of School X were randomly divided into four groups:

Group A was trained and motivated to produce as many ideas as possible.

Group B was trained and motivated to produce quality ideas.

Group C was not trained but was motivated to produce as many ideas as possible.

Group D was not trained but was motivated to produce quality ideas.

All subjects in School Y were administered the same creative thinking task as the subjects in School X but did not receive the training and the specific instructions for quantity and quality of ideas.

TRAINING PROCEDURES

In each class in School X, Groups A and B meeting together were simply asked to develop ideas for improving a toy fire truck so that it would be "more fun for boys and girls to play with." The children's ideas were simply acknowledged with some indication of interest by the experimenter.

Then the experimenter set out to develop Osborn's questions, or principles. This was done through the use of a set of squares that had been modified according to the principles, as illustrated in Figure 1.

The experimenter showed the squares one at a time to the children. As each square was held up, the experimenter asked: "What have I done to the square here?"

The principle illustrated was then related to the suggestions the children had made for improving the toy fire truck. For example, most groups suggested adding something to the fire truck—a hose, a first-aid kit, and top lights. When the children identified the principles of addition illustrated by the squares, the examiner would say, "Yes, you remember you suggested adding a hose and a first-aid kit to the fire truck."

If any of the principles were not illustrated by the children's responses, the group was asked for responses related to those principles. For example, if no one offered suggestions illustrating the principle of combination, the experimenter would hold up the appropriate square and say, "I don't believe you suggested one for the fire truck like this. What could you put with the fire truck?" The children would then respond: "A fire house." "A board with a play town." "A fire hydrant." "A cardboard house in flames."

Finally the children were told that the questions could be used in "thinking up ideas about almost anything."

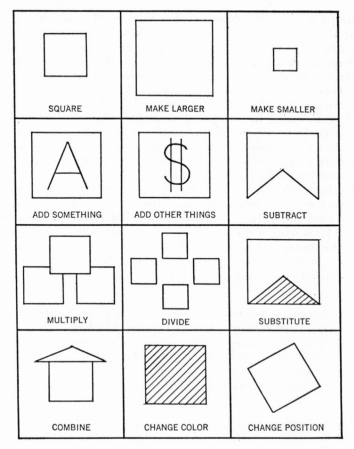

**Fig. 1. Changes in a Square Illustrate Principles
for Developing New Ideas**

All training sessions were conducted by the author. Each session lasted about twenty minutes.

TESTING PROCEDURE

Each subject was tested individually by a member of the staff of our Bureau of Educational Research, all of whom had had extensive experience in testing children with the type of task used.

The test task required the children to think of ideas for improving a stuffed toy dog so that it would be "more fun for boys and girls to play with." Each child was allowed eight minutes to dictate his ideas to the examiner. The time used in giving instructions was not counted in the eight minutes.

Groups A and C were instructed as follows: "I would like for you to see how many ideas you can think of to improve this little toy dog [*handing toy to child*] so boys and girls will have more fun playing with it. I'll try to write them down just as fast as you tell them to me. Tell me every idea you can think of; it doesn't matter how good it is or how crazy it sounds. Don't worry about how much it would cost."

An attempt was made to maintain motivation by offering a prize for the best performance in each group in each grade.

Children in Groups C and D were tested in separate rooms immediately after the experiment was explained to the entire class and the groups were formed. Children in Groups A and B were tested immediately after the training session described earlier.

The children's responses to the test task were scored on the basis of the number of ideas given (fluency), the number of principles or approaches used (flexibility), and the number of clever or unusual ideas offered. The scoring was done according to instructions in a previously developed manual (Torrance and Michie, 1959). An interscorer reliability of .93 was obtained between two judges, who followed the manual.

To illustrate the scoring procedure, let us take six responses from the

Table 1. Mean Scores for Four Experimental Conditions for Pupils Who Took Part in a Test of Creative Thinking

Grade and Condition *	Number of Pupils	Fluency Mean	Fluency Standard Deviation †	Flexibility Mean	Flexibility Standard Deviation †	Cleverness Mean	Cleverness Standard Deviation †
First Grade:							
Group A	18	12.61	4.60	5.50	1.95	5.89	2.85
Group B	15	14.07	6.95	5.33	2.80	6.80	5.52
Group C	19	11.11	6.66	4.32	2.03	5.32	5.17
Group D	16	11.31	6.45	4.62	2.06	6.19	4.11
Second Grade:							
Group A	20	14.15	6.04	5.90	2.10	6.15	4.29
Group B	17	20.35	8.66	7.53	2.85	11.29	6.26
Group C	21	10.00	5.19	3.52	1.68	3.81	4.26
Group D	17	11.59	5.94	4.12	2.61	5.47	4.23
Third Grade:							
Group A	18	16.56	6.26	6.56	2.03	10.61	4.82
Group B	11	21.18	5.88	8.18	1.53	13.09	4.01
Group C	19	16.68	9.23	5.53	2.23	8.47	6.89
Group D	13	14.46	6.23	5.62	1.69	6.15	4.85

  * Group A–Trained, motivated to produce large number of responses
   Group B–Trained, motivated to produce clever, unusual responses
   Group C–Untrained, motivated to produce large number of responses
   Group D–Untrained, motivated to produce clever, unusual responses
   † According to Bartlett's test, the variance is not significant at the 5 per cent level of confidence for any of the grades for any of the measures.

record of one boy in third grade who suggested the following improvements for the toy dog:

1. Give him feet that would go round so that as he moves he would dig a hole.
2. Make his tail longer.
3. Put a hero medal on him or a medal he won at a dog show.
4. Put a tiny tape recorder inside him so that what you say is recorded in dog language so he can answer you.
5. Put fleas on him—or flies.
6. Hook him up so that he can drink water from a bowl and so it will run down through a little tube and run back in the bowl and won't mess things up.

Each response received a point for fluency (score: 6). The first response illustrates the principle of "giving sensory appeal" (motion); the second, "magnification"; the third, "addition"; the fourth, "addition"; the fifth, "addition"; and the sixth, "combination." Thus, he received a score of 3 on flexibility. Only the second response, which was given by a high per cent of the children, was not judged to have qualities of cleverness. Thus he received a score of 5 on cleverness.

RESULTS

The data on the toy-improvement task are presented in Tables 1 and 2.

The general trends for the four conditions at the various grade levels are shown in Figure 2, which summarizes the data on total scores. The curves for the two trained groups are consistently above those of the two untrained groups. The curve for the trained groups that were urged to give interesting, unusual, and clever ideas is consistently above the curve of the other groups in each grade.

A two-way analysis of variance was performed to determine whether the observed effects of training and motivation can be accepted with confidence. The results show that the effects of training are statistically significant at better than the 5 per cent level of confidence for the second and third grades but not for the first. These results hold for all scores: fluency (number of ideas), flexibility (number of approaches), cleverness, and total.

The children who were asked to think of as many ideas as possible without regard to quality showed a consistent tendency to give fewer responses than the children who were asked to think of clever, interesting, and unusual ideas. The results are statistically significant only in the second grade, however.

Scores obtained by children in School Y were compared with those achieved by the untrained subjects (Groups A and C) in School X. No statistically significant differences were found in the average scores for any grade. Since other data available suggest that there were no differences in the quality of the pupils enrolled in these two schools, this result sug-

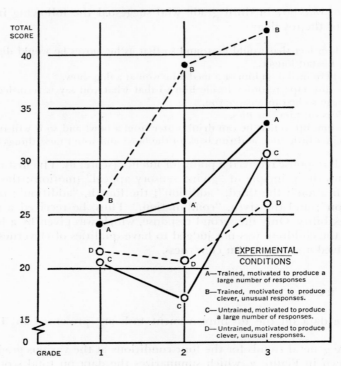

**Fig. 2. Summary of Mean Total Scores of Four
Experimental Conditions by Grades**

gests that the differences found in the basic experiment were due to the
teaching of the principles and the motivation rather than the warm up
and practice.

Except in the first grade, the children who had the benefit of the training procedures described in this experiment produced more ideas and
showed more flexibility and more cleverness in their thinking than the
children who had no training.

In the first-grade groups, the experimenter noted difficulty in getting
the children to follow the training program during the stage when principles were developed. All first-grade groups were active and productive
during the first stage of the training session; but during the second phase
interest seemed to diminish, and there were interchanges within the group.
A more effective technique or a more effective experimenter might have
produced more favorable results. Probably too many concepts were
presented in too short a time, or perhaps by the second phase the children
were tired.

Perhaps the most surprising finding of the study is that instructions to
produce a large number of ideas without regard for quality produced

Table 2. Total Mean Scores on a Test of Creative Thinking

Grade and Condition	Number of Pupils	Mean	Standard Deviation *
First Grade:			
Group A	18	24.00	7.37
Group B	15	26.20	14.23
Group C	19	20.75	12.85
Group D	16	22.12	11.44
Second Grade:			
Group A	20	26.20	11.16
Group B	17	39.17	16.52
Group C	21	17.33	9.98
Group D	17	21.18	11.41
Third Grade:			
Group A	18	33.73	11.22
Group B	11	42.45	9.32
Group C	19	30.68	17.36
Group D	13	26.23	11.42

* According to Bartlett's test, the variance is not significant at the 5 per cent level of confidence in any of the grades for any of the measures.

fewer responses than admonitions to produce clever, interesting, and unusual ideas. One would guess that instructions to think of "clever, interesting, and unusual ideas" tended to free the child for responses more than the admonition to think of as many ideas as possible, without bothering about "how good they are." If subjects had been threatened with penalties for "poor ideas" or instructed to give "only good, sound ideas," the results might have been different.

Since the training and the testing were both concerned with the improvement of a product, in this case a toy, it cannot be determined from this study whether the procedures used would be effective in training individuals to produce ideas for improving processes, situations, and interpersonal relations. It is quite likely, however, that the applicability is broad.

CONCLUSION

Results of this experiment indicate that pupils in the primary grades, with the possible exception of the first, can in a short period be taught a set of principles that will enable them to produce more and better ideas than they would have without training. The results provide no support for motivating pupils in the primary grades to produce a quantity of ideas without consideration for quality.

33 / Effects of Memory, Evaluative, and Creative Reading Sets on Test Performance

E. Paul Torrance and Judson A. Harmon

How can teachers help themselves, other adults, and children to think creatively and evaluatively? E. Paul Torrance and Judson A. Harmon of the University of Minnesota explore an approach to the problem of furthering creativity. The data in part indicate that "instructing mature students to assume various reading sets will have differential effects on the kind of goals achieved. . . . Those operating under the creative set, achieved the highest mean each week on the creative applications."

For several years the senior author (Torrance, 1950, 1951) has been experimenting with a variety of procedures which might increase the likelihood that students in mental hygiene courses will make use of scientifically developed principles of mental health in their work. Several recent experiments (Torrance, 1960) have been motivated by the belief that the failure of educators to make more effective use of such principles results from the fact that they have not been educated to think creatively or imaginatively about course materials. It soon became evident in this experimentation that many, perhaps most, students did not have the expectation that research results or scientifically developed principles *could* be applied imaginatively in solving many of their personal and professional problems. At best they were looking for specific prescriptions.

The rather shocking realization that students enrolled in a graduate course in mental hygiene did not even expect to be able to use the knowledge they were acquiring led the senior author to try to develop ways of establishing appropriate "sets." In one study (Torrance, 1960) random halves of two classes were asked to read research articles creatively or critically. Those who read and reported on the articles creatively were later more successful in developing a new idea of their own and in responding to a test of creative applications. These results stimulated the present study, an extension of "sets" to textbook readings.

The effect of appropriate preparatory sets in facilitating learning has been well-established (Johnson, 1955, p. 77). Usually a person's activities are integrated and he does not react to every event that stimulates his

Reprinted from the *Journal of Educational Psychology*, 1961, 52, 207–14, with the permission of the authors and the American Psychological Association.

sense organs. He is selective not only of what he responds to but also of what is produced and of the mental operation used in responding.

In designing the present experiment, the authors have been guided by Guilford's (1959) model of human intellect. Particular attention has been paid to his five mental operations: cognition, memory, convergent thinking, divergent thinking, and evaluation. By "cognition," Guilford means the operations involved in recognizing facts, discovery, and rediscovery. Memory involves the retention of what has been cognized. The two kinds of productive thinking, convergent and divergent, include the generation of new information from known information and remembered information. Convergent thinking leads to a conventional solution; divergent thinking leads to new and untested solutions. Evaluation refers to decisions as to the goodness, suitability, or adequacy of what we know, remember, or produce through convergent or divergent thinking. In this experiment a deliberate attempt was made to establish sets which would result in utilization of these operations.

METHOD

Subjects

The subjects were 115 students in a graduate level course in Personality Development and Mental Hygiene at the University of Minnesota during the summer of 1960. Seventy-six were males and 39 were females. Most subjects had had professional experience in one or more phases of education; 5 were public health nurses and 10 had had no professional experience. The average number of years of experience was 6.6 years and the range was from 0 to 30 years.

Subjects were assigned alphabetically to one or another of three groups (1, 2, or 3). The group number signified the reading set to be followed during a period of one week. This method of assignment to groups resulted in no biases due to sex, professional field, or number of years of experience. Some members of the original sample canceled the course or otherwise failed to participate in certain phases of the study, making the size of the three groups slightly unequal.

Description of the Reading Sets

The instructions of the memory, evaluation, and creative application sets were given to the subjects as follows:

Set A—Memory. When you read, it is important that you read with a set or intent to remember everything you read. In reading your assignments for the next three days, practice using this set. Try to make your mind act as a "sponge" and "soak up" as much as possible of whatever you read. Use whatever devices you like for trying to remember what you read. It may take some practice before you are really successful in assuming this set, but do not be discouraged. By the third day, you should find it easy to assume this set.

Set B—Evaluation. When you read, it is important that you think about what you are reading and evaluate critically the content. In reading your assignments for the next three days, practice using this set. As you read, ask: "Is what the author is saying really true? Does what he is saying agree with what I have experienced? Does what he is saying agree with what is known through scientific research?" Try to find defects in the reasoning of the author, in his factual presentation, and the like. Do not be concerned about errors in grammar, punctuation, sentence structure, and the like. It may take some practice . . . (etc., same as above).

Set C—Creative Application. When you read, it is important that you think about the many uses of the information which you are reading. It is especially important that you think of the various ways in which the information could be used in your personal and professional life. In reading, do not just ask, "What is the author saying?" Also ask, "How can I use what the author is saying?" Do not stop with just one use. Think of as many uses as you can of the important ideas presented. Jot down some of these uses for future reference. It may take some practice . . . (etc.).

Experimental Procedure

At the beginning of the first experimental week, subjects received reading-set instructions in accord with the group to which they had been assigned. Each subject received only one set during any one week. Thus, during the first week subjects in Group 1 received Set A; those in Group 2, Set B; those in Group 3, Set C; and so on—sets being shifted from group to group over the 3 weeks.

Each week each subject was provided an Evaluation of Reading Set Form upon which he was asked to report the degree to which he was able to maintain the assigned set, the degree of difficulty experienced in using that set, the number of minutes spent in completing the reading assignment for the last day of the week, and semantic reactions to the experience. Osgood's (1952) semantic differential technique was used in obtaining the latter. The following polar-adjective pairs were used with seven-point scales: good-bad, pleasurable-painful, labored-easy, wise-foolish, active-passive, fast-slow, cautious-rash, new-old, and interesting-boring.

Each Friday subjects were administered a 20-minute test which covered the reading assignment for that day.[1] This test included items which were defined as: cognitive (multiple-choice), memory (fill-in-the-blanks), divergent thinking (extensions from given facts, uses of facts, questions, hypotheses, etc.), and evaluation (decision making situations and justifications of decisions). It was at this time that the Evaluation of Reading Set Forms were collected.

[1] [The Friday reading assignments were as follows: first week, Shaffer and Shoben (1956), pp. 401–47; second week, Thorpe (1950), pp. 317–70; third week, Thorpe (1950), pp. 444–76. The three tests of reading sets are appended to the selection.]

Part-scores based on performance on these subtests were determined for all subjects and were reported to each subject at the beginning of the next week.

The following are samples of items presumed to involve cognition:

According to a recent study by two New York scientists involving tests of physical fitness, which of the following findings was obtained?
_____American children superior to European children
_____European children superior to American children
_____American children superior to Russian children
_____Russian children superior to American children
_____American children superior to Australian children
Which of the following is *least likely* to contribute to the prevention of paranoid behavior?
_____Training in straight thinking
_____Fostering attitudes of good sportsmanship
_____Finding available objects to blame
_____Developing self-ennobling attitudes toward sex
_____Facilitating social interaction

The following are examples of the memory items:

According to Wang, the primary factor in personality maladjustment is either _____ or _____ of the child's need for parental affection and sympathetic handling.

The experimenter who used a mechanical mother in laboratory studies at the University of Wisconsin is _____.

The following illustrate the creative-application problems:

If hunger needs are not satisfied during childhood, how is this likely to affect personality development? Assume that the child has been given enough food for subsistence but rarely enough to satisfy hunger. What kind of adult personality would you expect?

Research has shown that lower socioeconomic individuals have limited ability to delay gratification. List as many ways as you can think of for using this information in educational situations to promote healthy personality adjustment.

The following is a sample of the evaluative problems:

Assume that you are a member of the controlling board of the Minneapolis General Hospital which is considering the establishment of a children's psychiatric unit for mentally disturbed children. The treatment program will be quite similar to that described in the text for the Children's Psychiatric Unit at the University of Michigan and it is estimated that the cost of treatment per child will be $6,500. In deciding this issue, how would you vote?

_____Yes _____No

How would you justify your vote? Cite as many sound reasons as you can.

Analysis of Data

Analyses of variance were computed, comparing the effects of the reading sets of each of the different kinds of test performance (cognitive, memory, divergent thinking, and evaluation) for each of the 3 weeks. The evaluative-type item, unfortunately, was used in only one of the tests. Analyses of variance were computed for success in maintaining set, difficulty in maintaining set, number of minutes spent in completing the reading assignment, and each of the nine semantic differential scales for the three sets. Analyses of variance were also computed on Test Scores × Weeks and for Weeks × Groups in order to determine relative performance by weeks and by groups.

RESULTS

The data comparing scores on the memory-type items are presented in Table 1. It will be noted that only during the third week were the differential effects of the three sets statistically significant at the .05 level of significance or better, the memory set producing the highest score. The predicted trend occurred during the second week but was not statistically significant.

Table 2 presents the means and analysis of variance data for scores on the Creative-Applications or divergent-thinking items. It will be noted that the differential effects are rather strong for each of the 3 weeks and that in all cases those working under the creative set achieved the highest mean score. Those using the evaluative set consistently achieved the next highest mean score. On the third test all three groups tended to achieve higher scores than during the earlier weeks. This is probably due to the accumulative effects of the course which emphasized creative thinking concerning the course content.

The data concerning performance on the evaluative (decision making) items for the second week are shown in Table 3. The differential effects are statistically significant, with the evaluative, creative, and memory sets ranking in that order. Although this type of item was used at

Table 1. Comparison of Effects of Three Reading Sets on Performance in Memory Type Tests (Completion) for Each of Three Weeks

Week	Reading set	N	M	Between SS	Within SS	F ratio
First	Memory	40	6.04			
	Evaluative	38	6.24	3.9259	195.7898	2.226
	Creative	36	5.78			
Second	Memory	33	7.32			
	Evaluative	41	6.65	9.8958	420.2684	2.543
	Creative	37	7.20			
Third	Memory	38	8.30			
	Evaluative	34	8.15	12.7482	405.2544	3.429 *
	Creative	40	7.54			

* $p < .05$.

other times during the course, the only test in the experiment containing such an item was the one for the second week.

Table 4 presents the data for the cognitive items for each of the three

Table 2. Comparison of Effects of Three Reading Sets on Performance in Creative-Application Types of Tests for Each of Three Weeks

Week	Reading set	N	M	Between SS	Within SS	F ratio
First	Memory	40	4.25			
	Evaluative	38	5.43	72.4602	643.6542	12.496 **
	Creative	36	6.18			
Second	Memory	33	4.45			
	Evaluative	41	4.94	262.6431	372.4977	76.1493 **
	Creative	37	7.96			
Third	Memory	38	6.88			
	Evaluative	34	8.37	66.2446	524.4794	13.7613 **
	Creative	40	8.60			

** $p < .01$.

Table 3. Comparison of Effects of Three Reading Sets on Performance in Evaluative (Decision Making) Type of Test for Second Week

Reading set	N	M	Between SS	Within SS	F ratio
Memory	33	5.88			
Evaluative	41	7.54	39.1292	368.4517	11.469 **
Creative	37	6.70			

** $p < .01$.

Table 4. Comparison of Effects of Three Reading Sets on Performance on Cognitive Type of Tests (Multiple-Choice) for Each of Three Weeks

Week	Reading set	N	M	Between SS	Within SS	F ratio
First	Memory	40	6.21			
	Evaluative	38	6.52	1.9062	236.9290	0.893
	Creative	36	6.33			
Second	Memory	33	4.03			
	Evaluative	41	3.32	10.3007	200.9297	5.537 **
	Creative	37	3.43			
Third	Memory	38	4.68			
	Evaluative	34	5.06	7.3804	211.8738	3.797 *
	Creative	40	4.42			

* $p < .05$.   ** $p < .01$.

tests. It had been anticipated that subjects using the memory set would perform best on these items. This occurred only during the second week. The differential effects were also significant for the last test, but subjects working under the evaluative set achieved the highest mean score. It will also be noted that subjects using the evaluative set also had a slight edge during the first week but the differential effects were not statistically significant.

Test Performance by Group and by Week

Analyses of variance were also performed to study differential test performance by group and by week. It was found that the effects for groups are not statistically significant. The effects for weeks are statistically significant, total mean scores being higher for the third week than for the first two weeks. Thus, there is no evidence of the superiority of any one sequence of sets over the others.

Other Reactions to Assigned Sets

Failure to maintain an assigned set is obviously an important consideration in determining the effectiveness of a set in producing the desired results. Two questions on the Evaluation of Reading Set Form were designed to supply information concerning this problem. Responses concerning the completeness with which the set was maintained ranged from "not at all" (Point 1) to "almost all of the time" (Point 7). Responses concerning difficulty in learning to use the set ranged from "impossible" (Point 1) to "extremely easy" (Point 6). Weights were assigned arbitrarily. Means and F ratios are presented in Table 5 for the variables: success in using set, difficulty in using set, number of minutes spent in reading assignment for day, and for each of the semantic scales.

From Table 5 it will be noted that the sets had significant differential effects on both success and difficulty in using set but not on time spent on reading assignment. The memory set seems to have been the most successfully and easily maintained and the creative set seems to have been the least successfully and easily maintained. Subjects estimated that they maintained the memory set on the average about two-thirds of the time, finding it between "fairly difficult" and "fairly easy" to maintain. They reported that they were successful in using the creative set less than half of the time.

From Table 5 it will also be noted that on only four of the nine polar-adjective pairs are reactions significantly different among the three conditions of reading set. Those pairs are: fast-slow, cautious-rash, new-old, and interesting-boring. Subjects using the memory set tended towards fast, cautious, old, and boring. Those using the evaluative set tended towards slow and held to a middle position on the other pairs. Under the creative set the direction was towards rash, new, and interesting.

Table 5. Comparison of Effects of Three Reading Sets on Success in
Using Set, Difficulty in Using Set, Time Spent on Reading
Assignment, and Semantic Reaction for Three Weeks Combined

	Memory		Evaluative		Creative		
Variable	N	M	N	M	N	M	F ratio
Success in using set	106	5.18	109	4.06	105	3.79	63.35 **
Difficulty in keeping assigned set	106	4.54	110	4.10	105	3.97	26.72 **
Number of minutes spent on reading assignment	104	112.27	110	114.52	105	112.00	0.23
Good-Bad	105	2.47	109	2.92	102	2.59	0.59
Pleasurable-Painful	103	3.08	107	3.16	103	3.01	0.87
Labored-Easy	103	3.96	107	3.64	103	3.73	2.44
Wise-Foolish	103	2.45	109	2.37	102	2.36	0.30
Active-Passive	103	2.64	107	2.67	102	2.48	1.46
Fast-Slow	102	3.96	107	4.38	103	4.33	5.02 **
Cautious-Rash	102	2.86	107	2.97	102	3.13	3.27 *
New-Old	103	4.55	107	3.64	103	2.88	18.38 **
Interesting-Boring	103	2.76	107	2.25	102	2.13	17.11 **

$* p < .05.$ $** p < .01.$

In order to determine whether or not there are differential effects with
the passage of time, a comparison was made by weeks on the variables
listed in Table 5. Only four of the variables gave rise to changes with time
as data of analyses of variance showed. During the second week subjects
tended to report greater success in maintaining the sets than during the
other weeks. They also tended to spend somewhat more time on the
reading assignment during this particular week. Finally, there was a
consistent change towards fast and boring over the 3 weeks. Of these four
variables the time spent on the reading assignment was significant at
$.01 < F < .05$. The other three were significant at $< .01$ level.

DISCUSSION

From the data which have been presented it seems clear that instructing mature students to assume various reading sets will have differential
effects on the kind of goals achieved. This would seem to be especially true
if creative thinking and evaluative thinking are desired as outcomes. Although the students in the present study were able to maintain the creative and evaluative sets only about half of the time, attempts to maintain
these sets had measurable effects on performance on tests covering the
reading assignment.

Since most examinations given to large classes are of the cognitive
(multiple-choice) type, it is worthwhile to note that the memory set does
not uniformly result in the best performance on this type of test. In fact,

in only one of the 3 weeks does the memory set result in superiority on the cognitive type of test. The evaluative set tended to result in better mean scores during the other 2 weeks.

Because of the differential effects of the three sets on the four types of tests, one might also infer that instructors need to develop tests designed to measure different kinds of achievement, depending upon course objectives. If instructors expect their students to think imaginatively and evaluatively about what they learn, it is extremely doubtful that such goals are adequately assessed by the traditional multiple-choice and completion items.

The data indicate that students are more successful in maintaining the memory set and find it easier to maintain this set than the creative and evaluative sets. This probably results from the fact that they have had much more practice with this set than with the others. This hypothesis receives some support from reactions to the semantic differential. For example, subjects under the memory set tend to rate the experience in the direction of cautious, old, and boring. It is likely that, with practice, students will find it easier to maintain creative and evaluative sets and that better results will be achieved than those reported herein.

Finally, in interpreting the results, it should be recognized that the subjects are graduate students and that almost all of them have had rather extensive experience in various types of educational work.

SUMMARY

This experiment was designed to test the differential effects of memory, evaluative, and creative "sets" in reading assignments in a graduate level course on Personality Development and Mental Hygiene. The 115 subjects were arranged alphabetically and assigned to one of three groups. Each group was assigned in turn each of the three reading sets to be used in the assigned readings for a week. At the end of each week, a 20-minute test containing cognitive, memory, creative thinking, and evaluative items was administered. Subjects also estimated their degree of success in maintaining the set, difficulty in maintaining it, the number of minutes spent on the Friday's reading assignment, and their semantic reactions to nine polar-adjective pairs.

Analyses of variance indicated that the three sets produced differential effects on most of the tests for all 3 weeks. Those operating under the creative set, achieved the highest mean each week on the creative applications. Those operating under the evaluative set achieved the highest mean on the evaluative or decision making problem when such a problem was given (second week only). Those operating under the memory set achieved the highest mean on the memory tests (completion) only during the third week. The differential effects on the memory items were not statistically significant during the other weeks. Differential effects on the cognitive items were not consistent. Those operating under the memory set achieved the highest mean during the second week and those under the evaluative set led during the third week.

Subjects reported that they found it easier to maintain the memory set and rated themselves as more successful in maintaining this set than the other two. There were no differential effects on the estimated length of time spent on the reading assignment. On the semantic differential, subjects under the memory set tended towards fast, cautious, old, and boring. Those under the evaluative set tended towards slow and those under the creative set, towards rash, new, and interesting.

During the second week subjects generally reported greater success in maintaining sets than during the first and third weeks. On the semantic evaluations, there was a consistent and significant drift towards fast and boring. The three original groups did not differ significantly, giving no evidence of the superiority of any one sequence of sets over the others.

FIRST EVALUATION OF READING SETS

Name: _____   Reading Set: A____B____C____

PART I. Indicate the best answer to each of the following questions by checking the appropriate blank:

1. Which of the following characterized all or almost all of the approximately 40 wild children which have been studied? ____Crying and laughter ____Sense of modesty and shame ____Lack of anything resembling speech ____Ability to use tools ____Lack of ability to show violent anger

2. According to Mead, which of the following characterized the childhood of Samoan children? ____Complete freedom from responsibility ____No period of complete freedom from responsibility ____Well regulated changes according to an age schedule ____Emphasis on cleanliness and modesty ____Disregard for individual differences in learning

3. Which of the following is the best definition of socialization? ____Teaching of skills in interpersonal relations ____Teaching to act and think in culturally sanctioned ways ____Teaching the rituals and ceremonies of the social group ____Teaching to integrate personality needs and social needs ____Teaching good manners and social graces

4. Which of the following conclusions does Kardiner's study of Alorese personality support? ____Adult personality traits can be predicted with reasonable accuracy from knowledge of child rearing procedures. ____All adults in an isolated culture tend to have similar personality traits. ____Maternal neglect is likely to result in adult personalities characterized by confidence and freedom from anxiety. ____Maternal neglect is likely to result in adult personalities characterized by initiative and enterprise. ____Maternal neglect is associated with adult personalities intensely interested and curious about the world.

5. For what type of personality studies are Whiting and Child best known? ____Longitudinal ____Cross-sectional ____Cross-cultural ____Comparative ____Clinical

6. On the basis of cultural studies of personality, what characteristics are most likely to result from harsh and punitive socialization in childhood? ____Absence of feelings of anxiety and guilt ____Undue concern about food ____Rigorous suppression of aggression ____Guilt about aggressive impulses ____Perception of other people as potentially hostile

7. Which of the following social classes is characterized by anxiety about what others think of them and concern about respectability? ____Lower-upper ____Upper-middle ____Lower-middle ____Upper-lower

8. Which of the following is *not* used in Warner's Index of Social Characteristics? ____Type of occupation ____Amount of income ____Source of income ____Type of house ____Quality of neighborhood

9. Which of the following needs generally characterizes middle-class people? ____Achievement ____Affiliation ____Abasement ____Heterosexuality ____Aggression

10. Which of the following types of parental behavior is likely to produce children who lack originality, creativity, and curiosity? ____Overprotection ____Indulgence ____Possessiveness ____Domination ____Rejection

PART II. Answer the following questions by completing the blanks:

1. What types of sexual activity are most strongly disapproved by lower class families?
2. What is meant by a "nuclear family"?
3. What methods of home control differentiate delinquent boys from nondelinquent boys?

PART III. List . . . as many specific educational uses as you can think of for the fact that lower-class individuals place much greater emphasis upon immediacy than do middle-class individuals?

SECOND EVALUATION OF READING SETS

Name: _____ Set Assigned: A____ B____ C____

PART I. CREATIVE THINKING: If hunger needs are not satisfied during childhood how is this likely to affect personality development? (Assume that the child is given enough food for existence but never really enough to satisfy hunger.)

PART II. DECISION-MAKING: You are a member of the controlling board of the Minneapolis General Hospital which is considering the establishment of a children's psychiatric unit for mentally disturbed children. The treatment program will be almost identical to that described by Thorpe for the Children's Psychiatric Unit at the University of Michigan and it is estimated that the cost of treatment per child will be $6,500. In deciding this issue, how would you vote?

_____Yes _____No

How would you justify your vote?

PART III. MEMORY: Complete the following sentences by adding the correct word or words in the blanks.

1. According to Wang, the primary factor in personality maladjustment is either _____ or _____ of the child's need for parental affection and sympathetic handling.
2. The term used in referring to overt behavior towards an individual which leads him to believe that he is neither loved nor valued is _____.
3. The term which refers to a parent substitute is _____.
4. In humans and infra-humans, with real substitute mothers, the key to the child's mental health is the type of _____ relationship involved.
5. The experimenter who used a mechanical mother monkey in laboratory studies at the University of Wisconsin was _____.
6. The term which refers to intra-family sexual relations is _____.
7. A child's associates of the same status are termed "his _____ group."
8. A repeated twitch or muscular flexion associated with stress is called a (an) _____.
9. Enuresis is a term which refers to _____.
10. Fear of the dark, of animals, etc. is called _____.

PART IV. RECOGNITION. Check the best answer for each of the following questions:

1. Which of the following investigators discovered that deprivation of affective interchange during infancy is a serious handicap for development in every sector of personality? _____Margaret Lowenfeld _____Rene Spitz _____Harry Harlow _____Melanie Klein _____Anna Freud
2. Which of the following is *not* included by Thorpe as a "childhood condition" which contributes to the maintenance of emotional stability in later life? _____Adequate self-concept _____Opportunities for social experience _____Safety from traumatic experiences _____Secure home life _____Opportunities for self-expression
3. What term is usually used in referring to the process by which children in maladjusted families often learn or "pick up" similar behavior patterns? _____Identification _____Conditional _____Genetically determined susceptibility _____Projection _____Introjection

4. According to a recent study by two New York scientists involving actual tests of physical fitness which of the following findings was established? ____American children superior to European children ____European children superior to American children ____American children superior to African children ____African children superior to American children ____Russian children superior to American children

5. Which of the following is a unique characteristic of the small family in our society? ____Emphasis on togetherness ____Pressures for conformity ____Stereotype of roles ____Small degree of stress on achievement ____Upper-class values

6. Which of the following is most apt to choose a mate who represents a parent figure? ____Only children ____Oldest children ____Youngest children ____Middle children

7. According to Thorpe, how are most vocational choices determined? ____Through vocational counselors ____Through school counselors ____On basis of a teacher's suggestions ____On basis of suggestions and desires of parents ____By chance or accident

THIRD EVALUATION OF READING SETS

Name: _____ Set Assigned A____B____C____

PART I. Complete the following statements by adding the appropriate word or words.

1. Factors or traits which are related to ancestry are called _____ traits.

2. Hostility or aggression occurs when the individual is _____.

3. The term used to describe a person who is no longer in jail but who is checked on occasionally by a police officer or worker is a _____.

4. Four types of sociopaths are: (a)_____ (b)_____ (c)_____ (d)_____.

5. About _____ attempts at suicide are estimated to occur for every actual suicide.

6. Suicide is _____ frequent than murder.
         more, less

7. The suicide rate _____ in periods of depression and tends to _____ during cycles of business prosperity.

PART II. Indicate by checking the appropriate blank the best answer for each of the following questions.

1. According to Thorpe, why do sociopaths fail to respond to psychiatric treatment? ____They have defective egos ____They have uncontrollable ids ____They have defective superegos ____They are possessed of devils ____Their condition is hereditary

2. Which of the following makes important the famous Wickersham "Report on Causes of Crime"? ____It was based on empirical evidence

_____It supported the stimulus-response theory of behavior _____It emphasized study of the environment _____Suggestions made were quickly implemented on a national scale _____New methods of collecting data were employed

3. Which of the following is the most probable specific social influence towards repeated criminal behavior? _____Association with criminals _____Deteriorated ego integrity _____Intense need or tension states _____Genetically determined weaknesses _____Society's attitudes toward crime via mass media

4. Which of the following is a fundamental characteristic of psychopaths? _____High score on the MMPI psychopathic deviate scale _____Lack of socialization _____Preponderance of hostile behavior _____Psychosis _____Conflicts with parent of same sex

5. What is usually the most accurate prognosis concerning the success of psychotherapy with psychopaths? _____Almost complete success (almost all cases treated) _____Good chance of success (75 per cent "cures") _____Moderate chance of success (50 per cent "cures") _____Poor chance of success (20 per cent "cures") _____Very poor chance of success (about 5 per cent "cures")

6. What is the main criticism of case reports for decision-making concerning parole and probation? _____They include too much unimportant material _____They do not tell what should be done _____They are contrary to accepted principles of mental hygiene _____They do not aid in the isolation of pertinent personality dynamics _____They are written by social workers and acted upon by judges

7. Which of the following was *not* one of the characteristics Freud associated with hostility? _____Instinctive _____Necessary in many life situations _____Based upon primitive, inherited, psychic forces _____Temporally contingent upon need states _____Associated with early interpersonal relations with the mother

8. Which of the following is not included by Thorpe in his list of environmental conditions conducive to delinquent and criminal behavior? _____Glamorization of crime by newspapers _____Poverty and slums _____Make-up spread and fluctuations in population groups _____Divorce, separation, other adverse family conditions _____Poor police practices

PART III. On the basis of what you know about the causation of delinquency and crime, what conditions would have to exist in homes and schools to eliminate delinquent and criminal behavior? (How would parents and teachers have to behave?)

PART IV. Make a list of the specific questions you would want to ask in testing the hypothesis that psychopathic or criminal tendencies result from a lack of maternal love during infancy.

Personality Development

34 / Influencing Ethnocentrism in Small Discussion Groups through a Film Communication [1]

Leonard L. Mitnick and Elliott McGinnies

In the field of mental health education what can be the role of mental health films in discussion groups? After viewing and discussing a film such as "The High Wall," which treats group prejudice as a communicable disease and traces its origins in the family and community, do ethnocentric attitudes change, and if so, how much and how stable are the changes? These are some of the questions explored by Leonard L. Mitnick of the General Electric Company, Bethesda, Maryland and Elliott McGinnies of the University of Maryland.

The experimental literature dealing with persuasive communications has been summarized and given a theoretical orientation by Hovland, et al. (1953). Many questions, however, remain unanswered, among them problems concerning the relationships between certain aspects of group composition, interaction, and the direction and stability of attitude change under the impact of a persuasive communication. The present paper is concerned with learning and attitude change among the members of small, attitudinally homogeneous groups that experienced varying degrees of participation with respect to discussion of a motion picture film dealing with the problem of group prejudice and conflict.

Motion picture films may exert a significant influence upon the at-

[1] This research was supported in part by a special grant from the National Institute of Mental Health, National Institutes of Health, United States Public Health Service. The assistance of Dr. Willard Vaughan and Mr. Clagett Smith, our co-researchers, is gratefully acknowledged. Dr. Ray C. Hackman assisted in the design and statistical analysis. This paper is based upon portions of the doctoral dissertation of the first author.

Reprinted from the *Journal of Abnormal and Social Psychology*, 1958, 56, 82–90, with the permission of the authors and the American Psychological Association.

titudes and opinions of viewers (Hovland, Lumisdaine, and Sheffield, 1949; Peterson and Thurstone, 1933; Ramseyer, 1938; Raths and Trager, 1948). It has also been shown that group participation in decision-making is a more effective technique for generating acceptance than mere exposure to persuasive influences (Bavelas, 1947; Coch and French, 1948; Lewin, 1947). Active participation either imposed by the experimenter or allowed to develop at the initiative of the group members seems to encourage acceptance of the content of a communication (Janus and King, 1954; Lewin, 1947).

A difficulty in generalizing too confidently from such findings arises when one considers that active rehearsal of this nature is assumed to reinforce the content of the communication and, hence, might be expected to facilitate attitude change only in those situations where the participants concur with the communication content. In cases where the communication tends to counteract existing attitudes in the audience, it is questionable that active participation would provide the kind of conditions that would enhance the effects of the communication. It seems particularly questionable with respect to groups that are unified in their antagonism to the communication content. Prediction of the direction, extent, and stability of attitude change in groups predisposed in different ways toward a controversial film thus poses a problem. What, for example, would be the nature of attitude changes in groups composed homogeneously of individuals who have a positive, negative, or neutral bias toward the content of the communication when opportunity for discussion of the material is extended or withheld? The experimental literature in the field of communication and persuasion provides no basis for making clearcut predictions under several conditions described.

In one sense, as Hovland, Janis, and Kelley (1953) have pointed out, the effectiveness of a persuasive communication is a matter of learning. Any attitude change following exposure to a film, for example, may reflect the amount of new information conveyed by the film to the audience. Such change seems to be most effective with respect to those items that are covered specifically in the film content (Hovland, Lumisdaine, and Sheffield, 1949). A relationship between attitude and retention of information has been found by Doob (1953), who reports that intensity rather than direction of attitude facilitates retention of the content of a communication. If such is the case, then the familiar principles of learning do not apply without emendation to persuasive communication, since superior retention for pleasant, or acceptable, as opposed to unpleasant, or unacceptable, material has been reported in several studies (Edwards, 1941; Sharp, 1938; Watson and Hartman, 1939). A further problem intrudes here, namely the effects of initial attitude upon learning among the recipients of a persuasive communication. Does initial attitude influence the amount of learning from a relevant communication, and is attitude change related to such learning?

The problems suggested here become even more complex when one adds the variable of active participation to the audience settings, since it seems well-established that participation in a communication situation enhances learning on the part of those who participate (Kurtz and Hovland, 1953; Michael and Maccoby, 1953). The present study was designed to measure the relative influence of the factors of initial attitude and learning upon participation, the retention of information, and the direction, extent, and stability of attitude change.

METHOD

Subjects

Approximately 400 students from two high schools [2] responded to a slightly modified version of the California Ethnocentrism (E) Scale.[3] In each school, 27 students were selected from each extreme and from the middle of the distribution of E scores, which closely approximated a Gaussian curve. The three levels of ethnocentrism represented will be referred to as low E, high E, and middle E, indicating the portion of the score distribution from which the Ss were chosen. This preliminary testing took place about one month prior to the experimental sessions. Means and variances were determined for the students of the two schools and no significant differences between schools were found for either of these measures.[4]

Procedure

Within each category of ethnocentrism, nine Ss were assigned at random to each of three experimental conditions, designated as film-discussion, film-alone, and control. This was done within schools, so that a total of 18 groups, or 162 Ss, representing three degrees of ethnocentrism participated in the experiment. The film-discussion groups first viewed the film "The High Wall," which treats group prejudice as a communicable disease and traces its origins in the family and community. The members of these groups, representing low, high, and intermediate degrees of ethnocentric disposition, were given thirty minutes in which to discuss the film and related issues. The group members were free to participate in the discussion or not, and the discussion leader assumed a permissive, or nondirective, role. The same discussion leader served for all of the

[2] Miss Rowenetta Allen, Supervisor of Instruction of Prince George's County, Maryland, kindly granted permission for inviting two high schools to participate in this research. Mr. Allan Chotiner and Mr. Fred Wampler of High Point Senior High School, and Mr. Kalman Vozar and Mr. Ralph Angel of Bladensburg Senior High School cooperated generously in all phases of the study.

[3] [Appended to the selection under the heading Public Opinion Questionnaire E.]

[4]	Bladensburg High School	High Point High School
X	72.7	69.4
σ^2	519.16	397.33
N	81	81

Neither the F test for the variances nor the t test for the means showed significant differences at the .05 level.

groups. The discussions were terminated either at the end of half an hour or when it appeared that the group members had no more comments to offer. At the conclusion of the discussion, the Ss again answered the E scale.

Members of the film-alone groups viewed the film under comparable conditions but did not engage in discussion of it. They again filled out the E scale upon conclusion of the film showing. The control groups responded to the E scale at the same times as the experimental groups but without any intervening exposure to either the film or a discussion.

In order to determine the amount of learning of film content by the Ss, a 33-item multiple-choice Information test [5] covering factual material in the film was devised through pretesting and item-analysis. The items on the test covered such points as identification of characters in the film and details of the action in certain scenes. The items did not deal directly with the problem of prejudice. The Information test, therefore, was not a measure of attitude-related material but, rather, was an index of the sheer amount of detail retained from exposure to the film. Pretesting with this form would have been meaningless, since the pattern of responses would necessarily be random for Ss who had not viewed the film. This test was administered to each of the experimental groups (film-discussion and film-alone) immediately after the second administration of the E scale, following presentation of the film. Both the E scale and the Information test were readministered a final time one month after the film showing in order to determine retention of information and stability of attitude change during this interval. The control groups, of course, did not take the Information test at any time, since it dealt exclusively with the content of the film.

All of the discussions were tape-recorded, and the recording equipment was present whether a discussion was to follow the film or not. None of the apparatus was concealed from the discussion groups, but they were assured that all records would be held in confidence. Two other individuals were present in the experimental situation; they were the "spotters" who, from the rear of the room, recorded participation of an S in terms of S's seat by row and seat number. When an individual participated, his location was noted by both spotters in terms of these references. Thus, it was possible to maintain a running account of participation by each S, and to identify each comment with its source upon typed, verbatim transcripts of the recordings. This procedure is described in detail elsewhere. [see pp. 357–59.]

RESULTS

Attitude Change

The measure used to assess attitude change was a difference score determined by subtracting the post treatment score from the initial score on

[5] [Appended to the selection.]

the E scale. Since it is possible that a change of position on an attitude scale may be related to one's initial attitude, the correlation coefficient between initial attitudes and difference scores was computed and found to be 0.16, indicating that less than three per cent of the variability in the difference scores could be accounted for by the initial scores.

Table 1. Analysis of Variance of Attitude Changes

Source	df	Sums of Squares	Mean Squares	F [a]
Predisposition (P)	2	779.4	389.7	3.62
Treatments (T)	2	6506.9	3253.5	30.18 **
P × T	4	431.0	107.8	5.36 **
Within groups	153	3068.1	20.1	
TOTAL	161	10785.4		

[a] A single asterisk indicates rejection of the null hypothesis at the .05 level of confidence, and the double asterisk indicates rejection at the .01 level.

Table 2. Mean Attitude Change Scores [a]

	Low E	Middle E	High E
Control	32.5	35.9	37.8
Film-alone	44.9	48.5	54.7
Film-discussion	47.5	49.5	47.6

[a] For ease in computation a constant of +40 was added to all difference scores.

Data from the two high schools were combined for all statistical analyses. After Bartlett's test (Edwards, 1950, pp. 195–98) provided no basis for rejecting the assumption of homogenous variances, an analysis of variance was performed on the attitude change scores. As shown in Table 1, the F values for the treatment × predisposition interaction and treatment as a main effect were significant at the .01 level of confidence. Table 2 shows the mean values for each treatment and predisposition. Among the high E individuals differences in attitude change between the film-alone and film-discussion conditions were significant at the .05 level of confidence. The differences between the film-alone and film-discussions treatment for the middle E and low E groups were not significant. For the film-alone condition the high E groups showed significantly more change than the other two groups, but for the film-discussion treatment there were no significant differences among predisposition groups. It is evident, then, that giving the high E groups the opportunity to discuss the film counteracted some of the effects of the film, while for the low E groups a reversal of this trend was noted. The significance of treatment as a main effect was due to differences between control groups and both experimental groups;

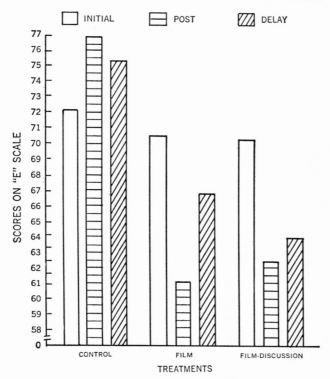

Fig. 1. Initial, Posttreatment, and Delay Scores on
the "E" Scale for Each Treatment

there was no significant difference between the combined film-discussion groups and the film-alone groups.

Fig. 1 presents the mean values for the initial, posttreatment and delayed administration of the E scale for all treatments. Since predisposition was not associated with attitude change, the various predisposition groups are combined according to treatment. The attitude change scores (initial-minus-post) for the film-discussion groups and for the film-alone groups both differed significantly from the control groups at the .01 level of confidence, but the experimental groups did not differ with respect to attitude change. In short, significant reductions in personal ethnocentrism were brought about by both the film-discussion and film-alone treatments, while the control groups showed no change in ethnocentric attitudes.

Ss were retested with the E scale one month after treatment, and an analysis of variance was performed on the differences between the initial scores and the delayed scores on the E scale. Inasmuch as some of the Ss were absent at the time of the delayed E scale, their scores were estimated by a procedure suggested by Cochran and Cox (1950, p. 98). Before performing this analysis, the correlation coefficient between this difference score and the initial score was determined and found to be 0.04, indicating that only 0.16% of the variability in the difference scores could be attributed to the initial scores. An examination of this analysis, shown in Table 3, shows that the obtained F value for treatment was significant at the .01 level of confidence. Fig. 1 presents the delay scores for each treatment. Differences between the retention of attitude change for the film-alone and film-discussion groups differed significantly from the controls at the .01 level of confidence, but these two groups did not differ from each other when compared with respect to initial score minus delayed score.

Table 3. Analysis of Variance of Stability of Attitude Change

Source	df	Sums of Squares	Mean Squares	F
Predisposition (P)	2	40.1	20.0	—
Treatments (T)	2	2563.3	1281.6	9.52 **
P × T	4	625.3	156.3	1.16
Within groups	139	18709.7	134.6	
TOTAL	147	21938.4		

A further comparison of the scores represented in Fig. 1 was made. Within each experimental condition, the scores on the posttreatment and delayed administration of the E scale were compared. Neither the control groups nor the film-discussion groups differed significantly on these two measures, indicating that for these two conditions there was no significant change one month after treatment from posttreatment scores. However, the film-alone groups showed a significant change on these two measures. At the time of the delayed measurement, the film-alone groups had moved significantly from their posttreatment score position in the direction of their pre-experimental position.

It was previously indicated that on the posttreatment measure the film-alone groups and the film-discussion groups did not differ significantly. A breakdown of the film-discussion groups was made into active and passive participants, with the active participants defined as those individuals who made one or more comments in the discussion regardless of length, and the passive participants defined as those individuals who made no contribution to the discussion. Of the 54 Ss who comprised the film-discussion groups, 37 were active participants and 17 were passive participants. Fig. 2 shows the mean values for three degrees of participation on each administration of the E scale. None of the changes from initial to posttreatment scores differed significantly from one another.

A comparison of the posttreatment and delayed E-scale positions had shown that the film-alone groups moved significantly from their posttreat-

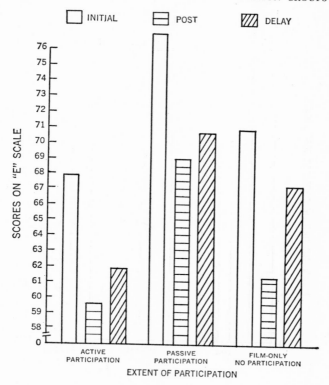

Fig. 2. Initial, Posttreatment, and Delay Scores on
the "E" Scale for Each Level of Participation

ment scores in the direction of their original position, while the control and film-discussion groups showed no such change. Is this difference attributable to greater attitude change among the active participants in the film-discussion groups, or does it result from the process of discussion influencing all members present, whether active or passive? In order to provide an answer to this question, the active and passive participants were compared on their posttreatment and delayed scores. Fig. 2 shows these differences graphically. The differences between the posttreatment and delayed E scores were not significant for either active or passive participants. That is, neither the active nor the passive discussion participants changed significantly from their posttreatment measures after an interval of one month. The film-alone groups on the other hand, regressed toward their earlier position. The stability of attitude change characterizing both the active and passive participants suggests that presence during a discussion is as effective as active participation in generating greater permanency of attitude change.

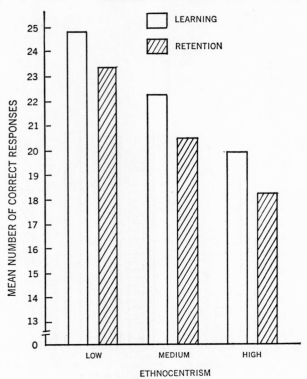

Fig. 3. Mean Scores on the Learning and Retention Test
for Each Predisposition Group

Learning

The relationship of amount of information learned from the film to
the major independent variables of the experiment was also evaluated by
analysis of variance. Since the relationship between learning and participation, however, was ascertainable only in those groups that held discussions, that analysis is presented separately.

Examination of Table 4 shows that the F value for predisposition was
significant at the .01 level of confidence. The mean scores for the three predisposition groups were: low E, 24.8; middle E, 22.3; high E, 19.8. All
differences between these means were significant at the .01 level of confidence, indicating an inverse relationship between initial degree of
ethnocentrism and learning of information specific to the film. Since
treatments were not a significant source of variability, it is apparent that
discussion following the film communication did not facilitate recall of
details from the film.

Fig. 3 presents the mean learning and retention scores of each predis-

Table 4. Analysis of Variance of Scores on the Information Test

Source	df	Sums of Squares	Mean Squares	F
Predisposition (P)	2	450.7	225.4	15.65 **
Treatment (T)	1	16.3	16.3	1.13
P × T	2	18.7	9.4	
Within groups	102	1468.0	14.4	
TOTAL	107	1953.7		

position group. It is evident that individuals who scored high on the E scale learned the least from the film, while those who were low on the E scale learned the most from the film. The middle E groups fell in between these extremes. Those individuals, in short, who were assumed on the basis of the E scores to be favorably disposed toward the content of the communication learned significantly more factual material from it than did those Ss who were antagonistic to the film's theme, even though the information learned was not directly related to the topic of prejudice. That this relationship was not confounded with differences in intelligence among the Ss was attested by the fact that the correlation between E scores and scores on the California Mental Maturity Test was not significant.

An analysis of variance was also performed on the retention of information scores to determine whether the experimental variables were reflected in differential retention of film content among the Ss one month after the first testing. The scores of the absentees were again estimated by the procedure suggested by Cochran and Cox (1950). Results of the analysis of variance which are given in Table 5 show that predisposition is sig-

Table 5. Analysis of Variance of Information Retention Score

Source	df	Sums of Squares	Mean Squares	F
Predisposition (P)	2	483.6	241.8	15.80 **
Treatment (T)	1	35.6	35.6	
P × T	2	90.7	45.4	2.97
Within groups	94	1436.5	15.3	
TOTAL	99	2046.4		

nificant at the .01 level. The differences in retention scores among the three predisposition conditions are presented graphically in Fig. 3. An increased degree of ethnocentrism, in general, is associated with a greater decrement in retention of information. It should be noted, however, that a correlation of .73 ($P < .01$) was found between learning and retention, so that the differences in retention of information may be ascribed to amount of material initially learned rather than to predisposition as such.

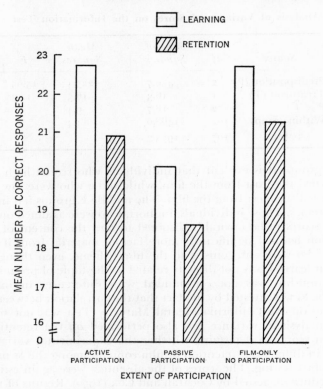

Fig. 4. Mean Learning and Retention of Information Scores for Each Level of Participation

Finally, an effort was made to determine whether those individuals who participated voluntarily in the discussions learned more from the film than those who did not participate. Fig. 4 shows the mean learning scores made by the active participants, passive participants, and film-alone *S*s. Evaluation by means of *t* tests revealed no significant differences between the active participants and members of the film-alone groups. Both the active participants and the film-alone *S*s, however, learned significantly more from the film than the passive discussion participants. This advantage persisted on the retention measure one month later.

In an attempt to determine whether attitude change was related to the amount of information learned, a correlation was computed between these two variables. The obtained value of .03 indicated that there was no significant relationship between learning of film details and attitude change.

DISCUSSION

Attitude change in response to a persuasive sound film was a joint function of opportunity for discussion of the film and initial attitude. Predisposition alone was not related to attitude change. It had been expected that in the low E groups a greater effect might be obtained with those members who held discussions, since these individuals had views that were essentially in accord with those contained in the film. (Even the low Es could show attitude change since the mean score of these Ss was 26.7 points below the ceiling of the E scale.) The discussion might reasonably have been expected to reinforce the initial attitudes of these Ss and thus facilitate a greater change in attitude than that produced among the low Es who did not hold discussions. In the high E groups, on the other hand, a possibility existed that expression of opinions at variance with those presented in the film might mitigate the film's effect, and that the nondiscussion groups might therefore show greater attitude change. Among the neutral or middle E Ss, no difference was expected between the film and film discussion conditions.

These hypotheses were generally supported by the data. Although the difference in attitude change in the low E groups under film-alone and film-discussion conditions was not significant, the trend was in the expected direction. The high Es showed significantly less change under discussion conditions. In general, it may be suggested that discussion of a persuasive communication does facilitate attitude change among those initially favorable to the communication content. On the other hand, discussion of a communication by homogeneous groups that are antagonistic to the content detracts from the effectiveness of the communication. This result may be attributed to the fact that discussion provides an opportunity for such individuals to express their initial views and thus partially to negate the persuasive effects that have been generated. Examination of the discussion transcripts supports this interpretation. The high Es devoted most of the discussion periods to expression of their antipathies toward Negroes, while the low E and middle E groups tended to examine the general problems of group prejudice raised by the film. The middle Ss having no clear-cut opinion either pro or con held very apathetic discussions and, therefore, neither reinforced nor mitigated the effects of the film.

While there were no differences in attitude change between the film-alone and film-discussion groups immediately following the communication, the film-alone groups regressed significantly from their posttreatment positions when measured one month later; the film-discussion groups and the controls showed no such change. The discussions probably gave those Ss present an opportunity to learn how other members of their group perceived the film and permitted the convergence of views toward a common norm. Apparently influenced by such a consensus effect, the film-discussion groups maintained their posttreatment attitude change. The film-alone groups, not having experienced this interaction, regressed towards their initial scores on the delayed measurement. Thus, participation in the form of group discussion following a communication may have some value in maintaining attitude changes produced by the communication, even when the initial gains are not measurably affected. Our results indicated that extent of participation was not a factor in determining initial attitude change. Participation, however, did influence the permanence of posttreatment attitude changes. On the delayed measurement neither the active nor the passive participants regressed significantly from their posttreatment scores, while the film-alone groups did show such a regression. Stability of the attitude change, therefore, cannot be attributable to active participation alone, but must be due in part to mere presence in a group discussion. Although active participation has been defined as verbal commitment, the possibility of nonverbal communication during the discussion must be considered. Reinforcement of opinion change may be the result of a number of aspects of the group discussion situation not limited to verbal interchange.

A decreasing amount of factual material was learned from the film in moving from the groups low in ethnocentrism to those high in ethnocentrism. This finding implies that those Ss whose attitudes were assumed to be congruent with the content of the film learned the most from it, while the Ss whose attitudes were in conflict with the film content learned the least amount of factual material. Our findings thus substantiate the hypothesis that learning from a persuasive communication is in part a function of initial attitude toward the communication content.

A content analysis of the discussion materials indicated that discussion in the low E groups tended to center about the arguments presented by the film, whereas discussion in the high E groups departed almost completely from the film. While it was not determined how much information in the film was reviewed in each discussion, the fact that more comments in the low E groups were related to the film increased the probability that specific informational items would be mentioned. Actually, the effects of discussion content and initial attitude are confounded in the discussion groups. In the film-alone groups, however, no such confounding of these two variables is present, and here the low Es also learned significantly more from the film than the high Es. In addition, the analysis of variance of Information test scores showed that treatment (discussion vs. no discussion) was not a significant source of variability. These considerations indicate that discussion of a communication does not necessarily alter the amount of information acquired from the communication. In the present instance, the discussion comments were not such as to involve rehearsal of factual content of the film. The probability that the amount of practice furnished by the discussion was slight would account for the lack of differences in learning between the film-discussion and film-alone groups.

Although there were no significant differences on the initial administration of the E scale between the active and passive participants, a significant difference was observed between these groups in amount of information learned. The fact that the active participants learned more than the passive participants agrees with the findings of Kurtz and Hovland (1953). In light of this, one might predict that the film-alone Ss, having no opportunity for participation, would learn less from the film than either the active or passive members of the discussion groups. However, the results showed that the film-alone Ss learned significantly more than the passive participants, and, in fact, did not differ significantly from the active participants. These findings seem to indicate that participation depended on amount of material learned, since the film-alone groups undoubtedly contained some individuals who would have participated actively in discussion given the opportunity. The presence of these potential discussants would tend to raise the average learning score in the film-alone groups above the mean of the passive members of the discussion groups. In other words, the mean learning score for the film-alone groups represents the joint contribution of potentially active and passive discussion participants.

Data reported by McGinnies and Vaughan (1957) support the contention that participation in a free discussion depends upon the amount of relevant information possessed by Ss. Their results indicated that the Ss who participated in discussions following mental health films rated themselves higher on a self-rating scale of mental health information than those who did not participate in the discussion. They also reported that the discussants had seen significantly more mental health films than the nondiscussants. Participation in a discussion appears to depend in part upon knowledge of the problem.

At the time of the delayed administration of the Information test, the low E groups obtained the highest scores, and the high E groups achieved the poorest retention scores. Although predisposition, or initial attitude, was not a significant source of variance when the retention scores were adjusted for initial learning, the predisposition × treatment interaction was nearly significant. In other words, the observed differences in retention of information among the several predisposition groups probably depended upon the occurrence or nonoccurrence of a discussion following the film. For the low E and high E groups, the more effective treatment was the film-discussion situation.

Retention of information was obviously unrelated to extent of participation in discussion, since the film-alone groups achieved retention scores equal to those of the active discussion participants and higher than those of the passive participants. Furthermore, no significant differences existed between the active and passive participants in this respect.

SUMMARY AND CONCLUSIONS

This study investigated the effects of ethnocentric attitudes and discussion participation upon the degree and stability of learning and attitude change in response to a persuasive communication. Twelve experimental groups, each composed of nine high school students, viewed a sound film "The High Wall." Six of the groups held discussions of the film, while the remaining six did not. The groups were formed on the basis of scores on the California Ethnocentrism Scale, so that two groups under each of the experimental conditions represented low, middle, and high scores on the E scale. Following experimental treatment, film-discussion or film-alone, all the group members were tested for attitude change and amount of factual information learned from the film. Six control groups were given pre- and posttests on the questionnaires without intervening exposure to either the film or discussion. One month following the experimental treatments, all groups were retested on the E scale, and the experimental groups were also readministered the Information test.

The major findings of this experiment may be summarized as follows:

1. Significant reductions in ethnocentrism, as measured by the E scale, were produced in both the film-discussion and film-alone groups. For prejudiced Ss, the effect was significantly less in the discussion groups than in the nondiscussion groups. Ethnocentric predisposition alone, however, did not affect the extent of attitude change induced by the film.

2. Stability of attitude change was a function of experimental treatment. The active and passive members of discussion groups, when tested one month later, had largely retained their posttreatment attitude gains, while the film-alone groups had regressed significantly toward their original attitudes.

3. Amount of information learned from the film was related to initial attitude. Those individuals who were low in ethnocentrism learned more from the film than those high in ethnocentrism. This trend persisted in the retention measures taken a month later.

4. Active discussion participants learned more from the film than passive participants. Analysis of this finding led to the conclusion that extent of participation in discussion depends upon the amount of learning that has taken place.

PUBLIC OPINION QUESTIONNAIRE E

On the following pages you will find statements which refer to opinions regarding a number of social groups and issues, about which some people agree, and others disagree. Please mark each statement according to your agreement or disagreement on the answer sheet as follows:

1. Strong opposition, disagreement.   4. Slight support, agreement.
2. Moderate opposition, disagreement.   5. Moderate support, agreement.
3. Slight opposition, disagreement.   6. Strong support, agreement.

There are no right or wrong answers, so answer according to your own opinion. It is very important that every question be answered so that slight differences in opinion will show. Do not spend more than a few seconds on any statement, for it is your first impression we want. If it is difficult for you to make up your mind, make the best guess you can, and go on to the next statement.

Please give your honest opinions. This questionnaire has nothing to do with your school work. Your answers will be kept strictly confidential.

1. The worst danger to real Americanism during the last fifty years has come from foreign ideas and agitators.
2. Negroes have their rights, but it is best to keep them in their own districts and schools and to prevent too much contact with Whites.
3. Foreigners prove that when people of their type have too much money and freedom, they just take advantage and cause trouble.
4. Now that the United Nations is set up, America must be sure that she loses none of her independence and complete power as a sovereign nation.
5. It would be a mistake ever to have Negroes for foremen and leaders over Whites.
6. Certain religious sects who refuse to salute the flag should be forced to conform to such a patriotic action, or else be abolished.
7. Puerto Ricans are all right in their place, but they carry it too far when they dress lavishly and go around with White girls.
8. Negro musicians may sometimes be as good as White musicians, but it is a mistake to have mixed Negro-White bands.
9. America may not be perfect, but the American way has brought us about as close as human beings can get to a perfect society.
10. Manual labor and unskilled jobs seem to fit the Negro mentality and ability better than more skilled or responsible work.
11. It is only natural and right for each person to think that his family is better than any other.
12. The people who raise all the talk about putting Negroes on the same level as Whites are mostly radical agitators trying to stir up conflicts.
13. The best guarantee of our national security is to have the biggest army and navy in the world and the most powerful hydrogen bombs in existence.
14. Most Negroes would become overbearing and disagreeable if not kept in their places.
15. The only guarantee of future peace is to wipe out as many as possible of the Russians and Red Chinese, and to keep the rest under strict control.
16. In times of national emergency, it is highly important to limit responsible government jobs to native-born, White Americans.
17. The most vicious, irresponsible, and racketeering unions are, in most cases, those having largely foreigners for leaders.
18. The Negroes would solve many of their social problems by not being so irresponsible, lazy, and ignorant.
19. European refugees may be in need, but it would be a big mistake to lower our immigration quotas and allow them into the country.
20. Any group or social movement which contains many foreigners should

be watched with suspicion and, whenever possible, be investigated by the F.B.I.

INFORMATION TEST

Please answer the following questions pertaining to the film that you have just seen. Read all of the alternatives before answering, and answer all questions. Indicate your answer in the proper space on the answer sheet.

1. The boys were in what hospital ward? 1) Ward 1; 2) Ward 2; 3) Ward 3; 4) Ward 4; 5) Ward 5.
2. Mrs. Gregory shopped at the Polish stores because 1) her friends shopped there; 2) of the low prices; 3) it was close to her home; 4) she liked Polish food; 5) none of these.
3. The man who visited the boys in the hospital was a 1) psychometrist; 2) social worker; 3) psychologist; 4) psychoanalyst; 5) psychiatrist.
4. The name of the case worker was 1) Jeff Holland; 2) Art Jackson; 3) Jim Ross; 4) Bill Hearn; 5) Dick Taylor.
5. According to the film, all newcomers into a society have a desire to 1) advance; 2) belong; 3) make money; 4) join new clubs; 5) none of these.
6. How far did the Gregorys live from the Polish section? 1) one block; 2) a few blocks; 3) a quarter mile; 4) a half mile; 5) a mile.
7. Tom's sister is named 1) Alice; 2) Joan; 3) Louise; 4) Laura; 5) Nancy.
8. Harold Gregory worked as a 1) lawyer; 2) office manager; 3) accountant; 4) bookkeeper; 5) personnel assistant.
9. Mrs. Gregory was described as a 1) social climber; 2) do-gooder; 3) tolerant person; 4) social worker; 5) none of these.
10. Harold Gregory smoked a 1) cigar; 2) cigarette; 3) pipe; 4) none of these.
11. Peter and Tom lived in what part of the city? 1) North side; 2) South side; 3) East side; 4) West side.
12. Prejudice begins 1) in the neighborhood; 2) on the streets; 3) at school; 4) in the home.
13. Prejudice spreads because it is 1) easy to acquire; 2) contagious; 3) difficult to spot; 4) unimportant; 5) impossible to fight.
14. As a child Tom played with the Polish children 1) never; 2) occasionally; 3) frequently; 4) all the time.
15. How long had Mr. Gregory worked for the company? 1) 10 years; 2) 13 years; 3) 15 years; 4) 18 years; 5) 20 years.
16. How old were Peter and Tom? 1) 15; 2) 16; 3) 17; 4) 18; 5) 19.
17. The man who interviewed the boys in the hospital was named 1) Mead; 2) Nordoff; 3) Hyde; 4) Scally; 5) Anderson.
18. In the hospital there were flowers beside whose bed? 1) Peter's; 2) Tom's; 3) Peter's and Tom's; 4) neither Peter's nor Tom's.
19. How did the case worker get from the Zerwitz house to the Gregory house? 1) streetcar; 2) bus; 3) cab; 4) car; 5) walked.

20. Mr. Gregory worked for a (an) 1) foundry; 2) automobile plant; 3) locomotive plant; 4) chemical company; 5) steel company.

21. Mrs. Gregory's first name was 1) Mildred; 2) Ethel; 3) Mary; 4) Edith; 5) Ruth.

22. What did Tom take out of the icebox after returning the knife to his father? 1) orange juice; 2) soft drink; 3) lemonade; 4) milk; 5) water.

23. Tom, on the way to Peter's house 1) drove the car; 2) sat in the front; 3) sat in the back; 4) stood on the running board.

24. The job of the case worker was to 1) interview the boys; 2) determine where the trouble started; 3) help the police; 4) find out how much damage was done.

25. Mr. Gregory was very strict with Tom because 1) he felt it was his duty as a parent; 2) Tom was a bad boy; 3) his wife was too easy on Tom; 4) his own father had been strict with him.

26. Prejudice is *not* 1) learned; 2) acquired; 3) inborn; 4) taught; 5) curable.

27. The medical report said the boys were 1) comfortable; 2) satisfactory; 3) restless; 4) critical; 5) none of these.

28. Tom broke the knife 1) to get even with his father; 2) so that he could get a new one; 3) accidentally while carving on the tree; 4) to gain attention; 5) because it was his mother's best knife.

29. When offered a cookie by Mrs. Zenwitz, Tom 1) hesitated and did not take the cookie; 2) hesitated, but tasted the cookie; 3) accepted the cookie but did not eat it; 4) accepted the cookie without hesitation.

30. To Tom, something is bad if it is 1) strange; 2) unusual; 3) different; 4) all of these; 5) none of these.

31. Recognizing symptoms of prejudice in ourselves is 1) difficult; 2) harmful; 3) easy; 4) unnecessary; 5) risky.

32. According to the film the best approach to prejudice is 1) to cure it; 2) ignore it; 3) immunize against it; 4) encourage it; 5) accept it for what it is.

33. The Zenwitzs and the Gregorys 1) were close friends; 2) knew each other quite well; 3) used to be friends before the fight; 4) knew of each other; 5) had never heard of each other.

A METHOD FOR MATCHING ANONYMOUS QUESTIONNAIRE DATA WITH GROUP DISCUSSION MATERIAL[6]

In view of the current interest of many social psychologists in discussion-group interaction and the number of research projects devoted to analysis of interaction variables, it may be helpful to investigators in this area to describe a technique for associating the comments made by discussion participants with biographical information obtained anonymously

[6] This matching procedure is used in selection 34. By Elliott McGinnies from *Journal of Abnormal and Social Psychology*, 1956, 52, 139–40. Reprinted by permission of the author and the American Psychological Association.

from them on questionnaires. These procedures have been devised as a means of securing data that will be used to describe the impact of mental health films upon community discussion groups.[7]

The aims of this research required that the following data be obtained: (a) verbatim recordings of group discussions following presentation of mental health films, (b) information concerning relevant socio-economic and other characteristics of the individuals participating, (c) written reactions of group members to the film, so that the views of those who did not participate in the discussion could be evaluated. In order to relate this information, it was essential that some means be found of identifying the group members with their transcribed comments as well as with their questionnaires. At the same time, we recognized the importance of assuring anonymity to the participants. Any forthright attempt to identify individuals with either their spoken or written comments could have reduced seriously both the spontaneity and the validity of their responses. It was also deemed necessary to record the discussions as inconspicuously as possible in order to further preserve the naturalness of the group sessions.

These various methodological problems were handled in the following ways. The groups to be studied met in their customary places. These ranged in size from school auditoriums to basement recreation rooms, depending upon the size and formal structure of the groups. Regardless of the physical setting, all groups were handled in substantially the same manner. Recording of the discussions was accomplished by placing from one to four microphones at strategic positions in the conference rooms. All microphones were of the semi-directional type. They fed into a standard commercial mixer, which made it possible to record from them individually through a twin-track tape recorder operating at $7\frac{1}{2}$ inches per second. To avoid cross-talk interference, only the microphone nearest a discussion participant was opened at any one time. All recording apparatus with the exception of the microphones was located in the rear of the room where its presence was not obtrusive. The group, of course, had been informed that the discussion was to be recorded.

Printed questionnaires were distributed at the beginning of the meeting, and the group members were asked to supply the indicated personal background information. They were told not to sign their names, since the answers were to remain anonymous. At the conclusion of the film they were asked to respond to an open-end question relating to film content. Finally, following a half-hour discussion of the film, the group members answered two questions pertaining to the discussion. They were instructed to leave their questionnaires upon their seats at the conclusion of the meeting. Identification of the questionnaires of individuals who spoke during the discussion, without violation of our promise of anonymity, was accomplished readily through some advance preparation by the experimenters. From a preliminary examination of the meeting place, we prepared a chart indicating each row by letter and each seat by number. Audience members were permitted to sit anywhere. When someone arose to speak during the discussion, his location by row and seat was recorded by two observers sta-

[7] This research was supported by Special Grant 3M9064 from the National Institute of Mental Health, United States Public Health Service. Mr. Irwin Altman, Mr. Willard Vaughan, and Mr. Clagett Smith assisted in developing the research procedures.

tioned at the rear of the room. An exact, seriatim account of the location of each participant was thus obtained throughout the discussion period. At the conclusion of the meeting, the questionnaires were collected in order, and each was identified by the row and seat of its owner.

In our laboratory, the taped recording of the discussion was transferred to an Edison Voicewriter disc for transcribing by a secretary. By listening to the tape with the transcription before us, we were able to identify each person who spoke from the records kept by the two spotters during the discussion. The first speaker, for example, may have occupied seat B4, the second speaker seat G6, etc. The first transcribed comment, therefore, was that of B4, the second comment that of G6. Thus, without knowing the names of any of the discussion participants, we were able to assign a symbol to each of them and to designate both their verbal comments and their questionnaires by that symbol. The fact that two observers recorded the order of participation enabled us to check the reliability of the procedure. Agreement between the spotters has consistently been around 98 per cent.

We hope that this methodological note will be helpful to those who are studying group interaction and who may require the type of information described here. From data such as we have acquired it is possible to compare individuals who participate in group discussion with those who do not participate. Sociometric data obtained from questionnaires can be used as predictors of individual participation and interaction in the discussion situation. Perhaps the main value of this approach is that of being able to study such relationships among persons who might be reluctant to participate if their names were used for purposes of identification.

35 / The Effectiveness of Unanticipated Persuasive Communications [1]

Jane Allyn and Leon Festinger

What are the effects of exposing two groups to the same communication, one group expecting a disagreeing persuasive communication and the other group not expecting a persuasive communication at all? The subjects are high school students who favor allowing teenagers to drive with few restrictions. The communication advocates strict control of

[1] The authors would like to express their thanks to Nathan Maccoby for his help in writing the persuasive communication and in the conduct of the experimental sessions. We are also indebted to John G. Caffrey and Curt R. Demele for their help and cooperation in obtaining subjects.

Reprinted from the *Journal of Abnormal and Social Psychology*, 1961, *62*, 35–40, with the permission of the authors and the American Psychological Association.

*teenage drivers. One group of students is oriented toward the speaker's
topic and contrary opinion; the other group is oriented toward the
speaker's personality and not told his topic or point of view. The
forewarned students change their opinions less and resist the
communication more than do the unprepared students. The process of
persistence and change of opinion to attempted persuasion is described
in terms of Festinger's (1957) theory of cognitive dissonance. The
authors are Leon Festinger and Jane Allyn of Stanford University.*

It seems plausible to suppose that an attempt to persuade a person to
change his opinion on some issue would be more effective if the persuasive communication were unexpected than if the person anticipated
the influence attempt. At least many people find this to be plausible.
Lazarsfeld, Berelson, and Gaudet (1948, p. 152), for example, state "If we
read or tune in a speech, we usually do so purposefully, and in doing so
we have a definite mental set that tinges our receptiveness. . . . This
mental set is armor against influence. The extent to which people, and
particularly those with strong partisan views, listen to speakers and
read articles with which they agree in advance is evidence on this point,"
and Festinger (1957, p. 158) says: "It seems clear that the avoidance and
evasion of material which might produce or increase dissonance depends
on anticipations (probably unverbalized ones) about the material or on
preliminary assessments of the material."

There are, however, virtually no data either to challenge or to support
such statements. A study by Ewing (1942) comes closest to being pertinent.
Ewing exposed two groups of subjects to a persuasive communication that
supported a very extreme point of view. The only difference in treatment
between the two groups was in the introduction to the persuasive communication. This introduction led one group to expect that the communication would support the extreme view which it actually espoused.
For the other group, the introduction led the subjects to expect that the
communication would agree with their existing views. The results indicated that those subjects who expected the communication to disagree
with their opinions were actually less influenced by it. In other words,
the persuasive communication was more effective if the audience falsely
anticipated that it would support their existing views. This study does
not deal with the effectiveness of a communication to an entirely unprepared audience, but it does point to the operation of some anticipatory
resistance by an audience which expects to hear a disagreeing speech.

One may, of course, raise the further question as to the exact nature
of the process by means of which the prepared audience is able to resist
the effects of the attempted persuasion.

Some understanding of this process may be obtained from Festinger's
(1957) theory of cognitive dissonance. We may say that a persuasive communication which argues for an opinion different from that held by the

audience creates dissonance in the listener. Specifically, dissonance is created between the opinion the listener holds and his knowledge of the arguments favoring a contrary view. Since a person who reads a persuasive communication, or is a listener in an audience, cannot attempt to influence the source of the communication, there are only two immediate ways in which he can reduce this dissonance. He can change his opinion to a position closer to that advocated by the communication or he can reject and derogate the communication and the communicator.

What, then, are the effects of being prepared or unprepared to hear a persuasive communication? If the conditions of exposure to a communication are such as to guarantee attentiveness, it seems plausible to assume that, hearing the same speech, the same amount of dissonance is introduced whether or not the person is prepared for it. In such a case, the effect of preparedness, if any, would be on the particular mechanism used to reduce the dissonance, namely, whether the person more readily changes his opinion or rather rejects the source of communication.

There is no rigorous derivation to be made here but one may argue that, if a person anticipates hearing a communication that will disagree with an opinion he holds strongly, he will approach the situation with hesitancy, suspicion, and perhaps some hostility. If he does approach the situation in this way, then it seems natural to expect that his first and easiest reaction will be to reject the communicator.

Thus, being prepared for the communication would not, in a sense, make the communication less effective. It would simply alter the way in which the dissonance is reduced. Those prepared for the communication would tend less to change their opinion and tend more to reject the communicator. The study by Ewing (1942) gives some support to this analysis of the situation. He found that the discrepancy between the subjects' initial opinion and the position they expected the communication to espouse was the major determinant of how biased they felt the communication to be. In other words, irrespective of what the communication actually said, if they expected disagreement, they later felt the communication to be more biased. Anticipation of disagreement seems to have led to more rejection of the communication.

The present experiment was designed to throw more light on this process by comparing two groups exposed to the same persuasive communication, one group expecting a disagreeing persuasive communication and the other group not expecting a persuasive communication at all.

PROCEDURE

A questionnaire was given to 128 students of the Palo Alto High School in order to discover a topic that was important to these students and on which their opinions were relatively extreme and homogeneous. This questionnaire was administered in the classrooms by the teachers who described it as a "Youth Survey." The subjects were assured that their replies would be confidential. The questionnaire included questions about the control of teenage drivers, teenage curfew regulations, and the treatment of communists in this country. All questions had four alternative answers: "agree strongly, agree slightly, disagree slightly, disagree strongly." The subjects were also asked to rank the three topics according to how important they were. On the basis of these rankings of importance and the clustering of their opinions toward one extreme, the issue of controlling teenage automobile driving was chosen for use in the actual experiment. The four questions concerning this topic on this questionnaire also served as our first measure of opinion.

Only 91 of these subjects were present at the experimental session 2 weeks later. The data from four of these were not analyzed; two arrived too late, and two were discarded because their responses were mainly attempts at humor. Of the remaining 87 subjects, 53 were females and 34 were males. The mean age was 15.7 years, with a range from 14–18.

The experimental session was conducted in the high school auditorium. As each student entered, he was given a questionnaire booklet. The students were asked to sit apart from each other and not to open the booklets until instructed to do so. The experimenter then explained to them that they were participating in an experiment conducted by the Stanford Psychology Department and assured them that their answers would be confidential and would have no effect on the grades they would receive in their classes. The subjects were then asked to open their booklets to the first page and read the printed instructions. There were two different sets of instructions and the booklets had been randomized in this regard when they were passed out. In one condition, "Opinion Orientation," subjects read the following:

> We are very much interested in studying the opinions and attitudes of high school students on the teenage driving problem. We particularly want to get your reactions to a talk by an expert on the subject. We have asked Mr. Nathan Maccoby, who is very well known for his reports and articles on this problem, to come here today and talk to you. In his articles, Mr. Maccoby has stated his very strong opinion that teenagers are a menace on the roads and should be strictly controlled by effective new laws. It is important that you pay close attention to him and to what he has to say, as you will be asked to give your opinions on the problem after he has finished his talk.

In the other condition, "Personality Orientation," subjects read the following:

> We are very much interested in studying how members of an audience form impressions of the personality of a speaker. We particularly want to see how high school students will "size up" the personality of an adult who is speaking to them on a serious subject. We have asked Mr. Nathan Maccoby, who is considered to be an expert in his field, to come here today and talk to you. We have asked him to speak on the topic that he knows the best, so as to put him more at his ease. It is important that you pay close attention to him and to what he has to say, as you will be asked to give your impressions of his personality after he has finished his talk.

When they had finished reading the instructions, the speaker was introduced. He delivered a speech that stressed the teenager's lack of a mature sense of responsibility and advocated stricter legal measures for the prevention and control of teenage driving. The communication was more extreme in the direction of control than the opinions of any of the students. After the speech, the experimenter thanked the speaker and instructed the students to answer the questions in their booklets. The booklets contained the same four questions on control of teenage driving which had been used previously together with other questions designed to measure rejection of the speaker, importance of the topic, and other items. These will be discussed in more detail under "Results." At the conclusion of the session the experiment was explained in simplified terms and any questions the students had were answered. The session took approximately 45 minutes.

RESULTS

Effectiveness of the Experimental Manipulation

The purpose of one of the sets of instructions was to create an orientation toward the personality of the speaker so that the actual persuasive communication would be unanticipated. The other set of instructions was intended to create an orientation toward the opinion of the speaker together with the expectation that the speaker would disagree with their own opinion. To check on whether or not the two different orientations were successfully created, the following question was asked:

> The psychologists who are doing this experiment are mainly interested in
> A. what kinds of opinions people have.
> B. how people judge other people's personalities.

If our manipulation was successful, we would expect the majority of Opinion Orientation subjects to check the first alternative and the majority of Personality Orientation subjects to check the second. Out of a total of 41 subjects who received the Opinion Orientation instructions, 80 per cent said the experiment was concerned with opinions. Out of the total of 46 subjects who received the Personality Orientation instructions, 63 per cent said the experiment was concerned with judgment of personality. The difference between the two conditions is, of course, highly significant statistically. Thus it appears that our experimental manipulation was effective in creating different orientations toward the speaker in the two groups.[2]

It should be noted in the instructions to the subjects that in each of the two conditions an effort was made to introduce the speaker as equally expert. This was done because we wanted to keep constant the magnitude

---

[2] There were no significant differences in the responses given by boys and girls on any of the measures in the study. Therefore, the data were analyzed for the group as a whole.

of dissonance occasioned by the persuasive communication. The following question was asked to check on this point:

When we introduced Mr. Maccoby, we said that he is considered to be an expert in his field. How much do you think he really knows about the problem he discussed?
  A. He is a real expert, who is very familiar with the problem.
  B. He knows quite a lot about the problem.
  C. He knows about as much as most people do about the problem.
  D. He knows less than most people about it.
  E. He knows very little, and a lot of his information is wrong.

The results show that we were successful in keeping the expertness of the speaker constant between the two conditions. In the Opinion Orientation condition 78 per cent said the speaker was a real expert or knew quite a lot about the problem. In the Personality Orientation condition the comparable figure is 80 per cent. Clearly, there are no appreciable differences between the two conditions.

Since the purpose of the experimental manipulation was to affect the orientation of the subjects but to keep constant the magnitude of dissonance, it is also important to know whether or not the subjects in the two conditions paid equal attention to what the speaker said. For this purpose a number of factual recall questions were asked. The results show no difference between the conditions in amount of material recalled. Since the two conditions were the same with respect to both attention paid to what the speaker said and degree of expertness attributed to him, we may regard the experimental manipulation as having created a difference in orientation or preparedness on the part of the subjects while holding constant the magnitude of dissonance introduced by the persuasive communication.

Comparison of the Two Experimental Conditions

We expected subjects in the Opinion Orientation condition to reduce dissonance mainly by rejecting the communicator and expected those in the Personality Orientation condition to reduce dissonance mainly by changing their opinion in the direction advocated by the communication. Change scores were calculated as follows: If a subject changed his answer to an adjacent category, e.g., from "agree strongly" to "agree slightly," he received a score of 1; if he changed to an answer two steps away, e.g., from "disagree strongly" to "agree slightly," he received a score of 2; since we used a four-point scale, the maximum possible change was 3. Changes in the direction of the position advocated by the communication were given a plus sign, and the changes were summed algebraically for the four questions to obtain a single score. Thus, if a subject changed from "disagree strongly" to "agree slightly" on one question in the direction advocated by the communication (a change of +2); changed from "agree strongly" to "agree slightly" on another question in the direction opposite to that advocated by the communication (a change of −1); and did not change at all on the other two questions, his opinion change score would be +1.

Rejection of the communicator was measured by the following question:

Do you think Mr. Maccoby covered all the facts pretty well, or do you think he was unfair or biased in some way?
A. He was very unfair and biased.
B. He was somewhat unfair; he didn't give all the facts.
C. He was very fair; he covered all the facts pretty well.

Table 1 presents the data for opinion change and rejection. Two indices of opinion change are presented in the table: the average change and the percentage of subjects changing appreciably (two or more points) in the direction advocated by the communication. Both of these measures show differences between the two experimental conditions in the predicted direction. Subjects in the Personality Orientation condition change their opinion more in the direction advocated by the communication than do subjects in the Opinion Orientation condition. While the difference in average change of opinion is not at all significant, the percentage who change appreciably is significant statistically (chi square = 5.71, p = .02).[3] The difference between the two experimental conditions on rejection of the communicator is also in the expected direction. Subjects in the Opinion Orientation condition are more likely to reject the communicator. The difference is statistically significant (chi square = 4.06, p = .05).

Table 1. Opinion Change and Rejection of Communicator for the Two Experimental Conditions

	Experimental Condition	
	Opinion Orientation ($N = 41$)	Personality Orientation ($N = 46$)
Average change of opinion	+.49	+.63
Percentage changing appreciably [a]	20%	43%
Percentage saying communication was very or somewhat biased	80%	61%

[a] An appreciable change is defined as a change of two or more points in the direction of the communication.

In other words, our expectations were borne out. If the subjects are led to expect that a persuasive communication will disagree with them, they reject the communicator more and are less influenced than subjects who are, so to speak, caught unprepared. The obtained differences, however, while significant statistically, are rather small. Let us, therefore, examine the data further to see what additional light can be shed on the process with which we are dealing.

[3] All p values reported are two-tailed.

Initial Opinion and Importance of Issue

The topic of teenage driving was chosen for the experiment because the initial opinions of the high school students were more extreme on this issue than on either of the other issues that we pretested. Theoretically, of course, we would expect that the differences between our two experimental conditions would be greater for people who held opinions very divergent from the position advocated by the communication since more dissonance is introduced for them. Although opinions on the issue of teenage driving were relatively extreme, still, only a minority of the subjects held entirely one-sided opinions on the issue.

The four questions used as the measure of opinions about teenage driving on both questionnaires were as follows:

1. Since most accidents involving teenagers happen at night, people between the ages of 16 and 20 should only be allowed to drive during the daytime.

2. Tests for obtaining a license to drive should be made much harder for teenagers and should also test for judgment and knowledge of the traffic laws.

3. I think that the minimum age for obtaining a driver's license in California should be raised to 18. [Note: present age is 16.]

4. If a person between 16 and 20 years of age receives a ticket for speeding or reckless driving, his license should be revoked until he is 21.

If we define an extreme opinion as disagreement (either strong or slight) on all four questions, we find that only 16 of the 41 subjects in the Opinion Orientation condition and 16 of the 46 subjects in the Personality Orientation condition initially held such extreme opinions.

Another variable that should affect the results of the experiment is the importance of the issue to the subject. The more important the issue of teenage driving is to a particular person, the greater should be the magnitude of dissonance created in him by the persuasive communication. In order to obtain a measure of the importance of the issue to each subject, we asked the following question:

How important is it to you to be able to have a license to drive a car?
A. very important
B. quite important
C. not too important
D. not at all important

Ideally we would have wanted to analyze the data from the experiment separately for the effect of extremeness of opinion and the effect of importance of the issue. Unfortunately, it turns out that there is a very appreciable correlation between these two variables. In both experimental conditions equally, those who hold extreme opinions also overwhelmingly state that the issue is important to them. Hence, we cannot look at the effect of each of these variables separately. Consequently the data were analyzed for those with extreme opinions versus those with moderate opinions on the issue, ignoring the specific responses on importance. It should be remembered, however, that these two go hand-in-hand in this sample. Since, theoretically, both of these variables should affect the data in the same manner, the interpretation will be, of necessity, slightly ambiguous. That is, the greater the difference between initial opinion and the position advocated by the communication, and the greater the importance of the issue, the greater will be the magnitude of dissonance introduced by the communication. Hence, we cannot separate the effects of these two variables in our data.

Let us, then, examine the data to see the effect of the combined action of both variables. Table 2 presents the data on opinion change separately for those who initially held extreme opinions and those who initially held moderate opinions for each experimental condition. It should be remembered that a subject was labeled as holding a moderate opinion if he initially agreed with the position advocated by the communication on one or more of the questions.

It is clear from Table 2 that the difference between initial opinion and position advocated by the communication is a major variable. For those who held extreme opinions initially (and for whom the issue was more important) there is an average change of $+2.31$ in the Personality Orientation condition as compared to an average change of only $+.81$ in the Opinion Orientation condition. The difference on the measure of percentage who change appreciably is also similarly large. Both differences are significant at better than the 2 per cent level. For those whose initial opinion was moderate (and the issue was less important) there is practically no difference between conditions and, indeed, practically no impact of the communication at all. The average change for the Opinion Orientation group is only $+.28$ and the average for the Personality Orientation group is even slightly in the opposite direction from that advocated by the communication. In other words, the entire difference that we found between the experimental conditions is attributable to those subjects for whom the persuasive communication introduced considerable dissonance.

Table 2. Opinion Change in Relation to Initial Opinion

	Experimental Condition	
	Opinion Orientation	Personality Orientation
Extreme Initial Opinion		
Average Change	$+.81$	$+2.31$
Percentage change appreciably	19%	60%
	($N = 16$)	($N = 16$)
Moderate Initial Opinion		
Average Change	$+.28$	$-.27$
Percentage changing appreciably	20%	30%
	($N = 25$)	($N = 30$)

We would also expect the difference between the two experimental conditions on the measure of rejection to be greater for those with initially extreme opinions. Surprisingly, however, this does not turn out to be the case. There are simply no differences between those holding extreme opinions and those holding moderate opinions in the percentage who feel the communicator was biased. In the Personality Orientation condition these figures are 62.5 per cent and 60 per cent, respectively, and the comparable figures for the Opinion Orientation condition are 81 per cent and 80 per cent. There is, of course, no reason to expect a difference in the Personality Orientation condition where dissonance was reduced mainly by changing opinion. There is reason, however, to have expected a difference in the Opinion Orientation condition. It is conceivable, however, that the over-all level of rejection was already so high in this condition (80 per cent) that a virtual ceiling had been reached as far as our relatively crude measure is concerned. This cannot, of course, be settled with the present data. The only thing that can be said is that, if there is not a ceiling phenomenon here, there is a theoretical difficulty involved in interpreting the rejection data.

SUMMARY

Eighty-seven high school students who were in favor of allowing teen-agers to drive with few restrictions were presented with a communication advocating strict control of young drivers. One group was given an orientation to attend to the speaker's personality and was not told the topic of the speech or the speaker's point of view. It was found that subjects who were forewarned of the nature of the communication changed their opinions less and rejected the communicator as biased to a greater degree than unprepared subjects. Differences in amount of opinion change between prepared and unprepared subjects were greater among those holding extreme opinions initially.

36 / The Effect of Prior Information on Susceptibility to an Emotional Appeal

Paul C. Lewan and Ezra Stotland

How to change social attitudes and how to develop attitudes that would resist change are important areas of research. The following article pertains to resistance to attitude change. Pupils who receive neutral

Reprinted from the *Journal of Abnormal and Social Psychology*, 1961, 62, 450–53, with the permission of the authors and the American Psychological Association.

information about an object are less influenced by an emotional
communication against the object than pupils who have not received
such neutral information. The authors, Paul C. Lewan of Wenatchee
Valley College and Ezra Stotland of the University of Washington,
interpret this finding in terms of attitudinal constancy and suggest
several possible limitations in generalizing from the finding.
Whether neutral information would also resist positive
attitudinal appeals awaits further study.

Considerable research has been done on the order of presentation of persuasive communications. A central problem of the research has been whether the earlier communication has any effect in reducing the effectiveness of the later communication (Hovland, 1957). In these studies, the communications have typically consisted of a list of arguments to support a given point of view of some object or issue. The present study is addressed to the corollary issue of whether a communication of neutral material about an object can influence the effectiveness of subsequent communications. In the present study, the second communication is primarily emotional in its appeal. In other words, the problem is, "Can the prior acquisition of neutral information concerning some object influence susceptibility to a subsequent appeal regarding that object?"

Studies such as Hartmann's (1936) and Janis and Feshbach (1953) have shown at least partially contradictory results. Hartman found that emotional appeals are more effective, while Janis found that extremely emotional appeals are not effective. One possible explanation for the somewhat inconsistent results may lie in the lack of prior information that the subjects had about the object of the appeal. The students of the Janis and Feshbach study may have been better informed about dental hygiene than the voters in Hartman's study were about public issues. The importance of prior information is also suggested by Cantril's (1940) finding that better educated persons, who were probably better informed, were less influenced by emotionally tinged communications. However, it remains unclear as to whether the lowered susceptibility to influence is a result of a greater fund of information or of greater critical ability. The present study is aimed at showing that regardless of the subject's critical ability, his possession of more information does in fact reduce the affectiveness of an emotional appeal. The following hypothesis was tested:

Persons who have received neutral information regarding a given object lower their evaluation of the object to a lesser extent after hearing an emotional appeal against it than persons who have not received such neutral information.

METHOD

Subjects

Ninety-seven pupils in four twelfth grade social studies classes were used as subjects for this experiment. Approximately 52 per cent of the subjects were male. The pupils in each of the four classes were seated in alphabetical order. No ability grouping by class was apparent to the experimenter; teachers described the classes in each case as "about average." [1]

Experimental Conditions

The experimental groups received an information sheet on the same subject matter area as the emotional appeal; the control group received information on a nonrelevant subject. The possession of relevant prior information by the experimental subjects was the only condition in the design which distinguished the experimental groups from the control groups.

Each class was divided into an experimental and a control group of approximately equal size. Since all classes used alphabetical seating arrangements, subjects were assigned alternately to the experimental or control group by alphabetical order.

Procedure

The experiment can be divided into four major steps: the presentation of the fact sheets, administration of the first attitude scale, presentation of the emotional appeal, administration of the second attitude scale. The experiment was given four times on the same day, once in each of the four twelfth grade social studies classes.

First, the teacher in charge of each class introduced the experiment by informing the students that they were to study a little-known area of Europe in a way somewhat different from the usual classroom routine. The pupils were told that there were to be some tests administered after they had an opportunity to look at some information sheets. The teacher, with the experimenter acting as an observer, handed out the "fact sheets" to the experimental and control groups. The experimental group received only information on Andorra (described below). The control group received only information of a similar nature about Etruria. The fact sheets consisted of items of information designed to be of a "neutral nature" on a subject matter area with which the students would not ordinarily be acquainted. From the time of the handing out of the information until the end of the experiment, intercommunication between pupils was not permitted. The subjects were instructed to read the fact sheets; when the

[1] The authors wish to express their appreciation to the teachers of Evergreen High School, Seattle, Washington, for their invaluable cooperation.

teacher had observed that all subjects had finished, the sheets were re-called.

Immediately after the reading of the fact sheets the teacher passed out scales exploring the attitude of both groups in the relevant subject matter area (the scales and their construction will be discussed more fully later). Half of each group received Scale A, the other half received Scale B on the initial attitude exploration. The scales in every case were identified by number only, the person responding remaining anonymous.

After the completion and handing back of the first attitude scales, the experimenter was introduced by the teacher as a guest speaker from the University of Washington who would like to present a few remarks about Andorra. The experimenter immediately presented the emotional appeal, which consisted largely of name-calling generalities presenting an unfavorable picture of Andorra and had been edited to present a mini-mum of factual information.

After the appeal the speaker retired once more to the role of observer and the teacher gave out the alternate attitude scales to both groups. Those students who had been given Scale A before the emotional appeal were now given Scale B and vice versa.

A comparison of the "change scores" (the difference between scores on the first and second attitude scales) for the experimental and control groups was used to test the hypothesis.

The Attitude Scales

In order to detect the expected changes of attitude in both the ex-perimental and control groups, two "Likert type" attitude scales were constructed.[2]

Each of the possible four responses for the 22 items on each scale was assigned a value of from one to four with the most unfavorable response (towards Andorra) being assigned the lowest value, the next most un-favorable responses being assigned the second lowest value, etc. The re-sponse categories in the scales were randomized in their order for each item to minimize the effects of position responses by the subjects.

The two forms, designed to be used as alternate scales, had been previously administered to a group of 26 eleventh graders (different from the experimental group) in a social studies class after the students had read the information sheet on Andorra. This class was characterized as an average class by several teachers and was composed of an equal number of boys and girls at the time of the testing, which was 5 weeks previous to the running of the experiment. The students were informed by their teacher, immediately before the passing out of the fact sheets, that this was to be a study of a little-known country of Europe and that some tests were to be administered after the reading. After the reading of the fact sheet, about half the class received the scales in the order AB; the other half received scales in the order BA. After completion of the scales the

[2] [Appended to the selection.]

experimenter answered a few general questions about the subject matter area. The students were not informed as to the intended use of the attitude scales in the later experiment.

The mean score on Scale A was 63.08, the mean score on Scale B was 62.73. A product-moment correlation of .91 (without correction for attenuation) was found to exist between scores on the two forms.

Fact Sheets

The information sheet on Andorra [3] received by the experimental groups was abstracted from *Collier's Encyclopedia* and carefully edited so that the items would be of a "neutral nature," i.e., unlikely to form marked attitudes towards or against the subject. The neutral information consisted of the following: a description of the geography, the agriculture, the industry and mining, the language and the use of the flag, the political system and the French representation in foreign affairs, the fiscal system, and the country's origin.

The control group received information of a similar "neutral nature," on Etruria [4] which was condensed from another work in the same source. The two fact sheets can be read in approximately the same length of time (about 8 minutes).

Emotional Appeal

The second "communication," the emotional appeal, was presented orally by the experimenter.[5] It consisted largely of name-calling generalities and was designed to present a minimum of factual information while presenting an unfavorable opinion of the relevant subject matter area (Andorra). The emotional appeal consisted of an attack on the Andorrese people as being ignorant, amoral, unworthy of membership in the United Nations or of American economic aid, undemocratic, weak, puny, potential dupes of the Communists in the United Nations, and dangerous to world peace.

RESULTS

The hypothesis of the study is based on the assumption that the information provided to the subjects prior to the initial appeal was neutral with respect to the object of the appeal, Andorra. This assumption does not, however, require that every bit of information given be neutral; rather the total effect of the information should not cause the recipients as a group to be more or less favorable to Andorra. The assumption can be tested by comparing the experimental and control groups in their attitudes toward Andorra as measured immediately after they received in-

---

[3] [Appended to the selection.]   [4] [Appended to the selection.]
[5] [Appended to the selection.]

formation about Andorra and Etruria and before hearing the emotional appeal. The mean attitude scale score was 60.54 ($N = 47$) for the experimental groups and 59.22 ($N = 50$) for the control groups, the difference not being significant by a t test. (The higher figure indicates more favorable attitudes.) Thus, the assumption about the neutrality of the information is supported.

The hypothesis was tested by first dividing the sample into three equal groups according to degree of favorableness of attitude toward Andorra prior to the emotional appeal, to control for the differential possibility of change from different positions of favorableness of attitude, and to check on any interaction effects between the experimental treatments and original degree of favorableness. The mean change scores were then computed for each of the three groups in each of the experimental conditions. These data are presented in Table 1. They show that for each degree of

Table 1. Mean Before-After Changes in Attitudes [a] to Andorra
($N = 10$ in each cell [b])

| | Favorableness or Attitude Prior to Appeal | | |
Condition	High	Medium	Low
Experimental	−12.7	−9.5	−8.8
Control	−17.5	−18.1	−12.5

[a] Negative changes mean changes to more unfavorable attitudes.
[b] Some Ns were dropped to equalize the Ns in the cells. The Ns to be dropped were those closest to the mean in each cell before equalization, thereby increasing the variance.

Table 2. Analysis of Variance of Changes of Attitude

Source of Variation	SS	df	MS	F
Experimental Condition	478.3	1	478.3	5.49 *
Original Attitude Position	209.4	2	104.7	ns
Interaction	66.1	2	33.1	ns
Within Cells	4793.1	54	88.8	ns

* $p < .05$.

original favorableness, the subjects in the experimental condition changed less after the negative emotional appeal than subjects in the control condition toward being more unfavorable to Andorra. The analysis of variance shown in Table 2 indicates that this difference is significant at the .05 level. The analysis of variance also shows no significant interaction, indicating that the experimental effect was the same for subjects at all levels of original attitude. The hypothesis is therefore supported. The acquisition of neutral information about Andorra did serve as a deterrent to susceptibility to an emotional appeal against Andorra.

DISCUSSION

One interpretation of these results would hold that the prior information creates a cognitive structure with regard to the object of the attitude, which then serves as a source of attitudinal constancy, since any change in the evaluation of the object tends to require support from the cognitive structure regarding the object. To the extent that such a cognitive structure contains elements inconsistent with the changed evaluation of the object, the person should resist changing his evaluation of the object of the attitude. This interpretation is consistent with the approach of Krech and Crutchfield (1948).

The results of this study concerned resistance to changes in a negative direction. The obvious question arises as to whether such information would also act as a deterrent to changes in a positive direction. If the process underlying the presently observed effect is simply, as just suggested, that information provides an anchor or a basis of constancy of attitude, then the information should prevent positive changes as well. However, other processes may underlie the effect. For example, as a result of their familiarity with Andorra, the subjects may have identified with it, and, thus, become resistant to any negative appeal about Andorra. If this interpretation is valid, it might be expected that the better informed subjects would then be more susceptible to a positive emotional appeal than the less well informed ones. The importance of the factor of familiarity with, and consequent identification with, the object of the attitude can be tested by a study in which familiarity is systematically varied without varying the amount of information given about the object. In any case, it is possible that the present results can be generalized only to resistance to negative appeals and not to resistance to positive appeals.

Another possible limitation to the generalizability of the findings derives from the fact that it is impossible to make an emotional appeal without at the same time communicating some "information," even if it is minimal and/or false. In some cases, this "information" may be contrary to the originally imparted, neutral information. In this case, the results would be the same as in the present study, the original information presumably having the greater effect, as in Luchins' (1957) study. In other cases, the emotionally communicated "information" may be consistent with the prior, neutral information, or may give the neutral information an additional context in which the prior information is no longer neutral but supports an extreme pro or con attitude. In these cases, the outcome would probably be the opposite of the present study, the prior information increasing the likelihood of later susceptibility to an emotional appeal.

SUMMARY

The hypothesis of this study was that persons who have received neutral information with respect to an object lower their evaluation of the object to a lesser extent after hearing an emotional appeal against it than persons who have not received such neutral information. The hypothesis was tested in an experiment done in high school classes, using an object with which the subjects had little or no prior acquaintance. The results confirmed the hypothesis.

INFORMATION SHEETS

Andorra

Andorra is an ancient European country of 191 square miles situated in the eastern Pyrenees between Spain and France. The country is rugged, full of narrow gorges, deep defiles and irregular valleys. The climate is cold in winter, cool in summer. Many small rivers course through the land.

Although the soil is largely unsuited for cultivation, tobacco is grown, as well as some barley and oats. The fields are generally small. Cattle, mules, sheep, and pigs are also raised. During the summer months the Andorrese trek to the villages high in the Pyrenees, where they herd their animals and gather their crops for the coming winter. Beginning in September, cattle fairs are held in most of the villages. Most Andorran festivals are held during the harvest season.

The Andorrese, numbering about 6000, live mainly in six winter villages. These people are mostly Spanish origin, although they speak Catalan rather than Spanish. The people call themselves "Andorrese" and unveil the Andorran flag during festivals and holidays. Outside of Andorra, however, the Andorrese flag is seldom seen.

Local industries include wool combing, wool spinning, processing of tobacco, sandal making. Trade with neighboring countries is important economically. Although the country is rich in iron and lead deposits according to surveys, the mines have not been developed extensively due to the high cost of transportation and lack of good roads. Some lead and iron is mined and some marble is quarried, however.

The internal affairs are handled by a General Council of Notables, four from each of the country's six parishes, elected by the heads of the landowning families. France usually represents Andorra in foreign affairs and has the right to maintain law and order in emergencies within the country.

The country has a small and balanced budget and uses both French and Spanish currencies since there is no such thing as Andorran coinage or money. Postal service is free within the country, being financed by the sale of Andorran stamps to stamp collectors. The Andorrese have almost no taxes but pay a small tribute every two years to the Bishop of Urgel (Spain) and the President of France, a traditional tribute which has been paid for almost 700 years.

The origin of Andorra is very old. It was probably one of the last surviving remnants of the buffer states established by Charlemagne to control and contain the Moslem advance into western Europe. In 1278 the French Count of Fois and the Spanish Bishop of Urgel reached an agreement known as the Pariatjes, which divided the responsibilities for the country between them while leaving the inhabitants of the country independent of either Spain or France. The compact still exists, the powers now residing in the President of France, as successor to the powers of the Count of Fois, and in the present Bishop of Urgel.

Etruria

Etruria is the name given in ancient times to an area extending for about 200 miles along the coast of central Italy. It may be described as a rough triangle, coming to a point at the south, bounded on the east by the Tiber River, on the west by the Mediterranean, and on the north by the Arno River. Etruria no longer exists as a country; the present descendant of Etruria is the present region of Tuscany in Italy, which occupies an area of 9000 square miles.

The Etruscans, the people who gave this area the name Etruria, were invaders who followed earlier peoples into this region; they probably arrived by ship and were attracted by the supplies of copper, and later iron, in this area and in the nearby island of Elba. The early cities in this region were situated on hilltops for purposes of defense. In time they became walled cities from which the inhabitants went forth daily to tend to their farming and herding on the slopes below.

From about 600 B.C. to 400 B.C. the Etruscans built a series of communities extending across the Apennines to the foothills of the Alps and south to the vicinity of Naples. Traditionally however there were in Etruria twelve leading towns which formed a loose religious and political confederation. During this period the Etruscans carried on commerce over the sea, particularly that portion of the Mediterranean enclosed by Italy, Sicily and Corsica. In the fifth and fourth centuries B.C. the Etruscans were dealt a series of blows by the Greeks of southern Italy, by the Gauls, and finally by the Romans. By 300 B.C. their political and economic power was negligible; however, historians believe that parts of their cultural tradition persists today in Italy.

Etruscan is today largely an unknown language but some progress has been made in deciphering the inscriptions and the mummy wrappings found in Etruscan tombs.

The Lucumones, whom their people believed to be endowed with god-like powers, were the rulers of most of the early Etruscan cities. The people they ruled were never very numerous and in time intermarried with the local population and lost their identity as a separate people. The Roman language and culture largely replaced the earlier culture until by the year 1 B.C. only small traces were left. The people of Etruria made statues, bronzes, reliefs, and paintings. Art historians believe that Greek influence could be found throughout Etruscan art.

The climate of this area does not lend itself to agriculture easily, with limited rainfall in the winter and early spring, the rest of the year being hot and dry. Vegetation consists of scrub forests, bushes and grassland. The soil is, on the average, rather stony and unproductive and yields a living only after much work. Grains, olives, citrus fruits, and herbs are raised along with a few livestock.

INSTRUCTIONS: Place your number on the test sheet. Then answer the following questions by selecting and checking the answer which best shows how you feel at this moment. Please answer all on the basis of what you know now.

1. How would you feel about the U.S. sending an ambassador to Andorra; would you: disapprove   strongly approve   approve   strongly disapprove
2. If an Andorrese (a citizen of Andorra) was coming to your school and you were asked if you would be a "buddy" until this student becomes better acquainted; would you: approve   disapprove   strongly disapprove   strong approve
3. The Andorrese is basically an honest hard-working person; do you: strongly disagree   disagree   agree   strongly agree
4. Andorra is a republic with a democratic tradition; do you: strongly agree   strongly disagree   agree   disagree
5. The Andorrese constitute a possible threat to the security of the free nations of the west; do you: strong disagree   agree   disagree   strongly agree
6. The benefits of extending U.S. recognition and sending consular personnel to Andorra would not be enough to offset the additional expense; do you: disagree   strongly agree   agree   strongly disagree
7. Andorra provides a poor future for economic development; do you: strong agree   strongly disagree   agree   disagree
8. How would you feel if a fellow were to say that Andorra is just a poor "musical comedy country"; would you: agree   strongly agree   disagree   strongly disagree
9. How do you feel about the Andorrese way of life; do you: strongly approve   approve   strongly disapprove   disapprove
10. If an Andorrese were to declare his intention to marry your sister, would you: approve   strongly approve   strongly disagree   disagree
11. Andorrese usually have narrow provincial opinions; do you: agree   strongly agree   disagree   strongly disagree
12. Andorra should be extended membership in the United Nations; do you: strongly disagree   agree   disagree   strongly agree

13. Andorrese membership in the U.N. would be a blow against Communism; do you: strongly agree   strongly disagree   agree   disagree
14. The Andorrese indirectly pose a threat to the world's peace; do you: disagree   strongly agree   agree   strongly disagree
15. Andorra would probably be worth a visit; do you: strongly agree   agree   disagree   strongly disagree
16. How would you feel if the U.S. was tentatively considering sending military arms to Andorra; would you: approve   strongly disapprove   strongly approve   disapprove
17. The Andorrese government is undemocratic; do you: agree   strongly agree   strongly disagree   disagree
18. If one of your ancestors had Andorrese blood, would you: strongly disapprove   approve   strongly approve   disapprove
19. Andorra would be at best an untrustworthy friend of the U.S. in the event of any conflict; do you: disagree   agree   strongly agree   strongly disagree
20. The admission of Andorra into the U.N. is probably a scheme being arranged by the bureaucrats for their own purpose; do you: strongly agree   strongly disagree   agree   disagree
21. The admission of Andorra would disturb the vital balance of power in the U.N.; do you: strongly agree   agree   strongly disagree   disagree
22. U.S. investments in Andorra should bring a profit; do you: disagree   agree   strongly disagree   strongly agree

INSTRUCTIONS: Place your number on the test sheet. Then answer the following questions by selecting and checking the answer which best shows how you feel at this moment. Please answer them all on the basis of what you know now.

1. U.S. diplomatic recognition should be extended to Andorra; do you: disagree   strongly disagree   strongly agree   agree
2. If an Andorrese (a citizen of Andorra) was taking the vacant apartment next door to you, would you: strong approve   disapprove   approve   strongly disapprove
3. Andorra is essentially a law abiding country; do you: strongly disagree   agree   strongly agree   disagree
4. Admission of Andorra into the U.N. could be the first step in the destruction of our way of life; do you: agree   strongly agree   disagree   strongly disagree
5. If your sister was considering marrying an Andorrese, would you: approve   strongly disapprove   disapprove   strongly approve
6. Andorra can not be counted on as a defender of democracy in the event of any diplomatic crisis; do you: strongly agree   strongly disagree   agree   disagree
7. The average Andorrese is limited in his outlook and does not care what happens outside his country; do you: disagree   strongly agree   agree   strongly disagree
8. How would you feel if you had an opportunity to visit Andorra;

would you: strongly disapprove   disapprove   strongly approve   approve

9. How would you react if a person were to say that Andorra is a corrupt political curiosity; would you: strong disagree   agree   disagree   strongly agree

10. How would you feel if the U.S. was considering sending economic aid to Andorra; would you: disapprove   strongly approve   strong disapprove   approve

11. Andorra could provide the final push that would bring on the most destructive war in history; do you: agree   disagree   strongly agree   strongly disagree

12. The people of Andorra are on the whole thrifty and industrious; do you: agree   strongly agree   strongly disagree   disagree

13. The industrial and economic outlook in Andorra is becoming promising; do you: disagree   strongly agree   agree   strongly disagree

14. The agitation for the admission of Andorra into the U.N. is probably the work of crackpots, radicals, and fascists; do you: strongly disagree   disagree   strongly agree   agree

15. If your family was found to be partially Andorrese in descent, would you: approve   strongly disapprove   disapprove   strongly approve

16. U.S. recognition should not be extended to Andorra as it will not bring to the U.S. any benefits of value; do you: agree   strongly disagree   disagree   strongly agree

17. The Andorrese would probably be a tool of the Communists in the U.N.; do you: strong disagree   agree   disagree   strongly agree

18. The time for the admission of Andorra into the U.N. is now; do you: disagree   strongly disagree   strongly agree   agree

19. How do you feel about the rights of the average Andorrese citizen; do you: disapprove   approve   strongly approve   strongly disapprove

20. The U.N. should admit Andorra; do you: strongly agree   strongly disagree   agree   disagree

21. How do you feel about the Andorran government; do you: strongly disapprove   approve   strongly approve   disapprove

22. It would be unwise to invest U.S. money in Andorra; do you: agree   strong disagree   disagree   strongly agree

EMOTIONAL APPEAL

An Argument against the Admission of Andorra to the United Nations

I would like to read to you some excerpts from an article in a well-known American magazine. It is entitled "Khrushchev Takes Notice of Andorra." The author states:

Recently there has been some agitation, peculiarly enough by both radicals and fascists, for the admission of Andorra into that great international organization, the United Nations. It is wise for us as thinking citizens and future citizens of our great country to examine this plot and see it for what it is —a scheme whereby the balance of power in the United Nations will be cunningly eased from the democratic nations of the west and wrapped as a gift for the power-seeking authoritarian governments of the world. This means that your freedom, yours and mine, is being given away, the gesture being cloaked in such high-sounding ivory-tower phrases as "democratic representation" and "a place among the community of nations." The "eggheads" and bureaucrats who persist in such an effort, who look no further than these high-sounding, democratic-appearing phrases, are selling us out.

How many of you believe that we can afford to give away, in these critical times, the balance of power? How many of you would enjoy life under the heel of the Communist dictator? Can we in all conscience spend the taxpayers' money to subsidize dictatorships and tyranny? It is our duty as future citizens to open our eyes to the threat of the "big give-away," the favorite device of big government, whereby we are in danger of being deprived of our rights to life, liberty, and the pursuit of happiness.

As heavy contributors to the United Nations we have a duty to perform. How many of you had heard of Andorra before today? Andorra itself is but another brick in the wall being built against democracy. Its government is not democratic but is very reminiscent of the proceedings of the Ku Klux Klan. Government in Andorra does not resemble the process of a responsible elected legislature, nor do you find an executive responsible to the will of the people. The average so-called "citizen" of Andorra has very little to say about law and government. This is a matter for the privileged few. When you consider these facts and weigh the evidence, I'm sure you all recognize the danger. The government of Andorra is bound to be a corrupt government; Andorrese votes in the United Nations will be bought and sold. Andorrese politicians will be the hirelings of the highest bidder.

It is clear that Andorrese membership in the United Nations will be a corrupting influence that would contribute to the destruction of the United Nations, our last-ditch attempt to keep peace and mutual understanding alive in the world. The threat of all-out war with possible total extinction looms before us. Radioactivity can sterilize the earth. Man's newest playthings in the arsenals of the great nations make peace a necessity, not a luxury. You have, I know, been haunted by the headlines in the newspapers, have all been startled by the air-raid alarms and have wondered if it were the real thing or just another grim rehearsal. We cannot, today, rock the boat: it would be dangerous, even suicidal, to sleep and let slip from our hands those guarantees which enable you to live your lives as *you* intend, not your masters.

We cannot, today, gamble nor compromise with our principles. The so-called "citizens" of Andorra are known throughout Europe, as backward, ignorant, unprincipled, provincial, undemocratic people. They are notorious for being poverty-stricken ne'er-do-wells, uncaring of what happens outside their principality, unchanging, feudal, cold, and remote to strangers. The Arkansas hillbilly would be a sophisticated "man of the world" compared to the average Andorrese. It is revealing that the national economy is based upon immorality, is based upon smuggling, black-market, and theft to a large extent. In fact, if you were to ask a well-informed person what is the one thing for which Andorra is noted, the answer would probably be "the absence of morality." In these times, when the world appears to be teetering on the brink of disaster, can we afford to give power to people of this sort? The answer must be no; we cannot and must not give to this degenerate country and its immoral people the power to manipulate our lives and destroy our freedom.

We are all taxpayers and will in years to come pay an increasing share of the cost of government. We support by taxation both the United States government and the United Nations. We must, for this reason, ensure that we have good government. We dare not waste our precious tax dollars when we need them for defense and winning the "Cold War." Can we afford to spend them on Andorra? What stake has America in this country? Of what interest or value is Andorra to the West? Would you ever think of visiting this miserable principality? Would you be interested in investing *your* money in Andorra? Would you be proud of your Andorran blood or heritage if you were of Andorran descent? (I can see by your faces that the answer is "No.")

Today, more than ever before, we need the assistance of staunch defenders; people who care about the democratic way of life deserve our aid and assistance. Andorra, of course, does not qualify. Its unreliable assistance would be weak, vacillating, puny, and inconsequential. We need friends we can rely upon, who cannot be bought, who will not waver with the passing winds. We cannot afford to waste our substance on the weak and vacillating, nor can we have it said that we are the supporters of tyrannical governments. The communists would gain an enormous propaganda advantage if we were to gather to our bosom this particular viper. Can we truly be said to be defenders of democracy when we think of giving aid and comfort to a ramshackle government which in no way resembles the democracies of the West? We must choose carefully in these times. For these reasons we cannot and must not admit Andorra to the United Nations.

37 / Attitude Change through Modification
of Attitude Structure [1,2]

Earl R. Carlson

> *Earl R. Carlson of Michigan State University finds in this controlled*
> *experiment that persons made aware that important values can be*
> *attained by changing their attitudes toward a social problem, tend to do*
> *so unless they are extremely prejudiced or extremely nonprejudiced.*

There is wide agreement that "attitudes" are complex, in that they are composed of a number of components, characteristics, or dimensions. Psychologists generally agree, also, that changes in attitudes may come through the operation of different processes (Sarnoff and Katz, 1954). There have been few studies, however, which have attempted to differentiate either components of attitudes or the processes of change experimentally. The present study is of this nature—an investigation of the importance of two independent sources of *affect* (the liking or favorableness-unfavorableness aspect) of an attitude.

The importance of the individual's system of general goals in life, or values, has been suggested by many theorists as of crucial significance in determining the affect associated with specific aspects of the person's experience. A recent study by Rosenberg (1953), building upon and improving the methodology and conceptualization of earlier experimental studies (Smith, 1949; Woodruff and DiVesta, 1948), demonstrated the relationship between attitudinal affect, i.e., the attitude position, or what is generally termed simply "attitude," and two components of "attitude structure." Rosenberg differentiated as structural components (a) the intensity of affect of a person's values, i.e., the expected satisfaction from these values, and (b) the perceived importance of the attitude object (situation, event) in leading to or blocking the attainment of the values. He measured "value satisfaction" and "perceived instrumentality" independently, and found each to correlate significantly with the attitude

[1] This study is one of a series undertaken by the Attitude Change Project at the University of Michigan. It was supported in part by the U.S. Air Force under Contract AF 33(038)-26646, monitored by the Human Resources Research Institute.

[2] The present paper is based upon a thesis submitted to the Department of Psychology of the University of Michigan in partial fulfillment of the requirements for the degree of Doctor of Philosophy. The writer wishes to express his appreciation to Dr. Helen Peak for her generous advice and assistance given throughout the study.

Reprinted from the *Journal of Abnormal and Social Psychology*, 1956, *52*, 256–61, with the permission of the author and the American Psychological Association.

of the person. The best predictor of attitude, however, was found to be an index of "affective loading" which combined the two measures. The results clearly indicated that value satisfaction and perceived instrumental relations were separate and important components of the attitude structure.

Attitude change, it follows from this theory, should result from changes in either the expected satisfaction from goals, or in the instrumental relationship perceived between the attitude object and the goal. The present study was designed to test this latter hypothesis—that changes in attitude (affect) result from altering perceptions of the attitude object (situation or event) as leading to the attainment of valued goals. This hypothesis is consistent with experimental findings on animal and human learning, but has not been clearly tested in the area of social attitudes.

A second important source of affect is hypothesized to be mediated through generalization from affect associated with related attitude objects or situations. Following principles of generalization developed in learning studies, tests were made of two further hypotheses: (a) attitude change generalizes to related issues, and (b) the degree of generalization is a function of the similarity of the attitude objects or situations.

METHOD

The experimental procedure of the study was designed to increase the subjects' perception that "allowing Negroes to move into White neighborhoods" would be a means for attaining four specified goals, or values. The attitude issue of Negro housing segregation was selected as the vehicle for studying attitude and attitude structure change, since the subjects varied widely in attitude on the issue, the attitude was relatively stable, yet some change could be produced using a limited experimental procedure. Attitudes on five related issues were also measured in order to test for generalization of attitude change.

The four values discussed in the experimental communication were (a) American prestige in other countries, (b) protection of property values, (c) equal opportunity for personal development, and (d) being experienced, broad-minded, and worldly-wise. These values were selected on the basis of their probable importance for this issue.

The data were collected in three major stages. Early in the semester experimental and control Ss were given attitude and value measures during regular class periods. Code numbers were used to maintain anonymity for the Ss. The experimental change procedure was administered to the experimental Ss in two parts: the first consisted of an assignment given by the instructor to be completed outside of class, one to two weeks after the initial measures were obtained; the second, five to ten days later, consisted of a prepared discussion given orally by the experimenter. After a further interval of three weeks the attitude and value measures were readministered to both experimental and control Ss. Finally, a follow-up questionnaire was given a few days later to obtain judgments of the perceived similarities between Negroes, Jews, and Mexicans.

In order to minimize the Ss' awareness of the nature of the study, the change procedure was presented as a separate experiment by a person not involved in the measurement of attitudes and value. The follow-up questionnaire indicated that Ss did not attempt to distort their responses deliberately.

Attitude Measures

The measures of attitude toward the primary issue of study, Negro housing segregation, and the five related attitude issues required the S to rank six alternatives (ranging from "I am completely opposed to allowing Negroes into White neighborhoods" to "I am completely in favor of allowing Negroes into White neighborhoods") in terms of the degree to which they represented the person's own opinion.[3] The measure of the person's attitude position used in the analysis was coded directly from the S's first choice of the six alternatives. The measure of attitude change was obtained through coding the first three ranks given of the six alternative positions; using only transitive rankings, the three ranks gave a 16-point scale, ranging from position 1 (subject choosing alternatives in the order ABC), to position 2 (BAC), position 3 (BCA), and on to position 16 (FED). The Negro housing segregation measure had an uncorrected reliability of .67 for the control group.

To test the hypotheses concerning generalization of attitude change, five attitude issues similar to the Negro housing segregation issue on two dimensions were also measured in the same manner before and after the change procedure, these being (a) Mexican housing segregation, (b) Jewish housing segregation, (c) command of White enlisted men by Negro officers, (d) command of non-Mexican enlisted men by Mexican officers, and (e) command of non-Jewish enlisted men by Jewish officers.

Value Measures

The measures of "value satisfaction" and "perceived instrumentality" required the Ss to rate each of the 25 value items given in Table 1. Two items, using different words but identical in meaning, were used within the set to measure each of the four areas selected for experimental change. The four sets of experimental items were items 5 and 19, items 8 and 11, items 10 and 22, and items 6 and 17. The remaining 17 values were selected to cover the broad range of further general goals in life that individuals regard as important in some degree. The items were presented on cards in random order, with a randomly assigned number on the card being used to record judgments of the value.

The value satisfaction index was obtained from Ss' ratings of the extent to which each value represented goals from which the S gets, or would

[3] [Appended to the selection.]

get, satisfaction. Each value was judged independently in terms of 11 categories on a graphic rating scale. The scale of positively-valued goals was defined by three descriptive phrases: "No satisfaction from the goal" (Category 0), "Medium satisfaction from the goal" (Category 5), and "Maximum satisfaction from the goal" (Category 10). One further category was for judgments of "Dissatisfaction from the goal." [4] The index of value satisfaction for the four experimental values was then obtained through arithmetic summation of the ratings of the eight items, coding "dissatisfaction" ratings minus 5. This index yielded an uncorrected test-retest reliability of .79.

The measure of "perceived instrumentality" required the Ss to judge each value in terms of the "probability that the goals will be attained by allowing Negroes to move into White neighborhoods." The judgments

Table 1. Value Items Used in the Satisfaction and Instrumentality Ratings

Value Item
1. Everyone being assured of a good standard of living
2. People sticking to their own groups
3. People looking out for the welfare of others
4. Being looked up to by others
5. America having high prestige in other countries
6. Being well-rounded, enlightened and sophisticated about life
7. Serving the interests of the group to which one belongs
8. Security of the value of one's real estate
9. Having power and authority over people
10. All persons having the chance to realize their potentialities
11. Having the value of property well-protected
12. Self-discipline—overcoming my irrational emotions and desires
13. All human beings having equal rights
14. Complying with the wishes of persons in authority
15. Being like others in general; having the same interests, opinions and ways of behaving as other people have
16. People having strict moral standards
17. Being a person who is experienced, broadminded, and worldly-wise
18. The open expression of disagreement between people
19. People in other nations respecting our principles and standards
20. Being allowed to maintain the privacy of one's opinions and beliefs
21. Being with other people; socializing
22. Everyone having opportunity to develop himself and his capacities
23. Letting others make their own decisions
24. People being strongly patriotic
25. Not being ashamed of one's own feelings and behavior

were made on an 11-point graphic rating scale defined by three descriptive phrases: "Maximum probability that the goal will be blocked by allowing Negroes to move into White neighborhoods" (Category −5), "Allowing

[4] [Appended to the selection.]

Negroes to move into White neighborhoods is irrelevant to achieving the goal" (Category o), and "Maximum probability that the goal will be achieved by allowing Negroes to move into White neighborhoods" (Category +5).[5] The index of perceived instrumentality was a summation of the ratings of the eight experimental value items, and had an uncorrected test-retest reliability of .66.

An index of "affective loading," used by Rosenberg to predict attitude, was computed separately for the total set of 25 value items, the eight experimental items, and the 17 nonexperimental value items. Since, according to the theory, attitude is a function of both value satisfaction and perceived instrumentality, attitude change should covary with change in an index combining measures of these separate components. The index of affective loading was computed by algebraically summing, over the set of values, the products of the satisfaction and instrumentality ratings of each value.

Change Procedure

The change procedure was designed to increase the Ss' awareness that "allowing Negroes to move into White neighborhoods" would tend to bring about the attainment of the four values. This procedure consisted of two parts: (a) a task which was presented as a "Test of Objectivity," and (b) a verbal discussion which ostensibly reported the results of the test. The "Test of Objectivity," completed as an assignment by the students outside of class, was introduced as a test of one's "ability to take a certain viewpoint and support it logically and objectively regardless of your own viewpoint." It was presented as a small experiment illustrating the scientific method, studying whether men or women were better able to take an objective viewpoint in reasoning. The test required the Ss to support four propositions, each stating that "allowing Negroes to move into White neighborhoods" would lead to one of four values listed above.

In the second part of the change procedure the experimenter, in reporting the results of the study on objectivity in reasoning, presented a prepared discussion of the four propositions. The discussion, covering each of the values in 350 to 400 words, attempted to make clear several important and reasonable points which would be accepted by the Ss, and which demonstrated the instrumentality of "allowing Negroes to move into White neighborhoods" for attaining each of the four values.

Subjects

One hundred eighty-three students in eight introductory psychology sections at the University of Michigan participated as experimental Ss; 126 of these received both parts of the experimental procedure (the "Test of Objectivity" and the verbal discussion of the test results), and 58 re-

[5] [Appended to the selection.]

ceived only one or the other of the two parts. The analyses reported in this paper are based upon the combined group of 183 experimental Ss.[6] Thirty-eight students in two classes participated as control subjects. The experimental and control groups were equated for initial attitude toward Negro housing segregation, and for both groups initial attitudes approximated a rectangular distribution.

RESULTS AND DISCUSSION

Effects of the Experimental Procedure

Before testing the basic hypotheses of the study, it must first be shown that the experimental procedure in fact altered both attitude and attitude structure as anticipated. The proportion of Ss changing attitude in a positive direction (toward less prejudice) on the Negro housing segregation issue was significantly greater for the experimental group than for the control group. Similarly, a significant proportion of experimental Ss changed in the predicted direction on instrumentality ratings of the eight experimental value items ($\chi^2 = 9.91$, $p < .01$).

Change in the value satisfaction ratings was not predicted, since the experimental procedure was directed only toward change in perceived instrumentalities, and no change was found. A significant proportion of experimental Ss, however, changed on the indices of affective loading based upon the eight experimental items ($\chi^2 = 17.79$, $p < .001$) and on the total set of 25 items ($\chi^2 = 4.19$, $p < .05$). Although not predicted, this change is consistent with the theory and with the rationale of the index, which is a direct function of instrumentality ratings as well as value satisfaction ratings. No systematic change was observed for the control group on the Negro segregation attitude scale or on any of the attitude structure measures.

It was anticipated prior to analyzing the data that Ss with different initial attitudes toward Negro housing segregation would react differently to the experimental procedure, but specific predictions were not made concerning the form of the relationships. No systematic differences were found for attitude structure changes, but the data clearly indicated a curvilinear relationship between initial attitude and attitude change for the experimental Ss, as shown in Figure 1. Tests comparing positive changes against the combination of no-change and negative-change Ss indicated that a significantly smaller proportion of Ss at position 1 (extreme prejudice) changed positively than Ss at positions 2 ($p < .05$) and 3 ($p < .05$); at position 4 the difference was at the .10 level. Similarly a

[6] Separate analyses for the experimental subjects receiving both parts of the experimental procedure and for those receiving only one part demonstrated the same relationships throughout (Carlson, 1953). The subjects receiving only one part generally showed less total change, as would be expected, but since the relationships between types of change were identical for both groups, the analyses reported here are based upon the combined group.

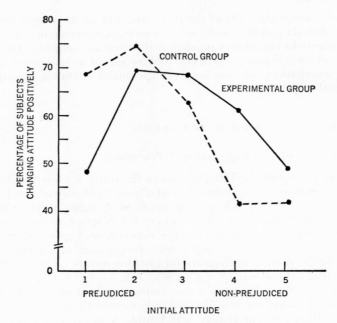

Fig. 1. Relationship between Initial Attitude
and Attitude Change

significantly smaller proportion of Ss at position 5 changed positively
than at positions 2 ($p < .01$), 3 ($p < .01$) and 4 ($p < .02$). The Ss at the
moderate positions (positions 2, 3, and 4) were found to be significantly
influenced by the experimental procedure, while extremely prejudiced
(position 1) and extremely nonprejudiced (positions 5 and 6) persons were
not found to change systematically. An analysis of change in the control
group is not meaningful as a result of the small number of Ss at each
initial attitude position.

A study of change on the five related attitude issues also supports this
curvilinear relationship. Combining the data from all six scales showed
that experimental Ss at position 1 were significantly less likely to change
positively than Ss at position 2 ($p < .01$), position 3 ($p < .01$) and position
4 ($p < .01$), and that Ss at position 5 were also significantly less likely to
change than those at position 2 ($p < .001$), position 3 ($p < .001$) and position 4 ($p < .05$). A further analysis of change for the generalization scales
studied separately indicated basically the same curvilinear relationship for
all six scales.

For the control group, however, the more prejudiced Ss changed
more in attitude than those at less prejudiced positions. A significantly
larger proportion of Ss at positions 1 and 2 combined changed positively
than Ss at positions 4 and 5 combined, suggesting the operation of other
change influences during the period of the study.

What accounts for this curvilinear relationship between initial attitude and change? The smaller proportion of positive changes at the nonprejudiced positions can be explained by the fact that the Ss already largely agreed with the change communication, and by the ceiling placed on change by the measuring instrument itself. The finding for experimental Ss of fewer positive changes in attitude for prejudiced Ss than for those at intermediate positions can be accounted for in terms of the possible wide range on the attitude continuum over which Ss at this extreme position may be spread. Some prejudiced Ss may have actual attitudinal positions far below the cutting-point between positions 1 and 2, and the same amount of actual positive change would result in fewer position changes than for Ss initially at other positions.

These findings indicate the importance of considering the possible interaction of initial attitude on effects of attitude change techniques. In the present study the absence of attitude change for Ss at the extreme positions prevented tests of the major hypotheses for these Ss. Consequently the analysis of relationships between attitude structure change and attitude change, and the generalizations from the findings, must be restricted to persons with moderate initial attitudes toward the issue.

Relationships of Attitude Change to Attitude Structure Change

The hypothesis that Ss who changed in perceived instrumental relationships would also change in attitude was clearly supported by the data. Experimental Ss with moderate initial attitudes (positions 2, 3, and 4) who altered their perception of the relation of segregation to the values discussed also tended to change their attitude toward Negro housing segregation, this difference being significant at the .01 level ($\chi^2 = 24.01$, $n = 69$, $df = 9$).

Changes in the value satisfaction measures, if occurring, should covary with changes in attitude, but the amount of value satisfaction change was too slight to enable an adequate test of this relationship. Changes in attitude, however, were significantly related to the indices of affective loading, which reflected both instrumentality and value satisfaction changes. The relationship for the total set of 25 value items was significant at the .02 level ($\chi^2 = 5.27$, $n = 69$, $df = 1$), and the relationship for the eight experimental items was significant at the .05 level, measured in terms of a correlation coefficient ($r = .27$, $df = 68$), but not significant tested by chi-square analysis ($\chi^2 = 1.43$, $n = 70$, $p < .15$). A relationship found between attitude change and change in the index of affective loading for the 17 nonexperimental values ($\chi^2 = 5.47$, $n = 70$, $p < .01$) is also consistent with the theory, since the basic relationship between perceived instrumentality and attitude should hold for all values, whether experimentally manipulated or not.

What are the implications of these findings? This test does not account for all of the variance of attitude-affect change, certainly, but it has tested experimentally the significance of *one* important source of affect of an attitude. The role of perceived instrumental relations was demonstrated for Ss with nonextreme attitudes, but was not tested for persons extremely prejudiced or extremely nonprejudiced. The underlying theory would predict that changes in value satisfaction would covary similarly with changes in attitude, but this hypothesis was not tested in the present study.

Generalization of Attitude Change

The data demonstrated generalization of attitude change to certain related issues, but the hypothesis of a gradient of generalization varying as a function of the similarity of the attitude objects or situations was not confirmed. Comparison of the proportions of Ss in the experimental group changing attitude positively, not changing, and changing negatively with changes in the control group indicated generalization of change to the Jewish housing segregation issue ($\chi^2 = 5.15$, $p < .03$), the Jewish officer issue ($\chi^2 = 8.43$, $p < .01$), and the Negro officer issue ($\chi^2 = 3.38$, $p < .07$). Because of the limited change in attitude for Ss with extreme initial attitudes, the analysis here was also restricted to Ss with initial positions 2, 3, and 4.

A sign-test analysis of positive changes compared to negative changes, i.e., discarding the no-change cases, rejected the null hypothesis (of no change in the positive direction) at the .05 level for all six attitude scales. A significant proportion of control Ss summed over all six scales changed positively ($p < .05$), and a significant proportion changed positively on the two Mexican issues taken together; the other control group comparisons, however, were not statistically significant.

Judgments on a follow-up questionnaire item of "Which group do you believe is most like Negroes? ____ Jews ____ Mexicans" indicated that Mexicans were judged as "most like" Negroes by almost all Ss, but, as reported, generalization of attitude change was not demonstrated for the two Mexican issues, though it was for the two Jewish issues. Actually significant proportions of experimental Ss did change attitude positively on the Mexican scales, but the proportion changing in the control group, though less, was also significant. With the relatively small number of control Ss the differences between groups were not statistically significant.

The failure to confirm the hypothesis of a gradient of generalization can be accounted for in terms of recognized limitations in the measure of "similarity" used in the study. Conceptual similarity between these issues is undoubtedly multidimensional, and the dimensions used by the Ss in judging similarity may differ considerably from those over which generalization took place. Also several sources of evidence indicated that the Mexican issues were not well-structured or stable for these Ss, and that changes occurring on them were due more to this lack of structure, and consequent instability, than to influence of the experimental procedure.

Further study of the process of generalization of change of social attitudes will depend upon systematic analyses of the gradients of conceptual similarity involved. Methodology for handling this problem has not been thoroughly developed, though an approach formulated by Osgood (1952), using a combination of associational and scaling procedures, may provide a systematic basis for such measurement and dimensionalizing of conceptual meaning.

SUMMARY

This experiment was designed to test the hypothesis that attitudes toward an object, or situation, may be changed through altering the person's perception of the significance of the object as a means for attaining valued goals. It sought further to test whether attitude change generalizes to related objects, and whether the degree of generalization is a function of the similarity of the objects.

One hundred eighty-three experimental Ss responded to three sets of measures before and after a change procedure: (a) measures of attitude toward "allowing Negroes to move into White neighborhoods" and five related issues, (b) a measure requiring ratings of 25 general values in terms of the expected satisfaction from each, and (c) a rating measure of the 25 values in terms of the probability that "allowing Negroes to move into White neighborhoods" would lead to, or block, the attainment of each of the values. Thirty-nine control Ss took the same measures but did not receive the change procedure. The change procedure was designed to increase the Ss' awareness that nonsegregation would lead to the attainment of each of four important values.

The experimental procedure changed perceptions of the role of Negro housing segregation in attaining the four values, and changed attitude toward Negro housing segregation for Ss with moderate initial attitude on the issue. Insufficient attitude change was produced in extremely prejudiced and extremely nonprejudiced subjects to permit tests of the hypotheses for these Ss. Satisfaction ratings were not affected by the change procedure.

Changes in attitude were related significantly to changes in perceived instrumental relationships, and to changes in an index based upon both satisfaction and instrumentality ratings. Attitude change generalized to three related attitude issues, but not to two further issues. The exent of generalization of attitude change was not shown to vary with the similarity of the attitude issues.

RANKING OF ATTITUDE MEASURES

In many parts of the country today there has arisen the question of whether Negroes should be allowed to move into neighborhoods that have previously been occupied only by Whites. Please *rank* the following statements according to how close they come to representing your own opinion on this issue. For these questions we would like you to respond as follows:

Place the number 1 before the statement which *most* agrees with your position.

Place the number 2 before the statement which *next best* reflects your position.

Place the number 3 before the statement which *third best* reflects your position.

Place the number 4 before the statement which *fourth best* reflects your position.

Place the number 5 before the statement which *fifth best* reflects your position.

Place the number 6 before the statement which *least best* reflects your position.

_____ a. I am completely opposed to allowing Negroes into White neighborhoods.

_____ b. I am much more opposed to allowing Negroes into White neighborhoods than I am for it.

_____ c. I am slightly more opposed to allowing Negroes into White neighborhoods than I am for it.

_____ d. I am slightly more in favor of allowing Negroes into White neighborhoods than I am against it.

_____ e. I am much more in favor of allowing Negroes into White neighborhoods than I am against it.

_____ f. I am completely in favor of allowing Negroes into White neighborhoods.

SATISFACTION RATINGS

INSTRUCTIONS: We would like you to judge the cards into 12 categories according to how close the goals described represent goals from which you personally get, or would get, satisfaction. Column o stands for "gives me neither satisfaction nor dissatisfaction" and column 10 stands for "gives, or would give, me maximum satisfaction." The columns in between represent, then, the in-between steps, and the column on the left is for goals which represent dissatisfaction for you.

Record the number on the back of the card into the column best fitting your judgment of the amount of satisfaction the goal represents. Be certain that *all the cards* (from 1 through 25) are judged carefully and recorded.

Dissatisfaction from goal	*No satisfaction from goal*				*Medium satisfaction from goal*					*Maximum satisfaction from goal*
—	o	1	2	3	4	5	6	7	8	9	10

RATINGS OF EFFECT ON ACHIEVING THE GOAL

INSTRUCTIONS: Here the cards are to be judged in terms of the degree to which the goal that is described would be reached if Negroes were allowed to move into White neighborhoods. If you think that allowing Negroes to move into White neighborhoods would lead to the full achieve-ment of a certain goal, then the number of that card should be written in column +5, which stands for "maximum probability that the goal would be attained by allowing Negroes to move into White neighborhoods." If you think that allowing Negroes to move into White neighborhoods would definitely tend to lead to the blocking of nonachievement of a certain goal, then this number should be written in column −5. Column o then represents "irrelevant to achieving the goal," and the other columns represent the in-between steps.

Be certain that *all the cards* (from 1 through 25) are judged carefully and recorded.

Maximum proba- bility that goal blocked by allow- ing Negroes to move into White neighborhoods	Allowing Negroes to move into White neighbor- hoods irrelevant to achieving the goal	Maximum proba- bility that goal achieved by allow- ing Negroes to move into White neighborhoods

−5	−4	−3	−2	−1	o	+1	+2	+3	+4	+5

38 / The Influence of Interracial Contact on Social Acceptance in a Newly Integrated School

Staten W. Webster

Does six months of interracial contact in a newly integrated junior high school increase social acceptance? What is the relationship between precontact social acceptance scores and later friendship choices? These two provocative questions are studied by Staten W. Webster of the University of California (Berkeley). Pertinent to this experimental investigation of modification of interracial attitudes and behavior is the discussion of the factors which may account for the results.

Does interracial contact lead to improved attitudes and increased social acceptance among the participants? This question has been the subject of

Reprinted from *Journal of Educational Psychology*, 1961, 52, 292–96, with the permission of the author and the American Psychological Association.

a number of investigations, most of which have involved white and Negro adult subjects.

Data reported in these studies have been contradictory. A number of investigations (Brophy, 1945; Deutsch and Collins, 1952; Neprash, 1952; Wilner, Walkley, and Cook, 1952) have indicated the successful influence of interracial contact in reducing prejudice. However, a number of negative findings have also been reported (Mussen, 1950; Rose, 1947; Young, 1932).

Those who argue against the positive effects of contact cite the restrictive influence of racial and ethnic group norms upon individuals in such situations. The existence of such frames of reference has been clearly documented by Bogardus (1959). While the impact of racial or ethnic group membership upon the individual has been established, there is also evidence that under certain conditions individuals and groups do modify their interracial attitudes, feelings, and behaviors. An analysis of successful contact situations seems to reveal three important requisite factors: equal status of the participants in the situation, contact of sufficient duration and intimacy, and the sanction or support of a higher authority.

PROCEDURE

Problem

In view of the dearth of contact research involving public school settings, this investigation sought to study the effects of interracial contact in a newly integrated northern California junior high school.

Specifically, two major questions were investigated: Does interracial contact, over a 6-month period, between white and Negro subjects, lead to increased expressions of social acceptance of one group for the other? Are precontact social acceptance scores (as measured by a social acceptance scale) associated with the eventual making of interracial friendships?

SETTING

The school board of a high school district in the San Francisco Bay Area reached a decision in the spring of 1959 to effect certain changes in the boundaries surrounding its junior and senior high schools. These realignments were made necessary by overcrowded conditions in some schools, and the unequal distribution of children in terms of socioeconomic status.

Prior to the boundary modifications, which became effective in September 1959, Jackson Junior High School [1] was populated by an all white student body. The composition of the school population was altered greatly by the boundary changes, with some 300 Negro children being integrated into the school's present total of some 1,400 students. This school, its feeder elementary schools, and its surrounding communities served as

[1] Actual school names are not used in this report.

the setting for this study. While there were some socioeconomic differences between the white and Negro communities, a study of the personal histories of the children revealed these to be minor in nature.

SUBJECTS

When the new school boundaries were announced late in the spring, it became obvious that most children in two elementary schools would be attending, in the fall, a truly integrated school for the first time. Walker Elementary School, which was all white, sent 60 sixth grade graduates to Jackson Junior High in September. From the almost all Negro Newell School came 44 transfers. (This school contained, in addition to some 400 Negro students, 17 children of Indian and Mexican-American extraction.)

A socioeconomically similar control group comprised of 55 whites and 53 Negroes was also selected. An all white community and junior high school, in a neighboring city, provided the white control subjects. The Negro control subjects were selected from an almost all Negro junior high school in another nearby city; with the exception of 9 Mexican-American and white children, the latter school's student population of 450 was composed entirely of Negroes.

HYPOTHESES

Four hypotheses were investigated in this study; they were as follows:

Hypothesis I: White and Negro subjects who have experienced intergroup contact in a school situation will express significantly more social acceptance of each other after a 6-month period of time.

Hypothesis II: The postcontact social acceptance scores of the white and Negro experimental subjects will display significantly more out-group acceptance than will the noncontact scores of the control subjects.

Hypothesis III: The precontact social acceptance scores of the experimental subjects will be significantly associated with their later friendship choices.

Hypothesis IV: The retest social acceptance scores of the experimental subjects will be significantly associated with their interracial friendship choices.

These hypotheses are interrelated. Hypotheses I and II seek to measure the impact of contact upon the experimental subjects, in light of the data on the control subjects. Hypotheses III and IV are designed to seek additional data on the effects of contact and on the validity of the social acceptance scale used to gather these data.

Method

The test-retest design was deemed most appropriate for this type of study. Both experimental groups were tested initially in June 1959, while they were still attending their particular elementary schools, and were retested at Jackson School in March 1960. Because of the time factor, it was impossible to test the control groups in spring 1959. The failure to obtain these data is, admittedly, a weakness of the study. However, since their elementary and junior high schools were relatively homogeneous in racial composition, it seems valid to assume that their single test scores (spring 1960) on a social acceptance scale (see below) would not differ significantly from the precontact scores of their matched experimental groups.

All testing sessions were conducted by members of the subject's racial group. To avoid the possibility of inhibiting the responses of the children, they were told that the questionnaires were anonymous. However, although the experimenter entertained some reservations about the procedure, invisible ink markings were used on the social acceptance scale to identify the respondents.

To measure social acceptance, a nine-item social acceptance scale was constructed. The respondent was asked to rank his willingness to accept members of four groups (Chinese, Japanese, Mexicans, and whites or Negroes) in nine social situations. The social situations ranged from the less intimate (e.g., working in the same factory) to the very intimate (e.g., living next door). Scale scores from 0 to 9 were possible, with the higher scores representing the greater acceptance. The scalability of the instrument was established in keeping with the criteria suggested by Guttman (1950). The coefficient of reproducibility was .92.

In addition to the social acceptance scale, a brief sociometric friendship questionnaire was used. The subjects were asked to indicate their six best friends in the school and to give the ethnic or racial backgrounds of these friends. These data were obtained after the retest of the experimental subjects.

To test the above hypotheses, it was necessary to validate the assumption that both experimental and control groups were initially similar in levels of social acceptance. The two-tailed application of the Kolmogorov-Smirnov two-sample test (Siegel, 1956) was used in this analysis. Since the KS test is sensitive to differences in central tendency, dispersion, and skewness, it seemed especially appropriate for this purpose. The comparison of the experimental subjects' precontact scores and the single test scores of the control subjects revealed no significant differences.

RESULTS

Table 1 contains a summary of the basic test data on the experimental and control groups. The reader will note the great discrepancies between the scores of the Negroes and the whites. Bogardus (1959) has reported similar distributions in one of his studies of social distance.

Hypothesis I. The Wilcoxon matched-pairs signed-ranks test (Siegel,

Table 1. Test and Retest Scores of Experimental and Control Groups on a Social Acceptance Scale

Subject	Group	N	Range	$\overline{X}$	Mode	SD
Experimental:						
Pretest	White	60	0–9	1.85	0	2.32
(June 1959)	Negro	44	0–9	6.05	9	2.86
Posttest	White	60	7–0	1.48	0	2.02
(March 1960)	Negro	44	9–0	6.32	9	2.61
Control:	White	55	0–9	2.54	0	2.24
(March 1960)	Negro	53	0–9	5.98	6	3.97

1956) was used to test the first hypothesis.[2] This nonparametric test makes use of comparisons between pairs of scores and takes into consideration both the magnitude as well as the direction of the differences between the sets of scores. Change for the white subjects was in the negative direction and significant ($z = 3.96$, $p < .05$). Change for the Negro subjects was positive and significant ($z = 2.12$, $p < .05$). Thus, the predicted hypothesis was confirmed only in the case of the Negro subjects.

An equal number of Negro subjects changed in each direction. However, the magnitude of change was greater for those subjects whose gains were positive.

Hypothesis II. The testing of Hypothesis II involved comparing the postcontact scores of the experimental groups with those of their controls, in an attempt to see if the contact situation had produced significant differences among the groups.

The one-tailed application of the KS test revealed a significant difference between the scores of the white experimental and control groups ($\chi^2 = 7.23$, $df = 2$, $p < .05$); however, this difference was in the nonpredicted direction. The obtained difference between the scores of the Negro experimental and control subjects was not significant ($\chi^2 = 2.16$, $df = 2$, $p > .05$).

Hypothesis III. This hypothesis is based on a suggestion by Neprash (1952). He speculated that the making of out-group friendships in a contact situation may be simply a matter of favorable precontact attitudes toward that group and not a result of contact. To test this assumption the precontact scores of the experimental subjects were dichotomized at the median and a comparison was made of the number of out-group friendships indicated by each group. The χ^2 test was used in the analysis and the findings were not significant. The median, in this case, happened to fall close to the derived zero intensity point (discussed later).

These findings seem to indicate that, in this study, precontact attitudes played little or no part in the willingness to make out-group friendships in the contact situation. The making of interracial friendships, it appears, was related to the effects of contact itself.

[2] The .05 level of significance was used in testing all hypotheses.

Hypothesis IV. It was predicted in Hypothesis IV that the subjects' retest social acceptance scores would be significantly associated with their reported interracial friendships. In testing this assumption, use was made of the intensity measure suggested by Guttman (1954) and his associates.

While the method of deriving this score will not be fully discussed, a brief description will be given. The zero or low intensity point is a measure that seeks to establish a psychologically meaningful point of low intensity on an attitude scale. Through the use of the extreme responses of the subjects to each scale item (Answer Categories 1 or 4), it is possible to trichotomize the respondents into three general groups: intensely positive subjects, intensely negative subjects, and indifferent or low intensity subjects.

In the case of the social acceptance scale used in this study, the zero intensity point was found to be located at the scale score of four.

The subjects were dichotomized on the basis of their intensity scores, and an analysis was then made of the number of out-group friendship choices reported by each group. The obtained result was significant ($x^2 = 10.56$, $df = 1$, $p < .01$) and Hypothesis IV, was thus confirmed.

DISCUSSION

The positive effects presumably associated with interracial contact were not confirmed in this study. What, then, are some factors which seem to account for the obtained results?

Although the three-part criterion presented earlier in this paper was met in this contact situation, it is possible that only more general and intimate contact between interracial groups (Brophy, 1945; Deutsch and Collins, 1952; Wilner et al., 1952) results in significant modifications of attitudes. It should be remembered that the subjects, while attending the integrated school, continued to live in racially closed communities. It is possible that integration within the total social environment is necessary, for the attitudes and values which can be developed in the school setting are probably contradicted by the realities of the restricted community.

The length of the contact situation in this instance could be another factor that partially explains the failure of the contact hypotheses. A 6-month period of time could very well be inadequate to allow for the necessary intergroup adjustment of the subjects. Although this period of contact was longer than that reported in a number of studies, subsequent investigation may show that the initial assumptions associated with contact experiences are valid.

The social acceptance scores of both white and Negro subjects provide another possible explanation. Social distance (acceptance) research by Bogardus (1959) and others has documented the existence of a hierarchy of racial preferences. These normative frames of reference appear to be held both commonly and consistently by members of various racial or ethnic groups. Traditionally, whites rate Negroes in their preferences low on a social distance scale, while Negroes tend to rate whites quite highly. The data obtained in this study reflect these phenomena. While social distance measures have proven to be both reliable and valid, it is possible that they are not sensitive enough to measure less noticeable changes within individual attitude structures. Methods and instruments which assess interracial attitudes with greater depth and precision would seem to be needed.

An interesting finding of the study was the significant association of interracial friendship choices with postcontact social acceptance scores but not with pretest scores. This finding seems to suggest caution in accepting the responses of subjects to social distance and other types of attitude measures as predictors of behavior. Many subjects whose precontact responses were favorable or highly accepting of the other group failed to make eventual interracial friendships, and in a number of cases completely reversed their scale scores from high acceptance (scores of 7–9) to high rejection (0–2).

The data obtained in this study seem to suggest a critical reappraisal of the contact hypothesis. Factors external to the setting of the interaction as well as those associated with racial and ethnic group membership must be considered.

SUMMARY

This study tested three major hypotheses relating to interracial contact, in a California junior high school, between white and Negro subjects. It was held that (a) a school contact situation of 6-months' duration would lead to increased interracial social acceptance by members of the two racial groups, (b) that a comparison between experimental subjects who experienced interracial contact and similar control subjects who did not would reveal greater interracial acceptance among the former group, and (c) that precontact social acceptance scores of the experimental subjects would be associated with out-group friendship choices made in the contact setting.

The test-retest design was used with 60 white and 44 Negro subjects, and 55 white and 53 Negro control subjects. A single administration of the social acceptance scale took place with the control subjects. All tests were administered by adults of the particular subjects' racial groups.

Contact had a negative effect upon the white subjects; they became significantly less accepting of Negroes. The findings were inconclusive in the case of the Negro subjects, but did tend to indicate that change was greater in the direction of more acceptance of whites. Precontact social acceptance scores were not found to be associated with later friendship choices. However, postcontact acceptance scores were associated with actual out-group friendship choices at the .01 level of confidence.

Social Behavior

39 / Superordinate Goals in the Reduction of Intergroup Conflict [1]

Muzafer Sherif

In a relatively natural setting, a boy's summer camp, Muzafer Sherif of the University of Oklahoma finds that intergroup conflict is reduced by introducing goals which are compellingly shared by members of the groups and which require the collaborative efforts of all. It would be useful to test this method of reducing group conflict with different groups and in other situations, such as cliques and factions in a classroom, between students from different classrooms or divisions, sororities and fraternities, clubs and other organizations.

In the past, measures to combat the problems of intergroup conflicts, proposed by social scientists as well as by such people as administrators, policy-makers, municipal officials, and educators, have included the following: introduction of legal sanctions; creation of opportunities for social and other contacts among members of conflicting groups; dissemination of correct information to break down false prejudices and unfavorable stereotypes; appeals to the moral ideals of fair play and brotherhood; and even the introduction of rigorous physical activity to produce catharsis by releasing pent-up frustrations and aggressive complexes in the unconscious. Other measures proposed include the encouragement of co-operative habits in one's own community, and bring together in the cozy atmosphere of a meeting room the leaders of antagonistic groups.

[1] The main points in this paper were presented at the Third Inter-American Congress of Psychology, Austin, Texas, December 17, 1955.

Reprinted from the *American Journal of Sociology*, 1958, *63*, 349–56, with the permission of the author and the University of Chicago Press. Copyright 1958 by the University of Chicago.

Many of these measures may have some value in the reduction of intergroup conflicts, but, to date, very few generalizations have been established concerning the circumstances and kinds of intergroup conflict in which these measures are effective. Today measures are applied in a somewhat trial-and-error fashion. Finding measures that have wide validity in practice can come only through clarification of the nature of intergroup conflict and analysis of the factors conducive to harmony and conflict between groups under given conditions.

The task of defining and analyzing the nature of the problem was undertaken in a previous publication (Sherif and Sherif, 1953). One of our major statements was the effectiveness of superordinate goals for the reduction of intergroup conflict. "Superordinate goals" we defined as goals which are compelling and highly appealing to members of two or more groups in conflict but which cannot be attained by the resources and energies of the groups separately. In effect, they are goals attained only when groups pull together.

INTERGROUP RELATIONS AND THE BEHAVIOR OF GROUP MEMBERS

Not every friendly or unfriendly act toward another person is related to the group membership of the individuals involved. Accordingly, we must select those actions relevant to relations between groups.

Let us start by defining the main concepts involved. Obviously, we must begin with an adequate conception of the key term—"group." A group is a social unit (1) which consists of a number of individuals who, at a given time, stand in more or less definite interdependent status and role relationships with one another and (2) which explicitly or implicitly possesses a set of values or norms regulating the behavior of individual members, at least in matters of consequence to the group. Thus, shared attitudes, sentiments, aspirations, and goals are related to and implicit in the common values or norms of the group.

The term "intergroup relations" refers to the relations between two or more groups and their respective members. In the present context we are interested in the acts that occur when individuals belonging to one group interact, collectively or individually, with members of another in terms of their group identification. The appropriate frame of reference for studying such behavior includes the functional relations between the groups. Intergroup situations are not voids. Though not independent of relationships within the groups in question, *the characteristics of relations between groups cannot be deduced or extrapolated from the properties of in-group relations.*

Prevalent modes of behavior within a group, in the way of co-operativeness and solidarity or competitiveness and rivalry among members, need not be typical of actions involving members of an out-group. At times, hostility toward out-groups may be proportional to the degree of solidarity within the group. In this connection, results presented by the British statistician L. F. Richardson are instructive. His analysis of the number of wars conducted by the major nations of the world from 1850 to 1941 reveals that Great Britain heads the list with twenty wars—more than the Japanese (nine wars), the Germans (eight wars), or the United States (seven wars). We think that this significantly larger number of wars engaged in by a leading European democracy has more to do with the intergroup relations involved in perpetuating a far-flung empire than with dominant practices at home or with personal frustrations of individual Britishers who participated in these wars (Pear, 1950).

In recent years relationships between groups have sometimes been explained through analysis of individuals who have endured unusual degrees of frustration or extensive authoritarian treatment in their life-histories. There is good reason to believe that some people growing up in unfortunate life-circumstances may become more intense in their prejudices and hostilities. But at best these cases explain the intensity of behavior in a given dimension (Hood and Sherif, 1955). In a conflict between two groups—a strike or a war—opinion within the groups is crystallized, slogans are formulated, and effective measures are organized by members recognized as the most responsible in their respective groups. The prejudice scale and the slogans are not usually imposed on the others by the deviate or neurotic members. Such individuals ordinarily exhibit their intense reactions within the reference scales of prejudice, hostility, or sacrifice established in their respective settings.

The behavior by members of any group toward another group is not primarily a problem of deviate behavior. If it were, intergroup behavior would not be the issue of vital consequence that it is today. The crux of the problem is the participation by group members in established practices and social-distance norms of their group and their response to new trends developing in relationships between their own group and other groups.

On the basis of his UNESCO studies in India, Gardner Murphy concludes that to be a good Hindu or a good Moslem implies belief in all the nasty qualities and practices attributed by one's own group—Hindu or Moslem—to the other. Good members remain deaf and dumb to favorable information concerning the adversary. Social contacts and avenues of communication serve, on the whole, as vehicles for further conflicts not merely for neurotic individuals but for the bulk of the membership (Murphy, 1953).

In the process of interaction among members, an in-group is endowed with positive qualities which tend to be praiseworthy, self-justifying, and even self-glorifying. Individual members tend to develop these qualities through internalizing group norms and through example by high-status members, verbal dicta, and a set of correctives standardized to deal with cases of deviation. Hence, possession of these qualities, which reflect their particular brand of ethnocentrism, is not essentially a problem of deviation or personal frustration. It is a question of participation in in-group values and trends by good members, who constitute the majority of membership as long as group solidarity and morale are maintained.

To out-groups and their respective members are attributed positive or negative qualities, depending on the nature of functional relations between the groups in question. The character of functional relations between groups may result from actual harmony and interdependence or from actual incompatibility between the aspirations and directions of the groups. A number of field studies and experiments indicate that, if the functional relations between groups are positive, favorable attitudes are formed toward the out-group. If the functional relations between groups are negative, they give rise to hostile attitudes and unfavorable stereotypes in relation to the out-group. Of course, in large group units the picture of the out-group and relations with it depend very heavily on communication, particularly from the mass media.

Examples of these processes are recurrent in studies of small groups. For example, when a gang "appropriates" certain blocks in a city, it is considered "indecent" and a violation of its "rights" for another group to carry on its feats in that area. Intrusion by another group is conducive to conflict, at times with grim consequences, as Thrasher (1927) showed over three decades ago.

When a workers' group declares a strike, existing group lines are drawn more sharply. Those who are not actually for the strike are regarded as against it. There is no creature more lowly than the man who works while the strike is on (Hiller, 1928). The same type of behavior is found in management groups under similar circumstances.

In time, the adjectives attributed to out-groups take their places in the repertory of group norms. The lasting, derogatory stereotypes attributed to groups low on the social-distance scale are particular cases of group norms pertaining to out-groups.

As studies by Bogardus show, the social-distance scale of a group, once established, continues over generations, despite changes of constituent individuals, who can hardly be said to have prejudices because of the same severe personal frustrations or authoritarian treatment (Bogardus, 1947).

Literature on the formation of prejudice by growing children shows that it is not even necessary for the individual to have actual unfavorable experiences with out-groups to form attitudes of prejudice toward them. In the very process of becoming an in-group member, the intergroup delineations and corresponding norms prevailing in the group are internalized by the individual (Horowitz, 1944).

A RESEARCH PROGRAM

A program of research has been under way since 1948 to test experimentally some hypotheses derived from the literature of intergroup relations. The first large-scale intergroup experiment was carried out in

1949, the second in 1953, and the third in 1954.[2] The conclusions reported here briefly are based on the 1949 and 1954 experiments and on a series of laboratory studies carried out as co-ordinate parts of the program.[3]

The methodology, techniques, and criteria for subject selection in the experiments must be summarized here very briefly. The experiments were carried out in successive stages: (1) groups were formed experimentally; (2) tension and conflict were produced between these groups by introducing conditions conducive to competitive and reciprocally frustrating relations between them; and (3) the attempt was made toward reduction of the intergroup conflict. This stage of reducing tension through introduction of superordinate goals was attempted in the 1954 study on the basis of lessons learned in the two previous studies.

At every stage the subjects interacted in activities which appeared natural to them at a specially arranged camp site completely under our experimental control. They were not aware of the fact that their behavior was under observation. No observation or recording was made in the subjects' presence in a way likely to arouse the suspicion that they were being observed. There is empirical and experimental evidence contrary to the contention that individuals cease to be mindful when they know they are being observed and that their words are being recorded (Miller, 1954; Wapner and Alper, 1952).

In order to insure validity of conclusions, results obtained through observational methods were cross-checked with results obtained through sociometric technique, stereotype ratings of in-groups and out-groups, and through data obtained by techniques adapted from the laboratory. Unfortunately, these procedures cannot be elaborated here. The conclusions summarized briefly are based on results cross-checked by two or more techniques.

The production of groups, the production of conflict between them, and the reduction of conflict in successive stages were brought about through the introduction of problem situations that were real and could not be ignored by individuals in the situation. Special "lecture methods" or "discussion methods" were not used. For example, the problem of getting a meal through their own initiative and planning was introduced when participating individuals were hungry.

Facing a problem situation which is immediate and compelling and which embodies a goal that cannot be ignored, group members *do* initiate discussion and *do* plan and carry through these plans until the objective is achieved. In this process the discussion becomes *their* discussion, the

[2] The experimental work in 1949 was jointly supported by the Yale Attitude Change Project and the American Jewish Committee. It is summarized in Sherif and Sherif (1953, chaps. ix and x). Both the writing of that book and the experiments in 1953–54 were made possible by a grant from the Rockefeller Foundation. The 1953 research is summarized in Sherif, White, and Harvey (1955). The 1954 experiment was summarized in Sherif, et al. (1954). For a summary of the three experiments see Sherif and Sherif (1956, chaps. vi and ix).
[3] For an overview of this program see Sherif (1954).

plan *their* plan, the action *their* action. In this process discussion, planning, and action have their place, and, when occasion arises, lecture or information has its place, too. The sequence of these related activities need not be the same in all cases.

The subjects were selected by rigorous criteria. They were healthy, normal boys around the age of eleven and twelve, socially well adjusted in school and neighborhood, and academically successful. They came from a homogeneous sociocultural background and from settled, well-adjusted families of middle or lower-middle class and Protestant affiliations. No subject came from a broken home. The mean I.Q. was above average. The subjects were not personally acquainted with one another prior to the experiment. Thus, explanation of results on the basis of background differences, social maladjustment, undue childhood frustrations, or previous interpersonal relations was ruled out at the beginning by the criteria for selecting subjects.

The first stage of the experiments was designed to produce groups with distinct structure (organization) and a set of norms which could be confronted with intergroup problems. The method for producing groups from unacquainted individuals with similar background was to introduce problem situations in which the attainment of the goal depended on the co-ordinated activity of all individuals. After a series of such activities, definite group structures or organizations developed.

The results warrant the following conclusions for the stage of group formation: When individuals interact in a series of situations toward goals which appeal to all and which require that they co-ordinate their activities, group structures arise having hierarchical status arrangements and a set of norms regulating behavior in matters of consequence to the activities of the group.

Once we had groups that satisfied our definition of "group," relations between groups could be studied. Specified conditions conducive to friction or conflict between groups were introduced. This negative aspect was deliberately undertaken because the major problem in intergroup relations today is the reduction of existing intergroup frictions. (Increasingly, friendly relations between groups is not nearly so great an issue.) The factors conducive to intergroup conflict give us realistic leads for reducing conflict.

A series of situations was introduced in which one group could achieve its goal only at the expense of the other group—through a tournament of competitive events with desirable prizes for the winning group. The results of the stage of intergroup conflict supported our main hypotheses. During interaction between groups in experimentally introduced activities which were competitive and mutually frustrating, members of each group developed hostile attitudes and highly unfavorable stereotypes toward the other group and its members. In fact, attitudes of social distance between the groups became so definite that they wanted to have nothing further to do with each other. This we take as a case of experimentally produced "social distance" in miniature. Conflict was manifested in derogatory name-calling and invectives, flare-ups of physical conflict, and raids on each other's cabins and territory. Over a period of time, negative stereotypes and unfavorable attitudes developed.

At the same time there was an increase in in-group solidarity and co-operativeness. This finding indicates that co-operation and democracy within groups do not necessarily lead to democracy and co-operation with out-groups, if the directions and interests of the groups are conflicting.

Increased solidarity forged in hostile encounters, in rallies from defeat, and in victories over the out-group is one instance of a more general finding: Intergroup relations, both conflicting and harmonious, *affected the nature of relations within the groups involved.* Altered relations between groups produced significant changes in the status arrangements *within* groups, in some instances resulting in shifts at the upper status levels or even a change in leadership. Always, consequential intergroup relations were reflected in new group values or norms which signified changes in practice, words, and deed within the group. Counterparts of this finding are not difficult to see in actual and consequential human relations. Probably many of our major preoccupations, anxieties, and activities in the past decade are incomprehensible without reference to the problems created by the prevailing "cold war" on an international scale.

REDUCTION OF INTERGROUP FRICTION

A number of the measures proposed today for reducing intergroup friction could have been tried in this third stage. A few will be mentioned here, with a brief explanation of why they were discarded or were included in our experimental design.

1. Disseminating favorable information in regard to the out-group was not included. Information that is not related to the goals currently in focus in the activities of groups is relatively ineffective, as many studies on attitude change have shown (Williams, 1947).

2. In small groups it is possible to devise sufficiently attractive rewards to make individual achievement supreme. This may reduce tension between groups by splitting the membership on an "every-man-for-himself" basis. However, this measure has little relevance for actual intergroup tensions, which are in terms of group membership and group alignments.

3. The resolution of conflict through leaders alone was not utilized. Even when group leaders meet apart from their groups around a conference table, they cannot be considered independent of the dominant trends and prevailing attitudes of their membership. If a leader is too much out of step in his negotiations and agreements with out-groups, he will cease to be followed. It seemed more realistic, therefore, to study the influence of leadership within the framework of prevailing trends in the groups involved. Such results will give us leads concerning the conditions under which leadership can be effective in reducing intergroup tensions.

4. The "common-enemy" approach is effective in pulling two or more groups together against another group. This approach was utilized in the 1949 experiment as an expedient measure and yielded effective results. But bringing some groups together against others means larger and more devastating conflicts in the long run. For this reason, the measure was not used in the 1954 experiment.

5. Another measure, advanced both in theoretical and in practical work, centers around social contacts among members of antagonistic groups in activities which are pleasant in themselves. This measure was tried out in 1954 in the first phase of the integration stage.

6. As the second phase of the integration stage, we introduced a series of superordinate goals which necessitated co-operative interaction between groups.

The social contact situations consisted of activities which were satisfying in themselves—eating together in the same dining room, watching a movie in the same hall, or engaging in an entertainment in close physical proximity. These activities, which were satisfying to each group, but which did not involve a state of interdependence and co-operation for the attainment of goals, were not effective in reducing intergroup tension. On the contrary, such occasions of contact were utilized as opportunities to engage in name-calling and in abuse of each other to the point of physical manifestations of hostility.

The ineffective, even deleterious, results of intergroup contact without superordinate goals have implications for certain contemporary learning theories and for practice in intergroup relations. Contiguity in pleasant activities with members of an out-group does not necessarily lead to a pleasurable image of the out-group if relations between the groups are unfriendly. Intergroup contact without superordinate goals is not likely to produce lasting reduction of intergroup hostility. John Gunther, for instance, in his survey of contemporary Africa, concluded that, when the intergroup relationship is exploitation of one group by a "superior" group, intergroup contact inevitably breeds hostility and conflict (Gunther, 1955).

INTRODUCTION OF SUPERORDINATE GOALS

After establishing the ineffectiveness, even the harm, in intergroup contacts which did not involve superordinate goals, we introduced a series of superordinate goals. Since the characteristics of the problem situations used as superordinate goals are implicit in the two main hypotheses for this stage, we shall present these hypotheses:

1. When groups in a state of conflict are brought into contact under conditions embodying superordinate goals, which are compelling but cannot be achieved by the efforts of one group alone, they will tend to co-operate toward the common goals.

2. Co-operation between groups, necessitated by a series of situations

embodying superordinate goals, will have a cumulative effect in the direction of reducing existing conflict between groups.

The problem situations were varied in nature, but all had an essential feature in common—they involved goals that could not be attained by the efforts and energies of one group alone and thus created a state of interdependence between groups: combating a water shortage that affected all and could not help being "compelling"; securing a much-desired film, which could not be obtained by either group alone but required putting their resources together; putting into working shape, when everyone was hungry and the food was some distance away, the only means of transportation available to carry food.

The introduction of a series of such superordinate goals was indeed effective in reducing intergroup conflict: (1) when the groups in a state of friction interacted in conditions involving superordinate goals, they did co-operate in activities leading toward the common goal and (2) a series of joint activities leading toward superordinate goals had the cumulative effect of reducing the prevailing friction between groups and unfavorable stereotypes toward the out-group.

These major conclusions were reached on the basis of observational data and were confirmed by sociometric choices and stereotype ratings administered first during intergroup conflict and again after the introduction of a series of superordinate goals. Comparison of the sociometric choices during intergroup conflict and following the series of superordinate goals shows clearly the changed attitudes toward members of the out-group. Friendship preferences shifted from almost exclusive preference for in-group members toward increased inclusion of members from the "antagonists." Since the groups were still intact following co-operative efforts to gain superordinate goals, friends were found largely within one's group. However, choices of out-group members grew, in one group, from practically none during intergroup conflict to 23 per cent. Using chi square, this difference is significant ($P < .05$). In the other group, choices of the out-group increased to 36 per cent, and the difference is significant ($P < .001$). The findings confirm observations that the series of superordinate goals produced increasingly friendly associations and attitudes pertaining to out-group members.

Observations made after several superordinate goals were introduced showed a sharp decrease in the name-calling and derogation of the out-group common during intergroup friction and in the contact situations without superordinate goals. At the same time the blatant glorification and bragging about the in-group, observed during the period of conflict, diminished. These observations were confirmed by comparison of ratings of stereotypes (adjectives) the subjects had actually used in referring to their own group and the out-group during conflict with ratings made after the series of superordinate goals. Ratings of the out-group changed significantly from largely unfavorable ratings to largely favorable ratings. The proportions of the most unfavorable ratings found appropriate for the out-group—that is, the categorical verdicts that "all of them are stinkers" or " . . . smart alecks" or ". . . sneaky"—fell, in one group, from 21 per cent at the end of the friction stage to 1.5 per cent after interaction oriented toward superordinate goals. The corresponding reduction in these highly unfavorable verdicts by the other group was from 36.5 to 6 per cent. The overall differences between the frequencies of stereotype ratings made in relation to the out-group during intergroup conflict and following the series of superordinate goals are significant for both groups at the .001 level (using chi-square test).

Ratings of the in-group were not so exclusively favorable, in line with observed decreases in self-glorification. But the differences in ratings of the in-group were not statistically significant, as were the differences in ratings of the out-group.

Our findings demonstrate the effectiveness of a series of superordinate goals in the reduction of intergroup conflict, hostility, and their by-products. They also have implications for other measures proposed for reducing intergroup tensions.

It is true that lines of communication between groups must be opened before prevailing hostility can be reduced. But, if contact between hostile groups takes place without superordinate goals, the communication channels serve as media for further accusations and recriminations. When contact situations involve superordinate goals, communication is utilized in the direction of reducing conflict in order to attain the common goals.

Favorable information about a disliked out-group tends to be ignored, rejected, or reinterpreted to fit prevailing stereotypes. But, when groups are pulling together toward superordinate goals, true and even favorable information about the out-group is seen in a new light. The probability of information being effective in eliminating unfavorable stereotypes is enormously enhanced.

When groups co-operate in the attainment of superordinate goals, leaders are in a position to take bolder steps toward bringing about understanding and harmonious relations. When groups are directed toward incompatible goals, genuine moves by a leader to reduce intergroup tensions may be seen by the membership as out of step and ill advised. The leader may be subjected to severe criticism and even loss of faith and status in his own group. When compelling superordinate goals are introduced, the leader can make moves to further co-operative efforts, and his decisions receive support from other group members.

In short, various measures suggested for the reduction of intergroup conflict—disseminating information, increasing social contact, conferences of leaders—acquire new significance and effectiveness when they become part and parcel of interaction processes between groups oriented toward superordinate goals which have real and compelling value for all groups concerned.

40 / The Effect of Teacher-Pupil Contacts Involving Praise on the Sociometric Choices of Students [1]

Ned A. Flanders and Sulo Havumaki

Teachers can influence the choice value of students. Praise from a teacher that is supportive and constructive is likely to increase the acceptance of the student by his peers. This is the finding of the following selection by Ned A. Flanders of the University of Michigan and Sulo Havumaki of the University of Minnesota.

Many teachers have used sociometric data to assign a choice value to any individual in a group. The individual who receives the most choices has the highest choice value, and the rest of the group can be arranged in rank order. Very little has been said about how teachers can influence the choice value of a student.

The present study is an attempt to see if teacher-pupil contacts involving praise will affect the sociometric choices received later on. The hypothesis to be tested is that contacts involving praise, given by a prestige figure, will increase the choice value of the student.

The following conditions must be controlled to test this hypothesis:

1. The group situation must involve an attractive activity and the praise given by the prestige figure must be centered on the relationship between an individual's behavior and the major activity of the group; merely to talk about the individual per se would not be a fair test.

2. Information given to the group must be controlled by the teacher so that certain individuals can be singled out for attention.

3. Any acquaintanceship patterns existing in the group prior to the experimental discussions must be identified so that it can be demonstrated that the factor of personal acquaintance did not bias the results.

4. The criterion question used to elicit sociometric choices must be related to the major activity of the group and appear to have consequences in the future activities of the group. This eliminates such questions as, "Who contributed the most to this discussion?"

[1] The authors wish to express their appreciation to the Minneapolis and St. Paul school officials and students whose cooperation was essential to the success of the study. This research was carried out as part of the research program of the Laboratory for Research in Social Relations, University of Minnesota.

Reprinted from the *Journal of Educational Psychology*, 1960, *51*, 65–68, with the permission of the authors and the American Psychological Association.

5. The prestige figure controlling the flow of information must be liked by the group, or at least not disliked.

PROCEDURE

In a study conducted at the University of Minnesota, Laboratory for Research in Social Relations, 33 groups of 10 subjects each (hereafter referred to as Ss) were involved in an experiment in which sociometric choices were made. In all groups the Ss consisted of approximately an equal number of boys and girls from tenth-grade classes of Minneapolis and St. Paul high schools. It was the belief of these groups that they were to appear in a Quiz Kid contest between schools from Minneapolis and St. Paul. Each group was to decide whether their group would appear on a radio or TV quiz program, either alternative being possible. This discussion was led by a teacher-trainer, not known to any of the students, whose function it was to help the students reach a decision and then train them for the performance. Elaborate arrangements were made to impress all Ss that the Quiz Kid contest was an attractive and exciting experience. Practically all Ss approached the problem of choosing between radio and TV programs seriously. At the very end of each experimental session when all Ss learned there would be no contest, sincere expressions of disappointment were displayed in each group. Judging from the manner in which all sessions were conducted and the behavior of the Ss, there is no doubt in the minds of the authors that the prospect of participating in the contest was attractive and stimulating to the Ss. Thus, these group discussions satisfactorily meet the first half of Condition 1 mentioned previously.

Besides the attractiveness of the group's activity, Conditions 1 and 2 refer to the nature of the teacher-trainer and the method of giving this information. The teacher-trainer's behavior for 17 groups was individually oriented, that is, he called on certain individuals by name and praised their contributions to the discussion. The teacher behavior thus served to provide praise for certain individuals in the group by focusing attention on these individuals in the individually oriented condition. The individuals attended to in this manner were always those who happened to sit in the odd numbered seats around a U shaped table. The original choice of seats was up to the Ss. The procedure of calling only on Ss seated in the odd numbered seats effectively restricted all verbal communication to these Ss and the teacher-trainer. While many Ss seated in the even numbered seats raised their hands indicating a desire to speak, they were not called on. Thus the teacher-trainer's praise reactions were clearly centered on Ss who were easily identified during the individual approach.

In the remaining 16 groups the teacher-trainer behaved in a group oriented fashion and praised the group as a whole for the ideas contributed by individual members. He called on no individuals by name and anyone who wished to talk was allowed to do so.

The verbal behavior of the teacher-trainer was categorized from voice recordings of all the group discussions. These categories consisted of a simple analysis of praise statements made by the teacher-trainer in response to student contributions. In the individually oriented condition most praise statements were made with reference to specific individuals; in the group oriented condition the praise statements were never coupled with an individual's name and were interpreted in terms of the group whenever this could reasonably be done.

Praise statements became standardized during pilot runs prior to conducting the discussions reported here. Examples of statements used in the individual approach are: "I'm glad John mentioned that point because it is very important for this group to consider in order to make a good decision"; "That's a very good suggestion, Mary"; "That's very true. I think Jim will be a big help to this team." During a group approach it was not always easy to turn a praise statement away from the individual toward the group, for example: "That's an important point. This team has good ideas"; "Good! A second good point; can anyone [looking at the group] add any more?" Occasionally, during the group approach only, the teacher-trainer would be interrupted after saying, "That's a good idea . . ." before praise could be turned toward the group. Thus, some praise statements during the group approach were classified as individual praise statement. An example of a praise statement that is clearly group oriented is: "This group is going to make a fine team."

The comparison of the praise statements of the teacher-trainer's individual and group oriented behavior patterns shown in Table 1 indicates that neither pattern is 100 per cent consistent. Actually, the differences are greater than indicated in Table 1. For example, the data do not reveal such important aspects of the teacher-trainer's behavior as looking directly at an individual, calling on him by name, and praising his ideas in association with his name, as contrasted with looking generally at the whole group, not calling on any one individual, and never associating the name of an individual with praise. The two patterns of teacher behavior were clearly different to an observer and easily identified by the tape recording with 100 per cent accuracy.

Thus far the discussion has dealt with the first two conditions necessary to the study; next, Conditions 3 and 4 will be considered. After each group was seated, they were first asked to list the names of all the Ss with whom they were acquainted and, in addition, place an "X" beside the name of any person who was a good friend. For all experimental groups the indication of friendship was so infrequent (a total of six friendship pairs) that they are not reported here. This was undoubtedly due to the cooperation of school authorities who were asked to choose Ss for each group from separate homerooms. The pre-discussion acquaintanceship data show that 477 Ss were acquainted with the 85 Ss who sat in the odd numbered seats before the discussion started; similarly, 505 Ss were acquainted with those Ss who sat in the even numbered seats. Of the total (928) acquaintanceships reported, 48.6 per cent involved Ss in the odd numbered seats, 51.4 per cent involved Ss in the even numbered seats. The hypothesis that this difference is significant can be tested by chi square. Since chi square = 0.012, the difference is clearly not significant. In addition, the Ss seated in the even numbered seats are slightly better known, so that a more rigorous test of the main hypothesis is possible.

After each discussion the teacher-trainer collected sociometric information in response to the statement, "List five members of the group whom you think would be good program participants." It was explained that two teams, size 10 each, would result in 20 Ss being in the studio ready to answer the quiz questions, and this was far too many. Therefore, each team would have five program participants who would answer the questions and five helpers who could help the participants. The Ss were told that their own group choices would be used to identify the program participants. The results of their selection are shown in Table 2.

RESULTS

The data in Table 2 follow the prediction that Ss seated in the odd numbered seats in the individual treatment and given praise by the teacher-trainer would receive more choices than would occur by chance,

Table 1. Distribution of Teacher Praise Statements

	Individual Condition (17 groups)		Group Condition (14 groups) [a]	
	N	%	N	%
Praise to Individuals	114	79.1	28	30.1
Praise to Group	30	20.9	65	69.9
TOTALS	144	100.0	93	100.0

[a] Two groups lost as recordings were inadvertently erased.

Table 2. Distribution of Choices for Program Participants

	Individual Treatment (17 groups)		Group Treatment (16 groups)	
	N	%	N	%
To Odd Seats	496	59.3	384	48.6
To Even Seats	341	40.7	406	51.4
TOTALS	837 *	100.0	790 **	100.0

NOTE. Since some Ss made only four choices, * does not equal 5 × 17 = 850 and ** does not equal 5 × 16 = 800.

Table 3. Desire to Continue with Same Teacher-Trainer

	Individual Treatment		Group Treatment	
	N	%	N	%
Yes	141	82.9	136	85.5
Not Sure	27	15.9	20	12.6
No	2	1.2	3	1.9
TOTALS	170	100.0	159 [a]	100.0

[a] One S failed to answer this question.

and the same comparison in the group treatment would show no such trend. The significance of 59.3 per cent distribution compared with a hypothetical 50–50 split can be calculated by using the standard error of correlated proportions. Testing the significance of a 59.3–40.7 split by this method yields a critical ratio of 2.98, indicating a 0.0028 probability that this difference could have occurred by chance. If one ignores the probable interdependence of the choice data and uses a chi square test on the data in Table 2, chi square = 19.063, indicating a probability of 0.001 for one degree of freedom.

The fifth condition listed at the beginning of this article refers to the requirement that the Ss like or at least not dislike the teacher-trainer. After the discussions, the teacher-trainer would leave, and the students were informed by the host-experimenter that it was not necessary for them to continue with the teacher-trainer who had led the discussions unless they wanted to. They were instructed to indicate their feelings toward the teacher-trainer by checking the item, "Would you like to continue working with the same teacher-trainer?"

Table 3 indicates that there is little difference between the two conditions of teacher behavior as to the degree of liking or of disliking of the teacher-trainer. The data for 329 Ss are shown in Table 3.

The hypothesis that the distribution of answers for the individual treatment are not significantly different from the distribution of answers in the group treatment can be tested by chi square. A chi square = 0.966 for two degrees of freedom fails to reject this hypothesis.

SUMMARY

In a decision making experiment sociometric data were collected from 330 tenth-grade students after they had interacted with a teacher who praised their participation. In 17 10-man groups the teacher interacted only with Ss seated in the odd numbered seats. In another 16 groups, all Ss were allowed to talk and statements involving praise were directed to the group as a whole. In the former situation the Ss in the odd numbered seats received significantly more choices than did the Ss seated in the even numbered seats. In the latter situation, the difference between Ss in the odd and even numbered seats was not significant.

There are undoubtedly many different ways to increase the choice value of students in a classroom. The results of this experiment indicate that teacher-pupil interaction involving praise that is supportive and constructive is likely to increase the choice value of a student indicating greater acceptance by his peers.

41 / Effect of Sociometric Seating on a Classroom Cleavage

Mary Ann Dineen and Ralph Garry

The following selection illustrates an attempt to reduce the cleavage between children from different socioeconomic and cultural backgrounds through periodic sociometric re-seating. The authors, Mary Ann Dineen of the Public Schools, Rochester, New York, and Ralph Garry of Boston University, conclude that, "Proximate seating based on personal choice following sociometric tests weakens, but does not eliminate, the barriers."

The teacher could see the cleavage that existed in her first-grade class. Children from the well-to-do homes excluded the children from poorer homes from their activities. It was not unnatural or necessarily deliberate. The two groups came from two areas in the town which were sharply divided by a main highway, and the neighborhood groups carried over into the school. And this seemed to be true of the upper grades as well. Most of the children did not seem unhappy with the situation, especially in the lower grades, yet a number of children in each grade were obviously dissatisfied and desired intercourse with the other group. In each grade the children from well-to-do homes seemingly accepted the other group as it was, were not unkind to the members, but, in general, ignored the overtures made by some of the children from economically poorer homes. For the most part the children wishing to cross the cleavage line were those from the estimated poorer of the two groups.

The present study, prompted by this situation, rests upon the assump-

Reprinted from the *Elementary School Journal*, 1956, *56*, 358–62, with the permission of the authors and The University of Chicago Press. Copyright 1956 by the University of Chicago.

tions that group cleavages which are based upon artificial criteria, such as differences in economic status, are detrimental to the formation of the friendship patterns essential to the mental health of the group and that the school has a responsibility for fostering intergroup acceptance.

In the school systems of our country today each teacher has the opportunity, if not the obligation, to do as much as he can to establish democratic attitudes in children and to help provide for the development of the mental health of these children. In most cases the school offers children their first opportunity for organized group experience outside the family. As a result the classroom becomes a setting for the give-and-take so necessary to the process of learning to live with other people. The social interaction between children in the classroom should lead to natural acceptance of the idea of social equality—the essence of a democratic attitude—and should result in their gaining a positive emotional approach to living with people from different backgrounds. The classroom teacher is in an excellent position for determining the extent of the group's progress and for deciding what factors in the situation are deterrents to the ideal of democratic and satisfying human relations.

Chief among the factors necessary for developing a full life in a heterogeneous group such as a class of children is a satisfactory friendship pattern. When a child is with others who accept him and respond to him, that is, others with whom he wants to associate, he can contribute more and function better in the group.

It is, of course, not necessary for two persons who become friends to be of different socioeconomic backgrounds; the important consideration is that there should be no barrier except personality. There should be wide understanding and full communication within the group, with complete freedom for the individuals to choose their friends.

The fact that cleavages, interferences with communication, and other tensions usually limit the opportunity to develop group skills and that they absorb energy which could be used for positive achievement is stated by Jennings (1948, pp. 6–7):

> Many experiments in the project testify to the fact that when the emotional shocks due to inadequate or discordant group life are removed and advantage is taken of the existing psychological affinities, there usually results a heightening and release of children's intellectual abilities along with a redirection of their thinking processes. These outcomes are related not only to what happens to individual personalities, but also to the play of group or social motivation on performance. Positive interaction in learning allows members of a group to complement one another's capacities and hence contribute to greater total achievement.

Believing the cleavage in her classroom to be detrimental to the well-being of the children, our first-grade teacher wondered if it was possible to reduce the barrier that circumstances of birth and residence had created in her school. More specifically, would seating arrangements based upon interpersonal choice help eliminate the cleavage?

THE METHOD AND THE SUBJECTS

The experimental procedure was a simple one. The social status of each child in the six grades of the school was determined. The existence of the observed cleavage was established by showing that the per cent of choices received by the upper social-status group on a sociometric test was significantly greater than could be anticipated on the basis of chance. Three of the six grades were used as control groups, while the seating plans in the other three classes (the experimental groups) were arranged on the basis of interpersonal choices made in sociometric tests at four intervals during the school year. The level of significance of the changes which occurred in choices between persons belonging to the two socioeconomic groups at each interval was established by statistical procedures, and the results were evaluated.

The school in which this experiment took place is located in a wealthy suburb of Boston, a town of approximately 20,000 people. According to the data reported by the Massachusetts State Department of Education, the value of assessed property valuation per pupil in attendance exceeds $17,000, while the amount spent per child for education in the public schools exceeds $250 a year.

The school is located in an older section of town, one which is now predominantly composed of families of a lower socioeconomic level. However, the school also serves children from a section geographically adjacent, on the other side of a main highway, in which are families in the upper socioeconomic levels.

One hundred and seventy children in all six grades of this elementary school were used for the experiment. Grades I, III, and V, enrolling 91 pupils, were used as the experimental groups; Grades II, IV, and VI, enrolling 79 pupils, were used as control groups.

PROCEDURE

The first task was to establish the socioeconomic status of each child in the school and to determine the validity of the teacher's observations. The weighted scale for determining social status, as set forth by William Lloyd Warner in *Social Class in America* (1949, pp. 131–59), was chosen as a suitable means for accomplishing this task. The four determinants chosen by Warner are (1) occupations, (2) source of income, (3) house type, and (4) neighborhood. Each of these general classifications is given a weight, and each classification is divided into seven descriptive subclassifications. A total weighted score for each family is obtained by deciding which of the seven descriptive subclassifications is correct for each child's family, by multiplying the number of the subclassification by the assigned weight for the general classification, and by adding the four figures derived.

Warner's key translates these ratings into six social-status categories. For purposes of this study only two groupings, upper and lower, were used. The upper grouping included what Warner calls upper-middle and upper classes (scores 12–35), while the lower grouping included those which Warner designates as lower-middle and lower classes. Fifty-six of the 170 children were included in the upper group, and 114 fell in the lower group.

Table 1 shows the extent to which children in the upper group made a disproportionately high number of in-group choices on the first sociometric test when they were asked to choose seat companions. It was assumed that, if the proportion of in-group choices made by either the upper or the lower group was significantly greater than their proportion

Table 1. Expected and Obtained In-Group Choices of Upper and Lower Socioeconomic Class Children in Experimental and Control Groups on First Sociometric Test

	Experimental Group		Control Group	
	Upper Class	Lower Class	Upper Class	Lower Class
Number of choices	82	171	78	153
In-group choices:				
Per cent expected	32	68	34	66
Per cent obtained	66	70	72	60
Difference	34	2	38	−6
Standard error of difference	.03	.03	.03	.03
Critical ratio	11	.6	13	1.9

in the entire group, there was evidence of a cleavage. In both the experimental (Grades I, III, V) and the control groups (Grades II, IV, VI), the upper-class children, but not the lower, made a statistically significant greater number of in-group choices (beyond .001 level of confidence). This difference held true in all grades except the fifth.

SOCIOMETRIC TESTS

With the co-operation of the teachers, each child in each group was instructed to choose the three children in his grade near whom he would like to sit. In Grades I–III it was necessary to ask each child individually, since spelling of names is difficult, if not impossible, for children at those grade levels. In Grades IV–VI each child wrote his own choices on paper which was distributed by the writer. Previous to the writing of the choices in the experimental groups, a brief discussion was held with the children about the fact that people are happier if they are able to be near, and to work with, people whom they like. It was explained to the children that their seats would be rearranged so that each child would be able to sit near his first, second, or third choice. Previous to the writing of the choices in the control groups, the children were asked if they would be willing to help by giving the names of the three children near whom they would most like to sit if it were possible for the seats in the classroom to be rearranged.

The procedure followed was that described by Jennings and was in accordance with the criteria established by Moreno (1943, p. 327). He says:

> The requirements of a good sociometric test are: (a) that it reaches and measures two-way relations, (b) that the participants in the situation are drawn to one another by one or more criteria, (c) that a criterion is selected to which the participants are bound to respond, . . . (d) that the subjects are *adequately motivated* so that their responses may be sincere, (e) that the criterion selected for testing is strong, enduring, and definite and not weak, transitory, and indefinite.

The seats of the children in the experimental groups were then rearranged in order that each child might sit near his first, second, or third choice. In this process a special attempt was made to put as many lower- and upper-class children adjacent to each other as possible. The isolates were given their first choices and were placed as near as possible to the most-chosen children in the grade. The proportion of upper-class in-group choices limited the freedom of action in rearranging seating in order to provide each child one of his choices and, at the same time, intermix the two groups. The seats of the children in the control groups were not rearranged.

The complete procedure carried out in the first sociometric test was repeated two times at five-week intervals (second and third tests). Each time the situation probably became less real to the control groups, since no seating was changed. Their replies, however, showed considerable consistency. At the end of six more weeks a final measure was taken, although the seats of the children in the experimental groups were not rearranged as had been done previously.

In order to obtain outside corroboration and validation extending beyond the classroom, many spontaneous play groups were observed, and at the same time as the first and last sociometric tests in the classroom, each child in the experimental and the control groups was asked during an organized game period to choose the three children with whom he would most like to play.

RESULTS

On all sociometric tests the choices expressed were classified into in-group, out-group reciprocated, and out-group unreciprocated choices.

Table 2. In-Group Choices Made by Upper- and Lower-Class Experimental
and Control Groups on Four Classroom and Two Play-Group
Sociometric Tests

	Total Number of Choices		In-Group Choices			
			Number		Per Cent	
	Upper Class	Lower Class	Upper Class	Lower Class	Upper Class	Lower Class
First test (pretest):						
Experimental group	82	171	54	120	66	70
Control group	78	153	56	91	72	60
Second test:						
Experimental group	80	183	37	115	46 *	63
Control group	76	149	49	84	64	56
Third test:						
Experimental group	70	184	30	122	43 *	66
Control group	75	150	49	101	65	67
Fourth test:						
Experimental group	75	185	36	122	48	66
Control group	75	149	46	81	61	54
First play-group test:						
Experimental group	58		41		71	
Control group	54		36		66	
Second play-group test:						
Experimental group	49		26		53 *	
Control group	50		34		68	

* Net difference statistically significant at .001 level.

Table 2 shows the proportion of in-group choices made in both upper-
and lower-class experimental and control groups for each sociometric test.
The success of the experiment in reducing the cleavage hinges on the
extent to which the proportion of in-group choices among the upper-class
experimental group shows a statistically significant reduction from test
to test when compared with the control group, for the cleavage is the result of exclusion by the upper-class group alone.

The difference in in-group choices between the first sociometric test
and each subsequent sociometric test was computed. This provided, for
both control and experimental groups, three differences between four
tests based on choice for seating and one difference between two tests on
play choice. The net differences between control and experimental groups
were used in estimating the significance of change. Because the same
groups were being used in each test, the procedure described by McNemar
(1949, pp. 79–80) was used for estimating the significance of differences in
correlated proportions.

These data showed that the sociometric seating was followed by a reduction in the proportion of in-group choices made by the upper-class

group in both experimental and control groups during all the intervals, with a single exception. The exception was shown for the control group on the criterion of play choice. The experimental groups showed greater reductions of in-group choices than did the control groups. Three of the four differences in the decrease in per cents for the two groups were significantly greater than could be expected by chance at the .001 level of confidence. The nonsignificant difference between experimental and control groups occurred in the change from first to fourth sociometric test.

Another way of expressing the results is to state that, when sociometric tests were made six different times during a school year, the children from upper socioeconomic levels tended to restrict their choices to children from their own level. This choice pattern, which was significantly different from the pattern to be anticipated by chance, was less pronounced after the pupils were seated on the basis of their choices, with deliberate effort made to intermix children from different socioeconomic levels.

CONCLUSIONS AND IMPLICATIONS

It would be naïve to assume that the only factor which was working to overcome the cleavage created by the upper class in-group choices was proximity of seating. For instance, athletic prowess, especially in Grades V and VI, must be recognized as influential. Nevertheless, proximate seating of children from different socioeconomic groups increased the likelihood of intergroup choice, at least for short periods. Whether the lower level of the significance of the change from first to fourth tests means a regression is occurring or whether it is a chance fluctuation about a real difference is difficult to determine.

Although the seating was not rearranged after the fourth test, the children were not told this would be the case. The fourth test occurred six weeks before the end of the school year, so that the atmosphere of "closing time" had not yet pervaded the school. It is more likely that the mere rearrangement of seating, while having an initial stimulating effect, is not sufficient to eliminate a cleavage without additional means being utilized to change the interpersonal attitudes. Particularly where the out-of-school contact between groups was sharply limited by geographic barriers, the in-group choice was reinforced.

Certainly, if the original assumptions (that cleavages within groups based upon artificial criteria are detrimental to the mental health of a group and that the school has a responsibility for fostering democratic behavior) are valid, it is a reasonable conclusion that the success of the school in these areas should be evidenced in the observed behavior of the children. If the children in the school used in this study are typical, mere presence in the classroom of children from economically different levels does not overcome intergroup cleavages. Proximate seating based on personal choice following sociometric tests weakens, but does not eliminate, the barriers. Apparently more action than words will be required.

42 / Effects of Cooperation and Competition on the Cohesiveness of Small Face-to-Face Groups

Beeman N. Phillips and Louis A. D'Amico

This study by Beeman N. Phillips of the University of Texas and Louis A. D'Amico of the U.S. Office of Education tests the following hypothesis: "The cohesiveness of a small face-to-face group will increase under cooperative conditions and decrease under competitive conditions." The subjects are fourth grade children and the experimental task is to identify animals. The significant findings include: groups working cooperatively increase in cohesiveness; groups working competitively do not necessarily decrease in cohesiveness. Whether decrease occurs or not depends upon factors not specifically controlled in the experiment. These results imply that cooperative classroom groups can be used to improve interpersonal relationships, but that competition does not necessarily have undesirable effects on interpersonal relationships.

In most classrooms children are encouraged to work both cooperatively and competitively. They are encouraged to get along with others and are even given grades on their report card for "cooperativeness," "helpfulness," "concern for others," etc. But they are also encouraged to compete with others. Goals and standards are set that only a few can reach, and grades and promotions are given on a competitive basis.

This mixture of cooperation and competition has caused much concern among educators in recent years, and an array of conflicting data has been collected with regard to the effects of cooperation and competition on the performance of classroom groups. French (1951), Deutsch (1949), Stendler, Damrin, and Haines (1951) found that classroom groups performed better under cooperative conditions, and Hurlock (1927), Leuba (1933), Tseng (1952), and Whittemore (1924) found that classroom groups performed better under competitive conditions.

One of the questions which has been raised concerns the effect of cooperation and competition on group cohesiveness. Research by Mizuhara and Tamai (1952, 1953), Grossack (1952), and Deutsch (1949, 1949a) suggests that cooperation and competition are related to group cohesiveness, but the nature of this relationship is not entirely clear. One of the im-

Reprinted from the *Journal of Educational Psychology*, 1956, *47*, 65–70, with the permission of the authors.

plications of their findings is that the cohesiveness of a group should increase under cooperative conditions and decrease under competitive conditions. The effect of cooperation and competition on group cohesiveness was the subject of this study, and the hypothesis which was tested was as follows: the cohesiveness of a small face-to-face group will increase under cooperative conditions and decrease under competitive conditions.

PROCEDURE

The subjects used in this study were fourth grade children selected from two schools in a midwest city of 30,000 people. Eight groups were set up with five children in each group. There were four high cohesive groups and four low cohesive groups. These groups were randomly assigned to work under either cooperative or competitive conditions. Two high cohesive groups worked under cooperative conditions and two worked under competitive conditions. Similarly, two low cohesive groups worked under cooperative conditions and two worked under competitive conditions.

According to Festinger, Schachter, and Back (1950) the cohesiveness of a group may be based on personal attraction, prestige, and/or goal mediation. In this study group cohesiveness was based only on personal attraction, and high and low cohesiveness were produced by manipulating the degree to which members of a group were attracted to each other. Attraction was measured by a sociometric questionnaire in which each child was asked to choose three children in the room that he would like to sit by. The questionnaire was administered by the teacher at the beginning of the experiment and essentially the same questionnaire was administered at the end of the experiment.

The groups were formed on the basis of the choices made on the initial questionnaire. High cohesive groups were formed by putting together individuals who had selected each other on the sociometric test, while low cohesive groups were formed by putting together individuals who had not selected each other. Thus, it was possible for a group to have from 0 to 15 within-group choices. The actual number of within-group choices for the eight groups on the initial and final sociometric questionnaire is shown in Table 1.

A change in cohesiveness was defined as a change in the number of within-group choices between the initial and the final questionnaire. For example, if a group started out with 10 within-group choices and had 15 within-group choices at the end of the experiment this would indicate that the cohesiveness of the group increased during the experiment.

Cooperation and competition were defined in terms of how members shared in their group's rewards. In cooperative groups they shared equally and in competitive groups they shared in accordance with their relative contributions.

The experimental task was a modification of the game "Twenty Questions." The object of the game was to identify animals by asking the

Table 1. Number of Within-Group Choices on the Initial and Final
Sociometric Test for the Eight Groups in the Experiment

Group *	Class	Initial	Final	Level of Confidence
HC–CO	A	11	10	
HC–CO	B	9	11	.01
HC–CM	A	10	7	.01
HC–CM	B	14	14	
LC–CO	B	0	4	.01
LC–CO	A	0	3	.01
LC–CM	A	3	3	
LC–CM	B	0	3	.01

* HC = high cohesion; LC = Low cohesion; CO = cooperation; CM = Competition.

experimenter questions that could be answered yes-or-no. The animals were selected from third grade readers used in the schools. Participation was considered as a regular class assignment, and every pupil in each participated even though he may not have been part of an experimental group.

Each group was taken to the experimental room and was given the opportunity to identify five animals on each of four successive days. Two randomly selected lists of animals were used, and the order of presentation of the animals was varied. Twenty pieces of candy were distributed among members of each group after identification of each animal. In the cooperative groups each member received four pieces of candy each time an animal was identified. In the competitive groups a scale was used to determine the amount that each member received. The scale which was used is shown below :

Type of question	Points
Question identifying correct animal	5
Question identifying outstanding characteristics of the animal	4
Question identifying distinctive characteristics of the animal	3
Question identifying common characteristics of the animal	2
Question identifying an incorrect animal	1

Each question asked by a member of a competitive group was assigned a point value. These points were totaled and averaged for each member after an animal was identified correctly. The 20 pieces of candy were distributed in the following pattern: 6-5-4-3-2. The member with the highest number of points per question got 6 pieces, the one with the next highest number got 5 pieces, and so forth.

RESULTS

The results of the study are summarized in Table 1. The number of within-group choices on the initial and final sociometric test are shown for all groups. The symbols HC and LC indicate high and low cohesiveness, and the symbols CO and CM indicate cooperation and competition. Class A had 29 pupils and class B had 38 pupils. In determining whether or not the changes in the number of within-group choices were statistically significant at the one per cent level, only approximate probabilities were computed.

Two significant findings are revealed in Table 1. First, groups which worked under cooperative conditions during the experiment increased in cohesiveness. In three of the four groups the increase in the number of within-group choices was significant well beyond the one per cent level of confidence. This means that individuals who worked together under co-operative conditions liked each other better at the end of the experiment than they did at the beginning of the experiment.

The second significant finding is that groups which worked under competitive conditions did not necessarily decrease in cohesiveness. In two groups there was no change in the number of within-group choices, in one group there was a significant increase in the number of within-group choices, and in the other group there was a significant decrease in the number of within-group choices. The inconclusive nature of these results suggests that whether or not competition decreases a group's cohesiveness depends on factors not specifically controlled in this investigation.

An idea of the nature of such factors was obtained by a further examination of the data for competitive groups which revealed that rewards were fairly evenly distributed in the groups in which there was either no change or an increase in cohesiveness during the experiment. This suggested the hypothesis that the effect of competition on group cohesiveness is dependent on the effect that competition has on the distribution of the group's rewards. If competition results in more or less uniform distribution of the group's rewards the effect of competition on the group's cohesiveness may be similar to the effect that cooperation would have on the group's cohesiveness. But on the other hand, if one or two members receive most of the group's rewards the effect of competition may be to decrease the group's cohesiveness.

One of the implications of these findings is that classroom groups which are operated on a cooperative basis can be used to improve interpersonal relationships. Such a procedure appears to be potentially the most useful when boys and girls do not know each other very well, when it is desirable to break up cliques or transfer friendships, or when it is necessary to help a new pupil or a shy pupil to establish friendships.

Another implication of these findings is that competition does not necessarily have undesirable effects on interpersonal relationships. The effect of competition on a classroom group's interpersonal relationships seems to be conditioned by its effect on the distribution of the group's rewards. If the members are well-matched and rewards are evenly divided among them, competition appears to have fewer undesirable effects on interpersonal relationships than if members are poorly-matched and rewards are as a result not evenly divided among them. In view of this it may be important in setting up classroom groups on a competitive basis to put individuals together who are more or less equal in ability on the task that has been assigned. In this way it is possible to utilize the incentive of competition in group work without seriously affecting member relationships.

The possible effects of a different type of task, an older group, and a longer period of time in the experimental situation, need to be considered in additional studies of the effects of cooperation and competition on group cohesiveness. Additional research is needed not only to determine the effects of these factors, but in view of the tremendous increase in the amount of activity that is carried out in groups, there is also a need for additional research on other aspects of the behavior of individuals in group situations.

43 / The Isolate in Children's Groups: Changing His Sociometric Position

Edmund Amidon

The teacher can improve the position of a socially nonaccepted child, and it is useful to include in teacher education courses an understanding of group social structure and skill training which may help teachers in working with nonaccepted children. These are two of the practical implications of this study by Edmund Amidon of Temple University.

Many teachers in the elementary schools find that they have children in their classes who are apparently not accepted by the other class members. This lack of acceptance is often expressed in situations in which children ignore a certain child, refuse to play with him, constantly call him names, and, in extreme cases, display aggression toward him. Sometimes the non-

Reprinted from the *Journal of Teacher Education,* 1961, *12,* 412–17, with the permission of the author and the National Commission on Teacher Education and Professional Standards of the National Education Association.

acceptance is not manifested in overt action; nevertheless, it may still be present in the classroom. Although in these less obvious cases the teacher may not be aware of the situation, usually the child who is not accepted feels the lack of acceptance, and usually the class is aware of the situation. It is apparent, then, that the classroom teacher may have some awareness of an isolate, a child who is not accepted by any class member, or he may be completely unaware of the child's position in the classroom group.

Whether or not the symptoms of a specific case of an isolate are obvious, the condition of non-acceptance is one which is of concern to all good teachers. Some teachers feel that if a child is not accepted by his peers in the early grades, he will not be able to develop normal interpersonal relations as he grows up. There is a good deal of research which tends to support this idea (Bonney, 1943; Moreno, 1934). There is also some research which indicates that the child who is not accepted achieves at a lower level than other members of his elementary-school class (Buswell, 1953).

Although no research has identified the exact causes of isolation, several factors appear to be closely related. In general these causes appear to be of two kinds: (1) those factors present in the relationship of the child to the group and (2) certain individual factors present in the child himself. In the first category such factors as group norms play an important part. Whether a child violates an important norm through ignorance or with conscious knowledge of the violation, the consequences may be the same. Sometimes the child may not be accepted because of certain factors present in the classroom culture. This kind of situation occurs particularly when a child is a new member of a very cohesive classroom group. There is some evidence, also, that teachers underestimate the popularity of individual children whom they themselves do not like; if a teacher communicates dislike of a child to the class, this may contribute to a child's isolation (Gronlund, 1950). This seems to be particularly true in the early grades where the teacher has great influence with the children.

The second category of factors contributing to a child's isolation includes personality attractiveness and other individual characteristics. Bonney (1943) found significant differences in personality between over- and under-chosen children. Northway (1944) found that the under-chosen child was likely to be rebellious, socially disinterested, or listless and recessive. It is probable that both the individual factors and the interpersonal factors interact with one another to cause most cases of social isolation in the classroom. It is important, therefore, that both individual and group characteristics be taken into consideration in providing a remedial program for changing the position of a child who is an isolate.

Several studies have been concerned with attempts to change the sociometric choice received by a particular individual in a group. Flanders and Havumaki (1960), in a laboratory situation, found that teachers could affect the frequency with which a certain child was chosen by directing supportive praise toward him.[1] McCleary (1956) attempted to change

[1] [See selection 40 in this volume.]

the social structure of a particular class. At the beginning of the year there were three cliques in the class and five isolates. After a period of time during which the teacher had used certain planned techniques designed to make the students aware of classroom structure, there were no clearly distinguishable isolates and cliques. Another case is reported by Shoobs (1947) who used assignment therapy and counseling to try to improve adjustment of isolates in a classroom. Zeleny (1941) reported that after isolated college students were exposed to sociometric regrouping and guidance there was a general increase in the number of times they were chosen. Moreno and Jennings (1944) discussed regrouping of individuals in a correctional institution and gave some indication that changes in social structure occurred. Kerstetter and Sargent (1940) discussed the use of assignment therapy and its success in changing classroom structure. Pre and post measures of sociometric choice show an increase in choices received and choices given after such therapy. Northway (1944) helped to improve the position of the isolate, as well as to identify certain behavioral characteristics that were common to such a person.

A large number of the studies discussed have demonstrated that it is possible to improve the position of a socially non-accepted child or of group members; hence, it seems appropriate, even necessary, to include in teacher education courses some understanding of social structure and skill training which may help the teacher in working with the child who is an isolate.

PROCEDURE OF THE PROGRAM

In the study described here an attempt was made to present some of the previous research findings as integral parts of a teacher education course in order to prepare teachers to facilitate the isolate's integration into the group. The study was conducted in a preservice elementary education course at Temple University in the spring of 1960. Seventy-nine elementary education juniors were enrolled in the course, which was designed to help the students understand the elementary classroom group. As part of the course requirement, each student acted as a leader of a small group of from seven to fifteen children in a social-work agency.

These seventy-nine elementary education students were divided randomly into two instructional groups. Each of the two instructors used a different procedure to try to help the student leaders improve the position of any isolate in their groups. These two different instructional approaches embodied two different approaches to the education of teachers. The one group of students was taught to use those techniques which, on the basis of research reviewed, seemed to have been successfully used to help the isolate become an integral member of the group. In the other group the instructor emphasized the diagnostic approach to the classroom. In this group student leaders were asked to analyze the social-psychological factors present in their groups before deciding on a technique to use. The purpose of comparing the two approaches was to determine the most effective way of using techniques to help the child who is an isolate.

In the technique group the instructor used three class periods to try to demonstrate some techniques which might be useful in helping the isolate. The techniques were as follows: (1) praising his work; (2) allowing him to emphasize that which he does well; (3) giving him important tasks to perform; (4) allowing him to work with class leaders; (5) having individual conferences with him; (6) allowing him to work in groups with students he likes; (7) using role playing to help him and the class gain insight into problems; (8) changing his seat so he is not near those that reject him; (9) communicating the teacher's acceptance to the class and to the isolate; (10) giving a sociogram to identify the problem.

The instructor using the diagnostic approach spent three class periods discussing five steps that a teacher should follow in helping the isolate. The steps outlined were as follows: (1) developing understanding of the classroom social structure; (2) collecting data on the class (such data would include sociometric attitude, observation, and informal clues which the teacher may get); (3) developing hypotheses (based on the data) as to why children are not accepted; (4) applying techniques that seem appropriate, such as role playing, group discussion of a problem, small group work, counseling, and reassignment of seats; and (5) evaluating the usefulness of the hypotheses using another sociometric measure and some informal observation.

Other than these three periods spent on the isolate and social structure, both groups covered the same course content. This course content included a discussion of the classroom as a unique type of group, group properties such as norms and cohesiveness, and an analysis of teacher behavior and its effect on the class.

RESULTS OF THE PROGRAM

Since the purpose of the study was to determine change in the position of the isolate, only those student leaders who had isolates in their groups could be considered in the analysis. On the basis of sociometric measures administered at the beginning of the spring semester, fifteen of the student leaders in each group found that they had isolates in their groups. Changes in isolate positions in the small groups of children were measured by a pre- and post-sociometric question: "What children would you like to work with in a small group?" An isolate was a child receiving no choices on this sociometric test. At the end of the semester when the second sociometric measure was administered by the student leaders in both groups, three students in the diagnostic group and nine in the technique group found that they still had isolates in their groups. In the technique group, therefore, the number of students having isolates was reduced from fifteen to nine; in the diagnostic group the number of students having isolates was reduced from fifteen to three. In the technique group six out of fifteen students and in the diagnostic group, twelve out of fifteen students were apparently successful in helping isolates to become integrated into their groups.

Using a contingency analysis and computing a chi square, the groups were compared statistically on the relative number of isolates before and after the course. The results were statistically significant at the .05 level of confidence, indicating that the fact that the student leaders in the diagnostic group were more successful was probably not due to chance alone but was related to the type of training of this group.

The two groups of fifteen students each were also compared on several factors which were thought to be related to a student leader's ability to help an isolate. These factors included general knowledge of an isolate, social sensitivity to the classroom social relations, attitude toward the isolate, and achievement in the course. None of these factors seemed to be related to the differences between the students in the two groups on their ability to help the isolate become an integral member of the group.

A second attempt to identify reasons for differences between the two groups was based on a content analysis of the case study which each student leader did on his isolate. This analysis of the case studies indicated several differences between the technique group and the diagnostic group. First, in the case studies written by members of the technique group, the student leaders spent a great deal of time discussing the techniques used to help the isolate, most of them of the direct counseling type, in which the student leader took the child aside and talked to him about his problems. Student leaders in the diagnostic group, on the other hand, discussed fewer but more varied techniques than those used in the other group. The members of the diagnostic group not only tried to counsel the isolate but also tried to relate the whole group to the problem in order to help the child become an integral member of the group.

A second difference between the two groups was evident in the manner of identifying the isolates. The members of the technique group, according to their case studies, were less concerned with identification of the isolates with a sociogram than they were in identifying them on the basis of the student leaders' own subjective judgment. When the judgment of these leaders differed from the results of a sociogram, they tended to rationalize the difference and maintain that the subjective judgment about the isolate was the more accurate. The members of the diagnostic group always accepted the isolates identified on the basis of a sociogram. Both groups administered the sociogram, but the members of the diagnostic group accepted the identification and tried to work with the isolates they had identified, whereas the technique group members were more likely to use their own judgment.

The third difference lay in the way in which the members of the diagnostic group tried to relate the behavior of the isolates to the techniques used, while the members of the technique group seemed to try certain techniques regardless of the problems indicated. Members of the technique group more often stated that since the isolate was shy and withdrawn they felt that it was necessary to give him a chance to be with as many children as possible, and that he needed to be talked to in order to be encouraged to be more outgoing.

SOME IMPLICATIONS FOR EDUCATION

On the basis of the results of the study several implications for teachers emerge. In the first place, it seems possible for a leader or teacher to improve the position of a child who is an isolate in a small group. Secondly, the process of identification is central in the attempt to help the isolate. Once the teacher or leader accepts the fact that a child identified in the sociometric test is an isolate, then she is in a position to try to determine why the child is isolated and do something about it. If the teacher accepts the sociometric identification on a halfhearted basis or attempts to rationalize, she will not be able to be enthusiastic in attempts to help the child. Finally, it seems to be more effective to relate analysis to technique than simply to become acquainted with various group techniques.

The steps which are indicated by the results of the study are (1) identification of the isolate; (2) collection of data formal and informal (including such data as careful observation of the isolate's behavior in the class as well as at play, attitudes that children hold about the group and the teacher, group properties such as atmosphere and class norms, and teacher attitude and behavior); (3) development of some hypotheses about what action to take; (4) utilization of those techniques which seem to be appropriate; and (5) evaluation of results of the action and revision of hypotheses if necessary (this will include readministration of the sociometric test).

On the basis of the present study it seems necessary that a group leader or teacher fit the technique to the dynamics of the situation. Before techniques are used the teacher ought to have a clear understanding about why she is using the techniques, some well-thought-out hypotheses about how the techniques will affect the group, and a formal or informal procedure which can be used for evaluating the success of the technique.

SOME IMPLICATIONS FOR EDUCATION

Part Three

IMPROVING PARENT AND

TEACHER EFFECTIVENESS

School Practices

44 / Basic Changes Needed to Serve Individuals Better

J. Lloyd Trump

The self-contained classroom and the rigid organization of the school day, according to J. Lloyd Trump of the National Association of Secondary-School Principals, are "the two most significant deterrents to recognizing individual differences among teachers and students in today's elementary and secondary schools." Among the proposals offered are: (1) Allocation of school time: the average student about fourteen years of age should spend about 40 per cent of his school time in independent study, 20 per cent in small group instruction, and about 40 per cent in large group instruction. (2) Teachers should have a variety of assistants: instructional assistants, general aides, and clerks. (3) A flexible arrangement of admittance to the elementary school and progress through school should be instituted. (4) Individual programming for subjects and activities should replace standard group procedures commonly used today. (5) Programmed instruction devices should be used to provide for individual differences and to encourage motivation by immediate reinforcement of learning.

What are the effects of mass education on the individual student? That old question in American education is sounded more loudly today than ever before. The hue and cry is strong against such developments as mass technology, teaching machines, easy solutions, automation, yielding to pressures, and national systems, to name a few derogatory terms frequently found in articles concerned with educating individuals.

The scientific study of education in this country has been progressing quite systematically since around 1890. These seventy-plus years have

Reprinted from *Educational Forum*, 1961, *26*, 93–101, with the permission of the author and Kappa Delta Pi, owners of the copyright.

taught us much about the differences among students and the factors that relate to student development. Both emotionally and scientifically most teachers and administrators react sympathetically to pleas for more attention to the differences among students.

Unfortunately most of the pleas for more attention to students as individuals fall short of realization because they largely ignore two important factors: (1) individual differences among teachers; and (2) the educational setting which makes possible significant attention to individual differences among students. Observe if this is not the case the next time you read or listen to some exhortation along this line. Let us examine this thesis in some detail in an effort to develop some hypotheses for further testing.

THE PROBLEM WE FACE

The two most significant deterrents to recognizing individual differences among teachers and students in today's elementary and secondary schools are: (1) the self-contained classroom, and (2) the rigid organization of the school day.

The self-contained classroom, especially in the secondary school, limits educational opportunities for students by restricting through the accident of the schedule the potentially stimulating contacts with different teachers that could be provided for students. For example, instead of receiving inspiration and instruction from the best teacher, in or outside the school, of writing, of speaking, of poetry, or of some other aspect of the English language arts, the student may only have one teacher with whatever strengths and weaknesses that teacher possesses. The situation is comparable in other subjects. The teacher is forced to instruct in all phases of the subject even though some aspects are less interesting to him and in others he is less competent.

Educational opportunities in the self-contained classroom are also limited because usually it is not financially feasible to provide in each room in a school all of the material aids to instruction that modern technology has given today's teachers and students. It is unreasonable to expect that every room will have an overhead projector, sound-film projector, slide and film-strip projector, tape recorders, television sets, radios, and all the other kinds of available aids that technology increasingly offers. And schools have found relatively little use of these aids when they are placed in specialized rooms so long as the philosophy of the self-contained classroom makes it difficult for students to get out of these classrooms.

Teachers try to recognize individual differences in self-contained classrooms, but the setting inhibits what they can do. Elementary teachers divide their classes into such groups as the robins, bluebirds, and crows. Secondary school teachers organize committees and various sub-groups. But the numbers of students and groups prevent teachers from giving undivided attention to different individuals and groups. And the setting fosters mass instruction—even though the mass may be only 25–35 students. Students need to get out of these self-contained classrooms into workrooms, laboratories, and libraries, in and outside the school, to work as individuals on matters that are important to them and that are within the scope of their individual talents and motivations. The students also need the personal individual help of specially trained teachers and instruction assistants in the different subject areas.

The rigid organization of the school day also limits attention to individual differences. School bells in the secondary school punctuate the day and keep individual students from caring very deeply about anything. So does the notion that a student must sit in a class 50 minutes a day, five days a week, for a semester or year in order to "take" a given subject. Even worse is the idea that able students must mark time, aided by busy-work sometimes called enrichment, while the slower students finally catch up, or are removed to a remedial class.

A PROPOSED SOLUTION TO THE PROBLEM

The proposals offered by the writer in two pamphlets, *Images of the Future* (1959) and *New Directions to Quality Education* (1960), and in a new book, *Focus on Change—Guide to Better Schools* (1961), urge basic changes in schools in order to cope better with individual differences among students and teachers. Let us note some features of a school that is organized to pay more attention to individual differences.

The "average" student around 14 years of age will spend about 40 per cent of his school time in "independent study" in workrooms specially designed to facilitate learning in the different curriculum areas. These workrooms will be provided in all the subject areas: English, history and social sciences, mathematics, foreign languages, sciences, health-physical education-recreation, fine and practical arts, and the rest. They will contrast with today's classrooms, laboratories, and gymnasiums which reflect a dedication to mass instruction in self-contained classrooms where all students do much the same kinds of things all together or in sub-groups—with one teacher in charge.

The proposed workrooms will have the "tools of the trade" in each subject area so that individual students can follow different kinds of activities. This equipment will be portable to the maximum degree possible so that new relationships may be developed among subject areas. Space and storage facilities for individual projects will be provided.

The independent study will also include much personal learning activity by students at individual rates and techniques. Reading, viewing, listening, and working with a variety of programmed instruction devices (textbooks and machines) will help to provide this instruction geared to individual differences among students.

The "average" 14-year old student also will spend about 20 per cent of his time in classes no larger than 15 so he can learn better how to think critically and solve problems in small discussion groups—and so a competent teacher can observe his growth and development. Working effectively with these small groups will challenge the highest professional talents of teachers.

Today's classes are too large for effective discussion. They inhibit adequate participation by individuals and encourage individual isolation from the group. When there are 15 or fewer students in the group, each individual has the chance logistically to participate and the size of the group contributes to his involvement in it.

The school will save time for both students and teachers by transmitting information, demonstrating skills, and providing better motivation in the setting of larger-than-usual student groups, averaging 100–150 in number. Such groups will be taught by the most able teachers for a given phase of a subject—in person or on television, films, or recordings —a teacher from inside or outside the local school.

The amount of time spent by the "average" 14-year old student in these large groups will vary with the needs of different subjects, but all subjects have considerable material which can be presented effectively in this setting. The student will spend about 40 per cent of the time of the conventional school week in these larger-than-usual groups. Here is where individual differences among students do not matter so much. All need to be motivated by contact with the most interesting and able teaching it is possible to muster. All need to receive the best explanations and demonstrations that can be presented. All need to take some group tests to see how well they have achieved. The large group logistically permits all students to have contact with the best teaching of this nature that the school can provide.

The "average" teacher will be scheduled with groups of students no more than about 15 hours per week so he has time to prepare, keep up to date, evaluate, and do other professional tasks better, and have more time to work with individual students. Today's school treats teachers as if they were very much alike. Tomorrow's school will treat them as individuals, each teacher doing what he is most able to do in the educational setting wherein he is most comfortable.

These and other changes are logistically possible and financially feasible because teachers will have the use of a variety of assistants: clerks, general aides, and instruction assistants. They and the students will also have the use of modern technology in learning basic skills and essential knowledge. And both will have appropriate educational facilities in which to work.

These teacher assistants will help to create in the minds of the public and for teachers themselves a changed concept of the role of the professional teacher. Teaching involves much more than being physically present with a group of students in a classroom. In fact the quality of what teachers do in classrooms depends largely on the professional activities of teachers outside the classroom. Teachers need much more time, energy, training, and facilities than they have now to keep them up to date, plan better, confer with professional colleagues, develop materials, and improve evaluation. Teacher assistants can help make those activities possible.

Instruction assistants will be available in all subject areas. These are persons with at least a college minor in the subjects they teach. They are college students, housewives, professional and industrial workers, and retired teachers and others who usually want to work on a part time basis. The school will also use clerks for clerking and general aides for duties where subject matter competence is not essential.

The schedule and curricular organization of the future school will contribute to serving individual differences among students and teachers. Time will be available for individual study in depth in chosen subject areas. All students will not spend the same time in a subject as they do in the rigid schedule of today.

Two points should be emphasized in concluding this brief description of tomorrow's school. First, there need be no dichotomy between teachers' liking and understanding children on the one side and knowing subject matter on the other. A teacher must be intellectually competent if he is to deal effectively with individual differences among students and to gain the respect of a divergent group. Second, if teachers are to rise above the level of merely being purveyors of subject skills and knowledge —to be stimulators of inquiry and creativity and to work with students on individual bases—teachers must cast themselves in a new professional image. Professional teachers differentiate among their roles at different times when student goals change. Such teachers also know very well what they as professional persons must do and what can be done by technology, programmed instruction devices, and by personal assistants. They have professionally designed educational facilities and they use them. They recognize differences in teachers' abilities and responsibilities. They keep their knowledge and practices up to date. Professional teachers encourage and spearhead new ideas and conduct research to see if there are better ways of doing things that are important to do.

The school of the future thus reorganizes the setting and the clock of instruction, uses purposefully all that modern technology can provide, and develops professional teachers in achieving its basic goal of providing the best possible education for all individuals in this democratic society. Let us next observe more specifically how individual differences are better recognized in this school than in the conventional school of today.

THE INDIVIDUAL STUDENT

At the risk of oversimplifying a complex process, consider the educational arrangements that are most likely to result in the maximum development of the individual potentialities of a student in an elementary or a secondary school. First, he must be motivated strongly to learn something. This is more likely to happen when he is in contact with the most stimulating teacher possible for him who understands his potential interests and capacities. Since teachers as well as students differ, the task of the school is to bring together the best teachers for a given group of students, or for an individual student, for a particular learning goal. The conventional school says this can be done by one teacher for a given grade or subject, for 25–35 students, usually for a school year. Few teachers have talents so diverse that they can perform these tasks best for all students. So some students are frustrated by being the captive of one teacher for a year, subject to that teacher's shortcomings (as well as areas of strength). School for both the students and the teacher may be dull and tense for considerable periods of time in that situation. Several teachers carefully selected can provide better motivation if each does what he is most interested in and most able to do, working as a team, each spreading his influence over a larger group of students. Thus the individual student has a better chance to "catch fire" from contact with an exciting teacher who is both very competent in his subject and in his knowledge about the students he faces.

Motivation is also encouraged by reinforcement of learning, the more immediate the better. Programmed instruction devices with individual pacing are designed to provide such reinforcement. Thus the school should make maximum use of these materials for teaching each student at his level the essential facts and skills of various subjects. Instruction assistants can evaluate some parts of student work and thus give the results to students more quickly than is the case in the conventional school where teachers are overburdened, and sometimes bored, with correcting routine student work.

Motivation also results when students are permitted to work on projects that seem important to them personally. The proposed school of the future permits students to work for extended periods of time in workrooms for all subject areas. The nature of the work and the amount of time devoted to it by individual students are subject to professional decision by counselors and teachers in the teaching team. Moreover, the school facilities are open to students at times when the conventional school's doors are locked. Thus a highly motivated student can work in a science laboratory or a social studies workroom 20 or more hours a week on investigations that seem important to him and his teachers.

Motivation is stimulated by discussion among students of like interests and talents. Small discussion groups involving no more than 15 students are scheduled in the school of the future. Moreover, arranging the individual schedules of students so that group discussion sessions are followed by independent study makes it possible to prolong the discussion if the teacher and students feel this is desirable. Today's school with its rigid bell schedule makes this impossible—and the large classes of 25–35 inhibit effective discussion among students.

Progress through school is also an individual matter. Today's school admits students to kindergarten or first grade by a clerical decision based on the student's chronological age. Then the school tries to fit him annually into pre-determined grades, and in the secondary school, into pre-determined subjects. When he has accumulated a given number of credits, a clerical decision says he may graduate and in some cases go on to college. This rigid setting causes schools to adopt such arrangements as homogeneous grouping, or heterogeneous grouping with sub-groups, or so-called remedial and enrichment programs in an effort to deal with individual differences among students locked into these pre-determined compartments. The school of the future will change these arrangements as it treats students as individuals.

Students will be admitted to the elementary school by professional decision and they will progress through school the same way. This contrasts with today's entrance at age 5 or 6 and dismissal at 18 years of age. A professional decision is based on facts collected by measuring devices and interviews, but it also applies professional know-how to the growth and development needs of the individual student. The curriculum is organized around stages or steps rather than by today's artificially created segments that are 9 months in length, one for each calendar year. Thus a talented and relatively mature student may be admitted to school at age four or so and may be ready for college at 15 or 16 while another is admitted at age 5 or 6 and is ready for college at 16 or 18. Another student is admitted at 5 or 6 and by age 15 is in school part time and working part time. There are many variations which result from professional decisions made in the best interests of the individual student (and society also as is shown in the next section of this paper).

Professional decisions also determine the nature of the individual student's program in school. Today's decisions are largely clerical: for example, students are required to take a given number of subjects for a given time; they may play on an athletic team if they pass a given number of subjects; and so on. The future school will determine for each student how much time he spends in large group instruction, small group discussion, and independent study, and the nature of each. Individual programming for subjects and activities will replace standard group procedures commonly used today. Of course, there will be togetherness in the school of the future when appropriate, but the amount of time spent that way will be less than today.

Learning by doing will occupy a more prominent place as the school of the future recognizes individual differences among students. Today's school can only make gestures in that direction because it is so difficult for students to break out of self-contained classrooms and rigid schedules to find ample time to work creatively on individual projects. Today's homework remains too largely a matter of doing more and more of the same kinds of teacher-assigned work. Professional teachers are indispensable in stimulating creative work by students. Their suggestions to students can encourage oblique and new solutions and ideas rather than the parroting of assignments.

Individuals not only need to learn the ways of the mathematician and scientist, but they must also learn how the individual functions in a democracy. These understandings are not learned by a student passively in a self-contained classroom in a school which regiments his day, makes most of his decisions for him, and generally mothers over him. These skills are not learned merely by reading books and passing examinations. Nor are they learned in make-believe committees in a social studies class. The basic emphasis must be on the individual, his needs, his purposes, and his activities as he relates himself to a divergent society.

NATIONAL GOALS

American democracy strives constantly to attain a workable balance between individual and societal rights, responsibilities and goals. The school in this social order also tries effectively to achieve that balance if students are to carry on our cultural traditions.

Society now places a number of requirements on schools. It requires about one-half of the secondary school subjects. The trouble is that in today's schools students work at a specified time in their lives to meet the requirements and then the system lets them forget about the specifications. One of the basic principles of learning calls for constant reinforcement. Yet the curricular organization of today's school permits a student to "take" a course at certain grade levels and then forget it providing he has memorized enough facts to pass the examination at the end of the course or year.

Tomorrow's school will plan so each individual student will learn to his capacity the basic understandings needed by good citizens in all areas of human knowledge. So long as the individual is in contact with the school that knowledge will be reinforced and kept up to date. For example, there will be no such a thing as merely requiring students to take United States history in the eleventh grade. The essential understandings in United States history will be taught in a planned sequence starting in the kindergarten and continuing throughout the years a student is in school. During the upper years this teaching will involve examination of the present social scene in relation to the past. This social studies part of his basic education in the upper years will take about one and one-half hours per week for the "average" student plus the time he devotes in related activities in the community. The other areas of knowledge will receive comparable treatment. Basic education thus for an average 15–16 year old student will occupy about one-third of the time the student spends in systematic school work. The balance of the time will be spent in depth study in the areas of his special interest and competence. Thus society insists that individual students are well educated for their roles in a democracy that increasingly requires higher levels of competency of its citizens.

PRESENT STATUS AND FUTURE DEVELOPMENTS

The ideas presented in this paper have come from many sources. Chief among these are the experiences which teachers and school administrators had during studies of better staff utilization sponsored from 1956–1960 by the National Association of Secondary-School Principals. About one hundred junior and senior high schools were involved one way or another in these studies. Persons in the schools reported their experiences in these studies in four issues of the *National Association of Secondary-School Principals Bulletin* (1958, 1959, 1960, 1961).

Other schools independently and in association with several major universities have also conducted comparable studies. A recent survey by the NASSP Committee on Staff Utilization, to be reported in the January 1962 issue of the *Bulletin* of the Association, indicates considerable spread in such practices as team teaching, large group instruction, small group discussion, independent study, flexible scheduling, use of assistants, and use of technological aids to instruction. Similar studies also have been conducted at the elementary and higher levels of education.

Although most of the studies are segmented in nature, they foretell the coming of the school of the future, a school that will be different in many ways from today's school. Sufficient confidence has been generated by the studies that a few schools today are making substantial steps in the directions which the proposals generated by the studies suggest.

No blueprint for the school of the future exists. Much more experimentation, both in educational laboratories and in schools, needs to be conducted to find better ways of doing things. Since all phases of the educational enterprise are completely interrelated, the studies need to be more comprehensive in scope. Trying to meet individual differences with team teaching and without schedule modification is bound to produce only limited gains. So it is with the other suggestions presented in this statement.

The proposals urged in this paper and elsewhere suggest hypotheses for further testing. The major point of certainty is that present schools cope inadequately with individual differences among students and largely ignore individual differences among teachers. And all of the platform pleas and leaflet assertions by those who defend the status quo or urge minor adjustments in schools can not alter the present picture. Basic changes in the educational setting are needed to enable schools to treat students and teachers as individuals who differ widely in what they can and should do.

Sound leadership is not characterized by looking only backwards. Nor does it ignore what has been learned in the past. Those who lead must be prepared to seek new patterns and settings for teaching and learning which are logically related to present goals. Old forms may be static forms not to be defended just because they were the best that could be devised. Nor is change advocated just to be different. Further gain in quality education demands creative and courageous leadership.

45 / The Dual Progress Plan—After Two Years

George D. Stoddard

In the Dual Progress Plan, the elementary-school child spends a half day with a teacher studying language arts and social studies in a "grade" just as he does in the conventional self-contained classroom. The other half day, spent with several specialized teachers studying mathematics, science, music, art, and other specialties, the child is not assigned to a specific grade but is encouraged to advance as rapidly as his talents in each subject permit. George D. Stoddard of New York University describes the principal features of the plan, outlines a program of teacher preparation for it, presents the course of events in the two school systems experimenting with the plan, and the reactions of teachers, parents, and students to the trial run.

It will be recalled that in the summer of 1956 the School of Education of Syracuse University celebrated it fiftieth anniversary by presenting a series of lectures under the general heading, "Perspective in Elementary Education." My lecture in this series was called "New Ways to Reach the Mind of the Child." The whole series of addresses was edited by Clarence W. Hunnicutt and published in a paperback book entitled *Education 2000 A.D.*

The second part of my address outlined a new scheme for the organization of elementary education which now bears the designation, the Dual Progress Plan. Hence my remarks today could really bear the subscript "After Four Years." However, except in theory, all we know about the plan is based on practical demonstrations in two school systems during the school years 1958–59 and 1959–60.

To refresh our memory and also get clear on basic assumptions, it will be helpful to sketch the main outlines of the plan.

The principal features of the Dual Progress Plan are four:

1. the concept of *cultural imperatives* vs. *cultural electives;*

Reprinted from Vincent J. Glennon, ed., *Frontiers of Elementary Education*, 1961, 7, 1–12, with the permission of the author and Syracuse University Press. Copyright 1961 by Syracuse University Press.

2. a grade progress of pupils based exclusively on the language arts and social studies (the cultural imperatives);

3. a vertical, upgraded progress in mathematics, science, music and art, the pupils advancing according to aptitude and achievement;

4. a reorganization of the curriculum and of teacher preparation (all teachers, including those in the grade or core segment, becoming specialists).

What is the nature of the cultural imperatives which are so important as to determine the total grade placement of the pupil—in theory, from the first grade through the eighth? It is held that there are only two massive ingredients, namely language and the social studies. Language in this context refers to speaking, reading, and writing in English. These abilities furnish most of the general communication in current society and much of its context. In fact, the common factors as between reading comprehension and mentality are so predominant that tests of general intelligence heavily depend on vocabulary, the understanding of sentences, the following of directions, and the solving of verbal problems; the tests contain little of significance in science, and nothing at all in art or music.

The day-to-day life of adults in the United States bears out this supreme dependence on English and the social studies. (In Italy music is part of the common social experience, and in Japan, the graphic arts.) We speak, listen, read and write; above all, we converse. Since we must talk about something, we habitually choose the content of our immediate personal and social needs—the daily routine, as it were. Of course, we read newspapers, journals and books that lift our sights to economic, social and political events, and to the world of fiction. The small store of mathematics and science we learned in school is rarely called upon. Similarly, for music and art: we talk *about* them endlessly but, considering the adult population as a whole, we are not given to drawing, painting, composing or performing. We indulge our tastes by listening and enjoying, often becoming very literate indeed about sights and sounds and persons. Thus to be ignorant in music is not to shun the piano; it is to fail to know the difference between Chopin and Beethoven.

The classroom teacher should be well prepared to teach language and the social studies. He has studied them from the kindergarten or first grade and they have saturated his out-of-school life from about age one. In short, the cultural imperatives cover what most people, including teachers, know and practice and expect of others. They are truly a sufficient ground for any grade system. In this great area of learning no child should be allowed to perform below full capacity.

How different is the situation with respect to the cultural opinions or electives! It is indeed wonderful to discover special musical, artistic or mathematical talent in a child, and to bring this talent to high fruition. Still, if the child lacks special talent, failures along such lines should not be considered either as a mark of general deficiency or of social obtuseness. They should not be an occasion for holding him back in school.

What kind of school is it that sets for itself standards so different from those acceptable to mature adults? Everybody expects us to read and speak but nobody expects us to play the violin. Is it not logical, ethical, if you will, to divorce specialized achievement from grade placement?

In the Dual Progress Plan all specialized subject matter is taught in sections based on the ability and interest of pupils. Thus bright third-graders will be brigaded with older pupils who are at about the same level, let us say, in mathematics or science. In the core segment, which is the half day of the program given to language and social studies, pupils are sectioned on the basis of tests. Actually those who are bright and sufficiently advanced in language arts and social studies may skip a whole grade without reference to accomplishment in the specialized disciplines.

Obviously if an elementary school system is reorganized along these lines there will be changes in the curriculum and in the program of teacher preparation. Although a teacher is responsible for only one subject, some crossovers occur in the practical situation. Thus it is common for a teacher to combine science and mathematics. As the plan develops, many teachers will choose to teach the language arts and social studies, thus retaining their status as grade school teachers. A teacher may accurately declare, "I teach in the fourth grade," meaning that he is responsible for a two-hour class presentation in the language arts and social studies. (The short period assigned to physical education is carried on as a part of the grade system by special teachers in this field.)

On the other hand, the specialized teacher does not think of himself as a fourth-grade teacher, for indeed he is not. The teacher of mathematics, science, art, or music will have pupils of a wide age range, the common factor being the level of maturity in a subject. If you ask this teacher what he does, he may respond simply, "I teach mathematics in the public schools of Long Beach," or "I teach art in the public schools of Ossining"—these being the two city systems now completing the second year of a demonstration of the Dual Progress Plan.

Let us now back up a bit in order to recall the sequence of events. Returning to the School of Education of New York University in 1956, I discussed with some of my colleagues in the School and in several school systems the plan briefly presented at Syracuse. A growing interest in it led to the formulation of a proposal to the Fund for the Advancement of Education for financial aid to establish the plan in three school systems. The proposal called for an elaborate matched group experiment. The officials of the Fund felt that there should be set up an action demonstration program that would immediately predicate a substantial commitment on the part of New York University and the cooperating school systems. The suggestion called for intensive study and for preparatory steps. (At this point one school system dropped out.) In order to get started we were granted in the early summer of 1957 the sum of $15,000 in support of a working party.

This working party really worked! It called together about 25 persons from New York University, the Long Beach Public Schools and the

Ossining Public Schools, together with outside consultants from Harvard University, Columbia University and the University of Illinois. In a six months' period of consultation and staff work, it produced a document of 134 pages which was submitted to the Fund in February, 1958.

Under the new proposal an experimental teaching center was to be established in the School of Education in order to follow through on the Dual Progress Plan and to devise other experiments. The two cooperating school systems were to change over from the self-contained classroom to the Dual Progress Plan in grades 3 to 6 inclusive for a period of three years. Thereupon, in the summer of 1958, the Ford Foundation made a grant to the cooperating groups in the sum of $350,000. The Ford money permitted Long Beach and Ossining to employ a study co-ordinator and specialist consultants in curriculum and teacher education, and the Experimental Teaching Center to appoint a director together with specialists in curriculum, teacher education, and tests and measurements. Of equal importance was the vote of confidence on the part of an external group of advisers to the Fund. The project, in the eyes of some persons, was automatically removed from the "crackpot" category.

All of us know it is easy for schools of education to set up special projects, institutes and centers, provided a foundation will give the necessary financial aid. To reorganize all the elementary schools of a public school system, convincing administrators, teachers, and board members that something radically new should be attempted, is another matter. I am still amazed that two of our leading school superintendents were willing to take the plunge! Fortunately, both Dr. David Salten of Long Beach and Dr. Charles Northrop of Ossining had played an active role in the working party and had become convinced that the new plan was worth a trial. The school boards responded favorably. The teachers were distinctly divided as to the merits of the plan, but less so as to the desirability of running the experiment.

Let us now take a brief look at the course of events in the two school systems over the past two years.

The Long Beach system has about 2,700 pupils and 93 teachers in the elementary schools; it operates on a 6-2-4 plan. In order to allow enough time to prepare for the Dual Progress Plan, its actual inauguration was postponed until February 1959. In the previous fall there was much discussion and planning on the part of teachers, principals and the new staff available. A close contact was maintained with New York University. It is noteworthy that while the fall in-service program for the various Dual Progress Plan subject areas was on a voluntary basis, 90 per cent of the teachers enrolled in these courses. An elaborate testing program for grades 3 to 7 was conducted late in September, thus establishing a base line for later comparisons. In setting up the program, teachers were consulted about their new assignments. Usually agreement was reached.

It is clear from these brief remarks that the initial stages of the project in Long Beach were of a transitional nature. A "pure" application of the plan would have called for the importation of new teachers on a large scale but this, of course, was not practical during a given year. It can be said, therefore, that in Long Beach the new plan at first was not fully in effect. Nevertheless it will be feasible to combine the one and one-half years of the Long Beach experience and the two years at Ossining into a set of tentative conclusions. But first, let us turn to Ossining.

In the Ossining elementary schools there are 1,263 pupils and 51 teachers. Again, with the necessary concessions made with respect to a teaching staff previously on the unitary grade plan, there was a transitional period. However, Ossining was able to set up the Dual Progress Plan in fairly complete form by the fall of 1958. The reactions toward this first trial year of interest. About three-fifths of the elementary school teachers reported they favored it. For certain features of the plan the percentage of acceptance was higher. Thus, about two-thirds of the group liked the specialist teaching and thought that pupils learned more from such teachers than from the all-purpose teachers. Also, on the whole, they favored the ability grouping of pupils and the idea of teaching at several grade levels. As in Long Beach, teachers reported that their work load had been unusually heavy during the first year of implementation of the plan. (In this connection it may be said that some amelioration was introduced in the second year.) There is general agreement that every teacher should have one full free period, that improved curricular materials and examinations should be made available, and that the teachers themselves must make full use of in-service training programs.

Some teachers felt the plan did not serve well the needs of the slow learner, but I do not know the exact nature of this criticism. It is certainly a matter of importance. In theory, the slow learner should be allowed to remain slow except in the language arts and social studies. Even in the common core areas, the pupil who is persistently below average in mental status should not be pressed to get too far beyond the informational and descriptive aspects of the subject matter. Of course, I am speaking of the very slow learner whose defect is not remediable through physical, emotional or cultural acts. In that part of the vertical segment devoted to mathematics, who cares whether a dull student gets beyond skills and simple facts? Why confuse him at abstract levels which he will always ignore and detest? (Having for many years taught statistics to graduate students, I can assure you that many mature persons also seem to abhor the abstract portions of mathematics.) Certainly no truly dull persons in the population are going to become mathematicians, scientists, or scholars, although the chance to reach the higher skills in music, art or sports may not be ruled out. Doubtless if one aspired to be a good skater, dancer or trombonist, it would be helpful to have a high I.Q., but at the level of skill we need not postulate an unusual ability to do abstract thinking.

Understandably, teachers who have long prodded children to accomplish every task set before them (as if all tasks were equally important in later life) will have trouble in adjusting to this *laissez faire* attitude toward the specialized subject matter.

There is more than learning at stake. My feeling is that a failure to

recognize the difference between what is *required* by social custom and
what is expected if a child shows aptitude and interest is a source of bad
behavior and neurosis. Parents who, for themselves, care little about
mathematics, knowing practically nothing about it, are likely to inflict
upon the child a strong feeling of guilt for failure; yet, in this respect,
the child is much like his father or mother. Are not parents on stronger
ground when their concern is for the child's vocabulary, diction, speech,
and knowledge of society? These, after all, comprise a currency of communication which he will need throughout life. Language is not only our
chief channel of communication with one another; it is also a source of
imaginative power and achievement in many art forms.

As we know, there is over the country an insistence that the teaching
of mathematics and science be reorganized as to content, curricular unit,
and methodology. Leading universities and teachers colleges are well represented in this movement, as are some state departments and federal
agencies. Here at Syracuse University you have the leadership of Professor
Vincent J. Glennon and his colleagues; you have the Madison project in
which, I note with interest, algebra is regarded as a basis for arithmetic!
In the early stages of the development of the Dual Progress Plan, in addition to the experts at New York University, we called upon Dr. Max
Beberman of the University of Illinois and Dr. Fletcher G. Watson of
Harvard University.

With respect to mental hygiene and the behavior pattern of children,
the adequacy of the new plan is not as yet clear. We cannot reliably determine this, short of the five school years now allowed for the demonstration in the two school systems. (In July 1959, the Ford Foundation granted
an additional sum of $825,000 in order to permit an extra two-year trial
and to introduce some new features.) During each school day a pupil has
four teachers in addition to his teacher or leader in physical education.
(Under the previous unitary grade plan, he had one teacher all day, although specialists appeared for art, music and shop, and he generally
went to a gymnasium or playground for physical education.) Having
watched children make the shift from the grade teacher's room to the
specialist's room, I am impressed with their gaiety and self-reliance. The
first day or so the teachers were careful to accompany the children down
the hall or to another wing of the building, but they soon discovered that
children like to look out for themselves. It was clearly an exhilarating
experience for many of the children to enter a special classroom set up for
science instruction and to find there a teacher who knew a great deal
about science and could answer all their questions.

At this point let us bury a fallacy! The idea that if teachers know a
great deal about subject matter they therefore know less or care less about
children, is really a slander. Rather, it can be said with confidence that a
zeal for experience on the part of a teacher is consistent with, and often
conducive to, a greater sharing in the lives of his pupils. Who can forget
the electrical effect of Leonard Bernstein on children and youth? It is the
teacher of all subjects in the self-contained classroom who gets nervous

about the questions bright children may ask; if his pupils are eleven or twelve years of age, unconscious defense measures may take the form of child rejection. In any case, insofar as we can select new teachers, giving them at least two years of liberal arts and the usual supporting courses in psychology, philosophy, sociology, and the like, together with an adequate amount of practice teaching under observation, there is no reason to suppose they will be inferior on any grounds to teachers in standard classrooms.

One predicted side effect of the installation of the Dual Progress Plan in two school systems, and its general supervision by the staff of the Experimental Teaching Center, is this: every one is induced to take a hard look at the assumptions and accomplishments of the self-contained classroom. For example, how much individualized instruction does it involve? What attention is paid to measured differences in intelligence, interest or special aptitude? What arrangements are made for sectioning on the basis of ability? Where is the research evidence to support the claim that one teacher a day (aided by specialists) is a necessary condition of high pupil morale? If the self-contained classroom is so generally conducive to emotional stability and good behavior patterns among children, how do we account for so much school-centered frustration and delinquency? If it is held that no school can be expected to control such matters, why, then, is there so much concern *along these lines* about the particular form of organization in the elementary school?

Certainly a grade teacher has the opportunity not only to co-ordinate pupil learning but also to serve as a sturdy axis for the totality of the events of the day. In this sense, the teacher is regarded as a mother substitute, the classroom taking on the character of a friendly home situation. While nobody wants to reduce friendliness and companionship in any school group, the parallel to the home soon fades out. Whoever heard of a family of twenty-five children, all about the same age? What family assembles its children for five or six hours a day for 180 to 185 days per year, and otherwise pays practically no heed to them? What mother would abandon her children at year's end in order to take on a totally different group? All these phenomena characterize the self-contained classroom!

In such a plan, is there not the unspoken assumption that a teacher who spends all day with a child is *ipso facto* a good *emotional* influence? Now we know there are teachers who are not good by any standards thus far devised. There must be many more toward whom children show no real affection; in fact, many pupils must feel like captives. The Dual Progress Plan permits some escape from this sense of being hemmed in: the homeroom teacher is going to be replaced for several hours by somebody else, and there is at least a statistical chance for gain. Personally I feel this likelihood is enhanced by the very nature of specialized teaching, and most teachers in our school demonstrations seem to share this view; above all other features of the plan, they approve of specialized teaching.

Under the Dual Progress Plan what happens to pupils in succeeding years? Each pupil gets a new core teacher, but he may again be taught by the same teachers in specialized subject matter. This is something new in his life. For example, Miss Smith, who early discovered Johnny's aptitude for mathematics and taught him in a fast moving section, is again there to encourage him. In short, what the child lost by familiarity with one teacher during a given school year he now regains on the vertical side of the plan. This had led to the question: Why not altogether abandon the grade system? Well, this has been tried. My feeling is that it is better to have grades as recognizable plateaus, as long as they are based on the inescapable demands of a society. They do offer a measure of immediate security to the young child. They furnish a home base.

Another more subtle change (and I trust it may emerge as a superiority) is that, beyond the acquisition of computational and related skills in arithmetic, the descriptive aspects of science, and the appreciation of music and art, there is no constant pressure on the child to perform. True, there is an *allurement* based on the tested aptitudes of the child; if these turn out to be low, then, to use a slang expression, "the heat is off." Hence the long-range effect of the Dual Progress Plan should be to *increase* individual differences in performance. We hope the dull do not get duller as the bright get brighter. We do not regard dullness or disinterest as inherently obnoxious. Perhaps the long-range effect on the slow learner will be to decrease his sense of discouragement, his need to escape. For gifted students, by the time of high school, it will permit truly advanced work in English, social science, mathematics, science, art, music or a foreign language, or in various combinations of these subjects. (I should mention that a satellite program will be put into effect on an experimental basis this fall; it will set up the study of a foreign language in the fourth or fifth grade, on a voluntary basis for pupils who have an aptitude for it.)

A practical difficulty in conducting classes under the Dual Progress Plan occurs with respect to non-classroom activities such as special musical programs or field trips. The core teacher has his pupils only a half day and he cannot very well gather the pupils together after they have gone into the various classrooms under specialized teachers. The specialized teachers also have difficulty in scheduling such events. The situation is paradoxical, for the best guide for a field trip to woods or factory might be the teacher of science, while the social studies teacher, now himself a specialist, should be effective as a guide to government agencies. Similar statements can be made about music and art. Accordingly it will be necessary to resolve this impasse. Perhaps an extra "floating" teacher can be employed to take care of classes when they are out of the school. A more radical approach which I should like to see tried, is to face frankly the fact that children are in school only one-half the calendar year and that, even while school is in session, the school day occupies less than one-half the child's waking hours. Could not field trips and visits, like sports, be placed off the end of the school day or the school week, and further developed intensively during the long summer period? Here, at least, we have an opportunity to initiate an adjunct school program which would combine some of the features of scouting and outdoor education. This division of labor would permit the school, in good conscience, to concentrate on building the structures of knowledge, on opening intellectual vistas to the child, and on promoting the habit of systematic accomplishment. These virtues nowadays are not too common in home life or neighborhood activities. Life in the city frequently downgrades talent. There is much watching, listening, and responding; there is too little of first-order doing and thinking. As a transitional stage, schools might organize festival weeks in which the whole student body and teaching personnel would combine in a coordinated series of events, exhibits and productions. Such a festival could come between the two halves of the year; it might be regarded as an exciting prelude to the long examination periods which so many students will face later in high school or college.

At this time I am able to insert only a few general comments on the trial run of the Dual Progress Plan, together with a few observations on the second year status of the work in the two school systems.

1. After one year of the Dual Progress Plan at Ossining, Stanford Achievement Test scores were the same in 1959 as in 1956, 1957, and 1958, with respect to reading, spelling, arithmetic, science, and social studies.

2. Changes in STEP-4A tests were the same under the Dual Progress Plan as previously, but the 1960 STEP-4A tests in science and mathematics showed that pupils in grades 4 and 5 were superior to those of 1959.

3. The SRA "Junior Inventory" showed no differences in personal-social adjustment as between 1958 and 1959.

4. In 1960 at Ossining, 80–85 per cent of the pupils are "wholly or mainly in favor of the Dual Progress Plan." (Data are not as yet analyzed for Long Beach.)

5. Parents favor the Dual Progress Plan by a proportion of about four to one; however, the Ossining returns for 1960 show that 58 per cent of the parents oppose a promotion plan based solely on pupil status in English and the social studies.

6. Would teachers choose to return to the self-contained classroom? See data for 1960:

	Would return %	No preference %	Would not return %
Long Beach	46	9	45
Ossining	35	11	53

7. What is the over-all reaction of teachers to the plan?

	LONG BEACH		
	In favor %	Don't care %	Opposed %
Sept. 1958	69	7	24
June 1959		Not given	
June 1960	57	1	41

	OSSINING		
	In favor	Don't care	Opposed
	%	%	%
Sept. 1958	86	2	12
June 1959	54	6	41
June 1960	71	2	27

8. What is the reaction of teachers to the idea of specialization in one subject area?

	LONG BEACH		
	In favor	Don't care	Opposed
	%	%	%
Sept. 1958	70	14	16
June 1959		Not given	
June 1960	71	14	15

	OSSINING		
	In favor	Don't care	Opposed
	%	%	%
Sept. 1958	84	6	10
June 1959	78	11	11
June 1960	87	5	8

1. Even with the major dislocations caused by the new plan, the expected rate of academic growth is maintained.

2. The majority of parents favor the plan.

3. The majority of pupils like the plan and enjoy working under it.

4. The teachers are divided in their acceptance or approval of the plan, but with experience in it and the correction of certain defects, they increasingly register approval. In the first year most teacher difficulties revolved about the extra work required and the newness of curricular materials. It is clear that the plan calls for a vast amount of new work in curriculum, teacher preparation, and examinations.

May I insert into the record one subjective testimonial? In New York last winter Dr. Glen Heathers, Director of the Experimental Teaching Center, and I were on a panel program during which we explained the essentials of the Dual Progress Plan. A third member of the panel was Mrs. Lilian Chase, a teacher at Washington School in Ossining. When she announced that she had had forty years of teaching experience, both Dr. Heathers and I wondered what her reaction would be to something new. At this meeting Mrs. Chase said:

The children from third through the sixth grade were changing rooms and being taught by different teachers. They seemed to enjoy this fully. They felt very grownup, like their older brothers and sisters in junior high. The changing from class to class was done in an orderly fashion. Each child was issued a card giving him the names of the teachers, the subject and the room to which he was to report. By the end of the second day all was well. The children had a chance to work with and become acquainted with more children because the groups did not move as units from one class to another. . . . A period never seemed too long. In fact, all too often it seemed too short. The interest and enthusiasm on the part of the children was very real and became a great challenge for the teacher.

From the viewpoint of the teacher a new and interesting experience had opened up. Instead of teaching all subjects, she would now concentrate on the one of her choice. She undoubtedly put in more time and effort in research in her chosen field and in the preparation and planning of the day's work. Latent abilities were tapped and brought into use. . . .

Each child could now move at his own pace. The more talented in the field of science could work out more difficult and complicated projects, while the others could work out projects on their own level of ability. What a splendid chance for creativity! Experiments became the order of the day and even the youngest "eager beaver" kept the teacher on her toes. Most of all the wonder world of science was unfolding for the children. There were no limits on how far the child might advance. . . . The number of science books, microscopes, chemistry sets, telescopes, rock collections, etc. requested by the children for birthday and Christmas gifts pays tribute to the children's interest in science.

Doubtless we could find a disgruntled teacher who would counterbalance Mrs. Chase's enthusiasm. Nevertheless, this report from a teacher regarded as one of the finest in the system is not to be discounted. It shows what *can* happen!

I have indicated that, because of its insistence upon specialization, the Dual Progress Plan calls for a new program in the education of teachers. There is not time to say much about these new developments at New York University. Considerable progress has been made, and we now have a fifth year of teacher education structured on the liberal arts baccalaureate that includes a major in one of the three areas of specialization.

Four areas of study constitute the framework of a fifth-year program. These are:

A. Social and philosophical foundations of education
B. Psychological foundations of education
C. Elementary curriculum and methods
D. Field experience

Many fifth-year programs for liberal arts graduates throughout the country operate within similar frameworks. The principal changes with respect to the needs of the Dual Progress Plan teacher are in category (C).

A general outline of a 40-point program covering these areas, without specific reference to existing courses in the New York University School of Education, follows:

A. *Social and philosophical foundations* (8 credits)
    1. Current philosophies of education
    2. History of education

  3. Role of the school in American society
  4. Principles, aims, and organization of American education
  5. Others
B. *Psychological foundations* (10 credits)
  1. Human growth and development
  2. Educational psychology
  3. Thinking and self-directed learning
  4. Interpersonal relationships and groups
C. *Elementary curriculum and methods* (10 credits)
  1. Program, curriculum, and materials
  2. General methods of elementary education
  3. Special methods
  4. Dual Progress Plan theory and its implementation
D. *Field experience* (12 credits)
  1. Observation and participation
  2. Practice teaching

At New York University this general plan has been incorporated into a new graduate program for the preparation of elementary teachers with a specialty. It is given the number 888 in the School of Education. The main features of the program include: orientation to American education; psychological foundations; the total elementary program (curriculum, method and materials); a foundation of content courses in the specialty, with background courses in the same area; field experience; individual and group conferences. Through the use of scholarship funds provided by the Ford Foundation it is hoped that some of our best talent in scholarship and potential teaching ability will choose as a career teaching in the elementary schools. All agree that men may especially like the idea of teaching in the upgraded specialized fields.

The next steps to be taken in the three remaining years of the demonstration program are to some extent implied in my discussion thus far.

To sum up, we now need:

  1. New and improved curricular materials in every field.
  2. New tests not only in subject matter but also in creativity and personality. (Dr. Esin Kaya of the Experimental Teaching Center is developing a test of creative thinking in young children.)
  3. A comparison of the performance of pupils in the two cooperating school systems with what they probably would have accomplished under a standard plan.
  4. Affiliations with other school systems in order to test various segments of the program and to make comparisons between it and the self-contained classroom. (Such affiliations are being set up.)
  5. Tests of the value of the New York University *Program 888* and of similar programs that may be developed in the preparation of teachers.
  6. Measures of the relative cost of the Dual Progress Plan and the standard elementary school organization.

7. Tests of the Dual Progress Plan for its adaptability with respect to team teaching and the use of special facilities, such as motion pictures, radio and television.

8. Studies of the design of classrooms, laboratories, special rooms and school buildings as modified by the operations of the Dual Progress Plan.

If all this sounds like a rather ambitious five-year program, so much the better. There is no magic in a term of three years or five years of research on elementary education. The study of education, like education itself, is a continuous process. Let us all get on with it!

46 / Three Examples of Team Teaching in Action

Robert H. Anderson

Ideally, team teaching is a kind of unity. Members of the team plan together, collaborate in teaching and in sharing responsibility, develop and use evaluation techniques and devices, and revise and revamp programs. The flexibility that characterizes team teaching makes it difficult to depict how precisely a team works. Robert H. Anderson of Harvard University gives three examples of team teaching.

Ten years ago, American public education was a relatively stable condition, particularly insofar as school organization and personnel structure were concerned. As the Fifties drew to a close, however, such features as the self-contained elementary classroom, the graded school pattern, the standard setting of secondary school instruction, and certain architectural concepts geared to these phenomena were undergoing serious reexamination.

The national scene and the professional literature were characterized by an intensified concern for *quality*. There was an enlivened interest in new or different approaches to familiar problems, especially of personnel and instruction. There was a growing awareness that many existing arrangements were either archaic in concept, unsuitable to the present requirements, or impractical in the present sociological-economical environment.

As part of the healthy ferment that has followed these developments, there have appeared several discussions of the directions in which our

Reprinted from *The Nation's Schools*, 1960, 65, 62–65, 102, 104, 108, 110, with the permission of the author. Copyright by The Modern Hospital Publishing Co., Inc., Chicago.

present thinking seems to be taking us. The March and April issues of *The Nation's Schools* have featured the Newton Plan, the Wayland Plan, and the Perception Core school, all of which represent unusual patterns of instructional organization and of procedure for training, developing and assigning secondary school teachers. A textbook has appeared to argue the case for abandoning the graded school structure in the elementary school (Goodlad and Anderson, 1959).

There has been a veritable deluge of periodicals and other publications dealing with the general problem of pupil grouping in both elementary and secondary schools, and there is a rapidly growing literature on the related problem of the utilization of teacher competencies. The response to these and other writings, which a decade ago might have been blasted as heretic, has been remarkably positive on the whole. It suggests that the profession is in a state of increasing open-mindedness about the ways children should be brought together for instructional purposes, and the ways schools should make use of the differential talents that reside in the professional staff.

Especially at the elementary school level, the typical school today resembles an egg carton: a series of equal-sized spaces, each well insulated from the others, is set out in rows. By coincidence the typical egg carton resembles a two-section school of six grades, and by intent the content of each space is the same size as the others.

The answers to these and other questions will be formulated by Harvard research workers: specialists in such fields as curriculum, measurement, guidance and administration, who work alongside the team personnel under the general direction of a committee of school and university representatives.

The research design of the project calls for the collection of extensive data on pupil achievement, pupil adjustment, patterns of staff utilization, role development within teams, staff morale, and the like. Evaluation will necessarily be a long-term problem because results obtained during the developmental stage are less directly attributable to team teaching than they will be when a certain stability is achieved.

The Franklin School in Lexington was selected for this rather dramatic enterprise, partly because a building addition of 10 classrooms, a small library, and a gymnasium-auditorium were made available to supplement the original eight-classroom structure in the fall of 1957. Volunteers, including veteran Lexington teachers as well as newcomers and beginning teachers, served as the venturesome staff who first translated the team teaching theory into an operational pattern. This pattern includes some homeroom groupings, interchange (or redeployment) of pupils between teachers, large-group lessons, small-group lessons, use of unusual electronic and audio-visual equipment, use of self-teaching machines, and several other devices or procedures.

At present there are three teams in the Franklin School, each under the management of a team leader who receivs a substantial salary supplement in recognition of his added responsibilities. Team Alpha, the smallest team, consists of three first-grade teachers who share in the instruction of 75 pupils.

Unfortunately, Lexington does not offer kindergarten services; and this fact, plus Lexington's decision to proceed more cautiously with the youngest age group, has resulted in a slower development of team teaching at this level. Experience thus far has encouraged the staff to step up the pace since it now appears that the younger children have greater adaptability and resilience than had been presumed.

The two large teams are Beta, whose pupils membership is 187, in the custody of seven teachers of Grades 2 and 3, and Omega with 249 intermediate grade children and eight teachers. The hierarchy of the Beta and Omega teams includes a position of intermediate level leadership, known as the senior teacher. The senior teachers, one in Beta and two in Omega, receive a modest salary supplement.

The remainder of the teaching staff carries the customary title of teacher, which title connotes no less prestige and/or responsibility than the word "teacher" presently carries throughout the country. This is important since the intent of the project is not to diminish the status of regular teachers but to create new and more responsible positions such as senior teacher and team leader to which the truly outstanding young person may aspire, and through which the career teacher of high competency and responsibility may be more fittingly rewarded by society.

The project hopes that the building principal and the teachers who lead will, over the years, constitute a relatively stable and permanent corps of career officers in education. To a great extent this will protect pupils from the effects of the staff turnover so characteristic of teaching.

Two of today's major movements in elementary education are aimed at removing this egg-carton aspect of school organization. The first of these is *nongrading*, an effort to remove the firm insulation between classes that keep teachers from collaborating in planning and implementing that curriculum.

Nongrading can take place whether a school is organized on the basis of self-contained or egg-carton classrooms or on a basis such as team teaching. Quite probably, nongrading causes teachers to adopt more of a "team approach" to their tasks than does the graded structure. It is even more true that team teaching, or one of its variants, stimulates teachers to think and to act in nongraded terms. Therefore any plan which minimizes either the grade-to-grade lines or the class-to-class lines tends to minimize the other lines as well. Since nongrading has already been thoroughly discussed in the literature, I will discuss team teaching in particular, and several related plans through which the barriers between teachers are being removed. A subsequent article will deal with the administrative and architectural implications of these plans.

About a dozen places in the United States are now engaged in an exploratory project labeled "team teaching" or the like. In these places, the egg-carton pattern has been wholly or partially abandoned in favor of an arrangement in which two, three or more adults combine their energies and talents to instruct a larger number of pupils than the usual 25 to 30. Team teaching does not necessarily increase or decrease the school's pupil-teacher ratio.

Most of the plans are relatively new, are not yet fully developed, and suffer the usual growing pains of frontier projects. Under ideal research conditions these projects should be allowed to proceed carefully and quietly until conclusive evidence attests their virtue or denies their worth. However, the urgency of the times and the apparently intense nationwide interest in team teaching require that some reports of progress appear occasionally.

FRANKLIN SCHOOL PLAN: LEXINGTON, MASS.

Probably the first team teaching project to involve an entire large school was begun in September 1957 in Lexington, Mass. Lexington is one of three New England communities that joined with the graduate school of education of Harvard University to form an alliance known as "SUPRAD," the School and University Program for Research and Development. Its operations have been financed principally by substantial grants from the Ford Foundation, which cover a 10 year period ending in 1967.

Currently the largest of 11 SUPRAD projects, the Lexington team teaching venture, attempts to discover whether teachers can collaborate in new ways, and if so, what immediate and long-range effect such new ways will have upon the growth and welfare of teachers, and teacher training and curriculum development.

This corps of leaders supervises and instructs (by example as well as directly) the less experienced and somewhat more transient teachers who work within the teams. It is also hoped that the corps of career teachers can offer a superior kind of preservice guidance and instruction to apprentices, interns and subprofessional workers. Thus it may be that team teaching will lead to new approaches to teacher education.

Other personnel of the Franklin School Project are three clerical aides, who provide a total of 80 hours service to the teams each week; several part-time teachers who relieve team personnel for certain research development tasks; various specialists who serve not only Franklin but the other Lexington schools, and the Harvard-associated "resident staff" of research workers. One of the specialists is a former Omega teacher who is now developing team teaching procedures in the areas of art, music and physical education.

It is too early to evaluate the project, although subjective evidence from pupils, parents and professional participants is definitely encouraging. Objective data suggest that the new conditions of team teaching have in themselves created no problems of pupil adjustment or morale. It is hypothesized that the phenomenon defined as "pupil security" is not weakened by exposure to a greater number of teachers and classmates in a variety of situations of the sort found in this project. Similarly, achievement test evidence indicates that the children are making acceptable progress even during this period of relatively unsettled conditions.

A more valid demonstration of the project is expected to begin in 1961–62, when a new building designed specifically for team teaching will be available. . . . If successful, this particular pattern of team teaching holds promise of providing a flexible mechanism for instruction, for curriculum development and revision, for training of professional personnel, and for attracting and holding outstanding people in the classroom. The profession should watch this project with great interest, with an open mind, and with a certain degree of patience.

NORWALK PLAN: NORWALK, CONN.

Another exploratory project in team teaching is under way in Norwalk, Conn. The Norwalk Plan was begun in September 1958 with four teams and has been extended to seven teams in 1959–60. Like the Franklin School Project, it aspires to establish a new career opportunity (role of team leader) for teachers of particular competence and professional dedication. In the plan, each team consists of three adults (team leader, cooperating teacher, and teacher aide) working with a group of children about three times the usual size of a class (e.g. 69 to 85), in spaces equal to three regular rooms.

In the first year, there were two second grade teams and two fifth grade teams, each operating in a different building. These are now third grade and sixth grade teams, respectively. Three new teams, one at the fifth grade level, one fourth grade and one second grade, were added in 1959–60 in two additional schools.

The team leader receives a salary supplement of slightly more than $1000, in recognition of the greater responsibility and extra work involved. For similar reasons the cooperating teacher receives a salary supplement of slightly more than $500. The teacher aide, not a professionally certified person, receives about $2800. Therefore the actual salary cost to the community is about the same as it would be if the plan were not in operation.

The teacher aide is in all cases a person with strong personal qualifications and some training and/or experience with clerical work. Most are mature women with families of their own, who previously have worked with groups of children in summer camp or church school teaching. Although they do not teach directly, these women assist the teachers in several semi-instructional functions, such as supervision of seatwork, assisting with classroom control under teacher supervision, and operating electronic instruction equipment. Much of their time, of course, is allocated to record keeping, handling money, preparing typed materials and records, and so forth.

Freed of nearly all noninstructional functions, the two professional teachers conduct total-group (entire team) lessons several times daily, in each case with the teacher in charge who has the greatest competence in the subject matter involved. Other lessons involve average size classes (22 to 30) grouped either heterogeneously or homogeneously as circumstances warrant, and various smaller or larger groupings as desired. Independent work activities also represent an important part of the child's school day.

The Norwalk Plan is remarkable in the extent to which it has developed the use of such instructional aids as the tape recorder (with earphone headsets in series) and the overhead projector. Like the Franklin School Project, the child is regrouped a number of times each day and the staff is able to respond to his varying needs with much flexibility.

The research of the Norwalk Plan (Norwalk Board of Education, 1959) is quite similar to that of the Franklin School Project, and the results of the first year of operation revealed satisfactory pupil progress and general enthusiasm among participating adults, including the parents.

ENGLEWOOD PROJECT: ENGLEWOOD, FLA.

Another important pilot program is found in Englewood, Florida, where the Sarasota County School District is attempting, with the assistance of the Vanderbilt family, to provide educational opportunities comparable to those anywhere in the country. The program is now housed in a flexible school plant. . . . The Englewood Project is still under development, but already embraces many features of both nongraded organization and team teaching. It makes deliberate use of "combination grades" with class sizes varying according to need. The teachers work in a variety of team arrangements and bring together the children of various homerooms for specific purposes. On some occasions, from two to five classes may be combined as one class with from two to five teachers, and many kinds of subgroups are then possible.

Staff experience at Englewood confirms the discovery in other projects that new patterns in classroom organization lead inevitably to complications and changes in existing curriculum patterns, reporting practices, and personnel arrangements. The project by intent is proceeding with restraint because the staff and its consultants believe that each step toward the ultimate goal (nongraded team teaching organization) should be carefully planned and evaluated.

OTHER PROJECTS

Other exciting enterprises on the current scene which involve differences or changes in the ways pupils and teachers are brought into contact include:

1. The Team Learning Plan developed by Donald Durrell of Boston

University, both in Dedham and Wellesley, Mass. Children are divided into learning teams of two or three, and each team advances as rapidly as it can do the work.[1]

2. The Dual Progress Plan, both in Long Beach and Ossining, N.Y., in collaboration with New York University. Children spend about half of their time in nongraded classes for mathematics, science, music and art; they spend the remaining time in graded homeroom classes (Stoddard, 1958).[2]

3. The Catskill Area Project in Small School Design (Whitcomb, 1959, 1959a) a program in search of theory and technics that will improve the variety and quality of education in rural secondary schools. Notable are the use of multiple classes, a pattern of flexible schedules, use of school aides, uses of electronic equipment in teaching, and a plan of "shared services."

4. Several plans calling for multi-grade and multi-age class groupings, notably the Torrance Plan in California. Here children from three adjoining grade levels are combined in primary (Grades 1 to 3) and intermediate (Grades 4 to 6) classes. Two-thirds of each child's classmates are therefore a year or two younger or older than he, and the differences between the children are regarded as an advantage both academically and socially (Hull, 1958).

Other places not previously mentioned but engaged in noteworthy enterprises include: (1) communities associated with the University of Chicago in the School Improvement Program; (2) communities participating in the Wisconsin Improvement Program (teacher education and local school systems) now under way at the University of Wisconsin; (3) Duchesne, Utah, where a team teaching plan is being conducted in Roosevelt Junior High School; (4) San Diego City Schools, California, where an experimental project in staff utilization involves the use of preprofessional teacher aides at the secondary school level; (5) Flint, Mich.; (6) Fort Wayne, Ind.; (7) Carson City, Mich.; (8) Winchester, Mass.; (9) Greenwich, Conn.; (10) Oceano Elementary School District, California; (11) Oriole Park School, Chicago; (12) Evanston Township High School, Illinois; (13) Jefferson County Schools, Colorado, and (14) Auburn, Me.

SOME PREDICTIONS

In view of the numerous exciting projects scattered across the country at this moment, it seems justifiable to predict that many American schools will soon be giving serious consideration to rather fundamental changes in organization and structure. Espousal of at least the philosophy of nongrading is spreading rapidly; there is intense interest in various new mechanical and electronic aids-to-instruction; the use of teacher aides and resource persons is also likely to be adopted in many places; various forms of intrabuilding staff collaboration and shared teaching are already in

[1] [See selection 47 in this volume.]   [2] [See selection 45 in this volume.]

evidence and probably will expand; many schools are engaging in trials of new pupil grouping practices, including the occasional use of large-group class instruction. If these things are indeed happening, then it seems all the more likely that team teaching, a highly complex arrangement within which all of the foregoing procedures tend to operate, will appear to many as a goal toward which to strive.

It is therefore especially important for administrators and others to realize that *even the smallest steps toward team teaching must be taken with utmost care.* Few, if any, school districts are presently in a position to launch team teaching with less than one or two years of advance preparations. Team teaching remains a hypothetical concept that has yet to be fully and competently demonstrated, or proved to be a superior plan of school organization.

Manuals and guidebooks of team operation are not yet in the public literature. Procedures for determining basic operational characteristics are yet to be outlined, and the best ways of selecting, training and supervising the various leadership personnel (especially principals and team leaders) have not yet been discovered. Perhaps more important than these unanswered questions are those concerning the antecedent conditions within a school system upon which the success of team teaching may depend.

In discussing ways to establish nongraded schools, Professor Goodlad and I have counseled school systems. We suggested that unless there is concerted and unanimous staff concern with problems of promoting, reporting and individualizing instruction, it is probably too early in the development of that staff to begin serious consideration of nongrading (Goodlad and Anderson, 1959, pp. 170–90).

We also have stated that the establishment of a strong understructure via kindergarten services, which are still regrettably missing in more than half of the school systems in America, is a first priority problem. We have clearly implied that other environmental factors, such as enlightened and adequate leadership and excellent curriculum development and evaluative services, are prerequisite to the establishment of successful nongraded operations.

This advice, I now strongly believe, applies to the school system with its eye on team teaching. Any pilot program of nongrading and/or team teaching is certain to encounter trouble unless it has a staff deeply concerned about the individual's learning opportunities, a complete and healthy K-12 program, a significant headstart on the staggering curriculum problems that face American schools today, sufficient quality and quantity in school district leadership "across the board," and other environmental advantages.

OTHER ESSENTIALS

Other prerequisite conditions to be considered for team teaching are the following:

1. *The budget for clerical services of the kinds—audio-visual aids, textbooks and supplies, and other expendable materials—should be much higher* than the state and national averages, which averages are abysmally low and painfully suggestive of poor logic and penny pinching. The conditions of team teaching will inevitably cause teachers to require more abundant and varied resources. Of course this is a good thing, but most teachers do not yet fully realize that they are the only major occupational group in America deprived of adequate tools with which to work.

2. *The community and the school district should have enjoyed a harmonious and constructive working relationship* for a number of consecutive years. The board of education in such communities is usually of higher intellectual and moral caliber. The parents and influential citizens usually are well informed as to school policies and problems, and confident in the competence of the school staff. Parents and teachers usually know each other (because of parent-teacher conferences, for example) and work together. The conditions of team teaching, which could confuse or upset a less secure parent group, can probably be taken in stride in such a situation.

3. *There should be a history of sincere interest in, and efforts toward, the rewarding of superior staff service.* One reflection of such an attitude would be a high salaried and adequate administrative supervisory staff (superintendent, central office personnel, principals). Another would be efforts toward recognizing superior service in the classroom through merit pay or other devices. If such things have been going on, then the idea of elevating the teachers of highest competence to team leadership will be a natural and acceptable one, and the top authorities probably have more accurate and comprehensive information about their staff members' strengths and weaknesses than is usually the case.

4. *The school district and its officers should, over recent years, have developed rather strong ties,* through a variety of mutual studies and activities, with one or more college or university agencies of high caliber. The arrangement underlying Harvard's SUPRAD or Chicago's School Improvement Program is probably basic to any endeavor as complicated and significant as team teaching.

These are not all the precautions that should be taken, but they are probably the major ones. To those who may protest, "but this would be stacking the cards," I would simply reply that the cards must be "stacked" if we are to make real gains on our major problems. Some school systems haven't held a winning hand in years, and it seems high time that we learn how this game should be played. Everyone knows what the stakes are.

47 / Implementing and Evaluating Pupil-Team Plans

Donald D. Durrell

Pupil-team learning as it functions in an elementary-school setting is described by Donald D. Durrell of Boston University. Three essential aspects of the project are treated: accomplishing organizational change, conducting in-service education of teachers, and evaluating the program.

Pupil-team learning consists of combining children into pairs, threes, or larger groups for mutual aid in learning. It utilizes the natural tendency of children to work together. This desire should be encouraged whenever it promises to increase the amount and quality of learning; it should be avoided when it seems to diminish either.

Much school activity is based upon the theory that every lesson is a test of achievement, rather than a practice in learning. Each arithmetic paper, each written product, is marked by the teacher as though it were a terminal examination, rather than a single small step in the learning process. Pupil-team learning assumes that most school activity is practice toward achievement, and that mutual aid in this practice may be desirable. During learning practice, pupils may compare and correct answers, exchange ideas and evaluate approaches to problems, work together on plans or projects, and assist each other at points of difficulty. Sometimes they may present a team product rather than a collection of individual practice papers. Evaluation and analysis of the results of learning are, of course, based upon individual work.

The success of team learning depends upon the quality of the learning tasks in which it is employed. Good tasks are of a suitable level for the team, are clear and specific in requirements, and appeal to children as important. Every useful motivation should be employed to assure the learning disciplines satisfying to children. Allowing teams to progress as rapidly as they can master the material in arithmetic and spelling provides "knowledge of progress" motivation. Team use of study guides in social studies and science increases attention and emphasizes significant concepts, assuring the learner of mastery. Increased opportunity to respond to learning is provided when "taking turns" reciting is replaced with three-man-team responses to the same questions, with responses recorded by the team scribe. Team specialties in social studies, assigned six weeks

Reprinted from the *Journal of Educational Sociology*, 1961, *34*, 360–65, with the permission of the author and the Payne Educational Sociology Foundation.

in advance of the appearance of the topic in the course of study, produce displays which enrich the learning of all pupils. Remedial work, or intensive practice at points of common weakness, is suitable for learning teams, especially if self-directing, self-correcting learning "packages" are available.

The teacher is the key figure in the team-learning classroom. She sets the learning tasks and reacts to team products even though she does not mark them; she decides the make-up of most teams; she analyzes and evaluates the individual tests of achievement; she balances the day between team learning and whole-class activities; she plans the program of enrichment; she disciplines when non-working noise appears in a group, usually by having pupils work alone at the team task. The quality of her direction, planning, and enthusiasm determines whether team learning is vigorous and disciplined, or whether it results in confusion and disorder.

Pupil-team learning requires no change in school organization; it may be adapted to self-contained classrooms, to ability grouping by subjects, to departmental teaching, to television or other programs of mass presentation, or to teacher-team programs. Its most extensive use to date has been in self-contained classrooms, to which it brings many of the advantages of the ungraded elementary school, yet maintains the single teacher responsible for most of the instruction.

The major project to date in use and evaluation of pupil-team learning was in Dedham, Massachusetts, during the academic year 1958–59. A U.S. Office of Education contract enabled the study to be made in forty-seven self-contained intermediate-grade classrooms in eight elementary schools. The problems and techniques in the conduct of the Dedham program may be useful in setting up and evaluating similar ventures.[1]

Accepted protocol for initiating new educational ventures calls for enlisting the interest of teachers who then make the decision on acceptance. Another desirable method is that of starting new ventures in selected schools or classrooms, then spreading the practices as they appear to be valuable. Neither of these was used in Dedham. The superintendent had been a member of a university laboratory in elementary school supervision, in which the group of supervisors initiated differentiated instructional practices in classrooms of cooperating schools. During this experience it became apparent that a vigorous approach to pupil-team learning in an entire school system would be desirable. The decision to try the program for a year was made by the superintendent with the unanimous support of the school committee.

The critical period for any such educational venture is between the decision to make the change and the time of its inception in the classrooms. In Dedham, the announcement of the decision was followed immediately by demonstrations of pupil-team learning conducted by the research fellows who were to assist in the program. The advantages and possibilities of pupil-team learning in providing for individual differences

---

[1] A more complete description of techniques and outcomes of the Dedham study is found in Durrell (1959).

was presented. Since this was done in May, with a summer to elapse before the start of the program in September, there was an interval in which teacher doubts and fears might grow. This is illustrated by a story told by one of the teachers after the program was successfully underway: "The proposal seemed to upset my own ideas about effective teaching. Since I had reached minimum retirement age, I decided to resign rather than to subject myself to the change. Then I had a better idea—I would start the program, then resign in protest."

A fall workshop was conducted by the research fellows, with all teachers and principals participating. This was concerned mainly with pupil-team progress methods in arithmetic and spelling. These subjects were chosen to begin the program for a number of reasons: they had always worked well in previous trials of team learning, pleasing both pupils and teachers; they could be started on the first day of school, using job sheets to accompany the arithmetic books (McHugh and Manning, 1961); they required less work of the teacher than conventional methods of teaching these subjects. The research fellows offered to help any teacher start the program in her classroom if she were uncertain how to begin, but most teachers preferred to introduce the program to their pupils.

The research fellows were in classrooms every day during the school year, assisting teachers with problems and making adjustments to the varying needs that appeared. Since both research fellows had been superior elementary school teachers and had experience in supervision, their suggestions were readily accepted. After team-progress methods in arithmetic and spelling were running smoothly, team-learning procedures were introduced in other subjects. The great shortage was that of self-directing, self-correcting materials, desirable for disciplined team learning. Groups of teachers met with the research fellows to prepare study guides, to find ways of adapting materials to various levels, to develop exercises for remedial instruction, to provide challenging learning experiences for superior pupils. The production of materials was shared by teachers; materials were exchanged to avoid duplication of effort. Successful new practices were spread by the research fellows, and there were constant demonstrations of promising approaches (McHugh, 1959; Manning, 1959).

The major evaluation of the program was made by comparing the achievements of pupils under the same teachers prior to and following the experimental year. Metropolitan Achievement Tests were used for general achievement comparisons. Although such tests are limited to a few facets of educational growth and depend largely upon retention of facts and skills, they provide a basis for comparison. Average achievements in the team-learning year improved six months over the control year in grade six, and four months in grade five, but there was no significant improvement in grade four except in spelling. Data were analyzed for subject achievement of pupils of different levels of intelligence, for boys and girls.

Changes in affective reactions of pupils, teachers, and parents were discovered by the use of various scales. Attitudes of pupils toward school subjects showed a statistically significant improvement in grade five; grades four and six did not change significantly. Social distance scales used by pupils revealed no significant changes, nor were any changes found in teacher ratings of classroom behavior of pupils. Teacher attitudes toward various aspects of the program were obtained by anonymous reactions to a questionnaire; they felt that the programs in spelling, arithmetic, and reading were "superior," but they rated social studies and language arts instruction as "good." Parent reactions toward the program, obtained by anonymous returns, were definitely favorable, with 95 per cent reporting "very pleased" or "satisfied."

Perhaps the most novel feature of the evaluation program was that of a "Subject Service Analysis" based upon a standard interview with each teacher. Evaluation was made of the following adjustments to pupil needs in each subject; provision for levels of ability, provision for learning rates, special instruction for varying skills needs, self-direction and social learning, and enrichment of instruction. Each item was rated on a four-point scale, varying from routine uniform instruction, rated as "1," to major provision for the service needed, rated as "4." The analysis had undergone several revisions and was administered by outside experienced supervisors who were especially trained in evaluating differentiated instruction. The reliability of the scale is .90, based upon separate ratings of fifty teachers (Scribner, 1960).

The purpose of the use of this scale was to determine the amount of actual change in instructional services to pupils. The degree to which any program achieves its intended services varies; some programs are found only on paper, but not in classrooms. The maximum possible rating on the scale was 92, the minimum, 24. The average rating of teacher service to pupils during the control year was 29.6; in the experimental year it was 63.5, a marked improvement, but still short of the maximum possible rating. Improvement in teaching the separate subjects was rated from most to least, as follows: reading, spelling, arithmetic, social studies, language arts.

All sorts of frustrations beset the experimenter who attempts to evaluate changes in a total educational program. The experimental program contains so many variables that it is impossible to ascribe the change in achievement to a single variable. The gains in arithmetic may have resulted less from pupil-team learning than from the provision to allow pupils to progress beyond the grade; one-third of the pupils completed two-years' work during the year. The use of study guides, the improved quality of discussion questions, the wide employment of pupil specialties, and the marked increase in public library circulation among these pupils are important to the gains shown. Some of the experimental factors may have been detrimental to learning but were more than offset by improvement resulting from other factors. And there is always the fact that the measures employed failed to include many of the accomplishments which were presumed to be taught.

Although the teachers were the same both years, the intelligence and initial achievements of pupils were the same, and the textbooks and school organization were unchanged, there were other variables which may have influenced the energy of the teachers and the achievements of the pupils. Any new program is stimulating, especially when it receives wide public notice and attracts constant visitors. The daily contact with the research fellows, and the increased classroom supervision by the principals must also be considered. All that can be said with assurance is that the program was effective in increasing achievement in grades five and six. The evaluation of pupil-team learning as a specific factor requires much more carefully controlled studies and several of these are under way.

One of the tests of an experimental program is its continuance in the schools where it was employed. The pupil-team learning program has continued in Dedham in the two years following the study. Many of the techniques have spread to primary grades and to junior high school classes. The assurance of achievement under pupil-team learning has led to a "departmental day," with Wednesdays being devoted to extra instruction in music, art, dramatics, science, languages, and other areas in which teachers have special competence.

The demand for assistance in starting pupil-team programs in other school systems has been met by an area-centered "laboratory in team learning," offered each semester in different locations. Enrollment is limited to principal-teacher teams; no teacher may enter unless her principal is also enrolled. Demonstrations are given with full elementary classrooms in which pupils are unfamiliar with pupil-team activities. These demonstrations are followed by discussion of promising variations in methods and by exhibits of materials. A new school subject is demonstrated every two weeks. After each subject is introduced, teachers are required to use some form of differentiated instruction in that subject for the duration of the course. They report on success, variations, and problems; they prepare lessons cooperatively and exchange instructional materials. Principals are expected to go into classrooms of teachers not in the course to demonstrate pupil-team learning procedures. More than two hundred members of principal-teacher teams have attended the laboratory during the past two years. They have included teams from teacher-team schools, from ability grouped schools, and from schools with self-contained classrooms.

48 / University of Illinois High School, Urbana, Illinois, Experiments Further with Independent Study

David M. Jackson, W. L. Shoemaker,
and Paul Westmeyer

Independent study, geared to individual differences and directed toward increasing students' motivation and responsibility for their own learning, purports to be a significant approach in improving learning and retention. The selection describes several projects in self-directed learning conducted at the University of Illinois High School, of which the authors are faculty members.

Five projects directed toward increasing students' responsibility for their own learning were begun in the University of Illinois High School in 1958–59 under the auspices of the Commission on the Experimental Study of the Utilization of the Staff in the Secondary School. Three of the projects—those in the teaching of chemistry, advanced problems in science, and school-college articulation—were continued in 1959–60 with support from the Commission. Final reports for these projects are presented in this article. Two of the projects—those in the teaching of biology and of advanced French—were supported during 1959–60 by the Research Department of the office of the Superintendent of Public Instruction, State of Illinois. Brief summaries of these studies are included here, and final reports have been published by the office of the Superintendent of Public Instruction.

Something of the common aim which has unified these studies may be seen in the title of the first year's progress report "A Search for Practical Means of Improving Instruction by Increasing Students' Responsibility for Their Own Learning. . . ." Practical results were achieved in full measure as the experimental courses and administrative procedures became a regular part of the University High-School program. Elements of each of the five projects are now included among the program elements which we recommend for serious consideration by other school faculties.

Even beyond the immediate practical impact of the studies has been the impetus which the staff utilization studies have given to further in-

Reprinted from the *Bulletin of the National Association of Secondary-School Principals*, 1961, *45*, 199–208, with the permission of the authors and the National Association of Secondary-School Principals.

vestigation and more widespread dissemination of ideas which have developed out of the studies. The work on the teaching of chemistry is being continued under the auspices of the Chemical Bond Approach Committee whose members seek to develop and try out a reconstructed high-school chemistry course.

The work in biology, with its emphasis on self-directed learning, is continuing in several ways, including motion picture production during 1960–61 under a contract with the United States Office of Education. The motion pictures will serve as a demonstration of the use of film technique in teacher education under Title VII of the National Defense Education Act. Growth in the pupil's ability to devise and perform biological experiments is to be shown in the films, which will be given wide distribution.

AN INDEPENDENT STUDY COURSE FOR GIFTED STUDENTS IN SCIENCE

Introduction

The problem of this investigation was described in the preliminary report (1959) in some detail. In brief summary, it was to develop and test a course which would enable gifted students in science to pursue advanced study in their chosen fields independently of formal instruction. The student who has completed basic science courses in the high school and who is capable and interested might either broaden his field of scientific knowledge or study more advanced materials in a standard field—biology, chemistry, or physics—in such a course.

Such a course was designed and established in the schedule of University High School for a two-year study (1958–60). The course and the results of the study are described in this report.

Course Description

Advanced Problems in Science is offered to seniors who have taken the basic science courses. (In a few cases juniors have been admitted.) It is offered every hour of the school day and is available after school hours if necessary. The student desiring to enroll in A.P.S. makes application, on a form prepared for this purpose, preferably in the spring of his junior year. On his application, he must (1) state the problems or the field which he wants to study, (2) describe his grade record in high school, (3) state the method of scheduling he desires, (4) have a parent's signature to show that his plans are approved, and (5) present some evidence of his ability to work effectively without supervision.

Students are accepted or rejected on the basis of this information, data from the school records, recommendation from teachers, and a personal conference between the student and the supervisor of A.P.S. If he is accepted, the student may elect to work for one or one-half units of credit and his scheduled time must then be the equivalent of five or two and one-half hours per week. The credit given is the same as for an academic course; it is counted for graduation requirements and entered on his transcript.

The work done in this course is independent of instruction. The class does not meet with a teacher. Each student is assigned a desk and book shelves in a room which is used only for this class. Each student also is given a key to the room and the door is left locked when the room is unoccupied. This gives the students a place which they can truly call their own and where they can work undisturbed.

At the beginning of the year, each student has several conferences with the A.P.S. supervisor and with other teachers in the science department. Fairly detailed plans are drawn up for his study and a copy is placed in the student's file. It is then his responsibility to follow the plans and to ask for help when it is needed. (Plans may, of course, be changed in consultation with the supervisor of the course.) Laboratory space, equipment, and supplies are arranged for as needed.

Each student must keep two records and he is strongly encouraged to keep one more. He keeps a daily diary of his work, containing very brief description of what was done. He keeps a weekly reading record of articles and books which he has read outside the field of his own special study. And he is encouraged to keep a careful record of all that he does, both laboratory work and reference work, on his own study. In lieu of requiring that this record be turned in for grading, it is required that formal papers be presented at appropriate times during the year. These are published in a dittoed "A.P.S. Journal" and distributed to other students and teachers.

Bi-weekly seminars are held for the purpose of giving students an opportunity to discuss their work orally. Each student has a turn (or several) at giving a seminar discussion. This is done after school hours and lasts from 30 minutes to an hour. In addition to the paper and the seminar, students also have about three conferences (minimum) per year with the supervisor to enable him to follow the progress of their study. Grading is entirely an individual matter. No common subject matter is dealt with, so no tests are given which are common to the whole group. Students may, of course, elect to be tested in their own area, or the basis of grades may be papers, records, conferences, or project results. Student self-evaluation is also considered an important part of the course.

Evaluation Based on the Two-Year Trial

In answer to the question, "Does the course work?" descriptions were given in the preliminary report (1959) of the work of nine students. During the second year of the trial, four students were enrolled for one-half unit and eight for one unit of credit. Their studies were of comparable quality to those reported previously and are recorded in the course files. A consideration of these studies strongly suggests that this course ought to be of real value to the students. The real question of value, however, probably is related to effects upon college experiences of the students.

Students in the first-year trial of the course have been asked to say what effect they thought it has had upon their college experiences. (They, of course, have been in college only one year.) No one has made any adverse comments. All have felt that they have benefited from the course, and two have said that it was the most important part of their preparation for college.

Students have also been asked at the close of the year to express some evaluation of the course. While there have been many suggestions for improvements, the evaluations have always been positive. Students feel that they not only are able to learn effectively what they have worked at by themselves, but also that they have a great deal of fun doing it.

Those parents who have volunteered comments have agreed that A.P.S. is a valuable course for their students. And the final evaluation may be seen in the popularity of this course. Many students begin even as freshmen to plan so that they may be accepted into A.P.S. as seniors.

Conclusions

1. The course has proved worth while as far as University High School is concerned. It will remain a regular offering in the science curriculum.

2. It has been found in this two-year trial that a minimum of supervision is necessary in this course. (Careful selection of students is necessary to retain this as a valid conclusion.)

3. Since most public schools have only a few gifted students, such a course would be a most desirable, and inexpensive, way to allow them to have special experiences in science.

4. A course such as this can be operated with few funds and with a minimum expenditure of teacher time. It would be highly desirable, of course, that the teacher have as much time to devote to a course such as this as that devoted to other science courses.

5. The success of such a course will depend upon careful selection and early guidance of students, and upon the willingness of the supervisor to trust the students once they have been admitted.

A METHOD OF TEACHING CHEMISTRY IN THE LABORATORY

Introduction

The enrollment of students in high-school chemistry courses has been increasing during the past few years. With larger numbers in classes, the supervision of students during laboratory work periods becomes more difficult. The result in many cases may be that the laboratory portion of the course is greatly reduced. This is a very serious matter since it is in the laboratory that motivation is typically highest, and it is also in the laboratory that the learning which is likely to have the greatest transfer value takes place.

The most desirable solution of this problem would be to provide more teachers, more classrooms, and more laboratories. Since there will be a considerable lag before this can occur, however, another solution must be sought. The solution proposed at the beginning of this two-year study was that a para-professional assistant might be used to help the regular teacher supervise the work of students in the laboratory. The first year of the study was devoted to developing materials and operating a high-school chemistry course with the help of such a laboratory assistant. The second year of the study has been devoted to the testing of hypotheses which evolved from the first year's study. The problem, re-stated, has been to develop and test a method by which the larger numbers of students in today's high-school chemistry classes can continue to have meaningful, varied, and extensive laboratory experiences.

Preliminary Data [1]

At the beginning of the first year of this study, the 30 students in the experimental class were given the *Max Test on Interpretation of Data* (1) and the *Whole Truth and Nothing but the Truth Test* (2) on factual information. Both of these tests were also administered as post-course measures. The *ACS-NSTA Cooperative Examination in High-School Chemistry* (3) was used only at the end of the course. Results on the two factual examinations supported the hypotheses that there would not be a significant difference between the learning of students in the experimental course and that of comparable students in other courses and that a significant amount of factual learning would occur during the course. Results on the *Max Test* showed a non-significant (at the .05 level) trend toward increased ability to interpret data among students in the experimental course.

In order to test the original hypothesis (stated above in the Introduction), an assistant was employed to work with the instructor in supervising the laboratory. The laboratory work was planned in such a way that the students were given progressively more responsibility for planning and carrying out their own work. At the beginning of the course the work was carefully directed and closely supervised. After the first two months, the method of planning laboratory work was changed to one in which small groups of students wrote directions and helped supervise the rest of the class in carrying them out. (All students had several opportunities to be on such planning committees.) During the last two months of the course, the work was individual, consisting of qualitative analysis and individual projects. Each student was almost entirely responsible for planning and carrying out his own work.

With the help of the assistant, a complete diarial record of the course

---

[1] For a more detailed description of the first year's study, see Jackson, et al. (1960).

was kept. From this record and from the results of two scheduled interviews with students during the year, data were selected for ten case studies. It became evident during the course that there was much variation among the students on the effectiveness and efficiency of self-direction. At the end of the course, the instructor and assistant rated all students on self-direction. The five students rated highest and the five lowest were selected as subjects for the case studies.

The Major Hypothesis

It was demonstrated during the first year of this study that a large class can be effectively supervised in the chemistry laboratory by a teacher and a part-time assistant. But a better solution to the original problem seemed to emerge from the data. Since most students in the course were able to demonstrate a considerable degree of self-directive ability by the end of the year, it seemed reasonable to predict that some degree of self-direction might be expected of students from the beginning of a course. It was hypothesized that, by appropriate methods at the beginning of a course, students could be quickly trained to bear a large share of the planning and carrying out of their own laboratory work. If this were found to be true, the problem of supervising a large class in the laboratory would be greatly reduced. This hypothesis was tested during the second year of this study.

Method of Testing This Hypothesis

Laboratory procedures were so designed that, on the *first* experiment, students were required to locate reference material in order to complete the work assigned. For the *second* experiment, very limited directions were given and students were made responsible for planning procedures (or asking for help in planning if they felt it was needed). From the third experiment on, all that was given to students was a statement of the problem to be solved. Planning and carrying out the experiment was left to students. (Safety precautions were given as necessary, new techniques were demonstrated, and other help was given when it was requested.) Students were encouraged to ask questions of a theoretical nature, but procedural questions usually were answered by referral to a reference book.

During each laboratory session, a record was kept of the number of procedural questions and the number of theoretical questions asked by students. These data are presented in the next section.

Data for First Five Experiments

The following tables are based on records kept in the laboratory during the first five experiments (September 6–November 10):

While the total number of procedural questions asked by students decreased steadily (this is seen most clearly in the "per-day" column, since some experiments required more time than others), the number of theoretical questions remained about the same. It was apparent by the end of the fifth experiment that students were locating needed information for themselves rather than asking for it. It was also apparent that most students were much more personally concerned with their laboratory work than is usually the case.

Table I. Nature of Experiments

No.	Title	Description
1	Description of a Chemical	Given a chemical, describe it in as much detail as you can. Heating, chemical tests, etc., are encouraged.
2	Density	Determine the density of an unknown chemical.
3	Compound formation	Dissolve iron in various acids. Determine what compounds are formed.
4	Polarity	By solubility, determine the electrical polarity of substances supplied.
5	Thermal stability	How readily will heat decompose given substances? What products result?

Table II. Number of Procedural Questions Asked by Students

Experiment	Total Questions	Questions Per Day
1	49	25.5
2	32	16
3	37	9.25
4	33	8.25
5	15	7.5

Summary and Conclusions

It was found during the first year of this study that students could apparently be given a large share of the responsibility for planning and carrying out laboratory activities by the end of the course. Testing of the hypothesis that this responsibility could be given students almost from the *beginning* of the course was done during the second year. The results given above, together with the evidence of high factual achievement during the course, suggest that students can be led quickly to plan and direct their own work in the laboratory and that such self-direction can be quite effective.

Increased Responsibility for Seniors

In essence, the study of increased responsibility for seniors as a means of easing the transition from high school to college provided (1) procedures by which seniors were made responsible for managing their own time outside of regularly scheduled classes, and (2) a follow-up of the class of 1959 through their freshman year in college.

The procedures and the results as observed in the school were discussed in previous reports. The rules originally proposed by the students and accepted by the faculty have remained in force without modification, and the practice of assigning no senior to a study hall unless there are specific problems of achievement or behavior has become an accepted part of the school routine. The study has had the welcome practical result of making a significant reduction in the amount of teacher time devoted to study hall supervision.

Results of the Follow-up Study. During the summer of 1960, a questionnaire was sent to all members of the graduating classes of 1958 and 1959 who entered college. The following paragraph was incorporated in the questionnaire that was sent to the members of the class of 1959:

> Previous senior classes in University High School were assigned to study halls or to other teacher-supervised activities when not in class. Yours was the first class in which individual students were expected to manage their own time outside of class. We are anxious to know whether, in your opinion, this plan for student self-management helped or hindered your work during your freshman year in college. Will you please indicate your feeling on this matter, citing specific examples if possible?

A similar questionnaire was sent to the members of the class of 1958 explaining the plan that had been put into operation and asking whether, in their opinion, "such a plan for student self-management in high school would have helped or hindered your work during your freshman year in college?" In analyzing and tabulating the responses to the free-response question, the following categories were set up: 5–Favorable toward plan with evidence cited; 4–Favorable toward plan with no evidence cited; 3–Neutral; 2–Against plan with no evidence cited; and 1–Against plan with evidence cited. The results by classes are shown in Table III.

Colleges and universities attended by the class of 1958 were Boston, Chicago, Cornell, Illinois, Oberlin, Smith, and Swarthmore. Colleges and universities attended by the class of 1959 were Cornell, DePauw, Eastern Illinois, Franklin, Harvard, Illinois, Knox, Lawrence, Northwestern, Oberlin, Reed, Rice, Swarthmore, Trinity, Wellesley, and Wisconsin.

Typical responses from the class of 1958, which did not have the self-management plan, that fell in categories 2, 3, and 4 respectively, were:

> 2–I definitely do think that this is not a good idea. I believe it may have hindered my freshman year work if this program had been in effect when I was at University High.

3–Wouldn't have necessarily done one or the other.
4–This is a fine program, I feel. By the time you're a senior, you have your study habits formed and it is to your advantage to have this free time to budget for yourself.

Typical responses from the class of 1959, which had the self-management plan, that fell in categories 3, 4, and 5 respectively, were:

3–Student self-management neither helped nor hindered my work.
4–I feel that the plan helped me.
5–If I compare my work to the work of most freshmen at (name of College) who had had a background of many rules and regulations in a boarding school, I may safely say that the plan has been advantageous to me. Generally speaking, I found that those students who had been accustomed to strict controls imposed by administrative authority could not adjust to the uncontrolled, unguided college life. Even some of my classmates who expressed a desire and interest in better studying habits were not able to schedule their time satisfactorily, for they had never before been required to guide and push themselves independently, and many of them reacted to their new-found freedom with an uncontrolled joy and irresponsibility.

Conclusions

1. There was no significant difference between the two classes in college freshman grade-point average or in number of hours which they reported as spent in studying; hence this evidence does not indicate that the plan was either beneficial or detrimental from these viewpoints.

2. Since no negative opinions were expressed—48 per cent were neutral and 52 per cent were in favor of the plan—it is concluded that the plan was a success from the participants' viewpoint.

3. A significant reduction was made in the amount of teacher time devoted to study hall supervision.

4. The plan was judged by the faculty to be successful and the plan is being continued.

Table III. Questionnaire Responses

	Class of 1958	Class of 1959
1. Number attending college	23	36
2. Percentage of response	57	75
3. Responses by categories		
Category 5	0	9
Category 4	4	5
Category 3	8	13
Category 2	1	0
Category 1	0	0
TOTAL	13	27
4. Number of hours outside of class reported as spent on study	26	27
5. Freshman grade-point average (on a 5-point scale)	4.13	4.06

FRENCH

Can students in fourth-year French classes learn as much from two classes per week with the teacher plus three class hours of independent study as they can in the conventional five classes per week with the teacher? Evidently they can, for fourth-year students of Miss Pauline Changnon in 1958–59 and 1959–60 did as well as previous classes had. During the two experimental years, students used books and phonograph records, as well as twenty specially prepared tapes, during their periods of independent study. The subject matter of the twenty taped includes drama, short stories, poetry, criticism, nonfiction articles, descriptions of life in France, and historical and political material. The thirty voices are those of both men and women of varying ages representing all major regions of France.

We are so pleased with the results of this experiment, particularly in seeing the extent to which students can learn to work independently, that we have made the course, including two classes and three periods of individual laboratory work per week, a regular part of the foreign language program. Although the students who participated in this experiment were almost all of high intelligence, ranking, in most cases, above the 90th percentile on the *Differential Aptitude Test* of the Illinois Statewide Testing Program, we do not hesitate to recommend such an advanced course for use in public schools, as the pupils enrolled in third- and fourth-year foreign language courses are usually a selected population of better than average ability. As noted in the summary below, students' attitudes are crucial, and high intelligence and verbal ability would not, in themselves, guarantee success in a program in which independent study is necessary.

A detailed report, which describes the results of the two years of experimentation and presents Miss Changnon's materials and procedures in detail, is available from the office of the Superintendent of Public Instruction, Springfield, Illinois. The report is entitled, "Techniques in Learning to Hear, Understand, and Use a Foreign Language in High School."

In summarizing the skills needed to support a fourth-year course which requires much independent study, Miss Changnon lists in her report the following requirements for the students:

1. Considerable oral-aural work, some of it with records and tapes
2. Ability to take notes in French and transcribe French dictation
3. Strong foundation in French grammar
4. An extensive French vocabulary and well-developed dictionary skills
5. Resourcefulness in problem solving
6. Willingness to cooperate with the group and to discipline himself when necessary
7. Attitudes of self-reliance, so that he can bridge the gap created by the absence of a teacher to whom he may turn each time he has minor difficulties.

BIOLOGY

Major effort in the biology project was devoted to developing materials to be used by students to help them learn to work on their own in the laboratory, freeing the teacher to help on those problems which demand specialized knowledge and competence. An important practical value sought in this study was that of helping teachers maintain, in the face of rapidly rising enrollments, laboratory programs which encourage students to experience the psychological rewards of discovery through genuine scientific experimentation.

Two years turned out to be a very short time in which to develop the needed materials. The basic notion of locating and collecting information for student use in rearing, breeding, and experimenting with living organisms was found to be a very useful notion, but the task of locating this information in the tremendous variety of possible sources and the task of preparing the information for student use so that it did not raise more questions in students' minds than it answered turned out to be formidable. Nonetheless, a significant number of techniques and devices were located and sufficient experience was gained with this approach to establish its feasibility.

A report of this study tentatively titled, *Manual for Self-Directed Experimentation in Biology* is being published by the office of the Superintendent of Public Instruction, Springfield, Illinois. This report will include the following parts:

1. A description of the staff utilization study
2. An annotated bibliography for use by students and teachers on how to plan and conduct experiments
3. Illustrative techniques and devices and examples of student projects
4. A guide to statistics commonly used in biological sciences, with particular reference to those techniques which can be used by high-school students.

49 / A Comparison of Graded and Non-graded Elementary Schools

Robert F. Carbone

> *We need to know whether the experiences we are providing children and adolescents are having the desired effects. Specifically and especially, changes in school organization and practices, the curriculum, and*

Reprinted from the *Elementary School Journal*, 1961, *62*, 82–88, with the permission of the author and the University of Chicago Press. Copyright 1961 by the University of Chicago.

*teaching methods need continuous experimental evaluation. This
experimental research article on the effect of non-grading on
achievement and mental health presents evidence "in sharp
disagreement with almost all the literature on non-graded organization."
Robert F. Carbone of Emory University proposes six questions that
teachers and administrators can consider when discussing
educational programs for pupil progress.*

The literature of education has in recent years reflected a renewed interest in the problems of elementary-school organization. American education appears to be experiencing another attempt to modify the traditional graded structure of our elementary schools. Despite these attempts, however, the graded school has continued to be predominant (Goodlad, 1960).

Perhaps the most popular suggestion for school reorganization now being discussed by educators is the non-graded school. Many school systems have developed non-graded programs or variations of this idea, but there is a paucity of experimental research in this area. Thus the effectiveness of non-graded organization is yet to be empirically established. This gap in knowledge prompted a recent study to determine the effect of non-grading on the academic achievement and the mental health of pupils who had attended non-graded schools (Carbone, 1961).

Basically, non-grading is a plan to implement continuous pupil progress through a series of achievement levels usually covering the first three years of elementary school. Many articles have been written on the subject, but Goodlad and Anderson (1959) have presented the most comprehensive discussion of non-grading to date.

A number of authors have advocated the reorganization of schools to overcome problems associated with graded structure. For the most part, these writers have tried to build a case for non-grading by citing research evidence on the ill effects of non-promotion. In general, these data tend to show that pupils who at some point were not promoted did not make substantial gains in achievement and often showed greater incidence of social and emotional maladjustment than similar pupils who had been promoted regularly.

Many of these authors suggest that the non-graded school shows promise of promoting social and emotional growth as well as maximum academic achievement, of reducing emotional and social instability in the upper grades, of reducing children's anxieties about success in school, and of generally promoting psychological and mental health in pupils. Because of the lack of experimentation in this area, few of the articles provide convincing evidence that non-grading can actually accomplish such results.

However, it was possible to find a few studies that reported better achievement and better mental-health scores for non-graded pupils than for graded pupils. These studies were conducted in elementary schools that had some form of non-grading. Most of the studies were limited by local conditions or by the lack of rigorous experimental design. For example, it was generally the practice in the studies to compare test results of pupils in these schools before non-grading with test results of pupils after the establishment of a non-graded plan. Often no attempt was made to match pupils or to adjust test scores for differences in intelligence.

Thus, it seemed appropriate to seek more evidence on the effect of the non-graded structure on achievement and mental health. In addition, it was decided to investigate the relation between this plan of organization and the instructional practices of teachers in these schools.

Three hypotheses were established for investigation:

There are no significant differences in the achievement of comparable groups of pupils who have attended graded and non-graded primary schools.

There are no significant differences in the mental health of comparable groups of pupils who have attended graded and non-graded primary schools.

There are no identifiable differences in the instructional practices of teachers in graded and non-graded primary schools.

It was possible to identify two school systems that Goodlad and Anderson (1959, pp. 217–28) list in their survey of non-graded programs. All schools in these systems were categorized according to the socioeconomic level of their attendance area. One school in each of the upper, middle, and lower levels was randomly selected for the study. In each of these schools three classes were randomly selected: a fourth-grade class, a fifth-grade class, and a sixth-grade class. All pupils in these classes who had not attended primary school in either of these non-graded systems were eliminated from further consideration in the study.

Next, two school systems that had primary schools organized under the graded plan were identified. These two graded systems were in communities that were similar to the two communities that had non-graded systems—similar in population, socioeconomic structure, and geographic location. Thus, the four communities were considered to be matched for the purposes of this study. By using sampling procedures similar to those described earlier, it was possible to select a group of fourth-, fifth-, and sixth-grade pupils who had attended graded primary schools. Finally, all possible pairs of graded and non-graded pupils matched for age and sex were selected. This procedure produced a total sample of 122 non-graded pupils and 122 graded pupils. All comparisons of achievement and mental health in this study were based on this sample.

Individual pupils' scores on the Iowa Tests of Basic Skills were obtained from permanent school records. The Mental Health Analysis of the California Test Bureau was administered to all pupils in the sample, and five factors on this instrument were selected for analysis.

Further information on pupil adjustment was obtained by using an experimental instrument known as the Semantic Differential. This instrument contains a list of twenty-five polar word pairs that a respondent may use in describing a person or a concept.

In addition, a questionnaire designed to provide evidence on the instructional practices of teachers was developed and administered to all teachers of primary classes in the graded and the non-graded schools.

ACHIEVEMENT

A comparison was made of six scores that indicated the achievement of graded and non-graded pupils in relation to the national norms provided by the test publishers. Because there was a significant difference in the mean intelligence quotient of the two groups, analysis of covariance was used to adjust the mean achievement scores. Thus, intelligence was held constant in all comparisons.

The results of this procedure, shown in Table 1, indicated that in all areas of achievement (vocabulary, reading comprehension, language, work-study skills, arithmetic) and in total achievement graded pupils scored significantly higher ($P < .01$) than non-graded pupils when the original test scores were adjusted for intelligence. On the basis of these findings it was possible to reject the hypothesis of no significant differences. There was no evidence to indicate that pupils who had attended these non-graded primary schools achieved at a higher level during their fourth, fifth, or sixth years of school than pupils who had attended these graded schools. On the contrary, the differences were all in favor of the graded pupils. However, the data revealed that both graded and non-graded pupils in this study were achieving above the national norms in all six measures of achievement.

MENTAL HEALTH

Comparisons were made of the five selected mental-health factors that provided evidence of the social and emotional adjustment of the graded and the non-graded pupils. Because of the verbal nature of the instrument, analysis of covariance was also used to determine the significance of differences in mean mental-health scores; the procedure compensated for the differences in intelligence.

The results of this procedure, shown in Table 2, indicated that in four out of five mental-health factors there was no significant difference in the adjustment of these graded and non-graded pupils. The four factors were freedom from emotional instability, freedom from feelings of inadequacy, freedom from nervous manifestations, and personal relationships. However, in the fifth factor, social participation, the graded pupils scored significantly higher ($P < .01$) than the non-graded pupils. Thus, the hypothesis of no significant differences was accepted for the first four factors and was rejected for social participation.

Additional information was provided by the Semantic Differential. Regardless of the differences in intelligence, these graded and non-graded

Table 1. Achievement of 122 Graded and 122 Non-graded Pupils as Indicated by Mean Deviations from Expected Grade Equivalents on the Iowa Tests of Basic Skills

| Subtest | Graded | | Non-graded | | Graded | Non-graded | | |
	Unadjusted Mean Deviation	Standard Error	Unadjusted Mean Deviation	Standard Error	Adjusted Mean Deviation	Adjusted Mean Deviation	F	P
Vocabulary	.985	.008	.934	.008	1.224	.695	13.7	<.01
Reading Comprehension	.875	.007	.908	.008	1.133	.650	10.3	<.01
Language	1.132	.009	.763	.006	1.344	.552	35.5	<.01
Work-Study Skills	.789	.007	.691	.006	.978	.501	24.4	<.01
Arithmetic	.731	.006	.484	.004	.867	.348	41.4	<.01
Total Achievement	.896	.007	.753	.006	1.100	.548	29.5	<.01

Table 2. Mental Health of 122 Graded and 122 Non-graded Pupils as Indicated by Mean Scores on the Mental Health Analysis of the California Test Bureau *

| Mental Health Areas | Graded | | Non-graded | | Graded | Non-graded | | |
	Unadjusted Mean	Standard Error	Unadjusted Mean	Standard Error	Adjusted Mean	Adjusted Mean	F	P
Freedom from Emotional Instability	10.2	.084	11.0	.091	10.4	10.8	.02	n.s.
Freedom from Feelings of Inadequacy	10.8	.089	11.7	.097	11.1	11.4	.51	n.s.
Freedom from Nervous Manifestations	13.8	.114	14.0	.116	14.1	13.7	.81	n.s.
Social Participation	15.8	.131	15.2	.126	16.0	15.0	8.01	<.01
Personal Relationships	16.1	.133	16.0	.132	16.4	15.7	3.29	n.s.

n.s. = not significant.

* Highest possible score for each factor is 20.

pupils tended to describe their primary-school teachers similarly on thirteen of the twenty-five word pairs, but on nine other word pairs the descriptions were significantly different. The latter word pairs all connote a definite favorable-pejorative distinction, and in all instances non-graded pupils selected the more favorable word. More specifically, when using these nine discriminating word pairs, non-graded pupils tended to describe their teachers as bright, smooth, sweet, relaxed, big, quiet, interesting, soft, and good. Graded pupils described their teachers as little, loud, boring, hard, dull, rough, sour, stiff, and bad.

These findings offer an interesting contrast to the data on mental health reported here, but because the Semantic Differential does not have established validity as a measure of mental health, the conclusiveness of these results may be questioned.

INSTRUCTIONAL PRACTICES

To obtain information on the instructional practices of teachers, a questionnaire based on a set of criteria related to instruction was administered. The questionnaire was an attempt to determine whether teachers in the non-graded schools were using instructional practices that differed from those used by teachers in the graded schools.

Responses were received from seventeen teachers (30 per cent) in the non-graded primary classes and from fourteen teachers (24 per cent) in the graded primary classes.

Although some differences did appear, the evidence pointing toward areas of similarity was strong. Teachers in the non-graded schools appeared to operate much the same as teachers in the graded schools. Both groups of teachers reported that they instructed groups of about the same size, that they used similar books and materials, that they evaluated pupils in similar ways, and that they were equally aware of pupil differences. However, non-graded teachers more frequently transferred pupils to other classes where instruction was more suited to the pupils' needs. In addition, in non-graded schools, decisions leading to such transfers appeared to be based on the individual pupil's academic growth, while in graded schools the teachers gave more attention to how the pupil compared with other pupils in his class.

Because there were differences as well as similarities in instructional practices, the hypothesis of no differences was accepted only tentatively. However, it was possible to conclude that changes in organizational structure, in this case non-grading, do not produce major changes in the instructional practices teachers use. This evidence supports the contention of Goodlad and Anderson (1959, p. 59) that "the non-graded plan is a system of organization and nothing more."

DISCUSSION

The evidence presented in this study concerning pupil achievement and mental health is in sharp disagreement with almost all the literature on non-graded organization. Most authors in this field expressed extremely optimistic views of the potential benefits of non-grading. In this study the graded pupils exhibited higher achievement than the non-graded pupils although both groups were achieving above national norms. Thus, the lower achievement scores earned by the non-graded pupils cannot be taken as an indictment of this form of school organization. However, this evidence strongly contradicts the notion that a change in school organizational structure, such as non-grading, will in itself produce higher academic achievement.

The evidence on pupils' mental health suggests a similar conclusion. The mental health of non-graded pupils was not significantly different from that of graded pupils in four out of five comparisons. In the fifth area, social participation, graded pupils exhibited better adjustment. Even though these non-graded schools had eliminated non-promotion (or the fear of non-promotion), the only evidence attesting to the positive benefits of this policy was found in the pupils' attitudes toward their teachers as indicated by their descriptions on the Semantic Differential.

Further, it was concluded that the establishment of non-graded structure in these schools did not produce sharp differences in the instructional practices of teachers. This conclusion suggests that it is possible that the admonition to "recognize individual differences" has a common meaning for teachers regardless of the organizational structure of their schools. As a result, the instructional practices they use in allowing for individual differences are very much alike. In addition, it is possible that the textbooks and related teaching materials conventionally available for use in all schools determine the kind of instruction that takes place regardless of how the schools are organized.

The implications of these findings are clear. First, it is not realistic to expect improved academic achievement and personal adjustment in pupils merely on the basis of a change in organizational structure. Second, the attainment of high pupil achievement and good mental health is not a unique result of non-grading. The evidence presented here indicates that these goals can also be attained in an elementary school organized under the conventional graded system.

A third extremely important implication is suggested lest readers see this evidence as an indictment of the whole concept of non-grading. It seems clear that if any new form of school organization is to produce the benefits that its advocates envision, it must be accompanied by appropriate adaptations in the instructional practices of teachers. Changes in organizational structure alone are not enough.

What, then, must be done to help non-grading realize its potential? Certainly if schools are to be organized to promote the continuous progress of each pupil, instruction must become increasingly individualized. Teachers and administrators must learn to view each child in terms of his individual potential and rate of growth. Faculties in non-graded schools must determine the skills, the knowledge, and the understandings that are to be attained at each of the many levels through which pupils progress. Teachers must identify or create instructional materials that not only contribute to the attainment of these goals but that are also adapted to a more individualized instructional program. Many of the materials should be self-teaching or self-testing in nature, thus allowing pupils to work individually at an appropriate level of sophistication.

Finally, the whole area of evaluation must be given much more attention. If individual attainments are to be evaluated, teachers must identify or create appropriate evaluation devices based on the goals at each level and adapted to the individualized program of instruction in the school. In addition, improved means of collecting and recording such evaluative evidence on pupil attainment must be developed so that teachers and administrators will have the necessary tools in making decisions about the advancement of individual pupils.

Thus, it seems unrealistic to expect non-graded schools to realize the benefits their advocates hope for without first considering the demands that continuous progress implies. These demands may be expressed in a series of questions that teachers and administrators can consider in discussing non-grading or any other program of continuous progress.

First, do we have clear statements of our instructional objectives organized in a realistic sequence and covering the entire span of our program?

Second, do we have a sufficient variety of instructional materials on different levels of sophistication so that each teacher can adjust instruction to the range of abilities found in each classroom?

Third, are we able to move toward greater individualization of instruction so that pupils can actually progress at individual rates?

Fourth, are we willing to use grouping practices that are flexible enough to allow easy movement from group to group within a class or from class to class within a school?

Fifth, do we have evaluation devices, based on our instructional objectives, that will provide clear evidence of pupil attainments and thus facilitate our decisions on grouping and progress?

And sixth, are we sufficiently committed to that educational shibboleth—recognizing individual differences—to do something about the differences that we have so long "recognized"?

Attention to questions of this nature are necessary first steps in the development of any program for continuous progress. Without such basic considerations it is difficult to see how non-grading, or any other form of organization for that matter, can realize its potential.

Community Practices

50 / The Prevention of Mental Illness

Donald C. Klein

This selection describes a team approach in fostering mental health. For ten years in Wellesley, Massachusetts, a mental-health center has been joining forces with professional and nonprofessional community groups to strengthen services to the schools and to the community. The wide range of activities of the service include discussions with parents of children entering kindergarten, workshops for teachers preparatory to their first marking and reporting conferences with parents, consultation with teachers about individual pupils and groups of children, identification of children with problems, and short-term therapy. Donald C. Klein is a member of the Human Relations Service of Wellesley.

This discussion will concern itself with an approach to the prevention of mental illness evolved by Dr. Erich Lindemann (1953) and his associates at Harvard University during the past 10 years and exemplified by the Human Relations Service of Wellesley, a mental health center in a suburban community of 24,000 people outside Boston (Hunt, 1953). The focus of attention upon issues of mental health and illness in the community, while embracing many lines of inquiry, has not included several important areas of study carried on in different types of settings. Studies of constitutional and genetic factors and the transmission of the potentials for mental illnesses, increased knowledge of the intra-uterine environment of the fetus and attempts at the identification of specific toxic and illness-producing features of man's environment are all essential to a comprehensive attack upon the varied mental illnesses of mankind. Knowledge of the role of German measles in mental deficiency has alerted physicians

Reprinted from *Mental Hygiene*, 1961, *45*, 101–9, with the permission of the author and The National Association of Mental Health.

and pregnant women to the wisdom of attempting to avoid infection during pregnancy. Understanding of the connection between syphilis and general paresis has led to the marked reduction of this brain disorder in the population. Other examples could be cited, and new instances should be forthcoming as the result of other studies.

While recognizing the importance of physical, constitutional and genetic factors in the community and its population, the community mental health approach has concentrated primarily upon the interrelationships between the individual and his social environment. As a result, the team of people concerned with mental health issues has been expanded to include sociologists, anthropologists, social psychologists, public health workers trained in the study of the mass features of disease and, more recently, architects and city planners, in addition to the usual trio of the psychiatrist, psychiatric social worker and clinical psychologist.

The community mental health approach necessarily began with the study of individual cases of mental ill-health. Scrutiny of these individual casualties suggested areas of the social environment which deserved the attention of the mental health team. Consequent studies of certain common life predicaments soon led to the identification of groups in the community that served to help large numbers of people during times of stress. Gradually it became clear that the cause of community mental health could best be served by a concentration upon the *population* of the community rather than upon the individual case alone.

This shift in focus from the individual case to the population is basic to community-centered efforts towards prevention of mental illnesses. It has permitted important lines of questioning of an order not possible on the basis of the study of the individual case alone. One such line of questioning concerns the sequence of events whereby certain individuals become so emotionally distressed or abnormal in their behavior as to warrant psychiatric care. For example, an extensive study of suicide suggests that the attempt at self-destruction is a final stage in a series of progressively less successful efforts of the victim to establish an effective balance between himself and his social environment (Sifneos, Gore, and Sifneos, 1956). Another series of observations of delinquency has led to the formulation of a so-called delinquency process involving the individual in an increasingly wide region of alienation between himself and his family, his neighborhood and the officially sanctioned institutions and activities of the community.

Another line of questioning made possible by a population or ecological focus concerns the distribution of certain disorders in the community. It is hardly accidental, for instance, that child guidance clinics and others consistently find that among children with learning and behavior disorders boys outnumber girls by a ratio of two or three to one. Such a ratio may have little or no significance for the treatment of the individual boy or girl suffering from a behavior disorder. However, the more we know about the factors contributing to this ratio, the better-equipped we will be to carry on more adequate *preventive* mental health work with the child population. It may be that alteration of child rearing and educational patterns will reduce the number of male children with emotional problems. On the other hand, it may be that more effective case finding measures will identify the girls with less obvious emotional problems who show up in later years in centers caring for late adolescents and young adults. The characteristic rates of incidence or identification of emotional disorders are only beginning to be discovered. The reasons behind them will only be understood if mental health centers throughout the country undertake painstaking research at the population level.

The shift in focus from the individual to the population necessarily involves some major alterations in the patterns of operation of the mental health unit itself. The following paragraphs will delineate the requisite changes in perspective and functions in terms of a sequence of modifications—from the traditional clinic to the preventively oriented center:

1. Consider the position of the treatment-oriented mental hygiene clinic in the community. Such a clinic devotes most, if not all, of its time to the careful diagnostic study of sick individuals and to the treatment of those persons for whom outpatient psychotherapy seems either most urgently needed or most promising. In most such clinics the workers concentrate primarily upon the psychic malfunctioning of the individual casualty. The social workers are sometimes delegated the task of assessing the current social environment of the patient; they are also usually the ones responsible for interpreting to professionals and others in the community the policies, the strengths and limitations of the clinic. The basic responsibility is to the patient who has entered the doors of the clinic. The needs of those *unable* to get help because of waiting lists—and most clinics have them—or *unwilling* to get help because of misunderstanding of psychological problems or the nature of psychiatric help are not the responsibility of the professional staff.

2. An increasing number of treatment centers, including virtually all child guidance clinics, have extended their focus to include one or more members of the immediate families of their patients. Mothers—and more recently fathers—have been encouraged and sometimes required to participate in the treatment of the child patients. The aim of such treatment is, in part, an alteration of patterns of interaction between the family members in question. One of the basic ingredients of the community mental health approach—namely, the concern with the balance between the individual and his environment—is clearly present.

3. The therapist in the mental hygiene clinic, however, often hears of other spheres of environment-individual interactions beyond the family unit, thus becoming aware of a broader network of relevant social relationships of the patient. Many patients have particularly unsatisfactory associations with neighbors, fellow club members or potential friends in a variety of settings. Some seem especially restricted in such contacts. Limited as he is to the patient's interpretation of the social milieu, the therapist is usually not in a position to assess specific characteristics of the

social environment itself. He learns only how it appears to the patient. He does not usually know which features of the social environment could be modified to the patient's advantage nor is he in any position to effect such changes should he wish to do so.

4. As the therapist works with individual patients and their families, he is also often aware of the existence of other professional or semiprofessional people whose activities affect the life of the patient. Community-centered treatment clinics have become increasingly cognizant of the needs of these professional groups for an understanding of mental hygiene principles and the use of psychiatric resources. As was suggested above, the psychiatric social worker, responsible for the initial contacts with prospective patients, is usually the team member in most direct contact with the physicians, clergymen, educators and others who refer the greatest number of patients to the treatment clinic. The quality of the referral itself—the nature of the preparation given the patient by the referring person—may sometimes spell the difference between successful and unsuccessful care. Therefore, some clinics have devoted much time and attention to helping the various professional groups in the community learn how to recognize those needing psychiatric care and how to help them accept such need.

5. Having entered into contact with the professional groups in the community, the mental hygiene clinic has taken another major step in the direction of a preventive orientation. Even such dissimilar shapes as "triangle" and "circle" can be drawn in a series with such gradual changes from one to the other that it is very difficult to determine where the triangle stops and the circle begins. Similarly, there is no clear dividing line between a treatment and preventive orientation, even though the general outlines of one approach markedly differ—as has been discussed—from the general outlines of the other. Nevertheless, it is believed that a basic alteration in focus has occurred when the mental health team devotes a major part of its attention to the caretaking relationships between the professional or semiprofessional groups in the community and the individuals, family units and other clusterings of people in the population with whom they are in contact. In certain respects, the caretaking resources of the community, available to large numbers of people facing common life predicaments at different stages in their lives, are analogous in the mental health field to the sewage disposal and water supply systems in *their* function of maintaining a physically healthy community. Once having accepted this basic premise, the mental health team must determine whether or not to relinquish a primary treatment focus upon the individual patient-casualty in favor of a preventive focus designed to bring it into contact with the community and its population in other more strategic and appropriate ways.

6. Functions are like pie in that they can be cut from many angles and into any number of pieces. We have chosen to think of the mental health unit as having three major service areas: *clinical, consultative* and *educational.* Moreover, as indicated earlier, *research* operations are considered

to be an essential component which will ultimately reduce the size of the gap between present knowledge and skill and the preventive goals of such a center.

The more specific activities of a mental health center can be described first in relation to professional groups in the community and second in relation to nonprofessional segments of the population. There appear to be four kinds of joint pursuits in which the mental health center and professional caretaking groups in the community can join forces: (A) Consultation; (B) Inservice Training; (C) Study of Hazards; (D) Case Finding. The specific work with caretakers will be taken up in terms of the pattern of mental health operations developed in the Wellesley schools by the Human Relations Service. This selection is made because the school program illustrates all four types of functions in operation.

A. CONSULTATION

At the base of the collaboration with the schools is an interest on both sides of providing the healthiest possible emotional environment for all children, the healthy as well as the psychologically handicapped. At the classroom level, service is provided via consultation with teachers about individual pupils or groups of children. Mental health consultants visit each school on a regularly scheduled basis—at two or three week intervals —designed to provide help within a reasonable period of time without causing the teacher to become overly dependent upon the outside expert. These contacts are viewed as a collaboration between two peers from different professions. The emphasis is on arriving at an understanding of the psychological needs of the child and on helping the teacher enlarge her own abilities to meet these needs. The consultant is usually in a good position to support a teacher as she undertakes the emotionally demanding job of responding in a helpful fashion to irritating and baffling pupil behaviors and of avoiding the temptation to dismiss or stereotype the child as incorrigible, hopeless or beyond redemption. Consultation of this kind may lead to two desirable outcomes for the teacher, in addition to the help provided the children on whom consultation is focused.

First, it often frees the teacher from an irritating, frustrating and time-consuming interpersonal struggle with the pupil, which robs her of the time and energy that would be properly devoted to all the children in her class.

Second, it adds to the professional skill and personal empathy of the teacher, allowing her to be a more helpful adult with present and future pupils. It is believed to be helpful for the mental health consultant to come from a base outside the school system itself. Such a person is less subject to pressures from within the system and more easily able to maintain objectivity. The consultant is also less apt to be seen as a supervisor or a person whose evaluations may affect the teacher's professional career.

The classroom environment is itself affected by forces operating in the school building and the system as a whole. Interpersonal conflicts among teachers, teachers and principals, subject supervisors and classroom instructors, central administration and building personnel, older and younger educators or those with different educational philosophies and—hardly least—between the educators and the surrounding community may all set up tension systems leading to increased pressures on children and a disruption of the stability of the classroom itself. For this reason, consultation is extended to include all special personnel, building principals and central administration as well as the citizen school committee itself. A number of important issues involving interpersonal tensions, administrative problems and school-community relationships have been brought to the attention of the consulting team. The latter is helped in this phase of the work by the continuing inquiries of the mental health center into the socio-economic characteristics, attitudes and value orientations and neighborhood dynamics of the community and its various sections. By bringing sociological perspectives to the schools, the consultants have helped school personnel analyze and work constructively with pressures brought to bear upon them by parents and others.

B. INSERVICE TRAINING

The educational benefits of consultation are supplemented, when requested, by special inservice training programs for school personnel. Workshops on mental health subjects have been held from time to time. Special meetings have been arranged with groups of teachers to report back to them results of the center's researches bearing upon their work.

C. STUDY OF HAZARDS

The center's emphasis upon the importance of environmental hazards to emotional growth and development has been adopted with increasing vigor by the schools. Two years ago, for example, the guidance council composed of teachers, the school psychologist, remedial reading and speech personnel, a nurse and a physician, guidance counselors, building administrators, the superintendent and assistant superintendent of schools and the director of elementary education—devoted a school year to a study of major transition points in the educational career of the child. In addition to school entry, this group considered the special demands of the shift from the primary to intermediate curriculum, from elementary neighborhood schools to a centralized junior high, from junior to senior high schools and from high school to more advanced institutions. The needs of children at these different points in the life cycle were balanced against institutional demands and the shifting patterns of relationship between the school and the home as the children moved through the system.

Since 1950 the schools and the mental health center have been co-operating on a study of a group of children seen initially either prior to their entry into school or during their kindergarten year. Preschool assessments of children's ability to meet appropriate work demands have proved to be highly predictive of school adjustment during the kindergarten and primary years. The study is also concerned with the varied patterns or styles of adjustment shown by the children in relation to teachers, peers and the demands of the curriculum (Gruber, 1954; Lindemann and Ross, 1957; McGinnis, 1954).

D. CASE FINDING

The identification of troubled children for whom outside psychiatric treatment may be indicated is a responsibility shared by a number of different people in the school system. In the most strategic position is the teacher, who often is in a position to review a child's development with a questioning parent and to help the parent make use of the center's clinical services. In this work the teacher is able to rely not only upon the mental health consultant but also upon her principal as well as the school psychologist and reading specialist, who stand ready to carry out special studies of the child's intellectual, emotional and educational potentialities. A survey of case finding carried out last school year by the guidance council (mentioned above) indicated that screening for emotionally disturbed or handicapped children was also being carried on by the school nurse and physician, the guidance personnel in the secondary schools and those in charge of physical education.

Specific activities with nonprofessional groups in the community are considered separately only for convenience in presentation. These activities—(A) Special clinics; (B) Brief clinical services; (C) Mental health education; and (D) Preventive group counseling—are part of a total Gestalt involving an integrated approach to both help-seeking and help-giving groups:

A. SPECIAL CLINICS

An immediate example of the integrated approach is found in the fact that the schools co-operate with the center in a preschool check-up service for families of children about to enter kindergarten. This free service is offered to all prekindergarteners and is publicized through the schools. It is presented to the parents as an equivalent to the preschool physical and dental examinations. The so-called "check-up" includes a brief screening contact with the child in a structured playroom setup, observation of the manner in which the child and parent react to the separation from one another during the contact and one or more interviews with the parent to review the child's social and emotional development. Almost half the parents have come with long-standing concerns about some feature of their children's development. In some instances, the brief screening contact has led to a more protracted diagnostic study and later arrangements for appropriate treatment. Many parents have felt that the preschool service has provided a helpful opportunity to gain a new perspective on their children and themselves as parents; as a result, they have felt better prepared to present their children—and of course themselves—to the school.

B. BRIEF CLINICAL SERVICES

It was stated earlier that a treatment center usually cannot take responsibility for those unable to secure treatment because of limited professional resources or because they cannot bring themselves to make use of available help. The community mental health center, however, having been given sanction to concentrate upon the population of a community, must take responsibility, however limited, for these people as well as for those not yet in need of care or who may never need psychiatric treatment. At the Human Relations Service in Wellesley we have attempted to meet these responsibilities in several ways. In 1952 the staff made a most difficult decision to give up all long-term treatment of psychiatric disorders. It was possible to take such action only because the staff had already been developing some alternative means of deploying its clinical skills. A clinical service is maintained which provides for the diagnostic study of psychiatric problems and the appraisal of the settings in which they are found. Following such appraisals, a few cases are referred to treatment centers or are put on a follow-up basis, often in collaboration with a physician, clergyman or the local family agency. About 40 per cent are seen in treatment for brief periods ranging from a few weeks to a few months, during times of crisis. By limited use of staff time and avoiding long-term therapy, it is possible to maintain this service for all requesting help, without resorting to a selective intake or to waiting lists. In this way it is possible to keep in touch with a wide range of problems as they arise in the general population and to note any major fluctuations in the nature or severity of problems from season to season or year to year.

C. MENTAL HEALTH EDUCATION

Education in the mental health field—just as in the general public health area—of necessity involves the team in the profound process of culture change. To be successful, it must challenge and alter some cherished beliefs and well-accepted ways of behaving. Successful health education should provide useful and acceptable alternatives to such beliefs and behaviors.

The approaches to mental health education in Wellesley have reflected the population-oriented frame of reference developed in this presentation. Consideration has been given to the target groups, to the readiness of those involved, to the common life dilemmas faced by those with whom programs are developed and to the outcomes to be expected from the educational efforts. At the present time the Wellesley center initiates no educational programs of its own. It is, however, highly responsive to requests for such programs coming from other groups, organizations and institutions.

We used to believe that many requests for talks on mental health themes coming from PTA's, women's groups, service organizations and the like represented the culmination of a program chairman's efforts to come as close as possible to Kinsey at no cost to the organization. We were, therefore, pleased to discover that most program chairmen and their committees were delighted to spend several hours with mental health staff discussing the kind of program best suited to their members' needs. Indeed, often the request for a speaker has turned out to be an expression of genuine interest in some facet of the field by one or more of those planning the program. In some instances, the planning sessions have been more rewarding for all concerned than the subsequent large meeting. Face to face educational methods involving ample opportunities for two-way communication have been favored. Small group discussions are primarily used. Large meeting techniques and workshop methods developed by the group dynamics field and members of the adult education profession also have been widely employed.

D. PREVENTIVE GROUP COUNSELING

Preventive group counseling is a form of face-to-face education with therapeutic components carried out with those facing similar emotional hazards. Each year, for example, so-called human relations seminars are carried on with beginning student nurses at the local nursing school (Rosenberg and Fuller, 1955). These students, meeting 12 to 15 times in small, informal discussion groups led by a psychologist or psychiatrist, are helped to discuss the major strains experienced by most of them as they leave home and begin their training in an emotionally demanding field. Other instances of preventive counseling—or, as they are sometimes called, "crisis groups"—have included discussion series with parents of children entering kindergarten (Klein and Ross, 1958) and a workshop series for teachers preparing to hold their first marking and reporting conferences with parents.

To summarize what has been discussed so far: The distinction has been made between a treatment-oriented mental hygiene clinic and a preventively oriented mental health center. The former often is cognizant of the social environment of the patient and is in touch with key professional groups who may make the most intelligent use of the treatment resource. Nevertheless, its major responsibility is to the patient. The mental health center's primary emphasis is upon the state of the equilibrium between the individual and the social environment. It is especially concerned with the common life predicaments experienced by many or most individuals at all points in the life cycle. It seeks to work closely with those professional and semiprofessional caretaking people who play important roles in the development of the individual and who are in a position to offer support and guidance at times of stress. Its major responsibility is to a population of people, including those making use of direct clinical and educational services as well as those unable or unwilling to use these services and those not in need of them.

At this point let us return to an examination of the implications of the population focus alluded to briefly at the outset of this paper. It is no doubt apparent that the community mental health orientation presented here is not based simply upon the principle of bringing more psychiatry to more people. Community mental health is not conceived of as the wholesaling of a commodity which heretofore has been marketed at a retail level by the therapist to his patient. Rather, the community mental health team seeks access to populations of people and the social-emotional environments in which they live for purposes which, though easily stated, can more often be pursued than attained.

The mental health center, first of all, attempts to find ways to keep track of the varying distributions of emotional disruptions in different segments of the population.

Second, it tries to locate itself in such a way that it can observe and study the earliest possible stages of development of responses to a variety of life predicaments. It studies both the successful and unsuccessful patterns of response to stresses and seeks to identify those factors in individuals, social groups and the wider culture, which contribute to the adaptive or maladaptive resolutions. As it explores these questions with the many key groups and individuals in the community, it also attempts to develop conjointly with them specific approaches of a preventive nature, which it then must evaluate and refine. Increasingly, preventive programs appear to become more and more specific in nature, focusing on limited target groups with respect to particular issues of growth and development and to circumscribed events believed to be emotionally hazardous to certain people. Viewed in these terms, a community mental health program should be evaluated primarily in light of its short-term impact upon specific disruptions in specific groups of people at specific points in the life cycle. There is no evidence at present to suggest that we are close to an understanding of the ingredients for the long-range immunization of individuals against emotional breakdown. A "healthy" child may fall prey to an adult emotional disorder just as the child who is free from diphtheria may succumb to cancer as an adult. The foundations of the adult's emotional health or ill-health are usually clearly apparent in the retrospective analysis of the sick patient; prediction of adult stability or instability from the careful study of the child's emotional status, however, is not so certain.

Thus, the term "prevention" itself must be carefully defined. Indications are that mental illness is not a unitary disease but rather a term applied to a variety of maladaptive responses to particularly noxious environmental factors. Some of these factors are physical or physiological in nature, others are social and psychological. For the present, at least, it seems wisest to concentrate preventive efforts on the control of particular unsuitable reactions under defined stress conditions. It is not yet possible to plan a program for school age children, designed to insure health, wealth and happiness in adulthood. Yet it is certainly possible to plan a preventive program designed to help the greatest number of children make the transition from home to kindergarten with the least possible amount of undue tensions, tears or tantrums—on the part of child or parent.

51 / Mobilizing Community Resources for Youth: Identification and Treatment of Maladjusted, Delinquent, and Gifted Children

Paul H. Bowman, Robert F. DeHaan,
John K. Kough, and Gordon P. Liddle

"An average American community with its own resources of persons and finances can significantly improve the mental-health level and the extent of the use of the talent of its children when interested persons in the community are given information and training in scientific methods of human development." This is the basic hypothesis of the Quincy [Illinois] Youth Development Commission, a ten-year action-research program to discover and to help children with potential talent and children with potential emotional maladjustment. This article by Paul H. Bowman, director of the project, gives a brief account of the design and method of the experiment.

Many communities seek to give their children the best possible chance to grow into happy, useful citizens. Yet all communities know that every group of children suffers from wastage resulting from maladjustment and from failure to develop and use talents. Some of these children grow up to become delinquents and criminals, some become emotionally disturbed

Reprinted from *Supplementary Educational Monographs*, No. 85, 1956, pp. 1–11, with the permission of the authors and the University of Chicago Press. Copyright 1956 by the University of Chicago.

and maladjusted adults, and some with unusual talents fail to discover and make use of them.

The general motivation for a project such as the Community Youth Development Program springs from the growing national concern for the conservation and development of our human resources, especially the conservation of mental health and the development of talent. The cost of mental ill health is much larger than the country can afford. There is great concern about the heavy cost of crime and juvenile delinquency, the loss to industry from inept dealing with employees and their problems of human relations, and the difficulty of providing adequate education for citizenship in a democracy. Finally, the nation is beginning to realize the great loss to the world that occurs through failure to recognize and develop talents and abilities that exist in many persons often unknown to themselves and others.

The more specific motivation for this project stemmed from a seven-year observational study of the personal and social development of youth in a midwestern community recently completed by members of the Committee on Human Development at the University of Chicago. Those working with this study found themselves observing signs of maladjustment and signs of talent in young people and frequently saw the maladjustment develop into serious social problems and the talent go undeveloped, but, because of the observational nature of the study, they were not empowered to attempt remedial action.

At this point it was resolved to undertake as soon as possible an experimental project which not only would discover potential talent and emotional maladjustment but would also be aimed at a developmental and preventive program for those individuals in need of it. The project was to emphasize the early discovery of symptoms of maladjustment, so that many children could be given help that might prevent their becoming serious problems. Early discovery of special talents of children would make possible their fuller development through the provision of information, exploration of interests, and additional training.

AVAILABLE RESOURCES

Community facilities for help in these areas are usually inadequate. Most of the existing agencies are doing effective work, regardless of their particular name or theoretical orientation; but, as a rule, their budgets and staffs are limited. Clinics of all kinds (mental-hygiene clinics, counseling centers, child-guidance clinics, psychological clinics, marriage counselors, etc.) can point to a high degree of success in helping their clients to more effective and happy living. Such services need to be greatly expanded, but there are certain problems that the clinics will always have difficulty in meeting. For instance, the clinics that exist are reaching only a small percentage of the people needing services. Many persons do not seek help because of lack of knowledge of clinic services, because of misconceptions about their use, and because of fear of asking for help; and clinics usually have no means of discovering or making contact with those persons needing help who do not take the initiative to seek out professional assistance. Again, clinics exist in relatively few communities, and the supply of adequately trained professional persons is so limited that many communities cannot rely upon the possibility of establishing clinic services for many years to come. Nevertheless, at the present time clinics and practicing clinicians are our major resources for the improvement of mental health.

Other sources for professional help are the trained counselors attached to the staffs of various institutions in the community, such as industries, schools, hospitals, or courts. While the number of such positions is increasing, they face limitations similar to the clinics.

A largely untapped resource is that group of persons found in every community who are concerned about problems of human development and who work with people in personal and professional ways but who are relatively untrained in psychological areas. There are many of these people, such as public school teachers, nurses, social welfare agency personnel, Scout leaders, Sunday-school teachers, religious workers, and recreation and other group workers. They are aware of the needs of youth and have daily contact with the young people, but they usually feel inadequate to render assistance in personal and emotional problems.

HYPOTHESES TO BE TESTED

This background of thinking led the Committee on Human Development to form a research committee to plan and initiate an experimental program designed to throw light on questions such as these: What can communities do to help prevent, or to solve, the personal and social problems of their children? How can existing research knowledge and clinically developed techniques be made available to local communities in a usable form? Can a youth development program be devised, the operation of which will rely mainly on residents in the community and require a minimum of expenditure of funds?

Obviously, such questions could best be explored in an action-research project in an actual community setting, and the research committee undertook to design such a program.

The basic, general hypothesis might be stated in the following terms: An average American community with its own resources of persons and finances can significantly improve the mental-health level and the extent of the use of the talent of its children when interested persons in the community are given information and training in scientific methods of human development. Additional, more specific, hypotheses might be stated as follows:

1. Screening techniques can be devised that will successfully identify

the potentially maladjusted (withdrawn and aggressive) and the potentially talented children in the early elementary grades.

2. Capable volunteers can be recruited in a community to work with children in a youth development program.

3. These volunteers, when given appropriate training, can make a significant improvement in the mental health and talent development of the children they work with.

4. The efforts of the volunteer and professional staffs for these specially selected children will significantly improve the community youth-serving facilities.

DESIGN OF PROJECT

To test this general hypothesis, the following design was formulated for the experimental project:

1. The experimental group would include all children in the fourth grade of the public schools in the beginning year of the project. The control group would include all children in the sixth grade of the public schools in the same beginning year.

2. A battery of tests would be given to both experimental and control groups during the first project year to discover potential maladjustment in the children and the presence of special talents.

3. A staff of volunteer counselors from the local community would be selected and given a course of training. They would then be divided into counseling teams that would work with individual children.

4. Those children of the experimental group who scored highest in potential maladjustment and highest in special talents would make up the case loads of counseling teams that would study the children further and, from their own membership and from the community at large, muster all the aid possible to assist the children's development. Children in the control group would be given no special help other than that which the community would ordinarily have offered.

5. The experimental group would be studied and assisted for ten years by the counseling teams. Identical records on individual children and their development would be kept for both experimental and control groups.

6. At the end of ten years the experimental and the control groups would be compared on all possible measures indicative of the mental health and talent development of the two groups. Some of these would be: delinquency rate, divorce rate, academic progress, school drop-outs, percentage going to college, employment records, and creative and artistic productions.

7. Further evaluation of the project would be made by assessing the changes in the community itself and in the programs of the various agencies that could legitimately be attributed wholly or partially to the work

of the project. Changes in the programs of individual agencies, develop-ment of new or different methods of work, the increase of co-operative efforts among agencies, community demand for additional services, in-creasing use of existing services, additions to staff, improvement in the training level of staff personnel—all would be indexes of general com-munity change. However, in order to determine the role of the project in producing such changes, these measures might have to be compared with the youth-serving programs of neighboring cities.

DEFINITION OF EXPERIMENTAL AND CONTROL GROUPS

In an experimental study such as this, special care must be taken to define the experimental and the control groups and to make sure that the two groups are substantially alike in all respects except the differences in-troduced by the experiment. The problem of defining the two groups was complicated by the fact that some children were continually leaving the community and others coming in, so that, to a limited extent, the experi-mental and the control groups had shifting populations. A strict defini-tion of these two groups is given below. They are referred to as the "X Group" (experimental) and the "Y Group" (control).

The experimental group (X Group). Basically, the experimental group was composed of children who were in the fourth grade in the public schools in 1951–52. Thus, most children of this group were born in 1942.

Not all the children included in the experimental group were in the regular fourth-grade classrooms of the public schools. Of the children in the educable mentally handicapped rooms (EMH rooms) in 1951–52, the project included in the experimental group only those born in 1941. This exception was made on the assumption that all these children would have been retarded at least one year if they had been kept in the regular curric-ulum. Pupils in crippled children's classes (CC rooms) in 1951–52 were included if they were born in 1942, or if they were born in 1941 and had an intelligence quotient (I.Q.) below 90, on the assumption that the latter would be retarded one year. Children in sight-saving classes (SS rooms) who were born in 1942 were included in the experimental group.

Children from the fourth grade of a local Methodist-supported boys' school and of the Lutheran parochial school were included as part of the experimental group. Catholic parochial schools were invited to join in this study, but they found it inadvisable to do so.

The records of children in the experimental group who moved out of the city were put in a special file. Some will return to this city and re-enter the study. In any case, we shall know what percentage of children leaves the community during the study and what portion of these had been screened out as potentially maladjusted or potentially talented.

In general, we have added to the experimental group all children who entered school here from out of the city who were in the fourth grade in 1951–52. We added these in-migrants to the experimental group and noted the year they arrived, up to the beginning of the fifth project year. These later in-migrants will probably not be helped much by our study, but we plan to keep account of them, especially as they contribute to delinquency figures. In-migrants have usually been tested during their year of arrival and added to the special groups if they belong there.

The control group (Y Group). The same criteria of inclusion and exclusion were applied to the control group, made up of children in the sixth grade in 1951–52. This group consisted mainly of children who were born in 1940.

CHILDREN RECEIVING SPECIAL ATTENTION

To identify the children who would benefit from special help, the project has screened two general groups: (1) the maladjusted group and (2) the gifted group (those with special talents).

1. The maladjusted group. Two kinds of maladjustment are generally recognized: aggressive and passive.

a. *Aggressive maladjustment.* This is typified by the youngster who cannot control his impulses and who gets into trouble because he breaks rules, steals or destroys property, fights and quarrels, or defies his parents and teachers. This is the child who is often labeled "predelinquent." At least, he is vulnerable to delinquency.

b. *Passive maladjustment.* At the other extreme from the child who is aggressively maladjusted is the youngster who is pathologically timid, who withdraws from society, who is insecure and afraid, and who shows signs of the kind of behavior that may eventually result in placement in a mental hospital. This child has been variously labeled as "withdrawn," "overinhibited," or "schizoid."

Discovery of this child was often difficult, because he was so inconspicuous. Furthermore, maladjustment of this type cannot always be separated from a stable and healthy introversion exhibited by some children. But, when evidence was secured on both the social behavior and the personality characteristics of children, the maladjusted ones could be distinguished by disclosure of pronounced inferiority feelings, anxiety, and depression.

2. The gifted group. The gifted children are defined as those who have special abilities or talents of social value. These include: (a) high intelligence; (b) talent in the fine arts, such as painting, music, and writing; (c) special abilities in a variety of socially useful areas, such as mechanics, science, dramatics, athletics, human relations, social organization; and (d) creative talent, or the ability to make new and novel solutions to problems.

SCREENING PROCEDURES

The earliest age at which selection by group testing was practical appeared to be about nine, or at the fourth-grade level. Special abilities as well as problem behavior were fairly noticeable at this age, and children could read and write well enough to take group tests and answer questionnaires. The screening process was continuous from the age of nine, but every effort was made to do the first screening thoroughly, in order to select children and begin helping them as early as possible.

Thus, toward the end of Grade IV all children in the public schools of the community were brought into the project and were studied. Test data already available in the schools were used, and new tests, including sociometric tests, were given. Every child was treated like every other child in the program, up to the end of the first screening. Special tests were then given to selected children on whom more information was desired. At the same time the teachers and other adults acquainted with the children were asked to fill out check lists and rating scales on all the children in this age group.

Thus, the fourth-graders were screened, and those in need of special help were identified. Always the entire age group was under study, and the screening process was to go on less intensively during the years following Grade IV in order to discover talent and problem behavior which emerge at later ages.

To date all screening tests have been administered at least once, and some of the personality measures have been given three times. From these data we have made predictions of the high-priority children for maladjustment and talent. These instruments and procedures are described in Part I of this report, along with the results of studies of the tests that have been completed thus far.

TREATMENT PROGRAM

The program for helping the children who were discovered to be in need of help consisted in training a corps of local people to work with youth, and these people were assigned to work in teams with the children. This program proposed to help the community make more efficient use of the people and the facilities it already had for work with children. It was to be no added expense to the community.

The treatment program, as predicted, has used the facilities and techniques of existing agencies in the community. . . . The professional staff has also seen fit to initiate a number of activities which have not existed in the community in the hope that they will be taken up and used permanently. . . . Probably the most unexpected difficulty in the treatment program was that of establishing contact with selected children and initiating the action in their behalf, and we as a staff have learned much from these experiences. . . . Part III of this report describes the activities in which the treatment of individual children has involved consultation with community organizations about programs.

VOLUNTEER TRAINING PROGRAM

The local community volunteers consisted at first of about sixty persons—school teachers and church-school teachers, public health nurses, Scout leaders, YMCA and YWCA staff members, social workers, court employees, and parents. These people studied for nine months in a training program that met once a week under the guidance of the University consultants. They studied individual children by a case-study procedure, using cases of various kinds, with special emphasis on the three types to be served in the project. The case studies were drawn from other communities. Not until the end of the year did they begin to study local children.

Toward the close of the year the volunteers were divided into teams of five or six persons. Each team included persons of various skills and interests; for example, a teacher, a nurse, a Scout leader, a social worker, and a counselor. At first, consultants from the University were also members of these teams.

The team became the basic element in the treatment program. Each team had assigned to it a number of children, the talented as well as the maladjusted. The team studied its children, one by one, and devised plans for helping them. It then put these plans into effect, drawing upon its knowledge of the community and its knowledge of children to do the best job that could be done with the community's facilities. The team was to follow a child assigned to it from the start, when he was nine or ten years old, until he grew up.

Essentially, this program was one of discovering children with needs which might otherwise go unnoticed and putting them "on the conscience" of a small group in the community, who would keep on studying and trying to help the children until they grew up. The team used whatever methods it thought best. Seldom did team members actually talk with a child or his parents; more often they worked through his teacher, pastor, or Scout leader.

It is at this point, however, that the original design of the project underwent some revision. The teams were unable to function as effectively as it had been hoped. In our second monograph we reviewed some of the major difficulties they were having in following the original plan of work. (Bowman, et al., 1953) (1) Teams were having considerable difficulty in geographical overlap of their cases. The same teacher might be receiving visits from three or four workers from different teams, and she might feel harried and somewhat unco-operative. (2) There was considerable tension in the teams about trying to work in the background without any direct contact with the child or his family. There was a vague fear of what the parents would think if it was ever discovered that someone else was working "secretly" in the interests of their child. Furthermore, without any direct contacts with the child or family, the volunteers were denied the basic satisfactions that they needed to keep up their interest and feel accomplishment in their work. (3) Team members experienced another major difficulty in establishing contact with the child or people close to him. They were at times regarded with suspicion by those who knew nothing of the project, and they frequently had no previous acquaintance with the area of town or the family involved. And, too, the volunteers were very unsure of themselves and what they could or should do in this new and unique role. There were no precedents to follow. (4) There was a lack of community facilities where the children could be referred for remedial services.

During the second year the teams were reorganized to try to minimize some of these difficulties for the members. Teams were set up on an area basis, so that the same team would take all the cases in any one school. Team members selected the area in which they had the largest number of contacts with the school and the community. This made possible more permanent relations between the teams and the school and more natural contacts with people in the area.

The idea of working incognito was abandoned, and it was decided to establish direct relationships with all parents. An invitation was sent to the parents of every child in the experimental group, inviting them to a meeting to be held at their school where the work of the Quincy Youth Development Commission (QYDC) would be explained and where they could talk privately with a counselor about their own child. Interviews were held with 51 per cent of the parents. Profiles of the child's test scores were made up and shown to the parents, and they were given the opportunity to discuss anything of concern to them. Many parents asked for help with their children, and a follow-up of such cases was made as soon as possible.

In spite of these reorganizations of teams, they still had great difficulty in their work. Therefore, at the end of the second year we decided to disband the teams temporarily and give the professional staff the task of studying further two questions: how the community resources for children could be increased and what specific methods of approach volunteers could use in working with their cases. For the next two years the staff members themselves played the role of volunteers in working with a small number of cases in order better to understand the dimensions of the problem and to arrive at job descriptions of the volunteer role based on actual experience. . . . At the same time conscious effort was made to stimulate improvement in community resources for children. . . .

THE COMMUNITY

Basically, this is a community project. The community assumes moral responsibility and provides a governing body (i.e., the QYDC) made up of local citizens. This commission determines all major policies but invites the University to provide consultation services, to train the local community people who work on the project, and to record and publish an account of the project.

It is also a community project in the sense that it depends on the cooperation of all the agencies that serve youth—schools, churches, Boy Scouts, Girl Scouts, the YMCA, the YWCA, recreation agencies, service clubs, courts, and social agencies. These agencies have executives from their staffs on the Professional Committee, which helps the staff plan the various steps of the project.

The project was located in this particular city after about six months of exploration by the University faculty; the possible program was explained to some leaders of the community, and then they were asked whether they wanted it for their community. A group of community agencies created the QYDC to accept and govern the project, and funds were secured from a foundation to pay for the services of the consultants from the University and for the technical work which was essential in a pilot study of these dimensions.

DESCRIPTION OF THE COMMUNITY

The project is located in Quincy, Illinois, a city of 44,000, situated on the bluff overlooking the Mississippi River. The city owes much of its early development to the fact that it had a good land-locked harbor on the river. The community was first settled by New England veterans of the War of 1812 and experienced very rapid growth during the period from 1840 to 1870. During these years European immigrants comprised half of Quincy's population. Most of these immigrants were German Catholics or Lutherans. The Germans settled largely in one area of the city and maintained their language for a considerable period. The descendants of the New Englanders and of the German Catholics and the German Lutherans are still important and fairly distinct groups within the city.

In addition to the fifteen puplic elementary schools and a junior and senior high school, there are six Catholic elementary and one Catholic high school and a Lutheran parochial elementary school. About 2 per cent of the population are Negroes, and most, but not all, of their children go to an all-Negro grade school.

The rapid growth of the city ended about 1870, and since 1900 it has grown very little. As the river traffic became less important and rail transportation more important, Quincy's size, relative to other cities, decreased. The climate of opinion in the community is relatively conservative.

OUTLINE OF ACTIVITIES OF THE FIRST FIVE YEARS

	Testing	Volunteers	Treatment	Consultant Role
Year 1	All children in Group X and in Group Y tested on all measures	Selection and training of seventy volunteers		
	Special ability tests given to upper half of classes			
Year 2	"Who are They?" Test and Behavior Description Chart repeated on all children	Organization of volunteer teams and their work with teachers, parents, etc., of selected children	Through team efforts	Ministers' seminar
			Through trained volunteers in counseling, etc.	Recreational survey
	California Test of Personality given to all children	Conferences with parents		Sunday-school teachers' seminar
		Training courses in counseling for volunteers		
Year 3	Newcomers tested on all measures	Training courses in counseling	Staff working on individual cases as guardian role; courts, foster homes, etc.	Consulting with Scouts, YMCA, YWCA, schools
				Workshop for teachers
			Staff acting as therapists, individual and group	YWCA program for gifted
				School counseling program
			Recreational clubs for underprivileged	Welfare Council program
			Art training for gifted	Reading program in school

OUTLINE OF ACTIVITIES OF THE FIRST FIVE YEARS *(cont.)*

Testing	*Volunteers*	*Treatment*	*Consultant Role*
			Co-ordinators for gifted children
Year 4 WAT and BDC repeated on all children		"Marriage" discussions for underprivileged	Development of a mental-health center
		Parent discussion groups	YWCA gifted children program
			Curriculum Enrichment Committee
Year 5 Newcomers tested			
Sentence Completion Test and Activity Inventory given all children			

52 / Youth Participation in Community Affairs

Sara-Alyce P. Wright

> *By furthering active participation of youth in community activities, adults can make noteworthy contributions toward strengthening a democratic society. In this article, Sara-Alyce P. Wright of the Young Women's Christian Association describes the extent of youth work in community projects and the roles of adults in helping youth enlarge their scope in community participation.*

In a democratic society active citizen participation in all phases of community living is of major importance. Opportunity for young people to participate in community affairs is essential to the realization of this goal.

Reprinted from *Children*, 1959, *6*, 140–44, with the permission of the author.

It provides the training ground for the development of mature, resourceful adults capable of participating in a dynamic society.

Spurred to a realization of this relationship by the Midcentury White House Conference on Children and Youth in 1950 and by the increasingly obvious necessity of reinvigorating the institutions of democracy presented by subsequent world events, youth-serving agencies, schools, and civic groups have for the past decade been exploring ways in which young people might take more meaningful responsibility, not only for their own immediate interest but also in areas of concern to the total community. In fact, even before that youth-pervaded conference, during the years of World War II, an awareness of young people's potential for managing their own affairs and working with adults in community activities seemed to be on an upswing. Teen canteens developed throughout the country, with youth and adults functioning together in program planning and policy making. Community youth councils were organized in many places so that a widely representative group of young people could express their opinions, raise questions, and work on special projects of community-wide importance.

Yet the questions are still frequently raised: "Can teenagers really participate with adults?" And, if so, "How?"

Five years ago Y-Teens of the YWCA in 27 cities—6 in the East, 12 in the Midwest, 7 in the South, and 2 in the West—made a simple survey of approximately 3,000 other teenagers, on the question: "Do you think that teenagers have privileges and responsibilities as citizens even though we do not vote?" The interviews took place during leisure hours in neighborhood centers, youth canteens, and "hangouts" among the young people who happened to be there. In one instance a civics teacher became interested and had the survey made in several civics classes.

The overwhelming reply of these 13-to-16-year-olds was "Yes." Many of them cited the fact that the Bill of Rights offers nonvoting citizens the same protection as it offers voters. In regard to their comments the *New York Times* (April 19, 1954) reported: "The youngsters named freedom of speech and worship, educational and labor opportunities, and the use of public facilities such as libraries among their privileges. They predicted that a more liberal attitude by adults toward teenagers would bring them more privileges and responsibilities as citizens."

The questionnaire used in the survey asked further: "What have you done or are you now doing to make your community a better place in which to live?" Leaving spaces for checking *Am doing now* or *Have done,* it listed the following activities:

Take part in traffic-safety projects.

Work in Community Chest and other drives.

Cooperate with other groups in working for better schools (promote bond issues, teacher-education recruiting, academic freedom).

Work as an aid in hospitals.

Serve as aids to group leaders to help with activities for small children in community centers.

Volunteer for other school and community projects (give examples).

Hold a part-time job and function reliably as a worker.

Study the structure and function of government—local, State, and National —and work to enlighten others.

Study to understand the work of the United Nations and work to enlighten others.

Participate with adults in YWCA and community activities.

Take part in international projects (name).

Work with communications media to publicize the worthwhile things teen-agers are doing.

The replies showed that in one city all 400 teenagers interviewed checked that they are now working on or had worked on at least one of the community projects listed. In another city the 200 teenagers inter-viewed checked at least two activities which they had been or were pres-ently engaged in. More than 50 per cent of all those interviewed in the survey were now working on or had previously worked on one or more of the following activities: (1) traffic-safety projects; (2) community drives; (3) part-time jobs; (4) government study projects.

Approximately 50 per cent were now or had previously taken part in: (1) U.N. study projects; (2) school and community projects other than those listed; (3) community activities, working side by side with adults.

Less than 50 per cent were now or had previously worked as: (1) hospi-tal aids; (2) aids to group leaders in work with small children; (3) partici-pants in international friendship and exchange projects; (4) participants in efforts to publicize through the communications media the worthwhile things teenagers are doing.

ENLARGING THE SCOPE

As the foregoing shows, most community activities for youth have been of a service nature. Such activities should not be belittled for they help young people to explore vocational avenues, pursue new interests, discover the importance of understanding persons of many racial, cultural, and economic backgrounds, and find the meaning of citizenship. It is important that this traditional approach be retained.

Young people today, however, because of the extended use of the community as a laboratory in education, increased opportunities to participate in conferences, work camps, and international exchange, and the ready store of information available through radio, television, news-papers, and magazines, can effectively enlarge their field of community participation. They need help from capable adults to do so.

Movement in this direction was taken in April of 1958, when 60 teenage leaders met in New York City in a consultation called by the Committee on Youth Services of the National Social Welfare Assembly (1958) to discuss youth in community affairs. The young people were asked as consultants to help the committee obtain a view of young people's opinions about ways in which youth is presently participating or might be encouraged to participate in community affairs. In planning the consultation the committee, composed of adult representatives of national youth-serving organizations, sought to create an atmosphere in which the young consultants would be able to express their opinions and feelings freely, leaving the adults to listen, observe, and to serve as advisers on request.

As they talked to each other these young people came to the conclusion that "only a small percentage of youth are participating in community affairs," and they wanted to find out why. They also exhibited considerable concern about adult attitudes toward youth, the problem of understanding themselves, and how to achieve self-respect and status.

Their report records their belief that: "Young people like us *are* interested in community affairs, but we represent only about 10 to 15 per cent of the youth of our age. . . . . . . Another large group, probably 75 per cent of all teenagers, could be interested in programs which include community affairs, but 'they need a little push.' . . . Another 10 per cent would definitely not be interested. . . . . . . But even these *could* be reached 'because after all everybody has *some* interest and you can appeal to young people through whatever interest they have.' "

The few skeptics, such as the young man who asked, "why does everybody have to be interested in community affairs—adults aren't?" were far outnumbered by the young persons who expressed the conviction that it was "both appropriate and important for youth to work with others to improve community life."

There were, however, those who registered reservations about the extent to which young people should participate in community activities, pointing out that in these years schooling is most important and nothing should interfere with it.

Thus through directly consulting with young people themselves youth-serving agencies have been trying to see the strengths and weaknesses in their present programs, as well as new opportunities for enabling young people to take their place *now* in community life.

CONTRIBUTIONS OF YOUTH

Giving youth a place in community life is not entirely a matter of training young people for adult responsibilities. Today's adults have much to gain from the process. Says Max Wolff (1959), associate professor of sociology at New York University, "In periods of crisis affecting the fundamentals of society the vision of youth must be blended with the knowledge of experienced elders to create the new basis for tomorrow's social organization. Such a critical period exists today in the American community."

It is well then to take a look at life throughout the United States to see what are the major forces affecting the well-being of communities and then to ask, Can youth help? This does not mean to ignore those needs related to youth per se, such as the ever-present need for additional recreational facilities, but rather to accept the fact that any major public issue in one way or another not only has some bearing upon the degree to which young people can grow to their fullest stature as citizens but may itself benefit from the freshness and frankness of the young.

Among the many problems facing our country today are a number in which young people have a direct stake. In regard to public-school integration, they are the ones who have firsthand experience. Their awareness, insights, and hopes in relation to their own abilities might also be taken into account as plans are developed for improving educational opportunities and school curricula and facilities.

Our Nation's difficulties with other countries might even be eased somewhat if the natural openness of youth and their ability and willingness to see through outward differences to the inner similarities in people could be fostered. A 17-year-old girl, who spent a summer in Germany on a scholarship saw this when she said: "In 2, 3, or 4 years we'll be the airline hostesses, military personnel, trainees for diplomatic service, and tourists. If we could have more opportunities now to get to know youth in other countries who will also be moving into these areas of responsibility, we'd save a lot of time in achieving a wholesome working relationship, which is so essential to real international cooperation and good will."

Recently a group of 17 Y-Teens and 8 adults working on plans for the 1959 National Y-Teen Conference on Youth's Role in National and World Affairs emphasized the importance of young people's finding ways to express the goals of our Nation to the world in other than material aid. They pointed out that urging young people to build their skills in all the arts and languages could make a vital contribution in "presenting to the world the real face of America."

Some guidelines for analyzing how young people might appropriately contribute to any particular project might be found in estimating the degree of ability and knowledge required for various elements of the task; the quality and nature of experience necessary to bring reality to the approach; the abilities and skills needed to accomplish the goal; and the interrelationships that might enhance the work in process and bring the added benefits of good human relations and understanding at its completion.

SOME PROJECTS

Young people and adults are already working together in a number of projects to find ways of involving youth in local, national, and world concerns. Several national youth-serving organizations have advisory councils of youth constituents, which meet with national planning groups to evaluate program and participate in the development of new program. The National Council of Churches of Christ in the United States of America included young people as fully accredited delegates in a recent "high level" conference on the church and world order. Y-Teens are now recognized as full members of the YWCA, with opportunity to attend triennial national conventions as delegates. The Michigan Youth Advisory Council, composed entirely of young people, has initiated a program that bears on the well-being of the State as a whole, including projects to promote summer employment for youth; traffic safety; and improvement of the labor, educational, and recreational conditions of migrants.

The Wisconsin Youth Committee for Community Youth Participation, open to all young people through a county-district-State structure, is officially recognized as the channel for the expression of young people's opinions on public affairs. With adult consultation provided by the State department of public welfare the committee attempts to draw youth into community affairs by providing clearing-house services and by holding an annual State conference for the exchange of ideas and experience. Its State committee, chosen by the young people in district elections, works closely with the Wisconsin Committee on Children and Youth, a body of adults and young people appointed by the Governor, which has among its responsibilities the promotion of local youth councils. To help such councils inject vitality into adult-youth partnership, the youth members of the Governor's committee have prepared the pamphlet "Youth Participation on the March" (1958), containing pointers for successful youth participation with adults in planning.

For several years young people in California have participated in the planning and deliberations of the Governor's youth conferences. The 1958 Conference on Youth Participation in Community Affairs (Sacramento, Calif., Youth Authority, 1958) offered an opportunity to discuss a wide range of interests including the family, the school, the church, jobs for youth, the motor age, delinquency prevention, community affairs, accomplishments of youth, and youth fitness. The report of the conference indicates that youth and adults entered freely into discussion and that there seemed to be acceptance of the need for partnership on the part of each. Reported one work group: "Youth and adults have something to share with each other. Neither group has all the answers. The important thing is developing good relationships and moving together with mutual trust and respect."

PRINCIPLES FOR SUCCESS

As groups in towns and cities work to achieve more extensive and vital youth participation in community affairs, it is well to consider some of the factors that may help and those that may hinder their efforts. These might be identified by a consideration of the following questions:

1. What experiences in family living, school, church, and community

groups will help young people become ready and willing to take part in the real issues of living?

2. As young people are helped to participate in community affairs, what are their motivations and expectations?

3. If young people seem unwilling to take responsibility in various phases of community life, what is the basis for their reluctance? What can be done to help them discover their own potential for participating in community life in a way that will have meaning for themselves and be of benefit to the community?

4. If adults invite youth to participate, what are the adult motivations and expectations?

5. As youth participates, how much should adults expect of them?

The role of the adult—singly and as an identifiable segment of the community—is an important key in the discovery, release, and utilization of the skills and potential of youth. It is important for those promoting adult-youth partnership to understand and accept some of the natural breaches between adolescents and adults, and find ways for them to work together in spite of these. The natural idealism and enthusiasm of youth along with the fact that most young minds are as yet uncluttered by the fears and prejudices that beset adults can bring an effective enthusiasm, not usually supplied by adults alone, to the tackling of many important tasks. Adults working to bring youth into meaningful participation in community affairs need an understanding of adolescent behavior, hopes, and aspirations, as well as an understanding and acceptance of themselves and their own strengths and limitations. They also need to have a knowledge of the elements at work in the community that enhance or hinder effective relationship, and to possess skill in helping people to work together in groups.

In searching for methods for promoting youth participation some groups may turn first to the formal organization of a youth council. With on-going staff and adequate adult leadership, such a group can be an effective channel for young people's efforts, relating their concerns to those of the community at large. However, creation of a council does not have to be the first and only step toward increased youth participation in community life. A conscious effort ought to be made by both adult and youth leaders to examine the activities in which young people are already involved in relation to their effectiveness and satisfaction for youth and for the community. In the process new avenues of interest may be opened as unmet needs become apparent.

After such a review of the current scene young people and adults together might make a careful selection of some immediate goals as well as a long-term plan for including youth regularly in all phases of community effort and concern. Then a group of young people and adults, representatives of various youth and community groups, might consider when, how, and at what points young people of various ages—junior or senior high school or college age—can and should be given the opportunity to participate in specific efforts.

In its pamphlet, previously mentioned, the Wisconsin Youth Committee (1958) cites several basic principles for successful youth participation in program planning:

In predominately adult groups there must be enough youth to lend support to each other.

No youth group can function satisfactorily without mature adult support and guidance.

When youth are sitting in with adults, extra time must be taken to keep the youth informed.

Adjustments must be made in meeting times, places, and methods when youth are being brought into adult programs—but also the inverse is true.

Whether youth or adults, special effort must be made to stay in contact with the people represented.

Youth must assume responsibility for showing adults what is desired of them. Sometimes, the nonparticipation of adults is a conscious effort not to take over.

Time must be allowed for both planning and evaluation if youth are going to learn by participating.

"Adults need to pave the way for youth participation, but the real effectiveness will come when the individual youth accepts his privilege and assumes his responsibilities," the pamphlet predicts.

A look at communities generally does not show the vital quality of youth participation that is needed to pour new strength into our democratic way of life. Too often youth participates only in a phase of experience which has very little chance of penetrating or changing the total community. However, the fact that in the past few years young people have been taking more and more responsibility for various community drives and are serving as volunteers in many community services may indicate next steps in participation. As young people ask to help with community projects, adults must be willing to accept their offer and provide the guidance that will enable them to take responsibility meaningfully. A scheme for making ways of participating in community affairs available for all young people would provide widespread training so that the leadership necessary for dealing with the myriad problems of our society would be encouraged to emerge.

"Participation in the democratic sense is a complicated art;" writes Max Wolff (1959), "only a few are born masters, but many, most of the people, can learn it. The best method of learning is active and continuing practice. Three conditions must be fulfilled to induce individuals to try themselves out as participants. They must be sure that: they are really welcome by the coparticipants; they are asked to participate because of their qualifications as coworkers; their participation will be a meaningful contribution to the goal of the cooperative activity."

With proper encouragement, youth can be a positive force for bringing about the changes for good that a dynamic society must constantly seek.

53 / City-Wide Discussion in Cincinnati: A Parent Education Program

Anna Hayes Cooper and Helen L. Webster

This article describes the framework of a series of yearly study-discussion groups and leadership programs in child development. The groups culminate their activities in the annual home-school workshop sponsored by the Cincinnati public schools and the elementary and secondary councils of Parent-Teacher Associations. At the 1959 workshop seven hundred participants—parents, teachers, administrators, and interested members of the community—discussed the topic, "Youth Prepares for the Scientific Age." The authors are Anna Hayes Cooper of the Cincinnati Public Schools and Helen L. Webster of the Cincinnati Council of Elementary School Parent-Teacher Associations.

" 'Mommy, what would you do if I stuck this knife in your back?' an eight-year-old asked a friend of mine."

"What did the mother say?"

" 'Why, I'd bleed,' she said calmly. 'What did you think I would do?' "

As the group laughed appreciatively at this quick-witted response, a school principal remarked, "That shows you have to know when *not* to take a child's questions too seriously."

A teacher chimed in eagerly, "That's just what I meant when I said we have to determine whether a youngster is asking a question simply to get attention or because he really wants to know."

"But if we are to foster the inquiring mind, what attitude should parents and teachers take toward children's questions?" the discussion leader asked.

The group of twenty parents, teachers, school administrators, and interested members of the community pondered the question. They were just one of thirty such groups gathered in classrooms at Walnut Hills High School in Cincinnati on the evening of February 1, 1960. The topic for discussion was "Preparing Our Children and Youth for the Scientific Age." The occasion was the fifth annual home-school workshop sponsored by the Cincinnati public schools and our two councils of Parent-Teacher Associations, one composed of elementary school units, the other of high school P.T.A.'s.

Reprinted from *The PTA Magazine* (*National Parent-Teacher*), October 1961, 56, 30–32, with the permission of the authors and the National Congress of Parents and Teachers.

Culminating each year in this city-wide project, study-discussion programs in Cincinnati flourish under council leadership, with the sanction and support of the school administration and the state department of education. Trained lay leaders for P.T.A. discussion groups on child development and home-school relations are provided through a lay leadership training program. This program was initiated jointly eight years ago by the Council of Elementary School P.T.A.'s, the Cincinnati public schools, and the Ohio State Department of Education.

LEARNING TO LEAD

The leadership training program is conducted by a supervisor in parent-teacher relationships in the Cincinnati school system. Participants, selected by their P.T.A.'s, meet for two-hour sessions twice a month from October to April. Under the supervisor's guidance they study and practice discussion techniques. They learn a good deal about Cincinnati schools and how to find out more about them later. They also receive information about community agencies, especially those which can supply resource persons for small groups that have no funds to pay for such assistance. And, of course, major purposes of the program are to provide prospective leaders with basic information about the development of normal children and to promote understanding between home and school.

Publications used in the course include *The PTA Magazine, New Hope for Audiences,* and other carefully selected materials. Their cost is covered by a small registration fee paid by the local unit for its representatives in the program.

Each person who takes the course is expected to lead a discussion group in her own unit the following year, during which in-service help is provided through a follow-up, advanced program. The new leaders, meeting once a month with the supervisor of parent-teacher relationships, receive additional information—for example, on program materials, including new films, pamphlets, and books. They discuss their on-the-job problems and exchange ideas and experiences. It is exciting indeed to sit in on one of their meetings and learn what is being done in parent education throughout the city.

In many ways the annual home-school workshop is the highlight of the year's study-discussion programs. It is a demonstration of the methods used in the local unit discussion groups and a splendid example of home-school cooperation. It not only sparks interest in study-discussion groups among parents but also stimulates teaching and administrative personnel to encourage the organization of groups in schools that have not previously had them. In addition to these benefits, the workshop provides the only opportunity in the year when parents and teachers from all over the city can meet face to face to discuss common concerns.

The project is an arduous but wonderfully satisfying enterprise, involving large numbers of people and close teamwork between school personnel and parent members of the P.T.A. Co-chairmen are the parent education chairman of the Council of Elementary School P.T.A.'s and the supervisor of parent-teacher relationships in the Cincinnati schools. Their planning committee includes the associate superintendent of schools, the director of adult education, and the presidents, vice-presidents, and program chairmen of the two councils.

The smooth functioning of the workshop depends on many committees—arrangements, art, coatroom, dinner, display, Founders Day (the workshop usually takes place in February), invitations, hospitality, information, program and tickets, and publicity. The work of these committees in assuring a successful dinner meeting is familiar to P.T.A. members. However, there are three additional committees whose functions are distinctive to this meeting. All three share responsibility for assuring profitable discussion and lively participation by parents, school personnel, and community representatives.

GROUNDWORK FOR GROUP DISCUSSION

The committee on leaders and recorders has the task of providing a qualified discussion leader and competent recorder for each of the discussion groups in the workshop. It tries also to maintain a reasonable balance between professional and lay people selected for these important jobs. For half the groups the discussion leader is a professional person and the recorder a layman. For the other half the roles are reversed. The professional people include teachers, principals, supervisors, and other members of the school staff. The lay leaders are council board members and others who have had lay leadership training.

The intricate, time-consuming, important job of handling reservations and setting up balanced discussion groups is the assignment of the reservations committee. Invitations are apportioned equally among parents and school staffs. On his reservation, each person indicates the school level he is particularly interested in—elementary, junior high, or senior high—so that he can be assigned to a group on that level. Groups are set up so that each one has roughly equal numbers of parents and teachers, as well as representation from various areas of the city.

Guests include presidents of nearby area councils, officers of the Ohio Congress, and members of the Cincinnati Board of Education. Also invited are representatives from the Red Feather agencies. Since these agencies provide resource persons for P.T.A. discussion groups, they are familiar with the parent and family life education programs published in *The PTA Magazine,* and they welcome the opportunity to participate in the city-wide discussion project.

Good questions are the key to good discussion. Our third special committee therefore is a committee to formulate discussion questions. The purpose of the questions, as the group leaders are informed, is not to limit discussion but to keep it moving briskly in all the groups within a framework pertinent to the topic. This committee, like the others, is a lay-professional one. After determining the general area of discussion the lay

and professional workers separate to prepare questions independently.
When they come together to combine and edit their work, it has always
been surprising to discover how similar their questions are. The differences are usually in words, not ideas.

TIMELY TOPIC

For the 1960 workshop our discussion topic came from the article
"Youth Prepares for the Scientific Age," by Evelyn Millis Duvall, in the
April 1959 issue of *The PTA Magazine*. Our discussion question committee based its questions on the article and study-discussion guide. It was
our good fortune to have Dr. Duvall accept our invitation to be the key-
note speaker.

We started off at four o'clock with a general assembly, at which Dr.
Duvall's stirring address generated keen interest in our topic and stimulated the thinking of the seven hundred workshop participants. Dinner
was followed by lively, profitable group discussion for two hours. At nine
o'clock, through the hard work of a committee on information, the findings of the groups were assembled and presented in a brilliant summary
by a news analyst from Cincinnati Station WKRC-TV. Thus our fifth annual workshop came to a satisfying close, with increased understanding
of the challenge of preparing children and youth for the scientific age and
with increased appreciation of the values of home-school cooperation and
group discussion. Now we look forward to our sixth city-wide discussion
program.

Parent education has long been recognized as the most effective means
for achieving the Objects of the parent-teacher organization. But successful parent education programs, we know, require organized effort, trained
leadership, and professional help. We in Cincinnati are fortunate in possessing all three. They enable us to provide more study-discussion groups
and programs each year to assure that in "The Eventful Drama of Growing Up" our children will have an able supporting cast of parents and
teachers.

54 / Youth Conduct Codes

Robert P. Capes

*Communities are discovering that youth, parents, and teachers can
agree on ground rules—or standards—for youth conduct. A purpose of*

Reprinted from *Youth Service News*, December 1958, *10*, 6–11,with the permission of
the Division for Youth, New York State Executive Department.

such codes is to achieve cooperative effort and mutual agreement for a
safe and acceptable program of social activities for young people.
Interesting is Minnesota's statewide code for junior and senior high
school students included in this selection.

Although youth conduct codes are not rivalling the popularity of the
"hula hoop" there is evidence that an increasing number of communities
and schools are interested in the establishment of such codes. Youth conduct codes set standards of behavior in certain areas which are acceptable
to both youth and adults.

Most of the youth codes which have been prepared follow a similar
pattern. Plans for the establishment of a code, age groups covered and the
types of items included in the codes reflect some agreement as to the manner
in which their establishment should be approached and the problems of
youth which should be considered.

The youth codes have been given impetus by a recognition that youth
need some "ground rules" covering certain areas of their conduct which
are acceptable to them, their parents and their teachers. Perhaps there is
an awareness that there is little total agreement on standards of youth
conduct among youth or between youth, their parents and their teachers.

Some believe that youth are trying to outdo each other in bizarre behavior in a sort of "can you top this" manner with a great majority of
youth being forced into the game.

For years, parents have been called "old fashioned" and pressured by
the statement of their children that "everybody else is doing it." Some
parents want to find out what is par in youth behavior and what others
think are acceptable behavior standards for youth.

The fact that there has been so much agreement among youth and
between them and their elders on the standards set forth in so many youth
codes would suggest that there is greater agreement than was suspected.
All that is needed is a better understanding of each other and their problems which can be achieved by a thorough airing and discussion of the
various points of view.

PERSONS PARTICIPATING

Youth codes have resulted from the joint interest and efforts of youth,
their parents and, in some instances, their teachers. It is generally recognized that the objectives of youth codes cannot be achieved without
both youth and adult participation. In some communities and schools
youth and adults have prepared separate codes which have been reconciled
and consolidated at subsequent meetings of both groups.

Other codes have been originally written by youth with subsequent
adult guidance. Under these and other approaches to the establishment

of youth codes, there has always been provision for the interchange of ideas, discussion and agreement by both youth and adults. Some believe that one of the principal benefits to be derived from a code is the finding out what each group expects of the other.

PENFIELD, N.Y.

The small community of Penfield, New York established youth conduct codes for junior and senior high schools. This community approached the problem of establishing codes in the following way: First, it was determined that interest existed in developing codes by discussing the possibility with teachers, students and parents.

A committee was formed to draft the codes. The student council, parent-teachers association and school faculty were each asked to appoint representatives to the committee. This committee had five meetings to work out the basic principles of the codes, and during these meetings the youth codes established by other communities were reviewed.

Each student was given a copy of the code and asked to take it home, read it carefully, talk it over with his parents and vote on the code at the next assembly. A written vote was arranged by the student council to be taken at the assembly.

After the code was approved by the youth, it was decided to hold a meeting to which parents and students both were invited. The high school parent-teacher association and the student council arranged for this meeting which was well-publicized in the local paper and by flyers sent home from the school.

The committee which drafted the original code acted as a panel at this meeting and the code was read aloud by the student council president and simultaneously flashed on a screen. After the code had been read through once, each section was discussed and questions were directed at members of the committee. After considerable discussion a vote was taken and the code was passed by a large majority of the participating youth and adults.

This latter meeting in which both youth and adults participated was felt to be of great value, in that it provided an opportunity for open discussion. Many of the problems faced by both youth and adults were brought into the open, and the young people on the committee answered all questions directed to them with frankness and honesty. Both youth and adults left this meeting understanding each other a little bit better.

CODE COVERAGE

Some communities have adopted two separate codes—one for the junior high schools—grades 7, 8 and 9, and another for the senior high schools—grades 10, 11 and 12. Some codes set different standards for the older junior high school and senior high school pupils than those set for the younger ones. Some youth codes have set conduct standards for only the senior high school group, feeling that there is little need for a code covering the behavior of the younger children of the community. Generally, youth codes provide a basis for determining acceptable conduct regarding: (1) parties; (2) use of the car; (3) suitable hours; (4) appropriate dress; (5) problems of party crashing; (6) proper respect for the property and rights of others; (7) smoking by teen-agers; and (8) drinking of alcoholic beverages by teen-agers.

BENEFITS OF CODES

It is difficult, if not impossible, to objectively measure the effect which the establishment of youth codes has upon the behavior of youth. However, generally, communities and schools which have adopted codes feel that they have had a beneficial effect and claim the following results:
1. The discussion between youth and adults which precedes the adoption of a code provides for a better understanding of each other.
2. Improved youth conduct in the areas covered by the code.
3. Gives parents support for the enforcement of standards set forth in the code.
4. Lessens the "everybody else is doing it" pressure on parents.

MINNESOTA'S CODES

Minnesota's teenage codes for junior and senior high schools are unique in that they are the only statewide codes which have been adopted. The Minnesota code resulted from the joint participation of over 600 youth and 300 adults and was promulgated to serve as a basis for community and school codes recognizing that such codes might depart from some of the standards set forth in the statewide codes because of local conditions. These statewide codes are intended to stimulate and guide communities and schools in the preparation and adoption of youth codes.

Over 231 Minnesota schools have discussed conduct codes using the following Minnesota teenage codes as a guide.

MINNESOTA TEEN-AGE CODE: JUNIOR HIGH SCHOOL (GRADES 7, 8 AND 9)

Basic Rule

Parents should know where their sons and daughters are while away from home, what they are doing, and with whom they are spending their time. Parents should also know what time their young people return home.

Parent-Youth Planning

A. An allowance should be planned together, based on a discussion of financial ability, needs and management of money.

B. Family plans should be organized so that: (1) necessary transportation for all members of the family can be provided; and (2) individual members can be reached in case of emergency or change of plans.

Home Entertaining

The home should be the center of young people's social activity. To accomplish this, the cooperation and support of parents is needed. Young people should be encouraged to bring friends into the home and to accept invitations to the homes of friends. Parents should welcome the opportunity to meet their sons' or daughters' companions and friends.

A. Social activities in this age group should be limited to weekends and holidays. It is important that invitations be clear as to type of function (for appropriate dress), the time of beginning and ending of a party. It is the responsibility of the guests to leave at the designated time.

B. It is important that a parent or responsible adult be home and on call at all times when young people entertain.

C. Young people and their parents feel more comfortable if some plans for entertainment have been made in advance. Boredom and confusion lead to undesirable results. Well laid plans for a party are disregarded only by a rude guest. A considerate guest will follow the plans of the host.

D. Party crashing is an inexcusable custom and presents a problem for the host and other guests. Crashers should not be admitted.

E. "Lights out" has no place in a well-ordered party.

F. Parents should be sure that transportation is provided for young people at the designated time of return.

General Dating

A. Some eighth and ninth graders "date" in addition to parties and dances. The home should be offered and encouraged as a possible place for dating. Parents should cooperate by providing an agreeable measure of privacy. Public entertainment puts a strain on a teen-ager's allowance.

B. Dressing according to the occasion makes a person feel more comfortable.

C. Young people and their parents should agree in advance on a definite time for return from a date. A boy should be given an opportunity to meet the parents of the girl and to discuss expected time of arrival at home.

D. Group, or double dating, rather than single dating, is to be encouraged. Parents can assist in making this attractive to young people by helping to arrange for trips to places of recreation or entertainment.

E. "Going steady" at this age should be discouraged. Young people profit by a variety of contacts.

School Dances

A. Transportation should be provided by parents. This can be a shared responsibility.

B. Plans should include dances that provide for an exchange of partners.

C. Parties after dances seem neither necessary nor wise in this age group.

Hours

If boys and girls of ninth grade walk home from an early function, a definite time should be set for arrival at home. The following are suggested hours for the termination of functions:

	Grades		
	7th	8th	9th
Formals		11:30	12:00
Informals	10:00	10:30	11:00
Home parties	10:00	11:00	11:00
General dating		10:30	11:00

Inasmuch as formal dances are infrequent in this age group, midnight is considered a reasonable hour, provided that boys and girls are transported directly home.

Driving

Ordinarily young people are not eligible to drive at this age. It is illegal for a parent to permit his or her son or daughter to drive on a public highway when such young person is under the age of 15. If such young person is older, he or she cannot drive, even with a parent in the automobile, unless he or she has a driver's license or a learner's permit. A licensed driver must accompany a person with a learner's permit.

Drinking

This ordinarily is not a problem at this age. Circumstances sometimes arise, where it becomes one, particularly when eighth and ninth grade girls "date" senior high school boys. The dangers under these circumstances are apparent.

Minnesota State Law prohibits sale of liquor or 3.2 beer to minors (under twenty-one years of age), and forbids serving it to them, or consumption by them.

Smoking

Minnesota State Law prohibits sale of cigarettes and tobacco to persons under 18 years of age, and prohibits such persons from smoking except in their own homes with their parents' consent.

MINNESOTA TEEN-AGE CODE: SENIOR HIGH SCHOOL (GRADES 10, 11 AND 12)

Basic Rule

Parents should know where their sons and daughters are while away from home, what they are doing, and with whom they are spending their time. Parents should also know what time their young people return home.

Parent-Youth Planning

A. An allowance should be planned together, based on a discussion of financial ability, needs, and the management of money.

B. Family plans should be organized so that: (1) necessary transportation for all members of the family can be provided; and, (2) individual members can be reached in case of emergency or change of plans.

Home Entertaining

The home should be the center of young people's social activity. To accomplish this, the cooperation and support of parents is needed. Young people should be encouraged to bring friends into the home and to accept the invitations to visit the homes of friends. Parents should welcome the opportunity to meet their sons' or daughters' companions and friends.

A. It is important that invitations be clear as to type of function (for appropriate dress), the time of beginning, and ending of a party. It is the responsibility of the guests to leave at the designated time.

B. It is important that a parent or responsible adult be at home and on call at all times when young people entertain but should provide an agreeable measure of privacy.

C. Young people and their parents feel more comfortable if some plans for entertainment have been made in advance. Boredom and confusion lead to undesirable results. Well laid plans for a party are disregarded only by a rude guest.

D. Party crashing is an inexcusable custom and presents a problem for the host and other guests. Crashers should not be admitted.

E. "Lights out" has no place in a well-ordered party.

General Dating

A. The home should be offered and encouraged as a possible place for dating. Parents should cooperate by providing an agreeable measure of privacy. Public entertainment puts a strain on teen-agers' allowances.

B. Dressing according to the occasion makes a person feel more comfortable.

C. Young people and their parents should agree in advance on a definite time for return from a date. A boy should be given an opportunity to meet the parents of the girl and to discuss expected time of arrival at home.

Hours

In deciding on a satisfactory hour for a young person's expected arrival at home from a social engagement, two factors have to be considered: (1) What time will the affair be over? (2) What is a reasonable amount of time to allow for arrival home following the affair?

1. What time will the affair be over? The following is a suggested guide for:

a. Non-school nights:

	Grades		
	10th	*11th*	*12th*
Formals	11:00	12:00	12:00
	12:00	1:00	1:00
Informals	11:00	11:00	11:00
	11:30	12:00	12:00
Home parties	11:30	12:00	12:00
General dating	11:30	12:00	12:00

b. School nights: 10:00 except for special events, such as school, church or other recognized activities.

2. What is a reasonable amount of time to allow for arrival at home? (If transportation is provided by parents, this is no problem.)

a. An invitation issued for refreshments following a dance or other late social function should include a definite time for beginning and ending. One hour would seem adequate for an occasion of this type but is subject to regional conditions.

b. Young people should come directly home from a function unless other plans have been approved by parents. If a young person is delayed for any reason, he should telephone home.

c. Parents should know when young people arrive home.

Driving

A. Parental consent for the driving privilege should be based on: (1) Possession of a driver's license; (2) young people's proof of ability to control themselves and the car; (3) a healthy attitude regarding the rights and welfare of others.

B. Because it affects the lives and property of others, teen-agers should be allowed to drive a motor vehicle only with a license (or permit) issued by the Drivers' License Division of the State of Minnesota. A licensed driver must accompany the teen-agers driving with a permit. State law prohibits anyone from allowing another to drive a motor vehicle without a driver's license.

C. Trained instruction is urged. Careful driving, as well as good driving attitudes, can save lives and secure the economic welfare of an entire family.

D. It is the duty of parents and youth to make certain that any car driven by young people is in safe operating condition.

E. Young drivers should be expected to assume their portion of responsibility for the maintenance and appearance of the shared car.

F. Parents should be firm in their decision to take away the car privilege when it is abused. On the other hand, they should be generous in their praise of proper driving attitudes and careful handling of the car.

G. Young people should understand that overcrowding of a car is dangerous.

H. Riders have a share in the responsibility for safe driving. Dares and jeers from riders have been responsible for more than one death.

I. Young people should understand that it is wise to refuse to ride with a reckless driver. Call your parents, or call a cab.

Drinking

Drinking among high school students represents a serious problem in which parents and youth must consider their responsibilities. Young people confirm that a number of parents serve alcoholic beverages (beer, wine and whiskey) to young guests in their home. It is well known that alcoholic beverages are brought to parties by guests, and are served by the guests themselves.

A. No one has the moral or legal right to serve any alcoholic beverages to other people's children. The adult who does so may be charged criminally and is directly responsible for any one of the serious consequences which may result.

B. Minnesota State Law prohibits sale of liquor or 3.2 beer to minors (under 21 years of age) and forbids serving it to them and consumption by them.

C. Parents should impound any alcoholic beverage which is brought to a party and notify the parents of the offender. No alcoholic beverages should be accessible to young guests.

D. Young people should understand that it is not a disgrace to decline an alcoholic drink.

E. Young people should understand that it is foolhardy to ride with a driver who is under the influence of alcohol, and should instead seek safer means of transportation.

Smoking

A. Minnesota State Law prohibits sale of cigarettes and tobacco to persons under 18 years of age and prohibits such persons from smoking except in their home with their parents' consent.

55 / Helping Unemployed Youth:
A Community Approach

Saul S. Leshner and George S. Snyderman

What shall we do for the young people who drop out of school without having developed skills and specific interests to find useful places in society? Here Saul S. Leshner and George S. Snyderman of the Jewish Employment and Vocational Service, Philadelphia, whose job it is to help young people to become work-oriented, present their views of the needs of school dropouts and the kinds of services a community should provide to assist them in attaining an industrious and constructive future.

The decades following World War I were accompanied by an unprecedented growth of our large cities, a growth stimulated and facilitated by advances in transportation, communication, and shift of population from rural to urban centers. While it is evident that marked changes in behavior patterns and personal values occurred in all classes of our population, youth were particularly affected. Removed from a simple to a complex society, many young people developed disorganized patterns of behavior.

We can predict that delinquency and other problems which constitute the "Youth Problem" will increase during the sixties, if for no other reason than that there will be more and more young people between the ages of 16 and 21. During this decade some 26 million young people will enter the labor market, and of this number 7,500,000 will not have completed high school.

Students of behavior agree that the youth who does not complete his schooling is likely to have other difficulties. Whether dropping out of

Reprinted from *Children*, 1961, *8*, 213–18, with the permission of the authors.

school is the cause or the effect of these difficulties is of little consequence. The point that needs underlining is that school dropouts do contribute more than their share to problems like delinquency, illegitimacy, and even narcotics addiction and alcoholism. And there is also no doubt that these young people have greater difficulty getting and holding jobs and have a higher unemployment rate than high school graduates. This fact is central to both the problem and the solution.

Work in our middle-class culture is the most significant way of achieving success. No goal, youth is taught, is impossible—if one works hard enough one can even become President of the United States. Work, then, is not just the means of earning a living; it is also the way one acquires social status. The image of success in our work-centered society is the person who starts at the bottom and works his way up through the shop and office until he becomes the head of the firm. He does this honestly without taking unfair advantage of his fellows, and while he is achieving success, he is contributing his knowledge, ability, and money to community enterprises.

This ideal, of course, is not attainable by many Americans, no matter how hard they try. The individual who is not fortunate, and who has considerable difficulty finding and holding a job, becomes something of a pariah, an object of contempt. His feelings, already bruised by his circumstances, are further assaulted by the culture heroes of the movies and television who, without working, live a life of ease and revelry. The youth who has not acquired middle-class beliefs in the intrinsic value of work cannot see why he should "sweat for it" when there are so many "easier and faster ways of making a buck."

What we are saying is that the goals of all youth are governed by what is real for them. Deprived youth are aware of their lack of opportunity, and they set goals which they think are rightfully theirs—goals which they can achieve, no matter how. Often they do not care what they will become, or they create problems because they do not try hard enough or because they use ways to attain their goals which are not socially acceptable. Their behavior is a reaction to a negative cultural setting, and only real understanding and a positive desire to help will stimulate these youth to wish to change themselves.

When personal success is life's most important goal, the close interpersonal relations needed for effective modern day living become difficult to attain. The youth who is driven to reach impossible heights is likely to say, "Why should I?" He is in danger of losing his sense of balance in the drive for individual success and to divert any remaining urges to cooperate into unsocial channels.

BACKGROUND FOR DELINQUENCY

In every metropolitan area of this country, many delinquents are recruited from the school dropout group. School, court, police, and public employment office records indicate that many school dropouts get into

trouble because they have nothing to keep them busy. Tragically, however, schools and community agencies, although recognizing this fact, have
neglected to set up well-rounded, closely integrated programs to help
these young people become equipped to participate constructively in
adult society. Where there are efforts they *are* usually made with a piece-
meal approach.

The idea that any single agency or institution can help these young
people to "mend their ways" is erroneous for it fails to consider fully
either the nature of their problems or the highly individualized basis for
each youth's failure to conform. The choice of other views involves one's
ability to disengage oneself from customary ways and means of resolving
problems. The writers of this article subscribe to the view that these
young people are everyone's concern; that all community agencies, voluntary and public, have a role to play and a job to do if our troubled
youth are to be helped to find a path out of the jungle which demands
social cannibalism to survive. The important task, therefore, is how to
mobilize and channelize all the resources of our communities to help
these young people develop an image of themselves as "good workers"
and then to take their place in society as such.

Society in America is to a certain degree stratified along socio-economic class lines and most of these delinquent youth come from the lower
socio-economic groups. These classes are, in a sense, subcultures with
their own traits, standards, and values. Thus, the middle class places great
values on close family life, good education, "proper" use of leisure time,
the church, and other community institutions. The middle class, accordingly, values morality, respectability, and "striving" to better oneself and
family. The class from which most of the school dropouts come requires
different responses of its young in terms of learning and goals. It punishes
or ridicules what the middle class rewards. Social skills in this class are
quite different and aggression is usually approved behavior (Polsky, 1959;
Teeters and Reinemann, 1950; Witmer and Kotinsky, 1956).

The hostility, defiance, resentment, and deep feelings of not being
wanted of many disadvantaged young people result in unsocial acts because this is the only way they have of expressing their feelings. Their
need to talk with and work with someone who will ask and not blindly
demand must be recognized. The trauma of school failure can only be
ameliorated by the use of interdisciplinary skills, close individualized
supervision, and the establishment of clear expectations, and these are not
found in the usual school setting. In short, while the schools have a responsibility to adjust their programs to keep potential dropouts in school insofar as possible, training young people to develop attitudes and motivation for work can be accomplished more effectively in a work-oriented
environment by persons with particular skills and orientation.

THE PHILADELPHIA PROGRAM

To illustrate this point it will be useful to review quickly what can
be done to help young people find their way into the world of work. We

cite what is going on in Philadelphia because there a progressive city administration has been attempting to resolve many of the problems, because the school counseling program is competently administered, because there is an effective employment service which has proved that many school dropouts can be placed in employment, and, lastly, because there is a network of voluntary agencies, which if properly mobilized and fully used could add the necessary impetus which thus far has been absent.

On one occasion all agencies of the community supported the efforts of the local office of the State Employment Service to help the "hard-core youth," that is, the out-of-school, unemployed, and untrained young people, aged 16 and 17, living in a neighborhood ranking highest in the city in delinquency, crime, illiteracy, poverty, desertion of children, and illegitimacy. Seven hundred and eighty-two boys and girls were dealt with by just two counselors, with rather striking results because for the first time someone actively involved these youth in their own rehabilitation. This experience shows that young people like these can be helped, that they desperately want to be helped, and that some suffer anguish because of their failure to adjust. Altogether 242 of these youth (31 per cent of the total) were placed in competitive employment through the provision of considerable counseling (2,511 interviews) and a tremendous number of phone calls and visits to employers (5,839). The small number of youth (3) who failed to accept an employer's offer of a job indicates how much help the counselors gave and how much these youth learned. More important, none of these youth created a serious disturbance at his place of employment.

The Philadelphia counselors found that these young people need constant stimulation. If allowed to drift, they revert to their old habits; but if they learn to seek stimulation, they adopt the approved standards of our society. They are more realistic about their status and role with respect to work than we assume. Generally, they aspire to and will perform best in low-paying entry jobs which are not sought by mature, experienced persons, so that any fear that the placement of youth will displace married men is ill-founded.

Another noteworthy fact emerging from this project is that, for these youth, vocational goals are meaningless unless placement in a job follows quickly. Unless the boys and girls see the results in terms of at least a referral to a paying job, they become impossible to reach.

THE SCHOOL'S ROLE

An additional conclusion may be drawn from the employment service's experience. Even in the subculture in which so many of these unemployed youth live, some kind of work is essential. Since a person's adjustment to work depends on his life's experience, these youth are handicapped because their previous experiences had been thwarting and negative. The community must find some way to help these youth become good workers. Young people who are potential school dropouts need to be identified by the schools at age 14 or 15 and referred to a community agency which is equipped to give specific help and professional attention to each youngster while he is still in school. The help these youngsters need cannot be given in classrooms or schools because they have already failed to adjust to the institutional setting which is the school. This failure accounts for much of their anxiety and hostility. The school, however, has an obligation to re-examine its program to find ways of making these young people's school experience at an earlier age an interesting rather than a frustrating experience.

The schools, of course, should have a responsibility for these youngsters until they are 18, but there is some question whether schools typically are able to cope with and help them. It would seem, therefore, that the schools' responsibility can be wisely exercised by referring these youth to a community agency which is noninstitutional and which is adult in character. Work in a realistic setting where authority is permissive, and where the youth have an opportunity to develop skills and habits in terms of their own achievement, will help them to adjust better. In this type of environment, their basic needs for self-determination and independence are met, and they gradually develop the self-image of a "good worker."

Formal institutional training usually fails with these youth because the youngsters themselves cannot be categorized. More important is the fact that institutional training symbolizes a continuance of the dependency which the school setting incurred. This is, perhaps, the most important reason why many of these youth fail to enroll in trade or business schools when they leave school.

SOME SUGGESTIONS

Several general solutions are often suggested for the youngsters who cannot accommodate themselves to school. They may be summarized as follows:

1. *Removal of the youth from school to prepare him for work* in a real work setting as a trainee or apprentice. In a nonschool environment the youth has a chance to develop skills, learn to get along with other workers, develop personal responsibility for his productivity, build tolerance for work pressures, develop such work habits as punctuality and observance of rules. Since these factors constitute the American image of a good worker, this solution would help some of these drifting young people.

This way, however, is not suitable for most of these youth because they are not ready to work—they first need to be helped to see that they can work. Moreover, there are few on-the-job training opportunities for youth generally, and disadvantaged youth are simply not able to compete for them. The proposed Federal "on-the-job training" program would increase the number of such opportunities.

2. *Additional vocational training in a school setting* either directly or cooperatively with industry. This is an extension of the school's authority against which these youth have already rebelled. As a matter of fact, it has been observed that traditional vocational training programs usually exclude the "low-level" youngsters because they do not have the "aptitudes" or "interests."

3. *A public works program.* This, in the opinion of most persons concerned with unemployed youth, is a necessity. Such a program requires considerable planning, supervision, and money. As of this writing, the City of Philadelphia has been able to provide work for only 200 youth. The results achieved in cutting down delinquency and truancy among those so employed have been gratifying.

4. *Work-adjustment training.* This involves removing the youth from their pattern of failure by introducing them to adult work, thus breaking the pattern of resistance and immaturity and nurturing maturation of personality. For many young people this type of program may lead ultimately to a return to school during the evening because the school will have a meaningful supplementary value. Many others may also be helped through this means to become "good workers" and contribute to the welfare of their families and communities.

Work-adjustment programs are relatively new and are sometimes known as "job adjustment" training. Generally, work-adjustment centers represent for disadvantaged youth a greater opportunity to learn and see how they can compete. The centers enable them to test themselves in a variety of work settings, achieving on many real work tasks, until they build tolerance for pressure and ability to integrate and organize their energies.

WORK ADJUSTMENT TRAINING

The Philadelphia Jewish Employment and Vocational Service, a voluntary community agency, has operated a work-adjustment program since 1957. Conducted in an industrial workshop with a true work environment, it is used to assess work tolerance and capacities. With the aim of rehabilitating persons of all ages who have emotional and mental handicaps, the program is supported by the Office of Vocational Rehabilitation as a research and demonstration project.

In the program a good work personality is developed by controlling and manipulating psycho-social factors and working conditions. Dealing with youngsters with all kinds of behavior problems has shown that these youth create an emotional shell over their feelings because they cannot tolerate their own anxieties. When confronted with rigid authority they break through this shell with highly explosive reactions. The programs of the Work Adjustment Center of JEVS provides a benign authority and enables the trainees to relate with and develop a trust in authority. It permits them to express healthy natural dependency feelings. The freedom of being without conflict in a wholesome, modulated work environ-ment helps them to begin to channelize their energies toward constructive ends.

Placed in this environment, the individual youth receives encourage-ment, praise, and direction from an industrial foreman who is firm, con-sistent, and understanding. The youth begins to work through his prob-lems of learning to be a "good worker." He takes an interest in his productivity. His interest is reinforced because he receives pay for the quantity and quality of work he produces. He learns that in competitive industry one must be able to produce and get along with supervisors and peers. He learns this positively through praise, monetary rewards, and negatively through loss of pay and privileges. This is the pattern of American industry. Unless the individual learns these lessons well, he is not ready to plan for vocational training, work, or return to school.

AN INDIVIDUALIZED PROCESS

Work-adjustment training is a highly individualized process since all youth do not react alike. Included in the process are supplementary tech-niques such as individual and group counseling, and the auxiliary services rendered by other agencies—family casework, psychiatric treatment, and job development and placement. Parents or other responsible family members are helped to understand, cooperate, and participate by inter-views with the psychologists and counselors. They can be involved with-out feeling threatened, for there is nothing punitive or legalistic about the program. Contrast an invitation to see Johnny working, being ac-cepted, and trying to succeed, with an order to come to school because he is failing, is truant, and generally troublesome.

Work includes much more than skills. Persons fail to secure or hold jobs because of factors other than occupational skills in the ordinary sense. The problem of placing the youth, therefore, requires that the counselor help the youth demonstrate to a prospective employer that he is the kind of person who can perform the required tasks and can become a member of the production "team." In the program the young person is prepared for this by being exposed to a variety of work tasks.

The rationale of the program is to make Johnny flexible first, then get him started in employment. If Johnny is really prepared by his shop experiences, he will have the psychological integration to stimulate him-self first to be a successful worker and then to seek advancement. Having successfully completed a work-adjustment program, finding a job be-comes easier. Johnny will use our placement facilities and those of the State Employment Service, the State Bureau of Vocational Rehabilitation, or any other agency or person, because he has developed a tolerance for work and a way to accommodate to his peers and supervisors. And most important, he has subdued or learned to live with his anxieties.

Vocational counseling in this program capitalizes on all the gains and growth which the individual has made in the program. The counselor starts at the point the youth has reached as a result of his work-adjustment training. The counselor recognizes that Johnny is a unique individual who must learn to make his way in a complex world which demands continuous interaction with others. Determining what Johnny needs to do to adjust, the counselor supports his efforts to learn more about himself as a worker. He teaches him how to define goals and find good ways of achieving them.

The responsibilities of the counselor do not end when Johnny is adjusted to a job of his own choice. Even after the youth succeeds, he often needs to be helped to take additional steps toward reaching a maximal level of employability. Will he need additional training, and, if so, when and where? Questions such as these are relatively easy to handle. In areas dealing with interpersonal relations, answers are usually not as obvious. But, only when the youth can find them will he be rehabilitated.

The reader will gather from this article that there is considerable work for every agency. A complete program for all youth will include adequate schooling and educational and vocational counseling plus work-adjustment programs as indicated.

A total program is now possible. We need, however, to find ways of defining lines of authority and responsibility. Agencies need also to learn to respect and use each other if they wish to help our youth.

A comprehensive, integrated program is not cheap in terms of money or agency prerogative. It is, however, an inexpensive way to bring better and happier lives for youth; and it will result in huge savings on maintaining institutions, courts, police, and other agencies concerned with social and individual breakdown. We no longer can afford the luxury of postponing cooperative efforts on behalf of disadvantaged youth.

56 / Raising Sights to Higher Horizons

Daniel Schreiber

The Higher Horizons program in New York City is designed to enrich the child's total experience by extending the educational environment beyond the limits of local streets to the whole of New York City and its arts and culture, and by reaching out to the children and their parents with sympathetic guidance and improved instruction in every segment of the curriculum. Started in 1956, the program, in January 1962, was functioning in sixty-three schools with 50,000 students. Success is measured by how all of the children in school have been

Reprinted from *Strengthening Democracy*, May 1960, *12*, 1, 4–6, published by the Board of Education of the City of New York.

*educated up to the limits of their particular talent and how the
community itself has been enriched and changed. Daniel Schreiber,
of the National Education Association, was formerly
coordinator of the Higher Horizons program.*

"Are these the same kids we had before?" a junior high school custodian-
engineer asked the principal several months after the school had initiated
its Higher Horizons program. "Yes," was the reply, "and in the six years
I've been here I've never seen the pupils as interested in their work, as
responsive, and as well behaved."

What had brought about this change?

The Higher Horizons program was set up because of the success of
the Demonstration Guidance Project at Junior High School 43, Manhattan, and George Washington High School. This project was originally
designed to identify, stimulate, and guide into college channels able students from low socio-economic status homes. Its aim was recently broadened to include raising the educational level of all pupils.

Begun in 1956, the study was planned for a six-year period to permit
follow-up of seventh-grade junior high school pupils through graduation
from high school. However, last September, when the project had run
only half its course, Superintendent of Schools Theobald expanded it
from 2 schools to 44 schools, from a junior-senior high school program to
an elementary-junior high school program.

This new Higher Horizons program is in effect in 13 junior high
schools and in 31 elementary schools that feed 9 of these junior high
schools. It now covers about 12,500 pupils.

ACHIEVEMENTS ON JUNIOR HIGH LEVEL

What specific accomplishments of the Demonstration Guidance Project at J.H.S. 43 changed the attitude of many pupils toward school and
encouraged the Superintendent of Schools to expand it into the Higher
Horizons program?

The median seventh-grade student in the guidance project, who was
1.4 years retarded in reading paragraph meaning in 1956, was graduated
from junior high school with a score 3 months above grade level. He
showed a growth of 4.3 years in 2.6 years, or an average growth of 1.7
years per year as contrasted with a previous average growth of .8 year
per year.

In 1956, about 20 per cent of the group was at or above grade level
in reading paragraph meaning; in 1959, the total was 54 per cent. Between 1956 and 1959, the number of students 2 months or more above
grade level rose from 28 to 78.

Project students who took the Otis Beta Intelligence Test in the sixth grade in 1955 and in the ninth grade in 1959 registered an average gain of approximately 4 points, with 21 per cent of the group recording gains of 11 points or more.

J.H.S. 43, Manhattan, has been above the junior high school city average in attendance during the three years of the guidance project, and during that period there has been an increased gain that reached 1.87 per cent above the city average in 1959. Translated into average pupil attendance, this increased percentage means that about 30 additional pupils were in school every day learning and, in the process, bringing the city additional state aid. The rate of increase of Children's Court appearances by pupils from J.H.S. 43 has been only one-half that of the city and one-third that of 6 comparable junior high schools.

PROGRESS ON THE HIGH SCHOOL LEVEL

The effects of the guidance project at George Washington High School, the receiving school for most pupils, paralleled the progress shown in the junior high school. Said Henry Hillson, the principal:

In the past, a large number of our most difficult discipline problems came from students from "43." More teacher and administrative time was spent on them than on any other group. Since the project began, few students in the project group have been reported to the dean's office for discipline. Today we consider the project students good school citizens.

A comparison of the I.Q. scores on the Pintner Test of General Ability (Verbal Series, Advanced Form 3), made by the remaining eleventh-year project group at George Washington in June 1959, with the results achieved by the same group in their eighth year at J.H.S. 43 on Intermediate Form B of the same test showed an average gain of 7 points. Forty out of 105 students showed gains of 10 points or more. Thirteen students, all boys, recorded increases of 21 to 40 points.

These results are even more impressive when considered in the following light: a 5-point change in I.Q. scores, plus or minus, would be considered normal. However, on the basis of past school experience, a drop in the I.Q. score would have been expected as pupils moved on to higher grade levels, since many pupils came from culturally deprived backgrounds and had a reading disability.

The academic record of the project group that entered George Washington High School has been far superior to that of the preproject students. Among the 1953 preproject students, 5 out of 105 passed all their academic subjects at the end of the first year, and 2 had averages of 80 per cent or better; in the 1958 project group, 43 out of 111 passed all their subjects and 16 had averages of 80 per cent or better.

In view of the culturally deprived background of many of the students, it was realized that, at the high school level, they would need considerable assistance in subject matter if any substantial number were to compile academic records that would assure college admission. Therefore, George Washington High School made these special provisions for project students: limited class registers in mathematics and foreign language to 10–15; organized double periods in English and restricted class size to 25; and set up classes in social studies, science, and other subjects with below-average registers. Also, where students needed help, tutorial groups of 2–6 pupils were formed and given assistance after school.

AIMS OF HIGHER HORIZONS PROGRAM

Unlike the Demonstration Guidance Project, which, because of its college admission orientation, began intensive work with the upper 50 per cent of the pupils in the junior high school, the Higher Horizons program aims to raise the educational and vocational sights of all students —bright, average, or slow—so that each can reach his optimum potential. As in the Demonstration Guidance Project, there is provision for additional services for guidance, teacher training, remedial instruction, and cultural enrichment. Also, the schools selected are generally located in less privileged areas where many children come from culturally deprived homes.

The Higher Horizons program functions through Associate Superintendent Joseph O. Loretan on the junior high school level, Associate Superintendent Florence Beaumont on the elementary school level, and the district superintendents. Associate Superintendent C. Frederick Pertsch of the High School Division is supervising planning on that level for the entrance of the present seventh-grade Higher Horizon classes into high school in 1962. Ethel J. Flanagan is serving in the program as guidance consultant and administrative assistant. The advisory committee of the Demonstration Guidance Project is acting in a similar capacity in the Higher Horizons program.

STRESS ON THIRD AND SEVENTH GRADES

Because latent talent usually does not develop to its full potential when early identification and stimulation are lacking, the Higher Horizons program is concentrating during the current school year on the third grade in the elementary schools and on the seventh grade in the junior high schools. While retaining its present grade coverage, it will move forward with the children from grade to grade, reaching the senior high schools in September 1962.

The Higher Horizons program on the seventh grade is substantially the same as that in effect in the Demonstration Guidance Project at J.H.S. 43, except for the inclusion in the program of all students on the grade. This program was fully described in "Operation Talent Search" (*Strengthening Democracy*, Mar.–Apr. 1957). Therefore, this article will concentrate on describing the Higher Horizons program on the third-grade level.

APPROACHES ON THE THIRD-GRADE LEVEL

One guidance position and an additional teaching position have been made available for each school, to be allocated at the discretion of the district superintendent. All districts are using the guidance positions in the same way: individual and group counseling of children and parents, consultation with teachers and administrators, conducting parent workshops, making and following up agency contacts.

Varied approaches are being followed in the use of the additional teaching positions. In District A, which already had the services of a remedial reading teacher in each school, the assistant superintendent, after consultation with the principals, assigned the extra teacher as a project assistant to work with the third-grade teachers.

The project assistant gives demonstration lessons, helps teachers prepare lesson plans, makes available audio-visual aids, works with one group in the classroom while the teacher works with another, coordinates trips, acts in a consultative capacity, edits the third-grade newspaper in each school devoted to Higher Horizons, works with parents, and meets with other project assistants and the district coordinator to exchange ideas and plan for future activities.

All third-grade teachers in this district took an in-service course on the third-grade curriculum, given by the specialists assigned to the district superintendent's office.

In District B, the assistant superintendent is using the additional positions differently. One teacher is acting as coordinator of trips and excursions. The other seven are serving as curriculum specialists: two each in reading and mathematics, and one each in science, music, and art.

These specialists visit the schools on a regularly scheduled basis. They give demonstration lessons, assist in the implementation of curriculum bulletins in the schools, and provide materials for use by teachers in the classroom.

Since each community has problems and resources that are unique, the program is community-oriented so that each neighborhood can meet its own needs. Uniformity is sought only in those areas that are common to all and that form the basis for evaluation and research—for example, progress in reading and arithmetic.

Reading, arithmetic, and group intelligence tests have been given to all children in order to identify their capabilities. And in some schools, the counselor has already held a conference with each child.

PARENT AND COMMUNITY COOPERATION

The parents and community are cooperating in the program, particularly in cultural enrichment activities. Many schools have instruction in learning to play the recorder, sometimes given by a parent. A neighborhood music school is giving concerts for the children on Saturday mornings. Parents in many schools have catalogued books, using the Dewey decimal classification, and have helped to set up a school library.

Public Education Association volunteers are serving as teacher aides in two schools. There are two volunteers for each class on the grade level. They check attendance, collect milk money, take groups to other places in the school to do research, work with small groups doing research, help pupils construct materials, and score standardized tests. Those volunteers with professional training are also able to give instruction in remedial reading, after orientation by a remedial reading teacher in the school or district.

SIGNS OF PROGRESS

Parent interest in the school program has burgeoned. Attendance at third-grade parents' meetings has skyrocketed. At one school, with a third-grade register of 250, an afternoon meeting drew 150 parents. Attendance at parent workshops has remained at a constantly high level. Parents are volunteering to take small groups of children on trips on Saturdays and Sundays. Increased understanding of Higher Horizons' aims has won their cooperation and participation in the school program.

The children's attitude toward learning has become more positive. For both parents and children, education has apparently become more important. Principals and teachers report that discipline in the halls and classrooms has improved, and vandalism has decreased. The change in pupil attitude has diminished tensions for the teacher. Since less time must be devoted to discipline, more time and energy are available for instruction.

SIGNIFICANCE OF HIGHER HORIZONS

The Higher Horizons program is a realization of the hopes expressed in the article in *Strengthening Democracy* (Mar.–Apr. 1957) on the Demonstration Guidance Project at J.H.S. 43:

The significance of this project extends far beyond the particular group under study. It is hoped that it will serve as a pilot project for the New York City schools and for nationwide programs to uncover the talent of young people who do not reveal their potentialities because of the absence of adequate identification techniques and lack of guidance, motivation, or information available to their families.

There is nationwide interest in Higher Horizons as a pioneer program. This interest is expressed in the constant stream of inquiries about the program from all parts of the country.

A number of divisions and bureaus in our school system are cooperating in order to reach toward Higher Horizons: the Bureau of Curriculum Research, the Bureau of Educational and Vocational Guidance, the Bureau of Educational Research, and the Housing Division. All of these agencies are working with the Elementary and Junior High School Divisions to help each child to raise his educational and vocational sights and realize his potentialities.

References Cited
in Selections

The date of each publication corresponds with the date given in a selection after an author's name.

Abel, L. B. 1936. The effects of shift in motivation upon the learning of a sensorimotor task. *Arch. Psychol.*, N.Y., *29*, No. 205.

Ackerman, N. W., and M. Jahoda. 1950. *Anti-semitism and emotional disorder.* New York: Harper.

Ackerman, W. I. 1954. Teacher competence and pupil change. *Harvard educ. Rev.*, *24*, 273–89.

Adorno, T. W., et al. 1949. *The authoritarian personality.* New York: Harper.

Alden, E. 1959. The effect on non-target classmates of the teacher's use of expert power and liking power in controlling deviant behavior. Unpublished doctoral dissertation, Wayne State University.

Anderson, H. H. 1939. Domination and social integration in the behavior of kindergarten children and teachers. *Genet. Psychol. Monogr.*, *21*, 287–385.

———. 1943. Domination and socially integrative behavior. In R. G. Barker, J. S. Kounin, and H. F. Wright (Eds.), *Child Behavior and Development.* New York: McGraw-Hill, pp. 459–83.

———, and G. L. Anderson. 1954. Children's perceptions of social conflict situations: a study of adolescent children in Germany. *Amer. J. Orthopsychiat.*, *24*, 246–57.

———, ———. 1956. Cultural reactions to conflict: a study of adolescent children in seven countries. In G. M. Gilbert (Ed.), *Psychological Approaches to Intergroup and International Understanding: A Symposium of the Third Interamerican Congress of Psychology.* Hogg Foundation, pp. 27–32.

———, ———. 1957. A cross-national study of teacher-child relations as reported by adolescent children. Paper presented at the Fifth Interamerican Congress of Psychology, National University of Mexico City.

———, and H. M. Brewer. 1945. *Studies of teachers' classroom personalities: I. Dominative and socially integrative behavior of kindergarten teachers.* Stanford: Stanford University Press.

———, ———. 1945a. *Studies of teachers' classroom personalities: II. Effects of teachers' dominative and integrative contacts on children's classroom behavior.* Stanford: Stanford University Press.

———, ———, and M. F. Reed, 1946. *Studies of teachers' classroom personalities: III. Follow-up studies of the effects of dominative and integrative contacts on children's behavior.* Stanford: Stanford University Press.

———, et al. 1957. Dominative and integrative teacher-child relations in five countries as reported by adolescent children. Paper presented to Michigan Academy of Science, Arts, and Letters.

Atkinson, J. 1957. Motivational determinants of risk-taking behavior. *Psychol. Rev., 64,* 359–72.

Ausubel, D. P. 1952. *Ego development and personality disorders.* New York: Grune & Stratton.

———. 1954. *Theory and problems of adolescent development.* New York: Grune & Stratton.

———. 1958. *Theory and problems of child development.* New York: Grune & Stratton.

———, et al. 1954. Perceived patent attitudes as determinants of children's ego structure. *Child Develpm., 25,* 173–83.

Bach, G. R. 1946. Father-fantasies and father-typing in father-separated children. *Child Develpm., 17,* 63–79.

Bain, W. E. 1934. A study of the attitudes of teachers toward behavior problems. *Child Develpm., 5,* 19–35.

Baldwin, A. L. 1948. Socialization and the parent-child relationship. *Child Develpm., 19,* 127–36.

———, J. Kalhorn, and F. H. Breese. 1945. The appraisal of parent behavior. *Psychol. Monogr., 58,* No. 3.

Bandura, A., and R. H. Walters. 1959. *Adolescent aggression.* New York: Ronald.

Barker, R. C., and H. F. Wright. 1954. *Midwest and its children.* Evanston, Ill.: Row, Peterson.

Bate, E. B. 1948. The effect of especially prepared materials in a learning program in human growth and development on the tenth grade level. Unpublished doctoral dissertation, University of Iowa.

Bavelas, A. 1947. Role playing and management training. *Sociatry, 1,* 183–91.

Beilin, H. 1957. The prediction of adjustment over a four year interval. *J. clin. Psychol., 13,* 270–74.

———. 1958. Effects of social (occupational) role and age upon the criteria of mental health. *J. soc. Psychol., 48,* 247–56.

———, and E. Werner. 1957. Sex differences among teachers in the use of criteria of adjustment. *J. educ. Psychol., 48,* 426–36.

———, ———. 1957a. Sex role expectations and the criteria of social adjustment for young adults. *J. clin. Psychol., 13,* 341–43.

Bird, C. 1931. *Effective study habits.* New York: Appleton-Century-Crofts.

Blair, A. W., and W. H. Burton. 1951. *Growth and development of the pre-adolescent.* New York: Appleton-Century-Crofts.

Blanchard, P., and R. H. Paynter. 1924. The problem child. *Ment. Hyg., N.Y., 8,* 26–54.

Bogardus, E. W. 1947. Changes in racial distances. *Intl. J. Opin. Attit. Res., 1,* 55–62.

Bonney, M. E. 1943. Personality traits of socially successful and socially unsuccessful children. *J. educ. Psychol., 34,* 449–72.

———. 1944. Sex differences in social success and personality traits. *Child Develpm., 15,* 63–79.

Book, W. F. 1927. Results obtained in a special 'how-to-study' course given to college students. *Sch. and Soc., 26,* 529–34.

Bowles, H. H. 1937. A study of nurses' attitudes toward behavior problems in children under hospital care. *Child Develpm., 8,* 282–88.

Bowman, P. H. 1953. Studying children and training counselors in a community program. Supplementary Educational Monographs, No. 78. Chicago: Univeristy of Chicago Press.

Boynton, P. L., and B. H. McGaw. 1934. The characteristics of problem children. *J. juv. Res., 18*, 215–22.

Brackbill, Y., and J. O'Hara. 1958. The relative effectiveness of reward and punishment for discrimination learning in children. *J. comp. Physiol. Phychol., 51*, 747–51.

Brim, O. G. 1957. The parent-child relation as a social system: I. Parent and child roles. *Child Develpm., 28*, 343–64.

Bronfenbrenner, U. 1958. Socialization and social class through time and space. In E. Maccoby, T. M. Newcomb, and E. L. Hartley (Eds.), *Readings in social psychology.* New York: Holt, Rinehart and Winston, pp. 400–25.

————. 1961. Some familial antecedents of responsibility and leadership in adolescents. In L. Petrullo, and B. M. Bass (Eds.), *Leadership and interpersonal behavior.* New York: Holt, Rinehart and Winston, pp. 239–71.

Bronson, W. C., E. S. Katten, and N. Livson. 1959. Patterns of authority and affection in two generations. *J. abnorm. soc. Psychol., 58*, 143–52.

Brophy, I. 1945. The luxury of anti-Negro prejudice. *Publ. Opin. Quart., 9*, 456–66.

Brown, A., J. Morrison, and G. Couch. 1947. The influence of affectional family relationships on character development. *J. abnorm. soc. Psychol., 42*, 422–28.

Brown, F. 1942. An experimental study of parental attitudes and their effect upon child adjustment. *Amer. J. Orthopsychiat., 12*, 224–30.

Burchinal. L. G., G. R. Hawkes, and B. Gardner. 1957. The relationship between parental acceptance and adjustment of children. *Child Develpm., 28*, 65–77.

Buswell, M. M. 1953. The relationship between the social structure of the classroom and the academic success of the pupils. *J. Exp. Educ., 22*, 37–52.

Cameron, W. J., and W. F. Kenkel. 1960. High school dating: a study of variation. *Marriage Family Living, 22*, 74–76.

Campbell, E. H. 1939. The social-sex development of children. *Genet. Psychol. Monogr., 21*, pp. 461–552.

Cantril, H. 1940. *The Invasion from Mars.* Princeton, N.J.: Princeton University Press.

Carbone, R. F. 1961. Achievement, mental health, and instruction in graded and non-graded elementary schools. Unpublished doctoral dissertation, University of Chicago.

Carlson, E. R. 1953. Attitude change through modification of attitude structure. Unpublished doctoral dissertation, University of Michigan.

Cartwright, D. 1959. Power: a neglected variable in social psychology. In D. Cartwright (Ed.), *Studies in social power.* Ann Arbor: University of Michigan Press.

Chwast, J. 1956. A study of the relationship between boys' perceptions of parental attitudes and their pre-delinquency. Unpublished doctoral dissertation, New York University.

Clark, C. H. 1958. *Brainstorming.* New York: Doubleday.

Clark, E. J. 1951. Teacher reactions toward objectionable pupil behavior. *Elem. Sch. J., 51*, 446–49.

Coch, L., and R. P. French. 1948. Overcoming resistances to change. *Human Relat., 1*, 512–32.

Cochran, W. G., and G. M. Cox. 1950. *Experimental design.* New York: Wiley.

Coleman, J. 1960. The adolescent subculture and academic achievement. *Amer. J. Sociol., 65*, 337–47.

Combs, A. W., and D. W. Soper. Publication pending. The helping relationship as seen by "good" and "poor" teachers.

Coulson, J. E., and H. F. Silberman. 1959. *Results of initial experiment in automated teaching.* Systems Development Corporation.

Crawford, C. C. 1926. Some results of teaching college students how to study. *Sch. and Soc., 23,* 471–72.

Crowder, N. A. 1958. Automatic tutoring by means of intrinsic programming. Paper read at the University of Pennsylvania Conference on the Automated Teaching of Verbal and Symbolic Skills.

Davidson, K. S. 1959. Interviews of parents of high anxious and low anxious children. *Child Develpm., 30,* 341–51.

———, et al. 1958. Differences between mothers' and fathers' ratings of low and high anxious children. *Child Develpm., 29,* 155–60.

Davis, E. A., and E. McGinnis. 1939. *Parent education: a survey of the Minnesota program.* Minneapolis: University of Minnesota Press.

De Leonard, C. C. 1956. Some psycho-cultural defense reactions of Mexican Indians. In G. M. Gilbert (Ed.), *Psychological Approaches to Intergroup and International Understanding: A Symposium of the Third Interamerican Congress of Psychology.* Hogg Foundation, pp. 50–56.

Del Solar, C. 1949. *Parents and teachers view the child: a comparative study of parents' and teachers' appraisals of children.* New York: Teachers College, Columbia University.

Deutsch, M. 1949. A theory of cooperation and competition. *Human Relat., 2,* 129–52.

———. 1949a. The effects of cooperation and competition upon group process: an experimental study. *Amer. Psychologist, 4,* 263–64.

———, and M. E. Collins. 1952. In G. Swanson, T. M. Newcomb, and E. L. Hartley (Eds.), *Readings in Social Psychology.* New York: Holt, Rinehart and Winston, pp. 582–93.

Diaz-Guerrero, R. 1955. Neurosis and the Mexican family structure. *Amer. J. Psychiat., 6,* 411–17.

Dickson, V. E. 1932. Behavior difficulties that baffle teachers. *J. juv. Res., 16,* 93–101.

DiMichael, S. G. 1943. Increase in knowledge of how to study resulting from a how-to-study course. *Sch. Rev., 51,* 353–59.

Doob, L. W. 1953. Effects of initial serial positions and attitude upon recall conditions of low motivation. *J. abnorm. soc. Psychol., 48,* 199–205.

Douglas, V. 1958. The development of two families of defense. Unpublished doctoral dissertation, University of Michigan.

Douvan, E. 1956. Social status and success strivings. *J. abnorm. soc. Psychol., 52,* 219–24.

Durrell, D., et al. 1959. Adapting instruction to the learning needs of children in intermediate grades. *J. Educ., 142,* 1–78.

Echelberger, E. 1959. Relationships between personality traits and peer status. Unpublished doctoral dissertation, University of Michigan.

Eckert, R. E., and E. S. Jones. 1935. Long time effects of training college students how to study. *Sch. and Soc., 42,* 685–88.

Edwards, A. L. 1941. Political frames of reference as a factor influencing recognition. *J. abnorm. soc. Psychol., 36,* 34–50.

———. 1950. *Experimental design in psychological research.* New York: Holt, Rinehart and Winston.

Ellis, D. B., and L. W. Miller. 1936. Teachers' attitudes and behavior problems. *J. educ. Psychol.*, 27, 501–11.

Entwisle, D. R. 1960. Evaluations of study-skills courses; a review. *J. educ. Res.*, 53, 243–51.

Epstein, L. J. 1941. An analysis of teachers' judgments of problem children. *J. genet. Psychol.*, 59, 101–107.

Ewing, T. 1942. A study of certain factors involved in changes of opinion. *J. soc. Psychol.*, 16, 63–88.

Ezekiel, M. 1932. Students' method for measuring the significance of a difference between matched groups. *J. educ. Psychol.*, 23, 446–50.

Ferster, C. B., and S. M. Sapon. 1958. An application of recent developments in psychology to the teaching of German. *Harvard educ. Rev.*, 28, 58–69.

Festinger, L. 1942. Wish, expectation, and group standards as factors influencing level of aspiration. *J. abnorm. soc. Psychol.*, 37, 184–200.

———. 1954. A theory of social comparison processes. *Human Relat.*, 7, 117–40.

———. 1957. *A Theory of cognitive dissonance.* Evanston, Ill.: Row, Peterson.

———, S. Schachter, and K. Back. 1950. *Social pressures in informal groups.* New York: Harper.

Fiedler, F. E. 1950. A comparison of therapeutic relationships in psychoanalytic, nondirective and Adlerian therapy. *J. consult. Psychol.*, 14, 436–45.

———. 1950a. The concept of an ideal therapeutic relationship. *J consult. Psychol.*, 14, 239–45.

Flanders, N. A., and S. Havumaki. 1960. The effects of teacher-pupil contacts involving praise on the sociometric choices of students. *J. educ. Psychol.*, 51, 65–68.

Freeman, F. N. 1939. *Mental tests.* Boston: Houghton Mifflin.

French, J. R. P. 1951. Group productivity. In H. Guetzkow (Ed.), *Groups, Leadership, and Men.* Pittsburgh: Carnegie Institute of Technology Press, pp. 44–54.

———. 1956. A formal theory of social power. *Psychol. Rev.*, 63, 181–95.

———, and B. Raven. 1959. The bases of social power. In D. Cartwright (Ed.), *Studies in Social Power.* Ann Arbor: University of Michigan Press.

Furfey, P. H. 1930. *The growing boy.* New York: Macmillan.

Gallagher, J. J. 1959. The gifted child in the elementary school. *What Research Says to the Teacher,* No. 17. Washington, D.C.: National Education Association.

Gatchel, D. F. 1931. Results of a how-to-study course given in high school. *Sch. Rev.*, 39, 123–29.

Geierhaas, F. G. 1955. Problems of reliability in evaluating story completions about social conflict by German adolescent children. Unpublished master's thesis, Michigan State University.

Gnagey, W. J. 1960. Effects on classmates of a deviant student's power and response to a teacher-exerted control technique. *J. educ. Psychol.*, 51, 1–9.

Gold, M. 1958. Power in the classroom. *Sociometry,* 21, 50–60.

———, and C. Slater. 1958. Office, factory, store, and family: a study of integration setting. *Amer. sociol. Rev.*, 23, 64–74.

Goldstein, A. 1960. Does homework help? a review of research. *Elem. Sch. J.*, 60, 212–24.

Goodlad, J. I. 1960. Classroom organization. In C. W. Harris (Ed.), *Encyclopedia of Educational Research.* New York: Macmillan, p. 224.

———, and R. H. Anderson. 1959. *The nongraded elementary school.* New York: Harcourt, Brace & World.

Gough, H. G., et al. 1950. Children's ethnic attitudes: I. Relationship to certain personality factors. *Child Develpm., 21,* 83–91.

Green, A. 1946. The middle class male child and neurosis. *Amer. sociol. Rev., 11,* 31–41.

Griffiths, W. 1952. *Behavior difficulties of children as perceived and judged by parents, teachers and children themselves.* Minneapolis: University of Minnesota Press.

Gronlund, N. E. 1950. The accuracy of teachers' judgments concerning the sociometric status of sixth-grade pupils. *Sociometry, 13,* 329–57.

———. 1955. Generality of sociometric status over criteria in the measurement of social acceptability. *Elem. Sch. J., 56,* 173–76.

———, and A. P. Whitney. 1956. Relation between pupils' social acceptability in the classroom, in the school, and in the neighborhood. *Sch. Rev., 64,* 267–71.

Grossack, M. M. 1952. The effect of cohesiveness, social influence, and communication. Unpublished doctoral dissertation, Boston University.

Gruber, S. 1954. The concept of task-orientation in the analysis of play behavior of children entering kindergarten. *Amer. J. Orthopsychiat., 24,* 326–35.

Guilford, J. P. 1942. *Fundamentals of statistics in psychology and education.* New York: McGraw-Hill.

———. 1959. Three faces of intellect. *Amer. Psychologist, 14,* 469–79.

Gump, P. V., and J. S. Kounin. 1959–1960. Issues raised by ecological and 'classical' research efforts. *Merrill-Palmer quart. of Behav. and Develpm., 6,* 145–53.

Gunther, J. 1955. *Inside Africa.* New York: Harper.

Gurnee, H. 1937. Maze learning in the collective situation. *J. Psychol., 3,* 437–43.

Guttman, L. 1950. The basis for scalogram analysis. In S. Stouffer, et al. (Eds.), *Measurement and Prediction.* Princeton, N.J.: Princeton University Press, pp. 60–90.

———. 1954. Principle components of scalable attitudes. In P. F. Lazarsfeld (Ed.), *Mathematical Thinking in the Social Sciences.* Glencoe, Ill.: Free Press, pp. 229–33.

Haggard, E. A. 1957. Socialization, personality, and academic achievement in gifted children. *Sch. Rev., 65,* 388–414.

Haggerty, M. E., W. C. Olson, and E. K. Wickman. 1930. *Haggerty-Olson-Wickman Behavior Rating Scales.* Cleveland: World.

Harrower-Erikson, M. R., and M. E. Steiner. 1945. *Large scale Rorschach techniques.* Springfield, Ill.: Charles C Thomas.

Hartmann, G. W. 1936. A field experiment on the comparative effectiveness of 'emotional' and 'rational' political leaflets in determining election results. *J. abnorm. soc. Psychol., 31,* 99–114.

Hattwick, B., and M. Stowell. 1936–1937. The relation of parental over-attentiveness to children's work habits and social adjustments in kindergarten and the first six years of school. *J. educ. Res., 30,* 169–76.

Havighurst, R. J., M. Z. Robinson, and M. Dorr. 1946. The development of the ideal self in childhood and adolescence. *J. educ. Res., 40,* 241–57.

Heber, R. F. 1955. A cross-national comparison of children's judgment of parent-child conflict in Germany, England, Finland, United States, and Mexico. Unpublished master's thesis, Michigan State University.

Heider, F. 1958. *The psychology of interpersonal relations.* New York: Wiley.

Heine, R. W. 1950. A comparison of patients' reports on psychotherapeutic experience with psychoanalytic, nondirective, and Adlerian therapists. Unpublished doctoral dissertation, University of Chicago.

Hendrickson, G., and W. Schroeder. 1941. Transfer of training in learning to hit a submerged target. *J. educ. Psychol., 32*, 206–13.

Hertzman, J. 1948. High school mental hygiene survey. *Amer. J. Orthopsychiat., 18*, 238–56.

Hildreth, G. 1928. A survey of problem pupils. *J. educ. Res., 18*, 1–14.

Hiller, E. T. 1928. *The strike.* Chicago: University of Chicago Press.

Hilton, T. L. 1955. Ego-involvement in teaching: its theory and measurement by a word completion technique. Unpublished doctoral dissertation, Harvard University.

Hoffman, M. L. 1953. Some psychodynamic factors in compulsive conformity. *J. abnorm. soc. Psychol., 48*, 383–93.

Hollingshead, A. B. 1949. *Elmtown's youth.* New York: Wiley.

Homme, L., and R. Glaser. 1958. Relationships between the programmed textbook and teaching machines. Paper read at the University of Pennsylvania Conference on the Automated Teaching of Verbal and Symbolic Skills.

Hood, W. R., and M. Sherif. 1955. Personality oriented approaches to prejudice. *Sociol. soc. Res., 40*, 79–85.

Horowitz, E. L. 1944. Race attitudes. In O. Klineberg (Ed.), *Characteristics of the American Negro.* New York: Harper, Part IV.

Hovland, C. I. (Ed.). 1957. *The order of presentation in persuasion.* New Haven: Yale University Press.

———, I. L. Janis, and H. H. Kelley. 1953. *Communication and persuasion.* New Haven: Yale University Press.

———, A. A. Lumsdaine, and F. D. Sheffield. 1949. *Experiments on mass communication.* Princeton, N.J.: Princeton University Press.

Hsia, J. C. 1928. A study of the sociability of elementary school children. *Teachers College Contributions to Education, No. 322.* New York: Teachers College, Columbia University.

Hull, J. H. 1958. Multigrade teaching. *Nation's Schools, 62*, 33–36.

Hunt, M. 1953. The Wellesley experiment: a pioneer undertaking in psychiatry for the community. *Harper's Magazine, 207*, 75–81.

Hunter, E. C. 1957. Changes in teachers' attitudes toward children's behavior over the last thirty years. *Ment. Hyg., N.Y., 41*, 3–11.

Hurlock, E. B. 1927. The use of group rivalry as an incentive. *J. abnorm. soc. Psychol., 22*, 278–90.

———, and L. C. McDonald. 1934. Undesirable behavior traits in junior high school students. *Child Develpm., 5*, 278–90.

Hurwitz, J., A. Zander, and B. Hymovitch. 1953, 1960. Some effects of power on the relations among group members. In D. Cartwright and A. Zander (Eds.), *Group Dynamics, Research and Theory.* Evanston, Ill.: Row, Peterson, pp. 483–92, 800–809.

Ives, O. L. 1949. A critique of teachers' ratings of high school boys as an indication of later neuropsychiatric rejection for the armed services. *Teachers College Contributions to Education, No. 950.* New York: Teachers College, Columbia University.

Jackson, D. M., et al. 1960. Five projects designed to increase students' independence in learning, University of Illinois High School. *National Association of Secondary-School Principals, Bulletin, 44*, 490–504.

Jackson, E. B., E. H. Klatskin, and L. C. Wilkin. 1952. Early child development in relation to the degree of flexibility of maternal attitudes. *Psychoanalytic Stud. Child, 7*, 393–428.

Jackson, J. 1952. Analysis of interpersonal relations in a formal organization. Unpublished doctoral dissertation, University of Michigan.

Janis, I., and S. Feshbach. 1953. Effects of fear-arousing communications. *J. abnorm. soc. Psychol., 48,* 78–92.

———, and B. T. King. 1954. The influence of role playing on opinion change. *J. abnorm. soc. Psychol., 49,* 211–18.

Jennings, H. H. 1943. *Leadership and isolation.* New York: Longmans Green.

Johnson, D. M. 1955. *The psychology of thought and judgment.* New York: Harper.

Jones, E. S. 1927. Testing and training the inferior or doubtful freshman. *Personnel J., 6,* 182–91.

———. 1929. The preliminary course on 'how to study' for freshmen entering college. *Sch. and Soc., 29,* 702–705.

Judd, C. H. 1908. The relation of special training to general intelligence. *Educ. Rev., 36,* 28–42.

Kelley, H. H. 1951. Communication in experimentally created hierarchies. *Human Relat., 4,* 39–56.

———, and J. W. Thibaut. 1954. Experimental studies of group problem solving and process. In G. Lindzey (Ed.), *Handbook of Social Psychology, Vol. 2, Special Fields and Applications.* Reading, Mass.: Addison-Wesley, pp. 735–85.

Kerstetter, L. M., and J. Sargent. 1940. Reassignment therapy in the classroom. *Sociometry, 3,* 292–306.

Kingsley, H. L., and R. Garry. 1957. *The nature and conditions of learning.* Englewood Cliffs, N.J.: Prentice-Hall.

Klausmeier, H., and J. C. Stanley. 1957. Opinion constancy after formal role playing. *J. abnorm. soc. Psychol., 6,* 11–18.

Klein, D., and A. Ross. 1958. Kindergarten entry: a study of role transition. In M. Krugman (Ed.), *Orthopsychiatry and the School.* American Orthopsychiatric Association, pp. 60–69.

Klugman, S. F., 1944. Cooperative versus individual efficiency in problem solving. *J. educ. Psychol., 35,* 91–100.

Kohn, M. L. 1959. Social class and parental values. *Amer. J. Sociol., 44,* 337–51.

———, and J. A. Clausen. 1956. Parental authority, behavior and schizophrenia. *Amer. J. Orthopsychiat., 26,* 299–313.

Kounin, J. S., and P. V. Gump. 1958. The ripple effect in discipline. *Elem. Sch. J., 59,* 158–62.

———, ———. 1961. The comparative influence of punitive and nonpunitive teachers upon children's concepts of school misconduct. *J. educ. Psychol., 52,* 44–49.

Kowitz, G. T., and C. M. Armstrong. 1961. The effect of promotion policy on academic achievement. *Elem. Sch. J., 61,* 435–43.

Krech, D., and R. Crutchfield. 1948. *Theory and problems of social psychology.* New York: McGraw-Hill.

Kuhlen, R. G., and B. J. Lee. 1943. Personality characteristics and social acceptability in adolescence. *J. educ. Psychol., 34,* 321–40.

Kurtz, K. H., and C. I. Hovland. 1953. The effect of verbalization during observation of stimulus objects upon accuracy of recognition and recall. *J. exp. Psychol., 45,* 157–64.

Landis, J. T., and M. G. Landis. 1958. *Building a successful marriage.* Englewood Cliffs, N.J.: Prentice-Hall.

Laughlin, F. 1954. The peer status of sixth- and seventh-grade children. New York: Teachers College, Columbia University.

Laycock, S. R. 1934. Teachers' reactions to maladjustments of school children. *British J. educ. Psychol., 4,* 11–29.

————, and D. H. Russell. 1941. An analysis of thirty-eight how-to-study manuals. *Sch. Rev., 49,* 370–79.

Lazarsfield, P., B. Berelson, and H. Gaudet. 1948. *The people's choice.* New York: Columbia University Press.

Leuba, C. 1933. An experimental study of rivalry in young children. *J. comp. Psychol., 16,* 367–78.

Levitt, E. E. 1955. Effect of 'causal' teacher training program on authoritarianism and responsibility in grade school children. *Psychol. Rep., 1,* 449–58.

————, and R. H. Ojemann. 1953. The aims of preventive psychiatry and 'causality' as a personality pattern. *J. Psychol., 36,* 393–400.

Levy, J. 1931. A quantitative study of the relationship between intelligence and economic status as factors in the etiology of children's behavior problems. *Amer. J. Orthopsychiat., 1,* 152–62.

Lewin, K. 1947. Group decision and social change. In T. M. Newcomb and E. L. Hartley (Eds.), *Readings in Social Psychology.* New York: Holt, pp. 330–44.

————, et al. 1944. Level of aspiration. In J. McV. Hunt (Ed.), *Personality and the Behavior Disorders.* New York: Ronald, pp. 333–78.

Lewis, G. M. 1958. Educating children in grades four, five, and six. *U. S. Office of Ed. Bull.,* No. 3. Washington, D.C.: Government Printing Office.

Lindemann, Elizabeth B., and A. Ross. 1957. A follow-up study of a predictive test of social adaptation in preschool children. In G. Caplan (Ed.), *Emotional Problems in Early Childhood.* New York: Basic Books, pp. 79–93.

Lindemann, Erich. 1953. The Wellesley project for the study of certain problems in community mental health. In *Interrelations between the Social Environment and Psychiatric Disorders.* New York: Milbank Memorial Fund, pp. 165–85.

Lindquist, E. F. 1940. *Statistical analysis in educational research.* Boston: Houghton Mifflin.

Lippitt, R., et al. 1952. The dynamics of power. *Human Relat., 5,* 37–64.

Lorge, I., et al. 1958. A survey of studies contrasting the quality of group performance and individual performance, 1920–1957. *Psychol. Bull., 55,* 337–72.

Lowenfeld, V. 1958. Current research on creativity. *Natl Educ. Assn J., 47,* 538–40.

Lowrie, S. H. 1956. Factors involved in the frequency of dating. *Marriage Fam. Living, 18,* 46–51.

Luchins, A. S. 1957. Primacy-recency in impression formation. In C. I. Rowland (Ed.), *The Order of Presentation in Persuasion.* New Haven: Yale University Press.

Lynn, D. B., and W. L. Sawrey. 1959. The effects of father-absence on Norwegian boys and girls. *J. abnorm. soc. Psychol., 59,* 258–62.

Lynn, K. S. 1955. *The dream of success.* Boston: Little, Brown.

McCandless, B. 1941. A study of selected factors affecting radio listening behavior. Unpublished doctoral dissertation, University of Iowa.

McCleary, L. 1956. Restructuring the interpersonal relations of a junior high school class. *Sch. Rev., 64,* 346–52.

McClelland, D. C., et al. 1953. *The achievement motive*. New York: Appleton-Century-Crofts.

MacClenathan, R. H. 1934. Teachers and parents study children's behaviors. *J. educ. Sociol., 7, 325–33.*

McClure, W. E. 1929. Characteristics of problem children based on judgements of teachers. *J. juv. Res., 13, 124–40.*

McGinnies, E. 1956. A method for matching anonymous questionnaire data with group discussion material. *J. abnorm. soc. Psychol., 52, 139–40.*

———, and W. Vaughan. 1957. Some biographical determiners of participation in group discussion. *J. appl. Psychol., 41, 179–85.*

McGinnis, M. 1954. The Wellesley project program of preschool emotional assessment. *J. psychiat. soc. Wk, 23, 135–41.*

McGranahan, D. V. 1946. A comparison of social attitudes among American and German youth. *J. abnorm. soc. Psychol., 41, 245–57.*

McHugh, W. J. 1959. Team learning in skill subjects in intermediate grades. *J. Educ., 142, 22–52.*

———, and J. C. Manning. 1961. Arithmetic job sheets to accompany growth in arithmetic. Cleveland: World.

McNemar, Q. 1949. *Psychological statistics*. New York: Wiley.

Mallory, V. S. 1943. *New plane geometry*. Syracuse, N.Y.: Sanborn.

Mandler, G., and S. B. Sarason. 1952. A study of anxiety and learning. *J. abnorm. soc. Psychol., 47, 166–73.*

Mann, J. H. 1956. Experimental evaluations of role playing. *Psychol. Bull., 53, 227–34.*

Manning, J. G. 1959. Differentiating instruction in the content subjects in intermediate grades. *J. Educ., 142, 52–66.*

Martin, A. R. 1943. A study of parental attitudes and their influence upon personality development. *Educ. 63, 596–608.*

Menger, K. 1958. New approach to teaching intermediate mathematics. *Science, 127, 1320–23.*

Michael, D. M., and N. Maccoby. 1953. Factors influencing verbal learning from films under varying conditions of audience participation. *J. exp. Psychol., 46, 411–18.*

Miller, D. R., and G. E. Swanson. 1958. *The changing American parent*. New York: Wiley.

———, ———. 1960. *Inner conflict and defense*. New York: Holt, Rinehart and Winston.

Miller, F. B. 1954. Resistentialism in applied social research. *Human Organization, 12, 5–8.*

Mills, H. C. 1934. How to study courses and academic achievement. *Educ. Administ. Supervis., 20, 619–24.*

Mitchell, J. C. 1942. A study of teachers' and mental hygienists' ratings of certain behavior problems of children. *J. educ. Res., 36, 292–307.*

Mizuhara, T., and S. Tamai. 1953. Experimental studies of cooperation and competition. *Japanese J. Psychol., 22, 124–27, 1952. In Psychol. Abstr., 27, 519.*

Moore, H. 1934. Training college freshmen to read. *J. appl. Psychol., 18, 631–34.*

Moreno, J. L. 1934. *Who Shall Survive?* Nervous and Mental Disease Monograph, No. 58.

———, and H. H. Jennings. 1944. Sociometric methods of grouping and regrouping with reference to authoritative and democratic methods of grouping. *Sociometry, 7, 397–411.*

Morgan, M., and R. H. Ojemann. 1942. The effect of a learning program designed to assist youth in an understanding of behavior and its development. *Child Develpm., 13,* 181–94.

Murphy, G. 1953. *In the minds of men.* New York: Basic Books.

Murray, H. A. 1938. *Explorations in personality.* New York: Oxford University Press.

Mussen, P. H. 1950. Some personality and social factors related to changes in children's attitudes toward Negroes. *J. abnorm. soc. Psychol., 45,* 423–41.

———, and J. J. Conger. 1956. *Child development and personality.* New York: Harper.

———, and L. Distler. 1959. Masculinity, identification, and father-son relationships. *J. abnorm. soc. Psychol., 59,* 350–56.

National Association of Secondary-School Principals Bulletin. Washington, D.C.: National Education Association. January 1958. *New horizons in staff utilization;* January 1959. *Exploring improved teaching patterns;* January 1960. *Progressing toward better schools;* January 1961. *Seeking improved learning opportunities.*

National Social Welfare Assembly, Committee on Youth Services. 1958. *Report of Consultation on Youth in Community Affairs.*

Neprash, J. 1952. Racial group contacts and social distance. *Phylon, 16,* 207–12.

Neumeyer, M. H. 1949. *Juvenile delinquency in modern society.* Princeton, N.J.: Van Nostrand.

Newcomb, T. M. 1956. The prediction of interpersonal attraction. *Amer. Psychologist, 11,* 575–86.

Newell, H. W. 1934. Psychodynamics of maternal rejection. *Amer. J. Orthopsychiat., 4,* 387–95.

Northway, M. L. 1944. Outsiders: a study of the personality patterns of children least acceptable to their age mates. *Sociometry, 7,* 10–25.

Norwalk (Conn.) Board of Education. 1959. *The Norwalk plan: a study designed to establish new careers for teachers.*

Ofschus, L. T. 1960. The effects on non-target classmates of teacher's efforts to control deviant behavior. Unpublished doctoral dissertation, Wayne State University.

Ojemann, R. H. 1946. The effect on the child's development of changes in cultural influences. *J. educ. Res., 40,* 258–70.

———. 1948. Research in planned learning programs and the science of behavior. *J. educ. Res., 42,* 96–104.

———. 1954. Personality adjustment of individual children. *What Research Says to the Teacher, No. 5.* Washington, D.C.: National Education Association.

———, et al. 1955. The effects of a 'causal' teacher-training program and certain curricular changes on grade school children. *J. exp. Educ., 24,* 95–114.

O'Malley, K. E. 1936. A psychological study of the annoyances or irritations of teachers. Unpublished doctoral dissertation, New York University.

Osborn, A. F. 1957. *Applied imagination.* New York: Scribner.

Osborne, K. In preparation. Saliences in students' perceptions of teachers. Unpublished doctoral dissertation, Wayne State University.

Osgood, C. E. 1952. The nature and measurement of meaning. *Psychol. Bull., 49,* 197–237.

Papanek, M. 1957. Authority and interpersonal relations in the family. Unpublished doctoral dissertation. Radcliffe college.

Parnes, S. J., and A. Meadow. 1959. Effects of 'brainstorming' instructions on creative problem-solving by trained and untrained subjects. *J. educ. Psychol., 50*, 171–76.

Pear, T. H. 1950. *Psychological factors of peace and war*. New York: Philosophical Library.

Peck, L. 1935. Teachers' reports of the problems of unadjusted school children. *J. educ. Psychol., 26*, 123–38.

Pepitone, A. 1950. Motivational effects in social perception. *Human Relat., 3*, 57–76.

Perlmutter, H. V., and G. DeMontmollin. 1952. Group learning of nonsense syllables. *J. abnorm. soc. Psychol., 47*, 762–69.

Peters, C. C., and W. S. Van Voorhis. 1940. *Statistical procedures and their mathematical bases*. New York: McGraw-Hill.

Peterson, R. C., and L. L. Thurstone. 1933. *Motion pictures and the social attitudes of children*. New York: Macmillan.

Polansky, N., and J. S. Kounin. 1956. Clients' reactions to initial interviews. *Human Relat., 9*, 237–64.

———, R. Lippitt, and F. Redl. 1950. The use of near-sociometric data in research on group treatment processes. *Sociometry, 13*, 39–62.

Polsky, H. W. 1959. Changing delinquent subcultures: a social-psychological approach. *Soc. Wk, 4*, 3–15.

Porter, D. 1957. A critical review of a portion of the literature on teaching devices. *Harvard educ. Rev., 27*, 126–47.

———. 1958. Teaching machines. *Harvard Graduate Sch. of Educ. Ass. Bull., 3*, No. 1.

Pressey, L. C. 1928. The permanent effects of training in methods of study of college success. *Sch. and Soc., 28*, 403–404.

Pressey, S. L. 1927. A machine for automatic teaching of drill material. *Sch. and Soc., 25*, 549–52.

———. 1926. A simple apparatus which gives tests and scores—and teaches. *Sch. and Soc., 23*, 373–76.

———. 1932. A third and fourth contribution toward the coming "industrial revolution" in education. *Sch. and Soc., 36*, 668–72.

Preston, G. H., and W. McL. Shepler. 1931. A study of the problems of 'normal' children. *Amer. J. Orthopsychiat., 1*, 245–56.

Pullias, E. V. 1934. How do you behave when the children misbehave? *Childh. Educ., 10*, 230–37.

Quinn, R. O. 1950. Psychotherapists' expressions as an index to the quality of early therapeutic relationships. Unpublished doctoral dissertation, University of Chicago.

Radke, M. J. 1946. *The relation of parental authority to children's behavior and attitudes*. Minneapolis: University of Minnesota Press.

Ramseyer, L. L. 1938. A study of the influence of documentary films on social attitudes. Unpublished doctoral dissertation, Ohio State University.

Rapaport, D. 1953. *Organization and pathology of thought*. New York: Columbia University Press.

Raths, L. E., and F. N. Trager. 1948. Public opinion and crossfire. *J. educ. Sociol., 21*, 345–68.

Riesman, D., P. E. Jacob, and N. Sanford. 1959. *Spotlight on the college student*. American Council on Education.

Rivlin, H. N. 1936. *Educating for adjustment.* New York: Appleton-Century-Crofts.

Robinson, F. P. 1961. *Effective study.* New York: Harper.

Rogers, C. R. 1942. The criteria used in a study of mental health problems. *Educ. res. Bull., 21,* 29–40.

———. 1942a. Mental health findings in three elementary schools. *Educ. res. Bull., 21,* 69–79.

———. 1961. *On Becoming a person.* Boston: Houghton Mifflin.

Rose, A. M. 1947. *Studies in the reduction of prejudice.* American Council on Race Relations.

Rosen, B. C. 1956. The achievement syndrome. *Amer. sociol. Rev., 21,* 203–11.

Rosen, B. L., and R. D'Andrade, 1959. The psychosocial origins of achievement motivation. *Sociometry, 22,* 185–217.

Rosenberg, M. J. 1953. The experimental investigation of a value theory of attitude structure. Unpublished doctoral dissertation, University of Michigan.

Rosenberg, P., and M. Fuller. 1955. Human relations seminar: a group work experiment in nursing education. *Ment. Hyg., N.Y., 39,* 406–32.

Rosenzweig, S. 1934. Types of reaction to frustration: an heuristic classification. *J. abnorm. soc. Psychol., 29,* 298–300.

Ryan, J. J. 1959. Factors associated with pupil-audience reaction to teacher management of deviancy in the classroom. *Amer. Psychologist, 14,* 378.

———, P. V. Gump, and J. S. Kounin. In preparation. An experiment on the effect of motivation to learn upon students' reactions to teachers' desist techniques.

Sacramento (Calif.) Youth Authority. 1958. *Report of Governor's Conference on Youth Participation in Community Affairs.*

Sampson, E. 1960. An experiment on active and passive resistance to social power. Unpublished doctoral dissertation, University of Michigan.

Sarason, S. B., et al. 1958. Classroom observations of high and low anxious children. *Child Develpm., 29,* 287–95.

———, ———. 1960. *Test anxiety in elementary school children: report of research.* New York: Wiley.

Sarbin, T. R. 1954. Role theory. In G. Lindzey (Ed.), *Handbook of Social Psychology.* Reading, Mass.: Addison-Wesley, pp. 223–58.

Sarnoff, I. 1952. Identification with the aggressor: some personality correlates of anti-semitism among Jews. *J. Pers., 20,* 199–218.

———, and D. Katz. 1954. The motivational bases of attitude change. *J. abnorm. soc. Psychol., 49,* 115–24.

Schachter, S. 1959. *The psychology of affiliation.* Stanford: Stanford University Press.

———, et al. 1951. An experimental study of cohesiveness and productivity. *Human Relat., 4,* 229–38.

Schrupp, M. H., and C. M. Gjerde. 1953. Teacher growth in attitudes toward behavior problems of children. *J. educ. Psychol., 44,* 203–14.

Scribner, H. B. 1960. A scale to rate teaching services in grades four, five and six. Unpublished doctoral dissertation, Boston University.

Seagoe, M. V. 1933. Factors influencing the selection of associates. *J. educ. Res., 27,* 32–40.

Sears, R. R., E. Maccoby, and M. Levin. 1957. *Patterns of child rearing.* Evanston, Ill.: Row, Peterson.

————, M. H. Pintler, and P. S. Sears. 1946. Effects of father-separation on pre-school children's doll play aggression. *Child Develpm., 17,* 219–43.

Seidman, J. M. and L. B. Knapp. 1953. Teacher likes and dislikes of student behavior and student perceptions of these attitudes. *J. educ. Res., 47,* 143–49.

Shaffer, L. F., and E. J. Shoben. 1956. *The psychology of adjustment,* 2d ed. Boston: Houghton Mifflin.

Sherif, M. 1954. Integrating field work and laboratory in small group research. *Amer. sociol. Rev., 19,* 759–71.

————, and C. W. Sherif. 1953. *Groups in harmony and tension.* New York: Harper.

————, ————. 1956. *An outline of social psychology.* New York: Harper.

————, J. White, and O. J. Harvey. 1955. Status in experimentally produced groups. *Amer. J. Sociol., 60,* 370–79.

————, et al. 1954. *Experimental Study of Positive and Negative Intergroup Attitudes between Experimentally Produced Groups: Robbers Cave Study.* University of Oklahoma.

Sharp, A. A. 1938. An experimental test of Freud's doctrine of the relation of hedonic tone to memory revival. *J. exp. Psychol., 22,* 395–418.

Shoobs, N. E. 1947. Sociometry in the classroom. *Sociometry, 10,* 154–64.

Siegel, S. 1956. Nonparametric statistics for the behavioral sciences. New York: McGraw-Hill.

Sifneos, P., C. Gore, and A. Sifneos. 1956. A preliminary psychiatric study of attempted suicide as seen in a general hospital. *Amer. J. Psychiat., 112,* 883–88.

Skinner, B. F. 1954. The science of learning and the art of teaching. *Harvard educ. Rev., 24,* 86–97.

————. 1957. The experimental analysis of behavior. *Amer. Scientist, 45,* 343–71.

————. 1957a. *Verbal behavior.* New York: Appleton-Century-Crofts.

————. 1958. Teaching machines. *Science, 128,* 969–77.

Smith, M. B. 1949. Personal values as determinants of a political attitude. *J. Psychology, 28,* 477–86.

Smith, W. M. 1952. Rating and dating: a re-study. *Marriage Fam. Living, 14,* 312–17.

Snider, B. C. F. 1957. Relation of growth in causal orientation to insecurity in elementary school children. *Psychol. Rep., 3,* 631–34.

Snyder, L. M. 1934. The problem child in the Jersey City elementary schools. *J. educ. Sociol., 7,* 343–52.

Soper, D. W., and A. W. Combs. Publication pending. The helping relationship as seen by teachers and therapists.

Sparks, J. N. 1952. Teachers' attitudes toward the behavior problems of children. *J. educ. Psychol., 43,* 284–91.

Spence, K. W. 1956. *Behavior theory and conditioning.* New Haven: Yale University Press.

Spillman, R. J. 1959. Psychological and scholastic correlates of dissatisfaction with school among adolescents. Unpublished master's thesis, University of Chicago.

Stendler, C. B. 1949. How well do elementary school teachers understand child behavior? *J. educ. Psychol., 40,* 489–98.

————, D. Damrin, and A. C. Haines. 1951. Studies in cooperation and competition: I. The effect of working for group and individual rewards on the social climate of children's groups. *J. genet. Psychol., 79,* 173–97.

Stewart, N. 1949. Teacher's concepts of 'behavior problems.' In *Growing Points in Educational Research.* Amer. educ. Res. Ass., pp. 302–10.

Stiles, F. S. 1947. A Study of materials and programs for developing an understanding of behavior at the elementary school level. Unpublished doctoral dissertation, University of Iowa.

———. 1950. Developing an understanding of human behavior at the elementary school level. *J. educ. Res., 43,* 516–24.

Stoddard, G. D. 1958. The dual progress plan. *Sch. and Soc., 86,* 351–52.

Stogdill, R. N. 1931. Parental attitudes and mental hygiene standards. *Ment. Hyg., N.Y., 15,* 813–27.

———. 1934. Attitudes of parents toward parental behavior. *J. abnorm. soc. Psychol., 29,* 293–97.

———. 1936. Experiments in the measurement of attitudes toward children, 1899–1935. *Child Develpm., 7,* 31–36.

Stotland, R., et al. 1957. The effects of group expectation and self-esteem upon self-evaluation. *J. abnorm. soc. Psychol., 54,* 55–63.

Stott, L. H. 1940. Parental attitudes of farm, town, and city parents in relation to certain personality adjustments in their children. *J. soc. Psychol., 10,* 325–40.

Stouffer, G. A. W. 1952. Behavior problems of children as viewed by teachers and mental hygienists. *Ment. Hyg., N.Y., 36,* 271–85.

———. 1956. The attitudes of secondary school teachers toward certain behavior problems of children. *Sch. Rev., 64,* 358–62.

———, and J. Owens. 1955. Behavior problems of children as identified by today's teachers and compared with those reported by E. K. Wickman. *J. educ. Res., 48,* 321–31.

Strang, R. 1955. Guided study and homework. *What Research Says to the Teacher, No. 8.* Washington, D.C.: National Education Association.

Strodtbeck, F. L. 1958. Family interaction, values, and achievement. In D. C. McClelland, et al., *Talent and Society.* Princeton, N.J.: Van Nostrand, pp. 135–94.

Sturgis, P. T. 1957. What are some of the positive reinforcers suitable for preschool children? Paper read at the Western Psychological Association.

Swanson, G. E. 1950. Development of an instrument for rating child-parent relationships. *Soc. Forces, 18,* 84–90.

Symonds, P. M. 1939. The psychology of parent-child relationships. New York: Appleton-Century-Crofts.

Taylor, D. W., and W. L. Faust. 1952. Twenty questions: efficiency in problem solving as a function of size of groups. *J. exp. Psychol., 44,* 360–68.

Teeters, N. K., and J. O. Reinemann. 1950. *The challenge of delinquency: causation, treatment, and prevention of juvenile delinquency.* Engelwood Cliffs, N.J.: Prentice-Hall.

Terrell, G., and W. A. Kennedy. 1957. Discrimination learning and transposition in children as a function of the nature of the reward. *J. exp. Psychol., 53,* 257–60.

Thibaut, J. 1950. An experimental study of the cohesiveness of underprivileged groups. *Human Relat., 3,* 251–78.

Thompson, C. E. 1940. The attitudes of various groups toward behavior problems of children. *J. abnorm. soc. Psychol., 35,* 120–25.

Thorpe, L. P. 1950. *The psychology of mental health.* New York: Ronald.

Thrasher, F. M. 1927. *The gang.* Chicago: University of Chicago Press.

Tiedman, D. V., and C. C. McArthur. 1956. Over and under-achievement: if any! *Thirteenth Yearbook of the National Council on Measurements Used In Education.* Cambridge, Mass.: National Council on Measurements Used in Education, pp. 135–45.

Tiller, P. O. 1958. Father-absence and personality of children of sailor families. *Nordisk Psykologis Monogr. Ser., 9.*

Torrance, E. P. 1950. The phenomenon of resistance in learning. *J. abnorm. soc. Psychol., 45,* 592–97.

———. 1951. Getting mental-hygiene practices into action through a college class. *Ment. Hyg., N.Y., 35,* 88–95.

———. 1960. Effects of induced evaluative sets on the development of new ideas among graduate students. In E. P. Torrance (Ed.), *Creativity: Second Conference on Gifted Children.* University of Minnesota.

———, and H. W. Michie. 1959. Explorations in creative thinking in the early school years: I. Scoring manual for a test of creative thinking. *Research Memorandum BER-59-1.* University of Minnesota.

Trump, J. L. 1959. *Images of the future.* Washington, D.C.: National Education Association.

———. 1960. *New directions to quality education.* Washington, D.C.: National Education Association.

———. 1961. *Focus on change: guide to better schools.* Chicago: Rand McNally.

Tryon, C. M. 1939. Evaluations of adolescent personality by adolescents. *Monographs of the Society for Research in Child Development, 4, No. 4.*

Tseng, S. 1952. An experimental study of the effect of three types of distribution of reward upon work efficiency and group dynamics. Unpublished doctoral dissertation, Columbia University.

Turrell, A. M. 1937. Study methods and scholarship improvement. *Junior Coll. J., 7,* 295–301.

Ullmann, C. A. 1957. Identification of maladjusted school children. *Public Health Monographs, No. 7.* U.S. Government Printing Office.

Unger, C. 1938. The relationship of teachers' attitudes to children's problem behavior. *Sch. and Soc., 47,* 246–48.

U. S. Children's Bureau. 1949. Juvenile Court Statistics, 1946–1949. *Statistics Series, No. 8.* U.S. Government Printing Office.

Wagner, M. E. and E. Strabel. 1935. Teaching high-school pupils how to study. *Sch. Rev., 43,* 577–89.

Wandt, E. 1954. A comparison of the attitudes of contrasting groups of teachers. *Educ. psychol. Measmt, 14,* 418–22.

———. 1952. Measurement and analysis of teachers' attitudes. *Calif. J. educ. Res., 3,* 10–13.

Wapner, S., and T. G. Alper. 1952. The effect of an audience on behavior in a choice situation. *J. abnorm. soc. Psychol., 47,* 222–29.

Warner, W. L. 1949. *Social class in America.* Chicago: Science Research Associates.

Watson, G. 1933. A critical note on two attitude scales. *Ment. Hyg., N.Y., 17,* 59–64.

Watson, W. S., and G. W. Hartmann. 1939. The rigidity of a basic attitudinal frame. *J. abnorm. soc. Psychol., 34,* 314–35.

Whipple, G. M. 1929. Experiments in teaching students how to study. *J. educ. Res., 1,* 1–11.

Whitcomb, M. 1959. A living laboratory for improving small high schools. *Nation's Sch., 63,* 53–58.

———. 1959a. Small high schools are worth retaining. *Nation's Sch., 63,* 63–66.

Whittemore, I. C. 1924. The influence of competition on performance: an experimental study. *J. abnorm. soc. Psychol., 19,* 236–53.

Wickman, E. K. 1928. *Children's behavior and teachers' attitudes.* Commonwealth Fund.

Wilkinson, F. R., and R. H. Ojemann. 1939. The effect on pupil growth of an increase in teacher's understanding of pupil behavior. *J. exp. Educ., 8,* 143–47.

Williams, R. M. 1947. The reduction of intergroup tensions. *Soc. Sci. Res. Coun. Bull., No. 57.*

Wilmer, D. M., R. R. Walkley, and S. W. Cook. 1952. Residential proximity and intergroup relations in public housing projects. *J. soc. Issues, 8,* 45–69.

Wilson, R. C. 1958. Creativity. In Education for the Gifted, *Fifty-seventh Yearbook, Part II, National Society for the Study of Education.* Chicago: University of Chicago Press, pp. 108–126.

———, et al. 1954. A factor-analytic study of creative thinking. *Psychometrika, 19,* 297–311.

Winter, J. E. 1936. An experimental study of the effect on learning of supervised and unsupervised study among college freshmen. *J. educ. Psychol., 27,* 111–18.

Winterbottom, M. R. The relation of need achievement to learning experiences in independence and mastery. In J. W. Atkinson (Ed.), *Motives in Fantasy, Action, and Society,* Princeton, N.J.: Van Nostrand, pp. 453–94.

Wisconsin Youth Committee. 1958. *Youth Participation on the march.* Madison, Wis.: Wisconsin Youth Committee.

Witmer, H. L. 1934. Childhood personality and parent-child relationships of dementia praecox and manic depressive patients. *Smith Coll. Stud. Soc. Wk, 4,* 287–378.

———, and R. Kotinsky (Eds.). 1956. New perspectives for research on juvenile delinquency. *Children's Bureau Publication, No. 356.* U. S. Government Printing Office.

Wolff, M. 1959. Youth must participate. *YWCA Magazine, 53,* 13, 30.

Woodruff, A. D., and F. J. DiVesta. 1948. The relationship between values, concepts, and attitudes. *Educ. psychol. Measmt, 8,* 645–59.

Young, D. 1932. *American minority peoples.* New York: Harper.

Young-Masten, I. 1938. Behavior problems of elementary school children: a descriptive and comparative study. *Genet. Psychol. Monogr., 20,* 123–81.

Yourman, J. 1932. Children identified by their teachers as problems. *J. educ. Sociol., 5,* 334–43.

Zeleny, L. D. 1941. Status: its measurement and control in education. *Sociometry, 4,* 193–204.

Zipf, S. 1958. *An experimental study of resistance to influence.* Unpublished doctoral dissertation, University of Michigan.

Zucker, H. J. 1943. Affectional identification and delinquency. *Arch. Psychol., N.Y., No. 286.*

CORRELATION OF

THIS BOOK WITH

REPRESENTATIVE TEXTS

Correlation of This Book
with Representative Texts

Bernard, H. W. MENTAL HYGIENE FOR CLASSROOM TEACHERS, 2d ed. McGraw-Hill, 1961	Bonney, M. MENTAL HYGIENE IN EDUCATION Allyn and Bacon, 1960	Carroll, H. A. MENTAL HYGIENE, 3d ed. Prentice-Hall, 1956	Coleman, J. C. PERSONALITY DY- NAMICS AND EF- FECTIVE BEHAVIOR Scott, Foresman, 1960

Text chs.	Related Selections in EDUCATING FOR MENTAL HEALTH: A BOOK OF READINGS			
1	16, 26, 50	16, 17, 25, 26, 50	16, 26	16
2	11, 12, 19	4, 5, 15	1, 2	1, 2, 5, 8, 11, 15
3	3, 7, 9, 10, 12, 43	14, 43	3	1–4, 8–12, 16, 25, 34, 38
4	5, 34, 38	14, 25, 38, 39, 41	4	9, 15, 52, 56
5	8–10	20, 27–30, 40	5, 9, 15	5, 10, 13, 14, 34, 37–43
6	25–26, 53	16, 44	11, 14, 43	26
7	10, 12, 43, 50, 51, 53	1, 3, 5, 10, 11, 15, 23, 30, 40, 54	10, 22, 27–43	10–15
8	7	1, 13, 42, 44–49	8, 11, 12, 14	8, 13, 18–21, 39
9	20, 22, 32, 33	14, 34, 42		16
10	19, 25, 39	19, 25, 37, 39, 52, 54		5, 10, 11
11	44–49	11–14, 50, 51	50–56	34–43
12	22, 29, 49	8, 47, 48, 52	25, 27–49	18, 21, 22, 27–33
13	13, 18, 21	9, 11, 22, 23	11, 22, 32, 33, 39–43	44–52, 54–56
14	22, 32, 33	3, 6, 39, 41–43	13, 18, 21	
15	22, 32, 33	2, 5, 45, 47, 53, 56	50, 55	
16	22, 32, 33	34, 38		
17	45, 50	45, 46, 51, 53, 56		
18	17			
19				
20	26			
21	16			
22				
23				

	Heyns, R. W. THE PSYCHOLOGY OF PERSONAL ADJUSTMENT Holt, Rinehart and Winston, 1958	*Kaplan, L.* MENTAL HEALTH AND HUMAN RELATIONS IN EDUCATION Harper and Row, 1959	*Katz, B., and Lehner, G. F. J.* MENTAL HYGIENE IN MODERN LIVING Ronald, 1953	*Klein, D. B.* MENTAL HYGIENE Holt, Rinehart and Winston, 1956
Text chs.	*Related Selections in* EDUCATING FOR MENTAL HEALTH: A BOOK OF READINGS			
1	1, 2		16, 17, 26	16, 26
2	10–12		10, 11	2, 4
3	14	10–12, 43, 55		1, 2, 4, 5, 6–10, 15
4	11–13	45–56	14, 43	
5	10	2, 4	1, 2, 4, 8, 55	
6	27–33	4, 15	11, 43	
7		25, 34, 38, 43		
8	1, 2, 4	2, 5, 11, 15, 21	2, 4, 25	5–10, 15, 40, 43
9	4, 25	11, 17, 26	3	1, 2, 10
10	6–11, 27–33	3, 14, 15		4, 50
11	2, 11, 40, 43	9, 10, 12, 43	3, 12	3, 39–43
12	3, 12, 15, 39	8, 9, 34–43, 45–49	50, 51, 56	1, 16
13		19, 22, 32, 33	6–10, 27–34, 37–43	34, 37, 38, 54
14		7, 11, 25, 28, 34, 38, 41, 42, 47, 56	13, 25	41, 42, 48, 52, 53, 56
15		44–49, 51	50, 56	11–14, 34, 38
16			55, 56	2, 3
17				5, 15–17
18			50–54	27–49
19				
20				
21			8, 11–14	
22			27–56	
23			34–40, 43	

Lehner, G. F. J., and Kube, E. THE DYNAMICS OF PERSONAL ADJUSTMENT Prentice-Hall, 1955	Lindgren, H. C. MENTAL HEALTH IN EDUCATION Holt, Rinehart and Winston, 1954	National Society for the Study of Education, Fifty-Fourth Yearbook, Pt. II MENTAL HEALTH IN MODERN EDUCATION Univ. of Chicago Press, 1955	Redl, F., and Wattenberg, W. W. MENTAL HYGIENE IN TEACHING, 2d ed. Harcourt, Brace and World, 1959
Text chs.	*Related Selections in* EDUCATING FOR MENTAL HEALTH: A BOOK OF READINGS		
1	17, 18, 21	6–8, 19, 26	6–10, 27–43	7, 9, 12
2	1, 2	1, 11–15	50	16, 17, 50
3	25	5, 9–10	9, 10, 19, 27–33, 43	8, 10, 11
4	4, 26	11, 16, 39–43, 51	2, 4	
5	7, 10–12, 39, 43	2, 7, 11	6–10, 13, 19, 25, 28, 34, 40–42	1–3, 47
6	11, 12, 43	5, 15, 55	50–56	1, 3–5, 34
7		16, 21–23, 39, 40, 42		11, 16, 26, 36, 37
8		8, 28, 39–43, 47, 52, 54	6, 7, 10, 19, 45, 46, 49	10, 27–31
9	2, 4, 15	8–12, 28, 40	19, 22, 28, 31, 32, 41, 42, 45–47, 49, 54, 56	7, 12, 20
10	8–14, 25, 27–33	13, 34, 37, 38, 42, 43	21, 29, 30, 47, 48, 52, 54, 56	11, 13, 14, 34, 38–43
11	11, 13, 14, 34–43, 56	7, 8, 23, 25, 27–33		7–9, 45, 46
12	55	7–12, 40	50, 56	6, 10
13	3	9, 19, 40	6–10, 22, 32, 33	25
14		2, 4, 53, 54, 56	45, 46	11, 17
15	6–12, 14, 17, 27, 34, 37, 38	1, 5, 12, 15, 25	17–19, 21, 24–26, 44, 50	11, 12, 20, 22, 32, 33, 43, 50
16	16, 26	17, 44–49, 50, 55, 56		18, 21
17		25, 50, 51, 56		51–54
18		13, 18, 21		6
19		16, 23		1, 50, 55, 56
20				
21				
22				
23				

	Rogers, D. MENTAL HYGIENE IN ELEMENTARY EDUCATION Houghton Mifflin, 1957	*Shaffer, L. F., and* *Shaben, E. J.* THE PSYCHOLOGY OF ADJUSTMENT, 2d ed. Houghton Mifflin, 1956

Text *chs.*	*Related Selections in* EDUCATING FOR MENTAL HEALTH: A BOOK OF READINGS	
1	6–10	8–12, 14, 18, 21
2	17, 26, 43, 50	10
3	7–11, 39, 40	1, 5, 8, 9, 12, 15, 28, 34–43
4	1–5	5, 10, 12, 14
5	2, 4	9, 27–34, 37–43, 51, 52, 56
6	8, 11, 14, 19, 38, 39, 41, 42, 52, 56	11, 14, 39
7	8–10, 12, 43	43
8	44–47, 49	
9	34, 37–39	
10	25, 29, 41, 42, 45, 47, 49	10
11	11, 13, 14, 28, 34, 37, 54	8, 11–13, 14, 34, 37, 38, 41, 43
12	13, 22, 32, 39, 41, 43, 56	
13	3, 8, 11, 12, 43	1–5
14	20, 22, 48	
15	7–10, 19	16, 26, 50
16	45, 46, 50	43, 56
17		19, 21, 23, 25, 27–34, 37–43, 45–56
18	17, 18, 21, 26	
19		
20		
21		
22		
23		

INDEX

Index

Names of contributors to this book are followed by inclusive references to their articles and by separate references to citations: for example, Armstrong, C. M., 229–32, 231.